T0213530

Compendium on Enterprise Resource Planning

Siar Sarferaz

Compendium on Enterprise Resource Planning

Market, Functional and Conceptual
View based on SAP S/4HANA

 Springer

Siar Sarferaz
SAP SE
Walldorf, Germany

ISBN 978-3-030-93855-0   ISBN 978-3-030-93856-7   (eBook)
https://doi.org/10.1007/978-3-030-93856-7

This Springer imprint is published by the registered company Springer Nature Switzerland AG
The registered company address is: Gewerbestrasse 11, 6330 Cham, Switzerland

Preface

In the digital age business processes can no longer be implemented based on spreadsheets. Thus, enterprise resource planning (ERP) systems are used to manage business information and processes. Essentially, an ERP system is a software solution for running the entire enterprise based on automated and integrated business processes. The complete process chain from research and development to manufacturing, marketing, sales, logistics, and services is digitalized. Due to central data management the cross-departmental visibility is increased, and it empowers organizations to analyze crucial scenarios and improve the efficiency of their business processes, which leads to cost savings and higher productivity. The ERP systems are composed of numerous modules which implement specific process components, for example, supply chain or manufacturing. The business data is synchronized and kept consistent among modules. For example, application data for the business process *product receiving* impacts immediately *inventory management*. Thus, data redundancies are eliminated, and efforts for maintaining data are reduced.

Another significant advantage is the improved efficiency and productivity. For example, ERP systems provide applications for routine transactions like *quality and cash management* or *sales realization*. Consequently, cycle times of the superordinated processes like *sales to cash* or *procurement to pay* are reduced. Furthermore, ERP systems support many decision-making capabilities, for example, simulation functionality or planning engines to improve the organization's demands. Therefore, resources as materials or headcounts can be effectively provided. Valuable is also the built-in analytics for identifying business insights which can be enhanced with ad-hoc reports.

In summary ERP systems build the backbone of companies and enable the digital transformation of daily operations, business decision-making, and tracking of enterprise's critical data. SAP provides with SAP S/4HANA the next generation of the intelligent and integrated ERP system. SAP S/4HANA is based on SAP HANA, which is an in-memory database providing analytical capabilities for evaluation and monitoring of key performance indicators in real time in addition to transactional processing.

The objective of this book is to explain the functional scope, the data model, the solution architecture, the underlying engineering concepts, and the programming model of SAP S/4HANA. In the first part the reader learns about the market view of the ERP solutions and vendors. The second part deals with the business processes for sales, marketing, finance, supply chain, manufacturing, services, procurement, and human resources, which are covered with SAP S/4HANA. In the third part the underlying concepts of SAP S/4HANA are described, for example, in-memory storage, analytics and search, artificial intelligence, process and data integration, security and compliance, lifecycle management, performance and scalability, configuration, and implementation. The book is concluded with a final chapter explaining how to deploy an appliance to explore the SAP S/4HANA system.

The target audience for the book are managers and business analysts who want to understand the market situation and the ERP future trends, end users and process experts who need to comprehend the business processes and the corresponding solution capabilities provided with SAP S/4HANA, architects and developers who have to learn the technical concepts and frameworks for enhancing the SAP S/4HANA functionality, consultants and partners who require to adopt and configure SAP S/4HANA.

The support of the following persons is sincerely appreciated and gratefully acknowledged: M. Alnaser, M. Angermeier, G. Beck, M. Benner, A. Berbescu, J. Bertrand, L. Blank, J. Eger, T. Emig, N. Fuerhaupter, L. Ganss, B. Grimm, T. Gross, J. Gruebener, T. Janson, T. Kessler, F. Klinke, D. Kossack, K. Krempels, T. Lorenz, N. Meffert, C. Meli, M. Mertens, P. Mischka, D. Neumann, A. Ochel, J. Pines, V. Popp, A. Richert, T. Scheuermann, A. Schweig, A. Siebert, P. Vittoria, M. Vonend, and J. Zecevic.

Walldorf, Germany   Siar Sarferaz

Disclaimer

This publication contains references to the products of SAP SE or an SAP affiliate company. The SAP products and services mentioned herein as well as their respective logos are trademarks or registered trademarks of SAP SE or an SAP affiliate company. For the SAP product screenshots included in this publication copyrights are reserved by SAP. All other product and service names mentioned are the trademarks of their respective companies. Data contained in this document serves informational purposes only. National product specifications may vary. SAP is neither the author nor the publisher of this publication and is not responsible for its content. SAP Group shall not be liable for errors or omissions with respect to the materials. The only warranties for the SAP Group products and services are those that are set forth in the express warranty statements accompanying such products and services, if any. Nothing herein should be construed as constituting an additional warranty.

Contents

About the Author

Siar Sarferaz is a chief software architect for the enterprise resource planning (ERP) solution SAP S/4HANA, working in the research and development department of SAP's headquarters in Walldorf, Germany. In this role, he drives the digital transformation by defining the solution architecture for the product and by providing inventive concepts scaling for mission critical business processes. For example, he is the lead architect for artificial intelligence implementations in SAP S/4HANA and is responsible for all conceptions how to add intelligence to business processes. In the context of ERP software, he owns 30+ patents. Furthermore, he is author of numerous ERP books and gives university lectures on ERP software. Siar had studied computer science and philosophy and holds a Ph.D. in computer science. He began his career as a method researcher at Siemens, before moving to SAP, where he has now worked for more than 20 years.

In this part the Enterprise Resource Planning (ERP) market perspective is explained. The ERP market size is constantly growing and diverges by the type of customers and deployment options. While traditional vendors continuously expand their footprint, new start-up companies enter the market due to changing technology and shifting paradigm. The challenges and characteristics of ERP systems are described as they have been evolving steadily in the last years. To be prepared for the future, upcoming ERP trends are summarized. The ERP market size varies by the type of customer use cases as depicted in Fig. 1. Services-based companies require mainly finance and procurement functionality. Manufacturing-based firms expected from their ERP systems in addition capabilities for digitalizing their factories. Generic features like human capital management or travel expense are typically needed in all types of enterprises.

In general, software architecture and technological innovations serve to provide business value and to best meet the needs of customers. Such requirements have shifted dramatically in the digital age. However, in order to understand the architecture challenges of modern ERP solutions, it is necessary to first look back at what made SAP's ERP software so successful. While addressing the needs of a constantly changing market, these qualities of the past must be retained by an ERP solution. And, without a doubt, they must be advanced in order to deal with emerging challenges and enable future business processes. Clearly, globalized and localized business process coverage, as well as industry variants, is an important factor in selecting SAP ERP software. However, there are architecture and technology drivers that are at the heart of SAP's success and have led to the adoption of its systems by thousands of businesses.

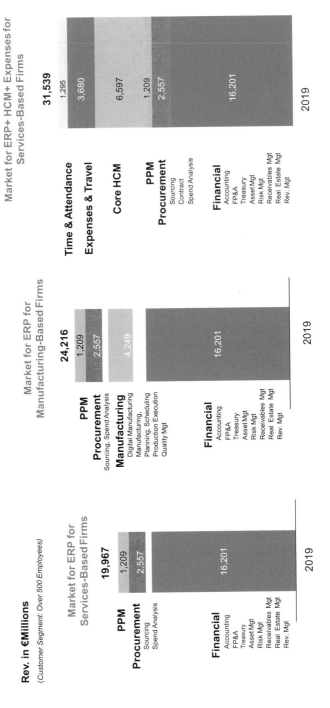

Fig. 1 The ERP market size varies by the type of customer use case

Challenges and Characteristics of ERP Systems

ERP systems are not new to the software market. But where does the need for ERP systems come from, and how have the systems and their requirements evolved? This chapter takes the reader on a journey through the history of ERP systems, demonstrating the systems' strengths and weaknesses as well as how providers, particularly SAP as the market leader, deal with the constant change in requirements.

Introduction

This chapter provides an overview of ERP systems, as well as challenges and key features. ERP is an abbreviation for Enterprise Resource Planning system. But what exactly is an ERP system? Enterprise Resource Planning (ERP) is a term associated with a multimodule software for managing and controlling a wide range of activities that assist a manufacturer or other business. Data capture, storage, product planning, parts purchasing, inventory control, purchasing, customer service, and order tracking can all be aided by ERP. ERP also includes finance and human resource management application modules. The implementation of an ERP system necessitates extensive business process reengineering and retraining. Because of the rapid progress of information technology and the ongoing digitalization of both the private and business sectors, the demand for highly sophisticated ERP systems is becoming an increasingly important issue. Reasons for this include the need for quick deliveries of goods and services, as well as a quick, easy, and secure way to conduct transactions across multiple instances. This chapter describes the evolution of ERP systems as well as the changes in requirements and features. In the area of challenges to modern ERP solutions, the focus is on SAP ERP system as SAP is actually the inventor of ERP solutions and since decades the leading vendor worldwide.

© The Author(s), under exclusive license to Springer Nature Switzerland AG 2022
S. Sarferaz, *Compendium on Enterprise Resource Planning*,
https://doi.org/10.1007/978-3-030-93856-7_1

ERP Evolution

ERP systems can be traced back to the 1960s or 1970s in the literature, depending on the author. Everything started with so-called MRP systems at the time. MRP is an abbreviation for Material Requirements Planning system. At the time, the manufacturing sector was the primary focus of MRP systems. It was defined as a system for calculating the materials and components required to manufacture a product (Essex 2020). The MRP system was invented in 1964 by Joseph Orlicky, an IBM engineer at the time. MRP systems have some flaws. Aside from the already mentioned narrow focus of the systems, there is also no possibility of providing feedback to the production plan in the event that the material plan was found to be infeasible due to a shortage of capacity. As a result, MRP systems have gradually improved. One thing quickly became clear: in order to have a functioning and comprehensive system, a holistic approach is required, which means that other processes, all the way up to the entire organization, must also be integrated. The continuous evolution crossed several barriers, including the establishment of links between manufacturing execution and production planning activities, known as the Master Production Schedule (MPS), among others. Other approaches, ranging from rough capacity planning to detailed capacity planning, have been developed to address the problem of capacity shortage. These approaches help with financial planning at the same time. These and other improvements resulted in a more advanced MRP system, the MRP II systems. These ideas and developments also resulted in market events, as various companies were founded in the early 1970s that also dealt with standard software for businesses. SAP was one of the start-ups, founded in Germany as "Systemanalyse Programmentwicklung" (in English, "System Analysis and Program Development"). The founding members were all IBM Corporation employees. The early stages of start-ups concentrated primarily on finance and the use of a single database, as well as real-time processing. The various systems were available at the time as mainframe software on large computers. Back-office processes such as human resources and accounting were gradually integrated. Until the 1980s, this development and integration were continued until all of a company's business functions were integrated. However, this was only possible because enormous progress was being made in the field of computer technology at the same time: both hardware and software were developing rapidly and steadily.

But let's get back to the MRP II systems. MRP II stands for Manufacturing Resource Planning and was created in 1983 by management expert Oliver Wight (1984). According to Wight, MRP II is a comprehensive market and resource-oriented planning of sales, production, and stock levels, beginning at the executive level. But what does this mean, and how did it come to be that several areas of a company were further developed and linked? Each department within a company has its own way of doing things. At the start of computer technology's introduction, each area attempted to map its own working methods using a system. As a result, each area had its own software and database that was tailored to its specific way of working. However, this did not exactly support the work done across all divisions within a company, because manufacturing planning and control activities are closely related to the activities of other functional areas such as accounting and finance, marketing and sales, product/process engineering and design, purchasing, and materials management (Sridharan and LaForge 2000). The attempt to connect different areas of a company suggests the idea of a uniform database and a single system, because double data management frequently leads to inconsistencies and increased time expenditure. This also leads to the fundamental concept of the MRP II's development and emergence: There is one physical system in operation in a company, and there is no justification for having more than one information system representing different dimensions of the physical system. With the advancement of computer technology, MRP II systems provided the ability to perform various simulations based on data sets in addition to a company-wide information base. Simulations do not alter data sets within the database, but instead work with fictitious numbers. They assist the company in making various operational decisions. This can include a wide range of decisions in various areas, such as examining individual trading positions, forecasting for best- and worst-case scenarios, and much more. By combining these functions, the company becomes more efficient and can serve customers better. So, based on the previous points, three key characteristics of MRP II systems can be deduced: interfunctional coordination, closed loop planning (from MRP systems to MRP II systems), and what-if analysis capability. In summary, an MRP II system is a business planning system because it connects various managers from different areas of the company through a single central information system. However, the MRP II system has a major flaw: all of the points mentioned, and the system's basic concept are always related to production. A company, on the other hand, consists of other sectors that are not directly related to production. Furthermore, there are not only manufacturing companies on the market, but also other sectors of the economy that do not find MRP II systems useful under these conditions. This is how the next stage of evolution arose: the ERP system, which was supposed to bridge the market gap.

ERP systems first appeared in the 1990s. According to Essex (2020) analysts at the research firm Gartner recognized the need for uniform naming and spearheaded its implementation. They were inspired by business software vendors such as SAP, PeopleSoft, Baan, and others. Despite the fact that the terms MRP or MRP II system are no longer commonly used, they are considered the forerunners of ERP systems. The various ideas and thoughts are still used in ERP systems today. MRP packages are typically integrated into ERP systems in most systems. But, exactly, what is an ERP system? ERP systems are cross-industry systems that support all major business processes across a broad range of company types. ERP systems thus map not only production processes, but also all other more general business processes. The peculiarity that should be highlighted is that ERP systems are intended for all industries, because every company, regardless of the sector or industry to which it belongs, has to write invoices and interact with other companies in some way. Simultaneously, ERP systems were confronted with the trends of globalization, global markets, international networks, and others, which presented new challenges. These new challenges reintroduced the need for multilingual and multicurrency systems, including conversions, to meet the global changing market environment and competition. ERP systems had to overcome several obstacles: Developing distributed systems, customized data views, and processing capabilities for various roles and employees. Engineering, Technical Change Control and Documentation, Procurement or Purchasing, Materials Management, Manufacturing, Human Resources, Cost Accounting, Finance, Marketing and Sales were typical functionalities that an ERP system had to support in 2000. With the introduction of the term ERP, system vendors began to reconsider as well. There was a shift away from mainframe computers and toward a server-client architecture. This enabled multiuser operation. Different user interfaces were gradually integrated to make work easier. At the same time, SAP switched over. SAP R/3 also made it possible to work with the software in real time at one's own workstation for the first time. Other features revealed at this time included a distributed relational database system with query and reporting capabilities, electronic data interchange capability to communicate with both suppliers and customers, decision support systems for managers, a graphical user interface, and standard application programming interfaces. However, the progress of computer technology did not stop in the year 2000. In the 10 years that followed, a new trend emerged on the market. Data should be accessible and retrievable at all times and from any location. Cloud computing is a term that came up frequently in this context. Cloud computing and the Internet enabled companies to communicate with one another in real time. Some businesses have shifted away from traditional desktop applications and toward browser-based user interfaces. From the 2010s to the present, there have been numerous new issues within computer technology advancements that have kept ERP system providers facing new challenges. This includes issues such as artificial intelligence and machine learning, blockchain, predictive analytics, and other emerging technologies that necessitate the cloud's superior computing power and Internet connectivity. The challenges and characteristics of modern ERP systems, as well as how they are addressed, are presented in the following chapter, which is based on the SAP's ERP product named as SAP S/4HANA.

Characteristics of Modern ERP Systems

SAP was one of the aforementioned start-ups during the transition from MRP systems to ERP systems. SAP is now the market leader in ERP systems. What are the characteristics and features of SAP SE solutions, and how have they been implemented in recent years? SAP S/4HANA is SAP's most recent generation of ERP systems. It is the evolution of SAP ERP into a simplified system of engagement, leveraging SAP HANA's in-memory capabilities such as embedded analytics, simulation, prediction, decision support, artificial intelligence, and machine learning in conjunction with mobile, social, Big Data, and deployment choice to deliver applications with a new user experience for people directly in the context of their lives. SAP's goal with SAP S/4HANA is to build on the previous success of its ERP systems while improving the features and principles. This chapter begins by describing the successful features of SAP ERP solutions. These are then supplemented by

SAP S/4HANA solution features. At the time, the unique selling points of SAP's ERP solution included not only adaptability to custom business process needs via the used ABAP-based system from SAP, but also a certain stability of the system. This was also true during the update period. SAP in year 1992, with the architecture of the so-called SAP R/3 system, was a pivotal point in the company's success at the time. It was a groundbreaking three-tier architecture that separated the front end, application server, and database, allowing for independent scalability. This architectural feature enabled SAP to stand out in the market by providing performance, robustness, and scalability. However, as time passed, customer requirements changed, posing new challenges for SAP and other ERP providers. SAP had a very clear idea of what features were and still are critical to customers. Seven key characteristics for modern ERP systems emerged (Saueressig et al. 2021b) high performance and scalability, user experience, extensible architecture, simple and standardized implementations, intelligent ERP processes, cloud and on-premise implementations, and security in terms of data protection, compliance, and data isolation.

The rapid technological development is responsible for the high performance and desire for scalability. As a result, there is a desire for high speeds and a high degree of adaptability to meet adaptations. This can only be accomplished through system scalability. But what exactly is scalability? Scalability is the ability of a software system to handle a higher load volume by utilizing additional resources. A modern ERP system's foundation is a future-proof architecture for constantly increasing system loads as enterprises collect sentiment data, sensor data, spatial data, market feeds, and experience data in unprecedented quantities. The digital era necessitates even greater speed and adaptability. Companies frequently encountered issues with multiple-batch run dependencies in ERP implementations over the last few decades, limiting scalability, and overall system performance. In-memory database systems enable a new generation of business applications that combine transactions, analytics, machine learning, and more, without the traditional complexities of persisted aggregates, redundancy, inconsistency, or latency imposed by standard database technology. The elimination of aggregate tables and indexes, as well as the use of insert-only models, lay the groundwork for significantly reduced processing time and greatly increased parallel throughput and scalability in modern ERP applications. The ability to run online transaction processing (OLTP) and online analytical processing (OLAP) applications on the same in-memory database system without replication results in significant cost savings and productivity gains. Real-time business processes, planning, and simulation also improve accuracy because reporting and analytics based on replicated, potentially outdated data can lead to poor decisions. Because of the elimination of application-controlled materialized aggregates, in-memory computing allows to avoid traditional batch programs, thus facilitating to create many innovative new business processes. The insert-only paradigm of in-memory databases enables lock-free, scalable software with significantly increased throughput. In-memory capabilities help to finally reimplement and simplify large portions of the application logic while meeting the scalability and functional requirements expected of a modern ERP system. Inventory management is an example of how the aforementioned batch-process scalability issues were addressed using in-memory capabilities. Inventory management in SAP ERP necessitates database updates on the aggregate table for quantity-in-stock information (table MARD). Due to the architecture of SAP HANA as in-memory database system, these updates can be removed in the simplified SAP S/4HANA data model. Intensive scalability tests with inventory management were performed to compare the performance and throughput of SAP Business Suite powered by SAP HANA and SAP S/4HANA. The results revealed a significant increase in throughput, which increased by a factor of 25 when a greater number of material movements were posted in parallel. This is a game-changing innovation, particularly for companies in the automotive industry, where backflush processes have a high number of common parts in the material documents. Column store of in-memory database systems enables data to be searched and analyzed without the use of additional indexes. This has a significant impact on the application architecture because it provides full-text searching for end users without replicating search-relevant data into an external instance, significantly reducing data volume in ERP systems. The desire for a good user experience stems from the fact that computer technology has now infiltrated many aspects of people's personal lives. Users' attitudes toward enterprise applications have shifted as a result of the digital era. Members of generation Y and Z, in particular, expect enterprise applications to be visually appealing, accessible from any device at any time, simple to use, responsive, and easily customizable. Applications that do not provide the same level of comfort that these users are accustomed to from consumer-grade applications or websites are frequently rejected and used less frequently. Thus, UX is concerned with meeting a user's needs in the most efficient and enjoyable manner possible. ERP systems should ideally be intuitive and simple to use without the need for extensive training. This necessitates a redesign geared toward an intuitive user experience, understandable terminology, and context-sensitive user assistance. The key requirement for applications today is that they be visually appealing, accessible from any device at any time, simple to use, responsive, and easily personalized. The properties of extensible architecture and simple and standardized implementations are inextricably linked. Many customers have customized the application's standardized processes to meet their specific needs. There must be a way to continue to provide this flexibility without jeopardizing upgrade capabilities and maintainability, as well as removing the fear of the next release. As previously stated, terms like artificial intelligence and machine learning, blockchain, predictive analytics, and other emerging technologies have also entered people's minds. This is something that various ERP providers are aware of. However, these can take advantage of the rapidly advancing computer technological development to provide the user with entirely new options. Integration of these technologies is a step forward in automation, which can lead to more efficient work. It is critical that a modern ERP solution allows for the integration and configuration of the capabilities that businesses require today and in the future. This necessitates that the ERP system be built on an extensible architecture, which is accomplished through flexible integration capabilities based on open standards on the one hand and powerful in-app extensibility mechanisms on the other. To ensure that upgrades do not break extensions or configuration, the system architecture must separate standard coding, custom extensions, and content. ERP products, of course, must provide standardized implementation packages. However, they must also provide options for tailoring the product to the specific needs of an organization without jeopardizing upgradability and long-term maintainability. Software architectures, particularly in the cloud, are distributed and service-oriented. Although extensions are frequently used to modify the standard system in the context of an ERP application, a modern ERP system embraces more and more extension capabilities through the integration of new cloud services. This approach is known as side-by-side extensibility. With this strategy, the system architecture transitions from less flexible, traditional, monolithic concepts developed on a single stack to federated services that allow for better service-level agreements (SLAs), such as scalability, availability, and resilience, and ensure maximum adaptability while ensuring update stability through separation via stable APIs. Customization of UI and business scenarios through field and process extensions, adaptations or extensions of business workflows, and open and flexible integration with third-party products via standardized APIs are critical requirements for both in-app and side-by-side extensibility and must be reflected in the software architecture. Most businesses have written a significant amount of custom code to enhance, partially replace, or even modify the ERP software implementation. Furthermore, they have heavily customized their systems. As a result, the IT landscape is disjointed, with a ERP system that is difficult to upgrade to the next release. As a result, massive modifications to standard software have locked enterprises in and are preventing them from taking the next step toward digital transformation. This includes reducing complexity by standardizing and simplifying business processes. ERP applications in the digital age necessitate the delivery of preconfigured packages that allow for rapid implementation. This necessitates a thorough understanding of the industries for which the business configuration content packages are designed. ERP configuration, particularly in the public cloud, must largely meet an organization's needs out of the box. This necessitates the use of a modern ERP to provide self-service implementation tools, which help to significantly reduce implementation costs. Tools that guide users through the implementation process step by step, as well as standardized data migration tools, are especially important. The aforementioned extensibility options can be used in cases where an organization's own practices are more beneficial. The desire to provide both cloud and SaaS solutions stems from the diverse needs of customers. There are several arguments in favor of and against each option. One reason why business may not want to use the cloud exclusively is that users do not want to entrust the security of their sensitive data to a cloud. They want to keep control of the situation. However, hybrid models are also an option. Hybrid models are not uncommon at this point. In terms of data protection and security, the use of the cloud, and thus the Internet, presents a new challenge. Operational processes, in particular, frequently work with data that could be critical to the company if third parties gain access. As a result, security is and will continue to be a critical issue for ERP systems in the future. SAP S/4HANA is also attempting to meet these requirements while adding new features. But what makes SAP S/4HANA so unique? SAP HANA was created to enable a new generation of business applications that combine transactions, analytics, machine learning, and more, without the traditional complications of persisted aggregates, redundancy, inconsistency, or latency imposed by standard database technology. To accomplish this, SAP S/4HANA provides an in-memory platform with an insert-only model that shortens processing time, increases parallel throughput and scalability, and allows transactions to be processed in real time. Six principles guided the development of the SAP S/4HANA application (Saueressig et al. 2021b):

- Stable but flexible digital core: A clean and stable core is established, allowing for faster software deployment and easier adoption of SAP software innovations as well as regulatory software changes. This lowers the costs of upgrade projects, resulting in a lower total cost of ownership (TCO). However, this does not imply that flexibility is in jeopardy. SAP S/4HANA aims to provide the same level of extensibility and flexibility as SAP ERP, but with significantly increased stability contracts to best support upgradeability. With the separation of concerns paradigm, the new concepts of in-app extensibility and side-by-side extensibility address this critical need. These flexibility mechanisms are built on a large set of publicly available APIs and objects with guaranteed stability contracts.
- Simplification with the principle of one: This is one of SAP S/4HANA's core architecture principles, and it describes the deprecation of redundant frameworks, data models, UIs, and other SAP ERP elements. The principle of one achieves simplification and reduced complexity in this manner. An important step toward addressing this is the significant simplification of solution offerings through the elimination of nonessential components in the simplified deployment. This is accomplished through quarantine and deprecation. The number of tables, data elements, and transactions in SAP S/4HANA has been drastically reduced by eliminating redundant functionalities.
- Open to innovations through service orientation: To avoid redundancies and achieve both efficiency and consistency, SAP S/4HANA introduces a virtual data model (VDM). As a result, it can create accurate cross-references between business processes and analytical scenarios. The user interface and application integration of SAP S/4HANA are based on a service-oriented architecture, which leverages web services built on open standards. The VDM in SAP S/4HANA provides a solid foundation for both RESTful UI services for SAP Fiori apps and integration APIs.
- Modularization into (hybrid) integration scenarios: SAP S/4HANA aims to support users in such a way that end-to-end processes are possible. It accomplishes this by integrating a container technology and a logical data model across all services. This SAP S/4HANA modularization is an important prerequisite for supporting hybrid scenarios, in which enterprises run parts of their SAP S/4HANA functionality in the cloud and other parts on-premise. As previously stated, hybrid deployments will be the integration reality for many ERP implementations for many years to come, providing enterprises with the flexibility to approach both digitalization and cloud migration with public, private, and hybrid approaches.

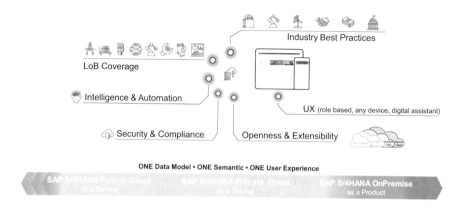

Fig. 1.1 SAP S/4HANA key capabilities

- Cloud first, but not only: There are numerous distinctions between a cloud-based SaaS solution and an on-premise application. Cloud architecture must be designed to take advantage of shared resources, enabling high availability and elastic scalability. SAP S/4HANA Cloud is a pure SaaS solution that incorporates every aspect of a modern distributed and service-oriented cloud architecture. Every customer tenant uses the same software stack. Large parts of the hardware resources, system data, and coding are shared across multiple tenants in multitenancy clusters for scaling effects. The solution provides fully dynamic tenant density, zero downtime for maintenance events, and complete automation of lifecycle management.
- Semantic compatibility to support evolution with the fewest disruptions: SAP S/4HANA supports the market needs for hybrid deployment models by providing homogeneous data models and integration points across on-premise and cloud versions. When an organization plans to migrate to a modern ERP solution such as SAP S/4HANA, new digital capabilities are always taken into account. The semantic compatibility of SAP ERP and SAP S/4HANA data models, as well as SAP S/4HANA on-premise and cloud deployments, enables enterprises to transition in a reasonable timeframe. Many of SAP ERP's extension points remain available with this compatibility paradigm, reducing the adoption effort for custom coding when migrating to SAP S/4HANA.

All of these features are combined and implemented by the market leader in SAP S/4HANA to provide users with the best possible ERP application experience. The named features are clearly summarized in Fig. 1.1.

Business Value

Enterprises face numerous challenges with ERP today, including a lack of integration, an inability to adapt to a rapidly changing business environment, the complexity of business transformation, change management, data conversion, and migration, and total cost of ownership (TCO). Furthermore, the COVID-19 pandemic necessitated radical ERP flexibility, for example, think cash management and financial agility, production and distribution changes, drastic cost cutting, customer demand changes, remote people management or working from home. While intelligent ERP is a growing market that is designed to address rapidly changing business needs, the crisis has altered the nature of many ERP transformation projects. As a result, value capture must occur quickly and incrementally. Installing or running an ERP system has an impact on business processes throughout an organization, which naturally creates a number of challenges. Long implementation projects can cost businesses a lot of money, not just in fees, but also in lost time to value. Furthermore, the knowledge and capabilities of a consulting implementation partner can have a significant impact on the project's success. These difficulties are exacerbated when complex, multifunctional systems that must integrate a wide range of tasks across an enterprise are introduced. Most organizations require from the ERP solution to support their mission-critical processes from start to finish. These processes can be divided into *commodity processes*, which seek maximum efficiency through standardization and automation, and *differentiating processes*, which generate competitive advantage and necessitate a high degree of flexibility to adjust and extend. Commodity and differentiating processes covering the core scenarios lead-to-cash, recruit-to-retire, design-to-operate, and source-to-pay which are supported by ERP systems and provide instant value. Lead-to-cash is concerned with following up on a customer's intent or interest in purchasing a product or service. Basically, it is how a company generates revenue from product or service sales covering the various stages of this process, such as the attract customer, offer, sell, fulfill, and collect phases. Recruit-to-retire oversees all aspects of the workforce involved in business operations. Functionalities range from workforce demand planning to staffing, onboarding, support during the working phase, travel, and payment for terminated work engagements. Source-to-pay encompasses and supports the sourcing and acquisition of goods and services covering the phases of sourcing and contracting, planning and forecasting, purchasing and delivery, and finally invoicing and payment. Design-to-operate aids in the design, manufacture, shipping, operation, and maintenance of products and services. For planning and manufacturing support, as well as the delivery process and continuous operation, various applications are combined. This process is a prominent example of the possible hybrid interaction between on-premise and cloud, with components that frequently run at the edge—close to controlled and monitored machinery and equipment. Organizations are increasingly requiring solutions that address specific scenarios or business problems or support dedicated processes, and companies are increasingly preferring to pay for what they use rather than pay for vendor-determined packages. This flexibility is possible, especially in the cloud, because traditional product boundaries are blurring and being replaced by highly flexible services. ERP is transitioning from a broad, fixed-scope solution that covers every critical business process a company may have to a commercial construct that bundles capabilities along predefined scenarios and end-to-end processes that organizations can consume as needed. While technically decoupled, this bundle still provides the most critical value for organizations that use ERP solutions in the first place: From the user experience (UX) to data and process integration, these solutions are highly integrated. Configuration flexibility is greatly increased, allowing for rapid adaptation of those services to meet the demands of a changing business environment. The current reality demonstrates that every industry participant must plan for the worst and strive for the best, including repaying technical debt and investing in a transformation strategy that is authentically focused on the consumer. SAP reflects this ethos by adhering to the fundamental principles of migrating to SAP S/4HANA and cloud-based digital transformation. Organizations have had to quickly recast key operational business processes, and this need for change is expected to be the new normal in the future. Business processes must be constantly read-jousted by shifting to automated, flexible, analytics-driven, project- and industry-oriented applications that play a role within a larger ecosystem. SAP's intelligent ERP offerings can help drive business by providing real-time insights, real-time planning, forecasting, simulation, and embedded analytics at each step of the way by recognizing those needs and meeting them with SAP S/4HANA. Business value can be divided into strategic and operational value. Both elements are critical for organizations to reap the full benefits of implementing a new ERP software system. Compared to the past of mostly monolithic ERP systems, today's IT environments are often driven by best-of-breed strategies, different technology stacks, and the move to cloud solutions from multiple vendors with unaligned release schedules. All these developments have made the job of IT managers much more challenging. At the same time, they are confronted with reduced IT budgets and skill gaps, while the demands from business stakeholders to implement new requirements in an agile way grow and timelines shorten. New regulatory requirements, data privacy laws, and cybersecurity threats do not make things easier. With SAP S/4HANA Cloud these IT operation tasks are offloaded to SAP as cloud service provider. The calculation of a financial business case is the starting point for every ERP implementation project. Multiple tools, approaches, and templates are provided by SAP and its ecosystem to complete this exercise and make the financial business case as standardized and convenient for organizations as possible. The standardization of business processes has more than just a positive effect on operations. With a solution based on industry best practices combined with preconfigured content, customers can implement ERP solution in the cloud much more quickly than ever conceived in the on-premise world. This standardization translates directly into lower project costs, faster rollouts, lower training requirements, leaner operations, and lower TCI. Currently the fastest SAP S/4HANA Cloud implementation was completed in 26 days. The cloud has substantially helped companies drive standardization, reduce implementation times for new ERP solutions, and increase the chances of a successful ERP implementation. In addition, they more directly see the implication of deviating from the standard, as the costs of integration and extension can explode and destroy the positive business case of moving to the cloud. Ease of use in software and simplicity can also help users accept compromises on functionality since people working with the software directly experience new possibilities and new analytical insights. The high degree of standardization across all dimensions—process definitions, infrastructure, implementation, operations, and updates—directly translate into TCO savings. In the initial TCO calculation, many companies forgot to integrate the costs of ongoing operations with their IT systems. Having the internal IT team and multiple contractors working constantly on the ERP system to keep the lights on is often seen as an unavoidable cost element and, in many cases, not directly assigned to one system. In addition, the costs of lost business user productivity because of system upgrades, integration into long-running IT projects, and missing analytical insights are rarely taken into consideration. As for upgrade costs, many organizations still using the SAP ERP application are on quite old releases of the solution and are afraid to upgrade because of expectations of huge costs and business disruption. Therefore, their users cannot take advantage of the latest innovations of software and may not be motivated to work with business software from the 1980s or 1990s in the year 2021 and beyond. The result is not only missing productivity and inspiration, but also workaround solutions in many areas. The costs for all these specific solutions attached to the large house called ERP are assumed directly by the business and are not attributed to the ERP system in most cases. If this cycle has continued for some years, a potential upgrade or change in the underlying ERP software gets more and more difficult which drives costs and requires extensive change management to transition end users who have gotten comfortable working with these legacy systems. Although a bit counterintuitive, unfortunately, ERP systems which were initially implemented to manage operational processes at scale and to support the growth of organizations, have become just the opposite—major change inhibitors—due to customizations and modifications over time. As described many organizations today look for cloud enterprise management systems for multiple reasons. One reason is a high degree of standardization, which again is the prerequisite for a high degree of automation. SAP has made major investments in recent years to increase the degree of process automation across all lines of business (LoB) to free users from routine tasks and allow them to shift their focus from transactional processing toward complex decision-making and from backward-oriented analytical tasks toward using predictive and simulation capabilities to determine the next best action based on situations that previously triggered an alert and to react to specific data patterns. One example of SAP S/4HANA shows how automation reduces redundancies for greater workforce productivity. For example, the Chinese branch of a worldwide leading manufacturer of polymer products relied on its in-depth knowledge of materials and extensive experience in technologies and manufacturing processes to meet the wide-ranging needs of its customers from across industries. However, to protect its status as a leader in polymers, this subsidiary knew it needed to create smoother customer experiences. One central element to change the customer experience was to revolutionize billing processes—ensuring billing occurs on time as well as with all the consolidation and flexibility end customers expect. By implementing robotic process automation (RPA) the company achieved greater process efficiency through automatic billing workflows and the automatic upload of a thousand financial accounting documents, turning 4 days of work into a 10-minute task.

Conclusion

Overall, ERP systems can be described as extremely powerful. The rapid development of computer technology, on the other hand, is constantly pushing vendors to their limits. To keep up with the competition, they must be creative and not rely on what they currently have. With SAP S/4HANA, SAP introduced a new generation of ERP systems to the market, which is continuously further developed. However, unlike many other systems, the new generation is already designed to be far more adaptable than the original MRP and ERP systems. Nonetheless, it is critical at this point that SAP does not rest on its laurels and keeps up with the times. Machine learning and artificial intelligence are constantly evolving technologies. Other technologies may also emerge and provide a breath of fresh air, necessitating additional action and innovation from ERP system providers.

ERP Market Analysis

2

This chapter describes the state of the ERP market. This includes revenue size, customer types, and vendor analysis. Depending on the cloud and on-premise deployment the figures can vary. In addition, different lines of business and regions develop diversely. This chapter also takes a look at the different market shares of the biggest competitors in ERP market and tries to give an answer why these competitors became so big. There will also be an outlook for the future growth in ERP market and how the different competitors try to achieve to go ahead of the others.

Introduction

Enterprise resource planning (ERP) is the software used to manage business processes. This allows organizations to plan their resources like human resources, technological resources, and other functions in a system of integrated applications. Therefore, an ERP system has different applications for different tasks. These applications run together as a complete product with a database, user interfaces, and specific applications to cover all facets of an operation like product development, manufacturing, sales, and marketing. While using ERP software a lot of data is generated. This data is useful for managers to evaluate success. Therefore, ERP software can also be used to get automated reports. Automated reports avoid the necessity of manual arrangement of data from different sources within the organization. For many companies, ERP systems are business critical, as they manage their processes. The company size can differ from small to large businesses. This is the reason why ERP systems have a growing market. ERP software can be used either on-premise, in a cloud environment, or as a hybrid solution between cloud and on-premise. Because of these different types of solutions there are different types of market volumes for on-premise or cloud-based ERP software. The market growth and the market shares are also different between these solutions. To get an understanding of the different market competitors in the ERP market a deeper look on the values for market growth, market shares per competitor, and market volume is

S. Sarferaz, *Compendium on Enterprise Resource Planning*, https://doi.org/10.1007/978-3-030-93856-7_2

needed. Another difference can be made by the different module types of ERP systems. To get an understanding how competitors became successful in the ERP market the history of the competitors is an important factor. To stay on top there are different strategies the competitors might choose. Based on the different strategies a future outlook can be given on how the market could behave in the next couple of years. One of the key factors of business success will be data. To satisfy customers a customer-centric and data-driven approach is key for competitors. Next to this, service offerings will become more important for customers, because they want to focus on their main business which is mostly not providing IT infrastructure for their used software. Therefore, cloud strategies must be offered by ERP software vendors. In the following chapter a closer look at the different mentioned topics is provided.

Market Volume

The market value of the ERP market was $35.81 billion in 2018. For 2020 the market size was expected to be $49 billion (Reinbolt 2021). In 2019, the top ten ERP software vendors accounted for nearly 32.1% of the global ERP applications market which grew 1.1% to approach nearly $94 billion in ERP license, maintenance, and subscription revenues (Pang et al. 2020). SAP led the ERP market in 2018 with a market share of nearly 6.8%. Oracle was on second place followed by Intuit, FIS Global, and Fiserv (Pang et al. 2020) (Fig. 2.1).

In 2019 the ERP market size was 53 billion euros. The biggest market competitors by share value are SAP with 10.8%, Oracle with 6.1%, Sage with 2.8%, Microsoft with 2.5%, and Inform with 2.4%. Together these companies nearly had a total market share of a quarter of the whole worldwide ERP market. Together with other big companies the total market share is again over 30% of the whole market. In comparison to the worldwide market share, SAP is only on second place in the North American market with 7.3%. Leading in the North American market is Oracle with 8.7%. For Europe Middle East Africa (EMEA) SAP has the biggest market share with 15.1% followed by Sage with 4.8% and Datev with 4.6%. Oracle is only on fourth place with 3.7%. The total market size of the EMEA market was 18 billion euros in 2019. For the Asia Pacific Japan (APJ) and China market, SAP had a market share of 10.1% of the total market size of 9.4 billion euros. On second place was Yonyou with 4.5% followed by Oracle with 4.2% and MYOB with 3.1%. For the Latin American (LA) market SAP was also leading with a market share of 17.5% followed by Totvs with 13.2% and Oracle with 6.5% of the total market size of 2 billion euros. According to these numbers the biggest players in the ERP market are SAP, Oracle, Sage, and Microsoft. The numbers also show that on different markets different vendors have the biggest impact. For most markets SAP has the biggest market share (Fig. 2.2).

In 2019 SAP had the most revenue in the most significant ERP modules compared to the biggest competitors Oracle, Sage, Microsoft, Inform, Salesforce, NetSuite, and Workday. The biggest revenue was in financial with 2217 million euros. On second place in financial is Sage with 986 million euros. Third and fourth

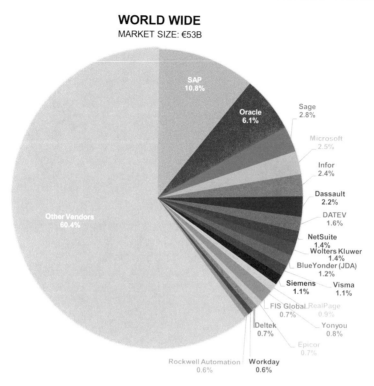

Fig. 2.1 Worldwide ERP market share in 2019

place are Oracle and NetSuite. The second most revenue was provided by travel and expenses. SAP led this category with 1768 million euros, followed by Oracle with 86 million euros. In core HR SAP made a revenue of 1048 million euro. In this field Workday is the biggest competitor with 1042 million euros followed by Oracle with 909 million euros. SAP's revenue was also leading in the fields of manufacturing with 774 million euros, procurement with 487 million euros, and sales management with 394 million euros. In service management Salesforce led the revenue with 860 million euros, followed by Oracle with 286 million euros. SAP was only at fourth place with 88 million euros. In the year-over-year comparison of the total revenue between 2018 and 2019 the ERP market size of the biggest players grew. The companies with a smaller market share mostly grew the most compared to companies with an almost big market share. Workday for example has a small market share with nearly 1% of 2019's market size compared to SAP, but therefore its growth rate is nearly as high as 50%. SAP has a market share over 10% and has a growth rate of a little over 10% from 2018 to 2019. Oracle's growth rate is under 10% and has a market share of over 5%. On the other end Infor shrank about 2% from 2018 to 2019 with a market share of approximately 2%. For cloud revenues the numbers look a little different. Microsoft made a growth of almost 55% with a market share of more than 2%. Workday and SAP also made a big growth with over

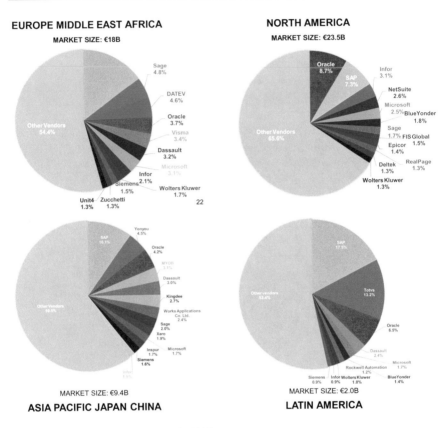

Fig. 2.2 Regional ERP market share in 2019

45%. The difference is the market share. SAP has a market share of approximately 6% and Workday has a market share of approximately 1.5%. Oracle has the highest market share in cloud revenue with over 6.5%, therefore the market growth was a lower with only a little over 20%. NetSuite, Sage, and Salesforce are in a different growth range around 20% to 25%. The difference between them is their market share, where Sage has the biggest market share compared to NetSuite and Sage. NetSuite and Sage have a similar market share of over 3%. The lowest growth rate and smallest market share have Infor. Infor shrank a little and has only a market share of under 2%. So far, the investigations were focused on ERP product license revenue. However, the neighboring market segments must be also considered. There are numerous businesses with high market volume around ERP systems as shown in Fig. 2.3. For example, implementation and consulting business, cloud operations and infrastructure services, hardware for on-premise deployment, analytics and business intelligence platforms for data warehousing and complementary third-party software must be taken into account.

Global IT Spending by Market Segment

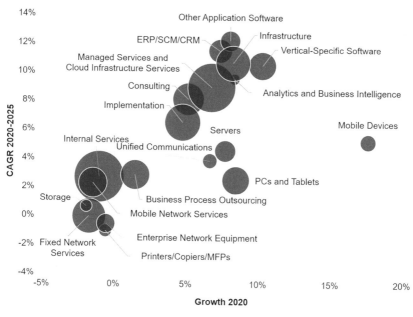

CAGR= compound annual growth rate

Fig. 2.3 ERP top vendor worldwide. Source: Gartner, 2021

Competitors

An approach to explain why companies like Microsoft, Oracle, or SAP have a higher market share than other vendors can be made from their history and other factors. Microsoft for example used dynamic product offerings and fully integrated tools to become successful in ERP market. Another aspect is acquisitions like Great Plains (Davidson 2020). SAP in comparison has been a leader in business applications since the launch of its first ERP system in 1972 (Davidson 2020). SAP has customers in over 180 countries and offers dozens of ERP solutions for almost every use case and every business size. The scalability of the software is also an advantage. Oracle is known for selling databases, software, cloud systems, and enterprise software products. They became a leading ERP company after some acquisitions in the early 2000s. In 2016 Oracle acquired NetSuite which was working on ERP systems in the cloud. Oracles cloud applications are based on machine learning (Fig. 2.4).

Sage has like SAP a long history in ERP software. They started in 1981 focusing on software for small businesses. Sage's ERP solutions are highly modular and customizable. Infor is one of the leading companies in cloud-computing after they aggressively modernized their product line since 2010. They also used acquisitions

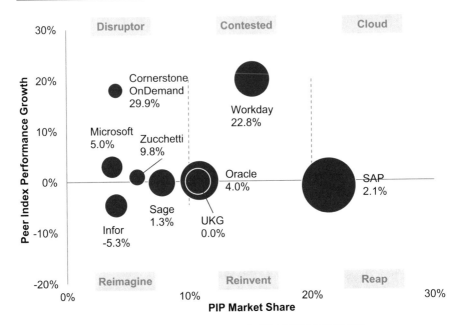

Vendor	PIP Market Share	PIP Growth	Revenue	YoY Growth
SAP	21%	-1%	8,584	2.1%
Oracle	11%	0%	4,373	4.0%
Workday	15%	20%	3,735	22.8%
Sage	8%	0%	2,206	1.3%
UKG	11%	0%	1,876	0.0%
Infor	4%	-5%	1,626	-5.3%
Microsoft	4%	3%	1,440	5.0%
Visma	52%	5%	1,286	20.6%
Zucchetti	6%	1%	830	9.8%
Cornerstone OnDemand	4%	18%	705	29.9%

The size of the bubble denotes revenue in millions of U.S. dollars. Percentages refer to the organization's overall growth rate, not the PIP growth rate.

Fig. 2.4 ERP top vendor worldwide. Source: Gartner, 2021

to provide ERP software for different industries (Davidson 2020). To get ahead of the others the market competitors have different strategies. These strategies can be divided into revenue growth, technology, and industry. Oracle plans to get a growth in revenue by migrating its legacy apps to the cloud. They also want to use synergies with their Oracle Cloud Infrastructure and PaaS. They want to acquire vertically and take shares of other competitors' customers. Their technology strategy is their cloud infrastructure stack and a unified cloud environment. They want to provide low- and no-code development (Fig. 2.5).

Another technology Oracle wants to use is analytics and AI. They focus on the industries' professional services, public sector, financial, oil and gas, healthcare, and manufacturing. Workday in comparison wants to achieve a revenue growth by migrating SAP's and Oracle's finance systems to their Workday Cloud. They also want to expand incrementally in their ERP segment. They plan to use technologies based on analytics and predictions. This is extended by the usage of AI technology and rapid implementation. They focus on the industry sector's public sector and government, higher education, healthcare, and professional services. Infor wants to grow their revenue with upgrading their customers to cloud. They also want to move their acquisition to the cloud. They focus on using rapid development and AI technologies. Furthermore, they target the automotive sector, aerospace and defense, industrial machinery, fashion, food and beverages, and distribution. Microsoft plans to bundle up their products and use azure as a key role in their enterprise strategy. For technologies, they focus on the Azure platform to provide development and deployment. They also plan to give developers the opportunity to build AI-based apps using AI as a platform. They focus on retail, public sector, telecommunication, life science, energy and utilities, insurance, and media and entertainment. SAP's strategy is also based on cloud business. It is planned to migrate users to SAP S/4HANA and cloudify the underlying IT infrastructure. Along this SAP plans to focus on customer experience using Qualtrics (Hackmann 2020) (Fig. 2.6).

This shows that all competitors have different strategies to get ahead. They have in common that they want to use upcoming technologies like AI and cloud services. Those technologies enable their customers to derive more insights from data and improve business processes. In general, the focus is very customer-centric and cloud based.

Market Forecast

The evolution of ERP software can be split into four big time slots. The first ERP systems from 1980s to 1990s had no focus on specific industries. The architecture was fragmented, and the integration was complex. Currently, there are only some buyers using this kind of systems. The time between 1990s and 2000s had focus on manufacturing and distribution industries. The architecture was mostly monolithical with the beginning of some architectural changes. The integration can be described as tight. Many companies are still using these kinds of systems. The postmodern ERP systems from 2010s can be described as service-centric and product-centric.

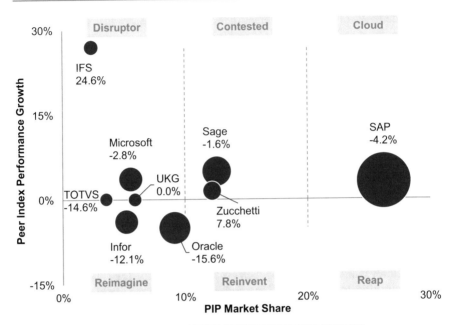

Vendor	PIP Market Share	PIP Growth	Revenue	YoY Growth
SAP	26%	3%	5,296	-4.2%
Oracle	9%	-5%	1,859	-15.6%
Sage	13%	5%	1,585	-1.6%
Microsoft	6%	4%	1,065	-2.8%
Infor	5%	-4%	1,057	-12.1%
Visma	56%	1%	855	13.8%
Zucchetti	12%	2%	651	7.8%
IFS	2%	27%	415	24.6%
UKG	6%	0%	347	0.0%
TOTVS	4%	0%	335	-14.6%

The size of the bubble denotes revenue in millions of U.S. dollars. Percentages refer to the organization's overall growth rate, not the PIP growth rate.

Fig. 2.5 ERP top on-premise vendor worldwide. Source: Gartner, 2021

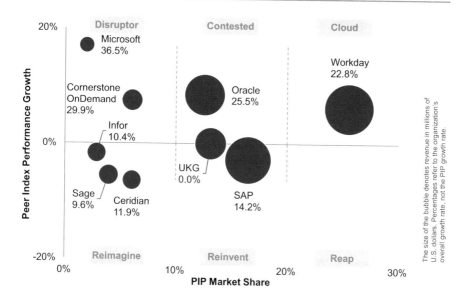

Fig. 2.6 ERP top cloud vendor worldwide. Source: Gartner, 2021

Systems of this kind use different kinds of architecture. The different applications are mostly loosely coupled. In general ERP system vendors are still highly relevant for this kind of system. For the future it is expected that the focus will be multiindustry and will suit the buyer as best as possible. The strategy for these systems is modular parts and end-consumer-centric. The architecture is expected to be cloud based on multiple clouds. On-premise systems are also used if there is a valid use case for it. The integration is expected to be self-connecting even if there are specific demands on different processes. In general, the cloud market of ERP is growing. Due to the pandemic the general growth paused temporarily. The pandemic had an impact on how ERP is used. Customers are using the system in a more flexible and analytic-driven approach. There are also current trends like AI and cloud, which are used more often in ERP. It is expected that the ERP cloud market growth will increase after the disruption of the Covid-19 pandemic in the year-over-year comparison. The growth of ERP cloud market dropped from 2019 to 2020 from 25.9% to 12.2%. From 2020 to 2021 there was also a slight drop to 10.3% growth in cloud. On-premise systems had an even bigger drop of growth from 2019 to 2020. The growth shrank about 15% to −9.9%, but it grew a little from 2020 to 2021 to about −6% growth. It is expected that the on-premise growth will raise to 0.2% to the year 2024. For cloud a growth of 22.1% is expected for 2024. In comparison to these year-over-year growths the absolute numbers of revenues of the on-premise revenue will shrink over the years. The cloud revenue is expected to grow linear from 15,815 million euros to 33,947 million euros in 2024. This means the revenue of 2024 in cloud market is expected to be more than two times the revenue of 2019. It should also be mentioned that it is projected that the cloud revenue will overtake the

Fig. 2.7 Trends impacting
the ERP market

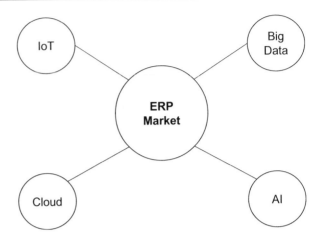

on-premise revenue in 2021. Which means that the cloud is a future trend of ERP systems. If the cloud revenue is split across different industries, there is big growth in banking, defense and security, healthcare, public sector, telecommunications, and utilities. Industries which shrank significantly from 2019 to 2020 are aerospace and defense, higher education and research, sports and entertainment, and travel and transportation. The shrink of some of these industries can directly lead back to the pandemic and the associated restrictions. Sports and entertainment and travel and transportation are industries, which were highly impacted by the pandemic restrictions. Therefore, a shrink is expected to happen. The ERP market size is influenced by different trends. The market size grows because businesses need operation efficiency and transparent business processes. An increase of the cloud market can be expected because companies using ERP software want to reduce their costs for computation. Mobile devices become more and more a part of the working culture. This leads companies to invest in cloud-connected mobile apps. With cloud-connected mobile apps information can be accessed anytime and anywhere. Together with trends like Internet of Things (IoT), Artificial Intelligence (AI), and Big Data this leads to a big growth in ERP market size (Valutes Reports 2020). The future trends in ERP market are shown in Fig. 2.7.

Other factors that influence the ERP market growth are for example shortages and digitalization. In the past many businesses used Word and Excel files to manage their business. On top often documents were kept as paper files (Balaban 2019). Today business owners start to think about how to use data more effectively in order to better see their strengths and weaknesses and also to provide better services to their clients (Balaban 2019). The shortage of staff on the other hand influences the usage of automation. Along with this, companies try to get rid of their use of human labor and use automation and standardization on their processes instead. New technologies can be used to avoid skilled workers doing routine tasks. ERP systems can free their workloads and allow these employees to focus on important things like solving business critical problems. In the future adoption of technologies like IoT, AI, and Big Data will provide further growth of the ERP market size. With these rising technologies it is expected that many opportunities will be generated for ERP market in Asia-Pacific countries. Small- and mid-sized businesses will increase the ERP market size in the future. During the forecast period until 2026 it is expected that North America will hold the largest market share. This is attributed to the constantly growing number of new businesses. It is also expected that these businesses will move to cloud-based solutions due to the lower costs for maintenance and hosting. For the Asia-Pacific region the biggest growth rate in ERP market is forecasted. This can be attributed to the growing number of small- and mid-sized businesses which start using ERP solutions for a more efficient management of their processes (Valutes Reports 2020). Studies point out that there is a positive correlation between data-driven decision-making and business outcome. This correlation also applies for pervasive analytics or AI-based approaches. However, not only the ability to generate more data and analyze it in a more efficient way than competitors leads to a higher business outcome. For a higher outcome it is needed that businesses can continuously learn, reflect, and adapt from the data in a better way than their competitors. The process of continuous learning and collecting information from different sources to get more knowledge and skills can be described as enterprise intelligence. This enterprise intelligence will define the winners in the market in the future. Additionally, it is necessary that employees become more and more data literate. For a better fail-safe it is important that processes in companies become more resilient in the future to prevent things like pandemics to have a big impact on the company (Vesset et al. 2020). Some predictions about the future of intelligence in the enterprise include that G2000 companies will use cloud computation to benefit from hyper-customization for AI and Big Data workloads. Next to this most of these companies will supplement their staff with social science experts. With this they want their data science and data engineering staff to work hand in hand with the social science experts for better recommendations in data analysis. It is predicted that by 2026 25% of the G2000 companies will invest in swarm intelligence solutions (Vesset et al. 2020).

Conclusion

The understanding of ERP systems changed over the years. Along with this the functionalities and customer requirements changed. In general, the focus became more customer-centric and service orientated. With this the ERP market grew over the years. The growth can also be explained because of the customers' needs to manage their business processes more efficiently. This can only be achieved if the collected data is analyzed. There is also a need to collect the data from processes inside the business. The usage of ERP systems makes it easier for customers to get everything under control, because data is stored in one system and there is no need to manually condense the different data sources. With this said there is also a need for ERP systems in the future. Next to this the current ERP market situation is based on some big players like Oracle, SAP, Microsoft, and NetSuite. These competitors got their position mostly with two strategies. The first strategy is building own ERP solutions for many years, which led to the superior role. The second approach to get a big player in ERP market is acquisitions. The way of acquisitions presupposes the possibility to buy other companies. Therefore, financial capacity is required which makes it easier to raise for big players in the market. The usage of synergies can help to speed up this process and make it more successful. This could be the reason why companies like Oracle became successful using their knowledge of databases and information technology systems. To achieve a continuous growth, the ERP software vendors have to adopt their strategies to their customers' demands. This means to offer more services and to provide the ERP software as a service. This is a big change, because currently many customers of the ERP software vendors have on-premise systems. Therefore, it is necessary to use future trends like cloud solutions, so customers can focus on their main business instead of operating ERP systems. Also cloud systems (public or private cloud) can better handle the growing amount of data in the period of Big Data. This data is generated due to the use of IoT systems and process monitoring. The pandemic depicted that customers ask for more flexible usage of ERP systems. There is a need for a resilient business which can easily adapt new features and technologies.

ERP Future Trends

3

This chapter depicts the future trends of ERP solutions. Customers are expecting due to the pandemic experience a more flexible, analytic-driven product. Composable applications, industry, and scenario-based applications are the future as they can realize these needs. Cloud and AI remain key technology drivers in the near term as they enable current trends.

Introduction

ERP systems have been an indispensable part of businesses since at least the 1960s. From material planning to finances—ERP systems lay the digital foundation of every successful business today. Accompanying businesses for several decades, ERP systems have undergone the same transformations as the businesses themselves. Especially the digital transformation in recent years gave the popularity of ERP systems an additional boost, strengthened even further by the Covid pandemic. Several other trends are already starting to take shape today. In the near future, and already happening today, ERP systems are expected to meet the ever-growing demand for flexibility. Alongside this, companies expect their IT to utilize the company's data to its fullest within the next 2 years, aiming for automation and AI-supported processes. Looking even further into the future, companies expect ever-increasing process modularity, providing businesses with custom-tailored and industry-specific applications. Companies expect IT products to provide modular services, enabling them to pay for what they need and quickly assembling applications for specific purposes, even further deepening this development in the next 2–5 years. Aside from these trends, ERP systems are also prone to change alongside the industries they are applied in. Trends such as Industry 4.0 and IoT will reinvent how people think about IT not just as business supporting but business-critical even more. Nothing changed human behavior quite so radically in the last few years as the Covid-19 pandemic has. While some of the observed changes have been a trend in years before, the pandemic has accelerated them greatly within little

S. Sarferaz, *Compendium on Enterprise Resource Planning*, https://doi.org/10.1007/978-3-030-93856-7_3

more than a single year. Especially the digital transition experienced more attention than it ever has. As a result, companies worldwide are forced to accelerate their digitalization measures to keep up with the rapidly changing demands of their customers and ever-evolving circumstances. Two examples that indicate an increase in mobility and flexibility of people are the increase in mobile phone usage during the past few years and an increase of people working remotely or from home. The first trend is supported by data on mobile phone usage in Germany. A survey from 2020 shows (Gentner 2020) that 89% of people own a smartphone, of which 95% use their device on a daily basis. While this is mostly for private usage, mobile access to work recourses is not negligible. Even among the age group of 65+ years, 79% own a smartphone, making it an essential point of contact between people and their work. An increase in flexibility is supported by another study from 2020 (Bockstahler et al. 2020) which depicts, that while most people are forced to work from home due to the Covid-19 pandemic, over 60% of respondents claim that their flexibility regarding spatial and temporal aspects of their work will increase in the future. This is supported further by the expectation of executives, who also believe that the future of work will shift toward being more flexible. To react to these rapid changes and the increase of flexibility, companies need to work faster as well. They need to streamline their processes and decisions and find ways in which to abandon the slow old and introduce the fast new. One implication of designing companies to act fast is to abandon slow-moving hierarchies and replace them with flat structures that decide fast. Reinventing the organization for speed comes with multiple consequences (de Smet et al. 2020):

- Faster decision-making: Companies need to abandon slow decision-making processes and replace them with newer and faster ones. By making decisions in just one meeting with a few involved people and recourses condensed to the most crucial part, not everything will take a few weeks to discuss and decide on.
- Leave it to the employees: By abandoning micromanagement and embracing employee responsibility, companies can leverage their workforce's true potential. Companies work at their best when everyone does what they do best, and goals and responsibilities are communicated concisely.
- Do not act alone: By trusting others and forming partnerships, companies can leverage mutual benefits. The ability to quickly work together with other businesses to achieve a common goal is vital in surviving in a fast world.
- Flat hierarchies: Instead of an endless stream of approvals and bureaucracy, companies need to design their hierarchies in a flat and lean way, such that they can respond quickly to emerging challenges and opportunities.
- Agile teams: Responsiveness does not stop at the hierarchies of a company. The teams themselves need to be organized in an agile way, each with concrete goals. Only then can the teams respond quickly, and their success can be measured.
- Hybrid work: As mentioned before, the days of everyone working on-site and from the same location every single day are over. Companies need to make way to both flexible workplaces and hours. Doing so increases employee satisfaction and thereby productivity.

- Value young talent: During the pandemic, companies are able to see who is ready to take action and take on responsibility—especially among the youngest employees. Seeing how employees act during a crisis gives executives insights into how the people in a company work in a very short duration of time.
- Adapt and learn: Together with agile teams, the importance of employees capable of adapting quickly has become ever so more important. Instead of experts that, by definition, are limited to their fields, executives put more value on talents who are—if needed–able to take on completely new challenges and adapt quickly to new tasks.
- Rethink leadership: Instead of typical leadership roles such as decide, command, and control, the role of executives is shifting toward enabling their teams to unleash their full potential.

To keep up with the ever-changing world, not only organizational structures need to be adapted but also the IT of companies. ERP systems play a major role in keeping businesses operational and need to be aligned with the overall strategy. Adapting to radical flexibility in the ways described above requires IT infrastructure capable of fulfilling flexibility expectations of the modern business. By connecting a large portion of working resources to the cloud, companies can quickly transition a large part of their workforce to remote locations while maintaining high levels of operability. An integral part of this is supplying employees with SaaS accessible from everywhere and a strong integration with HR processes. Companies need to be able to react quickly to challenges and opportunities with monetary measures. This includes preserving liquidity by actively monitoring cash flows and taking action when sudden changes in revenue are detected. Utilizing highly developed cash and treasury management solutions together with predictive analytics enables companies to react quickly to these changes. Enterprises need to be able to quickly adapt the way in which their products are built, packaged, sourced, and shipped. Picture the first lockdown during the pandemic 2020: on a moment's notice, companies were not able to sell their products via traditional channels, such as retail, anymore. Instead, only companies that quickly managed to sell their products online and ship them directly to the consumer saw their business growing even among the pandemic, requiring tight integration with flexible sourcing and material management, highly operational warehouse and distribution management, and functioning alignment with the entire supply chain of the business and its suppliers. This could only be achieved using proper IT systems. As described above, companies need to be able to react to sudden changes regarding their business. This requires quick action to keep their business operational and the ability to cut cost quickly while simultaneously preparing for a return of workforces and business. Implementing organizational changes to design a business for speed comes with multiple consequences regarding HR and talent management. Companies are expected to experience high fluctuations in employee count to meet the demands of business reality. Depending on the projects that are realized at any point in time, companies might frequently change their talent and workforce requirements. An ability to do so needs to be tightly integrated with HR, talent, and project management. Enterprises implementing measures in both organizational structure and their IT to meet demands of radical flexibility will quickly see benefits in rapidly changing times. They will be able to preserve existing customers and meet the needs of new customers quickly. By acquiring new customers and beating their competition when it comes to responsiveness and adaption to shifts in demand, they ensure long-term success. In contrast, companies failing to embrace the need for radical flexibility will experience much more difficult project management and completion, leading to potential loss of not only customers but employees and talent as well. Moreover, suffering from financial viability, companies risk losing their market share to their competitors. In the next sections some of the key ERP trends are listed and explained.

Data Fabric

All major trends that significantly changed people's lives in the past two decades are, in one way or the other, related to the digitalization of everything. Business, entertainment, and everything else people do in their private and professional life have undergone a major shift toward utilizing digital systems to increase efficiency and streamline processes. It is the nature of these digital systems that causes the abundance of data to increase every year. In 1965 Gordon Moore, the cofounder of Intel, famously predicted that the number of transistors within a set volume of integrated circuits will double every 2 years (Moore 1965). While Moor's Law in this context can be interpreted as the increase in data processing power, similar trends can be observed for the capacity of storage devices, such as hard drives, the number of pixels on a display that can be acquired for a set amount of money, and many other developments of computer hardware (van der Aalst 2016). The overall amount of data, the digital universe, which includes all digital data created, replicated and consumed in a single year, is estimated to be about 40,000 exabytes or 40 zettabytes in volume in 2020 (Gantz and Reinsel 2012). An incredible volume of data that would need 40 billion commonly used hard drives of 1 terabyte size for storage. Compared to 2012, this volume signifies a growth by a factor of 300. Furthermore, just like the trend of ever-faster CPUs and larger storage mediums, this trend is also observed to be exponential. While most of the data seems to be in an unorganized form, more and more companies start to see value in extracting information from data. In this context, data can be divided into three categories (Gantz and Reinsel 2012):

- Private data, the data everyone has on their personal computers, tablets, and phones, such as photographs and text messages. This kind of data is usually inaccessible for further processing by companies since it is protected by being private people's property and by physical barriers. However, the latter one has seen a significant decrease in recent years through the increasing popularity of cloud storages.

- Organizational data which includes all data directly accessible to a company, as it is created by the company itself. This can include a wide range of different data, such as roadmaps, white papers, and datasets on employee information.
- Data created through the interaction of companies and customers, this data is believed to hold the most value for companies since it includes potential information about customer needs, trends, causal relationships, and correlations between variables. The processing of this data is a challenge, at least. Data protection regulations such as the General Data Protection Regulation (GDPR) in the European Union prevent companies from freely accessing all their accumulated data for not predestined purposes. While data regulations are a complex topic for others to take a closer look at, it should be noted that it is an important factor companies need to consider if they want to extract value from their data.

While most of the world's data is unorganized and remains unexplored, the ultimate goal when talking about data shifts toward not collecting more and more of it but rather extracting value from already collected data. Data science is what drives customer satisfaction in modern systems. Whether it is about recommending content consumers might like on Netflix, product suggestions on Amazon or more industry-specific applications of data science such as predictive maintenance, data science is often taken for granted. However, the underlying truth is that companies need to acquire a deep understanding of their collected data before they can roll out features their customer will appreciate. This is exactly where data science comes into the picture (Shah 2019). Data science can be described as the application of scientific methods and principles, especially from the area of statistics to data collection, analysis, and reporting. The process of doing data science can be divided into multiple phases:

1. Project initiation and defining the problem statement.
2. Data acquisition, or rather collecting the data needed to achieve a solution to the problem defined in step 1.
3. Data preparation and quality check to ensure the collected data suits the purpose. Data science cannot extract insights from bad and low-quality data, but it definitely can do so if applied correctly to a dataset of sufficient quality.
4. Data modeling, meaning to formulate each step and technique to apply to the data to achieve the goal of the data analysis and executing these steps.
5. Reporting and communication of insights. Just like the following utilization of these insights, this step greatly depends on the results and insights extracted in step 4 and the target audience.

The goals of data science can be summarized in the two points: solving a concrete problem statement and gathering insight on a set of data, although the latter one is more of a means to achieve the first. Using data as a means to solve problem statements is becoming more attractive by the day. As stated before, the amount of data produced and stored is increasing exponentially, therefore creating more opportunities for data science to become the solution to problems. Big Data is often coined as the gold of the twenty-first century (Lukic 2015) and companies that showed an early adoption of this mindset could be observed to be successful today. The most prominent example probably being Amazon, which early on realized, that data science can be utilized to clarify how users interact with the web and how insights generated by data science can be used to inform critical business strategies. Since management decisions require as much high-quality information as possible, data science plays a vital role in providing such information to the management. Besides these strategic uses, data science also has applications in keeping a business operational. Both from a perspective of operating business processes—think predictive maintenance and automated anomaly detection—and operational controlling—think keeping the business competitive. Both these areas can profit majorly from the use of data science. Connecting data science principles with data gathered in ERP systems brings value to the data not only from the perspective of keeping processes operative but also by enabling companies to utilize the full potential of their data. By turning data into knowledge and insight, companies can achieve a deeper understanding of their customers and how their processes operate. These insights can be used to tune products to customer demands, improve processes, and gain valuable information on what factors drive a business.

Using the data that companies naturally generate in their ERP systems simply by operating their day-to-day business can help drive the digital transformation of companies and—as already mentioned—gain insights. Since ERP systems tend to contain a large amount of data about sales, it is only reasonable to assume that valuable insights can be derived from such data. Using the data to answer concrete problem statements such as: *How much material will most likely be needed for the next quarter?* or *Which factors influence the buy-decisions of our customers?* can be answered using classic statistical methods such as time series analysis and regression models. Using the same set of data, companies can analyze financial data and predict major financial events that require action in advance. With the transition to connected assets under the keywords Industry 4.0 and Internet of Things (IoT), there has been an ever-increasing amount of real-time sensor data. This opened the door to a multitude of new services relating to the maintenance and automation of assets, be it automated anomaly detection or predictive maintenance. Achieving useful services regarding this area is easier said than done. Applying data science to these problems not only requires a deep understanding of data science methods but also of the underlying assets and affected machinery. Utilizing natural language processing and computer vision systems, companies can automatically extract the information they need from documents such as invoices. This could be used to streamline the process of invoicing. Similar techniques can be used to classify documents, such as tickets and assign them to a responsible employee automatically. Using chatbots, employees untrained in querying databases can extract information from such data sources by linking the bot to queries of analytical tools. Just like the other examples, this requires a large amount of insight into how users interact with language and documents. Utilizing all the above, data science, in particular high-level reports with drill-down capabilities, can be used to communicate complex matters in a simple way to high-level management. This not only makes it easier for the management to access information but also increases ease of insight and data transparency. While both data science and ERP systems are nothing new, the synergies between them are. For many years, data science has been applied to ERP data to some degree, for example, using regression models to predict revenue, but the scale on which it is happening today is new. Diverging from such classical use cases, data scientists try to find meaningful insights from their data to help their companies. Additionally, the increase of research focusing on applying machine learning algorithms to data science problems in recent years has opened the door to many new solutions to old problems. Especially in the areas of automation and natural language processing, machine learning algorithms play a huge part in enabling systems and machine to act autonomously while communicating easier with humans. Utilizing data science effectively comes with several advantages for businesses. While increasing the return of investment by improving the operational efficiency and reducing (human-caused) errors, it also allows businesses to react faster to required changes in products and services, pricing or availability to stay competitive. Additionally, data science enables companies to work as a unit by enabling the top management to include more relevant information into their executive decision-making process. Failing to leverage the advantages of data science and the improvement of business processes that come with it means a potential decrease in customer satisfaction. Growing customer demands might not be met by a company but by their competitors who did not fail to do so. This, in turn, will lead to a loss in customers and market share. Additionally, not improving on processes might threaten the profitability of a business when compared to its competitors.

Autonomous ERP

The ultimate goal is to provide an autonomous ERP with self-directed business processes and self-diagnostic operations. In order to achieve this objective today's ERP systems must become more intelligent. Typically, intelligence is a quality that humans attribute to themselves and other living beings as the ability to learn, understand, and think logically about things. But what does the term intelligence in context of ERP systems mean? Despite a long history of research and debate, no universal definition of intelligence exists. Scientists have proposed various models for mathematical, linguistic, technical, musical, and emotional intelligence, but none have gained widespread acceptance. But how can ERP systems be made intelligent without knowing what this means? The operationalization method is used to resolve this quandary and make the term intelligence measurable by defining different automation levels, similar to how psychologists define IQ values. In the context of ERP systems, intelligence is not merely a means to an end. Rather, it is about increasing automation toward an autonomous ERP system in order to reduce total cost of ownership (TCO), such as through faster process runtimes or optimized resource consumption. As a result, the following equation holds true: the greater the level of automation of a business process or system, the greater the level of intelligence. ERP systems serve as a centralized management system for an organization's business processes. Understanding the common structure of all those business processes is essential for defining automation levels. As shown in Fig. 3.1a, there are four dimensions to consider for automation in a business process (Sarferaz and Banda 2020). This is an industry standard that has been adapted for use in ERP software. Each dimension's level of automation is rated from 1 (low) to 5 (high). The overall level of automation can be determined by determining the level of automation for each dimension of a given business process or system. As a result, the current and target levels of intelligence can be determined, and an execution plan for making the business process more intelligent can be defined. The process of entering data into ERP systems using devices such as a keyboard, scanner, disk, or voice is known as *data acquisition*. The following characteristics could be used to determine the various levels of automation for data acquisition: (1) Manual entry by user, (2) Manual entry and data integration, (3) Data integration and manual entry (exceptional), (4) Conversational AI and data integration, (5) AI-based data extraction and integration (e.g., PDF document is transformed to structured data and entered by robotic bot).

The process of studying and interpreting data in order to derive meaningful conclusions is known as *information analysis*. The following characteristics could be used to determine the various automation levels for information analysis: (1) Descriptive (what happened), (2) Diagnostic (why it happened), (3) Predictive (what will happen), (4) Prescriptive (what should we do), (5) Cognitive (autonomous self-learning analysis of happenings). The process of selecting a logical choice from the available options while taking into account the consequences is known as *decision-making*. The following characteristics could be used to determine the various levels of automation for decision-making: (1) User makes decisions manually, (2) User consumes system events and changes for decisions, (3) System provides relevant information to the user for making decisions, (4) System actively evaluates and recommends decisions, (5) System autonomously makes decisions that are traceable and auditable. The process of enforcing instructions to achieve a specific goal is known as *action execution*. The following characteristics could be used to determine the various levels of automation for action execution: (1) User performs actions manually, (2) User consumes system events and changes for performing actions, (3) System provides relevant information to the user for performing actions, (4) System actively evaluates and recommends actions, (5) System autonomously performs actions that are traceable and auditable.

To make a business process more intelligent, first the current level of automation based on the described methodology must be determined. This is the foundation from which solution managers can derive the target level based on business requirements. The next question is how to achieve the specified level of automation per dimension. To realize the specified intelligence level for the dedicated dimensions, there is not just one tool, but a number of concepts and technologies. However, as illustrated in Fig. 3.1b, techniques can be classified in order to accomplish different levels: manual, rule-based, and self-learning. Business processes can be carried out manually without the use of automation. To address this, various rule-based techniques can be used to boost automation and intelligence. Examples for

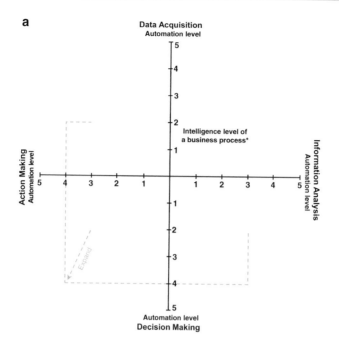

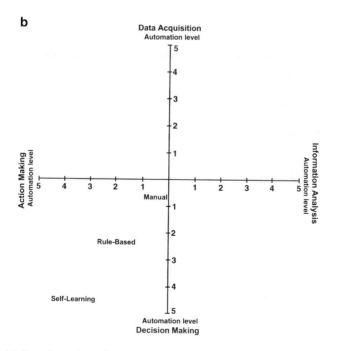

Fig. 3.1 (**a**) Four dimensions of process automation, (**b**) categorization of techniques based on automation level

rule-based technologies are Java code performing input or process validations and displaying error messages with resolution instructions to the user, a workflow for executing individual tasks/decisions moving from one step to the next until a predefined process is complete, an insight-to-action analytics scenario beginning with a key performance indicator (KPI) notifying the user about drifting trends. However, rule-based approaches are no longer sufficient for reaching level 5. They must be expanded to include self-learning techniques. Rather than programming explicit rules, these techniques make sense of raw data and discover hidden insights and relationships by learning from it. Some examples for this category of technology are deep learning for image recognition, conversational AI for natural language processing (NLP), bots to make decisions and perform actions autonomously. To infuse ERP systems with more intelligence, business processes must be moved to levels 4 and 5, targeting an autonomous ERP system. The majority of business processes in ERP systems are currently on those levels so that there is a long journey to targeting the autonomous ERP. Practically an autonomous ERP is most likely never achievable due to technical, legal, and functional limitations. However, already the interim steps—which means evolving individual use case to level 5— are valuable. For example, failure of high-tech equipment is a critical issue for manufacturers. The health of these machines can be predicted by combining sensor data with business information in ERP systems and applying machine models. Maintenance scheduling and logistics planning for spare parts and repair crew management can thus be turned into a proactive business process. A second example is, validating that a product was manufactured exactly according to its specifications and configuration is an important step in final quality assurance and readiness checks for product shipments. Image-recognition algorithms help with this by performing visual product quality checks. As a result, the accuracy and automation level of quality processes in production can be increased, resulting in fewer returns, higher customer satisfaction, and improved profitability. A third example is that as the foundation for ERP business processes, high-quality master data is critical. To ensure data consistency, artificial intelligence can automate the identification and implementation of validation rules. Autocompletion of attribute values based on artificial intelligence while maintaining master data simplifies interaction with end users and saves money by reducing manual activities. This kind of intelligent scenarios can be categorized into the following AI application patterns:

- Matching: Assigns relationships and detects similarities and anomalies in a given dataset, such as reducing the number of duplicates in the system during consolidation as a master data specialist. While manual matching takes a long time for users, intelligent systems can significantly speed up matching decisions by using artificial intelligence methods. To link similar objects, the system can present one or more strategies and their quality. Users only need to approve or reject the suggestions or modify them to meet their specific requirements.
- Recommendation: Makes suggestions for datasets or actions based on the current context, for example, a material requirements planner wants to see potential

solutions for resolving a material shortage issue. Intelligent systems can assist users by recommending relevant content or recommending an action or input that the user may prefer. The most common recommendation types are content, input, and solution recommendation.

- Ranking: Differentiates between relevant and less relevant datasets of the same type in relation to the current context. For example, a purchaser wants to see the top X suppliers for a specific product in the context of a given purchasing request. Ranking makes complex decisions easier for business users by displaying the best options first. Items in a group are ranked by comparing criteria relevant to the user's business context, such as a dollar amount, priority, or score. Two types are distinguished, ranking based on a predefined value and ranking based on a calculated AI score.

- Prediction: Forecasts future data and trends based on patterns found in past data, taking into account all potentially relevant information. A master data manager, for example, wants to estimate the number of change requests the team will need to process in the coming quarter in order to leverage the workload. Intelligent systems based on predictive models significantly reduce the cost of forecasting business outcomes, environmental factors, competitive intelligence, and market conditions for businesses. Predictive models are classified as either metric or nonparametric.

- Categorization: Assigns datasets to predefined groups (classes), for example, a service agent wants to classify the priority of incoming requests (high/medium/low) based on their content in order to improve customer service. It also finds new groups (clusters) in datasets, for example, segmenting customers for appropriate product offerings, targeted marketing, or fraud detection. Categorization is a complex task for which intelligent systems can aid in increasing automation by utilizing self-learning algorithms.

- Conversational AI: Interacts with the system using natural language conversation and enables the hand-free paradigm, for example, a purchaser wants to create a purchase order by talking to the system. The ability to converse with a digital assistant for business processes is an important part of the user experience for an intelligent application. Conversation AI (CAI) technology recognizes common natural language patterns to query for business entities using various parameters, look up a specific business entity by name or id, retrieve the value of a specific business entity's attribute, and create simple new entities, including line items.

ERP systems should provide for each pattern a standardized framework for implementation so that those AI application patterns can be applied as reusable building blocks by development teams for accelerating the implementation. Finally, to outline again, the autonomous ERP is a visionary direction which entirely might never be realizable. However, the interim step by infusing more and more intelligence into business processes is valuable as the degree of automation is increased and TCO reduced. Always there will be a symbiosis between human being and machine where the machine is going to assist the user and augment its capabilities.

Composable ERP

This trend is triggered by two business requirements. On the one hand, companies are faced with the challenge of having to react more quickly and flexibly to changes in the company and its environment in order to remain competitive. This was particularly outlined by the Covid 19 pandemic. But also, the advancing globalization, the associated increase in competitors, and the containment of climate change are forcing companies from a wide range of industries to continuously change. On the other hand, users expect personalized applications tailored to their activities. Solutions with a monolithic architecture, which contain superfluous program functions for the user's activity, overtax the user and lead to a poor user experience. From their everyday usage of smartphone apps, users are accustomed to using modular applications tailored to their needs (Gaughan et al. 2020). Composable enterprises shall meet both of these requirements, meaning they can respond quickly to change and deliver intuitively usable modular applications to their employees. They achieve this through packaged business capabilities (PBCs). These are modular building blocks of applications that are tailored to the roles of employees in companies. From a technical perspective, PCBs can be implemented by using a service-oriented architecture consisting of microservices. PBCs access microservices via application programming interfaces (APIs). PBCs do not always have to access exactly one microservice but can also comprise several microservices (Iakimets 2020). The key question is, what exactly is now the new aspect regarding composable ERP? The requirement for providing customers the ability to flexibly adapt business processes and incrementally implement them is as old as the first ERP systems. The only new aspects in this context is the controverse debate whether a monolithic or microservice architecture is better appropriated for resolving this requirement. To conclude on this, first both approaches must be discussed. Figure 3.2 depicts the basic architecture of monolithic- and microservice-oriented applications. In *monolithic applications* the database schema is shared by all modules. Table visibility is controlled by access grants between packages. When inserting or updating data from multiple modules, a single database transaction is used to ensure overall data and process consistency. Modules communicate by calling local functions. In most cases, a function call is served synchronously in the same process context. Furthermore, modules can operate on the same data (e.g., via accessing the same database tables). Upgrading a single component usually necessitates upgrading the entire system. Modules are made up of several packages that are then bundled together to form

Fig. 3.2 (**a**) Monolithic application, (**b**) microservice application

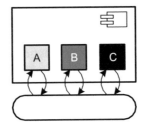 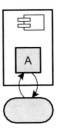 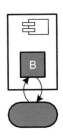

larger software components. Software components have specific version requirements in relation to the other software components on which they rely.

Microservices applications build the foundation for cloud native approach. Although microservices can share the same physical database/storage, they use separate logical schemas, resulting in decentralized data management. This also means that database transactions cannot be used for service coordination and communication. The interaction among microservices is based on REST APIs. Usually, there is no sophisticated middleware or mediator component involved, nor is there any business functionality (e.g., data conversion or key mapping). This also implies that services that are linked together must use the same message interface definition. A microservices-based solution, ideally, provides software vendors (particularly in the cloud) and their customers with a high degree of flexibility in configuring the system, such as supporting the use of only selected services or replacing a service implementation without disruption. In some cases, customers are willing to use their own implementation of a service. When traditional customizing is insufficient to provide the required flexibility, service toolboxes make a lot of sense. Customers must have a high degree of freedom in defining the user experience or supporting new sales channels in this case. However, for this to work, the interfaces and behavior of the respective services must be stable, regardless of how they are implemented. For highly standardized domains where regulations limit flexibility, providing configuration options via module-level customization can be simpler and more appropriate. Also, it is less likely that the customer will provide their own implementation for complex functionality.

While it is already proven that ERP software can be implemented based on the monolithic approach, still it is an open question whether microservice architecture is sufficient for this task. The microservices concept is geared toward high scalability on specific functionality. As a result, this architecture pattern's services are decoupled, independent, and small in size. Microservices provide the elasticity required for a load-adaptive and cost-effective operations model in cloud applications with highly fluctuating and partially unpredictable usage profiles. Scalability may be less of an issue for ERP systems that are not used for external-facing scenarios, such as web-shops. Scalability is more important for the entire application system than for isolated functionality when these systems serve complex and highly interdependent business processes. Thus, while the microservices-based scalability is definitely required for applications like Netflix, Spotify, Amazon Shopping-App, or Google Search, this is usually not the case for ERP systems. The usage patterns in ERP systems are deterministic and foreseeable. The hardware requirement for a particular ERP installation is known in advance. Even in very large ERP deployments the majority of the transactions are used by two to three persons, often not in parallel. Specific applications with high need of CPU-time, memory, and storage are known also in advance and mitigated accordingly, for example, by optimizing the underlying implementation or scaling the application out as a side car. Almost every business application requires data and process consistency in terms of atomicity, consistency, isolation, and durability (ACID). ACID transactions are an appropriate and proven method for ensuring this, so application developers have little to worry about. In essence, they only need to decide which operations should be covered by a single transaction. Because different microservices use different logical databases, a database transaction cannot span operations triggered by different services. When overall consistency is dependent on data managed by separate microservices, application developers must ensure data integrity in other ways. Typically, such systems can only guarantee eventual consistency, because updates from one microservice are only processed by another microservice managing dependent data after a certain amount of time. However, eventual consistency is appropriate for some application domains (e.g., streaming applications as Netflix, Spotify) but typically not for ERP systems. For example, finance transactions in ERP systems by legal obligations cannot be founded on eventual consistency. Furthermore, a microservice approach necessitates a thorough understanding of the business domain in order to define the appropriate service cuts for microservices. From the standpoint of application architecture, this is a challenge. An erogenous cut of services, in contrast to tightly integrated modules, results in the reimplementation of several services—and, more than likely, incompatible APIs. Even if data can be primarily managed locally by services for transactional scenarios, analytics frequently necessitates a holistic view in which data from various services is combined. All data required for analytics should reside in a single database schema in order to achieve good performance and support flexible drill-down into various aspects and levels of content. A common approach for microservices-based systems is to replicate service-local data into a single central schema for reporting. Replication is a common strategy for strategic reporting, where actuality is less important than access to historical data. However, replication is problematic in the case of operational reporting, which should ideally be based on the most recent application data. Not only does redundant information clutter the system, but permissions must be defined for the replicated data as well. Additionally, the information will be slightly outdated due to the replication delay. This excludes, for example, insight-to-action scenarios in which the user must identify issues to follow up on based on analytical data and immediately resolve them using a transactional application. Even minor differences between analytical and service-local (transactional) data can be extremely inconvenient if users frequently encounter false-positive issues that another user has already resolved. Analytics is just one example for cross-topics in context of ERP systems which are more complex to resolve with microservices. Extensibility, artificial intelligence, search, semantic data layer, localization, verticalization, legal compliance, lifecycle management, configuration, and implementation are additional cross-topics which are vital for an ERP system but hard to realize with microservices. Data privacy as an instance requires to delete and block personal data immediately when there is no purpose. Already in a monolithic system with one database this is very sophisticated to implement, in a microservice-oriented one the implementation becomes an even bigger challenge due to the distributed logical databases. Thousands of background jobs must be performed in order to determine end of purpose concerning personal data so that the scalability advantages of microservices might be depleted. Lifecycle management as a second example becomes more complex, for example, versioning dependencies or upgrades of thousands of microservices must be taken into account and reliably orchestrated. Extensibility as a third example for enterprise readiness requires more sophisticated concepts for microservices. Field extensibility as instance is simple to resolve with monolithic systems due to central persistency and uniform database schema. The storage of microservices is independent of each other. Thus, if a customer enhances for example the sales order object with additional fields, those must be propagated consistently and simultaneously to all related microservices persistency which is very challenging and hard to solve.

In summary, microservices-based architecture suites well for loosely coupled and heavy scalable applications, while monolithic approach targets tightly coupled and high consistent applications. The business processes covered by ERP systems are tremendously interdependent and therefore tightly coupled, for example idea-to-market, source-to-pay, plan-to-fulfill, lead-to-cash, recruit-to-retire, or acquire-to-decommission. Already an update on a status field (e.g., sales order status) has implications on numerous processes (e.g., material resources planning run, procure to receipt job). Customers expect that such kind of interplay among the business processes is performed in real time with guaranteed data consistency. The same is true also for the mentioned cross-topics (e.g., legal compliance, lifecycle management) which are crucial for ERP systems in terms of enterprise-readiness. Thus, the monolithic architecture very well resolves these requirements. However, the conclusion is to combine both approaches. The implementation of ERP core processes can apply the monolithic approach while specific decoupled applications with high performance demand can be based on microservices to leverage the scalability benefits. SAP S/4HANA for example follows this complementary approach and implements deep-learning use cases with the need of scalability based on microservices, docker, and Kubernetes technology. Finally, for the requirement described in the beginning of this section concerning the adaptability of business processes and their incremental implementation, not monolithic or microservice debate is relevant but to provide the necessary product qualities. Monolithic ERP systems can be incrementally implemented based on business scoping and the underlying configuration infrastructure. Thus, business processes can be implemented and consumed stepwise along with customers needs. SAP S/4HANA for example provides various in-app and side-by-side extensibility techniques and frameworks in order to enhance the business process from database level to user interfaces. Furthermore, SAP S/4HANA offers numerous configuration concepts, tools, and content so that customers can adopt the business processes to their industry- and regional-specific requirements including the ability of incremental implementation.

Industry 4.0

Until recently, supply chains were primarily assessed using efficiency metrics. Today, new trends are emerging that pose complex challenges and place supply chain and manufacturing at the heart of not only business success but also a company's differentiation strategy. Manufacturing companies face a number of challenges. In volatile markets, they must produce smarter products while maintaining high quality. Customers expect customized products down to lot size 1. Product lifecycles are becoming increasingly short. Staying competitive necessitates a faster time to market. The business model shifts from selling products to providing solutions. Many businesses see Industry 4.0 as a strategic priority for transforming these challenges into opportunities. Industry 4.0, also known as the Industrial Internet of Things (IIoT), is concerned with industrial transformation through the use of new digital technology that allows for the collection and analysis of data across machines and business systems, enabling faster, more flexible, and more efficient processes to produce higher-quality, individualized goods at a lower cost. This transformation will boost resource productivity and efficiency, increase agility and responsiveness, accelerate time to market, and allow for customization to meet customer needs. Industry 4.0, in more specific terms, refers to the intelligent networking of machines and processes for industry through the use of information and communication technology. The digitalization of the industrial production environment in factories, plants, and warehouses is being driven by technological innovations that emerged in the aftermath of the Internet and cloud revolution: IoT-connected devices; machine-to-machine communication; distributed computing; new edge and cloud technologies such as containers, microservices, and event-driven architecture; times series and BPM. Most large corporations and many mid-sized businesses have tested use cases to determine the business value of Industry 4.0. According to a recent McKinsey global survey (McKinsey & Company 2019) of discrete manufacturing customers, 68% recognize the strategic priority. While 41% are still piloting, 29% have begun to deploy at scale, with significant purchase decisions visible in the market. Companies that successfully implement Industry 4.0 at scale focus on business value rather than technology, mobilize and train their workforce on new technologies, and transition to an integrated IT infrastructure and automation technology stack. And they run the company through data-driven processes rather than transactional ones. Creating value from Industry 4.0 necessitates a sector-specific approach, as business objectives and challenges differ by industry and even by company. There is no one-size-fits-all approach to Industry 4.0. Based on the average lot size and the number of variants per factory, three distinct clusters can be identified for discrete manufacturing. *Engineer-to-order* production models, which are common in industries such as shipbuilding, high-end machinery, and aerospace, strive for high efficiency in manufacturing down to lot size 1. *Mass-customized* production, which is common in automobiles, agricultural equipment, and industrial components, aims to maintain high-sequence throughput and consistent quality in the face of increased product variances. In *high-volume* production, such as consumer electronics, commercial equipment, or semi-conductor chips, full automation (lights-out production) drives increased productivity, whereas changing product mixes necessitate greater flexibility or production line adaptation. In process manufacturing, lot size is converted to batch size, and variants per factory are the number of different formulas or recipes per plant. Multiproduct facility utilization becomes critical for *order-based* specialty production. Tailoring is now possible thanks to new technologies. Adapting products to individual needs, however, necessitates efficient use of manufacturing equipment. High throughput objectives are increasingly being combined with compliance, regulation, and traceability requirements in *mass-production, batch-oriented* industries such as fine chemicals, paper, metals, construction materials, food, or pharma. Asset efficiency of continuous flow production on a global scale drives further optimization for *commodities* such as petrochemicals, bulk chemicals, and ore in mining. The number of IoT endpoints worldwide grew by approximately 20% annually, from 3.96 billion in 2018 to 4.81 billion in 2019 (Gartner 2019). IoT endpoints are computing devices that are often microcontroller-based and perform a specific task or have specific functionality as a part of a process or a product. Many of these endpoints provide data which is often of great value to organizations because it can be used to make better decisions and automate processes. The value of this data only comes in combination with an ERP system designed to process the data. The role of ERP systems here is to act as a data hub for passing on IoT data to other systems. Additionally, the ERP system takes on the role of an interpreter and adds semantic information to make this data interpretable. The role of the ERP system is particularly central for industrial manufacturing companies that optimize their production processes through the IoT. Ideally, the IoT data is so extensive and the ERP system so well adapted that the ERP system is the digital shadow of the value chain. That means it maintains a digital image of the value chain. The merit of an ERP system that is a digital shadow is the optimal utilization of resources (Bitkom-Arbeitskreis Enterprise Resource Planning 2016). The key insight is that while the Industrial Internet of Things (IIoT) drives ERP innovation, a smart factory is only created by the combination of IIoT with other technologies inside ERP systems. IoT endpoints provide the data, but these can only be optimally used when they are processed in the ERP system with the support of data science methods and algorithms. Parts of the evaluated data remain in the ERP system and are used there, for example, by managers to make decisions. Another part of the data is fed back to IoT endpoints, for example to control machines. In this way, endpoints can perform tasks controlled via the Internet. This opens completely new possibilities in the area of ERP: Many business processes can be carried out directly by the interaction of IoT endpoints and the ERP system, and machines are thus increasingly replacing humans as the interface to the ERP system. Another part of the data is given to augmented reality and virtual reality glasses. These can be used to help employees perform tasks that cannot be fully automated yet. For example, service incidents, recognized through data from sensors on a machine, can be reported to technicians via their augmented reality glasses. The technicians can be navigated directly to the machine through the augmented reality glasses. Another innovation in the context of Industry 4.0 are digital twins. These are computer models that represent the behavior of physical assets in real time. To do this, they consume data from the ERP system, but also return important information to the ERP system. Applying digital twins based on ERP systems adds enormous value because operating manuals, diagrams, service instructions and records, performance records, and failure modes can be maintained and updated in near-real time across the

Fig. 3.3 Industry 4.0 themes

network, reducing manual effort and errors. Companies can build capabilities on this data to predict future states based on historical data, change behavior or performance by adjusting variables, and simulate possible outcomes by adjusting several variables to determine the best result before instructing the physical system. As shown in Fig. 3.3 four themes are driving Industry 4.0, each of which adds distinct value to the business. Intelligent products are designed and configured to precisely meet the needs of their customers. Intelligent assets are dynamically maintained and linked to all processes. Intelligent factories use data and intelligence to operate autonomously and deliver customized products at scale. People who are empowered have all of the tools and information they need to do their best work.

SAP S/4HANA Manufacturing for production engineering and operations as instance supports the intelligent product theme. SAP S/4HANA Extended Warehouse Management and SAP S/4HANA Quality Management for example facilitate the intelligent factory theme. SAP S/4HANA Asset Management as instance helps with the intelligent asset theme. With SAP S/4HANA Environment Health Safety for illustration enables empowered people theme. The promise, benefits, and value of the IoT have been extensively documented, but it also brings with it a slew of concerns about IoT security. It is unsurprising that the majority of IoT privacy and security failures occur in the consumer space. The industrial operator can put pressure on vendors and make educated decisions about how to implement security best practices. Environmental factors and physical constraints must also be considered depending on where the connected devices are deployed. Given the connectivity of equipment to cloud systems, all communication and access must be properly secured using end-to-end encryption. Modern security practices use a risk-based approach that takes into account both the ease of an attack and the impact if one occurs—providing a strong indicator of how much security you'll require. The promise of standards in smart manufacturing is critical in a fragmented market. It is difficult to transition existing machines and assets into the age of networked production. The success of Industry 4.0 is dependent on open standards. They enable lower integration costs, faster adoption, and scale, and they are the only way to enable seamless interoperability between multiple vendors. While technical lower-level standards are widely used in factories today, most providers have yet to implement higher-level standards that describe semantics, data models, data management principles, and part classification rules. Historically, the ecosystem supplying factory, plant, and warehouse owners and operators has been highly fragmented, with multiple players playing multiple roles at multiple levels within the factory.

Advancing Industry 4.0 necessitates close collaboration among ecosystem players. Nobody can do it alone, given the current market fragmentation, complexity of the shop floor, and digitalization expectations. SAP orchestrates with SAP S/4HANA a strong ecosystem with partners with complementary strengths and delivers Industry 4.0-relevant solutions to the owners and operators of manufacturing sites, plants, and factories in collaboration with partners.

Two-Tier ERP

Building a comprehensive enterprise software strategy capable of serving a large global enterprise has always necessitated some degree of compromise. The software and technology required to run headquarters operations have not always been the best choice for running subsidiaries and other smaller operating units within the enterprise. In many cases, software that can run headquarters was deemed too robust and expensive to be effective in a subsidiary operation, and the autonomy granted to many subsidiaries meant that it was easier to let these entities make their own choices rather than impose a solution that could be deemed overreaching, impractical, or both. As a result, many businesses adopted a two-tier ERP strategy that supported a standard enterprise system from one vendor in the headquarters and a multiple-choice ERP strategy for subsidiaries, effectively creating a multivendor, two-tier environment as shown in Fig. 3.4a. A large number of mid-market ERP vendors stepped up to the plate and created largely effective products that could be easily implemented in subsidiaries. These systems could provide some connectivity back to the headquarters, primarily for the purposes of consolidating financial, inventory, and other basic operational data across the enterprise. That model served well for many years, but its inherent limitations are beginning to emerge as the global business world shifts at an unprecedented rate to all-digital, real-time operations. Two-tier architectures that rely on integrating different vendor systems have become barriers to innovation, cost-containment, and operational efficiency, rather than a means of replicating the structural flexibility of the global enterprise. This has become increasingly true as the nature of subsidiary operations has evolved to necessitate higher levels of functionality and support for innovation. This is very much the status quo in the enterprise software industry, and until recently, it was a fact of life that businesses had to accept. However, the status quo is being challenged in the SAP enterprise ecosystem, and companies that run SAP in their headquarters now have the opportunity to reconsider whether running a non-SAP ERP system in their subsidiaries is the best strategic choice. This new opportunity is enabled by SAP S/4HANA's ongoing evolution, which is now available both on-premise and in the cloud, allowing organizations to leverage a consistent code line and data structure extending from a fully functional headquarters system running SAP S/4HANA on-premise to a flexible and adaptive subsidiary solution, also based on SAP S/4HANA, running in the public cloud. With the availability of SAP's PaaS solution, SAP Business Technology Platform extends this model even further by providing a platform for additional functionality not found in SAP S/4HANA, such

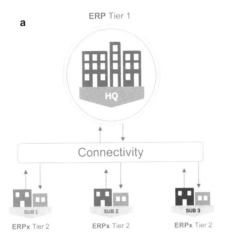

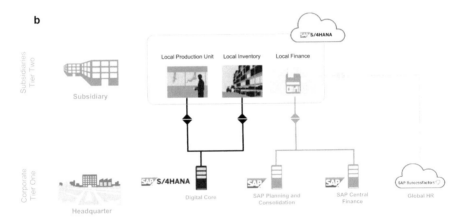

Fig. 3.4 (**a**) Two-tier ERP, (**b**) SAP S/4HANA Cloud and on-premise for headquarter-subsidiary scenario

as direct connectivity to other SAP cloud assets such as SAP Ariba, SuccessFactors, Hybris, and Concur, as well as a platform for developing net-new functionality. The ability to use the same product family—with its shared data structures, APIs, and extensibility platform—in a two-tier deployment allows for a better way to support a high level of operational integration between headquarters and subsidiary operations without sacrificing the autonomy and local requirements that many subsidiaries value. Indeed, the two-tier ERP opportunity will unleash a level of integration and business orchestration between headquarters and subsidiary operations that far exceeds what has traditionally been considered.

Figure 3.4b shows an example for two-tier ERP where the manufacturing plants run their local finance and consolidate back to the headquarter, whereas the manufacturing, inventory process runs locally only. This approach would equally apply for Warehouse management or Retail processes. Thus, hybrid scenarios in which enterprises run parts of their functionality in the cloud and other parts on-premise must be supported by ERP solutions. Hybrid deployments will be the integration reality for many ERP implementations for many years to come, providing enterprises with the flexibility to approach both digitalization and cloud migration with public, private, and hybrid approaches. Traditional constraints in document flows and workflows are resolved across those application areas to make each transaction atomic within an application area. Workflows in the digital age must be designed around the user's role and span end-to-end processes across solution components. This enables the rapid process changes required in the digital era. In case of public cloud ERP, a third-party cloud service provider owns and operates the system including the underlying hardware and software which are delivered over the Internet. In a public cloud, customers share the same hardware, storage, and network devices as other cloud tenants. A private cloud ERP is a collection of cloud hardware and software resources that are used solely by one organization. The private cloud can be physically located at customer's on-site datacenter or hosted by a third-party service provider. In a private cloud, however, the services and infrastructure are always maintained on a private network, and the hardware and software are solely dedicated to the customers organization. On-premise ERP system is deployed on a company's server, is protected by an internal firewall, and operated by the customer. Crucial for enabling two-tier ERP is semantical compatibility between the involved private, public, and on-premise ERP systems. This starts with a homogeneous data model which makes business semantics available for external use, analytics, search, and key user extensibility. Semantic compatibility applies also to the business processes concerning the different deployment options. This can be optimally achieved by having the same code line as for example SAP ERP and SAP S/4HANA (public, private, and on-premise edition) do. A subsidiary can run a separate instance of the cloud assets or connect to an enterprise-wide instance, depending on the business model. Furthermore, both the headquarters and subsidiaries can add new functionality as needed, providing a single-vendor option for integrating key business processes in areas such as finance, human resources, talent management, contingent labor, time and expense billing, customer interaction, and procurement. Two-tier and multitier offerings are an important refinement to the notion that local subsidiaries must be given the option of running whichever ERP system is realistic in their local setting, or that a low-cost ERP system from a third-party vendor is sufficient to meet the needs of a subsidiary operating in today's global economy. Rather, the strategic choice that really matters at this point in the evolution of business and technology is about changing, adapting, or implementing new business processes enabled in software—whether they are enterprise-wide processes or those specific to a local or micro-vertical need—without requiring extensive customization that would break the cloud model. This is a far cry from the argument that local autonomy trumps interconnectivity and synchronization of business processes with headquarters. This new definition of choice necessitates that local subsidiaries capitalize on the new opportunities available in the cloud—while using the same single-vendor platform and software to ensure business continuity across the entire enterprise. The ability to leverage processes, data, and analytics across the enterprise without having to maintain the interoperability of subsystems that would be required to accommodate the complexity inherent in a multivendor n-tier system defines this continuity. SAP S/4HANA is poised to change the stakes in two-tier and n-tier enterprise software systems by making this functionality available from a single vendor's code base, data model, and platform. This new model of two-tier functionality brings with it a slew of new capabilities. The knowledge gained from implementing in one tier can be used to accelerate implementation in another. Attributes established in one tier, such as master data, enterprise wide KPIs, and business processes, can be easily transferred to the other. Indeed, once the configuration of a specific tier has been finalized, it can be used as a template to quickly bring on other subsidiaries. The semantic compatibility of SAP ERP and SAP S/4HANA data and process models, as well as SAP S/4HANA on-premise and cloud deployments, enables enterprises to transition in a reasonable timeframe. Many of SAP ERP's extension points remain available with this compatibility paradigm, reducing the adoption effort for custom coding when migrating to SAP S/4HANA.

Conclusion

The world of ERP is changing rapidly due to technological progress and changing business requirements. ERP systems will become more modularized. From the business perspective, ERP systems will cover increasingly more specific industry and scenario-based applications. When it comes to implementation, there is a need to engage early across all levels and offer more sustainable and better-targeted training in the future. The market maturities of various innovative technologies like the blockchain, the Internet of Things, and virtual and augmented reality are driving some other trends. Industry 4.0 enables factories and businesses to become smarter. Due to the increasing number of cyberattacks and stricter privacy regulations, ERP systems must become more secure across all levels from the architecture to the users. Not only the characteristics of an ERP system itself but also the process of its implementation determines the success that a company derives from the ERP system. Therefore, and due to frequent budget overruns, time overruns, and implementation failures, companies will also strive for improvements of the implementation. Implementation here refers to the entire process from the decision to deploy, replace, or upgrade an ERP system to the point where the organization is using the system.

Part II

Functional View

This part deals with the functional scope of SAP S/4HANA. All enterprises run the business processes, develop products and services, generate demand, fulfill demand, and plan and manage the enterprise. Those business processes are described and mapped to the solution capabilities of SAP S/4HANA. The application features and architecture are elaborated along the SAP S/4HANA modules for sales and marketing, finance, manufacturing, supply chain, service, research and development/engineering, sourcing and procurement, asset management, and human resources. Main master data entities and industry verticalizations are also covered.

SAP S/4HANA is rich in functionality and covers the entire business processes of enterprises as illustrated in the next figure (Fig. 1).

Idea to Market supports the ideation, requirement analysis, and design of products and services. The outcome is used in the context of *Source to Pay* to contract suppliers, to procure the necessary materials and services, and to pay the corresponding invoices. *Plan to Fulfill* covers receipt and inspection of goods, manufacturing products respectively provisioning services. Marketing activities for generating leads, transferring opportunities to quotes and orders are ensured with *Lead to Cash*. In addition to those core processes corresponding supportive processes are necessary to serve an enterprise. *Recure to Retire* manages the complete lifecycle of employees starting with recruiting and onboarding, following with developing and rewarding, to retirement. *Acquire to Decommission* enables planning, acquisition, onboarding, operating, and offboarding of assets like manufacturing machines. Companies must manage risks and compliance, identity and access, cybersecurity and data privacy, IT infrastructure, trade, and tax regulations. Those are ensured by the supporting process *Governance*. *Finance* covers invoice to pay and cash, managing treasury and real states.

The described core and supporting processes are implemented based on application modules in SAP S/4HANA as depicted in the next figure. The application architecture founds on different software layers. As database system SAP HANA is used to store configuration, transactional, and master data. The semantic layer *Virtual Data Model* is provided for accessing the application data in a unified and simplified manner. The software modules on the application server provide reusable

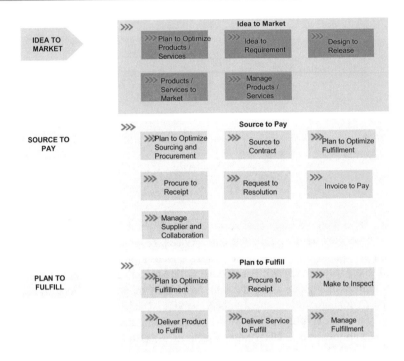

Fig. 1 The SAP S/4HANA business processes

functionality to realize the business processes. There is not a bijective mapping between the application modules and the core/supporting processes. Usually features of multiple software modules are required to realize one core/supporting process. In addition, extension components are used for the implementation as *SAP Ariba*, *SAP Fieldglass*, *SAP Integrated Business Planning*, *SAP Concur*, and *SAP SuccessFactors*. *R&D and Engineering* implements major parts of the core process *Idea to Market*. The software components *Procurement*, *Supply Chain*, and *Manufacturing* cover the core processes *Source to Pay* and *Plan to Fulfill*. The core process *Lead to Cash* is covered principally with *Sales* and *Services*. *Recruit to Retire* is managed with software modules *Human Capital Management* and *SAP Concur*. *Acquire to Decommission* is primarily realized with *Asset Management*. The supporting process *Finance* is mainly handled with the component *Finance*. For *Governance* various technical features of the SAP S/4HANA platform are used, for example, SAP Identity & Access Management, SAP Information Lifecycle Management, SAP Process Control, or SAP Risk Management.

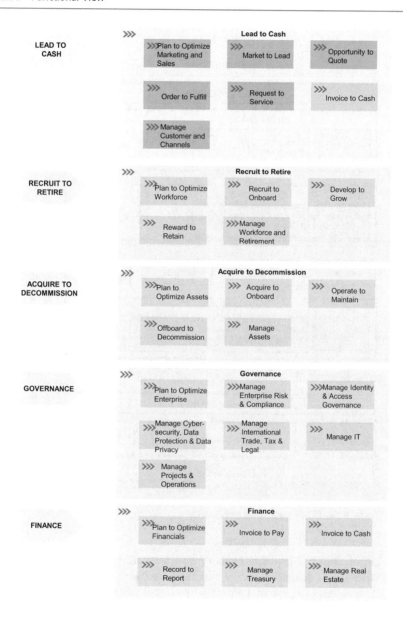

Fig. 1 (continued)

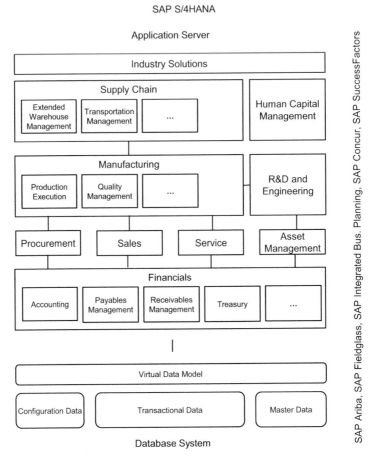

Fig. 2 The SAP S/4HANA application architecture

On top of the core modules *Industry Solutions* are provided. Thus, the core functionality is enhanced with industry-specific features for around 25 verticalizations. Covered are industries like Retail and Fashion, Banking, Insurance, Oil and Gas, Utilities, Waste and Recycling, Automotive, Public Sector, Defense, or Professional Services (Fig. 2).

Functional Departments and Enterprise Domains

4

This chapter deals with the functional departments of the enterprise domains: product and services, customer, supply, and corporate. The basic organization structure of enterprises and how this is managed by SAP S/4HANA are explained. Firstly, several significant terminologies such as the value chain, functional departments, domains and processes are explained. In accordance with that, the technical term organizational form is defined and some organizational forms such as the divisional organization or the line organization are expounded.

Business Requirement

The Value Chain and Domains

The value chain describes the total amount of processes of an enterprise. The value chain can be used for a first analysis on how to identify and create strategic competitive advantages. In the context of the value chain all interrelated activities for providing products or services are considered as components in a complex chain. Each component of the value chain causes costs and contributes to the value of the final product. As a consequence, it is necessary to analyze each component of the chain. The activities of a company are divided into two categories, the primary activities and the support activities. The primary activities deliver an immediate value-adding contribution for generating a product or a service. The support activities contribute to efficiency and effectiveness of the primary activities. The primary activities comprise inbound logistics, manufacturing, outbound logistics, marketing, sales and service, whereas the support activities include procurement, technological development, human resources management, and enterprise infrastructure. The value chain is divided into four different enterprise domains: the customer domain, the supply domain, the corporate domain, and the products and services domain which are depicted in Fig. 4.1.

© The Author(s), under exclusive license to Springer Nature Switzerland AG 2022
S. Sarferaz, *Compendium on Enterprise Resource Planning*,
https://doi.org/10.1007/978-3-030-93856-7_4

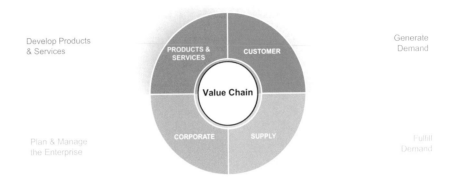

Fig. 4.1 Enterprise domains

The functional departments aligned to the products and services domain are responsible for developing products and services. In contrast, the functional departments aligned to the customer domain are relevant for generating demand. The functional departments being part of the corporate domain are responsible for planning and managing the enterprise and the responsibility of the departments aligned to the supply domain is fulfilling the demand of the customers.

Functional Departments and Processes

This section explains the functional departments and the corresponding processes that are assigned to the enterprise domains. The functional departments aligned to the corporate domain comprise finance, indirect procurement, asset management, human resources, corporate strategy, and corporate operations. The finance department is in charge of accounting, annual financial statements, treasury management as well as risk and compliance management. The department being called indirect procurement has the objective to reduce the product costs by large lot sized and fix demand planning. The department human resources focuses on choosing, hiring, and motivating employees and is responsible for training courses and compensations. The departments in the customer domain include marketing, sales, customer service, and omnichannel commerce. The marketing department is responsible for market research, advertising, public relations, trade shows, corporate identity, product flyers, and other activities leading to a higher recognition of the enterprise by its customers. The objective of marketing is to strengthen the brand and market share. The sales department is competent for the new customer acquisition, the process from an inquiry to the sales success, defining a sales strategy to convince the customers of the corporate products and the customer relationship management. The functional departments aligned to the supply domain contain supply chain

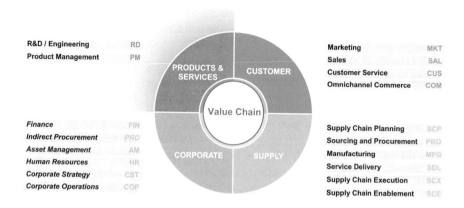

Fig. 4.2 Functional departments assigned to enterprise domains

planning, sourcing and procurement, manufacturing, service delivery, supply chain execution, and supply chain enablement. The manufacturing department comprises the business processes production planning and production execution. The business process production planning itself contains sub business processes such as bill of material, production requests, production orders, production schedule or production inventory. The business process production execution includes sub-business processes as well such as transferred material to production floor, machine usage or returned material to warehouse. The supply chain planning as one of the two main functions of supply chain management comprises demand planning, procurement planning, production planning, and distribution planning. The other main function of supply chain management being called supply chain execution refers to order fulfillment varying from transport processing and production processing to warehouse management. The products and services domain comprises the departments product management and research and development. The product management has the objective to optimize the product portfolio by introducing new products and optimize the assortment, whereas research and development is responsible for optimizing products by product tests and product changes. Figure 4.2 illustrates the assignment of functional departments to enterprise domains.

Organizational Forms

There are numerous external as well as internal requirements concerning organizational forms of enterprises which have to be fulfilled. The external prerequisites comprise a market and competition orientation, flexibility, and innovative capability. The internal requirements contain efficiency concerning leadership processes, service processes, human resources, and material resources. In the context of organizational forms, it can be differentiated regarding the formal organization of an enterprise between the organizational structure and the process organization.

Organizational Structure

The organizational structure portrays the static, hierarchical structure of an enterprise and arises by revolving the total creation of outputs, such as products or services, into single subtasks. Moreover, the organizational structure specifies task areas and the creation of positions. A position is the smallest organizational unit of an enterprise and executes multiple subtasks forming a certain task complex. Additionally, it summarizes positions into greater units, such as divisions or functional departments. The organizational structure is depicted in an organizational chart. The organizational structure is classified into one-dimensional and multidimensional forms. In the classical organizational chart, the upper level illustrates the management board, whereas the lowest level indicates the operational units. Besides, it is possible to establish staff positions in each of these organizational forms to relieve corporate management. Instances for one-dimensional organizational structures are the functional and divisional organization, whereas the matrix organization is assigned to the multidimensional organizational structures. These organizational forms are expounded in the subsequent sections.

Functional Organization

The way of contracts, instructions, and notifications is not determined by instance ways, but rather determined by the way of the concerning tasks in the functional organization. The functional organization depicts the initial form of an industrial enterprise. It was found especially in seller markets and still is widely spread in enterprises with a low product diversification. The decision for the functional organization is often justified in the growth of an enterprise, so that only one management level is not sufficient anymore. As a consequence, in smaller businesses in the level below the corporate management a technical and a commercial functional department with a clearly differentiated scope of responsibility arises. In case of further growth of the enterprise, further hierarchical levels are inserted, and the functional structure is retained in the third and the underneath levels. There are several conditions for the success of this organizational form. For instance, one condition is that the functions concurrently are the core competencies of the enterprise. Besides, there are no big differences between the customer segments. Additionally, the sales markets exhibit small disparities such as countries, languages, and cultural aspects. Moreover, the products are largely homogenous. The functional organization has several advantages, for example, clear functional responsibilities, the simple control enabled by the closed functional departments, and the easier recruitment due to the functional alignment of numerous skilled occupations. The drawbacks of this organizational form include a missing complete overview about the operations of the functional instances in many cases, power struggles, a missing profit orientation, restricted career opportunities, and a high need for communication

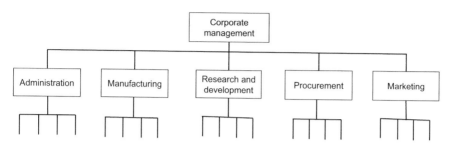

Fig. 4.3 Functional organization

and coordination. The following illustration shows a functional organization with the administration, marketing, research and development, procurement, and marketing as functions in the second level (Fig. 4.3):

Divisional Organization

The divisional organization forms relative autonomous departments which are also called business units, divisions, and lines of business. These divisions are set up in particular by products, product categories, markets, problem areas, or geographical considerations. It is also possible to form the divisions based on customers. The prerequisite therefore is distinguishability between customer segments, such as business customers and private customers. The managers of the divisions lead the businesses in their own responsibility. That is why the divisions take the responsibility for their area measured by their profit. As a result, the divisions are also denoted as profit centers. The created services between the divisions are exchanged by transfer prices. It is also possible to configure the divisions as cost centers or investment centers depending on the flexibility in decision-making. Divisions regarded as cost centers only have decision-making authority concerning the predefined cost budget, whereas the managers of investment centers determine the appropriation of profits in the context of reinventive measures. The lines of business contain the most significant functions of an economically independent unit, including for example sales, production, and funding. This means, that they are subdivided into functional areas again. It is possible to construct the divisional organization as a single line system or as the line-and-staff organization. The prerequisites for the success of the divisional organization are a sufficient size of the enterprise and a sufficient heterogeneity of the product segments. Besides it is necessary that the product divisions reckon as the core competencies of the enterprise and the selling markets of the divisions have to be varying, so that they don't have to compete with each other. On the one hand, the benefits of a divisional organization vary from the possibility of the holistic delegation of tasks and responsibilities and a better and faster decision-making within the divisions to the opportunity to react flexible on changes regarding the environment. On the other hand, the drawbacks comprise the risk of short-term profit and rentability focus, the possibility of a suboptimal resource allocation, and the necessity of central functions concerning the overlapping coordination of the divisions. The following figure indicates an instance for a divisional

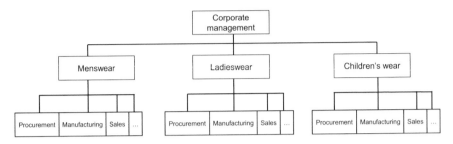

Fig. 4.4 Divisional organization

organization with the product divisions: menswear, ladieswear, and children's wear in the second hierarchical level (Fig. 4.4).

Matrix Organization

In contrary to the functional and divisional organization, the matrix organization belongs to the multidimensional organizational forms which means that in the matrix organization the organizational entities in the second hierarchical level are formed with concurrent application of two design dimensions. Therefore, the matrix organization is a multidimensional multiline organization. It is typical to usually form the matrix sites horizontal by functions and vertical by object-orientation, whereby however the application of other design patterns is possible. The matrix sites are directly subordinated to the corporate management and have the authority to issue directives toward the interfaces of the matrix. The matrix interfaces are responsible for the actual task execution as organizational units. The matrix interfaces can be management units to which other organizational units are assigned to or execution units. To each matrix interface there are two superior matrix units. As a consequence, this leads to competence conflicts which is why an equal coordination is targeted. The matrix interfaces don't have to consist of organizational units. It is possible that these matrix interfaces involve problem areas that must be solved together. The benefits of the matrix organization vary from short communication paths and a flexible adjustment of the organization to requirements concerning the market and the competition to a diverse range of opportunities regarding the human resources development. The drawbacks include the risk of too many trade-offs, the necessity of high information processing capacity, and a high need for qualified executives. The matrix organization is depicted in Fig. 4.5.

Process Organization

The process organization structures the enterprise in comparison to the organizational structure from a different perspective. The process organization considers the dynamic, time logical processes of an enterprise. The outputs of enterprises are generated in processes. As a result of this it is necessary to design the processes of an

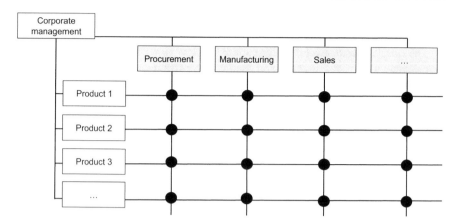

Fig. 4.5 Matrix organization

enterprise. Suitable methods for modeling processes are event-driven process chains or the business process model and notation.

Solution Capability

Organizational forms and structures are technically implemented with SAP S/4HANA Organizational Management which is described in this section. Organizational Management maintains the master data for the client, respectively the organizational structure by identifying manpower requirements, creating new jobs, assigning responsibilities, and managing performance and compensation. Organizational Management is a component inside the module SAP S/4HANA HCM and helps to maintain timely and correctly reports including organizational plans, hierarchical structures, and the positions of the employees, which is crucial for every enterprise. Organizational Management determines the relationships between workforce by using certain objects, for example, organizational units, positions, jobs, and cost centers. This means that organizational hierarchies are turned into data by defining which task is executed by which employee, in which department and business area under whom. It must be considered that the first step in implementing SAP S/4HANA applications comprises determining the specific organizational structures of the enterprise in the SAP S/4HANA system. The first step consists of analyzing the structures and procedures in the enterprise, followed by assigning them to the SAP S/4HANA structures. Organizational units being provided for accounting, logistics, and human capital management functions comprise the following:

- The *client* as the highest-level element of all organizational units represents the enterprise or headquarters group.

- The *controlling area* contains one or multiple company codes and portrays internal business transactions.
- The *company code* represents the national tax law view of the enterprise, the fiscal calendar, the local currency, and the tax reporting requirements. The company code in the SAP S/4HANA system is a legal, independent accounting unit which represents the central organizational unit of financial accounting.
- The *personnel area* represents a subdivision of the enterprise and is organized according to aspects of personnel.
- The *personnel subarea* is defined as an organizational unit representing a specific area of the enterprise organized according to certain aspects of personnel. This means that a group of people work under similar employment conditions within a personnel subarea.
- The *sales organization* responsible for the sale and distribution of products and services is an organizational, logistical unit structuring the enterprise based on its sales requirements.
- The *division* delineates an organizational unit being responsible for sales or profits from saleable materials or services. Articles are assigned uniquely to one division, whereby divisions are assigned to sales organizations.
- The *plant* describes a place where either materials are produced or goods and services are provided.
- The *storage location* is an organizational unit differentiating between several types of stocks in an enterprise and represents warehouses.

Figure 4.6 illustrates how to assign the structure of an enterprise.

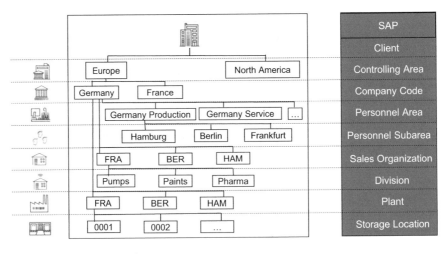

Fig. 4.6 Exemplary enterprise structure

Objects in SAP S/4HANA Organizational Management

The Organizational Management deals with objects which means that it uses an object-orientated data model for the representation of organizational structures whereby each individual object in the organizational structure represents components of the organization having their own responsibilities and tasks assigned to them. It is required to maintain the components in the structure referring to objects to maintain the hierarchical structure. It must be differentiated between several object types such as the object types: Organizational unit, job, position, cost center, task, task group, and legal entity. Every object type has a unique object key.

The following section describes the most important SAP-delivered objects:

- *Organizational Unit:* The Organizational Unit also known as Org. Unit is an object type referring to a department or a group of employees and is indicated by the object key "O." The Organizational Unit is a significant object type regarding the organizational structure because it contains the positions. An instance for an Org. Unit is financials.
- *Position:* The Position as an object type, for example, mechanic, relates to a job title and is described by the object key "S." It plays a significant role concerning the structuring of Organizational Management by designating the titles of individuals. The Position object is used as well for integrating Organizational Management and Personnel Administration.
- *Person:* The object type Person refers to employees in Organizational Management. This means that it indicates the name of the person holding a certain position, for example, the Person Johnson holds the Position Mechanic. The SAP S/4HANA user is redirected to Personnel Administration when creating a Person object in Organizational Management.
- *Job:* The object type Job concretizing the generic tasks executed by multiple Positions of the same level. For instance, there are multiple Positions in the management level of an enterprise such as HR Manager, Finance Manager, and Operations Manager and to each of these Positions tasks are assigned. On this occasion it must be mentioned that some of these tasks are common among the different Positions because they are all in the same hierarchical level of the enterprise. There is the possibility to group common tasks at the managerial level such as approving leaves and appraisals together under the job, instead of assigning them to each of the Positions so that the duplication of work is reduced. Besides, it is necessary to assign not common tasks separately. For instance, the task Hiring Planning is only assigned to the Positions HR Manager.
- *Cost Center:* The Cost Center object is the only external object in SAP S/4HANA HCM which means that it has its database in another module of SAP and is connected to other Organizational Management object types such as Positions or Org. Units through relationships. This means that it is not directly used in Organizational Management and belongs to the Cost Accounting module.
- *Task:* A task is defined as a duty and responsibility belonging to individual employees. A single task relates to a single activity having to be performed.

Therefore, the task object determines the work executed by a Person holding a position. A list of all tasks is available in the task catalogue.

- *Task Group:* The Task Group object refers to a row of activities or tasks having to be carried out in sequence. A Task Group is created by creating relationships between different rows of tasks.
- *Legal Entity:* The Legal Entity object in Organizational Management represents a company code which is the basis for the categorization within a client. These company codes are provided in Financial Accounting. It has to be mentioned that each of these company codes has an organizational structure. It is possible to connect the organizational structure to a Legal Entity object by using the General Structure tool.

Additionally, it is possible to generate further custom-delivered objects besides the SAP-delivered objects.

Relationships in SAP S/4HANA Organizational Management

Relationships connect the objects with each other to create a structure and rely on their object type. There are SAP-defined relationships for the objects delivered by SAP ensuring the structural accuracy in the organizational plan, and it is possible that one type of relationship occurs between multiple object types. Moreover, it is differentiated concerning relationships between two objects. These kinds of relationships include the hierarchical, lateral, and unilateral types of relationships. A hierarchical relationship distinguishes between the other types of relationships by a relationship of the manager with a subordinate position. In a lateral relationship the relationship exists between positions at the same level, such as the Quality Analyst and Quality Inspector. Unilateral relationships are relationships with only one direction, for example, a cost center is assigned to a position. The already mentioned SAP-delivered relationships consist of codes containing two components: the direction of the relationships being common to all relationships and a unique code for each relationship. The standard syntax of a relationship is "A/B 000." The most important relationships for organizational units are "A/B 002 Org. Unit to Org. Unit relationship," "A/B 003 Org. Unit to Position relationship," and "A/B 011 Org. Unit to Cost Center."[49] Org. Units play a crucial role in context of forming the organizational structure of an enterprise. Positions are assigned to Org. Units and are more specific entities than jobs. The most significant relationships concerning positions are "A/B 003 Org. Unit to Position relationship" and "A/B 012 Position manages Org. Unit." Jobs which define a Position because they are general sets of functions and assign tasks to a manager or secretary have a relationship with a position which is called "A/B 007." Persons normally depict the employees in a company holding a position which is why the most significant relationship to a person object type is the "A/B 008 Person to Position hierarchical relationship." A task as an individual responsibility has to be executed for a particular job or position. The most important relationship is the "A/B 007 Task to Job relationship." Cost centers either have relationships with Org. Units or with positions. The most important relationship concerning a cost center object is "A/B 011 Position to Cost Center." The letters A and B point out the direction of the relationship whereby A is used when someone is in charge of another and B indicates that someone reports to someone. This means that A represents a passive relationship and B indicates an active relationship.

Organizational Plan in SAP S/4HANA Organizational Management

The organizational plan in SAP S/4HANA Organizational Management represents the task-related structure of an enterprise and comprises of different objects and relationships between these objects. The organizational plan applies plan versions for planning purposes. The technical entity *plan version* enables creating and working with information and contains as well as the organizational plan the organizational structure. Moreover, it is possible that an enterprise requires multiple organizational structures, for example, as a result of acquiring a new company. As a consequence, it is possible to use plan version statuses which comprise the statuses: ACTIVE, PLANNED, SUBMITTED, REJECTED, and APPROVED whereby only one organizational plan is active at any time.

Conclusion

In all companies there are four enterprise domains to which functional departments are assigned to:

- *Products and Services* for developing products and services. The functional departments engineering and product management are aligned to this enterprise domain.
- *Customer* to generate demand. The functional departments' marketing, sales, customer service, and omnichannel commerce are aligned to this enterprise domain.
- *Supply* to fulfill the demand. The functional departments' supply chain planning, sourcing and procurement, manufacturing, service delivery, supply chain execution, and enablement are aligned to this enterprise domain.
- *Corporate* to plan and manage the enterprise. The functional departments' finance, indirect procurement, asset management, human resources, corporate strategy, and operations are aligned to this enterprise domain.

To implement the organizational and process structures SAP S/4HANA provides the solution Organization Management. This module offers all the necessary functionality for designing, maintaining, and operating organization structures. The component interacts with additional SAP S/4HANA solutions for facilitating supplementary capabilities.

Master Data of Business Partner

5

This chapter provides a detailed view on the business partner master data, which is relevant for most business transaction that companies process. For the business partner entity the challenges, the data model and the underlying concepts in SAP S/4HANA are described.

Business Requirement

Master data is information that is created to last for a longer period of time. The information which is maintained within the master data has huge implications for all day-to-day transactions. To put it more precisely, master data are business objects which are involved in business transactions. Master data is a vital part of any ERP system but also adds a lot of challenges like mergers and acquisitions, divestitures, corporate restructuring, business process optimization and consolidate IT landscapes (Fig. 5.1).

The way those challenges are resolved has implications all over the company. Most notably it has effects on the financials, company IT, sales, and supply chain. This includes for example the effectiveness of sales, the efficiency of the supply chain, the decision-making in procurement, the optimized utilization of assets, and the readiness of finance. Master data management ensures that there is complete and consistent master data available for the whole company despite business dynamics. Master data governance facilitates that the master data meets the company's standards concerning the data's quality. It handles the complete master data life cycle from creation, to changing and deletion. For business processes in context of ERP systems, the most important master data are business partner, product, and bill of material which will be explained in this and the following chapters.

© The Author(s), under exclusive license to Springer Nature Switzerland AG 2022
S. Sarferaz, *Compendium on Enterprise Resource Planning*,
https://doi.org/10.1007/978-3-030-93856-7_5

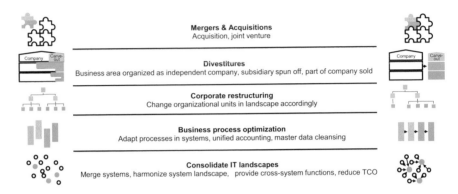

Fig. 5.1 Master data structural challenges

Solution Capability

Master data in SAP S/4HANA is maintained centrally and reused by all business processes. This is also the case for the master data of business partner with regard to various business transactions. This is especially necessary if a business partner has multiple roles for a company, such as sold-to party and ship-to party. Roles are used to classify a business partner from a business perspective. Business transactions built the basis for defining business partner roles. The attributes for the business partner role are specified to the needs of the respective business transaction. A business partner can be created in numerous roles and can take on further business partner roles over time. General data for a business partner which is independent on its function is maintained once to avoid redundancy. When a business partner is created, a business partner category must be selected. Based on the business partner category, specific set of fields must be filled with data. There are three business partner categories available:

- The category *person* denotes a natural person. This private individual has a defined role in the organization in which that person is employed. This could be a contact person for a particular project for example. For a business partner of the category person, person-specific data is entered. This information includes first name, last name, title, gender, address, birthdate, and language.
- The category *organization* denotes an egal person/entity or part of a legal entity, such as a department with which there are business relations. This could be a company for example. For a business partner of the category organization, attributes concerning an organization are maintained. These include organization name, organization title, legal entity, and industry sector.
- The category *group* allows to depict a more complex structure of a business partner. This could be a married couple or a joint venture for example. For a

Fig. 5.2 Supplier and customer as business partner

business partner of category groups attributes like address, two names, partner group type (marriage, shared living arrangement) are maintained.

The business partner is one of the most important business objects in the SAP S/4HANA system because master data for customers and suppliers is maintained based on this artifact. SAP ERP customers and suppliers were maintained differently but through an extension to the business partner model they still work with SAP S/4HANA. Thus, all departments of a company can work with the same business partners and ultimately in the same system. The change from the SAP ERP customer/supplier data model to SAP S/4HANA business partner model caused changes in business partner master data but also resulted in advantages. With SAP S/4HANA it is possible to maintain multiple addresses within one business partner. This is necessary to enter different addresses for shipping and for invoicing. To be able to view one business partner as customer and supplier the SAP S/4HANA business partner model gives users the opportunity to maintain different business roles. This results in one business partner being able to act as a supplier, a customer, and/or other roles at the same time. By being able to declare a single person as a business partner it is possible to offer business-to-consumer processes whereas in former SAP ERP versions with the customer/vendor data model that wasn't possible (Fig. 5.2).

Parts of the business partner data are time dependent in terms of being valid for a defined time period. This is the case for roles where relationships among business partners are maintained with the attributes *valid_from* and *valid_to*. Thus, for example a supplier will not further be considered as valid after a particular period of time. Similar to business partner roles, validity time period can be also defined for addresses. For example, after a specific date an address of a business partner can no longer be used for shipping and invoicing. Bank details can also have time dependencies, for example a bank account for a company is from a particular data on no more valid. This is also the case for payment cards which have an expiring validity period.

A relationship connects two business partners and is defined by business partner relationship categories. For example, a business partner of type person and a business partner of type organization can be connected with a business partner relationship to define a contact person for that organization. For this the contact person relationship with the relationship category *Is Contact Person for* must be created. For creating a relationship between business partners, a business partner relationship category to the business partner relationship must be assigned. The business partner relationship category represents the features of the business partner relationship. Attributes like company address for the business partner relationship can be assigned to a relationship to avoid redundant data storage. The relationship can also be time dependent in terms of defining a start and end date for the relationship. Thus, the history of periods in which specific business partners were contact persons for a company can be displayed. The following basic business partner relationship categories are provided: *Belongs To A Shared Living Arrangement, Has The Employee, Has The Employee Responsible, Is Shareholder Of, Is Activity Partner For, Is Identical To, Is Married To,* and *Is Replaced By.*

Data Model

The data model for the business partner master data is illustrated in Fig. 5.3. All relations of the business partner table (*BUT000*) with other tables are depicted. This contains the bank information of the business partners (table *BUT0BK*), the payment cards of the business partners (table *BUT0CC*), the roles of the business partners (*BUT100*), which were explained with their time dependency in the last section, and the business partner addresses (table *BUT020*) with their respective time dependent address usages (table *BUT021_FS*). Business partner identification information (table *BUT0ID*) are personal data, for example for an employee, regarding important information like social security number, driver's license number or passport number. The address information, which is maintained in table *ADRC*, can be divided into three categories: an organization/company address, a private address (for example of an employee), or a contact person address (for example the workplace address of that contact person).

The data model of the business partner relationship is shown in Fig. 5.4. Business partners can be linked via relationships. There are predefined relationship categories available but also own relationship categories can be created. Business partner relationship can be time dependent and displayed in form of lists, hierarchies, or networks.

Customer-vendor-integration mapper (CVI)—vendors were the earlier name for suppliers—integrates business partners that are customers and/or suppliers in their respective tables in the SAP HANA database. Within the SAP S/4HANA application the frontend components of business partner SAP Fiori apps and SAP GUI

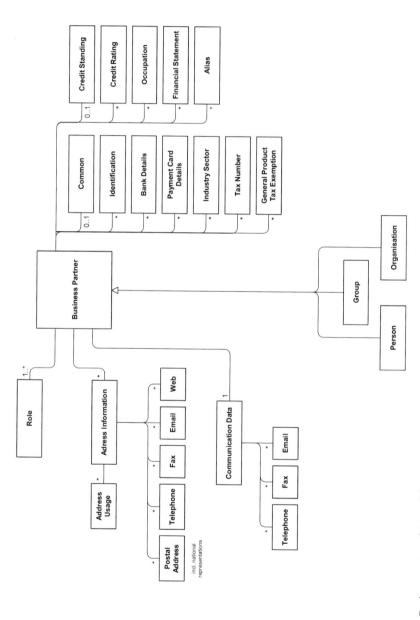

Fig. 5.3 Business partner data model

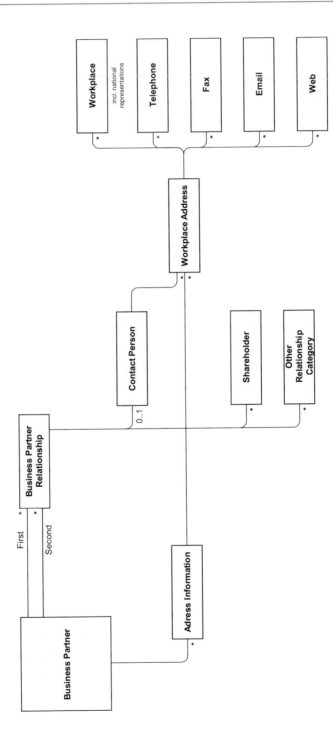

Fig. 5.4 Business partner relationship data model

transaction expose the information stored in the SAP HANA database. These frontend applications are the interaction point to the end user.

Fiori Applications

In Fig. 5.5 the most important apps for managing business partner master data are depicted and explained briefly in this section. There are also GUI transactions for business partner available which expose by far more functionality.

Manage Business Partner Master Data allows create, change, search, display, and copy business partner master data. With *Create Business Partner Master Data* a new business partner instance of type person or organization can be created. In this context information such as basic data, roles, or addresses can be maintained. The feature *Edit Business Partner Master Data* can be used to alter values and information of already saved business partner master data entries. A record can be selected from the list report page and displayed in draft mode in order to change values. *Copy Business Partner Master* Data facilitates efficient creation of new entries by using existing business partner as copy templates. A record from the list report page can be selected for copying. The prefilled values can be changed to meet the requirements of the new master data instance. In addition to these core features Manage Business Partner Master Data also provides further technical capabilities and options. *Role Based Navigation*, for example, allows the user to use the specific app when handling or maintaining business partner master data. When the role *FLCU01* for customer or *FLVN01* for supplier is chosen, the user can navigate to the corresponding app Manage Customer Master Data or Manage Supplier Master Data.

The Manage Customer Master Data application is very similar to the already explained Manage Business Partner Master Data. It ensures creating, editing, and copying of customer master data. While creating and editing are exactly alike, *Copy Customer Master Data* gives the user more options compared to *Copy Business Partner Master Data*. When copying customer master data all fields of an already existing record can be copied (*Copy All*) or just preselected fields (*Copy with Preselection*). This option can be triggered in a dialog box by clicking the copy

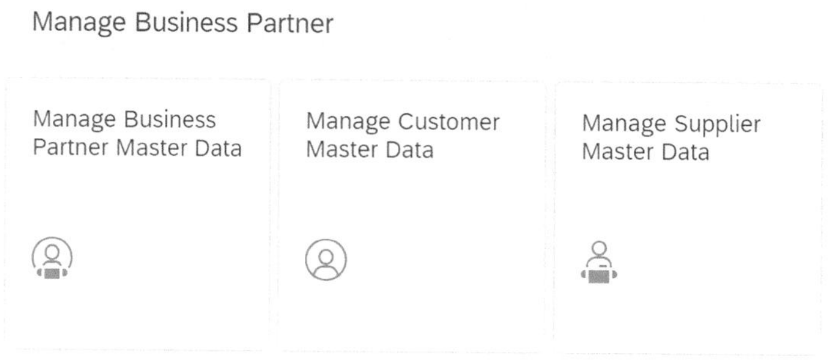

Manage Business Partner

Manage Business Partner Master Data	Manage Customer Master Data	Manage Supplier Master Data

Fig. 5.5 Fiori apps for managing business partner

button. In addition, *Copy at Facet* allows the user to copy information of customers at facet level, for example, address, bank accounts, sales area, or company code. The deletion at facet level (*Delete at Facet*) is also possible. Additionally, to these core features there are also more technical capabilities and options offered by Manage Customer Master Data application. These include for example *Time Dependency* for defining time validities, *Address Usage* for managing different addresses of a particular customers, or *Attachments* for adding corresponding attachments to customers.

Manage Supplier Master Data works analogues to Manage Customer Master Data. The core capabilities are the same, only they are concerned with managing of supplier master data. This means the following key features, technical functionalities, and options are the same as in Manage Customer Master Data only with supplier data:

- Create Supplier Master Data
- Edit Supplier Master Data
- Copy Supplier Master Data
    - Copy All
    - Copy with Preselection
    - Copy at Facet
- Delete at Facet
- Time Dependency
- Address Usage
- Attachments

Data Privacy

The business partner master data contains personal related information like name, postal address, telephone number, and email address. These are information that identifies individuals in terms of making them directly addressable or contactable. Therefore, General Data Protection Regulation (GDPR) must be ensured. The core requirements are to use personal data only for particular business purposes (e.g., order fulfillment) and to erase personal data as soon as it is not required anymore for the particular purpose (e.g., after 2 years when warranty is expired). Often personal data cannot be erased because of regulations in the form of legal retention periods (e.g., keep invoice documents 10 years for audit purposes). When legal retention periods apply personal data needs to be blocked as soon as the business purpose expires. Blocking means to restrict access to personal data and to prevent personal data to be used on a regular base. Only a few privileged users can have further access such as data privacy officers or auditors. Against this legal background SAP has to enable its customers to set up a legally compliant information lifecycle management in an efficient and flexible manner. Here the SAP Information Life Cycle Management (ILM) is an important building block to help SAP customers to comply with the various laws and regulations governing the retention of information. Information lifecycle management means managing a company's business data along its entire lifecycle—from the time it is created in the application system, through its long-term storage in a storage system, until its final destruction at the end of its lifecycle. Historically the business partner component provided data archiving for data volume management and a deletion report for test purposes. In order to enable customers to comply with legal requirements regarding the destruction of personal data a comprehensive destruction scenario for business partner based on the SAP ILM framework was provided additionally. Business data are stored in the database of SAP S/4HANA systems related to business objects such as business partner, sales order, article, contract, purchase order, material, payment, bank account, and loan contract. Business objects represent a specific view of well-defined and outlined business content. They can be classified for example into master data such as business partner, article, or material and transactional application data object. Business objects can use other business objects. For example, a sales order refers to a business partner as customer, a sales order item refers to an article, a bank account refers to a business partner as account holder, a payment order refers to a receiver account. When it comes to blocking, archiving, and destruction of expired personal data the dependencies between the business partner and business partner using applications have to be taken into account. For example, a business partner can only be blocked or archived if using applications do not need the business partner anymore, because the business with the business partner and the residence time ended already.

If retention time must be considered, personal data must be blocked when the business is complete, and the residence time is over in a way that regular users have no longer access and only a few authorized users can access this data. For blocking of business partners, a new preparation process was required. This process shall basically check end of purpose (EoP)—meaning whether business is complete, and the residence time is over—perform blocking and save the returned start of retention time (SoRT) for business partners with completed purpose. For the end of purpose check a new event was required. For this a corresponding interface has to be provided and implemented by the applications. Application components shall register their specific purpose completion check in corresponding customizing table. Thus, only if all registered application components raise the event *purpose complete*, the processed business partner record is considered for blocking, destruction, or archiving. When checking purpose completion not only applications deployed in the local system have to be taken into account, but for multisystem landscape scenarios application checks in remote systems have to be considered. When purpose is complete a particular business partner has to be blocked locally as well as in remote systems. Doing this new authorization roles had to be provided (e.g., for data protection officers). When the purpose is over access to business partner data has to be limited (blocking) in the database as well as in the archive if business partner data is archived after residence time. To resolve error situations unblocking also needs to be supported. However, unblocking shall be allowed only for authorized users. Blocking might not be required in all countries. Therefore, blocking is optional by customizing (e.g., configure residence time = retention time). The end of retention time (EoRT) for a business partner depends on the retention periods of the applications that refer to a particular business partner. Storage of start of retention time (SoRT) from each application perspective for a business partner is required.

Support regarding destruction of archived business partner data after retention time is required. Thus, the existing archiving process of the business partner was enhanced toward the SAP ILM standard in terms of considering blocked business partners and taking retention times into account. It has to consider start of retention time (SoRT) info from all relevant applications. SoRT info is part of archived data. Support regarding business partner data destruction in database after retention time is also required. Therefore, the existing deletion process for business partner was enhanced toward the SAP ILM standard in terms of considering blocked business partners and taking retention times into account. The structure of the destruction logs is customizable. One or more SAP ILM objects for the business partner had to be provided. Those objects are the basis for definition and evaluation of residence and retention time rules. It was ensured to maintain residence and retention time rules for the business partner from an application perspective. Usually the rules are defined by customers. Nevertheless, example rules were provided in the context of application documentation. Applications that use business partner data in their processes have to support the business partner data destruction scenario due to their dependencies—for example purchase order or bank account depends on business partner. The end of purpose check and the start of retention time are business process specific and vary from application to application. Thus, application components have to provide the new business partner end of purpose check. They also have to take care of business partners that have been blocked after residence time. And they should inspect their existing business partner checks *ARCH1* and *DELE1*. It is also necessary to check the SAP ILM enablement for those dependent business objects maintained by applications in regard to retention management. The handling of residence periods and blocking might also be required for dependent business objects.

Extensibility and Integration

The business partner can be extended from data model and functional point of view. Thus, specific requirements of customer can be met. For this the standard extensibility mechanism of SAP S/4HANA must be applied. The business partner can be extended by adding attributes to perform customer-specific evaluations or enter additional information. It is also possible to expand the roles of business partners. Conducting specific checks for business partner fields is also permitted as extension. For example, the check that a last name must contain at least three letters can be assigned. Finally, also relationships can be extended by including attributes. The following business contexts can be used to extend out-of-the-box SAP S/4HANA business partner master data:

- Business partner model with *BP_CUSTVEND1*
- Customer model with *CUSTOMER_GENERAL*

- Customer company code model with *CUST_COMPANYCODE*
- Customer sales area model with *CUST_SALES*
- Supplier model with *SUPPLIER_GENERAL*
- Supplier company code model with *SUP_COMPANY*
- Supplier purchasing organization model with *SUP_PURORG*

Business partner master data can be replicated to and from an external system such as SAP ERP that is connected to the SAP S/4HANA system. Different communication protocols are supported. SOAP APIs allow asynchronous business partner master data replication with data replication framework (DRF). OData APIs facilitate synchronous create-, read-, update-, and delete-operations (CRUD operations). And IDoc APIs enable communication format for the older SAP ERP version to ensure downward compatibility.

Conclusion

Master data plays a central role in SAP S/4HANA as it is the foundation for all business processes. To avoid data redundancies and achieve high consistency master data is handled centrally and reused by all transactions. Core master data are business partner, products, and bill of material. Business partner represents an organization (company, subsidiary), person, or group of people or organizations in which company has a business interest. With business partner master data different business relationship scenarios can be depicted (for example a business partner of type person can be a contact person for a business partner type organization). This business partner data model in SAP S/4HANA has evolved from the customer/vendor data model of the classic SAP ERP. This evolution comes with a couple of advantages, for example the ability of advanced maintaining of time dependencies and business roles.

Master Data of Product

6

This chapter tackles the product master data which builds the foundation for enterprises to offer services and solutions. For the product entity the challenges, the data model and the underlying concepts in SAP S/4HANA are described. Master data consists of a uniform and consistent set of identifiers and extended attributes to describe core entities and serve many different business processes in SAP S/4HANA as a single source of truth.

Business Requirement

In the context of SAP S/4HANA master, transactional and configuration data are distinguished. Master data refers to the characteristics of an object and remains unchanged over a longer period of time. They contain information that is required over and over again. Product is an example for master data. While master data is static, transaction data is dynamic and refers to all the transactions that are carried out. Usually transactional data is limited to a certain period of time and changes frequently.

Examples here is for data that arises in daily business processes, such as changes in purchase orders or invoices. Finally, configuration data corresponds to the technical information to control and customize business processes. Those are maintained during the implementation phase of SAP S/4HANA systems. Examples for configuration data are settings for organizational structures or fiscal years definition for finance.

Master data is the most important data object that is relevant for companies. The main characteristics of master data include long validity and temporal statistics. Master data is vital for both business administration and information technology. It contains the essential information about the objects that are relevant for business processes. Thus, it is data that plays a key role in the business activity and is needed in the long term. Accordingly, master data is referred to as master data or core data. The single objects of master data are also called master records, which are usually

© The Author(s), under exclusive license to Springer Nature Switzerland AG 2022

S. Sarferaz, *Compendium on Enterprise Resource Planning*,

https://doi.org/10.1007/978-3-030-93856-7_6

stored in SAP HANA. One of the most important characteristics of master data is its long validity. They are usually not related to time and schedule. This characteristic is accompanied by a time-independent statistic. Often, the data changes little over time. Companies often use their master data in several enterprise areas. They are broken down into partial master records and are used simultaneously in accounting, sales, materials planning, engineering, and purchasing, for example. For master data, the focus is on correctness and consistent maintenance. They need to be relied on because they serve as basic information for transactional data and many business processes. Therefore, data maintenance is essential to ensure the permanent correctness of the data. Last but not least, master data forms the basis for analytical evaluations. It is used for many analytical processes and is essential for online analytical processing (OLAP).

Solution Capability

The product master data is a vital element of central master data in SAP S/4HANA. It is the central source of information about all materials an organization procures, produces, and keeps in stock. Especially there are lots of information about the purpose of a material in a process. For example, analysis is provided to determine how a material is used in different processes, like procurement, planning, storage, or accounting. Regarding the process procurement, product master data holds information about the responsible purchasing group used for creating a purchase order in later stages. Furthermore, it can contain information about over- and underdelivery tolerances or the purchase order unit of a specific material. The material master also owns additional functionalities which were originally planned to be implemented in specific SAP solutions, for example, SAP for Retail or SAP Supply Chain Management (SAP SCM). The retail article master provides several retail-specific views and the ability to maintain various types of articles, prepacks, and display views. Processes like extended warehouse management (EWM) and advanced planning and optimization (APO) including demand planning or production planning are supported by SAP Supply Chain Management. SAP S/4HANA applies *principle of one* which supports optimization of processes by simplification. This means that there is only one solution for any business process. Therefore, the various functionalities of the material master in SAP S/4HANA are condensed into product master. For example, in the SAP Fiori application Manage Product Master Data there are various article types, like a single article, generic article, and structured article which can be easily maintained. Various supportive functionalities are offered such as variant matrix to configure generic article variants or bill of materials integration to fulfill the required integrations. While having a simplified user experience the complexity of the data model increases drastically. Since it may not be possible to fully define product master data in a single step there is a functionality enabling creating *drafts*. The SAP Fiori application Manage Product Master Data is a draft enabled solution. This means that the entered field values are persisted locally. The

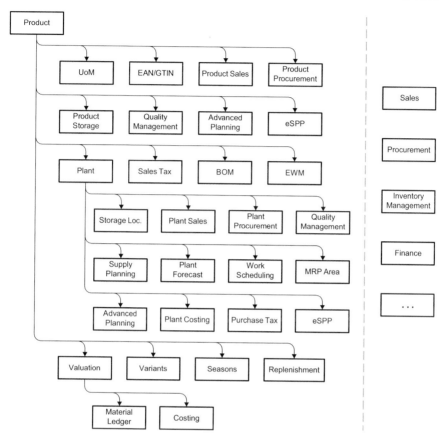

Fig. 6.1 Product master data model in SAP S/HANA

maintained data is not lost in case of a disconnection. Figure 6.1 depicts the Product Master Data Model in SAP S/4HANA (Saueressig et al. 2021b).

Firstly, the business object is organized as a tree-like structure. Thus, the root node of the data model is product. General behavior of the product is defined by basic attributes on root node level so that the product master can be already used in business processes. These basic attributes consist of the product type (impacts the user interface facets and fields), the base unit of measure, its dimensions, packaging data, danger classification from environmental, health, and safety perspectives. For each product several Units of Measure (UoM) can be defined. Instead of using base unit measures, there is also the possibility to use alternative units of measure defined for use in various processes. Purchasing could for example use a different UoM (order Unit) than sales (sales unit). The UoM in which products are issued from a warehouse (unit of issue) can be different from the UoM in which products are managed in warehouse management (WM unit). To be able to manage the inventory a conversion of the quantities entered in the WM unit to the base unit of measure will be executed. There are many ways to define a UoM depending on the underlying requirements. For example, if a product is normally managed using pieces as the base UoM, but the different pieces are being stored in a box it might be more reasonable to define a WM unit that is more suitable for purposes regarding warehouse management. The European Article Number (EAN) and Global Trade Item Numbers (GTIN) are unique numbers to identify products referring to a unit of measure or type of packaging. For each unit of measure defined for a product, one or more unique numbers (EAN or GTIN) can be assigned. There are a lot of downstream functions in SAP S/4HANA which are impacted by the elements of the product master data model. Since discussing all downstream functions in SAP S/4HANA would be too much a couple of important areas will be briefly discussed.

Finance

For strategic decision-making processes it is important that product inventory valuation data is accurately recorded in the organization's financial accounting system. There is a *valuation area*, which is usually a plant, where the product is valuated at organizational level. Several attributes determine how the inventory is valuated including the price control indicator. This is an attribute controlling if the inventory valuation is done using standard price or moving average price. Due to goods movements and the entry of invoices the moving average price changes. The calculation is possible by dividing the value of the product by the quantity of product in stock. This procedure will be automatically executed by the system after each goods movement or invoice entry. In addition, posting the stock values of products of the same product type to different general ledger accounts using valuation classes is facilitated. The decision of the valuation procedure is an accounting function. This evaluation class simply helps directing inventory value to the appropriate general ledger account. The structure of the general ledger is defined by the accountant or financial controller.

Sales

In the sales section, product master data defines the structure of the sales areas responsible for a product. It impacts sales functions like price calculation by defining classifications for country-specific taxes, specifying grouping terms like pricing group or rebate group. Additionally, it also defines quantity stipulations like the minimum order quantity. Furthermore, attributes which are relevant for the sales sector are maintainable both for the complete product and for specific sales area, defined as a combination of sales organization, distribution channel, and division. The distribution channel defines possibilities of how products or services reach the customer, for example as wholesale, retail, or direct sales. In contrast, the sales organization defines the organizational unit responsible for the sale of certain products. Finally, a division is a concept aimed at grouping similar products. For example, if a sales organization sells electric and nonelectric cars through both the retail and wholesale distribution channel, then it might be reasonable to further split into electric car and nonelectric car divisions.

Purchasing

In the purchasing area information is stored which supports the procurement processes, for example, the purchasing group which is available at the plant level identifying the responsible buyer for the procurement of a product or a class of products. Another important attribute is the purchasing value key which is defined at the product level. Providing a useful way of automating communication with the supplier the key also defines other attributes like reminder days, tolerance limits, or order acknowledgment requirement of the product being procured. To make sure product master data can be used adequately alongside multiple systems or modules in the SAP S/4HANA system there are various functionalities supporting different tasks and challenges.

Product Hierarchy

Offering a huge variety of products in sales processes, companies often organize products in product hierarchies allowing to structure products along multiple levels. Among others, product hierarchies play a significant role in sales. For instance, a product hierarchy can be used within price maintenance and calculation by adding a field in the pricing condition table to define the validity of a price of discount providing an input to the pricing application in all relevant documents, like sales orders or billing documents. In SAP S/4HANA hierarchies have been completely built from scratch and are not stored as a part of the product data model. Instead, there are hierarchy runtime tables storing information about product assignments to a hierarchy. Generally, there are no restrictions regarding the number of hierarchy levels in the new implementation. To visualize the product hierarchy in SAP S/4HANA Fig. 6.2 depicts the SAP Fiori application Manage Product Hierarchies. On the left side one notices the product Hierarchy ID and hierarchy version information. Furthermore, validity from and to dates are displayed. Product hierarchy information is not an attribute in the product data model. Moreover, it is displayed as a tree structure in the application (see right side of Fig. 6.2). Typically, products can be assigned at the leaf nodes in the tree structure.

Data Migration

When beginning to use SAP S/4HANA, migrating data is one of the first activities performed by companies. To allow an organization to efficiently handle the complex data migration process regarding product master data new migration objects have

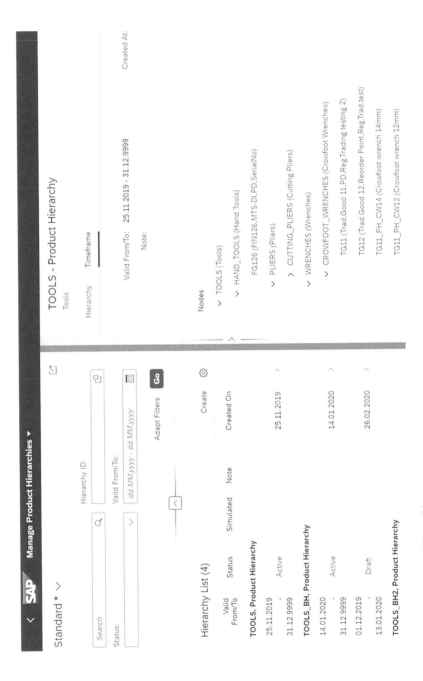

Fig. 6.2 Visualization Product Hierarchies

been provided. In terms of product master data there are two migration objects available both on-premise and in the cloud. One object is defined to create new products in SAP S/4HANA and the other one is used to extend existing products with new organizational data. When looking at migration extensibility, the data migration objects support all the extensibility business contexts in the extensibility registry of SAP S/4HANA. Therefore, field extensibility is supported while migrating for different components like product basic data, plant, and location.

Replicate Product Master Data Between Multiple Systems

There is the possibility to replicate product master data between multiple systems. Therefore, an asynchronous SOAP service has been provided based on the data replication framework defining which business object will be replicated to which targeting system using a specific interface. By creating an implementation for the outbound interface, one has fulfilled a prerequisite to be able to use the SOAP service due to the use of the push mechanism on the data replication framework. In terms of data replication filter objects and filter are important topics. A filter object defines the selection criteria used to determine the data object which needs to be replicated. A filter essentially carries out the comparison of a given set of objects against the maintained filter criteria. There are two different types of filters. Firstly, explicit filters are configured explicitly by the user. The user can define simple or complex filters. A simple filter is defined for attributed on a single entity root Table. A complex filter needs to be evaluated by certain function modules or methods, for example in merchandise category hierarchy. Using corresponding APIs, the semantic interpretation of complex filters is coded. Secondly, segment filters are special filters not limiting the number of objects. They are rather used to exclude segments of business objects from replication.

Maintaining Product Master

The SAP Fiori application Maintain Product Master can be used to search, display, edit, create, and copy master data for products and single articles, generic articles, and structured articles, effectively and quickly. The application guarantees that the master data displayed is always consistent. Furthermore, it can be also used to mark a product for deletion. For creating the product master, by default the industry sector M (Mechanical) is assigned to the new record. In case of editing, existing records belonging to any industry sector can be updated. Key features of the applications are automatic calculation of sales tax, attachment and reference handling, integration of supply change and extend warehouse management, classification, and variant matrix. Additional capabilities are for example compliance and subscription handling, just in time management, extended service parts planning, and the support of material ledger. Figure 6.3 shows some of the core functionality of this SAP Fiori application.

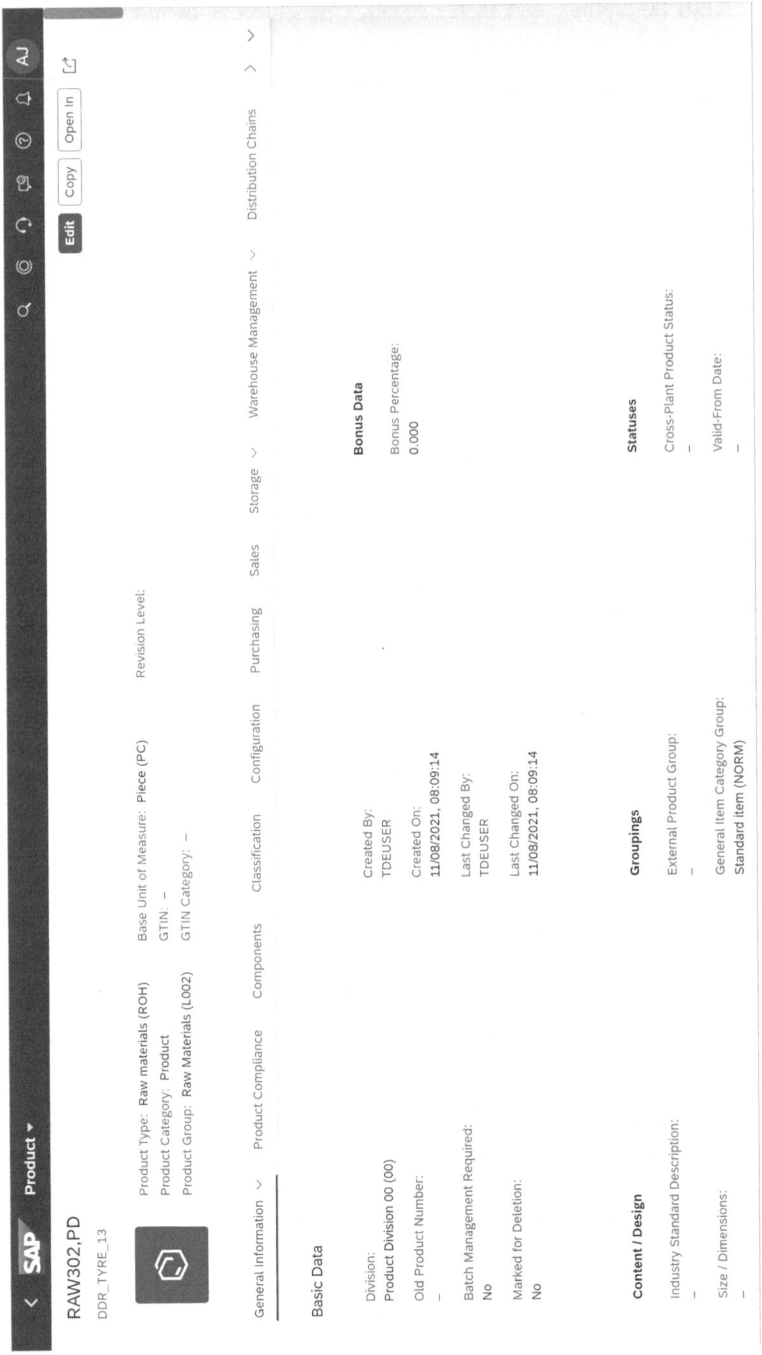

Fig. 6.3 Product master maintenance

Product Master Extensibility

In many scenarios organizations deploying SAP S/4HANA require adding custom fields to the product data model which needs to be supported from end to end. In the SAP S/4HANA Extensibility Registry there is the possibility to extend business contexts for product master data for product general data, plant, storage, and location data. Therefore, the corresponding database tables and ABAP Data Dictionary (DDIC) offer an *extension include* providing a stable anchor for field extensions. This activity is usually performed by a key user having additional authorizations to adapt artifacts like UIs, views on services, and so on. The key user can access the SAP S/4HANA Fiori launchpad to add custom fields to the required extensibility business contexts which are automatically updated in the UI by extending database tables, OData services, data migration objects and so on.

Self-Service Configuration

In SAP S/4HANA master data is used across multiple functional areas and modules. Therefore, master data needs to be configurable. That's why SAP S/4HANA provides various amounts of central configuration options. Firstly, attributes of the International Article Numbers (EAN) can be defined. For example, the number range object, interval assignment, and EAN length can be specified. Secondly, there is the possibility of defining valuation classes grouping different products with the same account determination. For example, if a user creates a product, the user must enter its valuation class in the accounting data. Afterwards, the system uses the entered values to check whether the valuation class is allowed for the product type. Thirdly, it is allowed to define the format for product IDs and specific attributes of product types. Regarding the format of product IDs there is the option of defining the length having a maximum length of 40 digits and the display template. In terms of product types there are different configuration alternatives when assigning a created master record to a product type. For example, the user departments (e.g., purchasing or accounting) or the price control (e.g., standard or moving average price) can be defined. It has to be noticed that these are just a couple of many configuration options available in SAP S/4HANA.

SAP Master Data Governance

Master data needs to be used across multiple modules in an ERP system. Therefore, master data needs to be well managed to make sure no errors occur when using across multiple modules. Master data management (MDM) is a process which creates a uniform set of data for various entities (e.g., business partner, products, or bill of material) from different IT systems. MDM helps organizations in improving data quality by ensuring the accuracy and consistency of identifiers and other key data elements enterprise wide. Many companies don't have a clear view of their customers because customer data differs from one system to another. Therefore,

MDM solutions enable organizations receiving a single customer view by consolidating data from multiple source systems into standard format. Duplicate customer records will be eliminated, giving data analysts, business executives, and operational workers a whole picture of individual customers without putting different pieces of information from different sources together. Furthermore, effective master data management enables organizations to use this information in business intelligence and analytics applications, increasing trustworthiness. Managing master data in an ERP system is very important because many different modules will rely on a single source of truth. Therefore, SAP Master Data Governance application has been implemented to consolidate and manage master data across the organization in SAP S/4HANA. It provides a unified, trusted view of master data across different domains. SAP Master Data Governance is an advanced master data management application, providing preconfigured, domain-specific master data governance to monitor and remediate possible data quality issues or centrally create, change, distribute, and consolidate master data across the complete enterprise system landscape.

The key features of SAP Master Data Governance are the following:

- Consolidation or central governance for consistent master data
  While enabling centralized governance, compliance, and transparency of master data, SAP Master Data Governance also provides consistent definition, authorization, and replication of key master data entities, thereby eliminating error-prone manual master data maintenance processes across multiple systems. Furthermore, through consolidation of decentralized master data in any enterprise system it supports the creation of records and key mapping between duplicates.
- Data quality
  SAP Master Data Governance enables processes like analyzing process quality, managing, and monitoring data quality and optionally integrating with platforms like SAP HANA smart data quality or SAP Business Technology Platform Data Enrichment.
- Integration and reuse
  Lastly the system enables native integration or integration of third-party services. In addition, SAP data models, already existing business logic, or configurations for data validation can be reused.

SAP Master Data Governance is part of SAP S/4HANA and enables end-to-end integration of master data in heterogenous landscapes. Figure 6.4 depicts different landscapes where master data is integrable but there are many more integration examples. Therefore, master data can be used in SAP S/4HANA (e.g., providing Master Data Governance for Central Finance), in Enterprise Resource Planning (e.g., usage of Material master data in purchasing, production, and so on), in Product Catalog and eCommerce (e.g., customer consolidation via open web service by synchronizing product master data toward product catalog and ecommerce solutions), in Business Analytics (e.g., export of MDG key mapping to SAP BI), or in Customer Relationship Management (e.g., allowing decentral look-up and ad-hoc replication or decentral creation and subsequent global governance) (Fig. 6.5).

Fig. 6.4 SAP master data governance—product overview

Fig. 6.5 End-to-end
integration in heterogenous
landscapes

Conclusion

Master data is an important part of every ERP system because it is a uniform and consistent set of identifiers and extended attributes that describe the core entities of the enterprise including customers, prospects, citizens, suppliers, sites, hierarchies, and chart of accounts. Therefore, it is no surprise that SAP S/4HANA is using master data to a large extent. In SAP S/4HANA one of the core master data entities is product master. This consists of different material data which is vital for an organization. It is the central source of information about all materials an organization procures, produces, and keeps in stock. Concerning the product master there is a data model implemented influencing several downstream functions, such as Finance, Sales, and Purchasing. To be able to support different modules adequately with product master data there are various functionalities implemented, such as data migration procedures, procedures to replicate product master data between multiple systems, specific self-service configurations in different business areas, or product master extensibility to add new fields in existing product master objects. SAP Master Data Governance has been implemented to consolidate and manage master data across the organizations in SAP S/4HANA. It provides a unified, trusted view of master data across different domains. The key benefits of SAP Master Data Governance are the consolidation or central governance for consistent master data, data quality, and integration and reuse. Using the SAP Master Data Governance solution, it enables end-to-end integration of master data in heterogenous landscapes.

Master Data of Bill of Material

7

This chapter focuses on the bill of material (BOM) master data, which is basically the list of the raw material for assembling products. For the bill of material entity the challenges, the data model and the underlying concepts in SAP S/4HANA are described. Particularly, the structure type of the BOM, the SAP classification system, and the variant configuration are explained.

Business Requirement

A lot of companies are using enterprise resource planning (ERP) applications to handle their business. For that, it is important that such a system supports all core business processes and functions of today's enterprises. The core task of ERP systems is managing the resources of a company, like material, money, or people. For this SAP S/4HANA includes various components like procurement, sales, service, asset management, manufacturing, research and development, supply chain, human resources, financials, and various industry extensions. The objective of those components is to implement the underlying business process. Particularly, all those business processes must have access to the required master data. Therefore, all the necessary master data is stored within SAP HANA which is the underlying in-memory database of SAP S/4HANA. From the SAP customer's point of view master data management is crucial as many of their business processes are based on master data. The customers are asking for integration across the SAP products as well as flexible integration with non-SAP products. Furthermore, they want an out-of-the-box integration and high extensibility and adaptability. Especially, the role of master data management is growing to be the core foundation of an intelligent enterprise. To help companies optimize their value chain, understand, and serve the customers and adapt to the globalizing world, it's important to provide them with access to trusted and high-quality master data. On the one hand there is the process of master data integration, which is all about synchronization of master data across all applications. It supports many domains out-of-the-box, but also provides integration

S. Sarferaz, *Compendium on Enterprise Resource Planning*,
https://doi.org/10.1007/978-3-030-93856-7_7

with third-party applications. On the other hand, the process of master data management ensures high quality for trusted master data across the enterprise. This is usually only applied to selected, relevant domains, as the investment both in cost and time, is relatively high. The typical approaches to master data management are consolidation, central governance, and data quality management. That means that master data is consolidated from decentral sources and these data will be centrally governed and distributed to the relevant parts of the system landscape. With central governance and consolidation, error-prone manual maintenance processes can be eliminated to achieve consistent master data in multiple systems. Apart from that, these functions deliver a consistent definition, authorization, and replication of key master data entities. The consolidation can be used to prepare high-quality and deduplicated master data. In contrast, central governance is used to keep high-quality data clean in the long term.

Typically, organizations rely on the help of stakeholders to serve its customers. Sales partner, suppliers, or employees are examples of stakeholders. All of them provide different inputs to the company, which will then be transformed into an output directly aimed at the consumer. This transformation process depends heavily on several types of data. The core data of an enterprise is called master data, which can fall into several categories. Two of the most important are product master data and business partner master data. Product master data describes various aspects of products purchased, sold, and produced by the organization. Business partner data on the other hand captures information about entities relevant to business. Besides these two there is also a master data type describing how products are characterized, composed, produced, and configured: Bill of Materials (BOM). This type of master data is considered more closely in the next sections.

Solution Capability

A company has the choice of manufacturing a product in-house or purchasing the product from an external supplier. This situation is known as the make-or-buy decision. Companies usually use quantitative analysis to choose whether making or buying is the best choice for them. If the organization decides to produce a product by themselves, all raw materials and assemblies used for creating the final product are listed in a BOM.

A product can have several variations of structure and that's why the same product can have multiple BOMs. One reason is that there are different phases of the product lifecycle. For example, in the first iteration the engineers structure a product in one way, in the second the manufacture team needs another structure of the product, so that it fits better into the factory line: this produces an engineering BOM and a product BOM. Adding to that, there are often different alternative ways to manufacture the same product, the most obvious reason being a different producing location, which leads to difference in availability of material, machinery, and knowledge.

Fig. 7.1 Bill of material
conceptual model

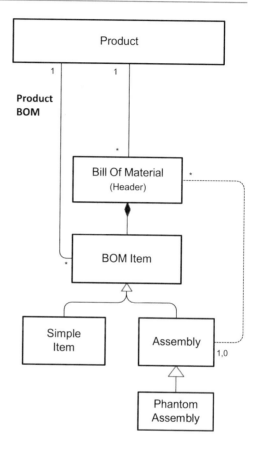

For a better understanding, Fig. 7.1 (Saueressig et al. 2021b) shows a simplified conceptual model of BOM. Only products produced by the company itself have a BOM. This BOM consists of two parts: the BOM header and the item list. The BOM header includes different properties about the BOM, like assignment to a plant or the validity period of the BOM. Every BOM header has a list of BOM items assigned to it. A BOM item includes the product's ID, component description as well as the quantity and units of measure. Also, a BOM item is either a simple item, which is a raw material, or a part purchased from suppliers, or an assembly, which is a produced product. This means that an assembly has its own BOMs. If a user wants the complete hierarchical structure of a product, the user must replace the assemblies by their own BOMs recursively, which is known as the BOM explosion process. Sometimes it's required to have phantom assemblies. These assemblies aren't physically in stock, they only exist in the manufacturing process.

Structure Types of Bill of Materials

After the general overview of BOM, a closer look at the two different main structure types is provided. One of them is the single-level bill of materials, the other one is called multilevel bill of materials. A single-level BOM is a simple and flat list of items for one product and is the more basic type of both. BOMs of this type list each component only once and state the required number of parts to produce the product. Also, it consists only of one level of children, such as BOM items or assemblies. One advantage of this type is that it's very easy to create, but it's not recommended for complex items, because single-level bill of materials gives no information about the relationship between parent and child components. In case of the product failing, it's difficult to find the right part to be replaced or repaired. Multilevel BOMs are more complex than single-level BOMs. This type of BOM structure offers more detail and specificity on the parent and child parts in the product. As with the single-level BOMs, the total number of required components is also shown in multilevel BOMs. In addition the multilevel structure is intended to show all items of the product that are in parent-children relationships. Figure 7.2 shows an example of both types.

Type of Bill of Materials

Besides the different structure types of bill of materials, there are also different types of bill of materials, depending on the lifecycle of the product. Each type of BOM describes the product with a different structure and level of detail. It can be distinguished between engineering, sales, and manufacturing bill of materials. An engineering BOM (EBOM) is developed by the engineering department using computer-aided (CAD) design or electronic design automation (EDA) tools. An EBOM defines all raw materials and assemblies and describes the product structure from a functional perspective. Normally one product has multiple EBOMs, because the design of a product is checked and improved several times, before it's produced.

Fig. 7.2 Single- and multilevel BOM structure

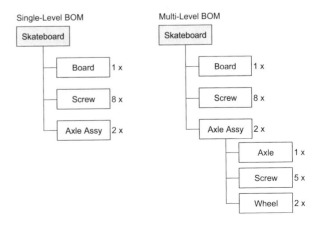

A sales document can include a BOM. These BOMs are called sales bill of materials (SBOM) and they represent the finished product and its individual components. A sales bill of materials defines a product in the sales stage. A manufacturing bill of materials (MBOM) describes a structured list of all raw materials or assemblies, which are required to produce a shippable finished product. MBOM contains the information about the individual components, as well as information about components, which must be processed before assembly, and information about the relationship between different components. All the information in the MBOM is shared with all business relevant systems, like procurement and manufacturing. In summary, three different types of BOM can be identified depending on the lifecycle of a product. Each type has different fields of application. The next section deals with the classification system of master data as well as important aspects of variant configuration.

Classification System

After the bill of materials has been described in detail as part of the master data, the classification system should now be introduced. Not all characteristics are described by the product master data, so different products can have various characteristics. With the help of a classification system, it is possible to define characteristics of products and to classify the products with the same characteristics. With using the classification system no changes to the software or database structure are necessary. Furthermore, the classification system allows the company to restrict the characteristics of a product. Such restrictions are called characteristic dependencies. For example, drills have the characteristic length, diameter, and material type. To describe them, the best way is to create a class. Whenever the company has a new drill to add as a product, it assigns it to the drill class and specifies the object with the correct characteristics. If one of the characteristics of a drill has a dependency, for example the length is restricted to 16 mm, this violation must not be allowed as all dependencies must be complied to. This classification system is not only used for product master data records, but also for bill of materials records or other documents. The classification system is used for maintaining the master data, because it is used to assign individual products, BOMs, or other documents to classes.

Variant Configuration

The BOM model described above doesn't consider the possibility that a product has different variations, which are based on several configurations. For example, as a customer of an automotive company, it is possible to configure your car by yourself. Popular properties to select are color, engine type, power, seat material, or drive assistance. For such configurable products, like a car or bicycle, a variant configuration is used. The system will create a concrete instance of this product, with the resulting BOM and the routing, based on the selected configuration values. The routing provides important information for the manufacturing process. In SAP S/4HANA there are two different variant configurators with which products can be configured in different variations: advanced variant configurator (AVC) and the traditional variant configurator. The AVC is based on a new configuration engine, which has been developed together with Fraunhofer Institute Kaiserslautern. It comes with an SAP Fiori-based UI and several other features. The AVC can be used in SAP S/4HANA on-premise as well as SAP S/4HANA Cloud. In contrast, the traditional configurator can only be used in SAP S/4HANA on-premise. The variant configuration uses master data, which is based on the following elements:

• Variant classes	• Object dependencies
• BOMs, super BOM, routings	• User interface/grouping
• Configuration profiles	

For a better understanding, these elements will be described in the next subsections.

Variant Classes

The classification system is used by the variant configuration to define the configuration parameters and their allowed values. A class reserved for variants is of a specific class type and called a variant class. Variant classes have configuration parameters as characteristics, that are selected during the configuration process. Each configurable product is linked to a specific variant class. Let's have a look at a specific variant class:

Variant Class Car	
Characteristic	Characteristic value
Engine type	Electric, petrol, diesel
Version	Standard, premium, sport

If a customer wants to order a car, the customer must decide which engine type and version are favored. The customer can't choose two different engine types in one configuration. A finished configuration contains the selected values of the variant class characteristics.

BOM/Super BOM

Since products can be configured differently, each configuration consists of diverse parts. To handle these different variant structures of a product easier, the company can create either super BOMs or BOMs with class items. A super BOM contains all selectable items of a variant class characteristic. All items of one characteristic have mutually exclusive selection condition. Looking at the car example above, a super BOM of a car has three values for the possible engines: electric, petrol, and diesel. The selection of one motor type excludes the other two. For example, when a car is configured with an electric engine, no further engine type selection is possible. The same applies to the different versions of a car. The second option to handle configurable products in BOMs is to use class items. Super BOMs include all selectable items, whereas a BOM can contain configurable placeholders for variable components. That means for different engine types, a BOM includes only one item, which refers to an engine variant class. The engine variant class is replaced with a concrete product of this class, during a BOM explosion.

Variant Configuration Profiles, and User Interface and Grouping

The configuration user interface and the interactive configuration process can be controlled by the variant configuration profile. It provides various settings for these. Furthermore, the variant configuration profile contains dependencies, that help consistency and automatic derivation of values. Besides that, the user interface and grouping help the user to handle complex configuration models with many characteristics by being able to create individual user interfaces or characteristic groups.

Object Dependencies

The variant configurator uses object dependencies. This ensures consistency of the configurations, controls whether a selected value of a characteristic violates another choice, and determines the actual structure of the product based on the selected values of the configuration. The object dependencies are very useful and important for complex configuration products like a car. The higher the number of different variations of a product are, the greater the complexity, which imposes greater risk that the final configuration is valid. To counteract this causality, the object dependencies are used. The variant configuration consists of many different parts, which are related to each other. It is an important part of the data governance and should be carefully maintained.

Fiori Applications

There are numerous applications available in SAP S/4HANA to manage and create version controlled BOMs and use additional features for converting engineering BOMs to manufacturing BOMs, for example, display BOMs, to create planning BOMs with items for long-time components, or to create assembly BOMs for serialized materials. To just provide an impression of those features two exemplary SAP Fiori Applications are described in this section.

Maintain Bill of Materials facilitates to display and manage all BOMs. Using the available filters allows to find and view existing BOMs, drill down to the required level of detail, and perform the necessary actions, for example, copy or delete BOMs or assign change records to BOMs. The application helps to create new BOMs whether classical, version-based, or alternative BOMs. Furthermore, it inserts the relevant components along with the required data, including attachments. BOMs can be searched for using a variety of filter criteria such as material, plant, BOM usage, and alternative BOM. The transfer of engineering bills of material (EBOMs) to manufacturing bills of material (MBOMs) is also supported. It is possible to create BOMs for configurable materials and maintain object dependencies using the classic application. Additionally, the application ensures to take tentative decisions while working on a BOM and save changes as a draft. Assigning BOMs to a change record and navigation to change instances using the change timeline are facilities. The

Fig. 7.3 Maintain bill of materials and detail view

solution helps to create a change number and assign it to a material. Documents or
files can be attached to a material. The application supports to create a version BOM
for manufacturing and operations. Software and the corresponding versions can be
defined in a BOM. International systems of units can be used to calculate BOMs.
The hand over to bill of material components to the SAP Asset Intelligence Network
is provided. In order to increase effectivity engineering change numbers (ECN) are
created automatically (Fig. 7.3).

Manage Multilevel Bill of Material facilitates to display and maintain the hierarchical tree structure of a multilevel BOM. The application enables to view the BOM
header of the multilevel BOM followed by the nested list of components, assemblies,
and materials. It helps to expand the subassemblies in a multilevel hierarchical tree
structure. Each level offers details of the usage in the production and the parent-child
relationship among the subassemblies. The application allows to search for a BOM
by making entries in the key fields. Subassemblies of a multilevel BOM are
displayed in a hierarchical tree structure by using the application. Additionally, the

Manage Multi-Level Bill of Material

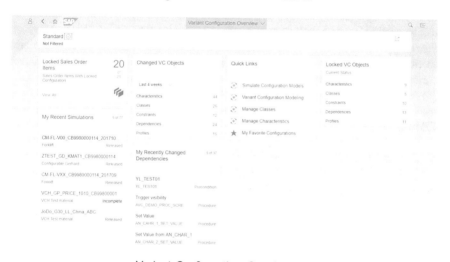

Variant Configuration Overview

Fig. 7.4 Manage multilevel bill of material and variant configuration overview

engineering change numbers (ECN) associated with the subassemblies can be viewed. With or without ECNs single or multiple BOM items in the hierarchical tree structure can be changed. Especially, existing BOM items can be added to single or multiple components. The draft mechanism is support so that single or multiple subassemblies can be deleted in draft status. Variants of the BOM items table views can be created to save personal settings and favorites. The columns of the BOM item table view are enabled for sorting, filtering, and freezing. The subassemblies are displayed in the same usage as the root BOM. If BOM for that usage doesn't exist, the system chooses minimum usage by default. Toggling between multiple alternatives to view the subassemblies is provided. The application supports different devices like desktops, tablets, and smartphones (Fig. 7.4).

Variant Configuration Overview facilitates to display an overview for variant configuration. Navigations to changed or locked variant configuration objects such as locked sales order items, recently changed object dependencies, recent configuration simulations, and favorite configurations are supported from the overview page.

The main cards of the application are *locked sales order items* and *locked/changed variant*. A list report is launched, when navigating to locked or changed variant configuration objects. On the list, individual line items are shown, from where the item's corresponding app can be opened to maintain the object. Navigation to different variant configuration objects is supported, for example, characteristics, classes, constraints, dependencies, or profiles. With quick links the navigation to further applications is provided, for example, simulate configuration models, variant configuration modeling, manage classes, or manage characteristics. Thus, searching for configurable products and configured objects and starting a configuration simulation with them are facilitated. Moreover, also searching for and opening previously created and saved simulation are supported. The simulation can be used to test and analyze configuration model by configuring objects based on the integrated characteristic value assignments and check whether the dependencies work appropriately. Especially, simulation for single-level and multilevel configurations is enabled.

Conclusion

Master data is a big and important part of SAP S/4HANA. This chapter gave an overview about master data and in particular bill of materials. BOMs can be used in different phases of the product lifecycle and can have different structure types. In addition to the default BOMs, it is possible to use the configuration system to configure BOMs with predefined characteristics and create different variants of BOMs. The various elements surrounding them have been introduced and explained for better understanding of the configuration system. As mentioned in the introduction the core capabilities of a company need access to the required data as well as to ensure data quality. SAP S/4HANA enables the customer to apply processes for getting trusted and high-quality master data and for distributing this data in the system landscape across the enterprise.

Process of Idea to Market

8

This chapter describes the business process idea to market consisting of the subprocesses plan to optimize products/services, idea to requirement, design to release, products/services to market, and manage product/services. Additionally, the application capabilities of SAP S/4HANA to resolve those business processes are explained.

Business Process

The general process of idea to market is depicted in Fig. 8.1 and explained in detail in the next sections.

The process from idea to market can be divided into five individual processes. It starts with the Plan to Optimize Products/Services which focuses on the portfolio management in terms of defining an appropriated product/service strategy, creating the portfolio, planning, and monitoring the investments. Ideas for products/services are validated and corresponding development requirements are derived from them. Those requirements are transferred to concrete design for products/services. In this context prototypes are implemented, and dependencies identified. Based on the detailed design the product/service delivery is prepared. Furthermore, the go-to-market offering including the pricing is defined. Supportive tasks like managing intellectual property, compliance requirements, or maintaining product/service data are also in focus of this end-to-end process. Comprehensive set of solutions and capabilities for ideation, portfolio management, and project management are required which can be used as a crowdsourcing tool to collect and evaluate ideas in order to implement the *right* ideas based on customer desirability, technical feasibility, and market viability. Based on corporate strategy, innovation managers can manage the fuzzy front end by creating campaigns to request the submission of ideas, which can lead to collaboration to improve on ideas, evaluating them before they become concepts and are chosen for implementations as projects or changes in a product or service. The ideation process can be sped up, which saves money. The

© The Author(s), under exclusive license to Springer Nature Switzerland AG 2022
S. Sarferaz, *Compendium on Enterprise Resource Planning*,
https://doi.org/10.1007/978-3-030-93856-7_8

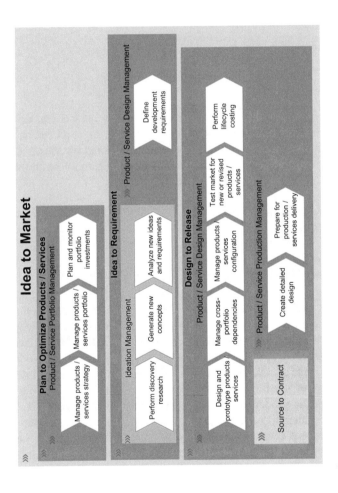

Fig. 8.1 Process idea to market

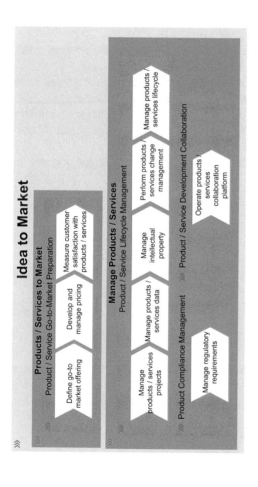

Fig. 8.1 (continued)

recipe development serves as the foundation for product development in process manufacturing industries such as food, beverage, chemicals, life sciences, and consumer goods. This process must address the entire product development, beginning with ideation, requirements, and trials and continuing through formulation and development to the handover to the enterprise, including manufacturing and supply chain. The specification management allows for the creation and maintenance of specifications which represent substances, packaging, and their properties. Recipe developers create optimized formulas based on existing specifications for the following activities:

- Perform calculations, such as determining a product's nutritional value, costs, composition, and loss calculation.
- Define processes as sequences of chemical, physical, or biological activities that result in the production of a product or intermediate products.
- Ensure product compliance by performing compliance checks using quantitative or qualitative constraints, such as identifying prohibited substances and ingredient thresholds.
- Distribute recipes to manufacturing, developing master recipes for use in production.
- Label sets with recipe information can help with final product labeling and artwork.

Businesses in the discrete manufacturing industry frequently use various authoring systems, such as mechanical and electronic CAD systems during the detailed design phase of product development. The basic scenario for CAD entails the creation and management of master data from the CAD structure.

Plan to Optimize Products/Services (Fig. 8.2)

The Plan to Optimize Products/Services covers in general the Product and Service Portfolio Management. The portfolio management is in charge of the following tasks:

1. Collect and describe portfolio elements
2. Characterize and evaluate portfolio elements
3. Compare and decide on portfolio elements
4. Monitor portfolio elements

Fig. 8.2 Plan to optimize products/services

These tasks are performed using various metrics and are used for comparison. The implementation of the individual elements will take place later in the project management. So, in conclusion the Product and Service Portfolio Management is in charge of managing the products and services strategies and the products and services portfolio and planning and monitoring the portfolio investments.

Idea to Requirement (Fig. 8.3)

The Idea to Requirement process includes Ideation Management and Product and Service Design Management. The first one is ideation management. The focus of ideation management is on recording systematically new ideas for products/services or product/service variations and even to record systematically new ideas for existing products/services, to improve or adapt them. Ideation management not only includes the recording but also the viability valuation. For the valuation several evaluation criteria are necessary such as cost and competitive analysis. It is important to perform a discovery research first before the new concepts get defined. After that the new ideas and requirements are analyzed. With the completion of ideation management Product and Services Design Management can start which includes the definition of the requirements. It is necessary here to keep in mind the Business Process Segment which is the group of the business activities and the business capabilities. Those cover the creation of a defined value or outcome for a stakeholder.

Design to Release (Fig. 8.4)

The Design to Release process is divided in three subprocesses. The Product and Service Design Management which already takes place partly in the Idea to Requirement process, the Source to Contract, and the Product and Service Production Management.

With the completion of the main requirement analysis the concept and detailing phase can start. An initial structure is created, which is constantly improved and adapted. It is possible to create an independent structure or to combine the functional, conceptual, and development structure into one. In order to carry out the subsequent validation, a prototype is necessary, on the basis of that the product or service validation is proofed. The developed products or services are normally very complex and must achieve strict quality and efficiency standards. In general, the assurance is the planning, control, and execution of examinations of the outcome, for

Fig. 8.3 Idea to requirement

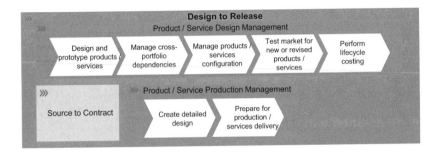

Fig. 8.4 Design to release

example, a prototype. Every malfunction or error must be documented and closed in order to guarantee success. It is important to identify every malfunction because in the end they would cause additional costs and negatively impact the quality of the product or service. The product or service validation depends on the previously defined requirements and objectives. All insights if they are conflicts or a success must be incorporated into the product or service improvement. It is necessary to make a validation in every product or service development step. The goal of the validation is to make sure that all quality standards are reachable and to optimize the process. The budget of employees and other costs should be monitored regularly. Product validation is a combination of several components. The combination includes document administration, quality management, process management, product management, and operational maintenance. It shows that advance planning is very important for the validation and that the validation is needed to be checked on a regular basis during the whole process. In conclusion services and products must be designed and prototyped, the cross-portfolio dependencies and configurations must be managed, a test market for revised or new products must be found and the lifecycle costing must be performed and monitored. All that happens before the Source to Contract and the Product and Service Production Management take place.

The Product and Service Production Management includes the detailed design of a product or service and the preparation for the actual production or the delivery of a service. It is the integration of the development and the actual production of a product. The bills of material (BOM) during a production must be monitored and controlled systematically. The bill of materials (BOM) is a list of all materials required in a process, along with the quantities required. The administration of the BOM is a basis to implement other concepts like digital factories and Industry 4.0. Digital factories are connectors between product development, planning, and production. They connect the data from the production with the development data for manufacturing. Tools for modeling and various methods for simulation and visualization are also necessary. The goal is to work digital and to construct the products three-dimensional. Industry 4.0 does not provide the tools and various methods; it supports the digital factories in real time and takes care of the operation and optimization of digital factories.

Products and Services to Market (Fig. 8.5)

After the product or the service is provided and designed the market entry can be planned. That means the go-to market offering needs to be defined, the pricing needs to be developed and managed, and the customer satisfaction with the products or services needs to be measured. That is all included in the process Products and Services to Market and describes the process of the market entry and the preparation of it.

Manage Products and Services (Fig. 8.6)

The fifth and last process of Idea to Market is the Management of Products and Services. That includes the Product or Service Lifecycle Management, the Product Compliance Management, and the Product and Service Development Collaboration.

The Product and Service Lifecycle Management supports projects, intellectual property, performance and lifecyle for products and services. The Product Compliance Management handles the regulatory requirements. It is important to always have an eye on the requirements. Next to the Product Compliance Management is the Product and Service Development Collaboration which covers the operation of the products or services collaboration platform. The establishment of a proper project structure by the project manager or a project financial controller serves as the foundation for all project-related planning, execution, and monitoring activities. Project creation process covers structuring of simple projects involving single accounting objects to complex project that may include a hierarchy of work packages, depending on the needs. Cost planning for a project at an early stage usually

Fig. 8.5 Products/services to market

Fig. 8.6 Manage products/services

necessitates a significant amount of effort. Furthermore, because expertise is based on personal bias or strategic considerations, it is frequently inaccurate or even skipped entirely.

Solution Capability

The end-to-end process Idea to Market is mainly implemented by SAP S/4HANA R&D/Engineering and SAP Enterprise Product Development (EDP) as depicted in Fig. 8.7. While SAP S/4HANA R&D/Engineering covers the core functionality SAP EDP includes extended features for engineering, visualization, collaboration, connected products, and partner applications.

The Extended Enterprise Portfolio and Project Management increases efficiency and automation for gaining insights for products and projects into cost, time, scope, resources, and quality performance. Product Lifecycle Management handles product information holistically and efficiently across the complete lifecycle, ensuring end-to-end visibility from requirements to design manufacturing to service in process and discrete industries. Product Compliance ensures compliance of products and chemicals to secure the right to market, sell, and ship products. Furthermore, it provides safe and compliant transportation of hazardous materials. Product Engineering provides a 360-degree view of all relevant aspects in the early stages of a product's life, from first product idea through design to handover to manufacturing. Enterprise Portfolio and Project Management gains insight into cost, time, scope, resources, and quality performance of products and projects.

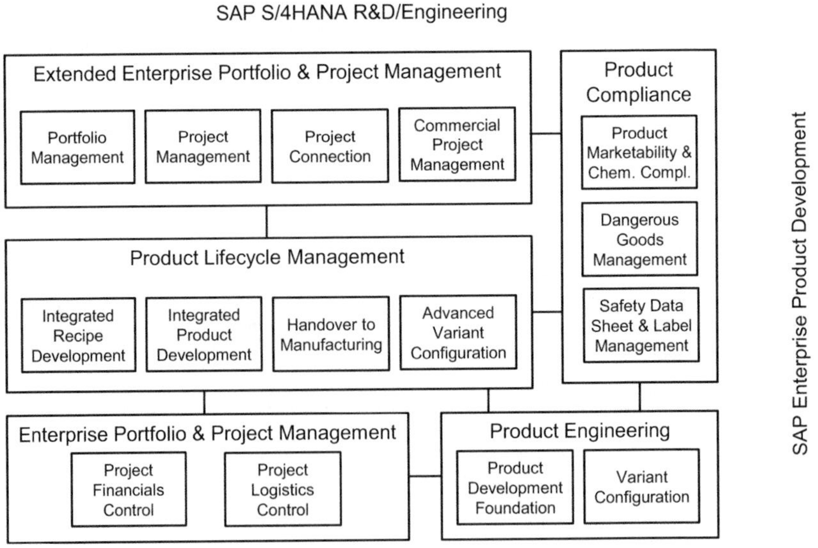

Fig. 8.7 SAP S/4HANA R&D/Engineering—functional architecture

Enterprise Portfolio and Project Management

This module is part of the R&D/Engineering solution in SAP S/4HANA. The Portfolio and Project Management is divided in two parts, the Project Financials Control and the Project Logistics Control. The Project Financials Control is for planning and monitoring costs and budgets. It supports tracking costs which are tightly integrated with core business processes. With this capability it is possible to define work breakdown structures (WBS) which are a basis for hierarchical project accounting. With the cost and budget tracking it is possible to avoid extra costs and to protect the project. This capability includes 13 key features, such as maintenance of standard WBS, milestones, operative and group WBS. Furthermore, changing projects, networks, project versions, and many more are supported (Fig. 8.8).

The Project Logistics Control is integrated with previous capability Project Financials Control. It enables defining project structures consisting of work breakdown structures and network structure, plan and schedule project activities, control all procurement processes integrated with the core business process, and provide an insight into all logistic related execution aspects of a project. Every step is simplified and designed for easy handling. This capability includes seven key features. These cover for example the maintenance of standard and operative networks, defining of network schedules, assigning materials to project and grouping requirement.

Product Engineering

This module is divided in two parts, the Product Development Foundation and the Variant Configuration. The Product Development Foundation provides a product innovation platform as basis for the whole development process. It is possible to integrate innovations and also to manage and translate them, to promote the product design, initiate master data and product structures, and also to integrate the change and configuration management. The embedded software management can be used for a unified product modeling. The Product Development Foundation also includes the bill of material (BOM). The BOM is a list of all materials required in a process together with the required quantities. The administration of the BOM builds the foundation for implementing other concepts like digital factories and Industry 4.0. In general the Product Development Foundation covers BOM handling, product structure management, embedded systems development, engineering change management, classification, document management, attachment service, and variant configuration (Fig. 8.9).

Variant Configuration is part of Product Lifecycle Management (PLM) and is also referred to as product configuration, as it allows customers to create their own model of a product. The users of SAP Variant Configuration define all rules and designs of the product themselves. At the same time a suitable work plan and a bill of materials for production are created. The software also offers other functions, such as price calculation. With the help of variant configuration, the customer or sales representative can specify the product and ensure that the product can be manufactured in the desired way it can be manufactured. The configuration allows not only specified products, but also supports seamless sales and manufacturing processes.

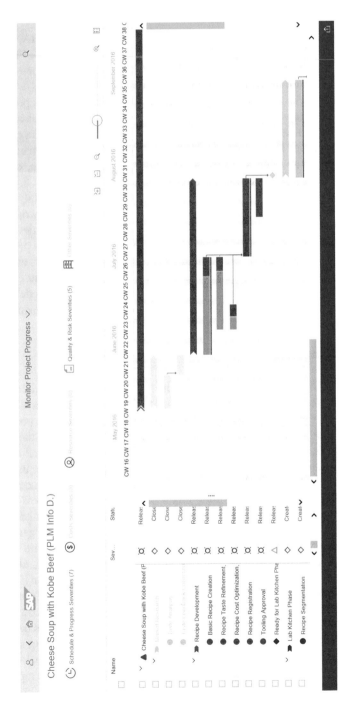

Fig. 8.8 SAP S/4HANA R&D/Engineering—monitor project progress

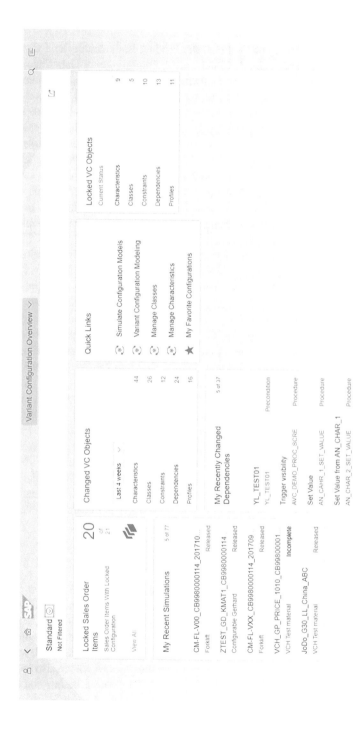

Fig. 8.9 SAP S/4HANA R&D/Engineering—variant configuration overview

Product Compliance

This module includes three subsolutions, the Product Marketability and Chemical Compliance, the Dangerous Goods Management, and the Safety Data Sheet Management and Hazard Label Data. Product Marketability and Chemical Compliance assists in the management of material and ingredient information as well as meeting legal and customer requirements. It collects compliance data from suppliers and customers and makes compliance information available to the public. In addition, this application automatically tracks volumes of regulated substances and assess and verifies products and materials for different compliance requirements including required registrations and tracked-versus-allowed quantities. This solution includes five key features. These are management of compliance requirements, management of compliance assessment processes, compliance controls embedded in business processes, compliance explorer and monitoring, and the management and publishing of compliance documents (Fig. 8.10).

The Dangerous Goods Management handles dangerous goods information centrally for all products, regions, and modes of transport. It automates dangerous goods (DG) classification and provides regulatory content. Furthermore, the application ensures that all shipments are DG compliant through integrated dangerous goods checks, providing adequate packaging, accurate transportation modes and routing, and to automate the creation and provisioning of dangerous goods documents. This solution includes four key features. These are dangerous goods classification, dangerous goods processing, dangerous goods embedded into key business processes, and output of dangerous goods information (Fig. 8.11).

The objective of the Safety Data Sheet Management and Hazard Label Data is to manage substance and regulatory information centrally, streamline component and product classification, and automate safety data sheet and label creation. Furthermore, it uses regulatory content to reduce effort and ensure ongoing compliance and to automate label printing and safety data sheet shipping integrated in logistics processes. This solution includes four key features which are data management for safety data sheets and hazard labels, safety data sheet generation using templates, safety data sheet publishing, and hazard labels embedded into business processes.

Product Lifecycle Management

This module consists of Integrated Recipe Development, Integrated Product Development, Handover to Manufacturing, and the Advanced Variant Configuration (AVC). The Integrated Recipe Development is a tool to describe the manufacturing of products or the execution of a process. Recipes comprise information about the products and components of a process, the process steps to be executed, and the resources required for the production. There are recipe types which are also included in the recipe development. These recipe types help to create a description of the product by considering the instructions and create the product. By making the data of enterprise-wide recipes more concrete, customers are enabled to derive site- and plant-specific recipes from it (Fig. 8.12).

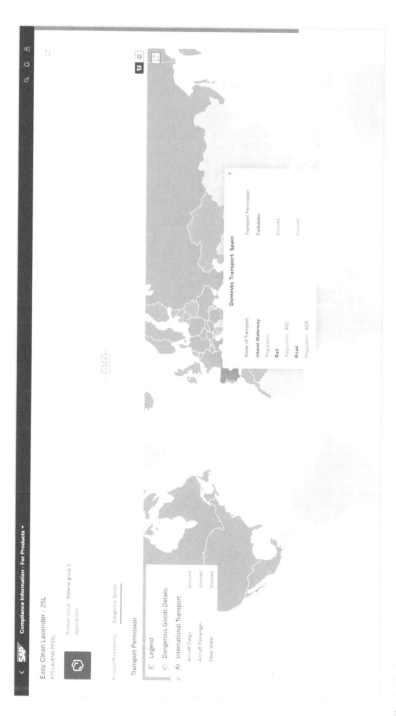

Fig. 8.10 SAP S/4HANA R&D/Engineering—compliance information for products

Fig. 8.11 SAP S/4HANA R&D/Engineering—classification of dangerous goods

Fig. 8.12 SAP S/4HANA R&D/Engineering—recipe analysis

The Integrated Product Development is for discrete manufacturing. It accelerates design by integrating product lifecycle management in a single, real-time environment. The solution validates and controls complex products structures, including the definition and management of hardware and software compatibility. It creates individualized products by defining and reusing variant product structures across the supply chain. In addition, this application differentiates the product from the competition and improves its reliability by collaborating with customers and end users and by incorporating real-time operational feedback into the product development processes. The Integrated Product Development includes embedded systems development, visual instance planner, visual asset planner, 3D visual enterprise manufacturing planner, access control management, engineering change and record management. The Handover to Manufacturing is the efficient handover from Product Engineering to Production Engineering by working in one integrated real-time solution. It minimizes product cost by thoroughly understanding product- and resource-related master data. The solution improves agility by deploying flexible manufacturing practices based on plant resources and capabilities. The end-to-end visualization helps to eliminate errors and improves quality. For the Advanced Variant Configuration, it is important to react quickly and to meet the demands of the customer. Variant configuration facilitates a simpler and faster exchange of information within the company up to delivery to the customer. It improves sales and product engineering performance for advanced variant configuration by implementing a new state-of-the-art configurator. This utilizes a comprehensive simulation environment for variant configuration models and enables user-friendly classification capabilities. The integrated advanced variant configurator supports multilevel variant configuration models. It efficiently manages constraints without coding, supported by a new tracing and inconsistency handling functionality.

Extended Enterprise Portfolio and Project Management

This module covers Portfolio Management, Project Connection, Project Management, and Commercial Project Management. It is based on Enterprise Portfolio and Project Management and was just extended. The Extended Enterprise Portfolio and Project Management help to increase efficiency and automation for gaining insights for products and projects into cost, time, scope, resources, and quality performance. It combines the four parts: Portfolio Management, Project Management, Project Connection, and Commercial Project Management.

Portfolio Management aligns portfolios with strategy while analyzing risk and performance in real time with SAP S/4HANA. It supports investing in the right projects and identifies those that can generate the most business value by instantly scoring and ranking proposals. Furthermore, the solution gains rapid insights into the performance of entire project portfolio through real-time analytics and monitoring. Project Management allows to plan, carry out, and monitor projects in real time to minimize deviations in schedule, cost, and scope. Thus, real-time insights into project cost, time, scope, and quality performance are possible. The solution manages the resources, schedule, and financial performance for each project phase,

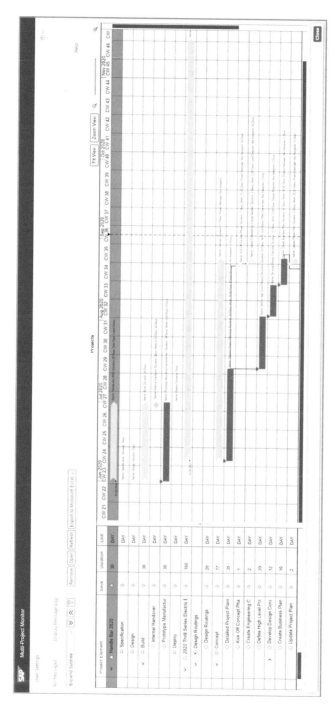

Fig. 8.13 SAP S/4HANA R&D/Engineering—project monitoring

from project initiation through closure. It minimizes delays and prevents business interruptions by monitoring the progress of projects in real time (Fig. 8.13).

Project Connection streamlines and automates a bidirectional exchange of project information with external scheduling tools. It oorchestrates exchange through business rules defining the sequence of creating and modifying project elements—dynamically, based on project types and other criteria. The application exchanges plant maintenance orders with third-party scheduling tools for full processing maintenance, from planning and scheduling to execution and progress tracking. Commercial Project Management covers multiple processes in an end-to-end scenario spanning the selling, planning, performing, monitoring, and controlling of projects. Companies that sell projects (e.g., in professional services or the engineering and construction industries) can so professionalize their core business processes and expand beyond back-office capabilities.

Conclusion

The Idea to Market is a core business process in companies for developing products and services. It starts with defining product and service strategy, portfolio management, planning of investments, and continues with transferring ideas to requirements and detail design. In SAP S/4HANA this end-to-end process is mainly covered by SAP S/4HANA R&D/Engineering component. This solution provides capabilities for portfolio and project management, product engineering, and compliance but also handles the whole product lifecycle management. The SAP S/4HANA modules are deeply integrated and frequently interacting so that also additional components contribute to handle this end-to-end process.

Process of Source to Pay

9

This chapter describes the business process source to pay consisting of the subprocesses plan to optimize sourcing and procurement, source to contract, plan to optimize fulfillment, procure to receipt, request to resolution, manage supplier and collaboration. Additionally, the application capabilities of SAP S/4HANA to resolve those business processes are explained.

Business Process

The general process of Source to Pay is depicted in Fig. 9.1 and explained in detail in the next sections.

Sourcing and procurement are critical functions in almost every organization. In general, a procurement process occurs when one organization purchases a good or service from another organization or individual. These procurement activities are classified as either direct or indirect. Direct procurement involves purchasing materials and services that contribute to the production or delivery of a product, whereas indirect, or supporting, procurement involves the acquisition of materials and services to keep the firm running. The Source to Pay refers to an end-to-end process handling purchasing, ordering, and paying for goods or services. The process starts with analyzing the spend profile and clarifying the purchasing requirements. Based on this information purchase quotas for products and services are defined and procurement contracts are negotiated. Purchasing requisitions are assigned to sources and purchase orders are created. Receiving products and services are prepared by coordinating dock and yard logistics. The process also covers supplier claims and return management. Furthermore, supplier invoices are processed and considered in account payable. Supportive tasks like certifying and validating suppliers, managing supplier catalogs, or evaluating supplier performance are enclosed.

© The Author(s), under exclusive license to Springer Nature Switzerland AG 2022
S. Sarferaz, *Compendium on Enterprise Resource Planning*,
https://doi.org/10.1007/978-3-030-93856-7_9

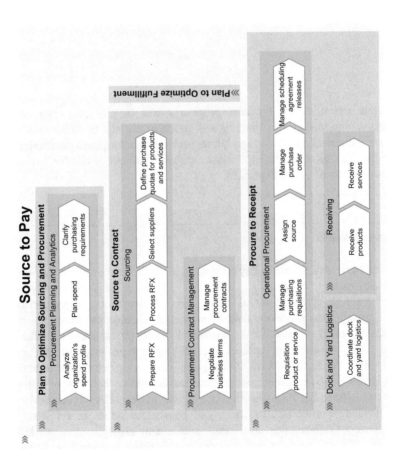

Fig. 9.1 Process source to pay

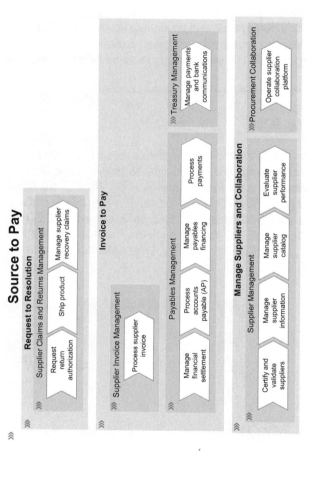

Fig. 9.1 (continued)

Plan to Optimize Sourcing and Procurement (Fig. 9.2)

An organization typically identifies and sources the requirement before purchasing a good or service. Sourcing is the process of matching the organization's needs with a supplier who can provide the necessary goods or services. Identifying and understanding the requirements, narrowing down the pool of bidders to the most viable suppliers, requesting information and bids from suppliers, awarding the purchase to the supplier with the best proposal, and then moving to the procurement process by creating a purchase order or contract are all steps in the sourcing process. The first subprocess deals with the analysis of the general purchasing strategies of a company. Thus, the organization's spending profile is investigated, expenditures are planned, and purchasing needs are clarified. The goal is to get an overview of the required purchases.

Source to Contract (Fig. 9.3)

The subprocess of the selection of the source takes place over a RFx. Request for x (RFx) describes a procedure, to organize an invitation to tender. Typically, RFx consists of three components: Request for Information (RFI), Request for Quote (RFQ), and Request for Proposal (RFP). Thus, the first step is to prepare and initialize the RFx. Usually, the RFx starts with the RFI and then passes through the RFQ and RFP. During the RFx phase the different potential suppliers are compared. The RFx phase ends once a company has decided on a source. Once a source is selected, the

Fig. 9.2 Plan to optimize sourcing and procurement

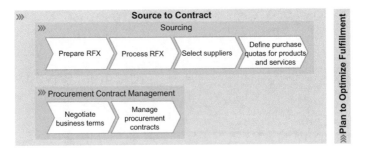

Fig. 9.3 Source to contract

final step is to define the purchasing quotas for the various products and services with the source. In context of Procurement Contract Management, the business terms are negotiated, and the contracts are created. The follow-up process to Source to Contract is Plan to Optimize Fulfillment. This process accompanies the most important steps to achieve optimal fulfillment of the orders. The activities involved in sourcing goods and services range from day-to-day sourcing requirements such as locating a supplier for office supplies to more strategic sourcing activities such as projecting and forecasting demand in a key spend category for the company and negotiating the best prices with an optimal supplier mix. Sourcing isn't always or even always only about price. A supplier may offer the best price, but if the supplier is unable to deliver on that price or is challenged by external factors, having the best price may be an unacceptable trade-off, resulting in a large-scale supply chain disruption or a degradation in the quality of the end product.

Procure to Receipt (Fig. 9.4)

Procurement usually picks up where sourcing leaves off, creating purchase requisitions and issuing purchase orders for goods or services to the supplier identified as the source of supply during the sourcing process. In general, the Procure to Receipt describes the process from procurement to goods receipt. The first intermediate step is the Operational Procurement. The objective here is to determine which products or services are needed for manufacturing. Based on information adequate sources are assigned to the individual required products and services. Once a source is selected, the next task is to create corresponding orders and release the scheduling agreement. Dock and Yard Logistics covers the coordination of the loading bays and the traffic on the plant premises. The last subprocess of goods movement is receiving the ordered goods. The Receiving of products and services differs. While services are consumed, products are stored in warehouse. Depending on the production strategy of the company and the capacities, incoming goods can also be processed immediately. In many industries, a growing trend is to move from traditional business models based on the production and selling of goods toward

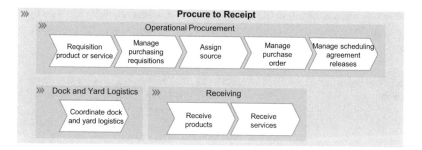

Fig. 9.4 Procure to receipt

bundling diverse offerings combining goods, warranties, continuous maintenance, and licenses into an overall service offering. A typical example might be selling a driving experience through lease options instead of selling a car, together with a service plan, guaranteed work, and standard repairs. As a result, services are infiltrating the heart of the business world more and more. Employees are the primary drivers of operational procurement. An employee recognizes a need and enters it into the system to place an order. Stock, consumables, and external services are the three main types of procurement conducted in operational procurement. Stock procurement is commonly used for direct procurement activities, and it entails purchasing stock items and storing them in inventory for management and distribution. A consumable item is frequently an indirect item that is consumed and replenished on a regular basis but is not managed as inventory in the system. Pens, paper, coffee for the office kitchen, and other consumables may be ordered by the office manager or directly by an employee who notices that the office is running low on a particular item. This type of indirect purchasing is typically of low value and high volume. Because of the high volume, it has a significant impact on an organization's overall spending. Consumable spending is also an ideal area to manage procurement using self-service processes in a system, allowing buyers to focus on strategic spending in the organization and allowing the requesting employee to select exactly what they require without going outside the organization's regular approval and spend processes. Purchasing services such as building maintenance, consulting, or other tasks suitable for contingent labor fall under the purview of external services procurement. External services are provided by individuals or groups who are not employees of the organization but are only involved in that specific scope of work. External services can be included in both direct and indirect procurement activities.

Request to Resolution (Fig. 9.5)

Failures can occur in the procurement of products or services. Thus, Request to Resolution deals with the handling of complaints and returns. Goods or services that don't meet the expectations result in claims. Once the claims are recorded and resolved with the supplier, the return process is triggered. In most cases, the provider of the goods must coordinate the return transport. Claims are in focus of analytics in order to identify gaps and continuously improve the processes and products.

Fig. 9.5 Request to resolution

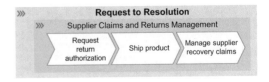

Invoice to Pay (Fig. 9.6)

Finally, the process concludes with payment, which includes receiving and processing receipts and invoices in subsequent processes. While payments are typically triggered at the end of a procurement process and the beginning of a sourcing process, some procurement scenarios are common enough exceptions to call a one-size-fits-all sequence into question. The Invoice to Pay is handled by the end-to-end process Finance. However, this is of course essential for the procurement of goods as it deals with the payment of the invoices. A supplier invoice is a payment document from a supplier for materials that were delivered or services that were performed. Supplier Invoice Management includes processing of supplier invoices which is about obtaining the invoice and to trigger the payment. Based on accounts payable the financial settlements are incorporated and financing payables initiated which performs the payments. The financial settlements are considered as the main element within the process. Starting from the financial settlements, the accounts payable are processed. Another element of the accounting office is the settlement of the open liabilities. Due to the integration in the process of goods procurement, the liabilities to the various suppliers are to be settled here. Treasury Management focuses on the communication with banks to process the payments. Treasury Management provides assistance with treasury processes such as cash and liquidity management, debt and investment management, and foreign exchange risk management.

Manage Suppliers and Collaboration (Fig. 9.7)

Manage Suppliers and Collaboration is divided into two subprocesses. The objective of the Supplier Management is to organize and analyze the existing suppliers. Thus, the first step is to certify and validate the existing suppliers based on internal criteria. Such an approach allows a better classification of the existing suppliers. Next the supplier information is managed which covers for example master data but also various RFx documents. An up-to-date and comprehensive listing of all relevant information is essential to be able to select the right supplier. Suppliers are categorized in a catalog. So, for the selection of the source this catalog with all important information can be used. A final step, which is carried out in connection with the

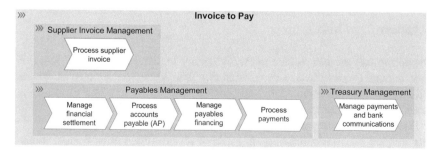

Fig. 9.6 Invoice to pay

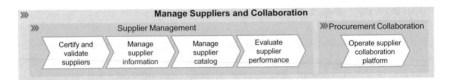

Fig. 9.7 Manage suppliers and collaboration

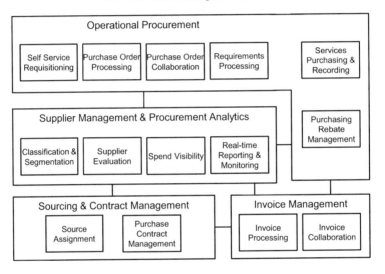

Fig. 9.8 SAP S/4HANA Sourcing and Procurement—functional architecture

suppliers, is the evaluation of the performance. This step allows the company to decide which source to choose for a new order based on the previous deliveries. Access to supplier networks is essential for which supplier collaboration platforms are used.

Solution Capability

The end-to-end process Source to Pay is mainly implemented by SAP S/4HANA Sourcing and Procurement as depicted in Fig. 9.8. While SAP S/4HANA Sourcing and Procurement covers the core functionality, SAP Ariba and SAP Fieldglass add extended features, for example, guided buying capability and catalog.

For practically every company the process of sourcing and procurement is vital. Procurement is about purchasing of goods or services from other organizations or individuals. While direct procurement refers to purchasing materials and services that contribute to a product being produced or delivered, indirect procurement is about acquiring materials and services to keep the firm itself functioning. The purchasing department must track the procurement process including purchase orders, goods and invoice receipts, and services entry sheets. Before companies purchase goods or services, they typically identify and source their requirements. Sourcing is defined as the process of matching the product and service needs with potential suppliers for provisioning. For this the requirements have to be analyzed in detail and winnowed down the pool of bidders to the most adequate suppliers. Furthermore, information and bids have to be requested from suppliers. Awarding the purchase to the supplier with the best proposal, and then moving to the procurement process by creating a purchase order or contract belong also to the core steps of the process. By integrating automated or manual functions, Operational Procurement streamlines the purchasing process. Analytic visualization embedded within transactional applications aids human decision-making. In addition, the solution determines the actual cost of product-based purchasing rebate agreements with suppliers. Sourcing and Contract Management ensures delivery of committed quantities and values. It finds, negotiates, and contracts the most qualified, reliable sources and suppliers efficiently. Invoice Management provides accurate invoices to accounts payable faster with electronic invoicing and automated verification. The solution improves the invoice processing lifecycle by increasing transparency and speed. Supplier Management and Procurement Analytics gains visibility to determine the right mix of suppliers, best serve to business objectives, and reduce overall supply risk. It reveals near-real-time insights into organizational spend, suppliers, and market information. Central Procurement integrates the SAP S/4HANA hub system with multiple SAP ERP and SAP S/4HANA back-end systems.

Operational Procurement

A purchase requisition is defined as a request to procure a certain quantity of a material or a service with a defined delivery time point. A purchase requisition builds the starting point in purchasing and can be created manually in SAP S/4HANA. However, also a demand from a material requirement planning (MRP) job can also result in a purchase requisition. Usually purchase requisitions are subject to a release strategy or trigger an approval process based on the workflow engine. A purchase order is defined as a request to an external supplier to deliver a specific quantity of material at defined time point, or to perform certain services within an explicit time period. Operational procurement is performed usually at the employee level. An employee identifies a requirement and creates an order. Stock, consumables, and external services are the main types of procurement. Stock is for direct procurement activities and entails purchasing stock items and taking them into inventory for distribution. Consumable procurement is about indirect items which are consumed and replenished on an ongoing basis but not handled in the inventory. Buying services, such as real-estate maintenance or consulting are covered by the category of external services procurement. External services are provided by persons or

Fig. 9.9 SAP S/4HANA Sourcing and Procurement—purchase order and monitor purchase order

organizations that typically are not employed by the company. External services can be in focus of direct as well as indirect procurement activities.

Self Service Requisitioning provides consumer-grade UX and cross-catalog search that enables employees to adopt procurement processes and policies. It supports enhanced workflow to complete purchase requisitions including workflow inbox Fiori app and notification center. Purchase Order Processing and Collaboration enable indirect and direct procurement leveraging integration with other business areas, automation, and harmonized UX. The solution provides analytical apps to monitor the status of purchase orders. Comprehensive business process integration with Business Network is also supported. Flexible workflow enhancements such as keeping purchase order deadlines or adding tax dates are provided by the application. Thus, increased visibility by including quantity delivery deficit situations is ensured (Fig. 9.9).

Requirement Processing allows control over automation and manual intervention where appropriate. In addition, human decision-making is supported by analytical visualization embedded within transactional applications. Service Purchasing and Recording provides harmonized UX for both goods and service purchasing processes. It simplifies limit (value-only) purchase order items to control over unplanned services and record details via Fiori service entry sheet application. Purchasing Rebate Management handles the purchasing rebate lifecycle, from planning to tracking, settling, and analyzing rebate agreements.

Sourcing and Contract Management

Sourcing of goods and services is about finding the optimal supplier but also covers more strategic activities for projecting and forecasting demand in a core spend category for the business and includes negotiating the best prices with the best supplier mix. However, even if suppliers offer the best price, they might not be selected due to quality gaps or delayed delivery time point. Thus, elementary for the procurement process is the Source Assignment. In practice, this is supported by SAP S/4HANA and SAP Ariba. SAP Ariba is an online business to business marketplace that can be used to identify new potential suppliers. SAP enables the seamless integration of SAP Ariba and SAP S/4HANA. In addition to integration, SAP S/4HANA also offers various analytics apps to monitor different RFQs or compare different supply offers. By the interaction of the SAP S/4HANA's core functions and the integrated SAP Ariba, the user is enabled to perform a complete source search. Purchase Case Contract Management provides analytic apps to manage the status of contracts and agreements. A purchase contract is an outline purchase agreement between the supplier and the company which procure special materials or services. In SAP S/4HANA an overview of all existing contracts is provided with various sorting and grouping functions. From the list of contracts, the renewing process can be triggered. Validity status of each contract including navigation into contract details are provided. To avoid manual activities the prices and conditions from the contract are copied automatically into the purchase order when referring to a contract. Contract template enables reusing data that is inherited from the template whenever new contracts are created. This reduces both the time and effort for spending on filling out the data. With flexible workflow approvers can easily approve or decline purchase contracts. This workflow process can be implemented based on automatic, one-step, or multi-step approval. Predictive algorithm allows to monitor contracts to help plan contract negotiations. Furthermore, templates and mass changes are offered to increase efficiency in managing a large number of contracts. Unplanned services are stored with reference to purchasing contracts to simplify the process.

Invoice Management

Supplier invoices are created after receiving the invoice from the supplier. They can be created with reference to a purchase order or without any reference. In case of references the corresponding delivery note or service entry sheet can be used. To ensure that the supplier invoice is correct, the invoice verification checks are performed. The supplier invoice can be simulated before posting the document to show the account movements. Furthermore, one clerk can park the invoice document while another clerk completes and posts the process. In case the invoice reduction functionality is activated during the creation of an invoice, output management is triggered automatically to inform the supplier. The output can also be scheduled based on a regular job. It is as well possible to post a supplier invoice to a purchase order limit item that defines a value limit either for unplanned materials or for unplanned services. In such cases, the invoice amount must be directly checked against the value limit. Supplier invoices can be searched, and the results used as a supplier invoice worklist. This worklist allows displaying the detail data, for example, showing a list of blocked supplier invoices for later release. Invoices can be released manually by selecting the blocked invoices using different filters. However, also automatic release of invoices is supported. For this, the system checks each blocking reason to evaluate whether it is still valid. Supplier invoices assigned to clerk can be performed by workflow. The clerk approves or rejects the corresponding work item. If necessary, work items are forwarded to a different employee for further processing. Invoice Processing and Collaboration enable uploading of supplier invoice attachments and allow fully automated implementation without user interaction. The solution helps to manage supplier invoices and payment blocks. Uploading scanned invoice copies for manual invoice processing with optional integration with OCR via OpenText is provided. Native integration with SAP Business Network is possible which is a cloud-based offering for cooperation with logistics partners. Thus, isolated supply chains are managed into a homogeneous, collaborative, and intelligent network that is barrier-free and centralizes data (Fig. 9.10).

Supplier Management and Procurement Analytics

The classification and segmentation of suppliers is an ongoing process in which suppliers are assessed and classified at regular intervals and allocated to segments of different importance. Purchasers can then focus especially on those suppliers that are strategically important and critical to the business, thus enabling them to develop and manage their business relationships. Purchasing categories enable buyers to manage suppliers based on specific types of goods and services, such as hardware and software or installation and inspection. The categories enable to monitor the pool of suppliers and optimize the purchasing process. Purchasing categories are as well a significant structuring element in the supplier evaluation process. They enable purchasers to compare the evaluations of all suppliers in the same purchasing category. A central overview of the master data is provided for each supplier, such

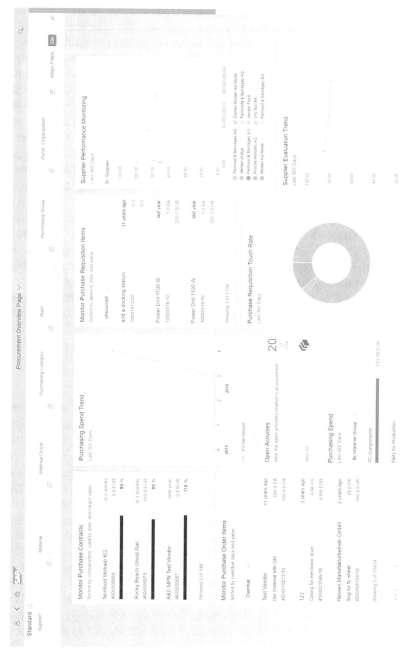

Fig. 9.10 SAP S/4HANA Sourcing and Procurement—procurement overview

as address details, contact person, bank, and tax data. In the context of supplier evaluation, corresponding requests are sent out to appraisers, asking them to fill out questionnaires about a supplier. The question and answer options are created first, and then they are included in one or more questionnaires. The questionnaires can be included in evaluation templates, which will be used to send out evaluation requests. Questions can also be created in the question library. For a better overview, sections can be used to structure the questions. Evaluation scorecards can be displayed that show the overall result of a supplier evaluation for one supplier. Classification Segmentation and Supplier Evaluation provide increased flexibility in supplier evaluation by defining individual supplier evaluation criteria like weighting and scoring. The solution allows for real-time analysis of the parts per million score in order to discuss potential quality improvement activities with the supplier. Real-time supplier evaluation analytics are generated automatically from transactional data. Furthermore, activities with suppliers or internal employee surveys to additional perspective on supplier evaluations are handled (Fig. 9.11).

Spend Visibility and Real-time Reporting and Monitoring enable increased transparency about the automation rate: high touch—low touch, how many documents were processed manually instead of automatically. The solution provides a real-time multidimensional spend report that can be manipulated like a pivot table and includes drill-down functionality. KPI tiles are provided so that at-a-glance exceptional situations can be identified and drilled-down for root cause analysis. With corresponding insight-to-action capabilities issues can be immediately resolved with the underlying transactional applications.

Central Procurement

This solution enables integration of the SAP S/4HANA hub system with multiple SAP ERP and SAP S/4HANA back-end systems. Contract management, purchasing, and requisitioning processes can be centralized with the hub system. Optionally leverage SAP Ariba solutions can be leveraged. Central Purchase Contract Hierarchy enables large enterprises to standardize requirements across multiple business groups. New updated source lists in connected back-end system are provided after central purchase contract distribution. Central Requisitioning allows employees to have a unified shopping experience where they can create self-service requisitions in SAP S/4HANA. Items for materials or services can be created which are extracted from external catalogs and from an integrated cross-content search based on SAP S/4HANA. Additionally, free-text items can be created if none of the materials in the connected system or the ones extracted into the hub system matches the requirements. This scenario also enables the user to confirm the ordered goods or services in the hub system. Central Sourcing facilitates purchasers to get an overview of all purchasing needs across various plants of the company and to source for all plants centrally. This results in an optimized procurement process and increases the overall savings. Purchasers can check all purchase requisitions in the connected systems and source for these purchase requisitions centrally. Central Sourcing

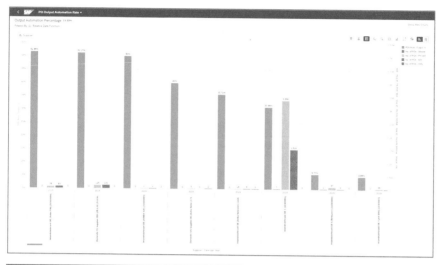

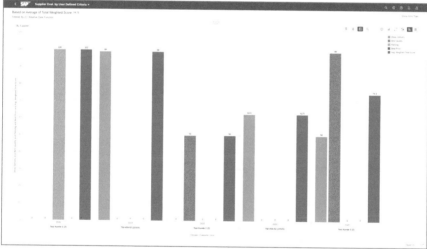

Fig. 9.11 SAP S/4HANA Sourcing and Procurement—automation rate and supplier evaluation

allows the creation of central requests for quotations, publishing them and after the bidding process is completed and providing supplier quotations on behalf of suppliers. Central Purchase Contracts facilitates the creation of central contracts which cover long-term agreements between organizations and suppliers regarding the supply of materials or the performance of services within a certain period as per predefined terms and conditions. The solution enables purchasers from different parts of a company in different locations to benefit from the negotiated terms and conditions. Central Purchasing provides a single point of access for viewing and managing purchasing documents. Purchase requisitions and purchase orders are examples of such documents. SAP S/4HANA supports the integration with external

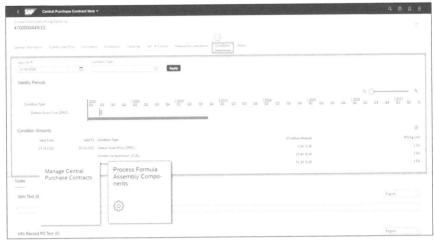

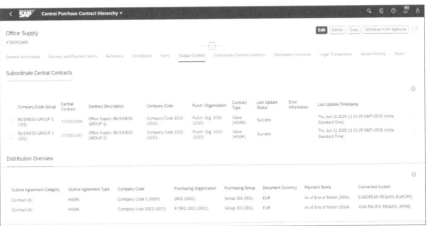

Fig. 9.12 SAP S/4HANA Central Procurement—commodity pricing and contract hierarchy

procurement systems (e.g., SAP Ariba Sourcing). If an external procurement system is integrated and supports the features below, central supplier quotations and follow-on documents such as central purchase contracts or purchase orders can be created automatically (Fig. 9.12).

Extended functionality with commodity management for procurement and sales processing is offered to enable advanced commodity pricing on procurement documents. It allows to create commodity sales contracts priced on market quotes, automate price calculations, and streamline invoicing by supporting provisional, differential, and final invoices. With the introduction of new commodity pricing, key users can easily apply complex pricing formulas, commodity weights, and price conditions in Central Procurement.

Conclusion

The Source to Pay is a core business process in companies for procuring materials and facilities that are required to manufacture products or provide services. For this, corresponding suppliers have to be sourced first. The process starts with planning and optimizing of sourcing and procurement and continues with sourcing and contracting suppliers. Receiving and payment of products and services are covered. In SAP S/4HANA this end-to-end process is mainly covered by SAP S/4HANA Sourcing and Procurement component. This solution provides capabilities for supplier management and procurement analytics but also handles operational procurement and invoice management. Furthermore, sourcing and contract management are also covered by the solution. The SAP S/4HANA modules are deeply integrated and frequently interacting so that also additional components contribute to handle this end-to-end process.

Process of Plan to Fulfill

10

This chapter describes the business process plan to fulfill consisting of the subprocesses plan to optimize fulfillment, procure to receipt, make to inspect, deliver product to fulfill, deliver service to fulfill, and manage fulfillment. Additionally, the application capabilities of SAP S/4HANA to resolve those business processes are explained.

Business Process

The general process of Plan to Fulfill is depicted in Fig. 10.1 and explained in detail in the next sections.

Planning and optimizing every step of a company's production are crucial for every product or service launch. Successful planning is key for cost and time efficiency and reduced man hours. Before launching a product or service, one has to derive every single step inside its supply chain, starting with a plan to optimize fulfillment, to making inspections, to further deliver the product or service to fulfillment and ending with the fulfillment management. Supply chain covers the planning, fulfillment, regulation, and tracking of supply chain activities, and includes also warehouse and transportation management. The various modes of production can be divided into the following categories:

- *Discrete manufacturing* is one of the most popular modes of manufacturing used by businesses that use production orders. A product can be assembled or disassembled and reworked in this mode of manufacturing, and it is typically manufactured across multiple work center operations. Manufacturing stages can be clearly distinguished between one operation and the next. Manufacturing begins with a production order, which is created to meet demand based on forecasts in a make-to-stock (MTS) scenario or sales orders in a make-to-order (MTO) scenario. A production order is so important in this type of manufacturing that direct materials, indirect materials, labor and overheads, and scheduling

© The Author(s), under exclusive license to Springer Nature Switzerland AG 2022
S. Sarferaz, *Compendium on Enterprise Resource Planning*,
https://doi.org/10.1007/978-3-030-93856-7_10

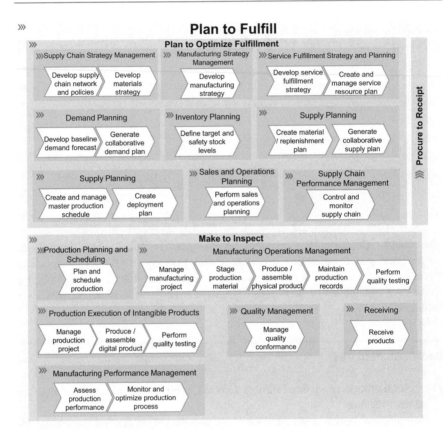

Fig. 10.1 Process plan to fulfill

information are all captured within the production order to provide a clear picture of the actual time, material consumption, and production costs.

- *Process manufacturing* is a common manufacturing method used in the chemical, consumer products (food/beverage and home care products), and pharmaceutical industries. Within these industries, process manufacturing integrates various stages of production, from filling and mixing silos or tanks with inbound materials, to actual production, to filling the finished product in tanks or containers for transportation. This type of manufacturing also takes into account materials that are fed into the process via pipelines, thus covering a wide range of process possibilities. Process manufacturing is typically done in phases and spread across resources, but it is not always possible to distinguish one phase from another. The majority of these industries employ batch-managed manufacturing driven by a process order. Process orders, like production orders in discrete manufacturing, play an important role in process manufacturing, for example, by providing a view of the actual factors of production.

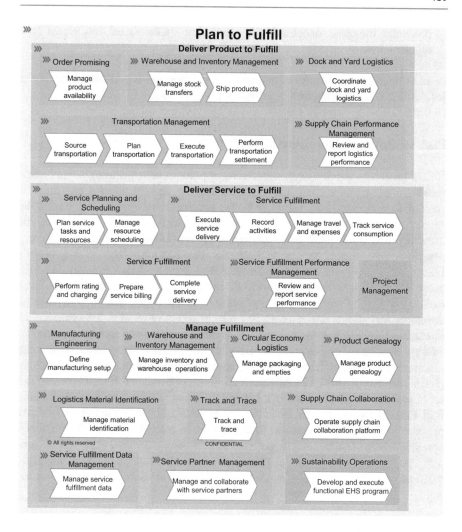

Fig. 10.1 (continued)

- *Repetitive manufacturing* is a mode of production in which similar products are produced repeatedly and continuously on a set of work centers. The primary distinction between repetitive, discrete, and process manufacturing is that repetitive manufacturing is driven by times and quantities in production rather than orders. In this mode of production, the rate at which each product is produced is an important metric. Planned orders are the result of a material requirements planning (MRP) run. Planned orders determine the run schedule, which determines production quantities and times. Material consumption is typically done in retrospect, via periodic backflushing. Depending on the material being produced, the costs associated with production are calculated and settled on a regular basis.

In addition to these modes of manufacturing, there is also lean manufacturing or just-in-time (JIT) manufacturing, primarily via Kanban.

Plan to Optimize Fulfillment (Fig. 10.2)

Before launching service or manufacturing a product corresponding supply chain network must be developed. This network includes several policies that must be applied. In addition to that, a strategy for the materials must be defined. Planning the supply chain helps to anticipate and manage the demands of the customers, the inventory and operational risks and opportunities. Developing and managing a manufacturing strategy is key to keep the manufacturing stage of a product's lifecycle organized and structured for the future. Manufacturing Strategy Management gives the user the opportunity to record a manufacturing strategy for a particular business unit and plan according to it. First there has to be a strategy developed how the service of a company is supposed to be fulfilled. This strategy has to contain all the necessary resources to achieve a successful fulfillment. When a strategy has been developed it is necessary to estimate which and how much resources are required. For that reason, creating and managing a service resource plan is also part of Service Fulfillment Strategy and Planning. Demand Planning is a set of processes and functionality that revolves around demand management, statistical forecasting, promotion, and lifecycle planning. It is an integral part of any organization's Sales & Operations Planning Process including the development of a baseline demand forecast and to generate a collaborative demand plan. With Inventory Planning organizations can plan the optimal stock of products at a specific location. The company considers whether it is better to stock or destock at a location,

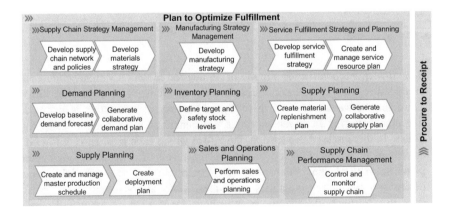

Fig. 10.2 Plan to optimize fulfillment

and calculates the economic order quantity in conjunction with safety stock for each location product. As a result, the company keeps stockholding costs as low as possible and reduces ordering costs. At the same time, it ensures a high level of customer service. The main task of Supply Planning is to balance demand with supply within the company's supply chain. This includes the creation of a material and replenishment plan, the generation of a collaborative supply chain, the creation and management of the master production schedule and deployment plan. With effective supply planning, companies are able to optimize inventory levels and resource utilization, as well as achieve customer satisfaction with the on-time delivery of orders.

Sales and Operations Planning is a versatile forecasting and planning activity that allows sales, production, and other supply chain targets to be set based on historical, current, and projected future data. Rough-cut planning can also be used to determine the quantities of capacities and other resources needed to meet these targets. Sales and Operations Planning can be used to streamline and consolidate a company's sales and production operations and is particularly suitable for long- and medium-term planning. The Supply Chain Performance Management helps companies to make their supply chain more effective and responsive in the face of complex and fast-changing market conditions. By focusing on the right process metrics, companies can track performance, identify bottlenecks, and uncover opportunities. It enables both departmental and organizational performance management. Thus, end-to-end supply chain visibility is provided for enabling both departmental and organizational performance management.

Make to Inspect (Fig. 10.3)

Material requirements planning ensures the availability of materials and performs basic production planning. Sufficient supplies have to be planned to cover

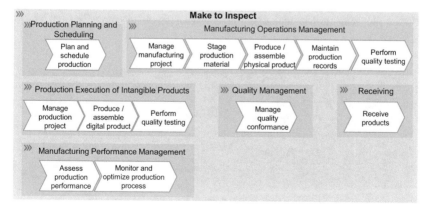

Fig. 10.3 Make to inspect

requirements—whether from sales orders, stock transfer orders, or from production. The goal is to ensure that both costumer and production demands are available on time and to avoid any disruptions due to missing parts. Manufacturing Operations Management has the objective to manage the manufacturing project. This includes staging production materials, producing and assembling physical products, maintaining productions records, and performing quality testing.

Production Execution of Intangible Products focuses on immaterial assets like services and has therefore only the objectives to manage the production project, produce and assemble digital products, and perform quality testing. Production materials aren't required here and therefore no staging. Quality planning ensures the quality of products, processes, and services right from the start. It is important during early stages of product design and development to implement appropriate quality-planning strategies inside every process. Receiving is about obtaining products in stores by displaying and posting incoming handling units. In this context checks are performed regarding the content of handling units with the expected and actually received product quantities. Manufacturing Performance Management has the objective to assess the production performance and to monitor and optimize the production process.

Deliver Product to Fulfill (Fig. 10.4)

Customers have high expectations when it comes to order promises. They want their products as fast and as reliable as possible. Customers are no longer willing to buy something without knowing the exact delivery date. Managing the product availability is therefore the main objective of Order Promising. Many companies run production facilities in different regions. They have to evaluate which facility handles the request. Other companies may evaluate alternatives for an out-of-stock product. All these factors must be taken into account when promising an order, in order not to run the risk of breaking the delivery promise. Inventory Management addresses the recording and tracking of materials on a quantity and value basis. This includes planning, entry, and documentation of stock movements such as good

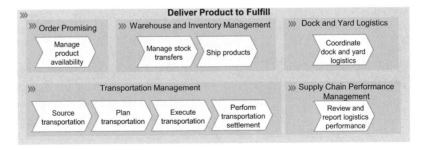

Fig. 10.4 Deliver product to fulfill

receipts, goods issues, physical stock transfers and transfer postings as well as the performance of physical inventory.

While Inventory Management handles the stocks by quantity and value, the Warehouse Management component reflects the special structure of a warehouse and monitors the allocation of the storage bins and any transfer transactions like shipping in the warehouse. Thus, organizations manage their material flow, using advanced put away and picking strategies. It is important to get products and services to market faster and to improve customer service by identifying, avoiding, and solving potential issues. Dock and Yard Logistics accelerate gate-in and gate-out processes for executing activities faster and increasing yard throughput. Thus, resource usage, planning, execution and billing are optimized. Transportation Management reduces costs and improves service with streamlined transportation management processes. It supports the complete transportation management lifecycle for both domestic and international freight to improve customer satisfaction. Furthermore, transportation needs are met by planning, optimizing, tendering, and settling freight, booking carriers, managing forwarding orders, and adhering to international trade and hazardous goods regulations. Supply Chain Performance Management is important to review and report logistics performance. Bad performance can lead to extra costs and slower delivery. This can be avoided by analyzing the reviews and by taking corrective actions.

Deliver Service to Fulfill (Fig. 10.5)

Service Planning and Scheduling is required to perform optimized Just-in-Time productions. The company has to plan service tasks and required resources. Additionally, the resource scheduling has to be developed in order to have a working supply chain with as little downtime as possible. Service Fulfillment involves several jobs that have to be performed. This task manages the whole service fulfillment like executing service delivery, recording activities, managing travel and expenses, tracking the service consumption, performing rating and charging, preparing service billing, and completing service delivery. Service Fulfillment Performance Management focuses on reviewing and reporting of performance. Bad performance can lead

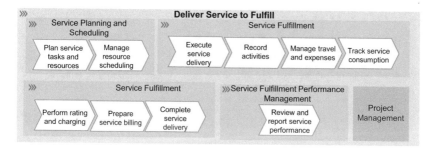

Fig. 10.5 Process plan to fulfill

to extra costs and slower delivery. This can be avoided by analyzing the reviews and by taking corrective actions.

Manage Fulfillment (Fig. 10.6)

Before starting the manufacturing step of the products lifecycle, it has to be established how exactly this step needs to take place. Manufacturing Engineering helps to establish and develop the manufacturing of a product and define the manufacturing setup for a smooth production. By focusing on inventory management, inbound and outbound processing, goods movement, physical inventory, and reporting, Warehouse and Inventory Management improves stock transparency and control. The process optimizes material flow control, yard and labor management, value-added services, kitting and cross-docking. Inventory management handles the mapping of physical stock in real time by logging all stock-moving transactions, allowing for real-time stock updates at any point in time. Not only are stock quantities and values updated with each goods movement, but related general ledger accounts for financial accounting are also updated via automatic account determination. This allows an inventory manager to view the current stock situation for a specific material as well as manage many of its own and external special stock forms. Warehouse Management helps users take control of their warehouse operations to keep up with changing demand while lowering costs. Circular business models reuse everything and cut waste to near zero. Sustainability, especially circularity, is one of the best paths for profitability. These practices are becoming more widespread as a result of growing urbanization and consumer preferences for products, services, and brands that demonstrate a commitment to sustainability. Managing packaging and empties is therefore the most important aspect of Circular Economy Logistics. Managing a products genealogy is vital including forward and backward traceability

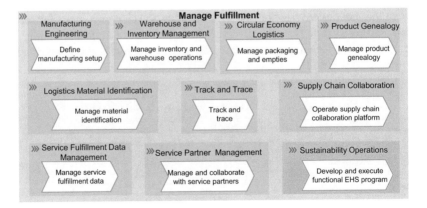

Fig. 10.6 Manage fulfillment

of the product from the main material to its subassemblies. The information displayed on products helps to identify what happened in certain operation activities. For example log of issues, as well as what actions were performed by the production operator are collected. Product Genealogy helps supervisors and quality engineers to identify quality issues in the manufacturing process or to detect if there were any missing or defective components. Material identification is managed in a production instruction sheet by way of dynamic methods. This includes completeness check, sequence check, automatic goods issue posting after the completeness check or sequence check, automatic transfer of data from material identification to the batch record, and a check for completeness of picking. Track and Trace is important to get real-time insights into the availability of materials and products to reduce supply chain risks and optimize costs. Traceability is a core capability to efficiently orchestrate goods to market and mitigate risks. Traceability of the entire supply chain includes visibility into both product creation and the movement of goods and assets across company and system boundaries. Track and Trace provides end-to-end process visibility and status monitoring, enhanced by multitier logistics network capabilities, for all types of logistics and execution processes, as well as serialized object tracking. The supply chain is changing dramatically as a result of technological advancements, improved processes, the availability of alternative resources, and the adoption of innovative business models. There are various stakeholders at various levels who are in charge of multiple tasks that require decision-making. People from various business units and organizations who may not have similar working styles or work environments must collaborate using various modern methods to achieve a common goal with high accuracy and speed. When all stakeholders work effectively together in a network, the organization benefits in a variety of ways. This is the objective of the Supply Chain Collaboration. During the process of service fulfillment data is collected to archive, record, and analyze the process. This leads to a large amount of data which has to be managed to be able to analyze the records. Therefore, Service Fulfillment Data Management helps its users to manage and organize the recorded service fulfillment data.

Service Partner Management focuses on optimization of partner relationship. Partners are individuals who are associated with the resellers, brokers, service providers, distributors, or other entities with which an organization collaborates. Theses collaborations can be useful to share ideas and to deliver superior content.

Sustainability Operations develops and executes a functional Environment, Health and Safety (EHS) program. Through ongoing analysis of operational data and the provision of relevant information, the process engages the workforce and identifies and acts on hazards before they impact safety. It also improves EHS performance by incorporating risk management into daily operations through integrated business processes, shared data, and workflows.

Solution Capability: Supply Chain

The end-to-end process Plan to Fulfill is mainly implemented by SAP S/4HANA Supply Chain and SAP S/4HANA Manufacturing. In this section capabilities of SAP S/4HANA Supply Chain are explained as depicted in Fig. 10.7. While this covers the core functionality, various extension modules like SAP Warehouse Insights, SAP Integrated Planning or SAP Global Batch Traceability are provided.

Logistics Material Identification manages batches, serial numbers, and handling units to increase efficiency and improve compliance across shipping and warehousing operations. Oder Promising generates accurate delivery date estimates during order creation and makes changes based on actual stock information to improve customer satisfaction. Delivery and Transportation orchestrates all delivery demands, plan and executes your transport, using functionality for basic agency billing and subcontracting. It ships the right products to the right place at the right time. Warehouse Management stores and handles goods and materials efficiently. It improves asset usage, increases throughput, and supports accurate on-time order fulfillment with a maximum of warehouse transparency. The component Inventory tracks and controls inventory and stock quantities in a transparent manner and ensure a streamlined material flow across all in and outbound logistics operations. Advanced Order Promising commits to orders quickly and accurately by automatically considering relevant stock in real time, all the while protecting business priorities and profitability goals. Advanced Transportation increases transportation efficiency by managing all inbound and outbound freight holistically. Advanced Warehousing optimizes orders by leveraging features such as cross-docking, workforce management, slotting, inventory optimization, transit warehousing support, and connectivity to warehouse automation equipment. Extended Service Parts Planning plans service parts inventory accurately across distribution networks,

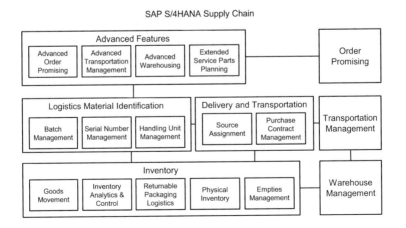

Fig. 10.7 SAP S/4HANA Supply Chain—functional architecture

based on parts volumes, velocity, and segments. It strategically calculates trade-offs between costs and service.

Inventory

Good warehousing helps to store and handle goods and materials efficiently. It improves asset usage, increases throughput, and supports accurate on-time order fulfillment with a maximum of warehouse transparency. Goods Movement uses simplified goods issue postings for transfer and scrapping. It experiences real-time, high-volume processing using sensor data. The solution benefits from locking elimination and material ledger valuation. Inventory Analytics and Control experiences the power of simplification by using state-of-the-art analytical apps, which take full advantage of the simplified data model and the 40-digit long material number. It optimizes inventory and material flows based on real-time information (Fig. 10.8).

Returnable Packaging Logistics tracks shipping and receiving of returnable packaging materials to and from business partners. It gains visibility in materials distribution and reduces overall volume of materials by integrating logistics information into a single version of the truth. Physical Inventory enables real-time reporting on warehouse stocks and inventory. It records the physical quantities of your warehouse stocks/own stock and other stock types. Additionally, the solution enables faster and more-efficient inventory adjustments. Empties Management tracks empties to and from business partners and processes high-volume transactions for empties returns.

Warehouse Management

Basic warehouse management facilitates real-time transparency into managing and processing material movements flexibly for optimized warehouse operations. Basic warehouse management helps organizations from the very beginning, starting with structuring the warehouse by defining physical structures, individual storage types and creating storage bins. The entire warehouse can be mapped into the system, down to storage bin level. Thus, an overview of the total quantity of each product in the warehouse is provided. Additionally, it is possible to always see exactly where a specific product is, at any time, in the warehouse complex. The product quantities can be managed in different stock categories at the following levels: At storage bin level, in intermediate locations, on resources, in handling units or in nested handling units.

A handling unit is a physical unit made up of packaging materials and the goods contained within it. It is always a blend of products and packaging materials. All of the information contained in the product items is stored in the handling units and is always accessible (Fig. 10.9).

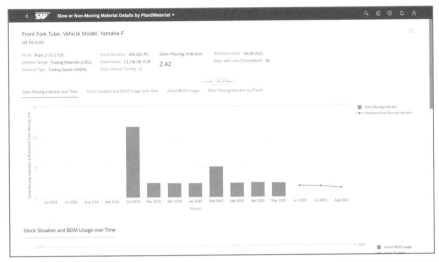

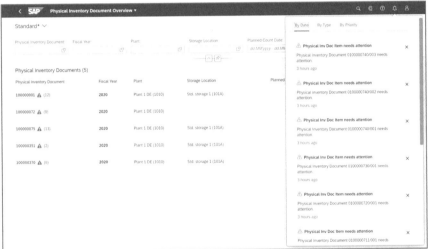

Fig. 10.8 SAP S/4HANA Supply Chain—inventory turnover analysis and physical inventory document overview

Inbound processing allows receiving products from vendors, production, other parts of the company, customer returns including unplanned returns. Warehouse capacity can be optimized and material flow by using put-away strategies. Thus, appropriate storage bins can be searched for incoming products by automatically determining suitable storage bins for the incoming products. Outbound processing allows to pick products and send them out of warehouses for example for sending ordered products to external customers or internal customers such as other plants, supplying products to production or returning products to vendors.

Fig. 10.9 SAP S/4HANA Supply Chain—pick by cart

Logistics Material Identification

Leveraging Batch Management improves product quality, ensures end-to-end traceability, and reduces customer and legal risks. The solution enables the creation of batch master records and the assignment of specific batch numbers, the classification of batches and the assignment of characteristics, the creation of a batch genealogy to automatically comply with legal requirements, and the tracking of batches. Serial Number Management identifies and differentiates between individual items of a material or equipment. It enables to create specific serial number profiles for materials, to create serial number master records to carry important data on the serialized material, and to identify single items to track in inventory management, physical inventory, and equipment. Handling Unit Management reflects packing-based logistics structures and tracks the movements of the entire handling units rather than each material individually. The solution manages materials that are relevant for segmentation in handling units from cartons to containers. It uses unit management in inbound and outbound business processes, goods movement, and transfer posting to improve product traceability. Additionally, the application expands on the existing packing function in shipping and warehouse processing (Fig. 10.10).

Delivery and Transportation

Delivery Management executes and confirms on transportation demands from all sources (sales order, purchase order, stock transport order) in an automated fashion. It leverages electronic collaboration to accelerate the process and avoids

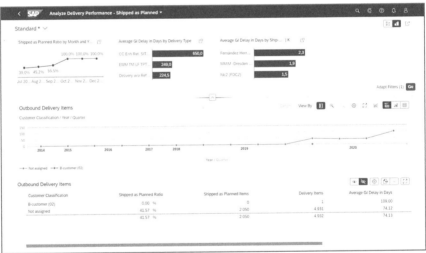

Fig. 10.10 SAP S/4HANA Supply Chain—manage outbound deliveries and analyze delivery performance

redundancies and human error. The goods receipt step for inbound deliveries is the final activity organizations complete before they receive goods. The substantial benefit of depicting the goods receipt process through the inbound delivery job is that many processes can be executed in advance, even before the actual goods receipt posting takes place. All the necessary information is available beforehand as the supplier notifies of the inbound delivery in advance. Thus, an effective and efficient inbound delivery process is ensured to plan for the put-away, packing, and storing of goods. Inbound deliveries are derived from a purchase order document or they are part of a two-step stock transfer process. The goods issue step for outbound deliveries is the last step to complete before companies send goods to customers. An effective and efficient outbound delivery process allows to plan for the picking, packing, and shipping of outbound deliveries.

Transportation Management

This solution supports the entire transportation chain and allows to manage the transportation demands by planning, tendering, and settlement of freight processes. Furthermore, it enables booking carriers in accordance with the requirements of hazardous goods. Transportation Management is used for domestic and international transportation not only for the shipper industry but also for inbound and outbound freight management. It enables to create and use central master data such as business partners and products for transportation-related processes but also for setting up transportation networks. Freight agreements can be used which are contracts between business partners that detail their commitment to conduct business with each other in an agreed manner. Furthermore, charges can be calculated for transporting goods between locations based on the rates maintained in a rate table or local rate table. When calculating transportation charges, this is based on master data such as agreements, calculation sheets, local calculation sheets, rate tables, and local rate tables. Transportation Management practices inbound or outbound deliveries to create freight units. Additionally, the logistics integration allows to continuously react to changes of original documents that occur in the system. Facilitating freight order management allows to create and edit freight orders and freight bookings which contain information required for transportation planning and execution, such as source and destination locations, dates or times, and product information, and resources used. With tendering fright requests for quotation can be sent out to one or more carriers. This can be handled manually or automatically by consuming the direct tendering process. Based on planning, freight units are created on the basis of inbound or outbound deliveries manually or automatically depending on the settings that are configured. Freight settlement enables to trigger the verification of an invoice, which has been received from a supplier or carrier, against a freight settlement document.

Order Promising

Advanced Features

Extended Service Parts Planning provides planning functionality specific to service parts as well as transparency throughout the supply chain, from the time demand occurs until the product is delivered. It enables forecasting, inventory planning, procurement, and large-scale distribution of service parts to customers. These capabilities ensure that the service levels that have been set are maintained. As a result, it is ideal for distribution-centric businesses that distribute large volumes of aftermarket service parts to multiple stocking locations. Advanced Warehousing provides tooling for delivering the optimal order by leveraging features like cross-docking, workforce management, slotting, inventory optimization and support for transit warehousing as well as connectivity to warehouse automation equipment (Fig. 10.11).

Advanced Transportation Management supports the entire transportation chain. By planning, optimizing, tendering, subcontracting, and settling freight processes, the user can manage transportation demands. Additionally, carriers can be booked in accordance with the requirements of international trade and hazardous goods. Advanced Order Promising helps companies to commit to orders quickly and accurately by automatically considering the relevant stock in real time, while protecting the company's business priorities and profitability goals.

Solution Capability: Manufacturing

The end-to-end process Plan to Fulfill is mainly implemented by SAP S/4HANA Supply Chain and SAP S/4HANA Manufacturing. In this section capabilities of SAP S/4HANA Supply Chain are explained as depicted in Fig. 10.12. While this covers the core functionality, there are various extension modules like SAP Digital Manufacturing Cloud, SAP Integrated Planning, or SAP Manufacturing Suite.

Production Planning enables planning products and components to initiate internal and external procurement using Material Resource Planning (MRP) live in memory for improved performance and more current planning results. Production Engineering designs products/resources and manages the change throughout the life cycle including master data as materials, routings, BoMs, recipes, work centers. Production Operations control manufacturing operations for discrete, process, and repetitive industry with fully integration with Supply Chain and Finance. Quality Management inspects production processes and goods receipts. It manages inspection lots and applies usage decisions to improve manufacturing output. Extended Production Planning and Scheduling extends core production planning and scheduling functionality (ePPDS) leveraging the visual planning board. The solution automates consumption bases replenishment through demand driven MRP and use simulation capabilities with predictive MRP. Extend Production Engineering and Operations engineers and operates the production processes. It bridges the gap between product engineering and manufacturing operations by converting product design into production process design, which serves as the foundation for production order management and shop floor execution.

Production Engineering

During the product engineering phase, products are designed and developed. New products or product lines are designed to take advantage of current process technology and to improve quality and reliability. Existing products might be changed due to shifting market or customer requirements. As the result of this product phase

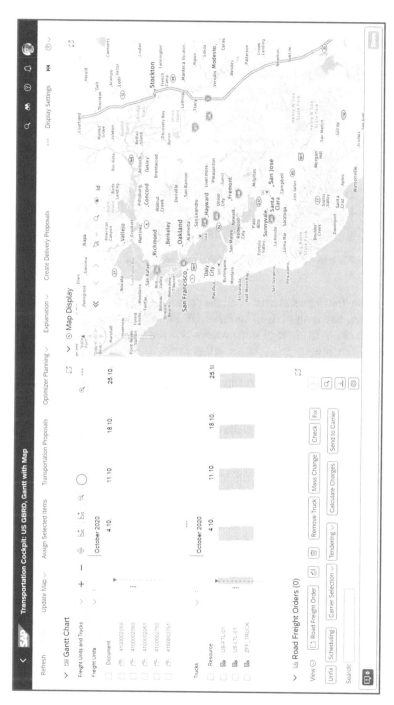

Fig. 10.11 SAP S/4HANA Supply Chain—transportation cockpit

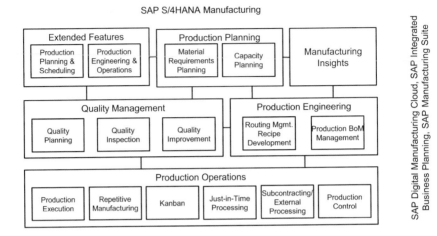

Fig. 10.12 SAP S/4HANA Manufacturing—functional architecture

corresponding drawings and a list of all the parts required to produce the product are provided. This list is the bill of material (BoM). Production BoM Management structures products to manage components and assemblies and defines separate BoMs for different areas (e.g., Engineering, Production, Sales and Services). The solution determines the valid BoM version for the respective date, production version, and purpose. Reporting function can be used to determine all components (assemblies and individual parts) in a product and displays them per low-level code. Reporting also helps to find out where an object (e.g., material) is used and the quantity that is required. During the process engineering phase, manufacturing equipment and production facilities are designed and continuously improved. Thus, the capabilities of the manufacturing equipment can be modeled, and the performance is monitored. Routing Management Recipe Development plans the operations during manufacturing activities. Operations provide the basis for scheduling dates, capacity requirements for work centers and material consumption. Recipes define the product formulation process and the development of manufacturing products. Work centers/resources are used to represent machines, production lines, employees, or groups of employees. In addition to BoM and routing/master recipes, the work centers/resources belong to the most important master data in the production planning and control system. They are used for scheduling, costing, capacity planning, and for simplifying operation maintenance.

Routing/master recipes describe the operations/process steps that must be performed to produce a material. Furthermore, routing/master recipes include details about the work centers/resources at which the operations/process steps are performed and the BOM components that are needed. In order to keep the production process running smoothly and efficiently the shop floor must be provided with up-to-date information. For this, it must be defined how the production process is to

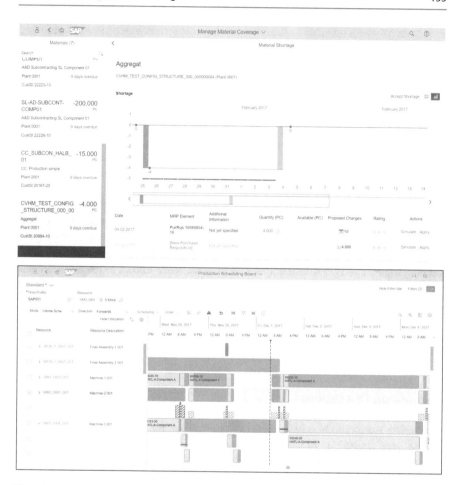

Fig. 10.13 SAP S/4HANA Manufacturing—MRP simulation and scheduling board

be executed and the data that have to be collected during production. By comparing this data with the existing one, continuous improvements to the process can be made (Fig. 10.13).

Production Planning

Production Planning has the objective to plan products and components to initiate internal and external procurement. Managers have to consider two aspects: Material Requirements and Capacity. Based on BoM explosion of finished product requirements companies have to plan raw materials. Additionally, proposals for internal and external procurement based on quantities and date requirements must be created. To plan the capacity the production planner must balance production requirements with available capacity of the respective work centers and shift calendars. Material Requirements Planning ensures the availability of materials and performs basic production planning. Usually this is performed by the MRP controller who monitors the material shortage and resolves any issues immediately. Furthermore, it guarantees that sufficient supplies have been planned to cover requirements. The objective is to allow that both customer and production requirements are available timely. The current supply and demand can be monitored and adjusted. Material shortages can be detected and also uncovered requirements and issues regarding process or production orders. Tools for automated solving of issues and communicating them to suppliers are provided. Planned orders can be converted into production orders or process orders. This can happen manually or automatically based on jobs. Material Requirements Planning (MRP) facilitates the coverage of demand by supply elements without considering the available capacity. It is the task of capacity planning to support the MRR planners in changing the production plan in such a way that the capacity constraints are considered while keeping the demands in time and quantity in mind. MRP allows to review when and how much capacity is available for a work center which is called the capacity definition. This definition can be managed for instance, by reducing the work time or by including additional work time. With MRP also the capacity load on work centers can be reviewed. Available and required capacities can be compared, thus the issues are identified which must be resolved (Fig. 10.14).

Production Operations

Production Execution bundles execution, controlling, monitoring, and confirmation of the manufacturing process with real-time data from shop floor, contract manufacturers, and suppliers. To do this, the production operator must transfer planned orders, release production orders, confirm operations, and track work in progress. Released production/process orders can be displayed by providing access to all the information required to produce the product including dates, times, and quantities. Repetitive Manufacturing processing can be simplified using mass processing and streamlined financial controls in periodic actions. In repetitive manufacturing, the material flow can be planned and monitored in a much higher level of detail. Planned orders are used to model, plan, and trigger material flow and product cost collectors to collect the costs. The product costs are collected based on the complete quantity produced during an accounting period. Deviations are aggregated. Repetitive manufacturing supports the make-to-stock and make-to-order production. The first one is controlled without a direct reference to the sales order while for the second scenario the system creates one or several planned orders which directly reference the sales order item. Using Kanban inventory enables to automatically replenish by implementing self-steering control circuits. This can be achieved for example with empty bins triggering the procurement process. Kanban is a methodic for controlling production and material flow based on physical material stock in production. The basic idea is to keep material that is required on a regular

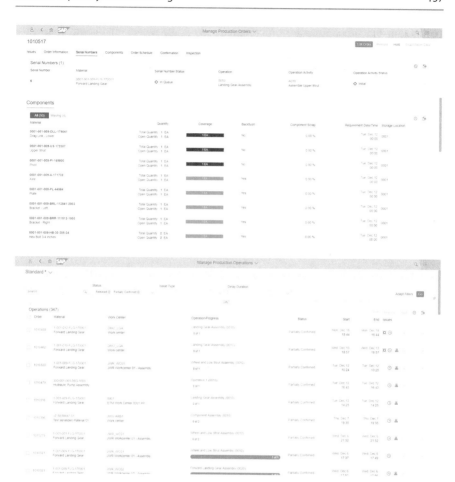

Fig. 10.14 SAP S/4HANA Manufacturing—manage production orders and manage production operations

basis available in small quantities in production. Thus, the replenishment or production of a material is only triggered when a certain quantity of the material has been consumed. Kanban approach ensures that the production process controls itself and the manual posting effort is kept to a minimum. This results in shorter lead times and reductions in stock levels. Production Control provides central cockpits to minimize bottlenecks and mitigate risks. Therefore, production operators must control full shop floor production for handling materials, BoMs, recipes, routings, components, work centers, and resources all the way up to the finished products. This process facilities to manage and regulate the manufacturing process. It is usually executed by the production supervisor who is in charge of dispatching production operations to individual machines. This person also decides on measures to mitigate machine breakdowns or missing components. Subcontracting can be used to outsource production via subcontracting procurement. To make use of this companies must provide components to the contractor according to the BoM structure. Additionally, companies have to manage and track component inventory and work in progress on contractor site. With External Processing organizations can even outsource production operations to third party providers or other production units within the cooperation. External operations in routings and production orders can manage this process. Just-in-Time Processing can avoid inventory buffers by delivering components and subassemblies directly to the production line of the customer. With just-in-sequence the assembly is delivered in sequence according to the requested specifications. Just-in-Time outbound processing allows to replenish direct materials required for manufacturing in the exact quantity and at exactly the time required. Just-in-Time inbound processing facilitates to produce and deliver materials in the exact quantity, for the exact time, and even in the sequence defined by the customer. For this scheduling agreements are used with delivery schedules for sales and production planning processes.

Quality Management

Quality Management provides tools to inspect production processes and goods receipts. The solution manages inspection lots and applies usage decisions to improve manufacturing output. Quality Management involves planning, inspection, and improvement of quality. Quality Planning is important to plan the quality of products, processes, and services. Therefore, control plans are used to perform an integrated inspection planning for goods receipt inspections and during production. Control plans, in conjunction with the Failure Mode and Effects Analysis, can be used to perform integrated inspection planning for goods receipt inspections and production inspections. The control plan depicts how products and processes are monitored. It includes tasks that are executed for each phase of the process. Quality-related master data like specifications and processes on a long-term basis must be defined as quality info records. Quality Inspection uses inspection lots to perform and record a quality inspection completed by the usage decision. Examples of usage decisions may be inspection determination, defects recording to record individual defect items, sample management for processing and managing samples, calibration inspection for test equipment, and quality certificates for inbound and outbound processes. The inspection planning function is used to define inspection criteria, for example, material to be inspected, how the inspection is to take place, characteristics to be inspected, required test equipment, work center, and inspection specifications. Quality notifications and root cause analysis allow to record and process quality problems and complaints and to execute the problem-solving process including root cause analysis. Corrective and preventive actions can be triggered in order to solve a problem and to prevent the issues from recurring. Nonconformance management enables to record and process defects. Quality Improvement focuses to improve the quality of products and processes. This can be achieved by quality notifications to carry out problem-solving processes and root cause analysis, corrective and preventive actions to solve problems and to prevent reoccurrence. Quality analytics and quality evaluations are provided based on inspection results or issue data. Audit management helps for determining, evaluating, and documenting quality defects.

Manufacturing Insights

This cross-capability helps to analyze manufacturing data for process improvements, decision support, and reporting and documentation purposes. The solution provides alerts for exception-based management. Real-time alerts based on production bottlenecks, such as time or component delays or resource bottlenecks, can be used to reduce shortfalls and scrap with high efficiency.

Extended Production Planning and Scheduling

This advanced solution has the purpose to create procurement proposals for in-house production or external procurement to cover product requirements and also to optimize and plan the resource schedule and the order dates/times in detail. The availability of resources and components must be considered here. It is used to plan critical products, such as those with long replenishment lead times or those produced on limited resources. Extended Production Planning and Scheduling is used to create executable production plans and to reduce lead times, increase on-time delivery performance, and to increase the throughput of products and reduce the stock costs, through better coordination of resources, production, and procurement (Fig. 10.15).

Extended Production Engineering and Operations

This advanced solution provides tools to handle highly engineered and complex products. It bridges the gap between product engineering and manufacturing operations by converting product design into production process design. This is crucial when producing highly engineered products that are subject to continual design changes. Furthermore, the manufacturing process can be modeled in great detail, including detailed work instructions for production operators. With the help of planning BoMs and planning routes, it is also possible to perform production planning concurrently with production engineering.

Conclusion

The Plan to Fulfill is a core business process in companies for manufacturing products or providing services. For this supply chain and manufacturing strategy has to be defined and the demand and inventory planning to be completed. Products are assembled and intangible services are provisioned, following strict quality

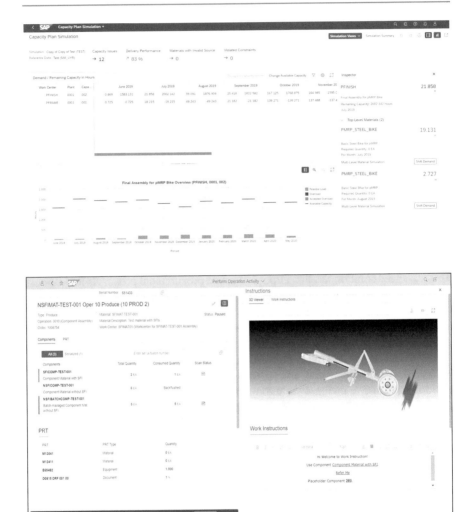

Fig. 10.15 SAP S/4HANA Manufacturing—pMRP simulation and operation activities

inspections. Products and services are delivered, and corresponding invoices created. In SAP S/4HANA this end-to-end process is mainly covered by SAP S/4HANA Supply Chain and Manufacturing components. SAP S/4HANA Supply Chain supports among others logistics material identification, order promising, delivery and transportation, inventory and warehouse management. SAP S/4HANA Manufacturing enables for example production planning, quality management, production engineering, and operations or manufacturing insights. The SAP S/4HANA modules are deeply integrated and frequently interacting so that also additional components contribute to handle this end-to-end process.

Process of Lead to Cash

11

This chapter describes the business process lead to cash consisting of the subprocesses plan to optimize marketing and sales, market to lead, opportunity to quote, order to fulfill, request to service, and manage customer and channels. Additionally, the application capabilities of SAP S/4HANA to resolve those business processes are explained.

Business Process

The general process of Lead to Cash is depicted in Fig. 11.1 and explained in detail in the next sections.

Lead to Cash begins with marketing and ends with revenue collection. First of all, strategy and budget for marketing must be defined. Sales forecasts and measurable goals have to be developed. In the context of marketing execution, the relevant customer profiles, sales prices, and promotional activities must be specified. Sale execution manages leads/opportunities, point of sales, bids and quotes and omnichannel presence. The order to fulfill process handles customer contracts and orders for entitlement. For delivered products and provided services corresponding supportive processes are enabled for managing customer complaints, processing returns, handling warranty claim and recalls. As final step, invoicing to customers is performed and accounts receivable processed for cash management. Frequently, the sales process begins with a sales inquiry from a customer, such as a request for a quotation or sales information without the requestor being under any immediate obligation to buy. An inquiry can be about products or services, terms and conditions, and, if necessary, delivery dates. The sales area that accepts the inquiry is in charge of the subsequent processing. Sales inquiries allow to manage all the important sales-related information that is used during the sales order processing process. Customers have the option to change or cancel the inquiry. However, ideally customers proceed from an inquiry to a purchase. In that case, the logical next step is for the customer to request an official quotation or to purchase the

© The Author(s), under exclusive license to Springer Nature Switzerland AG 2022
S. Sarferaz, *Compendium on Enterprise Resource Planning*,
https://doi.org/10.1007/978-3-030-93856-7_11

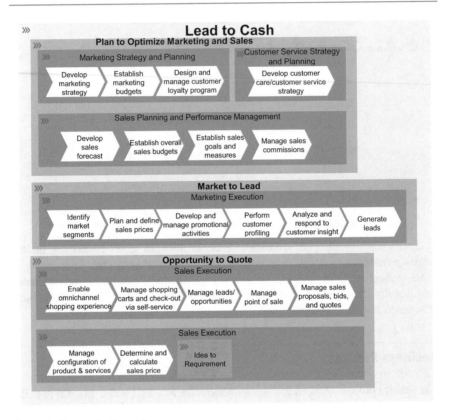

Fig. 11.1 Process lead to cash

products directly. A quotation is a formal set of business terms provided by the quoting company to the customer. The primary distinction is that a quotation can be referred to in a new sales order. A quotation is a legally binding offer to the customer to deliver a product or provide a service under specific conditions. This offer is only legally binding for the company for a limited time.

Plan to Optimize Marketing and Sales (Fig. 11.2)

In the subprocess of Marketing Strategy and Planning the first step is to develop a suitable marketing strategy and establish the corresponding marketing budgets. It is also recommended to design and manage a best fitting customer loyalty program. Customer Service and Planning helps to develop customer care and also customer service strategy for generating a unique customer experience. Sales Planning and Performance Management supports in generating a sales forecast. After that, an overall sales budget, sales goals, and measures can be established. In addition, sales commissions can be calculated and managed.

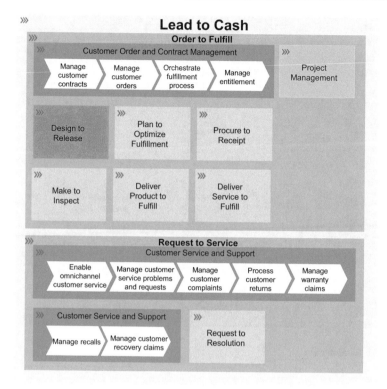

Fig. 11.1 (continued)

Market to Lead (Fig. 11.3)

Marketing Execution covers the main steps for implementing the marketing process. The market segments are identified, as well as the sales prices are planned and defined. At the same time, promotion activities are developed and monitored. Certain customer profiles are determined in order to reach a suitable target group. Based on that, the marketing activities can be carried out. The given results make it possible to analyze and react to customer insights, whereby interested parties who would like to purchase a certain product or service can be identified.

Opportunity to Quote (Fig. 11.4)

Sales Execution Process

Within the process of Sales Execution different channels, such as the Internet or local shops, are enabled and used for sales. In addition, the shopping carts and the checkout are managed by self-service. Also leads and opportunities as well as the

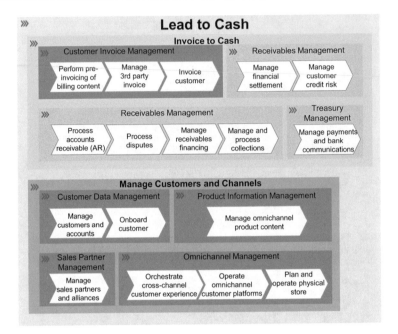

Fig. 11.1 (continued)

point of sale are managed by that. It is also necessary to check sales proposals, received bids, and quotes. In the course of this, the configuration of the products and services must be adapted and managed, whereby sales prices are determined and calculated.

Order to Fulfill (Fig. 11.5)

After a successful customer acquisition, it is necessary to negotiate and process a customer contract. Such a customer contract is defined within the subprocess of Customer Order and Contract Management and stored in the respective system. In this way, customer contracts and orders are managed, and the fulfillment process is then orchestrated. Ultimately, the entitlements can be managed. Once a customer order has been completed, the production processes begin. In the meantime, however, an order with special requests can lead to changes in the entire design. Order to Fulfill is also accompanied by processes such as project management. In the course of this, for example the optimization of the order fulfillment is planned and the product or the service is delivered for fulfillment. An internal sales representative's primary responsibilities are order capture and order fulfillment. In today's world,

Fig. 11.2 Plan to optimize marketing and sales

Fig. 11.3 Market to lead

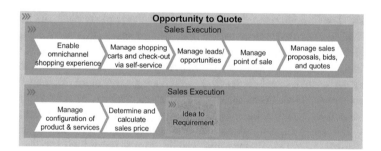

Fig. 11.4 Opportunity to quote

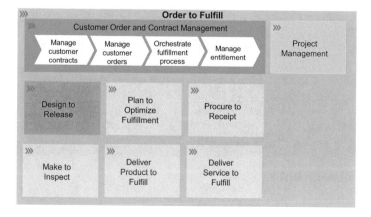

Fig. 11.5 Order to fulfill

where increasing order volumes and tight control of sales operations costs are critical contributors to a company's margins, efficiency, and effectiveness are key components of a modern order and contract management process. Unlike 20 years ago, the person in charge cannot manually capture all incoming sales orders and keep track of the statuses of open sales orders today. As a result, automatic sales order capture, low- to no-touch order management, integrated compliance with export and product regulations, credit and financial risk management, and exception-based working models are all critical. Contracts can help to sell more products and services while also ensuring that agreed-upon terms and service-level agreements (SLAs) are easily managed and taken into account during fulfillment.

Request to Service (Fig. 11.6)

Previously, the focus of brand building and loyalty was on designing and building excellent products. Of course, there is benefit to providing excellent service, but the primary focus of businesses has been on the products they sell. Service was frequently treated as an afterthought. The term *after-sales service* alludes to this. When things were broken, they were fixed. Offering good service was primarily used to drive the product's reputation and price, with the service itself being treated as a cost center. The limitations of the previous approach are today clear. As businesses demand end-to-end experiences rather than just products, the service function is becoming an integral part of the overall offering and value proposition, as well as a profit driver. Furthermore, in today's competitive environment, businesses cannot rely solely on reactive *break-fix* services, which are always more expensive and less profitable than a well-managed and effective service business. Service contracts that consider not only reactive but also predictive scenarios, combined with service offerings that are designed, planned, and managed as a profitable part of the company portfolio, are what companies require to maximize their service business and secure their customer base. Companies are changing the way the service department is integrated into their organizations to drive these changes. Service is

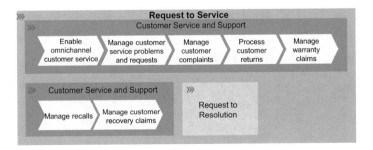

Fig. 11.6 Request to service

transitioning from a local cost center to a central business offering and must be planned, managed, and controlled as such. The transition from a purely cost-driven to a business-driven approach to service is currently underway, in tandem with a growing shift toward *solution selling*, with service being one component of this type of deal, which drives profitability through products, subscriptions, contracts, services, and even projects.

All support activities that are required after tangible or intangible products are provided to customers, are in focus of Request to Service. Such customer services can be offered via several channels like Internet or telephone hotline. Customer service issues and inquiries are managed in this process as well as customer complaints. Such complaints can result in returns which is also managed by Request to Service. Another far-reaching and important point is the management of warranty claims. In addition, recalls and customer recovery claims must be handled during the service process. Most businesses require not only a proper sales process, but also a dependable after-sales process that includes complaint processing, repairs, and returns processing. The returns process is expected to be of high quality, with transparent handling, efficient management, and an immediate refund process. The sale of returned, refurbished, or recycled products is gaining prominence and paving the way for a circular economy. Return and refund clerks face daily challenges in managing these complex processes. Accelerated returns management in sales is used to manage buyer and supplier returns and it offers a number of advanced functions for returns management. One of the most important aspects of gaining customer loyalty is customer satisfaction. As a result, in today's world, returns have become increasingly important because they are critical to success in satisfying the customer. Returns must be completed in a highly efficient manner because they can be costly and time-consuming.

Invoice to Cash (Fig. 11.7)

The process of Customer Invoice Management follows after a completed customer delivery, a successfully provided service or, in general, the fulfillment of a customer contract. This is succeeded by billing. The preparation of the prebilling of the invoice

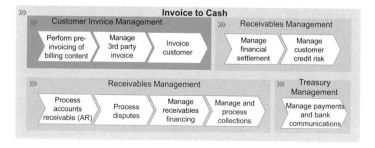

Fig. 11.7 Invoice to cash

content is covered by this step. The administration of third parties is included if subcontractors are involved. Ultimately, the invoice to customer follows. Receivables Management handles financial settlement, controls the customer's credit risk, and processes accounts receivables. In addition, disputes are also resolved. Furthermore, the receivables financing is managed, and collections are processed. Treasury Management covers payments and communication to the bank. This includes for example bank transfers. Billing documents are legal invoices created for the purchase of goods or services and can be emailed, printed, and mailed to customers. These documents also act as interfaces to financial accounting and serve as the foundation for financial postings. Billing clerks play an important role because they are in charge of the entire billing process. These persons collaborate closely with internal sales representatives, shipping specialists, and accounts receivable accountants to ensure that billing documents are created on time and that customers pay them without complaint.

Manage Customers and Channels (Fig. 11.8)

Customer Data Management handles all information regarding customers and accounts. Also, the onboarding of customers is considered. When multiple channels are offered, the product content must be provided multiple time which is supported by Product Information Management. Handling of sales partners and alliances is the main objective of Sales Partner Management. In the subprocess of Omnichannel Management the cross-channel customer experience is orchestrated. Additionally, it supports operating omnichannel customer platforms. Furthermore, a physical store is planned and operated.

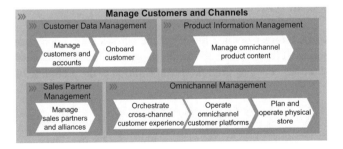

Fig. 11.8 Manage customers and channels

Solution Capability: Sales

The end-to-end process Lead to Cash is mainly implemented by SAP S/4HANA Sales and SAP S/4HANA Service. In this section capabilities of SAP S/4HANA Sales are explained as depicted in Fig. 11.9. While this covers the core functionality, there are various extension modules like SAP Marketing Cloud, SAP Sales Cloud, SAP Commerce Cloud, and SAP Customer Data Cloud.

Sales Force Support manages customer engagement cycles with embedded presales capabilities for lead, opportunities, and relevant tasks. Order and Contract Management ensures consistent master data, including pricing across the organization. It processes sales documents accurately and improves customer satisfaction. The solution provides access to real-time sales performance KPIs for supporting decision-making. Sales Performance Management (ICM) realizes strategic enterprise goals with effective monetary and nonmonetary incentives management. SAP S/4HANA Sales includes an extensive variety of sales processes, providing flexible business configuration for the integration with procurement, logistics, and finance. A product which is sold, can be either in stock, or can be produced/procured. Usually the sales process starts with a sales inquiry, succeeded by a quotation that is used as a reference to create a sales order. Alternatively, sales order can be created based on long-term agreements like sales contracts or scheduling agreements. Sales contracts basically specify which products are delivered in certain quantities or for a certain value within a certain time. Scheduling agreements define delivering products in a

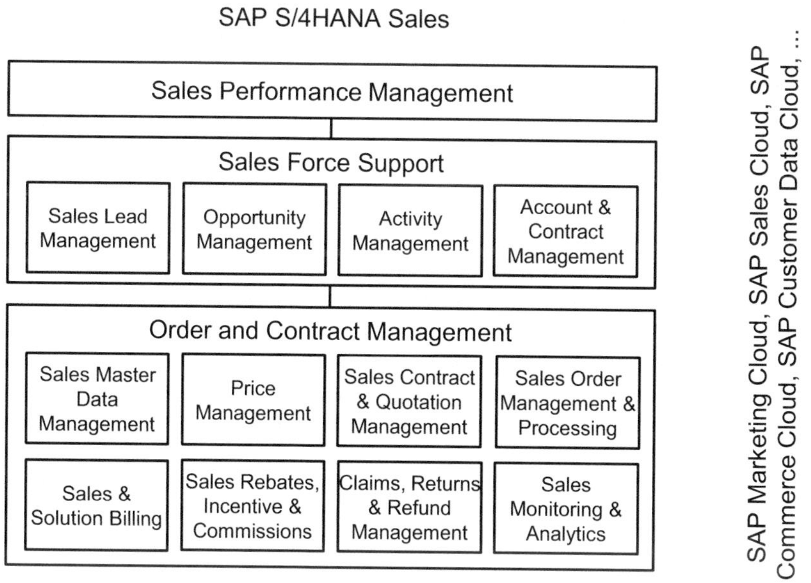

SAP S/4HANA Sales

Sales Performance Management			
Sales Force Support			
Sales Lead Management	Opportunity Management	Activity Management	Account & Contract Management
Order and Contract Management			
Sales Master Data Management	Price Management	Sales Contract & Quotation Management	Sales Order Management & Processing
Sales & Solution Billing	Sales Rebates, Incentive & Commissions	Claims, Returns & Refund Management	Sales Monitoring & Analytics

SAP Marketing Cloud, SAP Sales Cloud, SAP Commerce Cloud, SAP Customer Data Cloud, ...

Fig. 11.9 SAP S/4HANA Sales—functional architecture

certain quantity on regular basis. The final step within the sales process is billing which is about sending invoices to customers for payment. Billing documents are posted to financial accounting and consequently universal journal entries are created.

Order and Contract Management

Sales Master Data Management facilitates to leverage simplified data models and the central business partner. Sales master data is created, modified, or displayed in a harmonized user experience. Customer materials definition is used when customer products have identifications that differ from the number that the company uses. By maintaining material determination records the automated replacement of a product number entered in sales documents with a target product number is enabled. Material listing records and exclusion records can be maintained specifying which products customers can or can't buy. The Price Management controls the price master data definition and perform price calculation. This feature is used to set up the pricing process in business documents. This covers how price master data is determined and how net values are calculated. The solution allows to calculate and adapt accurate prices based on the price master data and the configuration of pricing.

Sales Contract and Quotation Management supports contract types, such as sales contracts, condition contracts for settlement management, scheduling agreement, or trading contracts. It is also possible to use real-time and predictive analytics to effectively manage sales contracts and sales quotations. This application enables to create, change, or display a quotation for customers. The process is triggered when a request for quotation (RFQ) is received from customers. In response to the customer's RFQ, a quotation is provided which is then either accepted or rejected by customers. This step assures the business partners that the product quantity at a specified time and price is delivered. In case of acceptance, the quotation is transferred into a sales order. Additionally, all quotations, expiring quotations, expired quotations, completed quotations, and incomplete quotations can be listed. Sales Order Management and Processing provides a 360-degree view of sales order execution. It maximizes low-touch order rate and leverages exception-based order management. It allows also to prevent overall delivery delay with embedded predictive analysis. The solution streamlines sales processes with workflows. This solution allows to execute business transactions based on sales documents, such as inquiry, quotation, and sales order, defined in the system. Within sales order management and processing, a sales document is entered based on customer requirements. When creating or changing sales documents, the system confirms dates and quantities. The sales documents to respond to customer questions can be displayed and changed. When a sales document is processed, the SAP S/4HANA Sales automatically carry out basic functions like pricing, availability check, transferring requirements to materials planning (MRP), delivery scheduling, shipping point and rout determination, and credit limit check. Sales and Solution Billing covers manual and automated billing and invoicing scenarios. External billing data can be combined with sales documents into one single invoice. Billing documents can be created, posted to financial accounting, and output to a variety of channels. But also billing-related documents such as invoice lists, preliminary billing documents, and billing document requests can be created and managed. Key features are debit and credit memo processing, billing document and invoice list processing, approval for preliminary billing documents, and invoice correction processing. The solution billing is used to combine billing data from sold products, services, and projects into a single, combined customer invoice.

Sales Rebates, Incentive and Commissions Management allows to handle business volume-based sales rebates with condition contract settlement. With the help of the Claims, Returns and Refund Management the customer service and support cost can be reduced by streamlining return processes and customer return analysis. The solution facilitates improved tracking, helps service organizations process requests faster, and reduces operational costs. The capture and handling of all complaints and returns are improved. Those trigger logistical follow-up actions such as inspection of returned products, resolution of issues, and claims and refunds management. Warranties are created and assigned with technical objects which enable manufacturers, importers, or vendors of complex products and their suppliers to better deal with many warranty claims. Claims with negative results of the automatic checks are included in manual processing.

The Sales Monitoring and Analytics enables to monitor and analyze core sales business processes, from quotations and contracts, to sales orders, including their fulfillment up to invoices. Sales planers set sales targets on various dimensions and can be created, changed, released, and displayed. It can be analyzed to what extent sales targets are being achieved and thus gain insights into current sales performance. Sales quotations can be analyzed according to flexible combinations of dimensions. The solution enables to focus on quotations with the highest net values and quotations with the lowest conversion rates. Drill down to quotation conversion rates by selected criteria are supported. Modeling-based predictions can be performed on quotation conversion according to selected criteria. It is possible to forecast the extent to which quotations will be converted into sales orders by comparing the actual and predicted results (Fig. 11.10).

Sales Force Support

This solution supports the entire presales lifecycle, from an appointment, through the creation of leads and then opportunities. The objective of Sales Lead Management is to collect any potential sales information at the beginning phase of the sales pipeline. The application ensures the company's chance to do business by automating the initial presales process and creating a link between first interest and sales. Whereas the Opportunity Management records the recognized sales possibilities and tracks the progress across the sales cycle. The solution allows to control the sales opportunity which describes the sales prospect, the requested products or services, budget, potential sales volume, and the estimated sales probability. Activity Management helps to plan, track, and organize sales activities

Fig. 11.10 SAP S/4HANA Sales—customer overview and sales order fulfillment issues

throughout the entire customer relationship lifecycle. It records all activities of the employees of the company. This includes making appointments and creating tasks. Account and Contact Management delivers sales force a holistic view of each customer with identified key contact and account data. It manages and provides easy access to accounts and contacts (Fig. 11.11).

Sales Performance Management

With the help of the Sales Performance Management sales forces can be motivated to increase revenue by provided incentive and compensation policies. The sales performance of the company can be improved with SAP software for incentive and commission management by implementing compelling variable compensation programs. Organizations can enable to handle programs for employees and partners,

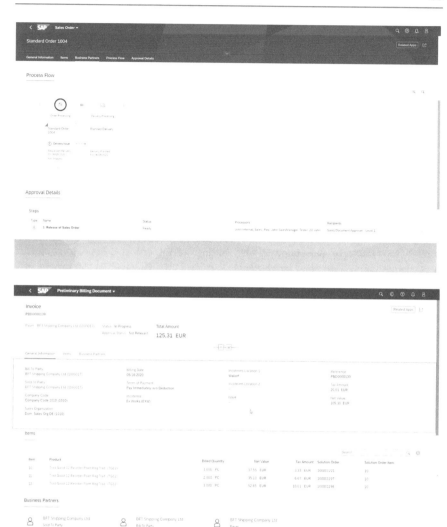

Fig. 11.11 SAP S/4HANA Sales—sales order transaction history and preliminary billing document

building and maintaining an accurate, strategically aligned incentive and compensation plan, so that the company can retain and motivate top performers and achieve corporate goals. Furthermore, industry best practices can be leveraged for the company's requirement.

Solution Capability: Service

In this section capabilities of SAP S/4HANA Service are explained as depicted in Fig. 11.12. While this covers the core functionality, there are various extension modules like SAP Field Service Management or SAP Asset Intelligence Network. SAP S/4HANA Service is in charge of the entire lifecycle of service management. Service Master Data and Agreement Management handles customer asset records, service history, and commercial agreements. It plans preventive maintenance services based on the relevant information readily available. The solution monitors operations and business outcome of services by holistically looking at the entire service processes. Service Operations and Processes engages with customers on multiple platforms for handling their requests, complaints, and any other interactions. It combines services and products as a packaged solution. The module performs services efficiently and effectively, with all the required material and human resources. In the scope is also billing customers in a timely manner in accordance with contractual agreements. Service Parts Management improves efficiency in parts fulfillment, planning, procurement, and warehousing with integration of core materials management, and finance functions. Subscription Order Management extends commercial service offerings with enhanced subscription management. Financial Shared Service Management leverages intelligent shared service capabilities with automation based on machine learning and artificial intelligence. Service orders capture the customer's request for the execution of a service. Service confirmations document and log the execution of service orders. In case of in-house repair, the service is provisioned in an internal service center. For regular execution of services corresponding service contracts are agreed on. Solution orders facilitate the bundling of one-time and periodic services including the sales of physical items.

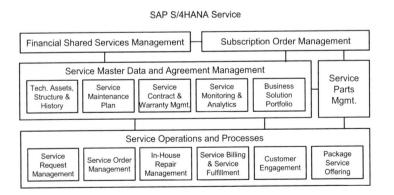

Fig. 11.12 SAP S/4HANA Service—functional architecture

Service Master Data and Agreement Management

With Technical Assets, Structure and History precise information on customer location and installed equipment can be provided to call center, field service, depot repair, and sales staff. It is also possible to plan and perform maintenance services with complete records of a piece of equipment or a system via equipment master data, maintenance plan, measuring point, task list, and bill of materials. Service Maintenance Plan allows to schedule service commitments and major maintenance events, like shutdowns and turnarounds, to enable preventive and predictive service activities, based on time, counter, condition, or risk. Service Contract Management and Warranty Management deals with service agreements, price arrangements, and customer entitlements in a single repository. It allows triggering of automatic periodic billing. Contracts are long-term service agreements between companies and their customers. They define the content and scope of the services that are guaranteed within specific tolerance limits for certain parameters, such as within a predefined timeframe. Service contracts contain detailed information regarding routing tasks for devices, prices for the routine tasks, objects for which services can be claimed, and conditions under which the contract can be canceled. Periodic billing plans can be used to schedule individual dates for the billing of service contracts, independent of the provisioning of the service. Typically, periodic billing plans have a start and end date. Fixed amounts are billed at regular intervals, for example, a recurring yearly maintenance fee. Warranties specify the scope of the services and parts usage which organizations perform in the event of damage or problems. This process ensures processing service deliveries with automatic checks for warranty agreements. With the help of Service Monitoring and Analytics and Business Solution Portfolio operations and business outcome of service businesses can be monitored by holistically capturing and measuring service performance and profitability using operational reporting and dashboards. Business solution portfolios pack service contract items, service order items, sales order items, and subscription contract items which are belonging to a solution and its corresponding customer. Thus, an overview of these items in the customer's business solution is retained. In case an external reference is added to a solution quotation, the system creates the business solution portfolio using APIs and automatically assigns the relevant service contract items, service order items, sales order items, and subscription order items. Overview information related to important key performance indicators of service transactions can be depicted. This comprises, for example, KPIs referring to service contract management and service execution process (Fig. 11.13).

Service Operations and Processes

Service Request Management lets the user create, track, and manage service requests with full visibility of current and historical service agreements and activities. It improves customer satisfaction by providing the frontline service agent with full view of customers, installed equipment, and service history is also part of that. Using

Service Management Overview

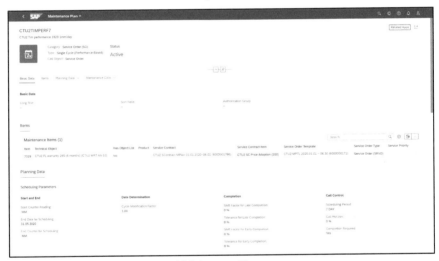

Maintenance Plan

Fig. 11.13 SAP S/4HANA Service—service management overview and maintenance plan

solution quotations enables to create quotations for combinations of different types of products, for example tangible products, services, and service contract items. These combinations of products are modeled as product bundles. For providing frontline field service teams with access to up-to-date information on service history and equipment configuration to expertly perform maintenance service work Service Order Management is responsible. The solution facilitates the entire lifecyle, from creating of service order quotations through to processing service orders and service confirmations. For example, customer service orders including technical details, prices, and ad-hoc service requests can be created. Furthermore, the execution of services can be planned, including required service parts and perform follow-on processes such as monitoring and confirming of services. Service order templates can be used for defining reusable sets of service-related data that minimize the amount of time required to create a service transaction. Service confirmations help to report working time, service parts, and expenses used while performing a service. Incidents can be used to report events to the service desk when something in the infrastructure is not working as expected. In-House Repair Management supports companies that offer an in-house repair and maintenance service for products. Planning and performing in-house repairs are more effective by integrating the repair process across various lines of business for greater transparency. The service is performed in-house at repair centers. The in-house repair process includes core repair and maintenance activities such as prechecking, quotation processing, planning, repairing, and billing for repair objects. The solution facilitates to create in-house repairs and then add repair objects, edit, and send out repair quotations, and to record whether the customer has accepted or rejected the repair quotation. Furthermore, it enables to schedule a repair and add the service employee who is to perform the repair. Also, triggering the billing process for the repair is supported. Service Billing and Service Fulfillment allows delivery services in the most efficient manner from simple to most complex services, through planning, scheduling, parts provisioning, service work, and billing. Thus, costs can get reduced with a complete logistical and financial insight. Customer Engagement supports efficient issue resolution through multichannel customer engagement and smart interactions. Packaged Service Offerings bundles items automatically and leads to corresponding follow-on processes all the way to the billing process (Fig. 11.14).

Service Parts Management

The use of Service Parts Management allows to facilitate the optimization of spare part stock processing according to usage and availability. In addition, improving efficiency in parts fulfillment, planning, procurement, and warehousing with integration with core materials management and finance functions as well as support for language and localization requirements is ensured. The solution covers all aspects of service parts management, including planning, execution, fulfillment, collaboration, and analytics. It comprises the service parts planning and service parts execution scenarios.

Subscription Order Management and Financial Shared Services Management

This component allows customers to offer their business solutions as a combination of products and subscriptions to services. Those can be recurring fees, usage-based charges, and one-off charges, based on consumption pricing model. The solution

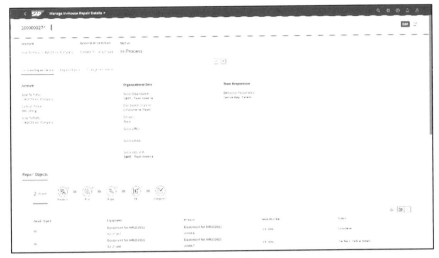

Manage In-House Repair

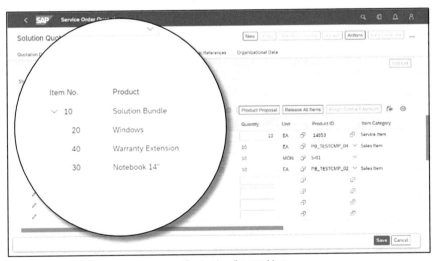

Product bundles used in a
solution quotation

Fig. 11.14 SAP S/4HANA Service—manage in-house repair and solution quotation

manages all parties involved in the business transactions and all data regarding subscription products. It handles products and product bundles consisting of various combinations of products and subscriptions. Business processes are supported which are required for the complete execution of customer orders using order management. The component supports change processes for existing contracts and a wide range of customer care functions using contract management are enabled. These include for example change and update of subscription contracts. The conditions that have been negotiated are implemented as partner agreements. The solution defines a contractual agreement with constituent parts for future single contracts. These include defining which legal unit can order which type of product for which price, the address to which the invoice is sent, and the conditions that must be met in order to be eligible for a special type of discount. Mass run functionality can be used to plan the creation or the processing of a preselected number of subscription orders and contracts and ensure high-performance execution, track the progress, and support monitoring of the results and further processing on the new or changed entities.

Financial Shared Services Management encompasses using service management capabilities natively integrated into end-to-end processes for generating synergies and improve efficiencies with a single working environment. The solution supports efficient, scalable operations by simplifying and automating execution of key financial processes across departments. It boosts quality and compliance by delivering standard, consistent, and repeatable services across diverse business systems. Furthermore, it reduces operational costs by replacing manual processes with automated processing of finance transactions.

Conclusion

The Lead to Cash is a core business process in companies for transferring opportunities to quote customer orders to contracts and invoices to cash. The process starts with developing a strategy for marketing and sales which includes planning budgets. Market segments are identified, prices are defined, and sales execution performed which at the end turn opportunities into quotes. Customer order contracts are orchestrated and fulfilled accordingly. Complaints, returns, and warranty claims are processed. For the delivered products or provided services invoices are created and sent to customers for payment. In SAP S/4HANA this end-to-end process is mainly covered by SAP S/4HANA Sales and Services component. The focus of SAP S/4HANA Sales is on managing orders and contracts, supporting the sales force, and realizing sales performance management. SAP S/4HANA Service handles service operations, service parts management, and the underlying master data and agreements. The solution is rounded up with capabilities for financial shared services and subscription order management. The SAP S/4HANA modules are deeply integrated and frequently interacting so that also additional components contribute to handle this end-to-end process.

Process of Recruit to Retire

12

This chapter describes the business process recruit to retire consisting of the subprocesses plan to optimize workforce, recruit to onboard, develop to grow, reward to retain, manage workforce, and retirement. Additionally, the application capabilities of SAP S/4HANA to resolve those business processes are explained.

Business Process

The general process of Recruit to Retire is depicted in Fig. 12.1 and explained in detail in the next sections.

The process supports the employee from recruiting and onboarding until the retirement. The process Recruit to Retire is divided into five subprocesses. The first one is Plan to Optimize Workforce which includes financial, strategic, and organizational management of all employees. The sum of the employees is called the workforce. The subprocess Recruit Onboard is responsible for recruiting new talents from advertising the brand over the interviews to the onboarding of new employees. Develop to Grow is the part where the employees set goals and learn or improve skills. Those skills help the employees' personal and the company growth. Reward to Retain focuses simply on the gratification of employees like financial compensation. Manage Workforce and Retirement provides supportive processes during employment phase. This includes the Human Resources (HR) administration keeping information about all employees, their contracts, and the time management of the employees including the absences, as well as the traveling expenses and the process of the payroll.

© The Author(s), under exclusive license to Springer Nature Switzerland AG 2022
S. Sarferaz, *Compendium on Enterprise Resource Planning*,
https://doi.org/10.1007/978-3-030-93856-7_12

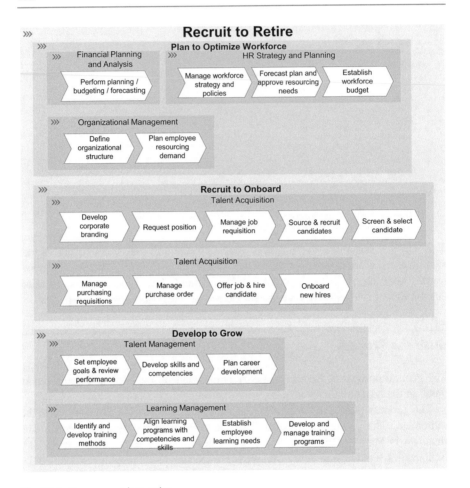

Fig. 12.1 Process recruit to retire

Plan to Optimize Workforce (Fig. 12.2)

The subprocess Plan to Optimize Workforce starts with planning and analyzing the requirements regarding financial and human resources. For this, goals are defined, and the necessary resources forecasted. Strategy and Planning of Human Resources covers the definition of the HR strategy which sets the direction for the workforce to achieve the specified goals. Furthermore, policies for the entire workforce are described and finalized. Before the workforce budget can be established, the forecasted human and financial resources must be approved by management. Organizational Management develops the organizational structure and the employee resourcing demands. This includes how many resources with which skills are needed to achieve the defined goals.

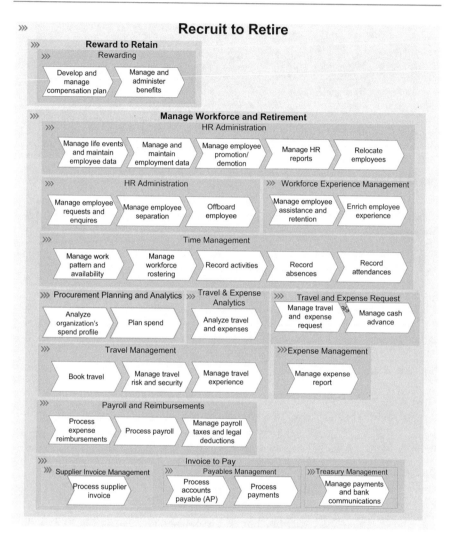

Fig. 12.1 (continued)

Recruit to Onboard (Fig. 12.3)

The objective of Recruit to Onboard is the acquisition of new talents based on the previous planning and optimization process. It starts with developing a corporate branding strategy for the company. Once the requested positions are approved, corresponding job requisitions are created which are the basis for the potential candidates to apply for vacancies. The received applications are matched to the open positions and the best fitting candidates are recruited. Purchasing requisitions and orders utilizes for example the necessary equipment for the new employees as

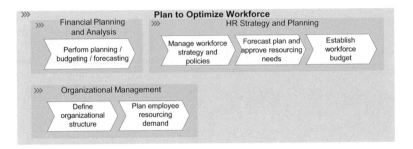

Fig. 12.2 Plan to optimize workforce

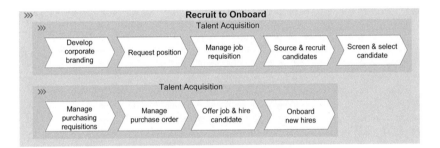

Fig. 12.3 Recruit to onboard

Fig. 12.4 Develop to grow

hardware or software. As soon as the candidates are hired, they are onboarded. In onboarding the tasks, the policies, the strategy, and everything the new employees need are explained so that they can become productive.

Develop to Grow (Fig. 12.4)

This process is around growth aspirations and development needs serving to plan the employee's own development, and to achieve the best possible balance between individual development goals and company and departmental targets. There should be a dialog between employee and manager to support each employee to develop in the near, medium, and long term so that they can apply their strengths and abilities to the best advantage of the company. The employee is in the driver's seat of their own development and the manager actively supports and provides the space for it. This is an iterative process consisting of establishing new development goals or adjusting the existing development plan, checking-in on the status of current development and reflecting on challenges, reviewing and archiving achieved development goals. All employees—regardless of their role—need to invest in their development for both current and long-term growth and success. Development isn't only about changing roles; it can also be about consciously building skills in a way that fits with competencies and intended direction for work life. There are different methods to train employees' skills, for example virtual classrooms or on the job training. Thus, the appropriated methods must be identified for the employee and aligned with learning programs and competencies of the employee. For this learning programs must be developed and managed.

Reward to Retain (Fig. 12.5)

Often the total target cash consists of the base salary which employees receive every month and variable pay respectively bonus. In some roles, the bonus is paid annually and in others, bonuses may be paid more often, such as quarterly. Bonuses are paid for outstanding achievements of a department or single employee. It is used to reward high performance employees. An example is to reward the employee with best achieved sales revenue. The goal of this subprocess is to focus on the employees and to retain them as workforce by rewarding them. In addition to direct financial compensation, companies may also offer a well-defined benefits package to inspire employees to perform at optimum and maintain a healthy work-life integration. Benefits offerings aim to improve health and productivity and protect employees against risks to future income. Benefits offerings can differ by country and include local statutory benefits and requirements, for example, sports facilities or health checks. Those benefits must be managed and administrated continually.

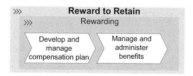

Fig. 12.5 Reward to retain

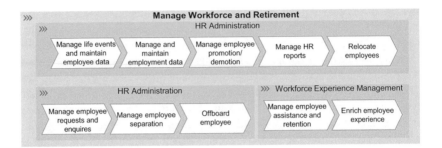

Fig. 12.6 HR administration

HR Administration (Fig. 12.6)

In the context of this process, employment and employee data are maintained. This not only includes administrative information like name, address, or age of the employee but also contractual data as full-time job, salary, or fixed-term contract. In accordance with the defined career development and achieved goals, employees can be promoted to the next career level or in worse case also demoted. The guiding principles for promotions must be transparently communicated to the employees and managers. To improve processes and serve better employee's need reporting and analytics are performed by HR departments on a regular basis. In a globalized world often, teams are relocated and reorganized. This might also result in physical relocation of employees to other regions. The process of relocation covers aspects like adjusting employment contracts, paying moving expenses, or changing pension contributions. In everyday work employees have numerous enquiries as questions to payroll, to contracts, or overtime hours. Such enquiries must be systematically handled by the HR administration. For example, ticketing solution could be used so that requests can be processed efficiently and effectively. Another important facet is the offboarding of employees. There are various reasons triggering the termination of the employment relationship, for example change of employer, retirement or fixed-term contracts. Finally, handling employee assistance and retention, including enriching employee experience is covered by this subprocess.

Time Management (Fig. 12.7)

This subprocess facilitates that employees record their working and absence times. This information is important not only for the financial and workforce planning but also for the payroll and labor laws. Different working patterns and availability must be supported, for example, part-time jobs. This is also valid for variability for workforce rostering, for example, night or weekend shifts. To enable accurate analysis and planning usually working hours are recorded on activity level. For instance, a software developer may record working hours along the activities design,

Fig. 12.7 Time management

Fig. 12.8 Travel and expense

implementation, and testing. Absence time due to vacations or illness must also be recorded.

Travel and Expense (Fig. 12.8)

Accurate analysis of the organization's spend profile and planning is the prerequisite for the travel management process. Employees must travel in order to visit customers and suppliers, attend conferences and trainings, collaborate with remote teams. Therefore, a corresponding travel and expense process must be established. This starts with analyzing the travel needs as hotel and flight bookings and concludes with managing the expenses. Thus, travel booking solution is required which must reflect the company's travel policies, for example, train trips to be preferred compared to flights due to carbon footprint and environment protection. There are expenses that are paid by the company in advance to the travel like hotel accommodation. However, there are also unforeseeable costs like taxi charges. Usually those are paid by the employee and must be requested back later based on the reimbursements process.

Payroll and Invoice Pay (Fig. 12.9)

As explained in travel expense management, unforeseeable and ad-hoc expenses are typically paid by the employee and requested back. For this the invoices must be

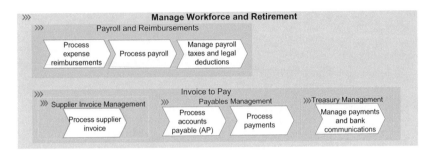

Fig. 12.9 Payroll and invoice pay

submitted and refunded based on the reimbursements process. The submission and processing of expense invoices are usually automated as the corresponding solutions are able to transfer the unstructured documents into relational system records. Besides the expenses the monthly salary must be paid to the employee which is enclosed by payroll process. During the payroll run taxes and legal deductions must be considered. For example, church rates, payroll tax, health insurance, and pension insurance must be held back and transferred directly to the corresponding parties. The Invoice to Pay process handles supplier invoices but also manages payables. Treasure Management leverages the actual payments with the bank. Here the communication with the bank is managed and salaries are wired to the employee's bank account.

Solution Capability

The end-to-end process Recruit to Retire is mainly implemented by SAP S/4HANA Human Resources as depicted in Fig. 12.10. While SAP S/4HANA Human Resources covers the core functionality, SAP Success Factors and SAP Concur include extended features for example for performance management, travel and expense management. The integration of SAP Success Factors is a recommended solution and gives different benefits. First it allows to link HR strategies with business strategies and analytics of the workforce. It reduces HR cost per FTE and a perfect engagement of talents across the organization.

Human Resources is the strategic and coherent approach to the management of people working for an organization. The goal of human capital management is to help an organization to meet strategic goals by attracting and developing employees and also managing them effectively. SAP S/4HANA Human Resources supports business processes in key areas. Talent management supports people during every phase of their employment—from recruitment through training, development, and retention. It helps in finding the right people, put their talent to the best use, align employee goals with corporate goals, maximize the impact of training, and retain top performers. Workforce process management automates and integrates critical workforce processes such as employee administration, organizational management, time

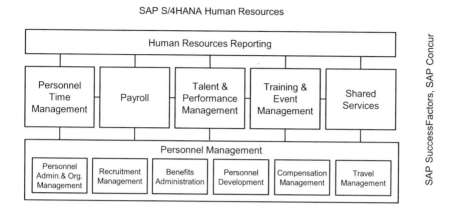

Fig. 12.10 SAP S/4HANA HR—functional architecture

management, benefits administration, payroll, and legal reporting. SAP S/4HANA Human Resources standardizes and consolidates all workforce-related processes and data onto a single platform, while also ensuring compliance with country-specific regulations and laws. Workforce deployment facilitates the right people with the right skills to the right positions at the right time. It enables the formation of project teams based on skills and availability, the tracking of project progress, the tracking of time, and the analysis of results for strategic decision-making. SAP S/4HANA Human Resources supports the assignment of workers to appropriate jobs, projects, and teams and the optimal scheduling of call center staff and retail staff.

Personnel Management

Personnel Administration deals with the administrative activities related to employee master data, such as employee personal data, address details, bank details, or work agreement information. Employee master data has multiple country-specific specificities and needs to be compliant to legal requirements. Examples are tax details, social security rules, and pension administration. The applications Benefits Administration and Compensation Management are based on Personnel Administration. Infotypes are the units of information. One infotype defines the data structure for semantically related data, which is stored together in the database and also displayed together on the user interface. Each infotype has its own database table structure in which all instances of the infotype are stored as records. In Personnel Administration data is typically valid for only a certain period of time. For example, the employee's bank details are valid from March 1, 2021, to October 30, 2021. Therefore, infotypes support the time-dependent storage of data. When data is updated, then old data is internally kept as time-delimited using a date-dependent validity of the record. Personnel actions facilitate basic personnel procedures within master data administration, such as hiring employees or performing organizational reassignments. Each personnel action specifies the data types that must be entered in relation to the action. Personnel action fast entry can be used for specific personnel actions, speeding up data entry. When you use the personnel action fast entry function, a view is displayed that only shows the input fields where data for the selected personnel action must be entered.

Organizational Management is used to create an organizational plan, which describes the functional structure of an enterprise. It includes organizational unit, position, task, job, and so on. Organizational Management is used, for example, to evaluate headcount, identify reporting structures, and assign agents to workflow tasks. So Organizational Management is integrated with Personnel Management bidirectionally in a way that the changes made in personnel data (e.g., change of position) is correctly reflected in the organizational plan and vice versa. The authorization concept uses Organizational Management too. The access rights of many objects within SAP S/4HANA Human Resources depend on the organizational structure of the enterprise. For example, a manager is only allowed to access data of employees reporting to the manager. It is possible to define authorization profiles based on the user's position and generate the corresponding authorization role and profile. There are infotypes available for defining the position-based authorization profiles. Organizational Management gives managers and HR professionals an overview about the budget and the organizational structure. Based on this data the cost planning can be done as well as creating job positions. The Organizational Management component covers various user group-specific modes and views to edit organizational plans. The organization and staffing view supports a simplified user interface for creating and editing organizational plans. The general structure view facilitates to edit organizational plans with any structure including self-defined object types. The matrix view enables creation and editing matrix structures.

With Recruitment Management, job applicants and candidates can search for job offers, register themselves in a talent pool, and provide their job applications online. Thus, the component supports the entire recruitment procedure, from creating applicant data to filling vacant positions. Recruiters can post job requisitions and also on external job boards via HR-XML interfaces. Applicant tracking and reporting functions help recruiters to process job applications in an organized way and to monitor the effectiveness of the recruitment department and process. Applicants not deemed suitable for a particular vacancy can be stored in the applicant pool, where they can be considered for future vacancies. This component facilitates to define a recruitment procedure that fulfills the needs of the company. Tasks can be distributed, and responsibilities assigned to different people involved in the recruitment process. Recruitment Management helps in dividing and assigning administrative and decision-making task areas. Tasks can be performed via mass processing parallelly. The component supports dynamic actions to enable automating many processes. When applicant data is entered, for example, the system generates a receipt confirmation in the form of an applicant activity and a letter confirming receipt of the application. Thus, the administrative tasks required of the HR department for applicant correspondence are reduced.

Benefits Administration provides services for queries related to the various benefits plans, like health plans, insurance plans, savings plans, credit plans, miscellaneous plans, stock purchase plans, flexible spending accounts, and flexible spending account claims. The business object modeled here is employee benefits administration. Benefits are vital in the total compensation that employers offer to attract and retain the best talents. This component provides employers a flexible framework for creating and managing tailor-made benefits packages for their employees. It supports configuration capabilities to offer a diverse range of benefits and to accommodate even complex plan definitions. By streamlining the administrative activities, for example, benefits inquiries are handled by employee self-services to minimize the volume of paperwork, it helps cut costs. Reporting capabilities support benefits staff and executives having direct access to structured benefits data to assist them in their analytical tasks. Numerous activities can be performed digitalized with component, for example enrolling employees in benefits plans and terminate enrollments, monitoring continuing eligibility for plans, displaying provision of evidence of insurability, viewing information about current benefit enrollments, printing enrollment and confirmation forms, transferring data electronically to plan providers and administering retirement plans.

Personnel Development deals with the activities related to employee development for example, capture employee potential and qualifications, career and succession planning, and creation of development plans. Personnel Development as well is based on infotypes. The component enables to plan and implement specific personnel and training measures to promote the professional development of employees. It also ensures that staff qualification requirements are met and planned. By developing qualification potentials, it is ensured that employees in functional areas are qualified to the standards required now and in the future. Career and succession planning scenarios are also a capability of Personnel Development. These can include measures to impart qualifications in order for employees to retain and keep up with technological advancements. With the solution qualification catalogs are structured and managed. Thus, profiles can be created based on the qualifications catalog and the organizational structure which can be used to manage, evaluate, and compare object characteristics. The component helps to plan, perform, and evaluate appraisals. Appraisals aid in the planning and monitoring of individual personnel development initiatives. In career planning, possible career goals can be identified, and career plans can be drawn up for employees. Such development plans are also used to manage short-term and long-term personnel development measures.

Compensation Management facilitates an enterprise for the implementation of novel reward strategies such as performance- and competency-based pay, variable pay plans, and long-term incentive reward programs. It also allows for the analysis and comparison of compensation packages using internal and external salary data to ensure market competitiveness. Compensation administration handles processes concerning compensation guidelines, planning, eligibility, reviews, granting salary increases, and bonuses. Long-term incentives cover functionality related to incentives like equity and stock purchase. Budgeting manages features regarding creating and monitoring budgets on the basis of organizational structures. The solution allows for differentiation between compensation strategies and those of competitors while maintaining flexibility, control, and cost-effectiveness. It provides a set of tools for strategic remuneration planning that reflects organizational culture and pay strategies, and it allows line managers to work within a flexible budget control framework. The component facilitates to control bottom-line expenditures and offer competitive and motivating remuneration, be it fixed pay, variable pay, stock options, merit increases, or promotion. The core functionality includes the ability to create centralized and decentralized budgets, plan and administer compensation adjustments at the manager level, plan and administer compensation adjustments within budget, perform job pricing, define pay grades and salary structures, and identify the internal value of jobs and positions within the organization. Travel Management covers all processes involved in handling business trips. The functionality is integrated with settlement, taxation, and payment processes. It includes the entire procedure to request, plan, and book trips, create expense reports, and transfer expense results to other business function areas. Travel request includes the general trip data, required travel services, cost estimates, and the manager's approval. Travel planning provides access to booking services (e.g., flight, hotel, rental cars, rail), applies travel policies for queries and bookings, sets up custom hotel catalogs, considers agreements with travel service providers, and stores travelers' personal preferences. Travel expense report supports creating general data for the travel expense report, settlement of travel expenses, payment of expenses via financial accounting and payroll.

Personnel Time Management

This component supports all processes related to planning, recording, and valuation of internal and external work as well as absence data. Time and labor data can be recorded centrally by a time clerk or by each employee himself or herself. Master data required for time management is stored in infotypes. Examples are absences (infotype 2001) and quotas (infotype 2006). For decoupled access to time infotypes, an additional business logic layer, the business logic processor layer, has been introduced. Time sheet enables an efficient way to record time and manage it. Employees can create and update time entries where they can fill in their working time and the absences. This can be a task, project, or nonproject time log, too. Managers have the ability to approve, review, and reject time entries of the employees. Time capture is for recoding of working time. Different formats for time recording are provided, for example, hours. Those can be displayed in weekly, monthly, and annual calendars. Time calculation allows to define and manage time elements for payroll schedules, and shifts. Work schedules can be created based on this information. An integration to payroll is in place. Absence management defines working calendars and vacation allowances for the employees. It allows integration with employee and manager self-services. Employees can create attendances and absences which are approved by the manager (Fig. 12.11).

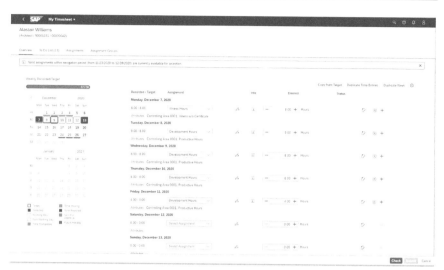

Time Recording

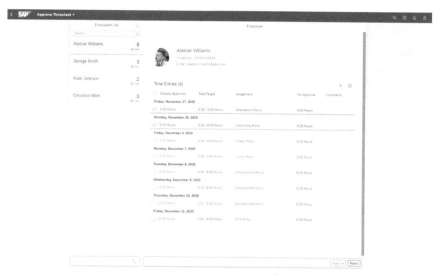

Approval Timesheet

Fig. 12.11 SAP S/4HANA HR—time recording and approval timesheet

Payroll

The component supports all processes related to the remuneration of employees. Based on the employee's time recordings and working contract, the payroll application calculates the gross and net pay, which comprises the individual payments and deductions that are calculated during a payroll period. The payroll result is generally transferred to SAP S/4HANA Financials, which posts the cost and triggers payment to the employee, for example, via check or bank transfer. Payroll administrators can configure payroll runs using the HR process workbench. The HR process workbench is a design time tool to design a process template for executing payroll runs and initiate subsequent activities like posting the results to financial accounting and providing pay slips for the employee. The administrator selects a process template, which defines the sequence of activities (e.g., payroll posting and bank transfer document preparation) to be performed before and after payroll runs. Payroll administrators can start, and monitor payroll runs manually using the HR process workbench. As payroll runs are executed regularly on a monthly basis, the administrator typically plans payroll runs as jobs starting at a defined point in time using the job scheduler. The payroll driver is the main program used to run the payroll. For each supported country version, there is a country-specific payroll driver. The payroll driver is configured by a country-specific schema and by rules. A schema is the central customizing object of the payroll application and defines the payroll functions and personnel calculations rules for one payroll run. Typically, a country-specific payroll driver uses only one main schema, but some companies use the option of different schemas for different processing units based on geographic and enterprise structures. Payroll functions provide logic for payroll calculations. Payroll functions access personal administration to retrieve information about the employee, the contract, and organizational information. In addition, the payroll driver calls payroll functions to calculate benefits, taxes, and net and gross amount. For example, there is one payroll function that considers employees' time data, which results from time evaluation driver. Payroll personnel calculation rules define which payroll operations are executed by the payroll driver and under which conditions. The rules contain the most basic logic used in payroll. Payroll operations are the basic operations that provide smallest possible granularity of operations like mathematical operands. Payroll operations are used to manipulate the wage types, which are basically the placeholders for storage of rates, amounts, and numbers. The properties of a wage type define how the processing happens on amounts and rates during a payroll run. An example for a payroll operation is to multiply the number of working hours by an hourly rate and store the result in the amount of a wage type. Payroll results are communicated to the employee using pay slip forms. These forms are defined as smart forms or Adobe forms using the HR forms tool. In addition, the HR forms tool can be used to define forms for legal reporting.

Talent and Performance Management

This component allows to flexibly develop and foster talents in enterprises. It aids in the hiring of personnel, further education and development of talents, the identification and formation of future management personalities, and the alignment of employees with enterprise goals and compensation.

Employee performance management helps enterprises define and monitor objectives for the entire enterprise, individual departments, and employees themselves. Objectives can be monitored using key figures and appropriate benchmarking. Performance Management helps in objective setting and designing appraisals that enable formalized and standardized appraisals. All of the standard phases for an appraisal process, such as the planning meeting, review, and appraisal, can be mapped. For example, in Performance Management, it is possible to map performance and potential appraisals, 360° appraisals, goal appraisals, references, or checklists. Workflows can be used to support the flow of the appraisal process. The appraisal catalog facilitates to create reusable appraisal templates. Appraisal documents can be generated centrally or individually. Objective setting agreements can be added to these appraisal documents either manually or automatically. Passing of qualifications to Personnel Development or the passing of rating results to Compensation Management can be automated.

Talent Management is used to perform the core processes such as succession planning or talent development for the employees. HR professionals and business leaders can give an objective assessment for the employee. The objective of skill management is the maximization of employee's utility and the company's needs. It helps in planning and measuring personal training. Qualified employees have an increased job satisfaction. Succession management helps to create careers. Careers are paths for the employee development. It makes sure that the company has a collection of qualified persons. The process of employee assessment is supported. Depending on the configuration, managers can evaluate the potential or competencies of employees, or nominate the employee as a talent. Talent management specialists can use the talent review meetings functionality to prepare, hold, and follow-up on meetings for discussing talents.

Training and Event Management

This solution has a wide range of powerful functions to plan and manage all kinds of business events from training events to conventions simply and efficiently. It provides flexible analytics and appraisal capability. Training and Event Management is the basis for extending and updating employees' skills and knowledge. Integration with Personnel Development allows to convert training proposals directly into bookings for employees with qualification deficits or needs. Due to integration into SAP Knowledge Warehouse direct access to a variety of training materials is enabled, for example, online training for self-study. Training and Event Management contains an extensive range of functions like business event preparation, setting up hierarchical structured business event catalogs, calculating business event costs and proposing prices, booking individual and group attendees, performing billing, appraising attendees and events, reporting for all events-related data. The component serves as the administration area for organizing, publishing, and booking classroom training. Training Management comprises course offering, which involves course planning and the creation of a course catalog, and training administration, which involves booking activities. The instructor portal is the user interface for instructors and tutors. Instructors can access their courses to manage the course participants. They can perform appraisals to get feedback from the participants. Achieved qualifications can be assigned to participants and are then stored in the corresponding infotypes. All offered classroom and e-learning courses are presented to the learners within the learning portal. The learning portal includes functionality to search course content and to book training courses. It also includes a content player for playing e-learning content. The content player loads the e-learning content from the content management system whenever a learner starts it in his or her Web browser. The separate offline player can be used to learn offline and synchronize the learner's progress with the central learning portal online.

Shared Services

The component standardizes and automates shared services processes and self-services for employees and managers. Throughout the enterprise, uniform processes and services can be implemented in order to reduce the lead times of operations and ensure a continuous high level of service. Self-services play a significant role in the interaction between a company's employees. The self-services solution enables the creation and operation of employee self-services (ESS) and manager self-services (MSS). Examples of employee self-services are employee personal information, leave and time management, benefits and compensation, and travel management. Examples for manager self-services are employee administration, compensation and budget planning, and project planning. To support managers in decision-making, self-services are provided to access information about the team birthdays, holidays, and deadlines. Managers also have graphical support and get information on the recruiting, talent management, planning, projects, organization, and reports. Employee self-service enables employees to control personal data. The employee can create, display, and cancel own bookings. Additionally, qualification management self-services can be consumed (Fig. 12.12).

Human Resources Reporting

For improving the processes and services complete and real-time analytics for human resources is required which is the focus of this component. As SAP S/4HANA Human Resources contains all relevant employee data, the necessary analytical operations can be performed to support decision-making. Numerous standard reports are provided that enable companies to report on data along hierarchical structures, and access standard analytics easily. Furthermore, cross-application reports can be created, and formatted according to the needs. Standard reports can be searched in individual applications, or across several applications. Application-specific analytical reports are offered in the info systems of individual human resources components. The reports are clustered together by content in the info system. For example, recruitment reports are organized in groups according to applicant, vacancy, or advertisement data. The standard reports are ready to use and

Benefits Enrolment

Changing Mail Address

Fig. 12.12 SAP S/4HANA HR—benefits enrollment and changing address

cover areas like personnel management, time management, payroll, training and event management, and organizational management.

Conclusion

The Recruit to Retire is a core business process in enterprises and covers the entire employee lifecycle. The process starts with recruiting and onboarding employees and continues with developing and growing staffs. To keep the employees satisfied and loyal to the company corresponding reward and retain processes are established. Travel and time management and also payroll and offboarding employees are included. In SAP S/4HANA this end-to-end process is mainly covered by SAP S/4HANA Human Resources component. This solution provides capabilities not only for personnel administration, organization management, recruitment and personnel development, benefits and compensation administration but also for time, travel, talent, and performance management. The SAP S/4HANA modules are deeply integrated and frequently interacting so that also additional components contribute to handle this end-to-end process.

Process of Acquire to Decommission

13

This chapter describes the business process of acquire to decommission consisting of the subprocesses plan to optimize assets, acquire to onboard, operate to maintain, offboard to decommission, and manage assets. Additionally, the application capabilities of SAP S/4HANA to resolve those business processes are explained.

Business Process

The general process of Acquire to Decommission is depicted in Fig. 13.1 and explained in detail in the next sections.

The Acquire to Decommission Process is an essential process for businesses which compromises the complete lifecycle of an asset, from acquisition to decommission. For manufacturing business, an asset could be a machine which is used for production, while an asset for a service-focused business might also be a company car or even a coffee machine. The core of this process is the managing of this asset. From its acquisition to managing its lifecycle by maintaining and finally decommissioning the asset. All this can be supported by digital processes. The Acquire to Decommission process consists of four subprocesses which are running partially in parallel. Plan to Optimize Assets is about defining the asset strategy including maintenance aspects. Acquire to Onboard refers to obtaining assets and assembling them if necessary. Operations to Maintain deals with asset maintenance planning and execution. Assets end of life is covered with Offboard to Decommission. In this context the asset is sold or disposed according to the exit strategy. Manage Assets mitigates risks and ensures environment safety. Maintaining physical assets allows to keep them as available as possible at the lowest possible cost, while also ensuring safe operations. For this comprehensive processes and seamless integration into other domains such as finance, sourcing and procurement, or workforce management are required. The availability of resources, such as technicians, spare parts, and tools, at the right time and place is critical, as is proper financial planning and cost settlement. Companies that rely on physical assets for business

© The Author(s), under exclusive license to Springer Nature Switzerland AG 2022
S. Sarferaz, *Compendium on Enterprise Resource Planning*,
https://doi.org/10.1007/978-3-030-93856-7_13

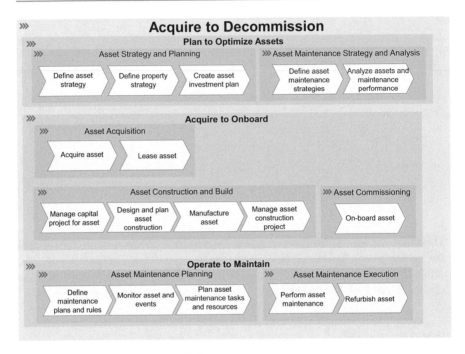

Fig. 13.1 Process acquire to decommission

operations may seek to improve maintenance management practices in order to increase profitability and productivity, as well as to achieve environmental and social goals. Assets are becoming increasingly intelligent. They are connected and can help answer questions such as *When is maintenance required?* and *What is required?* to mitigate potential failures or even avoid break-downs. This enables a broader range of maintenance strategies, from reactive to prescriptive, and necessitates a comprehensive approach as well as well-defined maintenance programs. Simultaneously, a shift has occurred in the roles of organizations involved in maintaining assets at peak performance. New asset-based business models necessitate a true collaborative approach with a single source of truth for data among business partners. Manufacturers and third-party service providers expand their businesses by providing equipment monitoring and maintenance as service (EQaaS) models.

Plan to Optimize Assets (Fig. 13.2)

To improve the maintenance processes and asset performance, enterprises should continuously assess and improve the effectiveness of their maintenance programs to support safe, dependable, and efficient asset operation. Reliability engineers assess the risk of the assets using best-practice methodologies such as reliability-centered

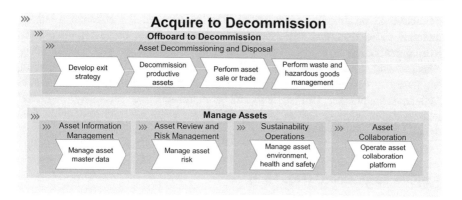

Fig. 13.1 (continued)

Fig. 13.2 Plan to optimize assets

maintenance to determine the best maintenance and service strategies that minimize maintenance costs and reduce the risk of failure for critical assets. By transforming them into data-driven processes, next-generation asset performance management refines and extends such long-standing methods in this area. Before the actual life cycle of the asset begins, the subprocess Plan to Optimize Assets is triggered. In this subprocess, the acquisition of the asset is planned, as well as the general acquisition strategy. This can further be categorized into two parts: The asset strategy and planning, and the asset maintenance strategy and analysis. The asset strategy and planning process defines the strategies to be set for acquiring new assets. Firstly, an asset strategy has to be defined for the company. Requirements from other processes, like the Governance process, are also important. Secondly, the property strategy has to be defined. It is decided on, whether an asset should be owned or leased. Here, consultation with the financial aspects is key. Finally, an asset investment plan has to be created. For the maintenance strategy, the asset maintenance policy needs to be defined. After that, the assets need to be analyzed, as well as the maintenance performance. The asset maintenance strategies are defined by reliability engineers. For that they perform an asset risk and criticality assessment to derive respective scores for own defined impact categories, allowing to focus on the most important assets. They decide and choose between the typical maintenance strategies based on detailed knowledge of the asset's potential failure patterns: reactive maintenance (also known as run to failure); time-, usage-, or condition-based maintenance; or predictive or prescriptive maintenance. The recommended maintenance strategy includes more than just dedicated repair work to keep the asset operational. Recommendations can also include the definition of inspection needs, design changes, and the like to reduce the likelihood of potential failures. A reliability engineer can decide to revise a maintenance strategy for better business results. Maintenance planner can review and comprehend the reliability engineer's recommended strategy and measures. The planner can use and implement these definitions in a collaborative process.

Acquire to Onboard (Fig. 13.3)

Next in the lifecycle of an asset is its acquisition and onboarding. The Acquire to Onboard subprocess compromises asset acquisition, asset construction, and asset commissioning. Firstly, the asset has to be either acquired or leased. This decision has to be run by the financial processes, as it influences the cash flow and/or the general liquidity of the company. This decision might also be made by lines of business departments with focus on functional and nonfunctional qualities. Sometimes assets must be constructed and built by the company itself. In some circumstances, this could make sense for a company, as there could be cost saving effects with building one's own assets. Perquisite is that the necessary skills and materials are available inhouse. Usually acquired or leased assets must be assembled. For that capital project for the asset must be managed. Furthermore, asset construction must be designed and planned. The construction project must be handled in order to assemble the asset. Before assets can be productively used, they must be onboarded in context of commissioning.

Operate to Maintain (Fig. 13.4)

One of the most important and probably the longest running subprocesses begins right after the asset has been onboarded. The Operate to Maintain subprocess consists of two mayor topics. These are asset maintenance planning and asset

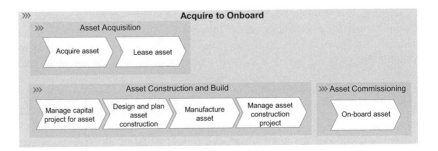

Fig. 13.3 Acquire to onboard

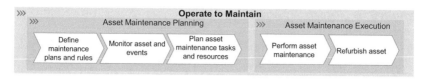

Fig. 13.4 Operate to maintain

management execution. When planning asset maintenance, several steps have to be taken. First, maintenance plans and rules have to be defined. This is also highly dependent on the asset itself, as different assets need different maintenance intervals. Next, the asset has to be monitored, as well as the events that concern this asset. Periodically, the asset maintenance tasks and allocated resources have to be planned. When a planned or unplanned asset maintenance has to be executed, there are two steps to be taken. Firstly, the asset maintenance has to be performed by qualified personnel. After that, the asset has to be refurbished. Operate to Maintain is running as long as the asset is in use respectively until it is decommissioned. Maintenance management enables to demand, plan, and execute maintenance to better meet the needs of a next-generation taskforce. In maintenance execution, end-to-end processes typically span multiple phases. The following phases are covered in an industry's best-practice scenario:

- Initiation by raising a work request
- Screening and approval of the work request
- Handover to detailed work-scope planning
- Order approval and release with subsequent scheduling and dispatching
- Work execution
- Work confirmation and closure

In traditional terms, proactive maintenance is scheduled for equipment before it falls out of tolerance or breaks, preventing costly scheduled repair or emergency repair and downtimes. A maintenance planner can plan ahead of time the work scope and time required for time- or usage-based measures such as inspections and maintenance work using maintenance plans and task lists. Moving away from a one-size-fits-all approach with traditional time- or performance-based maintenance plans, condition-based and predictive or prescriptive maintenance are applied. As a result, enterprises can transition to a much more individualized asset maintenance program, with optimized time windows and work scopes, for improved asset performance and availability.

Offboard to Decommission (Fig. 13.5)

The Offboard to Decommission subprocess marks the end of the asset lifecycle. If the asset is no longer useful or is getting replaced, this subprocess takes place. The subprocess contains the asset decommissioning and its disposal. First, an exit strategy has to be developed. Next, the productive assets have to be decommissioned. After that, the asset has to be sold or traded. Finally, the waste has to be taken care, as well as any hazardous goods that need to be disposed.

Manage Assets (Fig. 13.6)

The Manage Assets subprocess is the only one which runs parallel to the other processes from the asset's lifecycle point of view. One of the tasks in this subprocess is the asset information management. This task is about handling the asset master data which must be maintained consistently and kept up to date permanently. Another continuous task is to inherently review and manage the asset's risks. This process covers identifying, assessing, and controlling threats regarding assets. Based on the risk management plan mitigation procedures are performed if necessary. By considering potential risks systematically before they occur, a company can save money and protect their assets. Another very important task is the sustainability operation. This task is about managing the environment, health, and safety around the asset. Thus, the daily operation is made safe, the workforce is engaged to identify and act on hazards before they impact safety. By safeguarding the operations continuity, asset integrity is protected, and production is optimized by reducing unplanned downtime and outages through proactively identifying and mitigating safety issues. The last task is asset collaboration, which concerns itself with the operation of the asset collaboration platform. Another shift in the roles of

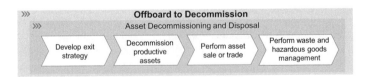

Fig. 13.5 Offboard to decommission

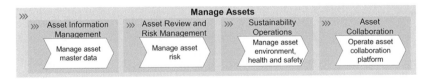

Fig. 13.6 Manage assets

organizations involved in asset operation and maintenance can be seen in the following ways:

- The operator does not always maintain the assets. Under EQaaS models, manufacturers or third parties offer to monitor and maintain assets.
- The processes for *in-house maintenance* by an operator and customer service by a supplier are merging. Third parties are increasingly responsible for the upkeep of complex assets.

These market trends drive a greater demand for collaborative business services and network concepts. Sharing asset data in a secure and standardized manner is critical to assisting peers in the maintenance and service business.

Solution Capability

The end-to-end process Acquire to Decommission is mainly implemented by SAP Asset Management as depicted in Fig. 13.7. While SAP S/4HANA Asset Management covers the core functionality SAP Intelligent Asset Management and SAP Geographical Enablement Framework include extended features for predictive asset insights, mobile management, or geolocation.

With Maintenance Management a holistic approach including planning, execution, improvement, and collaboration can be leveraged. Furthermore, it facilitates to combine material management and plant maintenance functionality to plan and achieve a holistic strategy for maintenance management. Tracking costs and conducting thorough damage analysis are also supported. Asset Operations and Maintenance extends core planning functionality with detailed scheduling capabilities and resource planning. Environment Health and Safety (EHS) ensures safety and business continuity. The solution mitigates health and safety risks by

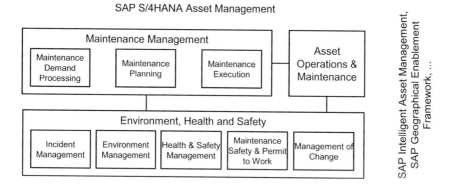

Fig. 13.7 SAP S/4HANA Asset Management—functional architecture

performing risk assessments, creating safety instructions, and managing incidents. Intelligent Asset Management is the newest offering in the field of asset management. It makes use of the newest technological trends to get the most intelligent asset management system possible. It uses state-of-the-art business processes which use new technologies to enable new asset management business processes anywhere and anytime. The solution allows to gain real-time insights on strategic, tactical, and operational levels. With connected assets, information from operational and business systems are combined, using the Internet of Things for scalable transparency. The component makes use of prediction, optimization, and simulation which allow to drive smarter decisions, improve reliability, and reduce outages. With collaboration throughout the asset lifecycle, asset information can be shared and enable business networks.

Maintenance Management

The maintenance master data builds the basis for various processes of asset management solution. The key features are structuring of technical objects in a hierarchical as well as a horizontal manner, creating master records for functional locations and pieces of equipment but also the creation of maintenance bills of materials. Additionally, reading measuring points and counters and creating measurement documents, accessing context-sensitive information and processing master data in the information center are supported. Furthermore, visualizing technical objects in the master data and viewing technical objects in the asset viewer are provided. With this set of features, asset master data can be maintained systematically and consistently. Maintenance Demand Processing allows users to create and process any type of work request, from classical corrective toward condition-based, predictive or prescriptive maintenance methodologies. Maintenance work can also be requested to be performed and mobile devices or a desktop can be used to describe the technical faults. This process can also be enhanced with SAP Intelligent Asset Management which allows to synchronize notification and order data. With Maintenance Planning, maintenance can be planned, and the ideal technician can be found to use appropriate tools and resources and perform maintenance activities. Also, a full view of asset status, maintenance cost, and breakdown causes are provided. Maintenance costs can be reduced by efficiently using labor, material, equipment, and schedules. Another function is classifying maintenance plans to allow for better searching and analyzing and monitoring maintenance costs. Operations can be classified into pre-, main-, and post-work. Key features that are offered in this solution are planning of complex maintenance cycles with strategies, processing maintenance plans, and planning recurrent maintenance work with task lists. Additionally, performing inspection rounds, accessing context-sensitive information, processing maintenance plans and items from a personal object worklist are supported. The solution facilitates selecting spare parts and viewing visual instructions in task lists and viewing relationships between maintenance objects in the asset viewer. After maintenance is scheduled, it has to be performed. With

Maintenance Execution, planned or emergency maintenance can be performed and the access of relevant information on any device enabled. Employees can access, transfer, complete, and manage assigned work orders remotely and can gain real-time insights of asset performance for timely, relevant decisions. They can also review ongoing maintenance activities with the ability to reschedule multiple times a day. Key features include the reporting of a malfunction using notifications and executing maintenance work using maintenance orders but also processing and confirming maintenance jobs. Furthermore, accessing context-sensitive information and processing maintenance documents in the order and notification information center are enabled. The selecting of spare parts and viewing visual instructions in maintenance orders and viewing relationships between maintenance objects in the asset viewer are also supported (Fig. 13.8).

Asset Operations and Maintenance

Maintenance Scheduling allows users to reduce excessive downtime and decrease costs by having the right systems and processes in place. It takes the availability windows for maintenance, work center capacity, and maintenance plans into consideration. The solution embeds resource scheduling. This means that insight into maintenance workload can be gained and available capacities for current and upcoming maintenance activities can be controlled. Additionally, the component facilitates to identify critical planning situations early and take action to improve planning relevant KPIs. Maintenance order can be planned efficiently based on work center utilization to make sure that all maintenance jobs can be completed. Alternatively, work center capacity can be adjusted quickly. Statuses to schedules can be assigned and work center capacity can be optimized. Maintenance orders are visualized in work centers to gain transparency about what needs to be done at which time. The solution allows to set up, share and monitor schedules, as well as provide feedback for a schedule and plan own work accordingly. The application provides a dashboard for monitoring key figures, such as work center utilization and number and priority of maintenance orders that are needed to work on. It also supports quick access to the schedules that are currently relevant. The utilization chart allows to visualize the current work center utilization by specific attributes, for example, to show the load caused by maintenance plans by using the processing status attribute. There are several options to manage the utilization of work centers. Order operations can be dispatched to confirm the planned dates and work center. If a work center is overloaded, it is possible to level work center utilization by moving order operations to another date or work center. Additionally, the available work center capacity for a specific target week can be adjusted. Scheduling of maintenance order operations usually covers multiple steps. First one or more schedule simulations for the target week are created. When the optimal schedule is determined, the scheduled order operations can be dispatched, and the final schedule can be frozen. When the target week has started, schedule execution can be tracked. One or multiple maintenance order operations can be assigned to a responsible person,

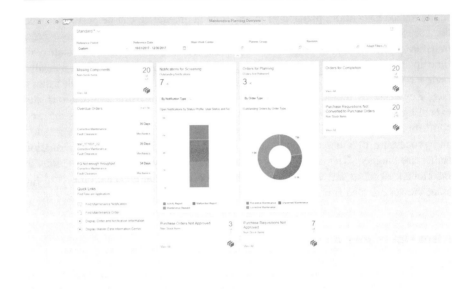

Maintenance Planning Overview Page

Maintenance orders and operations

Fig. 13.8 SAP S/4HANA Asset Management—maintenance planning overview and maintenance order

existing assignments can be changed or even deleted. With multiresource management, processes for defining and fulfilling project resource demands can be streamlined and automated. It also provides functionality for tracking, assigning and scheduling resources, collecting assignment approvals, and generating relevant reports like demand overview and resource utilization reports. This results in faster project staffing, improved resource utilization, more accurate demand forecasts, and increased project margins (Fig. 13.9).

Environment Health and Safety

The solution supports in managing business processes related to the safety of the environment and the health and safety of people. It enables to plan the required activities for managing the compliance of the company with emission-related environmental regulations. Additionally, the solution enables to record and process incidents, safety observations, and near misses. It helps to report the data to internal and external stakeholders to fulfill legal, regulatory, and company reporting responsibilities. Environment Health and Safety (EHS) enables to assess and manage risks in the organization. It can take the appropriate actions necessary to reduce risk to acceptable levels and prevent any harmful effects to the health and safety of employees and the environment. With Incident Management, EHS incidents, near misses, and observations can be recorded. Transparency and standardizations can be created with templates, task tracking, and analytical automated reporting. Injury, illness and incident rates can be decreased, EHS penalties and fines can be reduced, as well as unplanned downtimes. The component manages investigations, follow-up activities, and improves employee engagement. Role-based analytics provides insights into incident root causes. The process of incident management consists of the following steps:

1. An incident is reported by creating initial incident record.
2. The incident is processed and the formal reporting is performed. The following activities are executed during this step:
   (a) Inquiries are sent to get more details regarding the incident.
   (b) The financial impact of the incident is tracked.
   (c) Environmental releases are reported which occurred with the incident.
   (d) Equipment is assigned to the incident record and the damage is reported.
   (e) Incident is reported to authorities or for internal purposes.
   (f) Notices of violation are recorded that were issued to organization with regards to the incident.
3. Analyze and investigate the incident.
4. Analytics apps are used to get an overview of coherences concerning injuries and illnesses, and incidents.
5. Finally, corrective or preventive actions are implemented. Furthermore, the completion of actions and tasks is verified (Fig. 13.10).

Environment Management enables to forecast emissions data based on past emission data with the help of predictive learning algorithms and statistical methods. Greenhouse gas emissions, as well as other air or water emissions can be managed to

Maintenance Scheduling board

Schedule Maintenance Order Operations

Fig. 13.9 SAP S/4HANA Asset Management—maintenance scheduling board and maintenance order operations

fulfill legal requirements while fostering proactive data transparency and monitoring. This allows to reduce risk of environmental noncompliance and penalties. The application component enables companies to stay compliant with emissions-related environmental regulations. The solution supports the processes and subprocesses of managing compliance scenario activities to ensure compliance. These processes ensure to create and incorporate a strategy of managing environmentally related data from data collection, sampling, calculation, and aggregation of emissions into the daily operations within companies. Health and Safety Management supports to manage general and equipment-related safety instructions centrally and prevents incidents and reduces EHS risks. This is due to standardized, cost-effective approach

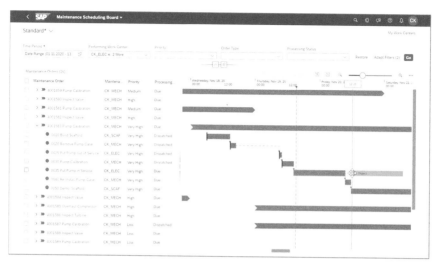

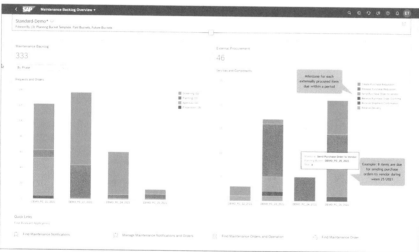

Fig. 13.10 SAP S/4HANA Asset Management—maintenance scheduling board and maintenance backlog overview

for managing operational risks. The solution helps to minimize workplace exposures and related health impacts. The component manages industrial hygiene, monitoring by planning and performing workplace sample campaigns and related measurements. Maintenance Safety and Permit to Work facilitates to control maintenance work through clear safety instructions and permits. It links EHS information to technical equipment and plant maintenance tasks. The component ensures flexible levels of permits natively integrated with the work-order process in enterprise asset management and automates the permit process and enforces fully auditable

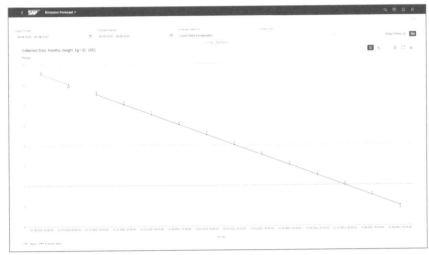

Emissions Forecasting

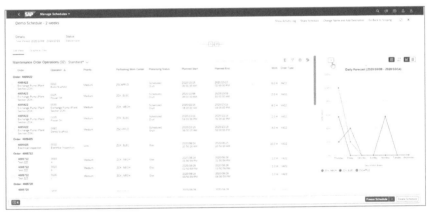

Manage Schedule

Fig. 13.11 SAP S/4HANA Asset Management—emissions forecasting and manage schedule

procedures that promote consistent behavior. Management of Change helps to streamline change requests. The solution automates the involvement of the right people to mitigate risks caused by changes to equipment, substances, operating conditions, and procedures. It manages operational changes with thorough review, risk mitigation, and documentation approval (Fig. 13.11).

Conclusion

The whole lifecycle of an asset is compromised in the Acquire to Decommission process. Furthermore, continuous tasks outside of the asset lifecycle are included. First, an asset acquisition strategy is planned, then the asset is acquired and onboarded. During the asset's life inside the company, a maintenance strategy is planned and executed. With the asset's end of life, it is decommissioned and disposed of. During the lifecycle of all the asset in a company, the assets are supported, regarding their master data, risk management as well as health, environment, and safety impacts. In SAP S/4HANA this end-to-end process is mainly covered by SAP S/4HANA Asset Management component. This solution provides capabilities for maintenance management, asset operations, environment health and safety. The SAP S/4HANA modules are deeply integrated and frequently interacting so that also additional components contribute to handle this end-to-end process.

Process of Governance

14

This chapter describes the business process governance consisting of the subprocesses plan to optimize enterprise, manage enterprise risk and governance, manage identity and access governance, manage cybersecurity/data protection/data privacy, manage international trade/tax/legal, manage IT, manage projects and operations. Additionally, the application capabilities of SAP S/4HANA to resolve those business processes are explained.

Business Process

The general process of Governance is depicted in Fig. 14.1 and explained in detail in the next sections.

The Governance process is one of the corporate processes. The goal of these processes is to plan and manage the company. This includes the departments of finance, indirect procurement, asset management, human resources, corporate strategy, and corporate operations. The Governance process consists of seven subprocesses. The main task of the process is to manage different areas: The enterprise's risk and compliance must be managed as well as the identity and access governance. Furthermore, handling of cybersecurity, data protection, and data privacy plays a big role to ensure that the data of the enterprise is safe and compliant. Moreover, the Governance process manages the international trade, tax, and legal as well as the IT. Additionally, the projects and operations of the company must be managed. Besides these managing tasks, another objective of the process is the optimization of the enterprise, which is the first subprocess of the Governance process.

© The Author(s), under exclusive license to Springer Nature Switzerland AG 2022
S. Sarferaz, *Compendium on Enterprise Resource Planning*,
https://doi.org/10.1007/978-3-030-93856-7_14

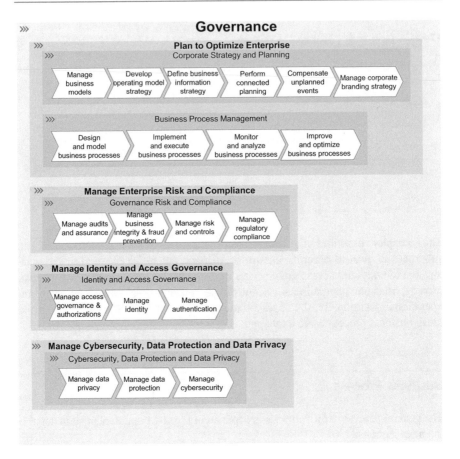

Fig. 14.1 Governance process

Plan to Optimize Enterprise (Fig. 14.2)

The Governance process starts with the subprocess Plan to Optimize Enterprise. This process starts with managing the business models because these are never static. A good example for that is the business model of Amazon: when Amazon was founded, they only sold books. Today Amazon is selling practically everything, from products to services. Therefore, their business model changed from only selling books to selling a lot more different goods. Therefore, it is important to always optimize and adjust the model of the business. To ensure this corresponding operating model strategy is developed. Moreover, it is significant to design a strategy to cope with business information as data of a company is sensitive and legally relevant and should not be accessible without appropriate authorization. The Governance process includes a global planning across all the end-to-end processes to facilitate an integrated planning. Specific attention is required for unplanned events.

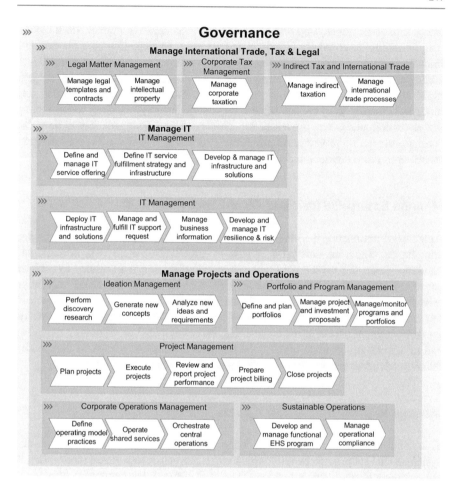

Fig. 14.1 (continued)

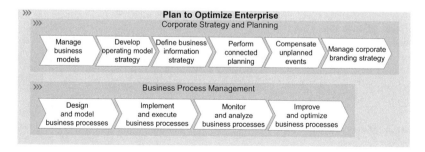

Fig. 14.2 Plan to optimize enterprise

These must be compensated and mitigated to avoid negative impacts on the company. Finally, the corporate branding strategy must be defined which for example impacts the reputation and public relations of the company. All business processes of a company are interrelated and must therefore be considered inherently to achieve high level of optimization. For that the business processes are designed and modelled globally to have a consistent foundation for implementing them. During the execution phase the processes are monitored and analyzed. Thus, they can continuously be improved and optimized. This helps in making the business processes even more efficient and it also eliminates bottlenecks.

Manage Enterprise Risk and Compliance (Fig. 14.3)

Apart from optimizing the enterprise, the Governance process manages risks and compliance. Thus, an enterprise is able to effectively handle risk, control, and assurance tasks. To reduce risks and ensure compliance it is necessary to perform audits and assurances. Business integrity must be managed, and fraud prevention measures are implemented. For global companies with locations in various countries this can be a challenging task due to cultural and mentality differences. Additionally, the company must manage and control risks by developing corresponding risk plans and mitigation procedures. Finally, the regulatory compliance must be handled by defining adequate action plans and execution processes.

Manage Identity and Access Governance (Fig. 14.4)

This subprocess is in charge of the technical access to critical infrastructure and systems. This subprocess handles which employee can access which information in the company through authentication. Thus, it is ensured that employees only know what they need to know and do not have access to everything. This can prevent security vulnerability. The entire lifecycle management of identities must be covered from provisioning to decommissioning. For these corresponding policies,

Fig. 14.3 Manage enterprise risk and compliance

Fig. 14.4 Manage identity and access governance

authentication mechanisms and corresponding implementation strategies must be defined. This is also true for the topic authorizations regarding data, processes, and systems. Apart from information identity and access governance must be also covered for additional assets like buildings.

Manage Cybersecurity, Data Protection and Data Privacy (Fig. 14.5)

This subprocess handles cybersecurity, data protection, and data privacy which are also key aspects of the governance process. There are more and more requirements for data privacy and security like the General Data Protection Regulation (GDPR) and the Consumer Privacy Act of California which must be considered in enterprises for legal compliance. Furthermore, business data is very sensitive and valuable and therefore in focus of cybersecurity. Successful security attacks can result in huge financial damages and can impact the public creditability of companies. Therefore, data privacy measures must be implemented to ensure legal compliance, data protection procedures must be applied to safeguard business data from unauthorized access, and cybersecurity mechanism deployed to defend the company from security vulnerabilities.

Manage International Trade, Tax and Legal (Fig. 14.6)

Another task of the Governance process is handling the international trade, tax, and legal. This ensures that the company does apply the international regulations. In context of legal matter management corresponding templates and contracts are defined and provided for reuse. For example, sales contracts need to be drafted

Fig. 14.5 Manage cybersecurity, data protection, and data privacy

Fig. 14.6 Manage international trade, tax, and legal

beforehand. Companies invent new products and services to have a competitive advantage. The underlying intellectual property must be protected and handled through the entire lifecycle. Companies must pay corporate tax on their profits. This covers the company's taxable income, which includes revenue minus cost. To be compliant with tax evasion laws, corporate taxation must be managed systematically. This is also true for indirect taxation which is collected usually by a producer or retailer and paid to the government. International trade is about exchanging goods and services between countries. Trading globally provides consumers and countries the opportunity to have access to goods and services not available in their own countries. International trading is subject of additional regulations and processes which must be managed for the company.

Manage IT (Fig. 14.7)

The subprocess Manage IT starts with defining and managing the different IT services offerings based on the company's requirements. The need of the IT services depends on the sector the company focuses on. To meet the IT requirements with corresponding services, fulfillment strategy and infrastructure concept must be defined. These are the foundation for developing and managing the IT infrastructure and software solutions. As companies have to cover the entire lifecycle of products or services, they usually deploy Enterprise Resources Planning (ERP) systems. The selection and the implementation of ERP systems require in-depth analysis and support of consultants.

While using IT solutions, problems or bugs can occur. The users must be able to report these and get help to fix the problems. For that IT support must be established which manages and fulfills the requests of the users. Enterprises handle large number of documents. Those must be created, updated, deleted, exchanged, archived, protected, and classified. Thus, corresponding strategies and procedures for handling business information must be provided. Finally, it is important to develop and manage the IT resilience and risk to ensure that the IT services have a high availability, and the risks are minimized and mitigated immediately.

Fig. 14.7 Manage IT

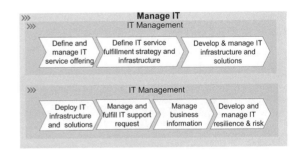

Manage Projects and Operations (Fig. 14.8)

The subprocess Manage Projects and Operations consists of five different processes. The first one is the ideation management. A company usually has many employees. Every one of these employees has their own thoughts and ideas. These ideas can be valuable for the company. The ideation management facilitates the submission of ideas by employees. Those ideas are grouped and prioritized by a central committee that also decides on the implementation. With ideation management employees are involved into the improvements of products, services, and processes. This increases the motivation of employees as their ideas are considered as relevant. It is also important to reward the employees whose ideas are implemented. Thus, the acceptance of the ideation management and the motivation of employees to submit ideas are increased. Portfolio and program management are crucial for enterprises as they have to deal with various products and services. Thus, portfolio must be defined and planned in accordance with the company's product or service strategy. Already the portfolio definition is a complex task with numerous involved stakeholders and objectives so that a program might need to be set up for successful execution. Programs consist of multiple parallel running projects which need orchestration and synchronization. There are many tasks in companies where programs must be established for execution. Thus, standardized methodology must be developed to harmonize the programs, make them comparable and more effective. Portfolio and program management require continuous monitoring and controlling to achieve the predefined goals but also to improve the underlying processes. As already mentioned, programs comprise several projects. The daily works in enterprises are often organized based on projects, for example, analyzing market opportunities, defining portfolios, or designing products. Thus, managing projects must be streamlined in companies concerning methodologies and tooling for planning, execution, and closing projects. This helps particularly in reviewing projects and reporting on their performance. Often projects are stuffed with third-party members. Therefore,

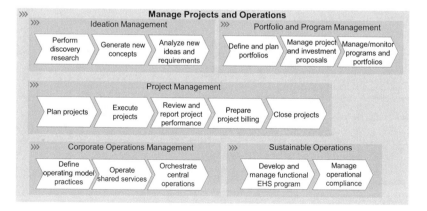

Fig. 14.8 Mange projects and operations

project billing must be considered. This can also be the case for project members from different cost centers of the company. In context of corporate operations management, the operating model practices are defined. Enterprises can decide whether operations are outsourced to shared services or handled internally. Typically, there is a hybrid strategy applied which combines both options. Anyhow the operations are distributed and must be orchestrated centrally.

The last subprocess of the Manage Projects and Operations process is handling the sustainable operations. For companies' sustainability is not only about protecting the environment but also improving the image and branding. Being a sustainable company also helps in being compliant to regulations and avoiding financial penalties. Therefore, it is important to develop and manage a functional EHS program. EHS stands for Environment, Health, and Safety, and it refers to laws, rules, regulations, professions, programs, and workplace actions aimed at protecting employees and the general public's health and safety.

Solutoin Capability

The end-to-end process Governance is not implemented with one SAP S/4HANA module but includes several, for example, the subprocesses Portfolio and Program Management as well as Project Management can be implemented with the help of the Enterprise Portfolio and Project Management solution of the SAP S/4HANA R&D/Engineering. However, core subprocesses of Governance can be implemented with the SAP Governance Risk and Compliance (GRC) solutions as depicted in Fig. 14.7. This solution is complemented with lines of business (LoB), industry and partner extensions (Fig. 14.9).

SAP GRC can be codeployed on SAP S/4HANA to lower the cost of operations for IT departments. Therefore, there is no need for data replication for mass data

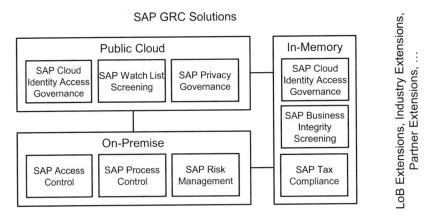

Fig. 14.9 SAP GRC solutions—functional architecture

analysis or plug-ins for extracting and transferring the required data. The plug-ins don't require complex connectivity setups to the business system anymore as it is directly embedded into the SAP S/4HANA processes. Enterprises which are using both are therefore enabled to have a real-time preventative compliance management. SAP GRC solution includes different public cloud, in-memory and on-premise solutions. These different technical capabilities depend on the business scenario and use case. The technical foundation of the cloud-based solutions is the SAP Business Technology Platform (SAP BTP). The cloud solutions include the SAP Cloud Identity Access Governance which governs access in the cloud, the SAP Watch List Screening which verifies business partner compliance, and the SAP Privacy Governance which addresses today's data privacy challenges. In-memory capabilities are used when high volumes of data must be analyzed and extracted from SAP S/4HANA. There are three solutions based on in-memory: the SAP Audit Management which transforms audit beyond assurance, SAP Business Integrity Screening which implements efficient fraud detection, and SAP Tax Compliance which complies with tax regulations. On-premise-based solutions rely on the SAP ABAP platform and are mostly used for the optimization of existing manuals and automated GRC processes and workflows while balancing implementation costs. There are three different solutions for SAP S/4HANA: the SAP Access Control which manages access risks, the SAP Process Control which ensures effective controls and ongoing compliance, and the SAP Risk Management which manages enterprise risk across the organization.

SAP Cloud Identity Access Governance

The SAP Cloud Identity Access Governance solution simplifies and manages the identity and access management in the cloud. To ensure that users get the necessary access they need as seamlessly and effectively as possible. The SAP Cloud Identity Access Governance solution provides key capabilities to solve the access management and compliance challenges for SAP S/4HANA. The Access Analysis Service helps to analyze flexible and extendable the access risk and get recommendations during the remediation process. Moreover, it enables to streamline access with real-time visualizations. Access Certification Service allows to review and certify access for on-premise and cloud source applications. This happens periodically, in order to identify changes in individual usage behaviors and prevent people from having unnecessary access privileges. Access Request Service enables to create self-service requests to applications. This helps with providing users only the access they need to perform their tasks and therefore preventing security breaches. Privileged Access Management Service handles the creating of self-service requests for emergency access to systems and applications. It also flags and monitors sensitive or administrative transactions as well as what is being executed with these authorizations. Based on self-learning algorithms it immediately flags suspicious activities by identifying anomalies and behavior changes. Finally, the Role Design Service handles the business roles of the processes. The service includes the creating and

Access Analysis Overview

Fig. 14.10   SAP cloud identity access governance—access analysis overview

optimizing as well as the maintaining of these roles. This helps in simplifying the role administration and the process of access assignment with machine learning-based role adoption (Fig. 14.10).

SAP Watch List Screening

The SAP Watch List Screening facilitates to verify the compliance of business partners by screening the names and addresses of these against sanctioned party lists. This ensures compliance with guidelines, regulations, and legislation. With SAP Watch List Screening, provider-defined sanctioned-party list can be uploaded to screen name and address information against the sanctioned-party list. The solution allows to resolve the hits found during screening by either confirming or rejecting them. The component integrates with other business processes and applications, for example, calling the screening service within the trade compliance document in SAP S/4HANA. To enable collaboration the decisions of the screening specialists are made available for further actions.

SAP Privacy Governance

This solution enables compliance with data protection and privacy regulations. It offers a single point of entry for the data protection officer (DPO) for everything related to data protection. SAP Privacy Governance handles the proper documentation of the organizational structure including the organizational hierarchy and units as well as the documentation of the business processes. Besides ensuring appropriate documentation it creates and distributes the organizational policies, manages legal and regulatory compliance requirements through regulation registry as well as the requests from data subjects for access their data. The application helps to ensure compliance as well and reduces risks by controlling the activities. SAP Privacy Governance has an extra risk framework which helps documenting and assessing potential risks to the organization. Moreover, it stores information about the processing of personal data while highlighting potential risks in those processes. The solution documents specific laws and regulations that are relevant for the organization's compliance with privacy legislation, creates and disseminates policies related to data protection, privacy, and security. The module allows to create records of processing activities (RoPA) surveys, publish surveys to gather RoPA information, use survey results to evaluate whether a data protection impact assessment is required. The application supports criticality of data protection and privacy (DPP) relevant processes with data privacy impact assessments and enables a lean risk evaluation to assess and monitor risks associated with DPP relevant processes. Finally, the solution facilitates managing automated procedures as well as monitoring their runs.

SAP Audit Management

With the help of the SAP Audit Management, it is possible to automate and improve internal auditing procedures. The auditing process is separated into five phases: planning, preparation, execution, reporting, and follow-up. These five phases include tasks such as building audit plans, preparing audits, analyzing, documenting, and communicating results, forming an audit opinion, and monitoring the progress. To plan audits corresponding audit engagement plans for a planning period are created and assigned to proper resources. Master data such as risks and dimensions are used to build a risk-based audit plan. An overview of risk coverage is provided by auditable items and audits. To prepare audits work programs are created manually, using predefined templates, or by copying them from previous audits. Mass uploading tools can be used to easily upload work programs. Test procedures, questionnaires, and automatic detection tasks are also available. Optionally, audit announcement letters can be generated and distributed to the stakeholders. To execute audits work packages are processed online or offline using Adobe forms. Working papers are managed, audit work is documented, findings are created, and action plans based are proposed on audit evidence. Audit reports can be prepared, reviewed, approved, and issued. Predefined report templates in multiple formats help to generate audit reports online. Follow-ups with auditees are supported so that the status of findings and action plans can be monitored. Historical action plans can be viewed to decide if further actions are needed (Fig. 14.11).

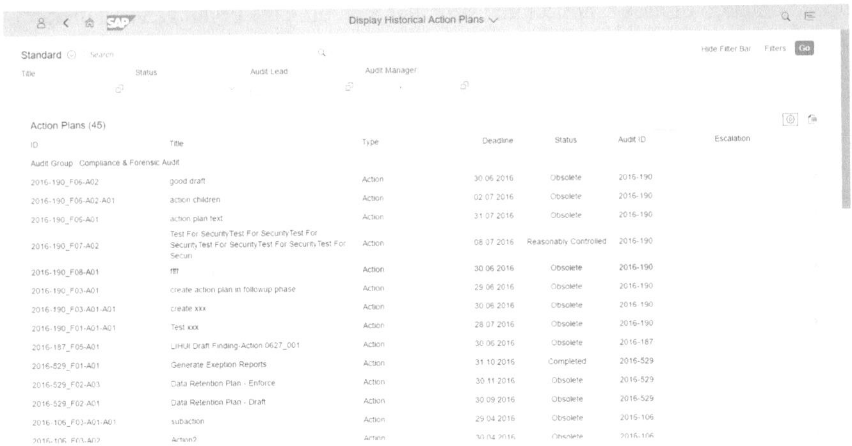

Display Historical Action Plans

Track Open Findings

Fig. 14.11 SAP audit management—display historical action plans and track open findings

SAP Business Integrity Screening

This solution implements an effective fraud detection that not only detects but prevents and deters fraud in big data environments by detecting, investigating, and analyzing irregularities in data. It helps enterprises to mitigate fraud risk and reduce losses. For the detection of fraud and irregularities, detection strategies are created. Master Data and business transactions are screened against screening lists. With the help of efficient alert management, detected irregularities are investigated. The detection accuracy is continuously improved by minimizing false positives with real-time calibration and simulation capabilities. This increases productivity of investigation team. It refines searches and improves fraud detection accuracy, even across very large volumes of data. The solution uses deterministic rules and predictive algorithms to identify common patterns. The number of false-positives is reduced by using what-if analyses on historical data and assessing which approaches are most effective. Quickly react to permanently changing patterns by leveraging machine learning. Multirule strategies to calculate risk scores and optimize analyses of fraud scenarios can be used. Analysis is supported to compare which approaches are most effective in deterring fraud and make better decisions. Reporting tools are provided to display a large range of key performance indicators on alerts. Investigation overview can be consumed to focus on outstanding activities for alert processing. Integration with other products is supported, for example, with payment proposals in SAP S/4HANA (Fig. 14.12).

SAP Tax Compliance

The last of the three in-memory-based solutions is the SAP Tax Compliance. It ensures that the enterprise is compliant with tax regulations to avoid fines and other penalties. To enable that, the solution helps to find and resolve tax compliance issues. The solution supports in gaining of transparency and insight into compliance or risk problems and therefore finding and resolving these issues quickly. It automates detection of the compliance issues and documents activities in resolving the issues. The application manages compliance checks on SAP and non-SAP data sources, across the company. Compliance checks are organized into compliance scenarios, in order to run them together. Compliance scenarios can be performed in simulation mode to test and evaluate them. However, job scheduling is supported to automatically repeat compliance scenario runs. Self-learning algorithms are used to find compliance issues and mitigate them using machine learning for decision-making as well as tasks and task lists. Workflow is used to process tasks which can be created-based task templates. Reporting capabilities are provided to analyze the number of hits over time for various checks and scenarios, and to relate the number of hits with the underlying.
amounts (Fig. 14.13).

SAP Access Control

The SAP Access Control helps to manage the access risk by controlling access and preventing fraud. This helps in minimizing the time and cost of compliance. The key capabilities of SAP Access Control are the monitoring of privileges such as emergency access and transaction usage, the certification of authorizations to check if access assignments are still warranted, the integration with connected systems, the analyzing of risks as well as the automated access administration and the maintaining of roles. To analyze risks comprehensive, predefined rule set can be used to perform cross-system analysis for enterprise applications in real time. If necessary, actions

Investigation Overview

Ad Hoc Screening

Fig. 14.12   SAP business integrity screening—investigation overview and ad-hoc screening

can be taken to remediate and mitigate access risks. To manage access self-service, automated access requests are provided based on workflow-driven approval process. Roles can be defined and configured in business terms and are aligned with business processes. Continues analysis and optimization of business roles are supported. Certifying role content and assignment to users are facilitated including automated periodic user-access reviews. Systemic monitoring privileges are supported allowing to manage emergency access, review user and role transaction usage details, get proactive notification of conflicting or sensitive action usage, and customize dashboards and reports.

Compliance Results Overview

Manage Compliance Scenarios

Fig. 14.13 SAP tax compliance—compliance results overview and manage compliance scenarios

SAP Process Control

The SAP Process Control is a solution for compliance and policy management and enables organizations to manage and monitor their internal control environments and when finding an issue to proactively remediate it. The solution ensures effective controls and ongoing compliance by identifying, prioritizing, and focusing on key business process risks. Moreover, it helps by managing the overall policy life cycle. Other key capabilities of the SAP Process Control solution are the unified repository for compliance, control and policy information, the embedded controls for strengthening business processes as well as improved compliance and control processes at optimal cost. These enable reduced costs of compliance, improve management transparency and confidence in compliance management processes. The solution provides a unified repository for compliance, control, and policy information. Thus, it ensures cross-function standardization and drive consistency across the company and manages multiple regulatory policies and compliance procedures with a single solution. The component optimizes the planning of control assessment and testing activities and aligns internal controls and policies with business objectives and risks. Key business processes are monitored and analyzed in real time. Thus, comprehensive online and offline control evaluations with flexible workflows and configurable forms are performed. Collaborative tools and surveys are provided. Issue management and certifications with workflows are standardized.

SAP Risk Management

The solution facilitates to manage enterprise risk across the organization. The module has four key capabilities. Firstly, it is important to create a risk strategy and plan. This includes identifying risk-relevant business activities, assigning risk appetite, risk owners and responsibilities as well as defining a key risk indicator (KRI) framework for automated risk monitoring. Next is the risk identification, where potential root causes and consequences of risks are documented. Risk analysis is about the likelihood of occurrence and the potential impact of an identified risk by running quantitative and qualitative risk analysis. Finally, a report with an analyzation on the company's risk situation is created. SAP Risk Management contains enterprise risk content and tools for industry-specific operational risk management. Graphical view is provided to create and analyze risks. Data monitoring controls and manages data from internal and external systems in real time. Starter kits include a library of standard business controls, basic regulations, direct entity-level controls, enterprise risks, risk drivers, and impacts. KRIs are classified according to risk drivers, risk categories, and industries. SAP Risk Management makes use of the various work centers in which all activities can be carried out. Work centers ensure easy access to application activities, and contain menu groups and links to further processes.

Conclusion

Governance is a core business process in companies for defining the corporate strategy and designing the corporate business processes. Governance manages enterprise risk and compliance, identity and access, cybersecurity, data protection, and privacy. Handling international trade, tax, and legal is also in focus of the Governance process. The entire IT lifecycle starting with developing the IT strategy to fulfillment and execution is covered by Governance. The processes and methodologies for ideation, portfolio, program, and project management are also streamlined in context of Governance. Key aspects of the Governance process are implemented in SAP S/4HANA based on SAP GRC solutions. This component governs access and enterprise risks, ensures process controls and compliance, addresses data privacy challenges, and enables fraud detection. The SAP S/4HANA modules are deeply integrated and frequently interacting so that also additional components contribute to handle this end-to-end process.

Process of Finance

15

This chapter describes the business process finance consisting of the subprocesses' plan to optimize financials, invoice to pay, invoice to cash, record to report, and manage treasury and real estate. Additionally, the application capabilities of SAP S/4HANA to resolve those business processes are explained.

Business Process

The general process of Finance is depicted in Fig. 15.1 and explained in detail in the next sections.

The Financial process has a supporting function in every value chain and keeps track of the finances in the company. The process starts with planning and analyzing which cover budgeting and forecasting for optimizing the financials. The process also includes management accounting which encompasses many aspects of accounting intended to improve the quality of information provided to management about business operation metrics, for example, the cost and sales revenue of goods and services. Invoice to pay process covers the entire lifecycle management of supplier invoices from receipt to payment. Invoice to cash processes customer invoices and ensures that they are paid. The financial close process comprises reviewing and reducing account balances beforehand the accounting cycle closes. It starts with recording the journal entry for all transactions that results to the review stage. Financial closing and financial accounting are performed in scope of record to report process. Handling payments and communication to banks are covered by treasury management. Companies have various real estates like office spaces or plants which must be acquired and operated. These facets are handled by the real estate management process. The Invoice to Pay and Invoice to Cash processes cover vendor- and customer-related finance processes. The Invoice to Pay process, also known as payables management, is the finance component of the larger Procure to Pay process, which extends from vendor relations and actual procurement all the way through to payment. The Invoice to Cash process, also known as receivables management, encompasses all financial accounting

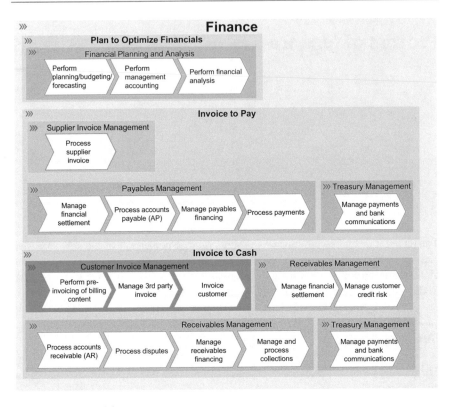

Fig. 15.1 Process of finance

operations pertaining to accounts receivable, such as billing customers and managing disputes, collections, and customer credit risk. Today's receivables managers must constantly strike a balance between the need to reduce days sales outstanding (DSO) and bad debt write-offs while providing excellent customer service. To meet margin targets, these managers must ensure that cash is available to fund business operations and new growth opportunities at a low cost.

Plan to Optimize Financials (Fig. 15.2)

The first subprocess in Finance is the Plan to Optimize Financials. The subprocess can be divided into planning, operational, and analysis phase. The planning phase includes which key performance indicators (KPI) should be recorded in the operational phase and for what period a budget and forecasting should be performed. To create a guide for the operating phase the budget for all departments is planned, and the spending and income forecasted. In the operational phase each department has its budget and should keep track of their books by having proper accounting management. The income and spending should be recorded. Management accounting is

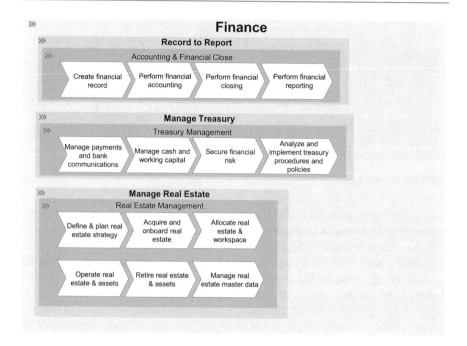

Fig. 15.1 (continued)

Fig. 15.2 Plan to optimize financials

about identifying, measuring, analyzing, interpreting, and communicating financial information to managers for tracking the company's objectives. Thus, managers are supported in making well-informed business decisions. Cost accounting is a subdivision of management accounting which particularly aims on capturing the total costs of production by considering variable and fixed costs. It helps managers to identify and decrease unnecessary spending and exploit profits. Finally, in the analysis phase the plans are compared to the recorded information in the operational phase. Thus, deviations can be determined, and corrective measure be taken.

Invoice to Pay (Fig. 15.3)

This objective of Invoice to Pay is to ensure that the bills are paid. It keeps track of the debt owed by the company. Supplier invoice management processes the invoices from suppliers, after a service was provided or a product delivered. Payables

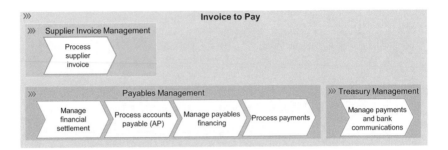

Fig. 15.3 Invoice to pay

management is responsible for keeping track of monetary assets. The process begins with managing financial settlements and continues to process accounts payables so that the company has a financial overview. The process also covers the payables financing which is in charge of clearing supplier's invoices and processing the payments to the right creditors. Accounts payable represents an account within the general ledger which denotes an organization's obligation to pay off a debt to its creditors or suppliers. Basically, accounts payable are amounts as a result of received goods or services from suppliers that have not yet been cleared. The total of the outstanding amounts owed to suppliers is depicted as the accounts payable balance on the company's balance sheet. Increase or decrease in total accounts payable from the prior period is reflected on the cash flow statement. Payable financing is a form of credit where companies borrow money from a supplier in order to purchase products and goods from the supplier. Companies that require additional working capital, payable financing is an adequate solution. With this type of financing, companies don't have to tap into their assets or resources to purchase additional inventory. Treasury management handles the payments and communication with banks. It aims to optimize a company's liquidity, while also mitigating its financial, operational, and reputational risk.

Invoice to Cash (Fig. 15.4)

This process is similar to Invoice to Pay process with the difference of owing the debt to the company by customers.

Customer invoice management performs the preinvoicing of billing content. Furthermore, third-party invoices are handled and if necessary, included in the invoice which is sent to the customer. Receivables management ensures that payments are received in an orderly manner. This subprocess starts with the management of financial settlements and continues with managing the customer credit risk. Accounts receivable and disputes are processed. Receivable financing and collection processing are performed. Accounts receivable represents the balance of money that must be paid by customers for received goods or services. Accounts receivables are recorded on the balance sheet as a current asset considering any

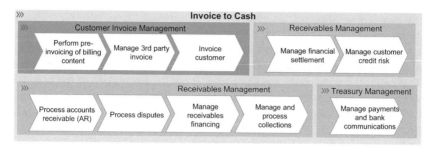

Fig. 15.4 Invoice to cash

amount of money owed by customers for purchases made on credit. Accounts receivable is comparable with accounts payable, but instead of money to be received, money to be owed is in focus. Accounts receivable can be analyzed with the turnover ratio or days sales outstanding to have an expectation of when the money will actually be received. Receivables financing is relevant when customers receive funding based on issued invoices. Those invoices due to purchased goods or service, but the payment hasn't been received so far. Treasury management handles the bank interactions and finalizes the payment process.

Record to Report (Fig. 15.5)

The subprocess is composed of creating a financial record, performing financial accounting, financial closing, and financial reporting. This process generates information which can be used by the management to examine the state of the company. Financial accounting is a subdivision of accounting which records, summarizes, and reports the myriad of transactions resulting from business operations over a period of time. These transactions are concised in the financial statements, the balance sheet, the income statement, and the cash flow statement. Financial accounting uses several established accounting principles. The relevant accounting principles are subject to the regulatory and reporting requirements of the company. For example, companies located in the United States of America must perform financial accounting in accordance with generally accepted accounting principles (GAAP). The GAAP provides consistent information to investors, creditors, regulators, and tax authorities. Financial closing is a periodic process in management accounting. Accounting teams prove and adjust account balances at the end of a defined period

Fig. 15.5 Record to report

(e.g., annually or quarterly) for creating financial reports for the company. The goal is to inform the management, investors, lenders, and regulatory agencies regarding the financial situation of the company. Closing the books encompasses consolidating transactions from various accounts, reconciling the data to confirm its correctness, and identifying irregularities and anomalies. It is vital that at the end the sum of all debts is equal to the sum of all credits. The general ledger accountant, the closing specialist, the business analyst, and the consolidation expert are the four main personas that ensure accounting accuracy and transparency.

Manage Treasury (Fig. 15.6)

Every company has bank accounts that deal with incoming and outgoing cash flows due to payments. These must be monitored and managed. In small businesses, accounting or even management takes care of it itself. However, the larger a company is, the larger and more complex payment transactions are usually. To manage it efficiently, a full-time position or even several is often needed: a treasurer or treasury department is hired or established. The main goal of treasury management is to control the liquidity of the company in such a way that it remains solvent at all times. In addition to cash or liquidity management, the tasks of Treasury Management are also risk management in the area of enterprise finance, as well as asset management and capital procurement. Treasury Management is a subdivision of financial management in many companies. While financial management focuses on managing financial resources so that revenue targets are met, treasury management focuses on ensuring liquidity at all times. Financial Management defines the financial plan that contains the strategies for achieving the financial goals of the company. Treasury Management ensures that the strategies defined for the short- to medium-term goals are implemented.

One task of Treasury Management is liquidity or cash management. It captures and controls the cash flows of liquid funds and is used for the internal and external financing of the company. The aim is to ensure solvency. Corporate financial risk management is also in focus of Treasury Management. For the success of a company, it is important that payment flows are managed in such a way that there is no deficit at any point in time that could cause the company to fall into late payment. To manage these cash flows efficiently, Treasury Management is required. It performs this task as part of liquidity management. In this way, a company ensures that working capital is used in an optimum and optimal way so that the long-term financial targets (revenue increase, cost reduction, and so on) are met.

Fig. 15.6 Manage treasury

Fig. 15.7 Manage real estate

Manage Real Estate (Fig. 15.7)

This process has one subprocess Real Estate Management which is responsible for managing the real estate of the company. The process to manage real estate begins with defining and planning a real estate strategy and continues to purchase and onboard real estates. Real Estate Management focuses on profit-oriented and value-based procurement, management, and marketing of real estate in organizations that do not have real estate as core business. Often these properties are also referred to as corporate real estate. After allocating the real estate and workspace the process of operations is triggered which covers for example paying rents and performing regular inspections and maintenance. Once the real estate is no longer needed, they are retired. Managing of the real estate master data is an essential task and also considered.

Solution Capability

The end-to-end process of Finance is mainly implemented by SAP S/4HANA Finance as depicted in Fig. 15.8. While SAP S/4HANA Finance covers the core functionality SAP Digital Payments, SAP Multi-Bank Connectivity and SAP Cash Application include extended features.

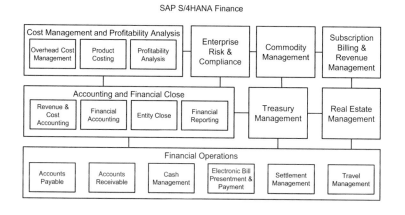

Fig. 15.8 SAP S/4HANA Finance—functional architecture

Financial Operations processes outgoing and incoming invoices and responds rapidly to fluctuating market dynamics. Advanced Financial Operations balances the need to decrease days sales outstanding (DSO) and bad debt write-offs, while maintaining superior customer service and reduced costs with automated exception handling, validation, and routing of invoices. Accounting and Financial Close simplifies corporate accounting and financial close, close books, creates financial statements, and manages according to IFRS as well as local legal regulations. Advanced Accounting and Financial Close drives a faster, compliant financial close with less cost and effort and a high degree of automation. Treasury Management improves the management of every activity associated with cash, payments, liquidity, risk, and compliance by simplifying working capital, risk management, and compliance. Real Estate Management performs activities from portfolio analysis and investment tracking to lead qualification, lease posting, rent escalation, and maintenance and repair service orders. Cost Management and Profitability Analysis collects, assigns, and analyzes costs by project, order, cost center, or business process. It evaluates the profitability of markets, channels, products, and segments. Enterprise Risk and Compliance manages risks, controls, and regulatory requirements in business operations, especially import and export compliance, as well as free trade agreements. Commodity Management identifies and qualifies financial risks associated with commodity price volatility in sales and procurement and mitigates by hedging them with commodity derivatives. Subscription Billing and Revenue Management leverages flexible models to include subscription and usage-based billing, partner revenue share, receivables management and payment handling as well as credit and collection management.

Financial Operations

Financial Operations is a function that keeps track of incoming and outgoing payments in real time. It provides an overview of the financial state of an organization by keeping track of all the financial operations in the company. The financial information is divided into different areas that each deal with their own topic. In Accounts Payable the way the data is recorded and managed is simplified. The money that is owed by a company to its creditors is presented as a liability in the company's balance sheet. This function provides a simple overview of the money owed and the due dates which help with management. Accounts Receivable manages customer accounts receivable efficiently. Accounts receivable involves money a company is owed from its clients or customers for goods supplied or services rendered. In Accounts Receivable the management of accounts that owe the company money is facilitated by automating invoice-to-cash processes which can be triggered automatically to accounts in response to changes in the general ledger. With this solution insights into the sales can be gained instantly in real time. If there are any problems the system will react and notify the person in charge who can react quickly and avert a crisis. With Cash Management the company can monitor everything that involves managing cash and liquidity centrally by monitoring the cash flow in real time to make sure that the company maintains sufficient liquidity. In today's digitalized world, an Electronic Bill Presentation and Payment is mandatory. This function provides an electronic bill and the option of paying online. This function also supports companies in creating electronic invoices for their customers according to company format guidelines. The solution improves service by empowering customers with a payment portal and e-billing. Electronic Bill Presentment and Payment involves presenting bills on the web and offering customers the option of paying their bills online. Settlement Management involves complex, high-volume financial payment processes that companies offer to business partners. To simplify this process SAP S/4HANA integrates core-business functions in the order-to-cash cycle. The Travel Management manages all processes involved with business trips and travel expenses. This solution keeps track of the expenses incurred and is responsible for reimbursing employees accordingly.

Advanced Financial Operations is an extension of the Financial Operations. By automating exception handling, validation, and routing of invoices the company can reduce costs and maintain superior customer service. Receivables management includes billing to customers and managing disputes, collections, and customer credit risk. Today, receivables managers must constantly balance the need to reduce days sales outstanding (DSO) and bad debt write-offs, though maintaining superior customer service. SAP S/4HANA Finance provides automated, integrated, and collaborative processes for receivables management. A streamlined payables management reduces costs and gains better control of invoicing. Furthermore, it integrates electronic documents into accounts payable process to ensure high collaboration, easy document exchange and archiving (Fig. 15.9).

Accounting and Financial Close

To keep the company's books clean and organized SAP S/4HANA Finance provides the Accounting and Financial Close module. The general ledger created in this function is the foundation of the company's finances. On the basis of that ledger insights into legal reporting and management profitability are provided. The solution supports the company by keeping all financial data in a central place so that reporting and accounting can be done properly. Revenue and Cost Accounting keeps track of the incoming and outgoing cashflow on a detailed level. The company can increase accuracy by keeping up with cost accounting changes on an ongoing basis. By automating the recognition of revenue and costs processes one can reduce audit cost, days to close the annual books, and the overall finance cost. The universal journal, SAP S/4HANA's general ledger is the heart of Finance as the single source of truth, providing the basis for instant insight into legal reporting and management profitability on a detailed level. Financial Accounting enables real-time reporting. This function streamlines financial processes which provide granular information. It enables financial reporting and real-time, self-service analytics directly from highly granular operational data, which support the management of assets and the closing of the books at the end of the year. Due to data model simplification, the asset worklist

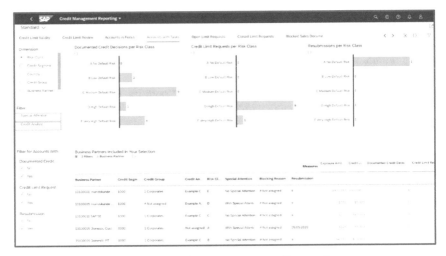

Payment Management Overview

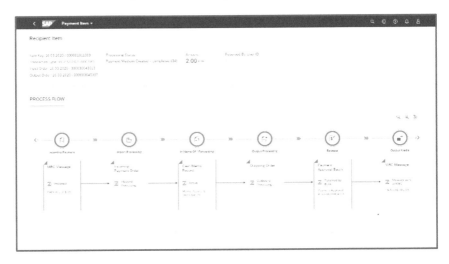

Process Flow Payment Item

Fig. 15.9 SAP S/4HANA Finance—payment management overview and process flow payment items

is included as central entry point. The solution improves extensibility for managing fixed assets and supports for year-end closing for multiple ledgers and company codes. At the end of the year the subprocess Entity Close can efficiently close the books and create a financial statement according to the preferred layout that complies with international financial reporting standards. The Financial Reporting provides information that discloses an organization's financial status to the management, investors, and government. The information helps managers make fact-based decisions as well as support the company with audits and compliance. The solution extends revenue accounting and reporting with additional value-add scenarios and optimizes integration with the universal journal.

Advanced Accounting and Finance Close provides financial insight and control through a faster, compliant financial close with less cost and effort, for example, efficiently close books on time and create financial statements at entity and corporate levels for International Financial Reporting Standards, U.S. GAAP, or other local requirements. Based on accounting data, together with logistic data, processes like central tax, central closing, and forecast analysis on group level are available on the single source of truth. The financial closing cockpit streamlines and orchestrates the full closing process. Companies can also use an approach to centralize their finance functionality in a central and separate SAP S/4HANA system, leveraging the procedures and replications on SAP Central Finance (Fig. 15.10).

Cost Management and Profitability Analysis

This solution keeps track of the costs and profitability of a service or a product. With the overview of costs and profitability, the company can adjust their product portfolio or optimize the costs for the products or services. It compares the costs to the turnover to create a profitability analysis. Overhead Cost Management provides high transparency and insights on the overhead allocation process with the speed of the universal journal. For cost centers (actuals and plan), profit centers (actuals and plan) and margin analysis are available. Overhead allocation assessment, distribution, and top-down distribution for actual data are supported. To keep track of the overall spending in the company the Overhead Cost Management calculates all the costs needed for a certain period. It then takes the plan and compares it to the actual spending in the period. SAP S/4HANA Finance provides the user with information displayed in graphs that highlight outliers. By flagging these discrepancies, an employee can react quickly and prevent damage to the company or eliminate the reason for the deviation. Product Costing enables the creation of financial statements on group level which means the costs created by the production of a single product or service can be calculated. This happens without extract, transform, and load processes so that a continuous accounting is facilitated. Profitability Analysis offers an overview of the profitability of products including the risks and the costs. The central storage of the company's data facilitates the process of analyzing the profitability in real time. This solution assists in creating the product portfolio of the company. It reduces risk and cost due to real-time financial reporting and multidimensional data analysis for accounting standards. For business reporting, for example, cash flow statement, semantic tagging is used (Fig. 15.11).

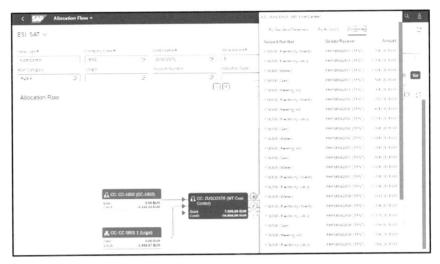

Allocation Flow

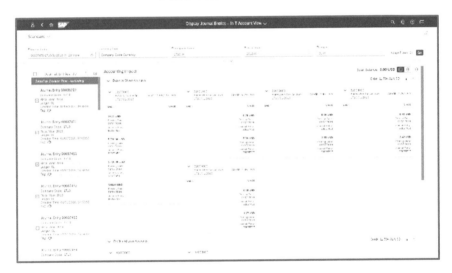

Display Journal Entries in T-account view

Fig. 15.10 SAP S/4HANA Finance—allocation flow and display journal entries in T-account view

Treasury Management

Treasury Management is responsible for the cash management and communication with banks. The solution enables cash, liquidity, and risk management as well as integrated financial reporting. It improves the management of every activity

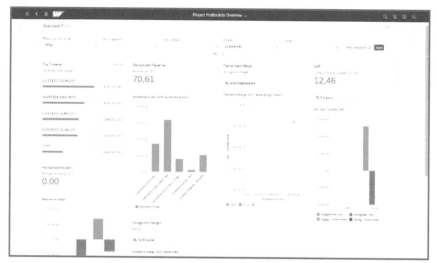

Project Profitability Overview

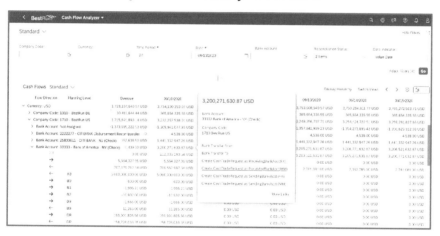

Cash-Flow Overview

Fig. 15.11 SAP S/4HANA Finance—project profitability overview and cash-flow overview

associated with cash, payments, liquidity, risk, and compliance by simplifying working capital, risk management, and compliance. Treasury Management gains complete transparency into and control over interrelated activities and automate critical processes to better understand the risks of those activities and how to mitigate them. The control over these complex demands ensures adequate liquidity to drive growth and innovation, while preventing exposure to the growing financial risks. The solution includes payments and bank communications, cash and liquidity management, debt and investment management and financial risk management.

Cash Flow Analyzer

Process Receivables

Fig. 15.12 SAP S/4HANA Finance—cash-flow analyzer and process receivables

The module provides enhanced reporting capabilities, expanded coverage of legislations in foreign currency hedge management and accounting for U.S. GAAP. Treasury Management allows to check the actual and forecasted cash positions to assist cash allocation decision-making. It supports to display, create, and change data about the banks that companies, their customers, and their suppliers use to transact business. Master data of the company's corporate or business bank accounts can be managed centrally, as well as house bank accounts. Additionally, future liquidity trends can be forecasted (Fig. 15.12).

Real Estate Management

The solution facilitates all processes across the real estate lifecycle. These include investment and construction, sales and marketing, lease and space management but also maintenance and repair. It performs activities from portfolio analysis and investment tracking to lead qualification, lease posting, rent escalation, and maintenance and repair service orders. Real estate objects management provides a dual view of master data, with an architectural view and a usage view. Furthermore, it creates and manages all types of real estate objects, including business entity, land, building, rental unit, rental space, and rental room objects. The contract management capability handles all contracts associated to real estate portfolio, including lease-in, lease-out, customer, and vendor contracts. Additionally, it assigns rental objects from diverse business entities, buildings, or company codes to contracts. Space optimization offers accounts for exceptional architectural structures, usage considerations, and technical amenities. Moreover, it defines space flexibly and rents them, extracting them from a larger available space, represents the real estate objects visually via data exchange with external graphic systems. With credit-side view of lease-in processes for example cash flow to the landlord can be controlled but also expense posting be organized. Various centralized business processes are supported, for example, integrated asset management postings and reports, real estate controlling, planning of new building developments, maintenance, and modernization projects.

Enterprise Risk and Compliance

This solution assists with managing risks, controls, and regulatory requirements in business operations. For the purpose of minimizing risk and checking compliance of all payments of any nature, incoming or outgoing, are checked based on Enterprise Risk and Compliance. If there are any issues the solution alerts the responsible automatically which shortens the response and reaction time. The solution provides the necessary information to make a quick and information-based decision to minimize the risk. Enterprise Risk and Compliance helps in ensuring compliance guidelines and identifying risks. For example, letter of credit keeps track of credit scores of customers and blocking shipment of products if the credit score is not compliant with company guidelines. The international trade management provides information and layouts for legal control and compliance in the international market. The solution improves business performance and decreases the cost and effort of managing governance, risk, and compliance—and provides transparency through compliance check results. The goal is to streamline and automate processes, anticipate and manage risk events, reduce compliance violations, and extend governance, risk and compliance programs into value-adding business activities. International trade classification allows for the classification of products using commodity codes, intrastate service codes, and customs tariff numbers, as well as product classification using control classes and control groupings for legal control. International trade

Compliance Run

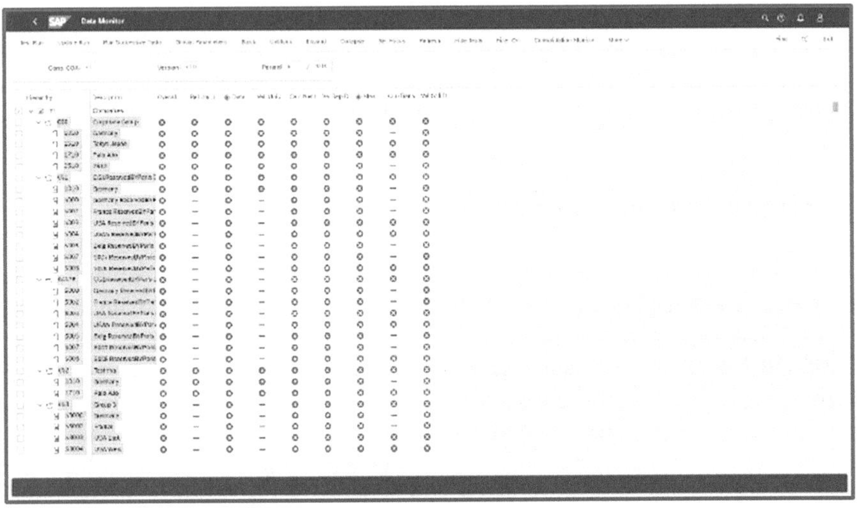

Data Monitor

Fig. 15.13 SAP S/4HANA Finance—compliance rung and data monitor

compliance manages licenses in accordance with legal control for export and import processes and controls statutory regulations for import and export. Furthermore, it handles blocked legal control documents, countries/regions under embargo and intrastate declarations and their master data (Fig. 15.13).

Commodity Management

Commodity Management is responsible for identifying and qualifying financial risks associated with commodity price volatility in sales and procurement. The solution helps to keep track of suppliers, resources, and the development of prices. This way the company can better decide on a procurement strategy for their resources or mitigate the risk by hedging them with commodity derivatives. Additionally, the exchange rate can be monitored for provided services in a different country with another currency. The module supports material management contracts from commodity pricing to risk analytics and makes mark-to-market queries including stock logistics documents and financial derivatives. Commodity procurement facilitates to enter, process, and manage purchasing contracts, purchase orders, goods receipts and invoices for commodities of all industries. It performs an easy-to-use formula-based commodity pricing, also for future dates and uses the market data management based on derivative contract specifications. Furthermore, commodity procurement helps entering and allocating price fixations, and performing period-end valuations. Commodity risk management deals with commodity futures, commodity forwards, commodity swaps, listed options, OTC options, and process the respective master and market data. In practice, option contracts are mainly traded on forward exchanges. This means that the purchaser and seller of an option do not interact directly with each other. As an alternative to this indirect, commercial execution, direct trade has established which is also referred as over the counter (OTC) trading. OTC options are contracts that are processed exclusively in direct trade. Commodity risk analytics helps in analyzing commodity price risks for commodity derivative and logistics positions. The commodity price risk-related information is derived from the document flows, commodity derivatives, and logistics transactions. Commodity Sales allows entering, processing and managing sales documents, deliveries and billing documents for commodities of all industries. It uses the market data management based on derivative contract specifications and allocates price fixations and performs period-end valuations.

Subscription Billing and Revenue Management

This function allows organizations to use flexible payment models to include subscriptions and usage-based billing. Subscription Billing and Revenue Management is the preferred subledger in SAP S/4HANA Finance for industries with high volume and high-performance requirements, as well as for service-based scenarios, for example, Utilities, Telco, and Insurance. It offers a lot of flexible and creative models to include subscription and usage-based billing, partner revenue share, receivables management and payment handling and credit and collection management. Key feature are subscription business models with recurring- and one-time charges, rating and billing of millions of usage transactions converged from multiple transactional platforms, complex, volume-based discounts and surcharges, revenue sharing and partner settlement. Subscription order management helps customers to

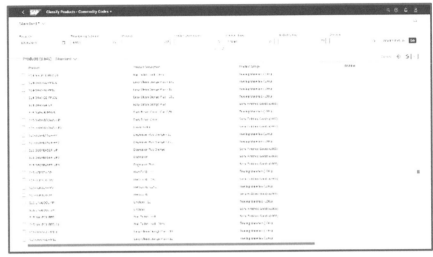

Classify Products Commodity Codes

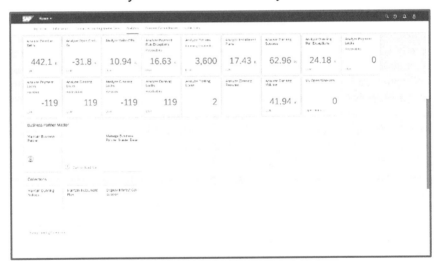

Finance Analytics

Fig. 15.14 SAP S/4HANA Finance—classify product commodity codes and finance analytics

provide their business solutions as a combination of products and services. It enables the customers to offer their products as-a-service and usage-based services with consumption-based pricing models. Convergent invoicing combines information from numerous billing streams as well as rated events. It allows service providers to consolidate charges into a single invoice and offer a complete view of the customer. Providers are able to accommodate partnerships with third parties and offer new services by outlining which party is accountable for any given charge.

Furthermore, they can handle sophisticated rules for invoice-level discounting. By significantly streamlining complex billing processes, providers can offer customers a single, consolidated invoice, while delivering better, more personalized services. Contract accounting allows to assign individual clearing strategies, automate payment reconciliation, and create reports which are aligned with accounting principles. Due to automated processing payments days sales outstanding is reduced. Credit and collections management offers credit scoring of new and existing customers based on historical customer data connected with external credit rating agencies. It automates routine tasks in the collections process for mass volumes of customers, for example, the calculation of interest payments. Collections strategies can be continuously optimized by using champion/challenger analysis. By providing an overview of the credit and collection history of new and existing customers the days sales outstanding and the risk of nonpayment can be reduced, while retaining loyal customers. Financial customer care facilitates customer service agents to manage customer financial inquiries efficiently and consistently (Fig. 15.14).

Conclusion

Finance is a supporting business process in the value chain that receives financial information from the other core processes. The process starts with performing planning, budgeting, and forecasting. Invoice to pay manages supplier invoices based on account payable. Customer invoices are handled with invoice to cash process based on accounts receivable. Accounting and financial close are also in scope of this supportive process. Treasury management covers payments and bank communications while real estate management deals with the entire lifecycle of real estates. In SAP S/4HANA this end-to-end process is mainly covered by SAP S/4HANA Finance. SAP S/4HANA Finance provides functionality for financial operations, enterprise risk and compliance, cost management and profitability analysis, accounting and financial close, real estate and treasury management. The SAP S/4HANA modules are deeply integrated and frequently interacting so that also additional components contribute to handle this end-to-end process.

Industry Solutions

16

This chapter tackles the verticalization specific functionality of SAP S/4HANA. Covered are the industries for the consumer, discrete industries, services, energy and natural resources, financial and public services. The switch framework is depicted, which enables the implementation of industry solutions.

Functional Scope

SAP S/4HANA offers more than 25 industry solutions that provide tailored industry-specific business processes. These solutions can be grouped into consumer industry, financial services, energy and natural resources, service industry, public services and production industry. As depicted in Fig. 16.1 the industry solutions are built by enhancing the S/4HANA core modules like R&D/engineering, procurement, supply chain, manufacturing, sales, service, finance, and asset management.

Key question is how those different industry solutions are isolated while they are enhancing the S/4HANA Core functionality? The underlying concept for this is the Switch Framework which enables switching code so that industry functionality can be implemented. Thus, customers can activate explicitly industry solutions in accordance with their business scope. In the next sections some of the industry solutions are briefly explained to provide an impression of their functionality.

Consumer Industry

This category covers the industry solutions for consumer products, life science, retail and wholesale distribution.

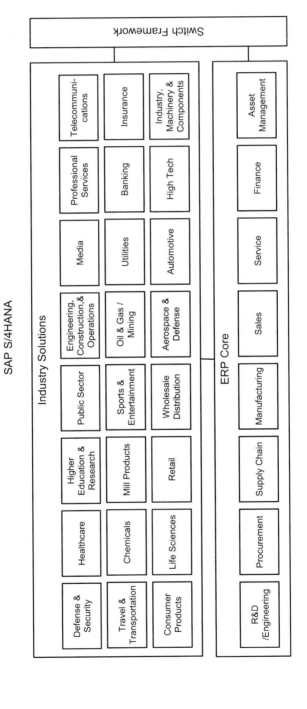

Fig. 16.1 SAP S/4HANA industry solutions

Consumer Products

Consumers of the current generation are demanding, spontaneous, and savvy. How can consumer products companies meet these demands and remain profitable? The answer is to target all aspects of business activities toward the end customer, that is, the consumer. With last-mile distribution, the process of distributing consumer products to the retail outlets and retail chains is supported. Manufacturers and suppliers can view and coordinate all phases of the sales process centrally. This industry solution provides many functions for route planning, execution, and monitoring.

Retail

Current trends in retail are online trade, new and innovative shopping opportunities, and sustainable businesses. Customers require a smooth shopping experience without interruption which is on the other hand as personalized as possible. To meet these high expectations, companies need to embrace intelligent and efficient digital solutions. Optimal master data management is therefore one of the key components of the consumer products industry. The associated industry solution enables companies to maintain products with all related product master data and context information, display them compactly, and navigate to related business objects from there. In addition, products can be grouped together across processes and products that meet selected criteria and can be adjusted quickly. Product hierarchies can be used to analyze how customers can find a product that they want to buy. Season management can use yearly periods as a time-dependent characteristic for products. Assortment management allows companies to create assortments and assign validity periods to them. This information can be combined with location information to deliver the right products to a store at the right time. Buying is also a key component. The industry solution supports best-order planning and processing, as well as collective order management, when combining several purchase orders from different stores and managing perishable goods. To save time, the industry solution forwards warehouse stocks and sales figures to vendors and manufacturers, so that they can optimize their material requirements and replenishment planning. It also supports the internal procurement processes and the industry solution as the basis for the replenishment process. Distribution curves define in which ratio different variants of a product are required. As a result, repeat orders are easier and more precise.

Solution	Functional scope
Agriculture	• Agricultural contract management • Third Party sales and purchase end-to-end process • Contract tolerances, flexible pricing, revenue recognition
Consumer products	• Last mile distribution for direct distribution • Route assembly based on freight orders • Settlement and route monitoring
Life sciences	• Drug formulation and recipe development • Clinical trial supply management • Strategic sourcing and procurement

(continued)

Solution	Functional scope
Retail	• Assortment management, merchandise buying, vendor-managed inventory, replenishment planning, demand forecasting, Inventory management • Retail for merchandise management, Store layout and retail price management, promotion management • Demand and supply segmentation, Supply assignment, Sales order management and processing • Manufacturing
Wholesale distribution	• Demand-side forecast collaboration • Invoice automation, extended warehouse optimization • Business network for logistics

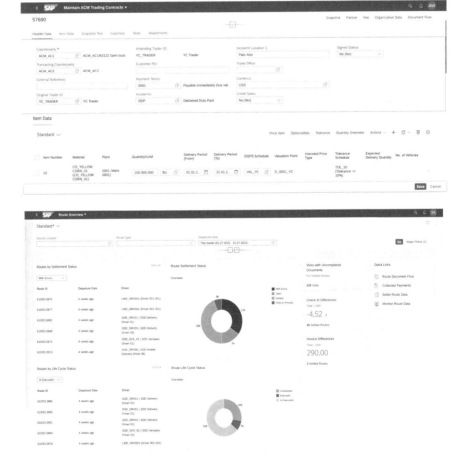

Agriculture—maintain ACM trading contract, consumer products—route overview

Production Industry

This category covers the industry solutions for aerospace and defense, automotive, high tech, travel and transportation, industry machinery and components.

Automotive

The automotive industry currently has two goals: on the one hand, it is important that traditional business remains profitable and continues to grow. On the other hand, it is important to find and implement innovative ideas and solutions in the new world of mobility. The industry solution in the automotive industry focuses on the wholesale and retail trade of vehicles. It supports the sale of vehicles that are in stock by searching for desired configurations and by reserving the results. It also supports delivery documents, trade-ins, and the buyback of used vehicles. In addition, it allows to order vehicles that have not yet been manufactured. The configuration is then forwarded to the manufacturer. Dealer vehicle orders for the warehouse are also supported with receiving the vendor invoice and posting. The industry solution also provides a web portal through which dealers can find and order vehicles and view the status. Spare parts can also be ordered and returned. Management of warranty claims and the related return delivery and recalls from manufacturers can also be managed.

Solution	Functional scope
Aerospace and defense	• Grouping, pegging, distribution • Transfer/Borrow loan payback • Resource-related billing and incoming orders • Project earned value • Inventory management, initial provisioning • Maintenance planning and stock calculation
Automotive	• Enhanced configuration management • Packaging logistics, just-in-time inbound and outbound • Planning, tracking and execution • Parts interchangeability, production backflush • Self-billing, evaluated receipt settlement, supplier workplace
Engineering, construction and operation	• Bill of services, equipment and tools management • Plant engineering and construction • Homebuilding, real estate sales
High tech	• Software license and installed based management • Contract management and billing process enhancements • Condition techniques in distributor reseller management, • Manufacturer and supplier processing • Distributor and reseller processing
Industry, machinery and components	• Product design with 3D visual and variant configuration • Predictive material requirements planning • Asset networks and predictive services

(continued)

Solution	Functional scope
Travel and transportation	• Passenger travel and leisure • Cargo transportation and logistics services • Billing and revenue management

Automotive—JIT delivery scheduling, travel, and transportation—travel and expenses

Energy and Natural Resources

This category covers the industry solutions for chemicals, mill products, mining, oil and gas and utilities.

Oil and Gas

Oil and gas customers have some requirements, for IT systems that other industries do not have. Throughout the entire value chain, it is necessary to comply with regulations and to pay customs duties and taxes, even when it comes to support and resale. The industry solution supports the management of all these requests. Volumetric reports can be used to prove compliance. Taxes can be calculated or proposed automatically for goods movements, purchase orders, and goods receipts and issues. In addition, the oil and gas industry uses volumes, mass, energy, density, and heating value as units. The industry solution provides functions for quantity conversion and the storage of values depending on environmental conditions such as pressure and temperature. Furthermore, silo and tank management can be used to read material stocks in silos on a regular basis. For prices, the industry solution offers some enhancements such as the storage of five decimal places, contract prices, generation of customer price lists, and time-dependent pricing. Load information can be forwarded to external systems via an interface. In addition, enhancements for the administration of checks and the grouping of goods into batches are part of the industry solution.

Utilities

In the utilities industry, retail is different compared to other industries. Customers consistently receive a service. This is measured and corresponding payable amounts are calculated based on this data. This calculation can be performed on a regular or event-based basis. The industry solution can be used to define products and their characteristics, and to create timelines for billing. Furthermore, payments can be simulated so that no unnecessary posting takes place later. Incidental costs are distributed over the entire delivery period. Typically, providers offer network-related services such as grid usage for other market participants. The provider then sends grid usage bills to the users. Electronic invoices can be created, notifications can be processed, and incoming payments can be posted accordingly, and payments can be allocated. Measurements can produce discrete data or equidistant time series values which are validated by the solution. Schedules are created and issued for the periodic meter reading orders. The module also provides functions for uploading and entering measurement data. Device management enables the handling of procurement, storage, and stock movements, as well as the installation, replacement, and removal of meters and other devices at the customer site. Separation and reconnection management is also part of the industry solution and enables automatic or manual separations and reconnections at the request of the customer or for other events such as forfeited claims. The industry solution also offers a web application template for customer self-services. Customers can manage their online account, as well as all personal and contact information, pension orders, and payments. Bills and consumption can be displayed and there are options for communicating with the utility company. Customer service employees can use a co-browsing function to help customers by considering the same information as a customer on their screen and thereby providing them with more precise support. There are also functions for regulations and requirements that apply in certain countries and regions.

Solution	Functional scope
Chemicals	• Embedded sample management including safety and products service quality • Scenario simulation toward assumptions, risks or business events • Physical assets and legal compliance
Mill products	• Original batch management and fast entry of characteristics • Reel calculation and characteristic-based packing in outbound deliveries • Classifying purchasing info records and cutting stock transfers, single unit batches and setting final delivery indicator • Delivery-related trading unit change, packaging material items in delivery • Enhancements in production planning and control • NF metal processing
Mining	• Maintaining and optimizing all mining processes • Collecting data on all mining processes • Planning long and short-term production objectives • Managing costs of entire supply chain • Managing distribution processes
Oil and gas	• Production and revenue accounting • Upstream operations management • Field data capture for upstream allocations • Downstream
Utilities	• Device management • Energy data management • Contract billing and invoicing • Customer service and work management • Intercompany data exchange and advanced metering

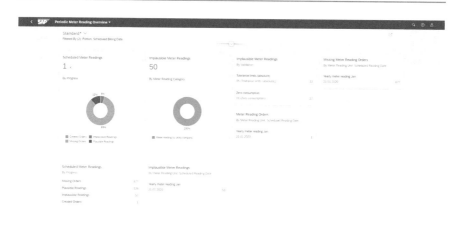

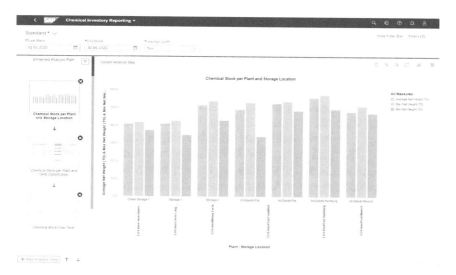

Utilities—periodic meter reading, chemicals—chemical inventory reporting

---

Financial Services

This category covers the industry solutions for banking and insurance.

Banking

The main business areas of banks are deposits, loans, and collateral. For all three, the industry solution module offers functionalities. Deposit management enables to manage checking accounts, fixed-term deposits, and savings credits. This includes various functions to support the lifecycle of deposit contracts and the management of master data. It is also possible to monitor payables and receivables, to manage business transactions such as the creation of debit memos and checks. Incoming and outgoing payments and standing orders can also be managed with the industry solution. Credit management includes structured loans like in area of retail loans as well as complex loans such as mortgage loans. The industry solution also supports the lifecycle of loan contracts and the management of master data. Cash flows can be calculated and various business transactions managed such as disbursement, waiver, write-off, borrower change, or disbursement. There are functions for billing processes for loans as well as for incoming and outgoing payments, such as repayments, interest payments, and disbursements. The module provides front- and back-end support in the area of collateral management. Integration into the operational transaction systems for customer information management, risk management, document management, and instruction creation are ensured. The solution contains capabilities for managing and monitoring the use of collateral. Integrated object management can be used to supply and evaluate data for various collateral objects, such as real estate, and to retrieve and consume credit information. This minimizes manual processing tasks and enables to assign simple and complex relationships between exposures, collaterals, collateral providers, and collateral recipients. Calculations such as collateral coverage, distribution of deposits, relationship of credit to value, calculation of free collateral, and under coverage of collateral are supported. In addition, the module helps to create, post, and manage cash impairments for balance sheet and off-balance-sheet transactions, and make proposals for individual loan officers. The component contains interfaces with which both SAP and non-SAP systems can be used as data sources. When the risk provision is posted, the system immediately transfers all balance-sheet-relevant data to financial accounting. Moreover, there are functions for regulations that apply in certain countries and regions.

Insurance

The industry solution for insurance supports policy management and allows to handle insurance contracts and contains capabilities along the lifecycle of a contract. This includes issuing policies and the current contract maintenance up to contract termination. The module enables life, claim, accident, and vehicle insurance. In the area of claims management, the industry solution maps the entire entitlement cycle to automate and manage the whole claim process from the first claim notification, to the adjustment of claims, and to financial reporting. The solution also supports additional types of insurances like liability insurance, health, and care insurance, as well as insurance for workers. Its features can be used to record loss notifications received through different channels and to create entitlements. As a result, relevant information can be maintained, and entitlements can be evaluated. The industry solution provides functions for payroll, and payment. Thus, collection and payment tasks can be performed centrally for various business areas, which enables more accurate payment processing and improves credit control. Functions related to collections and disbursements for reinsurers enable integration with the general ledger. Thus, almost nondisruptive end-to-end business processes are guaranteed, transaction costs of reinsurance business processes reduced, and improved customer satisfaction achieved. The accounting of open items, payment processing, correspondence, and dunning can also be carried out using this industry solution. In addition, broker accounting and coinsurance business can be mapped and the automation of business processes and integration with business insurance systems and back-office applications such as the general ledger are facilitated. The industry solution also offers features for compensation processes. Sales structures can be reproduced, and flexible incentive systems can be set up. Standard agreements can be used as the basis for creating individual agreements and processing commission cases. Compensation planning can be utilized to create consistent plans, to distribute the company strategy to specific sales targets, and to cascade plan changes. Thus, new organizations can easily integrate with sales composition and reward for selling redesigned products can be adjusted. Customer segments can be assigned to field service providers and commercial portfolio relationships. Employees are kept up to date with the latest rules and regulations. Internal and external sales targets can be aligned with the company's overall strategy and sales force compensation can be automated to achieve these targets. The industry solution also supports legal reporting to be provided by insurance companies. This is enabled through quarterly reporting and analytics on premium reserve funds. It is also ensured to create reports for capital investments in accordance with legal requirements and send them to BaFin. Required reports in specific layouts or electronic formats are provided to correctly record risks and portfolio data to national and international authorities. Forms or electronic formats from actual subledgers are created, and legal authorities can be preconfigured with relevant data for report layouts for country-specific/regional or international versions. The insurance product engine consists of a design time environment for product modeling and a runtime environment for product operations. Moreover, there are features for regulations and requirements that apply in certain countries and regions.

Solution	Functional scope
Banking	• Deposits and loans management • Collateral management • Reserve for bad debts
Insurance	• Collection and disbursements • Policy and claims management • Incentive and sales force management

Banking—manage restriction for debiting, insurance—claims supervisor overview

Public Services

This category covers the industry solutions for defense and security, healthcare, higher education and research and public sector.

Defense and Security

The internal and external security industry has some special requirements that are covered by the associated industry solution. An important task within the industry is the planning of deployments. This includes the creation of all available armed forces structures, organizational units, material planning objects, and personnel. By using hierarchical relationships, these can be displayed, and reference structures can be used as templates. Wartime functions can also be defined. When planning personnel, position, job, qualifications, and persons are available as additional characteristics. Staffing requirements can be represented by assigning positions to motorized elements. Scenarios can be used to structure capability-based planning and development processes and to compare possible scenario age native processes. Operations and exercise items with the characteristics of procurement, rotation, and readiness can also be defined and managed with the industry solution. Within the military supply chain, defense equipment management is an important task that also requires support from software systems. This includes comparing authorized and actual materials, managing personal and functional equipment, planning accruals for nonconsumable materials, and identifying materials using the manufacturer part number. Furthermore, maintenance can be planned, and critical status indicators be defined. The industry solution also provides support in the planning and execution of complex procurement of consumable goods and defensive materials. Nonetheless, the module offers support in the execution of replenishment procurement of consumable goods and defensive materials. The industry solution supports also defining explosive locations and all related characteristics to store explosive materials safely. In addition, information such as the net explosive weight for all of the explosive location and the compatibility status can be recorded.

Higher Education and Research

The industry solution focuses into a student information system. This includes functions for the teachers as well as for the students. The application and admission process are supported by creation and editing of forms using templates. The integration of admission processes in self-services is supported so that applicants can track the status of their applications. For curriculum management course or program catalogs enable students to book, change, or cancel course bookings online. Requirement catalogs can be created and managed to control admission to a course or the receipt of a degree. Students can execute what-if scenarios to indicate the requirements for a course. With centralized management of grades, students can review exam grades and make requests to change grades as needed. They can also monitor their academic progress and assess their graduation status. Administrators, consultants, and teaching staff can also view student progress and make better decisions, prepare support offerings, and accompany the completion process. Student administration can also be used to efficiently maintain and manage student data, and to organize all types of requests for the university and students, such as leave of absence or part-time study.

Public Sector

The industry solution for the public sector contains many features for the areas of funds management, grants, tax, and social services.

For funds management, the industry solution offers features around budget maintenance, budget execution, budget closing, and financial reporting. The objective of budget maintenance is on management and monitoring of public funds. Budgets can be transferred to other projects and departments and changes can be tracked and monitored throughout the entire budget cycle. Approved budgets can be uploaded to the system and rules for adjusting a budget increase based on revenue can be defined. It also contains monitoring functionality for budget overview, comparisons of budget versions and revenues increasing the budget. Budget execution focuses on integration of operational and accounting processes with the maintained budget. The industry solution enables real-time and parallel budget controls that can operate on multiple levels, helping to monitor and control funds while reducing procurement and operating costs. Parts of the available budget can be earmarked for expected revenues or expenditures. A separate cash ledge and a budgetary ledger for the creation of financial statements for governmental reporting are also available. There are also reports for a budget execution, an overview of budget availability, operational transactions affecting budget execution, a comparison of fiscal years, commitment and actual line items, the comparison of budget lines versus commitment and/or actual line items and earmarked funds journal available. Budget closing and financial reporting contains the planning, standardizing, scheduling, and monitoring of financial and budget close activities. Open remaining commitments, budget committed, and residual budget at the end of the fiscal year can be managed. Budgetary accounting data with financial and managerial accounting can be reconciled. Here are also reports available that support the monitoring of the commitment carry forward, cash flow reporting, and cash basis reporting.

The grants management is split into the areas: sponsor management, budget management, grants billing and receivables and closeout. Sponsor management covers functionality for defining sponsor master data, documenting sponsor communication, and all budgetary agreements. Available funds can be controlled by releasing budget in tranches throughout the fiscal year or lifetime of the grant based on sponsor defined rules. Reports on all attributes of a specific or series of sponsors and grant agreements can be created and the grants management keeps all information based on the sponsor perspective. Those are the sponsor's currency, time frames, and fiscal years. Budget management is about the maintenance and monitoring of grant budgets. The industry solution provides the functionality to enter and update grant budget data as required, to control the use of available funds and to define rules for when and how a budget increase is permitted. It also offers reports for a budget overview, comparison of budget versions, and an overview of revenues increasing the budget. Grants billing and receivables contain maintaining sponsor billing methods, ensuring proper accounting and timely reimbursement as well as documenting and automating many processes, including billing and receivables. It supports manual, resource related, milestone, and periodic billing. Reports of billable amounts based on status (open, partially, or completely billed) for one grant, group of grants, sponsor, or group of sponsors are available. Closeout contains functionality for creating customized closeout rules that meet sponsor guidelines and requirements. It helps ensuring that the grantee properly concludes all programs and projects according to sponsor specifications. Also, overhead, or indirect cost calculation can be run, and residual budgets transferred. Reports on all grants are offered. Public sector collection and disbursement are used to manage taxes, charges, and state benefits from or for taxpayers like business partners, citizens, and students. Contract accounts receivable and payable manage the business partners, their accounts, and contract objects, as well as the related business transactions. Also, the processing and management of mass data are supported by the industry solution. Tax identification and returns processing enable government agencies to administrate the complex and lengthy tax and revenue management lifecycle. This includes key processes such as registration, account maintenance, tax return filing and remittance processing, billing, correspondence and contact management, audit and compliance. With the capabilities of the industry solution, revenue types can be defined, the taxpayer registration enabled, tax return and registration capture used. Furthermore, automatic and manual form-based tax return processes are implemented, tax objects are processed, and invoicing is managed.

Investigative case management enables to handle investigation processes from start to finish. It allows to set up and run functions and processes for cases, activities, incidents, persons and organizations, objects, locations, documents, including all their relationships. The social services management solution helps social services agencies to receive benefit applications from their customers, determine an applicant's eligibility, and calculate the benefit entitlements. Eligibility and entitlement rules can be implemented without coding and are used to automate the decision-making process. The industry solution provides functionality for case management, benefit and deduction decision processing, payables management, payment handling, business rules processing as well as activity, business partner and document management. Multichannel foundation for Public Sector is a constituent-facing solution that enables public sector organizations to interact with their constituents using a set of standardized and reusable services. Thus, users can manage online accounts, constituent details, payments, and external users. Moreover, process forms can be created, billing information accessed, and communication displayed. Additionally. the industry solutions contain country and region-specific features.

Solution	Functional scope
Defense and security	• Material planning and operations • Military supply chain • Explosives management • Support for flight operations • Investigative case management
Healthcare	• Patient management • Ambulatory case management • Clinical systems
Higher education and research	• Student lifecycle management • Planning of academic offerings • Administration of fees and grants
Public sector	• Public sector management • Collection and disbursement • Tax, revenue and social services management • Multichannel foundation for public sector

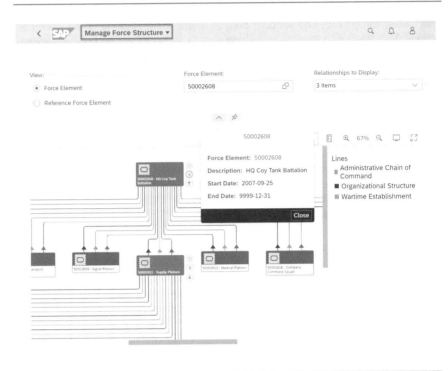

Defense and security—manage force structure, public sector—funds management

Service Industry

This category covers the industry solutions for engineering, construction and operations, media, professional services, telecommunications, sports and entertainment.

Professional Services

The industry solution for professional services consists of three parts: Project and engagements, resource management, and service management. Projects and engagement enable users to create projects with the creation of sales documents like quotations, contracts, or sales orders. Projects can also be created with the standard work breakdown structure. Resource management provides a range of tools and reports to establish links between employees and business objects, and thereby adjust processes and workflows to suit the size of the company and the spectrum of the services. These tools can also be used to manage assignments of employees to both client-facing and internal engagements. With the lean staffing feature the right professionals for engagements can be easily identified, selected employees can be assigned to engagements, the employee assignments can be monitored, and time recordings can be validated. Reliable reports and forecasts about employee utilization can be obtained and integrated functions for service-specific billing and financials can be used. With enhanced time recording, data for staff assignments from lean staffing can be displayed and used to perform automatic input checks during time recording and integrate service attributes to enhance the data record structure. Also, employees can plan their time, while documenting their availability in parallel. This improves the assessment of the employee commitments, raises visibility of employee utilization, and increases the reliability of the business forecast. In service management additional attributes can be used that allow flexible definition and capture of diverse requirements for service providers. These parameters are then available throughout the commercial service process, and can be used selectively in individual process steps, especially to control processes in resource-related billing. Work periods can also be used to add enhanced capabilities for billing services. In resource-related billing, the system consolidates work and cost assigned to a project and considers these values for invoice creation. With power lists, lean staffing can be combined with specific processes or used to invoke actions based on the information chosen to be displayed. Also, power lists can be used for staffing assignments, sales documents, and debit memo requests.

Solution	Functional scope
Engineering, construction and operations	• Pre-construction • Construction supply chain • Project delivery and asset management
Media	• Media sales and distribution, self-services • Advertising and campaign management

(continued)

Solution	Functional scope
	• Title lifecycle management, customer interaction center
Professional services	• Projects and engagement • Resource management • Service management
Telecommunications	• Contract accounts receivable and payable • Management of telecommunications services • Incentive and sales force management
Sports and entertainment	• Fan management • Venue and business operations • Teams performance

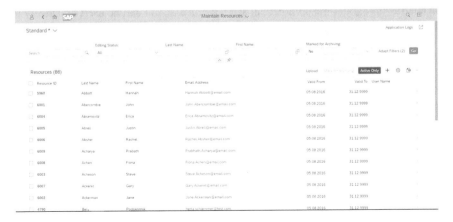

Professional services—project costs and maintain resources

Solution Concept

The Switch Framework builds the foundation for the implementation of the industry solutions in SAP S/4HANA. It allows users to externally control the visibility of repository objects or their components by means of switches. Since the Switch Framework is integrated in the ABAP Workbench and already contains all industry solutions, these no longer need to be installed before they can be activated. With switches, enhancements can be installed in SAP S/4HANA in an inoperative mode, without affecting the system behavior. Only when the switches are turned on, the corresponding enhancements become effective. This approach can be used to import mutually exclusive enhancements into the same SAP S/4HANA system, as long as only one is switched on afterwards. Typically, only one industry solution can be effective in the same system, but with the switch technology they can be installed into the same system in an inoperative state. Another feature of the switch and enhancement framework is the good performance, since in most cases enhancements and switching are handled by the ABAP compiler that generates corresponding code and thus avoids interpretation of meta data at runtime. A switch determines whether an associated switchable development object is effective or inoperative. Switches are repository objects. The difference between a switch and a field in a customizing table is that a switch can define which parts of the source code will be compiled—inoperative code will not be compiled and therefore will not be available at all. A switch determines

- whether data dictionary (DDIC) objects such as types are available in SAP S/4HANA,
- whether a development object, for example an enhancement implementation, is effective and can be used in the system,
- the visibility of maintenance views within view cluster and view fields in maintenance views,
- the visibility of screen fields and which modules are called in user interface flow logic.

There are various types of development objects that can be switched, but the possibilities to declare them so at design time differ slightly: Most types of objects, for example all enhancement implementations for ABAP are assigned to a switch indirectly by associating their package with a switch as shown in Fig. 16.2. Some development objects do not belong to a package; they can be associated with one or multiple switches, depending on the object type. Furthermore, switchable user interface elements can be specified whether they should be visible when the switch is turned on, or whether they are hidden. Although area menus belong to packages, their package switch is not used but switches can be defined per node. Thus, granularity of switching is increased, and switch definition is aligned with customizing which use the same hierarchy tool. A package can be assigned to exactly one switch; a switch, on the other hand, can be assigned to multiple packages. All switchable repository objects are affected by the package's switch state. Packages can be nested. The state of a switchable object depends on the switch assignment of its package; if there is none, then on the assignment of its super package, and so on. Therefore, a subpackage switch overrides a super package switch. Not all development entities can be switched in the same way. While it is simple to either compile or not compile a source code section, switching table definitions and other DDIC structures have to be treated carefully. Therefore, switches provide three states:

- Off: All associated objects are switched off. The system behaves as if the objects don't exist.
- Standby (enabled, but not effective): All declarative repository objects such as DDIC structures, tables, and static source code enhancements—that can only contain declarative statements—are switched on. All other repository objects are switched off. Standby has system-wide consequences.
- On: All associated objects are switched on. They are available in the system like nonswitched objects. This activation can be client- or user-specific.

At a given point in time, a switch has one of three states: OFF, STANDBY, or ON. Simply spoken, an object is not visible in the system if the switch is OFF, only visible at development time if the switch is STANDBY, and visible at runtime if the switch is ON. Except for DDIC switches and business configuration sets, switch states can be client-specific. A use case for standby switch state is when an industry solution requires some data types of an industry extension without having to activate the coding. In case a switchable object is not assigned to a switch—for example because neither its package nor super packages are assigned to a switch—then it is regarded as switched on. Since there may be many switches that have to be switched as a group to enable a new functionality, it is not possible to change the state of a switch directly. Instead, the concept of business functions has been introduced that map one specific business function to a set of technical switches.

Note that the sets of switches assigned to different business functions are not disjoint. The same switch can be assigned to multiple business functions. Even if some business function is switched off, some of the assigned switches may be on if they are controlled by other business functions as well. This might lead to surprising results if the switches and the switch assignment were not designed carefully. Switches are assigned to business functions either as an activation switch or as a standby switch. From an administrator's point of view, business functions are the most fine-grained units that can be turned on or off, thus changing the state of assigned switches. Initially, all switches are in state OFF. When a business function is set to ON, activation switches are turned to ON, and standby switches to STANDBY. When a business function is switched OFF, the framework has to check all assigned business functions. If one of them is ON, then the switch will not be turned off. Standby switch assignment is needed when packages with mixed content—for example type definitions and executable code—are needed by multiple business functions, and some of them only need the type definitions.

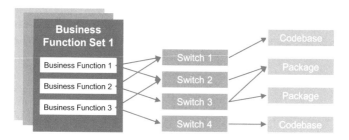

Fig. 16.2 Switch framework

A business function is a self-contained function from a business perspective that refers to a set of switches. A switch can be assigned to more than one business function. By activating a business function, all assigned switches are turned on or to standby respectively, depending on the definition of the business function. Business functions may be declared reversible if their switches don't affect the data dictionary. Only reversible business functions can be turned off again. However, this is not recommended in production systems. When assigning switches to business functions, it can be chosen whether a switch should be turned on or turned to standby when the business function is activated. A business function may depend on another business function as a prerequisite, or may be not allowed in conjunction with another business function. Those dependencies can be defined by developers and are checked before turning business functions on or off. A business function set is a group of business functions that usually corresponds to an industry solution. A business function can be part of multiple business function sets. Business function sets are used to bundle business functions that should work together in an industry solution. Business function sets can be nested, for example to include one industry solution in another. Therefore, they can be *insertable*, that is to structure business function sets only, and they can be *selectable*, that is they are able to be switched on. A business function set can be selected using the Switch Framework customizing tool. This provides a selection of industry business functions which can be turned on. The selection of the business function set can be only changed to a set that also contains the industry business functions that already have been turned on.

Conclusion

SAP S/4HANA provides a variety of industry solutions that extend the core ERP functionality. Some capabilities are quite common while some are specific and provide better workflows and full support for unique use cases. Additionally, the industry solutions contain features that were particularly developed for countries and regions with unique regulations or challenges. The Switch Framework enables the implementation of industry solutions so that they can be easily activated and used with minimal effort. The Switch Framework provides a structured approach for installing software in S/4HANA in an inoperative state, with the option to activate it later. In inoperative state the software exists in SAP S/4HANA but is not executed. The Switch Framework allows installing enhancements without activating them.

Part III
Conceptual View

This part describes the conceptual foundation of SAP S/4HANA applications. It presents the technology components and programming model that form the basis of SAP S/4HANA, both on premise and in the cloud. The section starts with the product qualities which are expected from ERP products and explains how they are implemented based on the SAP S/4HANA solution architecture as depicted in the next figure. From the database system, to application server and user interface layer the corresponding conceptual approaches are elucidated by clarifying the use case and defining the solution (Fig. 1).

SAP S/4HANA is available for on-premise, public, and private cloud deployment. However, SAP S/4HANA has basically one code line for different deployment options. Thus, the concepts are principally the same and are explained in the next chapter uniquely, even if there might be minor differences in the transition time. Usually, new features are developed first for public cloud and made available for on premise and private cloud later as shown in Fig. 2.

Being able to quickly grow the feature set and to address the scope that large-enterprise customers require is one of the key differentiators of SAP S/4HANA Cloud. So, what would be a better basis for a software-as-a-service ERP than the classic on-premise SAP ERP? SAP ERP alone has 80 million lines of code—the whole SAP Business Suite has more than 300 million—it supports 25 industry solutions, globalization, and localization for all countries—and all the best-practice business processes that made SAP successful. As a functional basis for a software-as-a-service ERP this is a valuable foundation. It is all there and just needing to be enabled. Thus, the path to SAP S/4HANA Cloud started with SAP ERP and was continued with S/4HANA On Premise. SAP began re-architecting and refactoring SAP ERP to benefit from SAP HANA's native capabilities—like, for example, combined transactional and analytical processing in one SAP HANA instance, getting rid of persisted aggregates and index tables. To be able to complete this journey, in 2015 SAP branched into a new SAP HANA-only product code line, which enabled even completely new processes on an SAP HANA-optimized model. For example, real-time inventory management in materials management, which is now built without any persisted aggregates and a lock-free, insert-only architecture

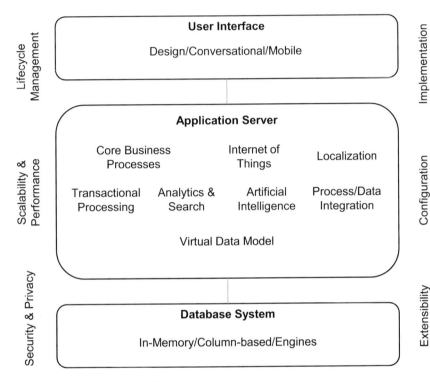

Fig. 1   The SAP S/4HANA architecture and concepts

Fig. 2   One code line for on premise and cloud

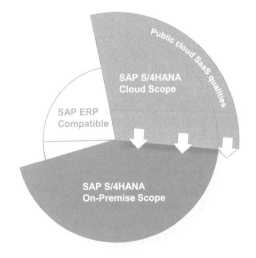

that drastically increases the throughput. It is important that with this new code line, SAP ensured *semantic compatibility*, which means that the semantic business data model is kept compatible to SAP ERP, so that especially integration interfaces like BAPIs and IDOCs are compatible to a large degree. Only exception here are so-called *deprecations* that SAP manages on a so-called simplification list.

So, what is now SAP S/4HANA Cloud? SAP S/4HANA Cloud is a full software-as-a-service ERP with Finance, Sales, Procurement, Logistics, covering more and more functionality from the former SAP ERP scope. And this scope is a subset of SAP S/4HANA On Premise. SAP S/4HANA On Premise and Cloud have the same code base—but of course this does not mean that the products are identical—but they are highly compatible, which is especially important for hybrid deployments. Scope of SAP S/4HANA Cloud can rapidly grow as features are already available under the hood in the code line; they just need to be cloud enabled. It is also clear that effort is required to prepare these business processes to work in a software-as-a-service (SaaS) deployment efficiently. The software and the application architecture must be prepared for cloud scalability like multi-tenancy, guided configuration and simplification, cloud extensibility, and integration. And, therefore, a large portion of development efforts is invested on public cloud qualities to make SAP S/4HANA Cloud a compelling SaaS offering.

Most customers start their cloud transformation with their commodity and non-differentiating business processes like HR, Travel Management, or Finance. Consequently, customers will have at least temporary hybrid landscapes requesting very good integration between on-premise systems and their cloud solutions SAP SuccessFactors, SAP Ariba, SAP Fieldglass, and SAP Concur. As SAP S/4HANA On Premise and Cloud have the same development code line, SAP can offer a native integration between cloud and on-premise applications. The APIs are just the same, and the business processes are semantically compatible. Thus, especially two-tier SAP S/4HANA On Premise to SAP S/4HANA Cloud scenarios are supported. An example is manufacturing plants running their local finance in SAP S/4HANA Cloud and consolidate back to the headquarters, which is running SAP S/4HANA On Premise, whereas the manufacturing, inventory process run locally only.

ERP Product Qualities: Customer View 17

This chapter deals with the qualities that an ERP system must provide from the perspective of a customer. The qualitative characteristics that make an ERP system useful and provide users with the desired advantages are described in detail. For this, the qualities are clustered and explained one by one.

ERP Qualities Expected By Consumers

Companies implement ERP systems for example to integrate their business processes, minimize interfaces, improve scalability, enable multilingual capability, centralize the system for reducing complexity, develop uniform data structures and processes, and ensure security. In addition, they want to significantly improve their productivity, service delivery, business network collaboration, and transparency. Thus, customers have a clear expectation regarding quality attributes and value of ERP systems. Figure 17.1 summarizes the most relevant qualities consumers require from ERP systems. Those are explained in detail in the next sections. Important to outline is that those qualities are interrelated. For example, higher response time is often achieved by data redundancy, on the other hand data redundancy results into a more sophisticated solution for legal compliance requirements like data privacy. Therefore, the qualities must be balanced and optimized as a whole. This is the task of the architects who design the solution concepts and enable the implementation of the qualities.

Data Isolation

Data Ownership and Isolation
Customer data that is exclusively owned by the customer. It must be separated from the data of other customers. There should also be techniques in place to ensure data and network isolation for tenant's service. To reduce total cost of ownership (TCO)

© The Author(s), under exclusive license to Springer Nature Switzerland AG 2022
S. Sarferaz, *Compendium on Enterprise Resource Planning*,
https://doi.org/10.1007/978-3-030-93856-7_17

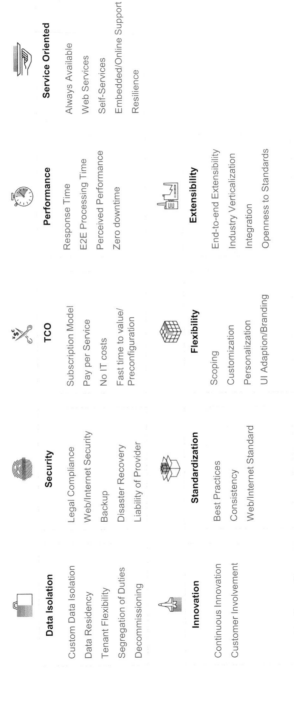

Fig. 17.1 ERP qualities expected by consumers

specially for cloud, network resources and common data are reduced to a minimum number of system deployments and databases. The concentration of data and resources introduces new risks, such as sharing the underlying infrastructure with unknown and untrustworthy tenants. To mitigate these risks, a cloud infrastructure provider or software as a service solution should provide strong guarantees for data isolation. Independent of the solution, a customer should be the only owner of their data.

Data Residency

This requirement is about the physical or geographic location of an organization's data or information. Data residency, like data sovereignty, refers to the legal or regulatory requirements imposed on data bases in the country or region in which they reside. For example, according to EUDP, cloud systems and services for European customers must be operated by a team located in EU. Furthermore, there must be full transparency of data center and data storage locations on request. Cloud computing, which enables businesses to deliver hosted services over the Internet, can raise concerns about data residency. Users of cloud computing are frequently unaware of the physical location of their data, as cloud providers store data globally across multiple data center locations. As a result, cloud service consumers must understand where their cloud provider's data centers are located around the world and how different data residency policies apply to each location.

Tenant Move

Reorganization that leads to the consolidation or split of IT systems and consequently to the moving, splitting, or merging of the application data of cloud services. Also, a box-move of a tenant from one data center to another should be supported. Often subsidiaries' or subcompany's businesses are the first to transition to the cloud which is referred as two-tier model. As the company grows, change is unavoidable, whether it is a reorganization, the acquisition of another company, or a merger with a competitor. Especially the move of legal business entities into another geographical area requires some flexibility in transferring data from one data center to another.

Segregation of Duties

Segregation of duties (SoD) is an internal control that ensures that at least two individuals are responsible for the separate parts of any task in order to prevent error and fraud. Sensitive data needs to be handled according to user role and duty. Consequently, different authorizations are needed. An application running with privileges more than what is required for the job, might be misused by attackers to gain unauthorized access to data and system resources beyond the direct control of the application. Apart from providing defense in depth, following minimal privilege rules helps classify data and define access to it. The principle is that no single individual is given authority to execute two conflicting duties. The requirement is even more important if certain administrative tasks are delegated to third parties, be it via complete outsourcing or by employment of third party resources.

Decommissioning/Offboarding

The automated formal process to remove or retire something from active service. Data return concept as well as a self-service scenario should be provided. After contract end or tenant move, there must be an option to return and destroy the data which is usually a legal requirement. The customer may request the export of their own data to an appropriate media and in an appropriate data format such as .csv or another standard format.

Security

Legal Compliance

Conformity with expected norms for security, breach prevention, privacy, operations in cloud computing. Customers should have access to these audited reports, certifications, and attestations. There are standards from bodies such as the ISO or the Cloud Security Alliance which are applicable to virtually all customers around the world. The next are regulations and standards that are based on regional or national needs or data protection laws. Finally, regulations that have been put in place for different industries. The cost benefits for cloud service providers come from the ability to scale multiple clients across shared resources. Compliance can be difficult as regulations frequently require encryption, auditing, and data separation, which increase hardware requirements and limit resource sharing. Cloud compliance requires a two-way partnership between the customer who owns the data along with the legal obligations for the handling of the data and the cloud vendor who acts as the data processor and must also handle the data in compliance with regulations.

Web/Internet Security

State-of-the-art web security standards must be ensured, for example, XSS, CSRF, SQL injection, URL manipulation, Faked requests and forms, Cookie visibility and theft, Session hijacking, Remote system execution, File-upload abuse, Denial of service, Phishing, Malware, etc. Malware prevention/management with SLA should be in place. Fast security patching. Web servers by design open a window between the network and the world. The care taken with server maintenance, web application updates, and the web site coding will define the size of that window, limit the kind of information that can pass through it, and thus establish the degree of web security.

Backup

Each component must ensure the capability of online backup for all business application data. Online backup means without shutdown of the component. To minimize the risk of data loss, customers need to back up their business data regularly.

Disaster Recovery

Possibility to recover data after loss. Recovery from backup must be possible also across distributed landscapes and data centers. This includes that replicated data needs special handling on application site, for instance data needs to be kept consistent. Backup and restore must not imply an unavailability during the process of data recovery. After a crash of one component within a scenario, it must be possible to restore to a consistent state of the complete scenario. This requires that, in addition to the component backup concept, the scenario backup concept must include information about data dependencies between components and necessary steps to come to a consistent state for the complete scenario.

Liability of Provider

For all services of the provider, security and data protection risks shall be identified and transparently managed to achieve a secure service lifecycle protecting customers and preventing liability risks. Consumer and provider should both agree and implement on a joint organizational interface including SLAs to discuss and to resolve assumed or happened information security incidents. Liability remains a cornerstone in the further expansion of cloud computing into all areas of business. For a company planning on moving its data and processing into the cloud two factors are decisive: risks associated and benefits to be gained. A right balance needs to be achieved between attributing rights and liabilities among the parties as well as diversifying the risks through cloud insurance. In addition, new approaches to the protection of intellectual property rights in the digital world are being developed with the respective obligations of cloud providers.

Total Cost of Ownership (TCO)

Subscription Model

With a subscription licensing model, consumers pay a per-user fee, either monthly or annually, which allows them to use the software during the subscription term. The customer doesn't own the software, instead it is leased. The subscription payment includes software licenses, access to support services, and new versions of the software as they are released. Subscription-based pricing model is applicable to all service models (IaaS, PaaS, SaaS). The traditional pricing models are not applicable in the Cloud as such for pricing of software products, for example, perpetual license, application bundles. Customers are not owning the software anymore but consuming services. There is a need for a clear and systematic pricing framework that allows a customer or organization to purchase or subscribe to a vendor's IT services for a specific period of time for a set price. Subscribers typically make a monthly or annual commitment to the services.

Pay per Service
This is about a model in which the customer begins with a zero account, provisioned cloud resources on demand, and is charged based on actual consumption (Pay-As-You-Go). To support the customer digital transformation and to offer more flexibility and quick access to new product functionalities, providers offer new usage-based commercial model (Pay-Per-Use) for cloud services.

No IT Costs
This requirement is about only paying for services instead of for hardware, software, power and the support for keeping these items secure, stable, and functioning properly. No additional costs for setup, maintenance, or upgrade of standard stack (SaaS model) or underlaying platform (PaaS) or infrastructure (PaaS) are considered. Upgrades are included in the monthly fees. Thus, no admin work and no IT skillset are needed. The use of cloud computing eliminates the need for on-premises servers. Customers no longer need to spend large sums of money up front on the hardware and software required to run their network thanks to cloud computing. In most cloud environments, these costs, as well as the cost of network maintenance, are included in a flat monthly fee. Furthermore, when the server and network backbone need to be upgraded, it is the cloud provider's responsibility to do so—at no additional cost to the user.

Fast Time to Value/Preconfiguration
Especially cloud deployment is the alternative to the do-it-yourself approach. In many companies the Lines of Business (LoB) are leading the discussions with specific insight to move into a cloud solution. The traditional internal-facing IT department can be quickly left behind by buy-and-go cloud service adoption, especially since the job of maintaining, patching, upgrading is all handled by the cloud provider. As a matter of fact, a company now wants to get its cloud computing arrangement off the ground in a very short time, with services running out-of-the-box. Thus, this requirement is about fast time to availability, timely provisioning of productive systems, fast go-live, predelivered content, best practice processes, services running out-of-the-box, guided configuration, seamless data integration, easy-to-use, intuitive, principle of one, low training effort, conversion/migration of legacy systems, and online tutorials.

Performance

Response Time
Single transactions, often represented by backend calls, should have acceptable response times even if the system is under load. An appropriate performance test mechanism should be in place to identify performance bottlenecks. Also, response times in production should be recorded. That is a good practice because none can

foresee and test all situations in a synthetic environment. Good response times are especially important when users must work interactively.

E2E Processing Time

This quality is about optimized end-to-end processing time of business services. This is the time to fulfill a task or a job, from login time until end of a process including network latency. The most important indicators for performance are response time and throughput. Good response times are especially important when users must work interactively. For example, web shops lose business if their users perceive the shop to be reacting too sluggishly. Also, network latency is the most significant factor in poor response times when using Wide Area Networks (WAN) because latency time adds significantly to the end-to-end response time.

Perceived Performance

This requirement refers to how quickly a software feature appears to perform its task. This is the total time to get a reaction of the system considering the quality of the outcome. Humans do not like to wait. Thus, the active and passive modes of a person using a website or application must be considered. During the active mode users do not realize they are waiting at all while during the passive mode their brain activity drops, and they get bored. When real performance cannot be increased due to physical limitations, techniques shall be used to streamline the end user's experience and increase the perceived performance. It's about how fast a user thinks the application is.

Zero Downtime

Zero downtime describes a quality with no perceived service downtimes from the end-user's perspective. Especially, updates or patches happen transparent to the user without moving the application into a maintenance mode. The application can be used by the users at any time. Any unplanned outage of the application can lead to frustration of the users. For business-critical applications, any outage can even lead to financial losses or potentially lost sales.

Service Oriented

Always Available

Services must be always accessible and available, ideally also on any device. If one service fails, then the remaining services continue running (service degradation). If one availability zone fails, then redirection to another. Also, the customer service center can be contacted at any time with immediate response. Customers have high demand of business continuity and need high availability of the computing infrastructure. This also includes the response time to users' requests. Especially in the cloud they expect 24/7 access to the business data and applications no matter the device or their location. There is also an increase in the use of mobile devices for business applications which outlines the importance of the requirement.

Web Services

Standard web access shall be provided for all applications and services, also for any kind of administration or auxiliary services like Output Management, Business Workflows, User Management. The SaaS distribution model provides applications via the Internet that are accessed from a web browser, while the software and data are stored on the servers. Web services are sometimes called application services. Web services are made available from a business's web server for users or other connected programs.

Self-Services

This requirement is about a system that allows end users to set up and launch applications and services in a cloud computing environment without the direct intervention of an IT organization or a service provider. Self-provisioning by users is applicable in public, private, and hybrid cloud scenarios. Examples for self-services are resetting passwords, changing personal details, or creating incident messages. End users want to be able to spin up compute resources on demand for almost any type of workload. This eliminates the need for IT administrators to provision and manage compute resources in the traditional manner. Also, cloud environment is a closed ecosystem in which access is very limited and should be restricted to few use cases and parameters which a key user is supposed to manage.

Embedded/Online Support

In many companies the Lines of Business (LoB) are leading the discussions with specific insight to move into a cloud solution. With cloud software, technical support is handled by the provider, hence LoBs can reallocate their limited resources to growing their business. Applications need to be designed to support nontechnical users. Thus, this requirement relates to enabling applications for business users without technical skills, intuitive design, high user grade experience, and self-explanatory. The application should provide an in-place capability to interact with the provider regarding technical issues or inconsistencies with the software. Furthermore, the application should collect essential context information to avoid unnecessary interactions with the support to clarify basic questions. For most of the incidents causing alerts, automated mitigations are in place. This requires the ability of the system or system component to gather information about its environment at any given time and adapt behaviors accordingly. Contextual computing, also known as context-aware computing, employs software and hardware to automatically collect and analyze data in order to guide responses.

Resilience

Applications should be designed to gracefully handle latency, inadequate response times, and service unavailability of downstream systems. The applications should be error tolerant and resilient to temporary problems, such as latency (time out, no activity, network slowdowns), peaks, outages, asynchronous interface call interruptions. Unavailability of application leads to unsatisfied users. For business-critical applications, any outage can even lead to financial losses or potentially lost sales. Enterprise applications are implemented in a distributed manner which can lead to multiple risks, such as network communication issue, lost message, long running requests, or even an outage of dependent systems. Resilience mitigates these critical situations. The goal is to achieve a reliable system made from unreliable components.

Innovation

Continuous and Fast Innovation

This requirement is about frequent delivery of new features, short release cycle, fast adoption of innovations, and short lead time. Every day, technology progresses further. Traditional IT processes are a poor match for today's speed. The success of the cloud and Software as a Service model reflects the users' demand for fast innovations. Computing is now driven by business needs that can be adapted with frequent software adjustments in any week or even through the space of a day. But today's business environment requires more than just speed, though. Innovation—the ability to develop new offerings, evaluate their potential market adoption, and then roll out the successful ones—is equally important. In this case, too, cloud computing is a far better fit than the traditional on-premise approach. Because cloud services are instantly available, it is simple to try out a new offering. Companies can get user feedback quickly, rather than waiting months for something to be tested in the market.

Customer Involvement

This quality focuses on early involvement, customer and stakeholder engagement, online feedback, embedded participation to ideation process, design thinking, agile development, innovation platform. Producing meaningful and usable software that meets the end users' needs is the goal of every stakeholder. With cloud computing the opportunity to influence software development decisions and adopt new innovations early on is much higher. Hosting the software, monitoring the activities, and sharing resources makes it easy to open for immediate feedback. Cloud services are shared by many and hence each inconsistency or misbehavior of the system has immediate impact on all consumers.

Standardization

Best Practices

Standard features should be available and should satisfy the customers' need from start to end. Predelivered best practice content, business processes, standard code lists shall be provided. Industry- and country-specific business best practices, legal compliance shall be supported out-of-the-box. The application should be compliant with standards and legal requirements. Customers want to reduce effort on standard LoB processes and focus on core competencies and differentiating tasks.

Consistency
Customer expects harmonized user experience, business processes, data integration, domain model alignments across all services since they don't want to consider all the technical background. Thus, approaches like principle of one are expected and not having for example multiple frameworks for solving the same problem.

Web/Internet Standards
The requirement is about state-of-the-art Internet standards, such as routing (no IP), caching, web protocols for application exits, stateless architecture, browser support, device support, web tools, business payment standards. Enterprise applications store and access data over the Internet. Especially in the SaaS model, providers install and operate applications while users consume the software via web interfaces. For this customer expects that all kind of web standards are met.

Flexibility

Scoping
Scoping is the process of selecting the required scenarios, business processes, and functionalities by the customer in a controlled way. ERP systems are very rich in functionality which brings new challenges in discovery and implementation. To address these challenges, advanced techniques are provided to assist customers in choosing appropriate services. Especially, in a consumption-based commercial model it is important to enable only those services that are requested.

Customization
This quality refers to configuration options, branding tool, and theme designer.
    Many organizations need to support similar processes. However, despite these similarities, there is also the need to allow for local variations and adaption to customers' needs. Therefore, solution must be provided to configure applications individually while sharing commonalities.

Personalization
This is about the capability for local settings and favorites handling. Users may become more demanding when receiving/consuming such services as they are exposed to a wide range of applications. Personalization is important in business applications, just as it is in web and/or mobile applications.

UI Adoption/Branding
UI adoption describes the process of adopting user interfaces or other assets that are delivered by the ERP provider out-of-the-box. Branding is the activity of connecting

applications with a particular color or layout in order to make users handle them easier. Capabilities for UI adoption and branding must be provided.

Extensibility

End-to-End Extensibility
This quality focuses on the ability of extending standard services and processes in all layers (table extension to UI field extension), as well as the extensibility of corresponding APIs. Thus, vertical extensions of processes or services are enabled. Partners extending core services may need an additional extension layer for their customers. Each extension should be independent of any other extension and safe from upgrades and updates.

Industry Verticalization
This quality allows enhancing the core functionality with industry-specific solutions (vertical market).

Industry customers are challenging ERP vendors when it comes to industry specifics. One size-fits-all software is starting to give way for more modular verticalized approaches. A clear trend has emerged in recent years aimed at replacing horizontal solutions with more customized solutions geared at specific industries from Healthcare to Retail. Furthermore, while in the past there was a clear assignment of a customer business to an industry solution, today's companies are investing in multiple industry businesses such as Oil & Retail, Manufacturing, and Utilities.

Integration

This quality covers anchor points, integration platform, integration out-of-the-box and communication arrangements. Traditionally data and process integration has been an exclusive task of IT specialists to connect systems with each other. As part of this exercise, the tools used to build integration solutions are complex and often require a programming background. In addition, they require a steep learning curve and are costly to maintain. However, today business users or so-called citizen integrators require integration out-of-the-box or want to accomplish the same tasks easily with integration tools. Furthermore, robustness of public APIs in terms of nonincompatible changes are required. Since applications that consume APIs are sensitive to changes, APIs also imply a contract. The contract provides some level of assurance that, over time, the API will change in a compatible manner so that the consuming application won't break.

Openness to Standards
This requirement is about providing public APIs, API management, open cloud development environment and extension platform, and support for standard programming languages (JAVA, JS etc.). Customers and partners want an extension

infrastructure for integration, portability, interoperability, and innovation. They would also like the possibility to combine services from different providers. To allow other solutions to integrate, the application should expose public APIs over standard web interfaces, for example, REST. There should be documentation listing all APIs and explaining their usage.

Conclusion

Ultimately, the goal of ERP providers is to create value for its customers. Therefore, the customer satisfaction regarding the usage of ERP systems plays an important role. Customers are happy when their expectations of a product or service have been met or exceeded. The individual quality characteristics of an ERP system are therefore founded on the wishes and requirements of the customers. These characteristics determine the quality and business success of the vendors and customers. Overtime customer needs change. As a result, the quality characteristics must also be adjusted and integrated by the respective providers.

ERP Product Qualities: Provider View

18

This chapter describes ERP product qualities which are expected from provider and are ensured by the SAP S/4HANA architecture. Covered qualities are operational efficiency, infrastructure, operations and monitoring, agility, and commercialization. The qualities are clustered and explained one by one.

ERP Qualities Expected by Provider

Enterprise Resource Planning (ERP) systems are considered as management information systems that streamline a company's business processes. Providing ERP software that meets the functional requirements of a company with an acceptable quality level is challenging. Cloud computing can help to resolve some of these challenges. Cloud providers not only build applications, but also run them under the software-as-a-service paradigm. Customers can just consume the software as a service by simply using a browser. Thus, IT departments on customer side no longer has to deploy and operate the ERP system. The provider of cloud services is the owner of the IT Environment. The primary task is to provide the services as declared in the contract. In addition, it's of utmost importance to provision and operate the services in an effective and efficient manner. The whole business in the cloud is driven by the goal of achieving a low TCO while delivering continuous innovations. This is an ongoing process as the request for new functionalities and system requirements is permanently changing. A platform is always designed for the current usages and needs. Additional features, different usages, upcoming technologies, the need to cover new businesses and markets, these are all points that require an environment both technical and organizational that is capable of continuous adaptation and refactoring of the IT and services. Thus, customers have a clear expectation regarding provider of ERP systems. Figure 18.1 summarizes the most relevant requirements regarding provider of ERP systems. Very important to outline is that in case of private cloud deployed ERP systems, the customer takes the role of the

S. Sarferaz, *Compendium on Enterprise Resource Planning*,
https://doi.org/10.1007/978-3-030-93856-7_18

Cloud Infrastructure	Operational Efficiency	Operations & Monitoring	Agility
Cloud Operations Design	Software Lifecycle Automation	Operation Tools	Agile Software
Data Center Management	Resource Sharing	Infrastructure Monitoring	Cloud Extensibility Platform
Infrastructure Independent	Content Lifecycle Management	Application Management	Ecosystem Support
Provisioning Tools	Simplification	Service Monitoring	
Global Scale	Scalability	Product Usage Analysis	
Dev-Ops Organization	Elasticity	Customer Activity Tracking/Turn-Out Management	
	Test Automation	Cloud KPIs	**Commercialization**
	Continuous TCO Improvements		Cloud License Models
			Partner License Model
			Customer Loyalty Program

Fig. 18.1 ERP qualities expected from provider

provider and is in charge for operations. Those are explained in detail in the next sections.

Cloud Infrastructure

Cloud Operations Design

Cloud Computing is a large-scale distributed computing paradigm that is driven by economies of scale, in which a pool of abstracted, virtualized, dynamically scalable, managed computing power, storage, platforms, and services are provided on demand to external customers over the Internet. Enterprises, service providers, and other organizations are all migrating to virtual data centers, or cloud architectures, including the new software-defined data center, as a result of the well-documented benefits of agility, efficiency, and cost control provided by technologies such as virtualization and cloud computing. However, the adoption of these new architectures calls into question traditional management tools and processes for ensuring the data center's effective operation. The need to improve data center operations is leading to the new concept of the cloud operations center. Thus, IT system needs to be designed to support SaaS qualities and decision on platform and architecture is required.

Data Center Management

Traditionally, data center strategies focused on keeping applications running, providing sustained and controlled growth, and doing so in a secure and fault-tolerant manner. Today, not only the typical location, power, tax, outsourcing, and employment base, decisions come into play, but new factors including cloud operations, green environmental initiatives, and legal requirements. Legal requirements must also be considered, such as the Chinese Cybersecurity Act or the European GDPR, which restrict data access to certain areas. Although most ERP systems have limited influence on the network between the customer's web browser and the cloud, data centers should be always selected according to an intelligent algorithm to minimize latency effects. Additional aspects of this quality are data center infrastructure, computing and noncomputing processes, and outsourcing strategy.

Infrastructure Independent

Cloud development and hosting environments should be independent of the infrastructure or platform. Application and data portability are a fundamental goal for cloud computing. Cloud infrastructures and platforms shall support business applications regardless of style, age, ownership, and location. It shall be possible to move to another cloud infrastructure or platform provider with minimal risk, short delays, and no loss of data. Regardless of how, when, or where they were implemented, applications should work with a standard set of underlying services. Virtualization and containerization are fundamental technologies that power cloud computing. The software tools separate computing environments from physical infrastructures so that multiple operating systems can be processed. Furthermore, it also allows to be independent of the underlaying infrastructure.

Provisioning Tools

Cloud provisioning is an important aspect of the cloud computing model that describes how a customer obtains cloud services and resources from a cloud provider. The cloud provisioning process can be carried out in one of three ways. Advanced provisioning, dynamic provisioning, and user self-provisioning are the three models. With advanced provisioning, the customer enters into a formal service contract with the cloud provider. The provider then prepares and delivers the agreed-upon resources or services to the customer. The customer is charged a one-time fee or is billed on a monthly basis. Dynamic provisioning allows cloud resources to be deployed in a flexible manner to meet a customer's fluctuating demands. Typically, deployments scale up to accommodate spikes in usage and scale down when demand decreases. The customer is charged based on the number of times the customer uses the service (pay-per-use). The customer purchases resources from the cloud provider via a web interface or portal with user self-provisioning, also known as cloud self-service. Additional aspects for this quality are tools and services to provision software on given infrastructure, app center offering, feature and content activation.

Global Scale

Companies looking to expand the global scale of their businesses are increasingly turning to the cloud. In order to minimize latency, instances need to be offered close to the access points. However, sometimes regional or DNS failures must be considered, hence it should be possible to quickly set up a new instance build. The benefits of cloud computing services include the ability to scale globally on a given infrastructure or across data centers. Thus, services need to scale on given infrastructure and data center should be distributed to decrease latency. Additional aspects for this quality are load balancing, no assumed IP addresses, geographic redundancy, no special nodes, automatic cluster join.

DevOps Organization

DevOps is a set of cultural philosophies, practices, and tools that improve an organization's ability to deliver applications and services at high velocity by evolving and improving products at a faster rate than traditional software development and infrastructure management processes. Development and operations teams are no longer separated in a DevOps model. Development and operations should be either combined in a single organization or closely coordinated to ensure close alignment. This speed enables businesses to better serve their customers and compete in the market. Software starts to create value once it is successfully used by end users. Therefore, software providers must ensure a high flow of work from the idea to the development and use of new versions. Teams should focus on small set of functionalities and release them as soon as possible to get feedback.

Operational Efficiency

Software Lifecycle Automation

In the classical on-premise world, the customer has the flexibility to apply updates in a self-defined time frame. Cloud computing offers the possibility for faster innovation cycles by releasing patches or new features more often, sometimes even multiple times per day because the provider operates the software and can update the software at any time. This requires a high automation of the update process, especially because an essential part of the update is to make sure beforehand that the new code fulfills the required quality level. When delivering frequently that is only possible with a high degree of automation. Software lifecycle processes have to be a nonevent from an effort and cost perspective. Continuous service delivery needs to be performed without manual operation task. Software lifecycle automation system is required to ensure high degree of automation everywhere, for example a build pipeline, to support upgrades, patches and migrations, independent of connected underlaying products.

Resource Sharing

Resources sharing leads to significant economic efficiencies. It allows development teams to write code once, implement features in one codebase without duplication, and serve multiple customers. By sharing a single codebase, cloud apps and data can be patched and updated much faster. A cloud provider may choose between multiple levels of resource sharing ranging from sharing same hardware using virtual machines to sharing the same process through clever programming. For this computing architecture is required that allows providers to share computing resources in a public or private cloud.

Content Lifecycle Management

The configuration data must be separated from the application data and system data. However, coding and content should use similar processes and infrastructures. Moving from support for initial activation to a complete product lifecycle, including introduction, maintenance, extension, upgrade, and possibly retirement, is a fundamental change that requires rethinking basic principles of configuration delivery. In cloud computing it is key to make business configuration as seamless and smooth as possible for development, partner development, cloud operations, and customers. The fast and simple setup of customer systems is only possible based on high-quality content and a high degree of automation. As there are no consultants who can intervene and have the knowledge to compensate defects, all standard content needs to be useable out of the box.

Simplification

The IT industry as a whole is forced to think *Simplicity*. IT departments want to shift their focus from the day-to-day demands of managing technology and concentrate on delivering the innovation that technology makes possible. Businesses want to reduce the complexity of their current network and data center and capitalize on the flexibility and efficiency the cloud offers. For cloud providers simplification is a prerequisite for operating an efficient cloud environment. Additional aspects of this quality are reduced complexity of data models, principle of one, standard tools, harmonization, intuitive user experience, and low data footprint. Companies typically have created a large amount of custom code that enhances and partially replaces or even modifies the ERP software. This leads to a scattered IT landscape with an ERP system that is difficult to upgrade to the next release. The massive adjustments to the standard software have therefore locked the companies and prevent them from taking the next step toward digital transformation. Now, in the digital era, standardization is needed, and even though companies try to avoid individualization wherever possible, they still demand a high degree of flexibility. This includes reducing complexity through standardization and simplification of business processes. ERP applications of digital time require the delivery of preconfigured packages that enable fast implementations.

Scalability

Applications need to scale horizontally by adding more instances of a service (scale out) or vertically by adding virtual CPUs or memory to existing instances (scale up). Traditionally, businesses were tied to physical constraints, such as hard-drive space and memory, all of which impeded scalability. The classic IT systems were optimized for the current situation and the customer needs. In the cloud there can be only one setup. With cloud computing, these constraints are replaced by an infrastructure that can scale up or down (typically up) and adapt in harmony with a business's needs. A scalable system is one in which the workload that the system can process grows in proportion to the number of resources provided to it, that is, its capacity scales with available resources. Additional aspects of this quality are auto-scaling, economy of scale, or capacity on-demand without significant service degradation.

Elasticity

This is about the ability to provide the same level of service regardless of current load. For this the system needs to adapt to actual workload changes dynamically and consider high frequency, peaks, low activity, and no activity. The platform/infrastructure itself shall support the on-demand and elastic nature of the cloud approach (*automated elasticity*), to be closely aligned as it expands and contracts with the actual demand, thereby increasing overall utilization and reducing cost. Elasticity is also important in Cloud environment where the resources are paid per usage. Elasticity usually requires a scalable system; otherwise, the additional resources have little effect. Elasticity is the ability to dynamically adjust the resources needed to deal with loads, adding more resources as the load increases and shrinking as demand decreases and unnecessary resources are removed. Thus, if the load increases, more resources need to be added to keep the unused capacity as small as possible while if demand decreases, resources must be constrained to keep the wasted capacity as small as possible. To avoid the effects of unexpected peaks, scaling must be as close to actual demand as possible, while keeping wasted capacity as small as possible.

Test Automation

Automated tests make use of specialized software to execute tests which are specified as code. In contrast to manual testing, alle test steps are automated. The tests are stored together with the application code. The tests usually consist of three phases: The test environment is built up, one or multiple actions are triggered, and finally the actual outcome is compared to the expected one. Everything can be run locally or fully automated in a build pipeline. Software should be tested before releasing it to customers. This is true for both, for newly added features as well as for existing ones. Verifying functional correctness is important for the consumer satisfaction. Executing these tests manually is a repetitive, error-prone, and expensive task. Especially, when delivering software frequently, as common in the cloud, it might not be possible to execute all tests manually multiple times a day. Furthermore, the humans could likely miss a test step. Lastly, this repetitive task will consume a lot of human resources and thus it is likely cheaper to automate the execution of the tests. Regression testing is a type of software test aimed at finding new software errors or regressions in existing functional and nonfunctional parts of a system after new development, patches, or configuration changes. The developer is responsible for writing tests for implemented features. There are multiple types of tests and for each type different tools exist: Unit tests refer to the idea if testing single small units, such as classes. Dependencies are usually mocked so that only the unit under test is asset. Unit tests are the type of tests for which the greatest number of tests should exist. Integration tests refer to testing the integration of multiple modules and even dependencies. End-to-end simulates the typical user flow by using the full application end-to-end.

Continuous TCO Improvements

New technologies, improved operations techniques, and changing business require a continuous improvement process in Cloud operations in order to keep the agility, flexibility, scalability, efficiency, and low TCO. As the IT infrastructures behind the cloud services are invisible for the customers, changes and migrations must be hidden without interrupting the current operations. At the same time this is also an opportunity to continuously adapt and improve the system. Infrastructure, operations, and development should be continuously revised to keep a low TCO. There is no final end state.

Operations and Monitoring

Operation Tools

Continuous Integration, Continuous Delivery, and Continuous Deployment (CI/DI) is a collection of techniques, processes, and tools to improve software development and delivery. CI/DI follows continuous integration and continues the feedback cycle in software development and delivery. In the CI/CD pipeline, the code is tested automatically to find any bugs early. Once validated, the code is automatically uploaded to a repository. The CD process includes merging code changes, in-depth testing, code releases, and providing production-ready builds of the software. The aim of CD is always to have a code base that is as up to date as possible. Therefore, it is important to integrate continuous integration with continuous delivery in the CI/CD pipeline. The essence of CD is to ensure that new code can be rolled out with minimal effort. Thus, operations tools are required to support the CI/CD processing. Furthermore, tools are necessary for managing costs, usage, and ultimately optimize the cloud. Additional aspects of this quality are logging, auditing, and exception handling.

Infrastructure Monitoring

There is nothing inherent in cloud implementation architectures that makes a cloud 100% reliable. The fact is, running a hugely scalable, automated, efficient service is a lot of work. There are lots of moving pieces and sometimes things go wrong. Hence, a tool is needed to keep the whole infrastructure continuously monitored. Such tools must monitor the system availability, outages, or connectivity problems. Continuous feedback from operations on how to improve operability is required.

Application Management

Software development and delivery in the cloud is different to the traditional world. In the cloud, new developed code is shipped to all customers (almost) at once, hence it has immediate impact on all instances. Furthermore, the changed behavior/new features may have to be released in different time frames or geolocation. Therefore, not only the resource locations must be known to the application, but the application must also know which instance of the resources to use based on factors like geolocation, and which it should not be using perhaps due to eventual-consistency jobs not being completed yet. Thus, adopted concepts are required for cloud application deployment, upgrades, new features activation (e.g., toggling), and software performance. This includes also restart and recovery of asynchronous interfaces. Moreover, the application must work using minimal resources while still delivering the level of service required in any given situation.

Service Monitoring

Observability is important to get an overview about the active services and to be able to immediately react on failures or inconsistencies. With multitenant solutions, debugging in production is hard and the real state of the application is in flux. Thus, it is necessary that applications write comprehensive log information not just to fulfil product standards (e.g., audit logs) but to easily analyze application failure states ex-post. In addition, traceability between services as well as services and the end users (e.g., based on correlation IDs) is an absolute necessity. Furthermore, applications should be easily monitorable at runtime to detect nonapplication failures such as slow networks or unresponsive downstream systems. Every service should be monitored in order to check its performance and allow for corrective actions in case of failure. Service Level Agreement (SLA) is usually employed to serve as a bilateral contract between two parties to specify the requirements, quality of service, responsibilities, and obligations. SLA can contain a variety of service performance metrics with corresponding Service Level Objectives (SLO). Therefore, the values of associated metrics must be measured which are defined in the SLA at the usage stage to monitor whether the specified service level objectives are achieved or not. Furthermore, service and resource usage must be metered and monitored on an as-needed basis to support a dynamic scale feature.

Product Usage Analysis

Provider needs to understand if the innovations that are delivered, have an impact on customer side and if the investment efforts are justified. Analysis and evaluation of this usage data enable product and portfolio decision-makers to better define the footprint in the market and to continuously improve product functionalities. By being able to focus on the right use scenarios/products, development capacity can be focused to the areas with higher relevance and benefit for the customers. Enriching product scorecards with high level usage metrics is required. Feature flags are in place to experiment and validate functionality with some customers before they are generally deployed.

Customer Activity Tracking/Turn-Out Management

The objective is to identify different customer usage behavior, to reduce activities, and to provide reminder options. Furthermore, telemetry is needed for monitoring a consumption-based commercialization (pay-per-use). The service/resource usage has to be metered, based on which the bill can then be calculated. Additional aspects of this quality are contract management, entitlement, feature/service control according to license and contract, and turn-out-management.

Cloud KPIs

Key performance indicators (KPIs) are selected key figures from reports that have been restricted by certain selections and for which reference and target values as well as threshold values can be defined. KPIs are often used to measure a certain measure of progress toward a goal or objective. The KPI value is often compared to a reference number to determine what is an improvement. Although cloud services abstract away and automate much of the underlying IT infrastructure, users still need an objective way to measure service performance and the effect it has on their business. To perform this kind of measurement, users need to define cloud performance metrics. Cloud KPI reporting and predictive analytics provide SaaS teams with an automated solution for consolidating cross-business data, developing accurate SaaS metrics, and providing insight. KPIs are required to track and optimize deployment, show operating status, service consumption, and activities. Additional aspects of this quality are built-In metrics, monitoring, and visualization capabilities like dashboards.

Agility

Agile Software

Monolithic architecture represents the architecture that consists of coarse-grained services and components that depend on each other. Monolithic deployment of a system represents a single point of failure, if the application fails for some reason, the whole set of services fails too. In conditions where monolithic architecture becomes a significant barrier to achieving business competitiveness and enabling scalability, flexibility, and other requirements such as fast development, short time to market, and large team collaboration. Agility is well supported by Microservices. Microservices are an emerging architectural design pattern that brings agility and scalability to enterprise applications. A key enabler to implementing microservices is the cloud. However, scalability and agility are not the only qualities that are expected from ERP systems. For example, high process consistency, compliance, and extensibility are qualities that are better to achieve with a monolithic approach.

Cloud Extensibility Platform

As long as the cloud code line follows the code density and standardization paradigms it is key to keep the core stable. Hence, own platform is needed to provide options for extending the cloud services and business processes and to unlock solution flexibility and innovation. Such an extensibility platform is required for implementing huge new modules while in-app extensibility can be used to enhance the core. In-app extensibility means that the extensions are implemented within the core application using predefined extension points. Both the kernel and the extension run on the same server and use the same database instance.

Ecosystem Support

While the core is highly standardized and needs to be kept stable, there is a need to fill white spaces and accelerate the innovation speed in the cloud by collaborating with partners. Today there are product and technology players, a highly collaborative and complexly orchestrated community. The result is a win-win situation for all involved parties, and a one-stop shop for customers, backed by a single service level agreement (SLA) and a single point of support. The trend of partner ecosystem in cloud computing has rendered obsolete the long-used concept of complete vertical integration coming from one organization. Thus, it is requested to allow partners to extend and operate services and solutions. For this lifecycle management dependencies, partner programming model, organizational setup, partner access, and authorization concept must be considered.

Commercialization

Cloud License Models

When people talk about cloud applications, they are talking about Software as a Service (SaaS). However, there are three main types of cloud service models: Software as a Service (SaaS), Platform as a Service (PaaS), and Infrastructure as a Service (IaaS). Due to the Cloud, customers begin to expect the ability to pay month-to-month and cancel at any time if they were not satisfied with the solution. These expectations led to the recurring types of licensing models. Monthly and annual subscription licenses are now standard in the Cloud. Technical advancements have enabled vendors to accurately track usage of their software and services, paving the way for a new type of license called Pay-As-You-Go. This means the customer pays only for the consumed solution. The usage can be measured in many ways, for example, service consumption, online time, size of database, number of used APIs or queries. Pay-by-Instance Licenses is the final type of license which applies more to Cloud services such as IaaS and PaaS. In addition to the on-premise to cloud transition, there is a conversion in the network licensing technology itself away from node-locked toward pooled. This transition is required because new virtualized and cloud/SaaS network service delivery models necessitate more flexible and responsive licensing technologies that allow entitlements to be quickly repurposed and reused. In this scenario, the customer pays for each server or server instance that the vendor spins up. Try-Before-You-Buy programs are ideal for introducing additional features to new and existing customers. It also helps to differentiate the SaaS model, improve the value of the software, and provide more predictable cash flows. License mobility, or moving licenses for applications and operating systems from one virtual environment to another, is also part of cloud licensing management.

Partner License Model

In cloud world computing resources, network and software are given as metered services. Based on the services provided, three types of service models are defined in the cloud: Software as a Service (SaaS), Infrastructure as a Service (IaaS), and Platform as a Service (PaaS). Usually month-to-month and annual subscription licenses are standard approach in the Cloud. For partner extensions require new OEM or VAR license agreements for cloud services including partner use rights for Cloud services, compliance obligations, service level agreements. OEM stands for original equipment manufacturer and is used by a company that takes components from other vendors to build a new product which then sold under its own brand. A VAR (value-added reseller) purchases a product from a manufacturer, adds value to that product somehow (e.g., adding a service), and then resells the product under its own brand. A VAR agreement defines the legal contract for that process.

Customer Loyalty Program

Cloud service providers get firsthand information about not only what their customers buy, but also which applications are actively used, by which user type, when and how long. Being able to view customer data via a cloud will help leverage the loyalty program to maximize up-sells and cross-sells. Cloud-based loyalty programs allow providers to find out what their customers want and are a great way to keep customers coming back (renewal). Beside customer retention programs, also internal user engagement programs shall be offered.

Conclusion

ERP software must meet specific software qualities. These are divided into two: customer and provider category. This chapter focused on the qualities that are expected from ERP providers for the cloud deployment. The qualities were clustered into cloud infrastructure, operational efficiency, operations and monitoring, agility and commercialization. The aim of those qualities is to reduce the TCO while delivering continuous innovation. Thus, there are conflicting goals which have to be balanced out accordingly. Important to outline is that in case of private cloud deployment, the customer takes over the role and obligations of the provider.

In-Memory Persistency

19

This chapter focuses on in-memory database system SAP HANA, which is used to store application data of SAP S/4HANA. Particularly benefits, architecture, underlying in-memory concepts, platform capabilities, and the application types of in-memory database systems are explained.

Business Requirement

In the past years there has been a revolution in data management systems due to in-memory technology. The main reason for this is that the prices per megabyte of main memory have fallen tremendously while the ability of parallel processing increased dramatically due to multicore processors. For example, the price for 1 MB of main memory in 2010 was 0.01 USD, which has decreased enormously compared to the price in 1960, which had been more than 1,000,000 USD. The idea behind in-memory database systems is to keep the complete dataset permanently in the main memory, enabling faster access to the data. Figure 19.1 represents a memory hierarchy in the form of a pyramid. It illustrated the slower the storage medium, the lower its cost and the greater its latency. So, when accessing data on a hard disk level, there are four layers between the accessed hard disk and the registers of the CPU, which takes a lot of time. For example, reading 1 MB of data from main memory takes 250.000 ns compared to 30.000.000 ns for hard disk.

During the last 30 years the performance of CPUs has developed enormously. This happened due to the high number of transistors built into CPUs and increased clock speeds. Due to the efficient production processes CPUs have become much cheaper.

Since the invention of the first multicore processor IBM POWER4 the CPU development industry has changed so that it is no longer focused on increasing clock rates but on growing the number of cores in CPUs. For example, while in 2001 the maximum number of cores was restricted to around 10 in 2016 already 1000+ cores were possible. Multicore processors help with in-memory data management

© The Author(s), under exclusive license to Springer Nature Switzerland AG 2022
S. Sarferaz, *Compendium on Enterprise Resource Planning*,
https://doi.org/10.1007/978-3-030-93856-7_19

Fig. 19.1   Storage hierarchy

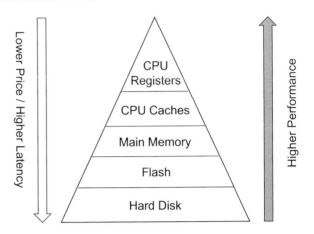

due to parallel processing on logical database partitioning. The application data stored in the database system is partitioned into individual subsets of data that are independent of each other. Those subsets of data are assigned to different CPU cores to allow parallel processing and increasing performance. Due to high performance of in-memory database systems capabilities like analytics, planning, predictions, or simulation can be performed on transactional data resulting from ERP business processes. Consequently, those capabilities add value to the business processes and allow rethinking them from scratch. That is the reason for having SAP HANA as the underlying in-memory database system for SAP S/4HANA.

Solution Capability

SAP HANA is a data management platform on which SAP S/4HANA is based on. The core of this data management platform is the SAP HANA database, an in-memory database management system which makes full use of the capabilities of current hardware to increase application performance, to reduce cost of ownership, and to enable new scenarios and applications that were not possible before. The SAP HANA database is a hybrid database management system that combines several paradigms in one system. It includes a full relational database management system where individual tables can be stored column-based or row-based in memory, and column-based on disk. It supports SQL, transactional isolation, and recovery and high availability. These capabilities are extended with for example analytics, text analysis and search, geo-spatial, time series, streaming and spatial processing. SAP HANA can combine and analyze all kinds of data within the same database management system which a core capability required by modern business applications. This enables developers to create new kinds of applications and it reduces complexity and cost, as no separate systems are required for analytical processing, searching, spatial data operations, graph data processing, or for planning and simulations.

In-Memory Concepts

The SAP HANA database is built for high performance applications. It makes full use of the main memory and processing power provided by modern hardware. All relevant data is kept in main memory, so all read operations can run in main memory. SAP HANA is also designed to make full use of multicore CPUs by parallelization of execution. Research showed that with in-memory column-based data stores performance improvements up to a factor of 1000 are possible in certain scenarios. With high performance for both read and write operations, the SAP HANA database supports transactional as well as analytical use cases. SAP HANA systems can be distributed across multiple servers to achieve good scalability in terms of both data volume and concurrent requests. Figure 19.2 summarizes the main concepts of in-memory database systems like SAP HANA.

In the past database management systems were designed for optimizing performance on hardware with limited main memory and with slow disk I/O as the main bottleneck. The focus was on improving disk access, for example the number of disk pages that were read into main memory was reduced when processing a query. Today's computer architectures have changed. With multicore processors, parallel processing is possible with accelerated interaction between processor cores. Very large main memory configurations are now commercially available and affordable. Server setups with hundreds of cores and several terabytes of main memory are a reality. Modern computer architectures create new possibilities but also new challenges. With all relevant data in memory, disk access is no longer a limiting factor for performance. As the number of cores increased, CPUs are enabled to process by far more data per time window. That means the performance bottleneck is now between the CPU cache and main memory.

Row and Column Store

From conceptual point of view, a database table is based on a two-dimensional data structure consisting of cells which are organized in rows and columns. However,

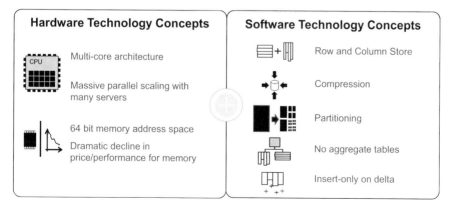

Fig. 19.2 In-memory concepts of SAP HANA

Table

Country	Product	Sales
US	Alpha	3000
US	Beta	1250
JP	Alpha	700
UK	Alpha	450

Row Store

Row1	US
	Alpha
	3000
Row2	US
	Beta
	1250
Row3	JP
	Alpha
	700
Row4	UK
	Alpha
	450

Column Store

Country	US
	US
	JP
	UK
Product	Alpha
	Beta
	Alpha
	Alpha
Sales	3000
	1250
	700
	450

Fig. 19.3 Table representation in row- and column-based storage

memory is structured as a linear sequence. For storing a table in linear memory, there are two options available as illustrated in Fig. 19.3. A row store stores a sequence of data records that contain the fields of one row. This is different in a column store where the data of a column is saved in successive memory locations.

SAP HANA supports two types of tables that store data either column- or row-wise. An existing table can be altered from columnar to row-based storage and vice versa.

Column-based tables are applied if

- On single or few columns, the calculations are executed
- Based on values of a few columns, the table is searched
- The table has a big number of columns
- Columnar operations (e.g., aggregate or scan) are necessary and the table has a big number of rows
- The majority of the columns consists of only some distinct values compared to the number of rows so that high compression rates can be realized

Row-based tables are applied if

- Only one single record must be processed at one time, for example many updates or selects of single records
- The complete record must be accessed by the application
- Compress rate is low as the columns encompass mainly distinct values
- Fast searching or aggregation is not needed
- The number of rows is low, for example, configuration tables

To ensure fast searching, ad-hoc reporting, on the fly aggregations, and to profit from compression, transaction data is usually stored in column tables. Master data is typically also put in the column store. Master data is frequently searched and often has columns with few distinct values. Master data is frequently joined with transactional data for analytical queries and aggregations. In SAP HANA this is most efficiently done using the analytical processing capabilities of the column store. The row store is used, for example, for metadata, for application server system tables, and for configuration data. In addition, application developers may decide to put business data in the row store if the criteria given above are matched.

Compression

The goal to keep all relevant data in main memory can be realized compressing the data. Due to columnar storage highly compression rates can be achieved without the need to apply sophisticated algorithms. There is data fragmentation by design as each column contains records with identical data type so that standard compression procedures like length encoding or cluster encoding can be easily applied. This is particularly efficient for SAP S/4HANA as most columns encompassing few distinct entries compared to the number of rows. Examples for this circumstance are country codes or foreign keys. Due to this degree of redundancy an effective compression is facilitated for column data. In contrast row-based storage contains data of different columns which results in lower data fragmentation and corresponding compression rates. Typically, with column-orientation compression factor of 5–10 can be realized compared to traditional row storage database systems. However, this is not always possible, depending on the characteristics of the data. Column-based storage is especially efficient for storing columns that contain only one distinct value. Such a column can be stored by just a few metadata and the single value. As mentioned, column-oriented data is stored closely together in blocks one after the other. Thus, there is no need to apply complex algorithms to locate the data first, then know the type of data and then compress the data. Thus, the data can be compressed at once and without complex algorithms, which results in a huge reduction of data size.

Partitioning

Furthermore, column storage facilitates parallel execution based on multiple processor cores. One advantage of the column-based approach is that data in a column store is already vertically partitioned by definition. That means operations on different columns can easily be processed in parallel.

If multiple columns are searched or aggregated, each of these operations can be assigned to a different processor core. Furthermore, operations on a single column can be parallelized by breaking it into many portions, each of which is processed by a different processing core, as shown in Fig. 19.4. Operations on single columns (e.g., searching or aggregations) can be performed as loops through an array stored in memory regions with columnar data organization. This process has a high spatial locality and makes good use of the CPU caches. The same operation is slower with row-oriented storage because data from the same column is distributed across memory and the CPU is slowed by CPU cache misses. Assuming that a row-based table is used to aggregate the sum of all sales amounts. Data transfer from main memory to CPU cache is always done in fixed-size blocks called *cache lines*, for

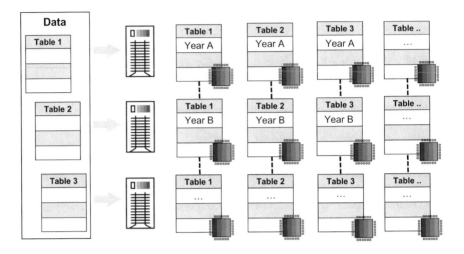

Fig. 19.4   Using partitioning to further leverage parallelism

example, 64 bytes. With row-based data organization, each cache line may contain only one sales value (stored in 4 bytes), while the remaining bytes are used for the data record's other fields. Each value required for the aggregation necessitates a new access to main memory. This shows that with row-based data organization, the operation is going to be slowed by cache misses, causing the CPU to wait until the required data is available. Because all sales values are saved in sequential memory with column-oriented storage, the cache line contains 16 values that are all demanded for the operation. Furthermore, because columns are stored in contiguous memory, memory controllers can use data prefetching to reduce the number of cache misses even further. As previously stated, columnar data organization enables highly efficient data compression. This not only saves memory but also improves performance. Data that has been compressed can be loaded into the CPU cache more quickly. As the data transfer between memory and CPU cache is the limiting factor, the performance increase outweighs the supplementary computing time required for decompression. If the operator is aware of the compression, it accelerates operations like scans and aggregations. Given a good compression rate, computing the sum of the values in a column will be much faster if the column is length encoded and many additions of the same value can be replaced by a single multiplication.

No Aggregate Tables

Materialized aggregates are used to improve read performance in traditional business applications. Additional tables are defined by the application developers in which the application stores the results of aggregates (such as sums) computed on other tables redundantly. Materialized aggregates are computed and stored at predetermined intervals or after each write operation on the aggregated data. Instead of computing the materialized aggregates each time, read operations simply access them. With scanning speeds of several megabytes per millisecond per CPU core, the SAP

HANA in-memory column store enables high-performance calculation of aggregates on large amounts of data on the fly. This eliminates the need for materialized aggregates in many cases. Financial applications, for instance, can compute totals and balances from the accounting documents when they are queried, instead of maintaining them as materialized values. There are several advantages to eliminating materialized aggregates. It simplifies data model and aggregation logic, which makes development and maintenance more efficient, it allows for a higher level of concurrency because write operations do not require exclusive locks for updating aggregated values, and it guarantees that aggregated values are always up to date, whereas materialized aggregates are sometimes only updated at predetermined intervals. In many cases, columnar storage eliminates the need for additional index structures. Storing data in columns already works as if each column had its own built-in index: The in-memory column store's column scanning speed and compression mechanisms already enable very high-performance read operations. Usually it is not required to have additional index structures. Eliminating indexes reduces memory size, can improve write performance, and reduces development efforts. However, this does not mean that indexes are not used at all in SAP HANA. Primary key fields always have an index and it is possible to create additional indexes, if required. In addition, full text indexes are used to support full-text search.

Insert-Only on Delta

SAP HANA supports history tables which allow queries on historical data which are also known as time-based queries. Applications may use this feature for example for time-based reporting and analysis. Existing records are not physically overwritten by write operations on history tables. Instead, write operations always insert new versions of the data record into the database. Current data refer to the most recent versions in history tables. All other versions of the same data object contain historical data. Each row in a history table has timestamp-like system attributes that indicate the time period when the record version in this row was the current one. Historical data is typically read by the execution of a query against a historical view of the database (SELECT ... AS OF time). *Alternatively, you can put a database session in history mode, so that all subsequent queries are processed against the historical view. In literature, data with time-based validity or visibility is known as temporal data. SQL:2011 covers support for temporal data, based on assigning time periods to table rows. The standard distinguishes two levels of temporal data support, which can be characterized as system-versioned and as application-managed. For temporal data versioned by the system, the timestamps are automatically entered and specify the transaction time when the data was current. New versions are automatically created by the system during updates. The history tables in SAP HANA correspond to system-versioned temporary data in SQL. The SQL:2011 concept of application time periods is different. Here the time period indicates the period of validity on application level. For instance, the planned assignment of an employee to a new department can be written to the database today, with a validity period that starts 3 weeks in the future. In this case two versions of the same employee record would exist, which are both current with respect to the transaction time but have different application-level validity periods. SQL:2011 includes several extensions for using application-level validity periods in SQL statements.*

Database Architecture

Traditional databases of online transaction processing systems don't make use of current hardware efficiently. It was depicted already in 1999 that with a memory resident traditional database management system, the CPU loses half of the execution time, for example in waiting until the data is loaded from memory into the CPU cache. A high-performance data management system for modern hardware must have the following characteristics:

- In-memory database: The data must be kept in main memory, so read operations can be executed without disk I/O. Disk storage is still needed to make changes durable.
- Cache aware memory organization, optimization, and execution: By design the number of CPU cache misses must be minimized and CPU stalls have to be avoided. One implementation option is to use column-based storage in memory. Search or operations which are applied on one column, are typically implemented as loops on data stored in contiguous memory arrays. This leads to high spatial locality of data and instructions, so the operations can be executed completely in the CPU cache without costly random memory accesses.
- Parallel execution support: In recent years CPUs did not become faster by increasing clock rates. Instead the number of processor cores was increased. Software must make use of multicore processors by allowing parallel execution and with architectures that scale well with the number of cores. For data management systems this means that it must be possible to partition data in sections for which the calculations can be executed in parallel. To ensure scalability, sequential processing—for example enforced by locking—must be avoided wherever possible.

The main building blocks of SAP HANA are depicted in Fig. 19.5. The servers for SAP HANA are certified by SAP. As mentioned before, SAP HANA is aware of the new hardware technologies and makes explicit use of advanced architecture elements—for example location of data in the different types of CPU caches. Because of this, it is important to ensure that only CPUs of the latest technology and types are used. In addition, for the overall processing a defined ratio of memory size to CPUs is important. Overall, with the certification approach SAP eliminates all potential issues of not-suitable hardware, this area of potential risks and issues is eliminated. At the same time, the SAP certification is open. With the advanced capabilities of SAP HANA in the area of parallelization and clustering it is possible to build high-end systems using commodity hardware. So, for high-end business systems it is no longer needed to purchase the expensive high-end Unix servers. SAP

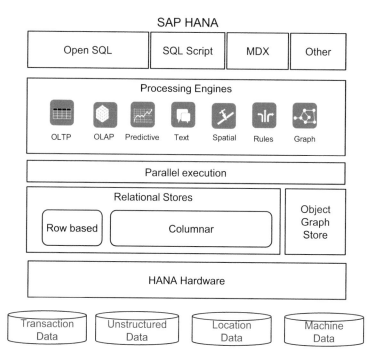

Fig. 19.5 SAP HANA architecture

HANA uses the commodity components to build a platform providing ultimate performance, scalability, and state-of-the-art high-availability and disaster recovery functions.

Now, let's move to the database layer. On the database layer, the already explained capabilities for row-based, column store, and parallel execution are implemented. The SAP HANA architecture is based on a parallel usage of completely independent services/processes. These processes have no interdependencies as SAP HANA uses a so-called *shared nothing* approach. With this approach scaling is possible very efficiently compared to traditional databases. The most important component in the layer is the index server. The index server comprises the in-memory data stores and the required engines for processing the data. The name server owns the information about the topology of an SAP HANA system. In a distributed system, the name server has the information about where the components are running, and which data is located on which server. In a system with multiple database containers, the name server has the information about existing database containers and it hosts the system database. In addition to providing database services, SAP HANA also provides the possibility to run code directly in the platform. There are so-called *engines* shipped by SAP. The principle is to run data-intensive operations close to the data. Before SAP HANA, typically calculations are done on the application server level. Sometimes this means that large amounts of data need to be transferred to the application server, where the analysis and calculation take place. And often, in the end a very small results set is generated. With SAP HANA, calculations which are data intensive are executed directly in the SAP HANA platform where the data resides. This dramatically reduces data movement and boosts performance. In this case SAP HANA returns only the result sets to the application server. There exists already a number of such SAP HANA engines including text analysis, predictive analytics, planning or OLAP. It also is possible to create custom code and *push it down* into the SAP HANA platform. SAP S/4HANA applications are a combination of business logic on the application server level and reuse engines as well as code-fragments executed directly in the SAP HANA platform. SAP HANA provides a broad range of open standard interfaces for applications. Starting from Open SQL or ODATA/JDBC/ODBC/JSON for data access there are interfaces for. Net connections, for the Java world, and for the Web world. This means that SAP HANA is not only a platform for SAP applications. It is easy to bring any type of third party or custom applications to SAP HANA. These applications benefit right away from the SAP HANA capabilities and over time, they can be optimized to leverage HANA even more, for example, by pushing down code to the platform.

Real-Time Analytics

The biggest advantage of the in-memory database SAP HANA is its capability of combining both online transactional (OLTP) and online analytical processing (OLAP) in the same system. Thus, the redundancies of analytical data are avoided, and real-time analytics provided. This approach is called hybrid paradigm, which allows to analyze data efficiently in the same database, so that there is no need any more to separate between systems, which has the disadvantage of using more processing power, time, and costs. This integration of both OLTP and OLAP in one server allows us to develop applications capable of providing fast and innovative solutions to business processes in enterprises. Figure 19.6 illustrates the difference between the traditional analytics and the hybrid transaction/analytics processing (HTAP) paradigm.

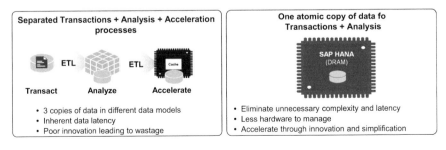

Fig. 19.6 Traditional analytics versus in-memory analytics

The traditional separation of OLTP and OLAP systems results in a complex, expensive, and maintenance-intensive analytics processing. OLAP systems are filled with the relevant data by extraction, transformation, and load (ETL) processes from OLTP systems. ETL processes are fault-prone and expensive to develop and operate. Extracting the data from an OLTP system creates a considerable load on the OLTP system which negatively impacts the performance of the transactional processes. The transformation of the data must ensure consistent results, especially when merging data from different sources. Usually the data loaded in the OLAP systems is already no more up to date as they might be already updated in the OLTP source. Thus, the analytics result is accordingly inaccurate. There are specific analytics use cases where the response time of the OLAP systems is not sufficient. Therefore, the data for such scenarios must be replicated based on ETL processes to accelerators to achieve the demanded analytical performance. Thus, the application data is copied three times which causes increased hardware and software costs. In addition, the data is not up to data which results in poor analytical conclusions. These challenges can be resolved by using SAP HANA to combine OLTP and OLAP. This reduces the effort for creating ETL processes, and allows analytics based on real time. In addition, the underlying analytical data is no longer aggregated, which enables a detailed and seamless drill-down, for example. SAP S/4HANA makes use of the hybrid transaction/analytics processing (HTAP) to incorporate systematically analytical capabilities in business processes.

Application Development

The SAP HANA database provides several programming and modeling options for executing application logic close to the data. This is required to make full use of the parallelization and optimization capabilities of SAP HANA and to reduce the amount of data that needs to be transported between the database and the application server. SAP HANA supports, for example, procedures, user-defined scalar functions, table-valued functions, and calculation views, which extend the standard view concept of SQL. SAP HANA comes with several libraries and built-in functions, for example for currency conversion, financial math, and predictive analytics. Let's have a closer look at why it is easier and faster to develop new applications on SAP HANA. First of all, SAP HANA's hybrid transactional analytical processing capabilities allow to create a new class of applications that deliver intelligence inside a business process. Furthermore, these applications can perform complex workloads at in-memory speed and deliver sub-second responses to users no matter where they are and what device they use. To further improve performance, the SAP HANA platform can be used to benefit from rapid inter-process communication and avoid transferring data between a database and an application server over an independent network. SAP HANA support for open standards and APIs and protocols, together with the ability to use programming language of choice allows to leverage existing skills. Specifically, SAP HANA provides a variety of standard application development languages for client-side, server-side, and algorithms development. For client-side development any language that works with standard interfaces can be chosen, such as JDBC (Java Database Connectivity), ODBC (Open Database Connectivity), and RESTful Web services. For server-side development SQLScript, JavaScript, or C++ can be leveraged. Furthermore, multidimensional query expressions are facilitated, for example, ODBO (OLE DB for OLAP) or MDX (multidimensional expressions). Developers benefit from built-in tools and integrations to implement, perform version-control, bundles, transport, and install applications through the entire lifecycle management. With SAP HANA support for CDS and OData, it is easier to extend existing SAP application and to incorporate cloud microservices easily. SAP HANA comes with a wealth of packaged components that can be reused to improve both developer productivity and app performance, for example, AFL, PAL, or AFM. These components are optimized to run inside the database and automatically deliver superior performance. Application function library (AFL) delivers ready-to-use procedures that can be called directly from SQLScript. All AFL functions run close to the data inside the SAP HANA database, for improved application performance. Predictive analytics library (PAL) contains over 100+ algorithms that allow to embed data mining and predictive scenarios into applications. Application function modeler (AFM) is a graphical editor in SAP HANA studio that helps connecting to PAL and use visualization and drag-and-drop capabilities to decrease development effort. Algorithms and business logic can be leveraged using either C++ or R script. Figure 19.7 depicts the possible application architecture using SAP HANA.

SAP HANA allows to use the runtime environment that better suites the applications needs. If developers are extending SAP applications, they can use native constructs (e.g., CDS views) and data models and the full ABAP environment—on premise and in the cloud. This approach has been chosen for the implementation of SAP S/4HANA. If developers are developing in Java or in a. Net environment they can leverage any third-party application server and via standard interfaces (e.g., ODBC, JDBS). Developers can also use the SAP HANA application server and benefit from inter-process communications and avoid data swapping.

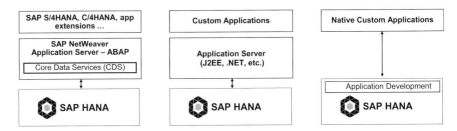

Fig. 19.7 Possible application architecture

Conclusion

SAP HANA is the underlying database system for SAP S/4HANA. This is an in-memory and column-based database management system. The in-memory technology is enabled due to price erosion of RAM and the increase of CPU cores. Thus, application data can be kept in memory for fast execution of database operations. Due column-orientation, partitioning, and compressing are improved which result in additional performance boost. Consequently, analytical processing is also reinforced which facilitates combining analytical and transactional data. Therefore, real-time analytical capabilities are incorporated into SAP S/4HANA transactional applications. This is a dramatical innovation compared to the traditional paradigm where transactional data must be replicated to data warehouses for analytics. Hence, hardware, software, and operations costs are reduced and more accurate analytics for decision-making is provided.

Virtual Data Model

20

This chapter focuses on the virtual data model (VDM), which is a semantical layer to access application data of SAP S/4HANA. Thus, the cryptical and complex data model is encapsulated and exposed in an understandable and reusable way for application developers and various frameworks. VDM consists of Core Data Service (CDS) views. Business data, which is stored in abstract database tables, gets exposed in a business-oriented way. This allows easier understanding and consumption of needed business data. End users can access needed data by using released CDS views. They can define custom views that are built on top of existing views delivered by SAP. With VDM, an understandable, comprehensive, and executable data model is exposed, ready to be consumed in analytical and transactional applications and external interfaces.

Business Requirement

The data model of ERP systems is historically grown and covers ten thousands of tables with complex network of relationships and cryptical field names. Thus, the data model is hard to explore and consume by developers, customers, and partners. Due to this circumstance the implementation of business processes results in high efforts and demands very specialized knowledge. To resolve this challenge a corresponding semantical layer is required on top of the data model in order to hide the complexity and allow a human-understandable and efficient access to the business data. Today even end users expect to query needed data by themselves, like in a self-service Business Intelligence system. However, this is tough to achieve in ERP systems due to data model hurdles in terms of finding data, providing adequate Query-Response times, and understanding the structures. Designing a virtual data model solves these issues and gives also end users access to data they need.

© The Author(s), under exclusive license to Springer Nature Switzerland AG 2022
S. Sarferaz, *Compendium on Enterprise Resource Planning*,
https://doi.org/10.1007/978-3-030-93856-7_20

Solution Capability

The *virtual data model (VDM)* represents the semantic data model of a business application in SAP S/4HANA. The goal is to simplify the complexity and provide business data in a way that eases its understanding and consumption for developers and end users. It abstracts data from the underlying database tables and exposes it based on business semantics. In order to ensure this, two requirements have to be fulfilled:

- Database views need to support more than SQL. Things like, for example, look up the last record, pivot the data, split data to process it differently, and data quality checks cannot be done in a single SQL query.
- The views need to return the data in sub seconds. The system will not be used if a good performance is not given.

SAP customers and partners can develop on released VDM views. VDM represents the data model and source for transactional and analytical applications and external interfaces. Benefits of VDM are a business-oriented, understandable and semantically rich, reusable, and stable data model.

Core Data Services (CDS)

The virtual data model is implemented by using Core Data Services (CDS). CDS helps developers to create semantically rich data models. It uses and extends SQL and allows to define and consume these data models in applications. The productivity, consumability, performance, and interoperability get improved. CDS is a family of domain-specific languages and services for defining and consuming such semantically enriched data models:

- **Data Definition Language** (DDL) for defining semantically rich domain data models and retrieve them. It extends native SQL means for higher productivity.
- **Query Language** (QL) for consuming CDS entities via platform embedded SQL. It is used to read data.
- **Data Control Language** (DCL) defines authorizations for CDS views and controls the access to data. It integrates with classic authorization concepts.
- **Data Manipulation Language** (DML) is used to write data.

CDS data models are defined and consumed on database level rather than on application level. CDS offers capabilities beyond traditional data modeling tools. They support SQL-compliant definition of views so that developers can use SQL features, such as *JOIN, UNION,* and *WHERE* clause. Relations between views can be modeled as associations. Aliases can be used to rename tables with an understandable name. CDS views also support the use of annotations to define metadata. For example, an annotation can define that a field with type *DateTime*

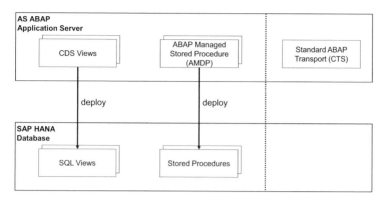

Fig. 20.1 Top-down approach

contains the time when the data was created or last updated. Other CDS capabilities used in VDM are parameters, view extends, easy exposure as OData services, and anchor for behavior definitions. Annotations of the virtual data model allow classifying CDS entities in terms of their admissible reuse options and provisioned content. This classification is used only for SAP internal structuring and interpretation of the CDS entities. It is envisioned to be interpreted for instance by view browsers and other capability which is based on the virtual data model. Re-leasing CDS entities for customers and partners is controlled by an additional dedicated internal classification of the entities.

CDS is fully integrated into ABAP, the proprietary programming language of SAP. It is embedded in ABAP SQL, which results in easier-to-understand SQL statements. CDS views are also integrated with the ABAP data dictionary (DDIC). The ABAP DDIC contains all metadata about the data in the SAP system including different views. Existing ABAP authorizations can be used, and the ABAP transport system is used. Figure 20.1 shows the connection of the ABAP Application Server and the SAP S/4HANA database when using the recommended top-down approach. Developers can work in their ABAP environment and still use the power of SAP S/4HANA.

The top-down approach uses the *Code Pushdown* technique. Code Pushdown means that calculations are performed on the database system instead of the application server. It only pushes down calculations for which it makes sense. For example, to determine the amount of all positions of invoices, an aggregation function (here: SUM()) could be used on the database instead of calculating the sum in a loop on the application server. This results in a fast retrieval of data and a better performance and response time of the application itself. The classic SAP ERP supported various database systems for which a corresponding data access abstraction was required. Therefore, business data was first transferred from database to the application server, looped for relevant records, and finally processed. Thus, usually more data was exchanged between database and application server as necessary. Furthermore, data intensive operations were executed on the application server instead of on the

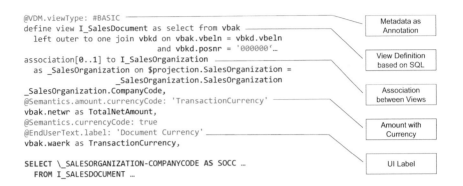

```
@VDM.viewType: #BASIC
define view I_SalesDocument as select from vbak
  left outer to one join vbkd on vbak.vbeln = vbkd.vbeln
                           and vbkd.posnr = '000000'…
association[0..1] to I_SalesOrganization
  as _SalesOrganization on $projection.SalesOrganization =
                           _SalesOrganization.SalesOrganization
_SalesOrganization.CompanyCode,
@Semantics.amount.currencyCode: 'TransactionCurrency'
vbak.netwr as TotalNetAmount,
@Semantics.currencyCode: true
@EndUserText.label: 'Document Currency'
vbak.waerk as TransactionCurrency,

SELECT \_SALESORGANIZATION-COMPANYCODE AS SOCC …
  FROM I_SALESDOCUMENT …
```

Metadata as Annotation	
View Definition based on SQL	
Association between Views	
Amount with Currency	
UI Label	

Fig. 20.2 Example for CDS view

database to achieve better performance. As SAP S/4HANA supports only SAP HANA as database, dramatic optimization could be realized. For each CDS view defined on ABAP level a corresponding SQL view on SAP HANA is generated. All SQL statements applied on the CDS views are pushed down to the SQL view and executed on the database level for optimal performance. For example, while authorization checks were accomplished in the past on the application server, with SAP S/4HANA they are pushed down to the database system by automatically enhancing the SQL statements with an *WHERE* clause. In-between several ten thousands of CDS views are available in SAP S/4HANA as all business processes are using VDM to access application data. Consequently, the performance of all those business processes have been improved systematically as all data access is pushed down to SAP HANA. CDS views can be defined with SQL statements but they can also be coded with SQLScript. ABAP Managed Stored Procedures (AMDP) are used for this. AMDPs are just ABAP classes containing SQLScript code instead of ABAP. During runtime the SQLScript coding is pushed down to SAP HANA for optimal performance. Whenever the logic of the CDS view is too complex to be expressed by SQL statements, the scripted approach is applied. From consumption point of view there is no difference between CDS views based on SQL or SQLScript.

CDS views are the most important CDS entity type. There are released CDS views ready for reuse in VDM. Customers can also define custom CDS views. For example, they can be used as the data source in ABAP select statements. Figure 20.2 provides an example for a CDS view concerning sales documents.

Authorizations for CDS Views

CDS views which expose sensitive or data privacy and protect relevant data must be secured. The access to CDS views can be restricted and is expressed by roles. A repository named DCL Source defines CDS roles. A CDS role is applied to one or more CDS views. Access conditions are defined with the key word *WHERE* and function as a filter for the corresponding CDS view. The access restrictions are automatically applied to direct ABAP SQL selects on their protected CDS views. If a single CDS view has multiple rules, the access restrictions are combined by a logical OR by default. It can also be explicitly defined as replacing DLCs or as using combination mode AND. This means that the results of querying a CDS view can be restricted by using DCL so that only users with a corresponding role can read the returned data. It is important to note that CDS access control only works if a program accesses directly the protected CDS view.

Stability Contracts for CDS Views

CDS views are the basis for defining a semantically rich VDM and exposing all business data of the SAP S/4HANA database in an understandable way. They are used for different purposes, for example, providing an interface between applications and add-ons in the same stack and for remote systems and applications. Customers can use released CDS views provided by SAP to create their own custom views. To fulfill these functions reliably, CDS views have to find a balance between two properties:

- Flexibility: CDS views have to offer a certain degree of flexibility for further development.
- Stability: Semantic and technical features should be kept sufficiently stable so that CDS views do not need to be adjusted after each upgrade.

Released CDS views for SAP S/4HANA view model provide a stable basis for customer extension scenarios, for example, creating custom views or analytical queries. They must support specific stability criteria to ensure that custom built objects are not affected when the SAP S/4HANA system is upgraded. SAP has introduced three stability contracts to ensure that released CDS views fulfill their tasks reliably. Each contract applies to different consumption scenarios of CDS views.

Key User Field Extensibility Contract (C0)
The contract for key user field extensibility ensures that changes to a CDS view do not break the anchors of field extensions. Key users can add a custom field using the Custom Fields and Logic app. Consumer can use extension fields like regular fields. Only CDS views that SAP has defined as extensible are available for field extension in the app. The anchors of the extension are elements that are kept stable for key user field extensibility. C0 is not expressed via the API state of a CDS view. Instead, it is defined by publishing a CDS view in the extensibility registry.

System Internal Contract (C1)
CDS views can be released either for system internal use or for remote API use. The majority of released CDS views follow the stability contract C1 for internal use. The contract's goal is to ensure sufficient stability so that custom CDS views still work

after an upgrade to the next software version, for example, from SAP S/4HANA 1809 to SAP S/4HANA 1909. Only SAP views released for C1 contract are available in key user tools for customer extensions. Such CDS views have the following properties:

- CDS views released for system internal use start with the prefix I_ (interface views) or C_ (consumption views). Not all these interface and consumption views follow the C1 contract.
- Field length extension is allowed and must be tolerated by consumers.
- They are available in several key user tools, for example, Custom CDS Views, Custom Fields, and Logic and Custom Business Objects.

Main stability criteria for C1-released CDS views are:

- No deletion of fields
- No renaming of fields
- Restricted changes of data typing of fields
- Semantic stability of view processing and fields
- Stability of selected view annotations relevant for data processing

Remote API Contract (C2)

Some CDS views need to be accessed by remote APIs. External services, such as OData, make this remote access possible. SAP releases such CDS views for the C2 contract. The views are not available in key user tools. Field length extension is not possible. This keeps more elements stable than the contract C1 for internal use. The main use case of remote API views is that they perform basic database functions (updating, retrieving, deleting) in scenarios in which applications interact with an external client. After release of such a view incompatible changes are forbidden. If necessary new view versions must be created and released.

Naming Conventions of VDM

The VDM is based on a set of common naming rules. Following rules guarantee consistent and self-explanatory names:

- Names should be precise and uniquely identify a subject. For example, a sale order document should be named *SalesOrder* and not *ID* or *Order*.
- Names capture the business semantics of a subject.
- Different subjects must have different names. If two fields use the same name it implies that their underlying value lists match.
- Names are generated from English terms in camel case notation with an uppercase first letter. Underscores are used in predefined cases only. Abbreviations should be avoided if possible. They can be used to stay within a given character limit. For example, *Query* can be abbreviated as *Qry*.

These naming rules apply to all CDS entities and their parts, for example, field names, associations, parameters, or CDS views. The basic pattern for VDM View Names is <VDM prefix> <semantic name> <?suffix>. VDM prefixes represent the VDM view type which are described in the next section. Examples are I_ for an interface view, C_ for a consumption view, and A_ for remote API views. The semantic name describes the business semantics of a single record returned by the view. Suffixes are optional. Example VDM view names are I_Customer or I_TaxCodeText for interface views and C_SupplierEvaluation or C_GoodsMovementQuery for consumption views.

Structure of the Virtual Data Model

VDM views follow a layered approach and are organized in a hierarchical structure. Upper layers select from and define associations to the same or lower layers. Lower layers cannot select from or define associations to upper layers. VDM views are assigned to layers by using a special CDS annotation @*VDM.viewType*. Figure 20.3 shows the stack of VDM views. There are two layers, the Interface View Layer including Composite and Basic Views and the Consumption View Layer including Consumption and External API Views. The interface view layer provides views to reuse. Consumption and external API views are based on the lower layers and built for a given purpose. The following paragraphs describe different views of VDM.

Basic Views
Basic views are the lowest level of the VDM view stack and placed on top of the database tables. They are the only views that access the database tables directly what makes them the most important component of the VDM. Basic views have the following main purposes:

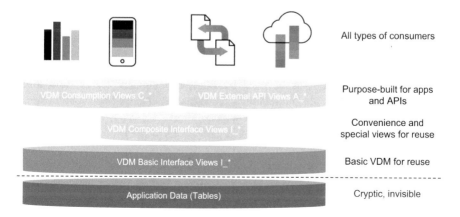

Fig. 20.3 Stack of VDM views

- All other views are based on them. Basic views serve as reusable building blocks for other nonbasic VDM views. This means that other views do not need to directly select from the database tables.
- Nontransparent, hard to understand names of table fields in the database layer are renamed in terms of business semantics. The result are more transparent and understandable field names.
- Basic views facilitate an abstraction from the database tables to semantically higher layers.

Composite Views

Composite views provide further functionality on top of the basic views. Primarily they serve as reusable building blocks for other views. They can also be defined to support a specific consumption domain. For example, analytical cube views can be defined, which consolidate data sources for usage in multiple analytical queries.

Transactional Views

Transactional views are special composite views. They define the data model of a business object and support defining its transactional processing-related aspects. Transactional views can have elements that support the transactional processing logic, for example, additional fields that preserve user input temporarily. The views are only used in the context of transactional processing.

Consumption Views

Regular basic views are defined independent of a specific use case so that they support any use case. On the other hand, consumption views are intentionally designed for a given purpose. They are expected to be directly used in a specific consumption scenario. For example, a consumption view can provide exactly the data and metadata needed for a specific user interface element.

Restricted Reuse Views

The described basic and composite views are part of the interface layer with the I_ prefix by default, which means they can be used by any SAP application. They can also be used by SAP customers and partners once they are released. Sometimes development teams define basic and composite views that are meant to be used only in their own applications. In such cases a restricted reuse view with the R_ prefix is defined. Such views cannot be used by other development teams from other applications. Examples are transactional processing-enabled views, which expose internal functions and operations of a business object.

Remote API Views

Remote API views can be consumed external and represent the functionality of a single business object model. The system internal VDM model, which can evolve over time, gets decoupled from its external consumers. A stable interface is established. To allow the use of the remote API views, OData services are defined.

The OData services get published and are ready to be consumed by remote applications.

Consumption Scenarios

The most used consumption scenarios supported by CDS entities are analytics, SAP Fiori UI applications, enterprise search, and remote APIs. The following figures show two typical VDM view stacks for analytical and transactional processing-enabled applications. Use case specific views are defined on top of reusable basic and composite views. The data model and functionality get adapted to the individual application needs.

Analytical Applications

Analytical applications are based on cube views and a network of associated views. They are used to monitor and analyze data. On top of the VDM stack in Fig. 20.4 are one or more analytical query views, which project the envisioned functionality from its underlying cube view. The cube view is associated to dimension views in the interface layer. These dimension views are associated to other dimension and text views within their own layer. The basic views select data from database tables. The analytical query views are not executed on the database but on selections from the cube.

Transactional Applications

Transactional processing-enabled applications represent a second consumption scenario. The model in Fig. 20.5 is based on transactional views. The transactional

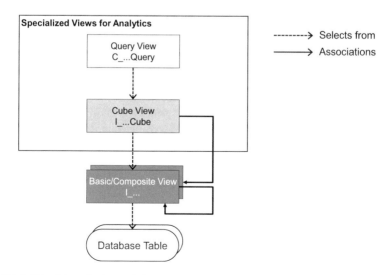

Fig. 20.4 View hierarchy for analytics

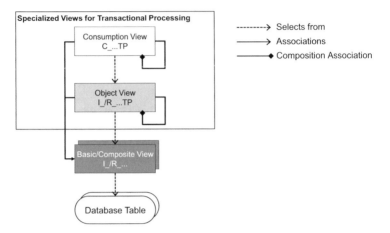

Fig. 20.5 View hierarchy for transactional processing

views are related through compositional associations and establish an entire business object. The consumption view pictures relevant functionality and expands the data model with annotations to render the UI application built on the view. The lower layers of the VDM stack select data from the database tables and provide them to higher layers. It is recommended to develop transactional applications by using the ABAP RESTful Application Programming Model.

Conclusion

The introduction of VDM allows end users to query the needed data in ERP systems by themselves. It has the character of a self-service business intelligence scenario. VDM exposes data from database tables in a business-oriented way to ease its understanding and consumption. It consists of CDS views. CDS views are based on Open SQL. The semantically enriched data model makes the model easier to understand. By given naming conventions it is declarative in nature and remarkably close to conceptual thinking. Another main advantage of VDM is the reusability. Once built and released, VDMs can be consumed by many different applications. Since the CDS views exist on the application layer, existing ABAP security can be used to protect CDS views. As coding is pushed down to the database server, calculations can be executed close to data. Thus, the response time and the performance of applications are improved. VDM provides a data model for applications, that is business-oriented, understandable, reusable, stable, and executed on the database. It uses well-known business terminology, documents relationships between entities, and enriches the entities with additional business semantics for better understanding.

Transactional Programming Model

21

This chapter focuses on the transaction programming model of SAP S/4HANA, which enables the implementation of business applications. Particularly data modeling and behavior, business services provisioning, service consumption, and business object runtime types are explained. Transactions are a key component of every ERP system and are the foundation for implementing business processes.

Business Requirement

Every system, which stores information, needs to manage how data is accessed. Especially systems which handle many concurrent actions are at risk of data corruption if the same data is accessed by multiple users or systems concurrently. ERP systems experience heavy and frequent data modification from many users simultaneously. Write operations can overwrite each other and thus corrupt data. This is especially problematic if more than one dataset is modified; hence invalid relations between different datasets can be caused. To prevent such corruption scenarios and protect data integrity, transactions are introduced. Besides system events, like system failures or power outages, a write operation can fail in a couple of scenarios:

- **Dirty Reads**: A dataset is read, while another user or system writes to the very same dataset. If the read happens after the dataset is modified but the write operation fails, the dataset is left in an invalid state and cannot be reverted. As soon as the operation needs to write the previously read data, the invalid state is again saved. There is no way for the system to revert the malicious write, and the database remains in a faulty state.
- **Non-repeatable Read**: Another problem can occur if an operation needs to read the same dataset multiple times in its execution time. If another operation writes in between the read operations, the following reads access the modified data even though the unmodified data is expected. This leads to undefined behavior and

© The Author(s), under exclusive license to Springer Nature Switzerland AG 2022
S. Sarferaz, *Compendium on Enterprise Resource Planning*,
https://doi.org/10.1007/978-3-030-93856-7_21

may produce inconsistent data as well as hard-to-reproduce errors during development.

- **Phantom Reads**: The problem describes a scenario like the non-repeatable read. In this case, data aggregation is performed on multiple datasets. The first time the data is loaded all entities are returned. If another operation adds or deletes a dataset, the aggregation may be invalid. If the same request is repeated, some entries might be missing or may be appearing for the first time. In ERP systems, this may also be very important, as analytics are often based on such aggregations and new datasets are added frequently.

Therefore, a robust approach for managing concurrent database access is needed, to prevent all kinds of problems and to ensure database integrity as well as database validity. One possible and the most used method is the use of transactions. The programming model for transactional applications must consider and resolve those anomalies. Furthermore, it must ensure an efficient and enterprise ready for implementing business applications from database design to developing the business logic and the user interfaces.

Solution Capability

Within the scope of computer science, a transaction describes operations, which are inherently small. Therefore, every process consists of several atomic steps. As these transactions cannot be divided, they may succeed or fail as a complete work unit. In no circumstance can a transaction be only partially completed.Transactions are primarily used in database systems to ensure that the saved data are always in a valid state, as partial writes to the database are impossible. If an invalid write is detected, the whole transaction needs to be aborted and may be retried at a later stage. Transactions adhere to the four pillars of the *ACID* principle:

- **Atomicity**: All changes which are introduced into a dataset by a transaction are atomic. Either all changes happen at once or none happen at all. Changes can be arbitrary operations working with the dataset, meaning all operations which read, process, modify, or write data.
- **Consistency**: The database is always in a consistent state. Every transaction starts from a consistent database. After the transaction is processed, the database is again in a consistent state. In case an error occurs, the stored database contents are not changed, in order not to violate any integrity constraint.
- **Isolation**: The transactions' execution is undetermined, and the transactions may be executed in parallel. Every transaction's execution is isolated from other transactions. Every transaction sees only the database at the start of this transaction as well as its own changes.
- **Durability**: If a transaction is successfully executed and the database is again in a consistent state, the changes are permanently persisted. Even in the event of a power outage or a system crash, the changes remain saved.

Even though transactions have benefits like allowing multiple users to access and modify data at once, there are some drawbacks, too. Primarily the setup and management costs of a transaction system can take a hefty toll on development and computational resources. As described by Jim Gray and Andreas Reuter, "a transaction processing system provide tools to ease or automate application programming, execution and administration of complex, distributed applications" with "a database representing some real-world state" (Jim Gray 1999, S. 10).

S/4HANA aims to ease implementation of such functionalities as well as accelerate development progress. As such S/4HANA incorporates a transaction model as part of the RESTful programming model (RAP). The programming model follows the ACID principle (SAP Help Portal 2021). The next chapter takes a closer look at the technicalities of S/4HANA's transactional programming model.

RESTful Programming Model

SAP S/4HANA is based on an architecture designed to support and rely on transactions and builds on top of them. All business logic and interfaces are intertwined with the transactional programming model through the ABAP RESTful programming or RAP for short. With changing requirements and technology changes the programming models of the ABAP application server have changed over time. Figure 21.1 shows a historical overview over the programming models. With these iterations, the way how data integrity is handled also changed.

Classic Programming Model

The initial programming model was the classic ABAP programming model, which was used in releases 7.5 and earlier. Developers created a basic data model. Data integrity was ensured by foreign key definitions, which referenced other parts of data. With NetWeaver 7.4 a major change was introduced: The Core Data Services (CDS). CDS views and the relations between them could be defined through the data model. However, CDS views were read-only, and the resulting developing abilities were limited. Transactional operations could not be used.

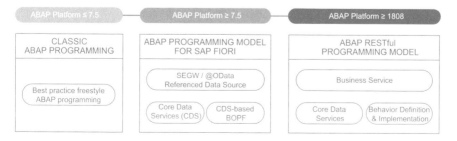

Fig. 21.1 Historical evolution of transactional programming model

ABAB Programming Model for SAP Fiori

With the release 7.5 and newer versions, the new ABAP programming model is available. For the first time, the model supports transactional applications. Special annotations can define connections between the CDS and Business Object Processing Framework (BOPF), which internally enable support for transaction-oriented behavior. Additional validations and actions could be implemented in ABAP. CDS views can be implemented through the SAP Gateway services and can be exposed as OData services. However, as both the CDS and the BOPF are model-frameworks, additional development efforts were needed, as both required to be maintained at the same time. Additionally, the frameworks acted very differently in terms of developer experience and error handling, further complicating the development of transactional applications.

ABAP RESTful Programming Model

With the release 1808 of the ABAP environment, the new RESTful programming model is introduced. The programming model aims to solve the previously mentioned problems. The RAP model uses the CDS views, and transactional services can be added through the behavior definitions. The logic which defines the data model as well as the behavior is exposed as business services and can be used by different applications and services like SAP Fiori.

Since the introduction of this programming model, it serves as the basis of SAP S/4HANA. Goal of this model is to separate the architecture in several layers. For example, the user interface is separated from the application logic, which itself is separated from the database. Figure 21.2 shows an overview of these layers.

First, a business object is defined through the already mentioned CDS views and its behavior. The data model is specified by entities and their structure. CDS entities, which define business object nodes, are referred to as transactional views. Additionally, relations can be expressed through compositions and associations to allow

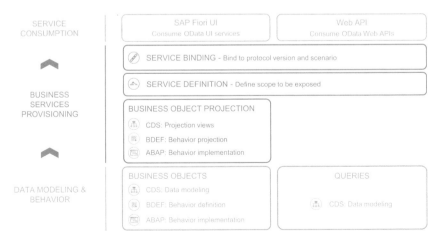

Fig. 21.2 RESTful programming model

transactional access. The behavior definition represents the transactional behavior by declaring all operations, which are accessible through the business object. Such operations cover create, update, delete actions, as well as other application-specific actions. The behavior definition also defines locking, authorization, feature control for declared operations, and ETag handling for HTTP consumption. ETags or entity tags are part of the HTTP protocol and help to determine changes of a resource, for example, in caching scenarios to minimize redundant data transfer. On top of this layer, business object projections and services can be defined, which are used by SAP Fiori and remote applications. The next chapter goes into detail on how the RESTful programming model and how the transaction programming model are used to guarantee data integrity.

Transaction Model

The transaction model as part of the virtual data model (VDM) serves as a foundation for all processes supported by SAP S/4HANA. All operations, which work with data, are handled through the online transaction processing (OLTP) and the transaction programming model. Goal of these approaches is the transparent handling of transactions without interruptions and without disturbing the user experience. In SAP S/4HANA a transaction defines changes between multiple states. Transactions have a buffer and a two-phase lifecycle, in which the phases or logical units of work (LUW) are managed through the ABAP runtime. The transactional buffer stores the current state and all modifications (Fig. 21.3).

Fig. 21.3 Transaction lifecycle

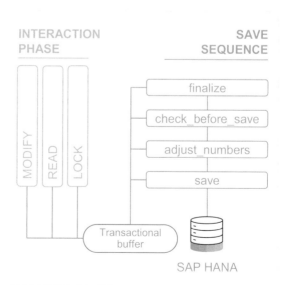

The lifecycle is split up into two phases, each having a special purpose. These phases are:

- Interaction Phase: The information contained within at least one entity of one or more business objects is modified. This phase can be invoked through a user or a service through OData APIs.
- Save Phase: The changed business objects are processed to achieve a durable, persisted state within the database. As a result, further application logic is executed to validate and ensure that data consistency is checked before the changes are finally committed to the database.

Internally, the phases are again subdivided into subphases which are controlled by the runtime. The runtime follows a sequence for processing all entities which make up the transaction.

The Interaction Phase

The interaction phase marks the beginning of an operation. As soon as the user opens a view, the interaction phase starts. The phase follows a set of structured steps, which are executed one after the other and are controlled by the runtime. Only if the previous step is finished successfully, the next step is started. In case there is an error, the whole save operation is aborted and no data is modified. As the name implies, the interaction phase is the last opportunity in which data can be modified by an application before it is written to the underlying database and persisted. Figure 21.4 illustrates these steps and their execution order.

Authorization Checks

The runtime checks if the modifying user has the necessary roles and permissions to be allowed to access this data or these operations. An example for these checks is the comparison of the role of the current user with the roles defined by the Data Control Language (DCL) of the current view.

Feature Control

The feature control oversees which operations (create, update, delete, actions, functions) are enabled for a given business object. During this step, the runtime checks if the data and the invoked actions are enabled. For this, static feature controls are checked, which define if an operation or field is available in general. For example, internal operations might not be allowed to be accessed by other actions,

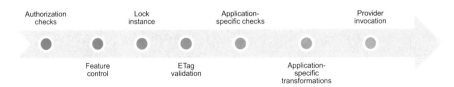

Fig. 21.4 Interaction phases

and fields are read-only. Global feature control defines if an operation is enabled or disabled independently of instances. Instance feature control, on the other hand, define accessibility by the instances itself.

Lock Instance
The entity is locked to prevent further, possibly conflicting, writes. Entities can be defined as *master* or *dependent*. In this case, even if a depending entity is accessed, the master entity locks the whole composition.

ETag Validation
This step checks if the ETag matches the currently stored ETag. The ETag or entity tag is part of the HTTP protocol and serves to determine if a resource was modified. As such, this step is only executed if the operation was invoked through an HTTP request. If data was modified in the meantime, the entity tag is changed and incoming ETag does not match anymore. In this case, a save cannot be performed automatically, and the data must be merged.

Application-Specific Checks
Every application can add additional checks. For example, an application can provide additional authorization checks or additional logic checks.

Application-Specific Transformations and Augmentations
If all previous steps could be completed successfully, additional data transformations and augmentations can be applied. This step is only executed for projections.

Provider Invocation
Finally, as the last step before the data can be saved, the provider can be invoked. The provider can execute different actions depending on its implementation and its type. These operations can include further checks, like authorization on a given instance or if instance feature control allows access to the instance action. Furthermore, the provider can invoke further actions, validations, and determinations.

The Save Phase
If all data modifications are concluded, the transaction can be finalized. For this, a commit is executed. The save phase consists of five steps following a *save sequence*, which focuses on saving the changed data as well as checking the data for validity. Each step is executed by the RAP runtime. Like the interaction phase, per step every entity is processed, before the next step can be started. Only if a precious step is succeeded, the next step can be started. Otherwise, the transaction aborts to protect database integrity (Fig. 21.5).

Fig. 21.5 The save sequence

Finalize

The save phase starts with the finalize step. In this step, every entity is executing validations and determinations. Application-specific logic can be executed to further enhance the validation. Target of this step is to process an entity to reach its final state, which can be stored in the database.

Check Before Save

The *check before save* step validates the consistency. It checks if the final state can be stored in the database. The finalize and this check before save steps have a special behavior if an error is detected. If the save was not invoked through an HTTP request but though the user interface, the save is rejected, and the user is returned to the interaction phase. This enables the user to correct invalid inputs before invoking the save once again.

Draw Numbers

Draw numbers adjust the numbering of entities, especially if gapless numbers or rather late numberings are enabled. This is necessary because of legal reasons.

Save

The save step oversees writing to the underlying database.

Cleanup

If all entity could be saved, the transaction is nearly complete. In the last cleanup step, the internal state is cleaned. This contains resetting internal states, as well as clearing the transactional buffer, which contained the now saved entities.

Thus, the consistency is checked multiple times spanning all phases of the transaction lifecycle. It is important to point out what happens in case the save phase detects an inconsistent state. In case of such an event, SAP S/4HANA prevents write operations as part of the save phase, hence ensuring the database is always consistent. Instead, the transaction returns to the interaction phase, thereby allowing changes to be made. If a transaction originates from a machine request instead of a user input, the request is considered faulty and the request is rejected. Even if there is an incident, after data is written to the database, consistency is not compromised. In this case a transaction rollback is issued, thus restoring a valid database state.

Application Development

Development on the SAP S/4HANA platform can take place in different forms, which differ significantly. In general, development can take the form of two approaches: A green field and a brown field approach.

Green Field

Green field or managed deployments signify the optimal usage experience with the platform. These are characterized by a fresh start. New implementations can use all functionalities to an optimal extent. One of these features is the managed provider. Managed providers can take over many of the steps involved in saving and checking data. Standard CRUD (Create, Read, Update, Delete) operations work out of the box, without developer intervention, thus accelerating development. If at any point additional business object-specific functionality or business logic is needed, the default implementation can be changed to support such cases.

Brown Field

Brown field or unmanaged deployments on the other hand are use cases, in which some parts already exist. This is typically the case when migrating from older versions. Unmanaged providers need to implement all the steps of the interaction phase, as well as in the save phase. To support the use of preexisting code and enable backward- compatibility, adapters are introduced. These adapters can be used to integrate these functionalities into the new runtime. Therefore, in unmanaged deployments, the developers are currently still in charge of the business object runtime and the CRUD operations.

Figure 21.6 shows the order of implementation. The starting point is the data model which is defined by the CDS. Next, the developer adds behavior, either by manually adding the required operations in an unmanaged provider or using validations offered by a managed environment. At that point, the lock object and authority object are available for use, for example, in the interaction phase of a transaction. Additionally, the now existing functionality can be tested by creating unit and integration tests. As the next step, the corresponding projections for both the data model and the behavior are added. The service definition is supplemented to specify which entities will be exposed, and finally the service binding is created. This also defines the necessary roles, which will be validated at the start of the interaction phase.

It is also important to point out that the development is accelerated as ABAP already implements many validators, which are ready to use. Especially in managed environments, validators can be implemented by writing only a small number of lines in a declarative way. The environment can then generate all the necessary implementations on its own.

Example

In this section an example is explained to demonstrate how these models are used. This example contains code snippets of an application which models travel plans. The main parts, which change with the new programming model, are the CDS behavior definition as well as the CDS behavior projection. In this example a simple service is defined:

```
define service ZMH_Travel_SD {
  expose ZMH_C_Travel as Travel
}
```

This service exposes a projection of a travel entity:

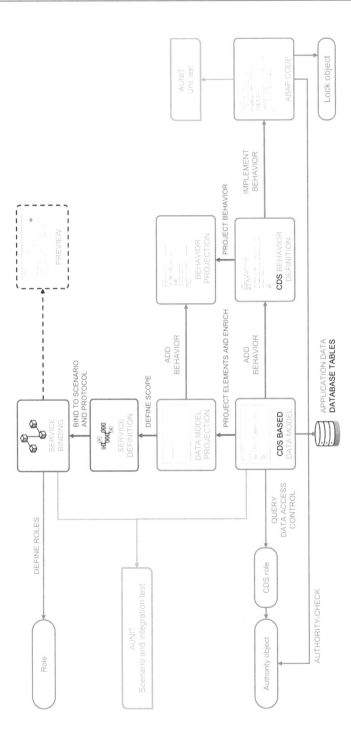

Fig. 21.6 Relations and development order

```
define root view entity ZMH_C_Travel
  as projection on ZMH_I_Travel
  {
    Key travel_id as Travel_ID,
```

The projection follows an interface view:

```
define root view ZMH_I_Travel
  as select from zmh_travel as Travel
  {
    Key travel_id,
```

With these basics, the next step is to create the missing CDS behavior definition. This example uses managed approach (greenfield). Other properties, which are specified, are the name of the class, the behavior name, which database to write to, and the locking behavior. The lock is engaged on the master if any changes are made.

```
managed implementation in class zmh_bp_i_travel unique;
define behavior for ZMH_I_Travel alias travel
persistent table zmh_travel
lock master
{
```

If a developer wants to add operations, the developer can declare which operation the behavior shall have. In this scenario, the operations create, update, and delete are specified.

```
managed implementation in class z_bp_travel unique;
define behavior for Z_I_Travel alias travel
persistent table z_travel
lock master
{
  create;
  update;
  delete;
```

To add the missing projection and to be able to use these operations in OData services as well as the user interface, a new projection is created for the view entity:

```
projection;

define behavior for ZMH_C_TRAVEL
{
  use create;
  use update;
  use delete
```

Like the behavior definition, operations can be made available simply be declaring them.

As part of the transaction lifecycle, additional validations, actions, feature control, and other features are checked. These can be added in a very similar way. Again, it is declared which validations and actions are included in the behavior definition.

```
managed implementation in class z_bp_travel unique;
define behavior for Z_I_Travel alias travel
persistent table z_travel
lock master
{
  create;
  update;
  delete;

  validation validateDates on save { field Begin_Date, End_Date; }

  action ( features : instance ) setBeginDate result [1] $self
```

Here a validation is declared on the fields *Begin_Date* and *End_Date*, which are executed when the underlying object is saved. Additionally, an action is defined to be able to set the begin date.

The underlying implementation of these actions and validations needs to be defined in the ABAP language. As these are very application specific and are standard ABAP source code, the implementation of these validations is not explained further. Important is however that validations can be added by simply declaring it on the behavior definition, and the execution of these validations is automatically managed by the runtime.

Like the CRUD operations, the newly created action can then be exposed through the behavior projection:

```
projection;

define behavior for ZMH_C_TRAVEL
{
  use create;
  use update;
  use delete

  use action setBeginDate;
```

Thus, SAP S/4HANA makes it extremely easy to integrate the described models in a declarative way. This eases development efforts, increases development productivity, and ensures harmonization of the applications.

Conclusion

In this chapter the ABAP RESTful programming model and its incorporated transactional programming model were explained. First, the challenges were described which can occur in ERP systems, especially through concurrent write operations. As a method to prevent data corruption, transactions were explained. For better understanding a transaction, the use case of transactions and how they help to ensure that a database is always in a valid state were depicted. With ABAP 7.51 a partially new and improved programming model was introduced. This chapter focused on the SAP S/4HANA system and how it uses transactions throughout its data management to ensure data is never in a corrupt or invalid state. For this purpose, it was described how the system enforces data integrity through different methods, like the two-phase lifecycle and special steps in the save sequence, which checks if data is ready to be saved without interference. Finally, it was explored how developers can use the transactional programming model in their software solutions. For this, the managed and unmanaged approaches for implementing providers were explained, and the differences between the diverse kinds of providers were highlighted. The managed implementation was finally used in an example demonstrating the use in a real-world application.

Analytics

22

This chapter explains embedded analytics concepts and tools of SAP S/4HANA. Due to the usage of in-memory database technology online transactional and analytical operations are combined and allow native integration of analytics into the transactional applications. Additionally, the use case and solution approach for data warehousing are explained.

Business Requirement

An ERP solution collects data with each business transaction. This data, over time, becomes a valuable asset that can be used for decision support, business planning, or simulation. Furthermore, the collected data can be used to automate business processes that were previously carried out through manual interaction steps. With embedded analytics actual transactional data can be used for real-time reporting, planning, and simulation without the delay caused by replicating the data into data lakes. In the context of ERP systems, the analytics use cases can be grouped into the following clusters:

- **Operational reporting**: The operational use cases support day-to-day business decisions. Operational reporting is about enabling the business to perform their daily work by providing detailed and real-time information on business processes. The use case focuses on collecting transactional data in order to enhance operational efficiencies. Operational reporting covers all business processes within a company (e.g., financial, material management, sales, or purchase) and is subject to constant additions, updates, and deletions. Operational reports are consumed by people with accountability for improving operations. These persons offer task-oriented line-item information on individual business processes at the very granular level of detail needed for operational management. The reports usually rely on data from one business application like a single ERP deployment, which is covering North America financial processes. Reports cover a shorter time frame in comparison to other use cases. Examples for operation reporting are list of open orders, material on stock, and education cost in a profit center.

- **Tactical reporting**: Tactical analytics is run by business professionals with little or no technical experience. They want to use analytical applications to drill down and drill through multidimensional objects and rely on architects to build commonly used data objects for their work. This use case could require combining data from multiple operational systems or store attributes that are not persisted in the operational ERP system as they are not needed for online processing. The use case includes historical data and structures, prepares and consolidates the data for multidimensional usage. In short, these reports put operational data into a business context for business users. It also may require complex data analysis or even predictive analytics including past trends. Tactical analytics aims for monitoring and responding rapidly to a variety of short-term circumstances and don't have a necessity for real-time data. The reported data is stable over a certain time frame so that results are consistent across reports from a variety of perspectives for the analysis duration. Examples for tactical reporting are days sales outstanding (DSO), working capital management (WCM), and liquidity forecasting.
- **Strategic reporting**: Strategic analytics mainly serves the management, who demands pre-consolidated and deeper structured and aggregated data as it is already delivered for tactical reporting. Very often there is no need for detailed information except when a root-cause analysis is required. Strategic reporting summarizes and structures business KPIs to support strategy decisions. It always includes a historic view and is dealing with longer time periods and combines data throughout the whole company to provide a holistic overview over the company's situation. Examples for strategic reporting are productivity by manufacturing unit and market share development for different product lines.

In addition, **planning and simulation** functionality must be supported for all the three explained use case types as well. There is an operational, tactical, and strategic plan within a company's planning cycle. Planning and simulation addresses the need to foresee the future of a business. It does not deal with actual business transactions, but it predicts the transactions of the future. The basic requirement for business planning is to create plan data either manually or automatically. Planners have to develop the information and understand the objectives of the corporation and the overall business environment to make sure the business plan developed is achievable and will move the company toward a successful result. Plans from different areas are interrelated very much, for example, a sales plan provides the basis for a production plan. Due to this dependency the creation of the plans for different areas typically follows a strict schedule in the company. As a consequence, support for steering and monitoring the whole planning process across the different planning areas is needed. Reacting to changes in the context of a business plan requires rapid generation of results, quick re-planning and re-budgeting, coordinated and swift implementation of the new budget across highly complex organizations. The plan data has to be separated from the actual data; however, for analytical processing it has to be accessible just like actual data, especially to allow actual-plan comparisons easily.

One of the most important operations in planning is distribution. This operation is used to distribute values from a coarse aggregation level down to a detailed aggregation level, for example, distribute planned sales revenue for Europe down to countries. The aim of software products in this area is to improve planning, consolidation and simulation frequency, accuracy, and effectiveness in order to reduce planning-cycle times and costs.

Solution Capability

Transactions performed by users in a system are processed by Online Transaction Processing (OLTP) engines. Thus, availability and performance of OLTP are key success factors for ERP systems. Typically, not large data volumes are processed but high number of transactions. Online Analytical Processing (OLAP) is a term used in the context of performing analytical operations. OLAP focuses on the analysis of data resulting from OLTP processes. For example, the data is aggregated, filtered, or KPIs are calculated for drawing insights and taking decisions. Conversely, this means that very large volumes of data are processed including historical data. Hence, the requirements for OLAP applications fundamentally differ from OLTP scenarios. Extract, Transfer and Load (ETL) is a process used to load data from one or more OLTP data sources into an OLAP target system. The data is extracted from the various data sources, transformed into the correct format, and loaded into the target data sources. As depicted in Fig. 22.1 in traditional analytics process, data must first go through a certain process in order to be analyzed in a meaningful way. In the first step data resulting from transactions are processed and stored using OLTP. After the data has been processed by an ETL solution, the data is prepared for OLAP so that analytics can be performed. This traditional analytics processing is inefficient and ineffective. The data must be replicated multiple times, which causes high hardware and processing costs. Furthermore, due to latency caused by the ETL process, the data for analytics are usually outdated as there might be updates or new records available in the source system. Analytics based on outdated information can result into incorrect conclusions which can cause additional costs for companies.

The analytics approach of SAP S/4HANA resolves these problems. SAP S/4HANA is based on the in-memory database SAP HANA and combines OLTP and OLAP in one system. As shown in Fig. 22.2, unnecessary replications are avoided as OLTP and OLAP sharing the same online database. Thus, the data for analytics is always up to date so that real-time and accurate reporting is ensured. This

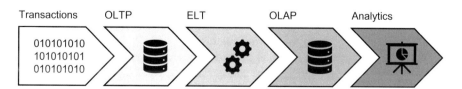

Fig. 22.1 Traditional analytics process

Fig. 22.2 In-memory based
analytics process

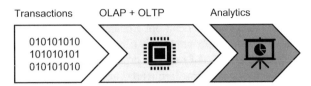

Transactions   OLAP + OLTP   Analytics

is a breaking through innovation and allows specially to incorporate analytics capabilities directly into transactional processes.

Analytics Architecture

In this section the solution architecture for implementing operational, tactical, and strategic analytics use cases is explained. The architecture is based on the following key business objectives:

- Reduced total cost of ownership: With SAP HANA in-memory data management concepts, the required analytical capabilities are directly incorporated into the operational systems. SAP S/4HANA becomes less complex and easier to maintain, resulting in less hardware maintenance and IT resource requirements.
- Innovative applications: SAP HANA combines high-volume transactions with analytics in the operational system. Planning, forecasting, pricing optimization, and other processes can be dramatically improved and supported with new applications in SAP S/4HANA that were not possible in the classic SAP ERP.
- Better and faster decisions: SAP S/4HANA's in-memory technology allows quick and easy access to information that decision makers need, providing them with new ways to look at the business. Simulation, what-if analyses, and planning can be performed interactively on operational data. Relevant information is instantly accessible, and the reliance on IT resources is reduced. Collaboration within and across organizations is simplified and fostered. This leads to a much more dynamic management style where problems can be dealt with as they happen.

Figure 22.3 summarizes the analytics architecture of SAP S/4HANA. The more data is processed during a single operation, the closer it should be executed to the database. Set-based processing operations like aggregations should be executed in the database, while single record operations should be part of the next layer. Thus, for analytics in SAP S/4HANA the pushdown paradigm to SAP HANA is used systematically. Hence, performance intensive operations are executed close to the data which results to an optimum throughput.

Very often the core data model is defined numerous times for different purposes only because minor metadata must be added. For example, technology solutions for integration, user interfaces, analytics, or transactions require unnecessarily their own data models. This increases total cost of development (TCD) as the same content

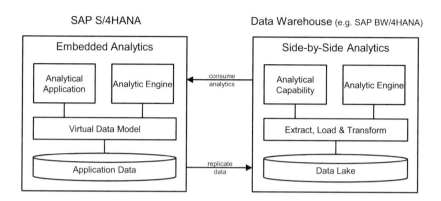

Fig. 22.3 Overview analytics architecture

must be provided several times. 'Due to the incompatible meta models', cross topics must be resolved multiple times, e.g. UI integration, extensibility, or authorization. This results in high TCO and encounters consumption of solutions by customers. Therefore, with the virtual data model (VDM), the core data model is defined once and reused in different contexts by specific enhancements. This simplifies the analytics architecture for SAP S/4HANA, avoids redundant data modeling, and allows solving cross topics uniformly. Operational reporting and partly also the tactical reporting can be implemented based on the embedded analytics of SAP S/4HANA, while for strategic reporting data warehousing is required (see Fig. 22.3). Especially for strategic reporting historical and cross-system data is necessary, which is usually stored in data warehouse solutions like SAP BW/4HANA. In essence, for embedded analytics the virtual data model is used to access the application data, process them with Analytic Engine and expose so analytics capabilities for integration into business applications. There is no need of data replication. The data is always up to date and ensures real-time analytics. Furthermore, analytics features can be built into transactional processes natively. This means to provide analytics to the right person, at the right time, and at the right place. For the side-by-side analytics, application data must be replicated to the data warehouse solutions based on ETL processes and made available for analytics. The reporting features must be integrated into SAP S/4HANA applications with remote APIs or with generic Business Intelligence (BI) clients. As far as possible open standards are used, and proprietary technologies are avoided. Open standards lower total costs and increase returns on investment by providing interoperability, vendor neutrality, efficient use of existing resources, lower and manageable risk, robustness and durability, and increased available skills. In the context of SAP S/4HANA analytics SQL, ODATA, INA, and MDX are the main open standards that are considered regarding access of data or integration into design/runtime tools.

Embedded Analytics

As already mentioned, embedded analytics aims to solve the operational and partly the tactical reporting use cases. As shown in Fig. 22.4 embedded analytics is based on the virtual data model (VDM) and the Analytic Engine. Reporting capabilities are incorporated into transactional applications allowing improved decision-making. In the past there was a rather strict separation between operational analytics and tactical and strategic analytics, which was about process optimization in an *ex post facto* mode: The business processes of the past are analyzed in a consolidated way, and the result of this analysis is fed back into the business processes (e.g., via planning and target setting), closing the loop. While these processes are still useful, the embedded analytics with SAP Fiori demands to overcome this separation on the level of tasks and activities of a particular user. Insight-to-Action involves a paradigm shift: Instead of gathering insight in the context of a specific business transaction or process, the insight is provided first in a summarizing and highly meaningful way. From this insight the end user decides which actions to take and takes them immediately in a seamless manner. This working model allows to respond to unplanned or systematic changes in the business and to appropriately (re-)prioritize tasks instead of working on a queue of business transactions. In order to achieve this goal, KPIs, analysis results, and analytical applications are offered to the end user in a very convenient way (e.g., on the home page, sometimes even involving active updates pushed to the UI), and the possible actions are provided as links or via a context menu, similar to contextual insight. So, Insight-to-Action implies per definition a seamless UI navigation from analytics to the relevant business transactions, and it typically has to be real time in order to show the effect of an action instantly.

The analytics model is founded on VDM and completely modeled in Core Data Service (CDS) views. The architecture leverages both SAP HANA and the Analytic

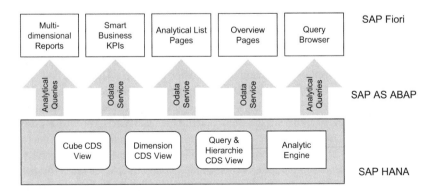

Fig. 22.4 Embedded analytics

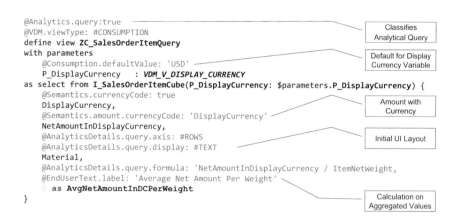

Fig. 22.5 Example for CDS query view

Engine. Embedded analytics enables multidimensional analysis with advanced functionality, for example, variables, restricted measures, formula aggregation, exception aggregation, and hierarchies. The reporting capability are exposed via InA and OData protocols for consumption. The embedded analytics consists of three layers. The lowest layer contains the database itself, which is in this case SAP HANA. The application data is stored in tables and exposed via the predefined CDS views of the virtual data model. The well-known analytics artifacts like cubs, dimensions, hierarchies, and queries are modeled as CDS views and processed with Analytic Engine of the SAP Application Server ABAP respectively the OLAP functionality of SAP HANA. Figure 22.5 illustrates an example for CDS query view. To display analytics results in the frontend there are various options available, for example, dashboards or analytics pages which are partially explained in the next section.

Reporting Frameworks

There are several frontend solutions for displaying analytics results but also for browsing CDS queries available in SAP S/4HANA. Those can be used in the context of embedded and side-by-side analytics. Some of the main frameworks are exemplary explained in this section.

Multidimensional Reports

Users can examinate analytics in different ways. One option to analyze the data is multidimensional reports. This approach allows to slice and dice, sort, and filter the data. Drill down and drill across are supported. With multidimensional reports swapping rows and columns are facilitated. Charts and tables can be displayed in personalized views. Finally, the navigation to other SAP Fiori applications is possible (Fig. 22.6).

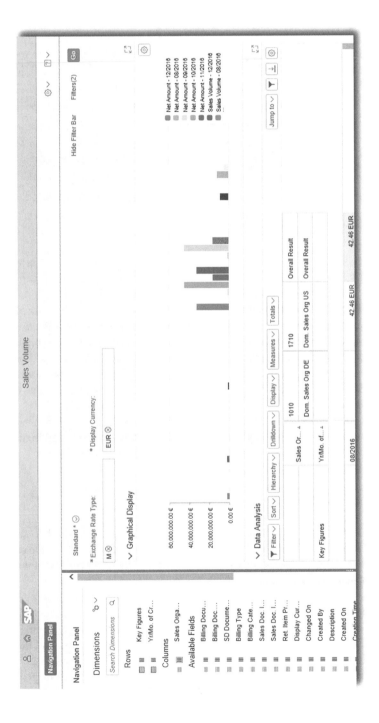

Fig. 22.6 Multidimensional reporting

Smart Business KPIs

This framework enables the provisioning of key performance indicator (KPI). In the SAP Fiori launchpad quantitative information is offered for KPIs. Thus, the end user can react immediately if a KPI drifts to unplanned direction. Clicking on the KPI tiles drill-down to various details is supplemented by selecting dimensions. Such KPI details can be personalized and saved as new SAP Fiori tiles for regular use. KPI details are the default navigation target of KPI tiles. However, this behavior can be reconfigured so that SAP Analysis Path Framework or other SAP Fiori Apps are reflected. Analysis Path Framework (APF) is a tool to easily build and enhance interactive analytical Fiori applications. APF-based applications facilitate business users to dig into data recursively by building up analysis paths covering a sequence of analysis steps. Selections made within a step of an analysis path take effect in all subsequent analysis steps (Fig. 22.7).

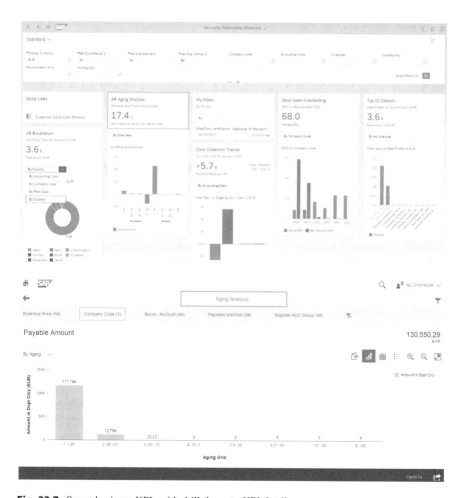

Fig. 22.7 Smart business KPIs with drill-down to KPI details

Analytical List Pages

The two analysis options in the previous sections are designed to generate individual key figures for a specific use case. The Analytical List Page is used when only the overview is needed and not the detailed information. For example, an employee can display all open receivables that have not yet been assigned to a processor. Analytical List Pages Visual provides filters to focus on the most important areas. The user can switch between complex, visual, facet filters. Personalized chart areas are offered for quick overview and drill-down. Additionally, details area for operational details are supported. Navigation is facilitated to other Fiori applications that are semantically linked to the data. Personalized views can be configured. Analytical List Pages are ideal for insight-to-action scenarios (Fig. 22.8).

Overview Pages

With Overview Pages the most important information can be presented at a glance instead of opening many different transactions. They combine analytical and transactional information and enable built-in analytics. More detailed information can be provided by clicking on the cards. Each card basically represents a business transaction where analytical data is the starting point of the end user's investigations, followed with concrete transactional activities. The entire page can be fully personalized. For example, it is possible to hide individual tiles or maps. Furthermore, the navigation to other Fiori applications that are semantically linked to the data are supported (Fig. 22.9).

Query Browser

The Query Browser is an SAP Fiori application that can be used to quickly and easily search for, browse, and tag the analytical queries. The Query Browser shows all the authorized analytical queries and customer queries to which the user has access. The queries can either be executed directly or be opened in Design Studio. The second option provides more functionality, for example, additional configuration options for dimensions, rows, or columns. For searching queries, information regarding views, tables, view descriptions, view column names, annotations, or tags is used. Those search options can be combined with each other. Filter options allow to sort or filter the views. The sorting of queries is founded on the CDS view names and the underlying application components in the system. The filtering of the queries is built on the user tags and the corresponding application component. The list of application components is illustrated as a hierarchy (Fig. 22.10).

Analytical SAP Fiori Apps

There are predefined analytical SAP Fiori applications that can be consumed directly. Those applications are implemented based on SAP Fiori floorplans and UI5 controls. These are individual and use case-specific analytical applications. Typically, this approach is applied for developing highly specific use cases where the already explained generic frameworks are not sufficient. Therefore, break-out solutions are required to fulfill the sophisticated functionality demanded for the scenario (Fig. 22.11).

Fig. 22.8 Analytical list page

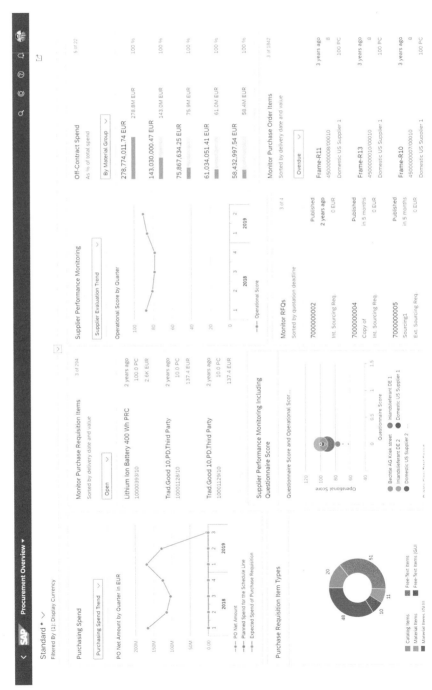

Fig. 22.9 Overview business page

Fig. 22.10 Query browser/custom analytical queries

Fig. 22.11 Analytical Fiori App

Data Warehousing

The operational analytics represents the majority of the analytical use cases and can be well handled based on embedded analytics. Partially, this is also the case for tactical reporting. However, as soon as historical data is required for analytics, a data warehouse solution is necessary. This is because usually in operational database of SAP S/4HANA the historical data for a restricted period are stored but definitely not for several years. Keeping historical data for long periods in the operational database would result in high volume of data. Thus, very soon hardware limitations would be achieved. Furthermore, negative performance drawbacks are expected as for each database operation, huge data volumes would need to be processed. For strategic reporting also cross-system analytics must be considered, which is also not in the focus of embedded analytics. Hence, for strategic and partially for tactical reporting often data warehouse solutions like SAP BW/4HANA are used as they enable historical and cross-system analytics. Figure 22.12 illustrates the architecture of SAP BW/4HANA. SAP BW/4HANA provides a complete view of business to satisfy the diverse needs of end users, IT professionals, and senior management. It combines business warehouse infrastructure, a comprehensive set of tools, planning and simulation functionality, and data-warehousing capability. This solution consolidates data across the enterprise and provides standardized data model for analytics. For this common semantics is defined, data values are harmonized, and a

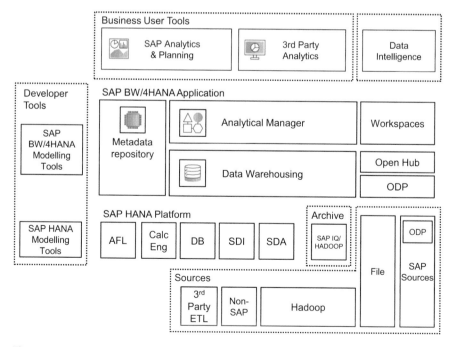

Fig. 22.12 SAP BW/4HANA architecture

single version of truth is established. While SAP BW/4HANA provides a single, comprehensive source of current and historical information, it keeps a copy of source data to ensure independency of source.

SAP BW/4HANA gains significant performance gain through pushdown of operations/calculations to SAP HANA. The OLAP Engine performs complex query calculations, for example, exception aggregation. Planning functions (e.g., disaggregation) and data management (e.g., transformation logic) are also pushed down for optimal performance. The modeling tools are based on Eclipse so that a unified and single user interface is provided for all development tasks. Following SAP Fiori design patterns, single point of entry for all administration tasks is offered with the Web Cockpit. Thus, a unified user experience is ensured. Additionally, own applications and groups can be included which consider user context and authorizations. SAP BW/4HANA simplifies data integration by offering comprehensive access to external systems. The number of source system types are reduced from 10 to 4 to improve TCO. Real-time replication of data is supported with SAP HANA SDI or SAP ODP-SLT. Furthermore, the data can be accessed virtually so that replicas can be avoided. For loading data optimized processing in SAP HANA is available. On the way from the source system to SAP BW4HANA data is transformed into a unified format and cleansed. The data-warehousing component is responsible for data replication, transformation, and storage on the SAP BW4HANA server. Data is stored in relational tables generated from the data models. The data models are stored in the Meta Data Repository. To cover archiving and data aging data might as well be stored in a near-line storage system. The Analytical Manager is responsible for reading and processing the data, which includes aggregation and calculation. Moreover, this also contains a planning engine which enables the write back of changed data. Various front-end tools like Analysis Office, Design Studio, and the Enterprise Performance Management (EPM) client allow the end user to access and analyze the data. The core data model comprises InfoProvider and InfoObjects. The main building blocks of the data model are the InfoObjects, which are divided into key figures (numbers or measures, e.g., revenue, quantity sold), characteristics (evaluation groups such as company code, product, customer group), and units (currencies and units of measure). Characteristics are very similar to business objects and therefore might have a link to a business object located. The InfoObjects only exist in a global scope—i.e., their properties are shared among all objects that are composed out of InfoObjects like InfoProvider and InfoSources. The most important entity is the InfoProvider, which is an abstraction for an object containing analytical data. The InfoProvider is one of the following concrete entities:

- DataStore Object is central persistence object in SAP BW/4HANA. It is used for reporting and determination of delta information.
- Characteristic refers to master data with their attributes and text descriptions.
- CompositeProvider represents a union or join of several InfoProvider.
- Open ODS View enables the user to define data models for objects like database tables, database views, or SAP BW/HANA DataSources for direct access. These

data models allow flexible integration of external data without the need to create InfoObjects. An Open ODS view can be a characteristic.

All front-end tools are based on queries which are always defined on exactly one InfoProvider. The query and the query view define a view (often a subset/projection) of the data available in the InfoProvider. In addition, some visual properties are defined as well, for example, which InfoObjects appear in the columns/rows or if hierarchies are used for the visualization. Based on one or more queries/query views applications are then build either for the web (Web-based front end) or MS Office (Office-based front end). Moreover, it is also possible to embed a query view in analytical Web Dynpro pattern. In the Data Warehouse layer modeling is used to transform and merge data from various sources into the InfoProvider. The inbound layer is always modeled as a DataSource. Data is then mapped into one or more physical InfoProvider via transformations. Since the warehouse might be modeled containing various levels of detail, it is also possible to model transformations between InfoProviders (e.g., from one DataStore Object into another DataStore Object). DataStore Objects are candidates for an information lifecycle management. They could optionally own a data archiving process which defines a partitioning schema for the data relocation to an archiving object (for offline usage only), a near-line Object (enabled for direct query access), or the combination of both (Fig. 22.13).

In addition to the static data model there are more entities for modeling the dynamic behavior of the SAP BW/4HANA system. The most important object is the process chain, which controls the scheduling and execution of several process types. Some very prominent process types are data transfer processes (DTP), InfoProvider administration (delete data, . . .), and execute a planning sequence. SAP BW/4HANA business content is one of biggest differentiators. A simple business content example is invoice and payment trends over time, or order delivery performance analysis. Building and maintaining complex analytical models across finance, procurement, human resources, supply chain, which source the right data from the right fields and then map them to data structures for analytics is really hard and time-consuming. SAP BW/4HANA provides analytics content which can be used out of the box.

Conclusion

Key use cases for analytics are operational, tactical, and strategic reporting. They cover demands for users performing their daily work to senior managers taking strategic decisions for the company. For the implementation of these use cases embedded analytics and data warehouse technics are applied. Embedded analytics is based on SAP S/4HANA's platform. In-memory concepts of SAP HANA are used to combine analytics and transactional processing. Thus, built-in analytics is facilitated in terms of offering analytics capability to the right person, at the right place, and at the right time. While operational and partially tactical reporting are well covered with embedded analytics, for historical and cross-system reporting data

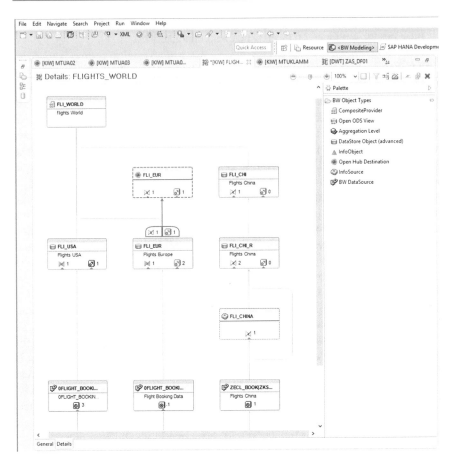

Fig. 22.13 SAP BW/4HANA—data flow modeling

warehousing is required. With SAP BW4/HANA as data warehouse solution data from across the enterprise and beyond can be integrated, and then transformed into practical, timely information to drive sound decision-making, targeted action, and solid business results. This product is also founded on SAP HANA and makes intensive use of in-memory computing and pushdown approach.

Search

23

This chapter focuses on enterprise search architecture and framework of SAP S/4HANA. Particularly different search types like in-app search and value help, search models and connectors, configuration, and managing of search models are explained.

The pushdown of search requests to SAP HANA is also briefly described as this impacts the response time of search engine.

Business Requirement

Especially in big and versatile ERP software it is important to ensure effective navigation and therefore good user experience. One way to provide effective navigation is to provide a powerful search. In the case of ERP systems, users should be able to get a quick overview of business objects. Also, this search feature should help them to navigate business objects across the entire enterprise network. Free-text search shall be provided to the users for specifying search requests. The search results shall be listed according to their relevance ranking. Best suited results must be itemized on the top of the list. In the context of ERP solutions, the search capabilities must be restricted to the authorization permissions of users, for example, only those sales orders shall be listed in the result list of the search query for which the user have the authorizations. In addition to this cross-application search capabilities, also in-app search features are required. Thus, within a business application and the underlying restricted business context, searching for entities shall be supported. Typically, ERP user interfaces contain code lists from which users must select the relevant codes. Search shall facilitate value helps for searching such code lists and simplifying the experience for the users.

S. Sarferaz, *Compendium on Enterprise Resource Planning*,
https://doi.org/10.1007/978-3-030-93856-7_23

Solution Capability

The search functionality is an integral part of SAP S/4HANA. There are three types of it, each targeting different application requirements. The first type, Enterprise Search, offers a free-text search for all instances of effectively any business object types. Furthermore, it offers this free-text search for SAP Fiori apps, which are available in SAP S/4HANA. It is important to point out that the search scope for each user is of course limited to only those objects and applications which are assigned to the user's roles. This Enterprise Search is accessible through the search field at the top of the page in the SAP Fiori launchpad. Enterprise search enables business users to get a quick overview of business objects and helps to navigate these business objects across the entire enterprise network, which is exactly what was required. It features *facets*, where users can narrow down the search result set and where users can select multiple filters which can be applied along certain discrete attributes of the overall data collection. Additionally, it gives a brief statistical overview of how data is distributed across the result set. Finally, all this information can be shown as a list, bar graph, or pie chart. Figure 23.1 illustrates the results of searching for *Products* in SAP S/4HANA using Enterprise Search.

The Enterprise Search also features *fuzzy search*. This provides search results based on similar search strings and helps in case of typing errors. Furthermore, the fuzziness threshold can be changed according to the user's needs. In addition, it features type ahead. It shows a suggestion list when the user enters a minimum number of characters and therefore improves the search experience.

Besides the Enterprise Search, which provides cross-application search, SAP S/4HANA features the In-App Search, where the user can search within a specific application. This search is integrated into a single SAP Fiori app and offers context-specific fuzzy search capabilities. It can be found through special search fields in the SAP Fiori list apps. If features value help dialogs and type-ahead input controls. Also, SAP S/4HANA provides a Value Help Search, which is used to offer input help for fields within the application. Finally, different roles can be assigned to different users so that the search results can be altered based on these assigned roles.

Search Architecture

The general search architecture has SAP HANA as the lowest layer. SAP HANA consists of two major blocks, where one is the actual database and the other is the XS-Engine, which acts as the application server. On top of SAP HANA, there is the ABAP-stack, which also acts as an application server. The very top layer is the client that consumes all the services. Here the client is likely to be a browser but might also be Microsoft Excel. The entire search architecture is based on the virtual data model (VDM), an overview of which is depicted in Fig. 23.2.

The enterprise search framework can be divided into two parts, one implemented in SAP HANA and the other implemented in the ABAP platform. The SAP HANA Enterprise Search Framework provides the core enterprise search capabilities

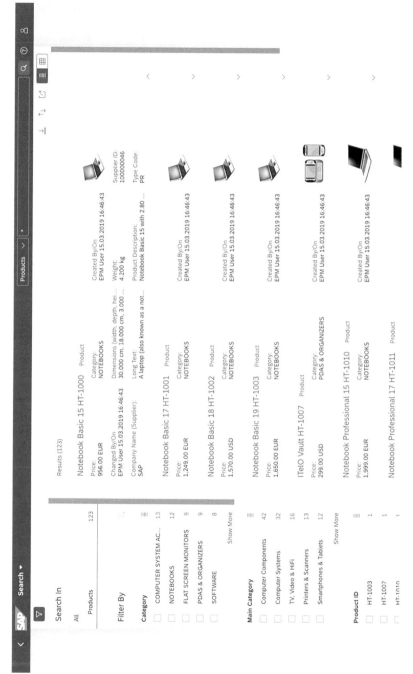

Fig. 23.1 Enterprise Search in SAP S/4HANA

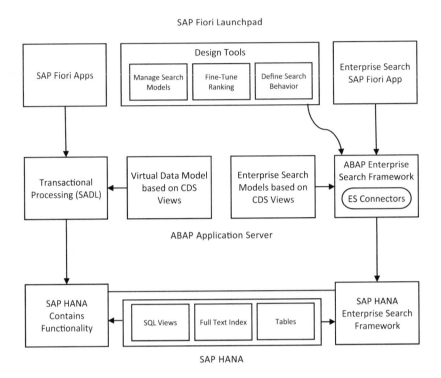

Fig. 23.2 Search architecture in SAP S/4HANA

through a set of database procedures. The second part of the enterprise search framework is the ABAP platform. The enterprise search in ABAP exposes its search via an ABAP-API and via a InA-service. Here InA (Information Access) is a proprietary protocol which comprises all features required by search and analytics. While the InA-service is used by the Fiori search exclusively, all ABAP applications are based on the API. Moreover, the ABAP Enterprise Search Framework is responsible for the integration with the Search SAP Fiori app and on the other it is responsible for processing enterprise search Core Data Services (CDS) models. Also, the service adaption definition language (SADL) framework is the infrastructure for the model-based processing of OData services in this ABAP platform. This is controlled by special annotations of the @*Search* domain, which are directly in the VDM consumption views. These Enterprise search CDS models are special CDS views which are annotated with @*Enterprise-Search.enabled: true*. Technically, the enterprise search models are not VDM views and can be created without the previous mentioned VDM rules. In SAP S/4HANA however, they are normally built on top of the VDM basic layer and therefore share the same business models with other VDM entities. Several sets of runtime metadata called enterprise search connectors are generated by the framework during the activation of an enterprise search CDS model. During runtime, these connectors are the main artifacts controlling the execution of the enterprise search queries. In the client part there are libraries for Firefly and sInA (simplified InA). Here Firefly focusses on the analytical scenarios and provides platform independence. sInA focusses on search. Nevertheless, Firefly can handle search requests and sInA can manage analytical requests, too. Both libraries communicate via InA with the server.

Search Models and Search Connectors

The enterprise search is based on predefined Search Models. A Search Model contains all information that is required in order to execute a successful search. Some of this information are listed here:

- **Request Fields** defines in which columns the search term could be found
- **Freestyle Search Request Fields** specifies which columns should be considered in a freestyle search
- **Relevance of Freestyle Search Request Fields** defines how relevant a hit is in each column
- **Facetted Search Request Fields** specifies which columns are relevant to a facetted search
- **Advanced Search Request Fields** define which columns should be enabled for advanced search
- **Auto Completion Request fields** decides which columns should use the auto completion feature
- **Response fields** defines which columns should be part of the search result
- **Title Response fields** specifies which columns are relevant to the title of a search hit
- **Authorization Checks** defines which authorizations are required to access which data
- **Boosts** decides which hits should be boosted or promoted
- **Field Semantics** specifies based on the semantics which appropriate search configuration is used

Search Connectors are required to execute a search. These Search Connectors are based on the Search Models and without the connectors there is no search possible. Just Search Models are not enough. A Search Model is a Design Time construct, it is well-considered developed by a domain expert, where as a Search Constructor is a Run Time construct which is created and activated by an administrator. Additionally, a Search Model is independent of the concrete system, it can be created in one system and then shipped to another system. A Search Connector is bound to a concrete system and it cannot be shipped or transported into another. An overview of this relationship is depicted in Fig. 23.3.

These types of Search Models and Connectors represent the Classical Search Models and Connectors. Classical Search Models can be created using the Modeler for Search and Analytics (ESH_MODELER). Based on the Classical Search Models

Fig. 23.3 Relationship
between search model and
search connector

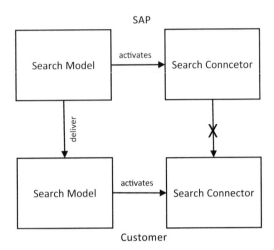

the Classical Search Connectors can be created. These can be created using the
Connector Administration Cockpit (ESH_COCKPIT) or via an Enterprise Search
Task List (SAP_ESH_CREATE_INDEX_SC). It is important to point out that
Classical Search Models and Connectors have been relevant in the past, and now
CDS-based Search Models and CDS-based Search Connectors are being used in
SAP S/4HANA Cloud. Classical Search Models are still used in SAP S/4HANA On
Premise. CDS-based Search Models are the future direction, and it is planned to use
them exclusively in both the Cloud and On Premise.

Like mentioned before CDS-based Search Models are just ordinary ABAP CDS
views with some special annotations (e.g., *@Enterprise-Search.enabled: true*).
Currently, there are three ways to create a CDS-based Search Model. First, these
models can be created with the Enterprise Search Model Migration Assistant. It is a
semi-automatic conversion of classical Search Models and is part of the Enterprise
Search. Second, these models can be maintained with the Create Search Model
UI. Here the user is guided through the creation of a CDS-based Search Model.
Finally, they can be created with the ABAP Development Tools (ADT), which is a
standard tool for the creation of ordinary CDS views. But due to *contains* limitations,
the usage is not recommended. CDS-based Search Connectors are created automati-
cally when a CDS Search view is activated. No Enterprise Search Task List (like
SAP_ESH_CREATE_ INDEX_SC) or Connector Administration Cockpit
(ESH_COCKPIT) is required.

Managing Search Models

SAP S/4HANA provides multiple apps to manage and adjust single search models in
order to meet the specific requirements of each organization and customer. The most
important apps for that are covered in this section. With the Display Search Models

app the user receives an overview of the models that are available in the system. Additionally, their status and the authorization are also displayed for each model. Here the user can also activate and deactivate the models (Fig. 23.4).

The Manage Search Models app offers plenty of functionalities for adjusting single models. Here, the user can, for example, change the appearance of fields in the search results. Also, the user can edit the weighting factors of the fields for rankings and exclude fields from the search scope. The following two features might be of special interest for the users. First, there is the possibility of inclusion of custom fields. The custom field extensibility of the search models works in a standardized way, when using the Custom Fields key user extensibility tool. Nonetheless,

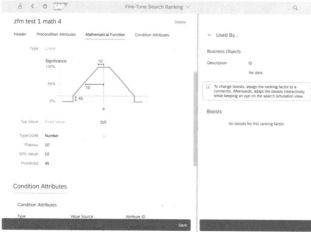

Fig. 23.4 Display and manage search models

adjustment of the search settings on these fields is only possible using the enterprise search modeler. Second there is the option to customize the search models. A key user can customize the fields of the model which are used for search requests and their appearance in the enterprise search UI. Furthermore, search-related settings of a model and rankings of the fields can be changed. As mentioned above it is possible to adjust rankings, which allows users to assign custom ranking factors to the models or to fine-tune the factors defined by the developer of the model. For example, users can boost the relevance of newly created objects or objects created in a particular region. In order to make these changes SAP S/4HANA features a special Fine-Tune Ranking application (see Fig. 23.5). With this application it is also possible to monitor the influence of these factors in real time.

Annotations of Search Models

Here, CDS means in the first place SQL, that is, the core-SQL in its DDL- and DML-flavors as supported by every DBMS relevant to SAP. This SQL is enhanced by annotations of an SQL statement, some keywords which can be resolved to core-SQL and some additional artifacts. With CDS as SAP HANA language, the search configuration is formulated as close as possible to the InA-search model. Also, the Enterprise Search ABAP-configuration can and shall be mapped to this format. So, a CDS-based Search Model is just an ordinary ABAP CDS View with some special annotations. These special annotations can modify the search behavior and can be classified into the following categories:

- **Basic/General** Annotations
- Annotations related to **Request Fields**
- Annotations related to **Response Fields**
- Annotations related to **Field Groups**
- Annotations related to **Descriptions**
- Annotations related to **Navigation**
- Annotations related to **Time and Language Dependency**
- Annotations related to **Full Text Indexes and Search Options**
- Annotations related to **Ranking and Boosting**

With these annotations it is very easy to build a CDS-based Search Model; the annotations just need to be added to the given CDS View. Here, not every view is necessarily a search view. Annotating @*Search* at any view is reasonable because this is leveraged by SADL, oData, and Smart Controls in UI5. Annotating any view with @*EnterpriseSearch* is not reasonable, because the views must be highly denormalized. It might happen that a view representing the object structure is being ruined this way. Therefore, there will always be a separate, dedicated search view on top of the actual object view. CDS also has defined inheritance rules when stacking them. Search views do fully participate in this mechanism. Annotations on view level are never inherited, while annotations on element level are always

Fig. 23.5 Fine-tune search ranking

inherited. Inheritance ca be switched off completely by the annotation @*Metadata.
ignorePropagatedAnnotations.*

Also, views can be enhanced, adding to their elements. Besides, Meta Data
Extensions (MDE) can be defined which do not alter the view structurally but do
only modify the annotation of domains released for this mechanism. For a view to be
enhanced by MDE, it needs to carry to view-level annotation @*Metadata.
allowExtensions.* Additionally, CDS-checks include Enterprise Search validations.
Errors from these validations are displayed as warnings. The core-activation with the
generation of the Data Dictionary (DDIC) view must succeed, no matter whether
appendixes like Enterprise Search issue errors. There are several levels of validation:

- On activation in ADT, a subset (performance-induced) of checks is carried out on
  the current document (view, view-enhancement, MDX). Errors are reported as
  warnings. In case of an error, no search connector will be generated.
- If none of them fails, the actual Enterprise Search activation is triggered. Here, the
  complete definitions across the whole view stack are considered and checked
  fully. Any error detected here results in an abortion of the activation. No search
  connector will be created.
- If no error is detected, a search connector is generated. Mind that the errors up to
  now are not reported in the Enterprise Search Cockpit since no connector is
  available for them.
- The system carries out some meaningful searches on the new connector. If any of
  them fails, the connector goes to status *Error while preparing.* The job log shown
  in the Enterprise Search Cockpit displays all information. The reason for changing the status is to take the connector out of the search scope, because otherwise
  each search in "all" would result in errors.
- On individual request or when releasing a transport request, ABAP Test Cockpit
  (ATC) checks are carried out. They comprise the full range of validations.
- On importing a CDS-search view in a system, Enterprise Search triggers the
  activation. Any validation error is reported in the transport import log.

An example with a Student CDS View can be found below. It is assumed that a
small CDS View already exists for students. When the annotations are added like
below it will be a CDS-based Search Model.

```
@AbapCatalog.sqlViewName: 'Student'
@Search.searchable: true
@EnterpriseSearch.enabled: true
@UI.headerInfo.typeNamePlural: 'Student'
@ObjectModel.semanticKey: ['MatrikelNumber']
@UI.headerInfo.title: {value: 'NameOfStudent'}
define view STUDENT
as select from STUDENT
{
    @EndUserText.label: 'Student'
    @UI.identification: { position: 1 }
    _STUDENT.fieldval as NameOfStudent,
    @EndUserText.label: 'Course'
    @UI.identification: { position: 2 }
    _COURSE.fieldval as COURSE,
    @Search.defaultSearchElement: true
    @Search.ranking: #HIGH
    matnr as MatrikelNumber
}
```

With *@Search.searchable: true* it is stated that this is relevant to search scenarios. With *@EnterpriseSearch.enabled: true* a Search Connector is requested, and with *@UI.headerInfo.typeNamePlural* the name in the dropdown menu is defined. *@ObjectModel.semanticKey* defines the key from the search perspective while *@UI.headerInfo.title* defines the title response field. *@EndUserText.label* and *@UI.identification* define the Response Fields which are displayed on the first and second positions. Finally, *@Search.defaultSearchElement* and *@Search.ranking* set the Freestyle Search Request Field to high relevance.

Configuration of Default Search Scope

In-application search is a built-in functionality and does not need any special configuration in order to work. The enterprise search however offers plenty of possibilities to adjust its behavior to specific demands. The enterprise search queries of each user are executed on the set of the enterprise search models. Of course, this only applies to the search models the user is authorized for. This set of models is called *search scope*. This search scope can further be restricted to a specific search model with a dropdown list which can be found near the search input field. There are two entries in this list which have a special meaning. All means that the full set of the models are available for the user. Apps on the other hand restricts the search only to SAP Fiori apps that a user has access to.

But by far the most powerful features of the enterprise search become clear when the user is searching within the *all scope*. If the user types a search term, a partial search term, an ID, or a combination of words, the user automatically gets an overview of fitting business objects and applications in the systems. These results are ranked according to the relevance of the user. Because of that, most of the SAP

S/4HANA users and customers are using the enterprise search as an entry point into the system. However, searching through the entire system has its downsides in terms of resource consumption. This is especially the case in the previously mentioned entry point scenario, where users are often interested in finding a specific application but often spend unnecessary computing resources by searching in all search models. Moreover, users search models included by the *all scope* instead of restricting the search scope only to the applications (with *apps*) they want to find. Due to this problem there are enterprise search-specific settings in SAP Fiori launchpad for controlling the default scope of the enterprise search. There are two options. One option makes all applications the default options instead of applications; here the user must explicitly select *all* if this is required to use. The other option is to completely remove the *all scope* from the enterprise search; here it is only possible for users to search in specific models like apps.

Personalization

Like already mentioned, the enterprise search returns the search results ranked according to the relevance for the user. When the enterprise search framework has the permission to collect and analyze data about the user behavior within the search scenarios, the relevance calculation can be dramatically improved. However, by default, the data collection is configured as an opt-in option. To allow the collection of data each user can go in the SAP Fiori launchpad settings and activate it. Additionally, the system administrator can change the default settings to opt out using the Configure Personalized Search app. If this is the case each user is still able to turn off the data collection. It is highly recommended by SAP that the collection of user data is enabled in order to get more accurate search results. It is important to point out that no data is transferred to SAP (Fig. 23.6).

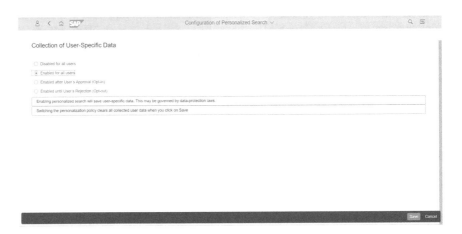

Fig. 23.6 Configuration of personalized search

Conclusion

This chapter provided an overview of the Enterprise Search in SAP S/4HANA. First, all search types were presented and compared. After this introduction, the document focused on the Enterprise Search, which is the most important search type for the user. For a general understanding, the search architecture was presented, and a brief explanation of Search Models and Connectors was provided. In the last part how a user can manage and configure these Search Models was explained, so that the search can be more effective and relevant for the user.

Artificial Intelligence

24

This chapter focuses on artificial intelligence (AI) to allow algorithms learning from data instead of being explicitly programmed by human beings based on rules. Thus, intelligence is infused into business processes, and the automation level is increased in SAP S/4HANA toward an autonomous ERP. In order to provide a deeper understanding of the topic, the basic concepts of this technology are being explained in the first part. In the following section the focus is on how artificial intelligence adds value to business processes in general, as well as the history of automation in different industries is briefly analyzed. Finally, the implementation of artificial intelligence in SAP S/4HANA is explained.

Business Requirement

There were and there always will be changes in the industries and the way how people work. It all began in the late eighteenth century, as the industrial revolution started in England. The manufacturing processes of the textile industry slowly started to be replaced by mechanical machines. Those machines kept rapidly improving and expanding to other industry sectors, especially after the start of the exploitation of coal as a new source of energy. This led to massive economical and productivity growths in the industrialized countries. Later in the 1960s, the efficiency was once more improved by implementing the first automation of repeating industry processes. In the late 1990s, the business processes themselves started to become the subject of the ongoing digitalization and automation. At the turn of the millennium it became clear: the future of every business lies in their usage of information technology, especially of the predictive artificial intelligence. The most innovative players have the chance of gaining massive advantages over their competitors by adopting these new technologies in their value chains early. Nowadays it is assumed that around 70% of all companies integrate or at least think about integrating artificial intelligence technology in their business processes, in order to boost the productivity of their workers or even fully automate them. As a logical

S. Sarferaz, *Compendium on Enterprise Resource Planning*,
https://doi.org/10.1007/978-3-030-93856-7_24

consequence, the market for artificial intelligence application for enterprise keeps constantly growing.

The term artificial intelligence is hard to define properly. One of the reasons for that is that the term *intelligence* itself is a not very well defined one. Intelligence is a characteristic that humans assign to themselves and other living beings. Intelligence describes the ability to learn, understand, and think in a logical way about things. Based on that, artificial intelligence is the discipline that tries to research and develop on building intelligent computer systems and programs. A system can be called *intelligent* when it is able to accomplish any task that would otherwise require the usage of human intelligence. Artificial intelligence is an umbrella term that covers many different areas and subdisciplines.

What Is Machine Learning?

Machine learning is a subdiscipline of the artificial intelligence focused on developing applications and systems that learn from given data and constantly improve without them being explicitly instructed to do so. These solutions are using self-learning algorithms that can be automatically fitted to a given dataset using their statistical properties, in order to make predictions or decisions based on new unknown data. The first step in developing such a solution is to choose and prepare the datasets, according to the use case. The second step is to choose and train an algorithm in order to find the best configuration and create a model. The last step is using the created model to make predictions on new data. The more the model is used, the better its accuracy gets, as it is gathering bigger amounts of data.

Types of Machine Learning

The machine learning methods can be divided into three different categories. In order to choose the right method, the use case and the provided data should be analyzed.

Supervised Learning

The supervised learning method is used when the provided datasets contain already known labels that can be determined by the system. This is one of the most used methods, as it is one of the easiest methods to comprehend and evaluate. In order to train such a model, the provided dataset must be split into training and test data. The best algorithm configuration is found using the training data. The quality of the created model can be evaluated by predicting on the test data and subsequently comparing the result to the given labels from the dataset. Figure 24.1 shows the process of creating and using a supervised learning model. The biggest bottleneck of this machine learning method is the gathering of data. Good labeled datasets can be very expensive to produce. Furthermore, supervised learning models undergo the

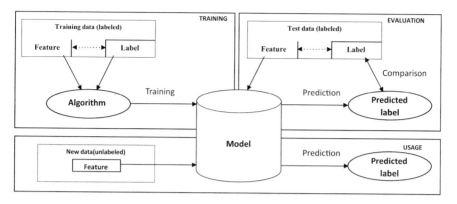

Fig. 24.1 Process of training, evaluating, and using a supervised learning model

risk of overfitting to their dataset, which means that the model is perfectly fitted to its training data but can still not make good predictions on new data.

Unsupervised Learning

Unsupervised learning is used when the provided dataset is unknown and unlabeled. With the help of this method a data scientist can gather relevant information about these unprocessed datasets. This method works by analyzing the statistical properties of the data, using different types of algorithms and configurations. The analysis process is called clustering and has the scope of finding hidden information in the data that cannot be directly seen by humans. The problem of this method is that the results can be hard to comprehend. They can also not be evaluated, as the provided datasets do not contain any labels. In fact, there is no right or wrong in the unsupervised machine learning. Each output can show some new properties of the dataset. The most important part of this process is to choose and interpret the results according to the use case. In order to achieve a meaningful clustering, the data scientist needs to have some basic knowledge of the use case. The results of such a clustering can be used as labels for the future development of a supervised learning model. Figure 24.2 shows the ideal outcome of a clustering process.

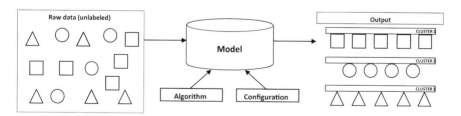

Fig. 24.2 Process of creating an unsupervised learning model

Reinforcement Learning

Reinforcement learning means training a model to make decisions, based on experience gathered in a controlled environment. The machine faces a game-like situation, where it needs to try different approaches for solving a problem and choose the best of them, based on the feedback given by the environment. The base of a reinforced learning system is its reward policy that can be seen as a set of rules for the game. The designer of the system needs to define these rules, so that the machine can understand the feedback as reward or penalty. The machine then uses trial and error heuristics to maximize its reward function, as shown in Fig. 24.3. The big challenge of the reinforcement learning is building the controlled environment. For simple tasks like playing chess this can be easily done, but this gets very complex with more advanced tasks, such as autonomous driving.

Solution Capability

Using the AI-enabled features of SAP S/4HANA allows enterprises to gain different advantages on multiple levels. SAP S/4HANA helps organizations from different industries to achieve higher business agility, to meet the rising expectations of the modern consumer, as well as to deliver new products while managing their resources efficiently.

Key Pillars for Intelligence

Figure 24.4 shows the four key areas of innovation that SAP S/4HANA uses, in order to increase the intelligence of an enterprise.

There are different intelligent technologies that are being offered from SAP in their portfolio as shown in Fig. 24.4. The Conversational AI is a digital assistant that helps to complete tasks more quickly. The assistant is context sensitive and is able to recognize different relevant business objects in the applications the user is currently working with. New objects can be added and created, as well as referenced to an existing object by simply talking to the Conversational AI. The assistant can be used on either mobile or desktop devices and can be as well integrated on external channels and platforms, making for a truly seamless digital assistant experience.

Fig. 24.3 Process of training a reinforcement learning model

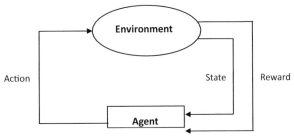

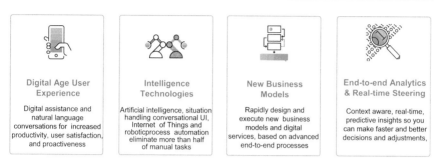

Digital Age User Experience	Intelligence Technologies	New Business Models	End-to-end Analytics & Real-time Steering
Digital assistance and natural language conversations for increased productivity, user satisfaction, and proactiveness	Artificial intelligence, situation handling conversational UI, Internet of Things and roboticprocess automation eliminate more than half of manual tasks	Rapidly design and execute new business models and digital services, based on advanced end-to-end processes	Context aware, real-time, predictive insights so you can make faster and better decisions and adjustments,

Fig. 24.4 SAP S/4HANA's key pillars for intelligence

Some of the features of the Conversational AI are natural language processing, contextual chats, creation and editing of business objects, as well as cross-application access. Robotic process automation (RPA) is a technology that uses software bots to execute different tasks, like interacting with user interfaces or making API calls. The SAP S/4HANA robotic process automation goes one step further and enables the inclusion of machine learning into existing tasks. There are two different types of bots: unattended and attended. The unattended bots work fully automated, without requiring the intervention of humans. They can work along with other applications. The attended bots are completing partially automated tasks, mostly supporting a human worker. The SAP S/4HANA robotic process automation solution consists of three components: studio, factory, and desktop agent. These components guide the user through the process of developing, debugging, and monitoring each of the bots, in order to deliver bots that are suitable to every business need. A business process is not always running smoothly from start to finish, even though it was planned throughout its course. The Situation Handling technology tries to recognize such unexpected situations and finds the issues in the business processes. When using this technology, analytics data is constantly collected in the background. This enables a true understanding of each business process and more efficient problem recognition, by integrating machine learning technologies in the process. The goal of the Situation Handling process is to detect an issue before it causes any further trouble or costs. If something unexpected happens, the right group of users receives a notification via e-mail or the SAP Fiori launchpad. The users can act immediately and prevent the problem from happening. The Situation Handling offers continuous improvement processes, for both human supported and automated business processes and can boost productivity in the long term. SAP S/4HANA offers an own implementation of different Machine Learning algorithms that suit the most needs of enterprise customers. The goal is to achieve a better performance, by optimizing the algorithms and the availability of the data by using the faster in-memory database. The SAP S/4HANA Machine Learning includes various features, covering the entire spectrum of the technology, from consuming intelligent services through training own machine learning models to deploying and using them in a productive manner. The main use cases covered by basic machine learning algorithms are rankings, categorizations, and predictions, and can be easily implemented without needing to allocate too much memory and CPU time. More complex tasks, like image recognition, sentiment analysis, and natural language processing, require the use of deep learning algorithms based on neural networks. These models require more GPU power, so they are managed by the SAP Business Technology Platform (SAP BTP), in order to avoid that the transactional processes in the SAP S/4HANA system suffer from resources-intensive machine learning jobs. Finally, the Internet of Things (IoT) defines a network of physical objects that are equipped with sensors for measuring data from their environment and transmit it. SAP S/4HANA helps to transform this raw data into valuable information for the business processes.

What Makes Business Processes Intelligent?

As already mentioned even after a millennium of research and debate, there is no standard definition for intelligence. Generations of scientists have developed and scrutinized various intelligence models for areas ranging from mathematics, linguistics, and technology to music and human emotions, but none of them are generally accepted. So how to design an intelligent ERP, SAP S/4HANA, without knowing what being *intelligent* really means in the context of ERP? To resolve this the term is made measurable by defining different automation levels—similar to how a psychologist calculates human IQ values. By using this operationalization method, making SAP S/4HANA intelligent does not become the goal. Instead, it's the vehicle for turning automation into autonomy to improve the total cost of ownership and return on investment, and to optimize the business processes. The higher the level of automation of a business process or a system, the higher the intelligence level. The approach to automation is based on the implicit understanding that automation is more than adopting a single tool. Instead, it's a combination of intelligent concepts and technologies that enable businesses to move ahead of their competition with differentiation. At the heart of this model is SAP S/4HANA, operating as the central system for organizational processes across the business. But first, automation levels must be defined based on a clear understanding of the typical structure of every business process across four dimensions: data acquisition, information analytics, decision-making, and action-making.

The automation level of each dimension is measured within a range between 1 (low) and 5 (high), as shown in Fig. 24.5a. By determining the automation level of each dimension for a given business process or a system, the overall level of business automation can be detected. With this approach, the current and target level of intelligence for SAP S/4HANA can be determined. Then, an execution plan for making business processes more intelligent can be defined for each dimension:

Dimension #1: Data Acquisition
The process of entering data into SAP S/4HANA is often completed using devices such as a keyboard, scanner, disk, or speech to text. The automation of this dimension ranges, from low to high:

Fig. 24.5 (a) Four dimensions of process automation, (b) categorization of techniques based on automation level

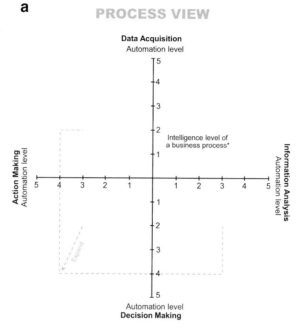

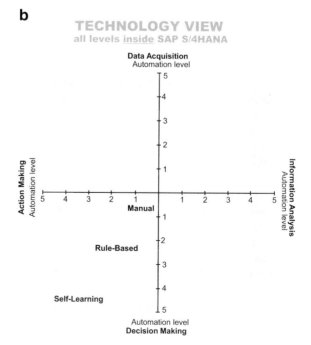

1. Manual entry by the user
2. Manual entry and data integration
3. Data integration and manual entry exceptional
4. Conversational artificial intelligence and data integration
5. AI-based data extraction integration—for example, the transformation of a PDF document into structured data and entered by a robotic bot

Dimension #2: Information Analysis
Automating information analysis requires an increasingly systematic approach to studying and interpreting data into meaningful findings, based on a scale of (from low to high):

1. Descriptive, detailing what happened in the past
2. Diagnostic, explaining why a particular event occurred
3. Predictive, forecasting what will happen next
4. Prescriptive, recommending next steps
5. Cognitive, automating self-learning analysis of past, current, and future events

Dimension #3: Decision-Making
Selecting a logical choice from available options requires a clear view of the impacts of each option. The following qualities could be used to determine the level of automation (from low to high):

1. Manual decision-making
2. Consumption of system events and changes
3. Relevant information generated by the business system
4. Technology enablement of active evaluation and decision recommendations
5. Autonomous decision-making with traceability and auditability

Dimension #4: Action Execution
The automation of enforcing instructions to achieve a specific goal follows a line of qualities for action execution (from low to high):

1. Manual action taking
2. Consumption of system events and changes
3. Relevant information generated by the business system
4. Technology enablement of active evaluation and recommendations of potential actions
5. Autonomous execution of actions with traceability and auditability

From manufacturing planning to contract consumption, SAP S/4HANA is designed to empower employees to spend more of their time taking action, instead of digging for information. The approach to intelligent automation enables the intelligent ERP to shed light on critical challenges and exceptions that most businesses miss and recommend actions that resolve or minimize the impact of such events. Consider the impact of this tactic on sales performance management. Creating a sales plan that lays out revenue goals and maps out the steps to meet those targets is traditionally a highly manual process that relies on analyzing historical data to forecast revenue. However, machine learning can significantly improve the process by predicting the forecast in terms of how sales could develop in the future and projecting how resources should be leveraged. This one update to the sales planning experience decreases the manual effort needed, while providing better insights to boost actual sales volume. To make a business process more intelligent, the current level of automation is first determined. This step is the foundation from where the target level can be derived by solution managers based on business needs. Various concepts and technologies can then be applied to achieve the specified intelligence level for the predefined dimensions. Technologies can be categorized to realize different levels of automation as shown in Fig. 24.5b. At the most basic level, business processes can be run manually without any kind of automation. Then over time, varied, rules-based techniques can be applied to increase the level of automation in respect to growing intelligence. For example, ABAP reporting can automatically perform input and process validations and display error messages with resolution instructions to the user. It can also trigger a workflow for individual tasks and decisions from one step to another until a predefined process is complete. An insight-to-action analytics scenario can also be applied, starting with a key performance indicator tile notifying the user about drifting trends. This capability enables users to perform root-cause analysis, execute corrective actions, and gain the necessary data to resolve and recommend amended actions.

Whenever it comes to achieving the highest level of automation (Level 5), rules-based approaches are no longer sufficient; they must be extended to self-learning techniques. This tactic helps make sense of raw data and discover hidden insights and relationships by learning from data, rather than programming explicit rules. Potential use cases include deep learning for image recognition, conversational artificial intelligence for natural language processing, and intelligent bots or applications based on machine learning models that support autonomous decision-making and action. Therefore, the focus of the next section is on machine learning, particularly as the techniques require new conceptual considerations.

Machine Learning Architecture

Depending on the requirements of a specific AI use case corresponding machine learning implementation approach must be selected. On the one hand, there is the embedded machine learning, running in the SAP S/4HANA backend. On the other hand, there is the side-by-side machine learning that uses the SAP Business Technology Platform (SAP BTP). Figure 24.6 illustrates the SAP S/4HANA machine learning architectures. Simple use cases like trending and forecasting require also common algorithms for their implementation, for example, regression, classification, or time series analysis. For the training of such kind of algorithms very limited data, CPU, and memory are needed. Thus, these categories of ML scenarios can be

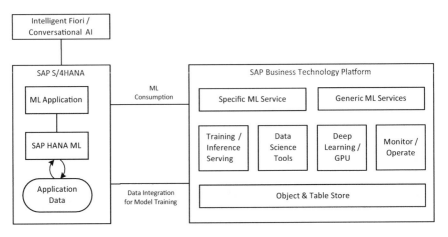

Fig. 24.6 The SAP S/4HANA machine learning architecture

implemented within the SAP S/4HANA platform based on the embedded machine learning approach. SAP HANA as the underlying database of SAP S/4HANA provides around 100+ machine learning algorithms which can be used in this context. Anyhow the application data is already stored in SAP HANA. Thus, for a specific machine learning question the adequate algorithms can be trained with those application data and exposed for inference. Hence, the machine learning capability can be deeply integrated into the business processes and user interfaces. What the relevant algorithm and the required training data are is in the focus of the data science exploration, which is the initial phase before the implementation of a machine learning application can start.

However, there are also more complex machine learning scenarios, for example, image recognition or natural language processing. These kinds of scenarios usually require more advanced algorithms like neuronal network and deep learning. This category of self-learning algorithms demands high data, GPU, and huge memory volume for training. To avoid system resources drawbacks for the transactional processes in SAP S/4HANA, these types of scenarios are scaled out to SAP Business Technology Platform. Here corresponding scalable and distributed infrastructure for training and inference is provided. Furthermore, advanced data science tools, deep leaning environment, GPU hardware, and reusable ML business services are offered. Thus, for a specific machine learning scenario, the necessary application data is replicated to SAP Business Technology Platform, the model is trained, and an endpoint for inference is facilitated. Remotely this endpoint is called by the SAP S/4HANA application in order to incorporate the machine learning feature into the business processes or the user interfaces. In addition to advanced algorithms and high demand of resources, external data is a third decision criterion for implementing a scenario based on side-by-side machine learning.

Embedded Machine Learning

The embedded machine learning is based on CDS views and uses the capabilities provided by the SAP S/4HANA system. The used algorithms can be processing intensive due to the high volumes of data, but their performance increases when the algorithms are processed close to the application data. SAP S/4HANA offers the predictive analytics library (PAL) and the automated predictive library (APL) that can be used for different statistical and data mining problems. The provided functions can be called from the SAP HANA database procedures, written in SQLScript. The data needed can be obtained from SQL views generated for the ABAP CDS views. The trained models are integrated into business processing by wrapping them with CDS views that are based on ABAP classes. These views can be combined with other CDS views and be presented to the consumers. Providing the machine learning services in this way efficiently reuses lots of already implemented concepts for CDS views like the authorization, extensibility, and the UI integration, making for a very simple yet efficient system architecture. The information gathered by the model is shown to the right user at the right moment and in the right place, making it a suitable solution for most of the SAP S/4HANA customers. Figure 24.7 illustrates the described process of embedded machine learning.

Side-by-Side Machine Learning

The side-by-side machine learning concept makes use of SAP Business Technology Platform for storing and managing the model data, even though the training data can

Fig. 24.7 Embedded machine learning

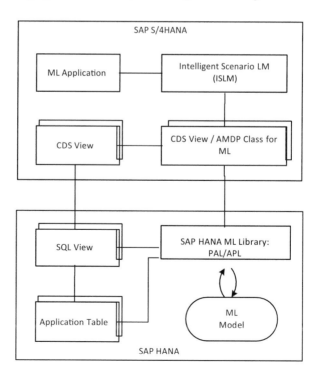

be extracted from SAP S/4HANA as well. In this way, more complex and performance-intensive models can be trained and used, without impacting the performance of the other SAP S/4HANA components. The processing of the application data is based on a pipeline engine, which offers the possibility of graphical programming for creating new scenarios, without needing to write actual code. This engine orchestrates a complex flow of data via multiple pipelines and is based on a scalable Kubernetes environment. For more advanced users, like data scientists, there is the possibility of data exploring and feature engineering using state-of-the-art technologies like Jupyter Notebook and Python. The SAP Business Technology Platform delivers the provided GPU infrastructure for training and managing the complex deep learning models. For implementing side-by-side machine learning use cases, each application must define its own scenarios and pipelines. The SAP Business Technology Platform then organizes each use case by artifacts. An artifact contains everything needed for the required implementation of a use case. They consist of multiple pipelines, implementing the training and inference processes. These pipelines can be run as either sequential or parallel tasks. The provided results can either be directly used in SAP S/4HANA applications or be served as a REST API service, allowing them to be integrated in multiple business processes. Figure 24.8 shows a graphical representation of the concept of the pipeline engine.

Exemplary Application

The machine learning applications in SAP S/4HANA are following the explained embedded and side-by-side programming model. For illustration one example application is briefly described in this section. The SAP Predict Arrival of Stock in Transit is based on the embedded machine learning architecture and predicts delivery delays. For companies issuing and receiving good from and to their plants, it is important to track the status of the materials in transit in order to take action in case of problems. The SAP Predict Arrival of Stock in Transit application gives an overview of the open shipments allowing the business user to take action. With machine learning the application predicts shipment dates for each goods movement

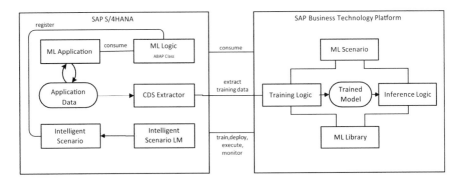

Fig. 24.8 Side-by-side machine learning

to allow users to react timely in case of delivery delays. Key features of the applications are:

• Predicting the arrival date of a shipment and classifying the status into different classes.
• Defining the predictive models, training and running the scenarios.
• Pre-built set of KPIs allows for robust analytics on SAP S/4HANA data with drill-down functionality.
• Early and efficient visibility for stock transport orders.
• Integration capabilities with SAP S/4HANA to gain real-time insights in produce scenarios with predictive analytics (Fig. 24.9).

Thus, machine learning optimizes and automates the business process of tracking stocks in transit. Overall, more reliable planning and scheduling of goods in transit processes are facilized. Enhanced usability for the businesses visualizing with predictions is provided and improves user satisfaction.

Lifecycle Management

An intelligent scenario refers to an ABAP representation of one machine learning business use case and runs through a specific lifecycle, from its planning to its final usage. The SAP Intelligent Scenario Lifecycle Management (ISLM) is a framework that helps a user to operate on different machine learning scenarios. It can be seen as a self-service multipurpose tool to be used for standardized implementation and operations of machine learning use cases. The Intelligent Scenario Lifecycle Management framework can be used in combination with both the embedded and side-by-side machine learning architectures. This framework includes the two SAP Fiori applications Intelligent Scenarios and Intelligent Scenario Management. Those two components include multiple functionalities like creating, displaying, training, deploying, and activating machine learning models. One of the operative advantages of this framework is that it offers a single access point for developers and administrators, allowing them to create and manage existing scenarios for the business. Furthermore, it proposes one standardized and comprehensive process for managing every given scenario. A big technical advantage consists in the framework's flexibility and orchestrating capabilities. The Intelligent Scenario Lifecycle Management can handle both combinations of machine learning architectures running in on premise or cloud environments (Fig. 24.10).

Creating Intelligent Scenario
Creating a new scenario requires some prerequisites. First of all, in order to create a new scenario, the specific Analytics Specialist permission role is needed. While creating an embedded machine learning scenario, it is important that the validity of the use case has been checked and that there is sufficient data in the training dataset. While using the side-by-side approach, the developer needs to make sure that the

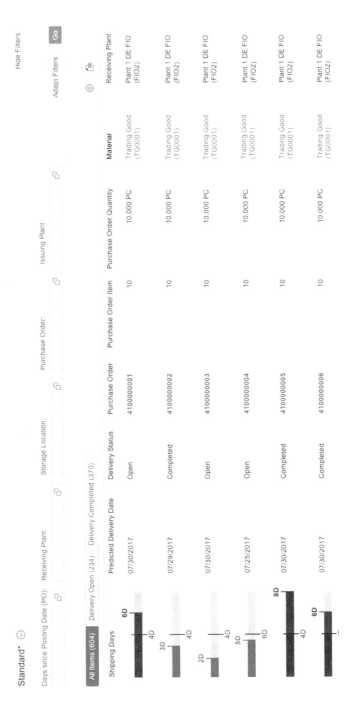

Fig. 24.9 SAP predict arrival of stock in transit with *predicted delay date* column

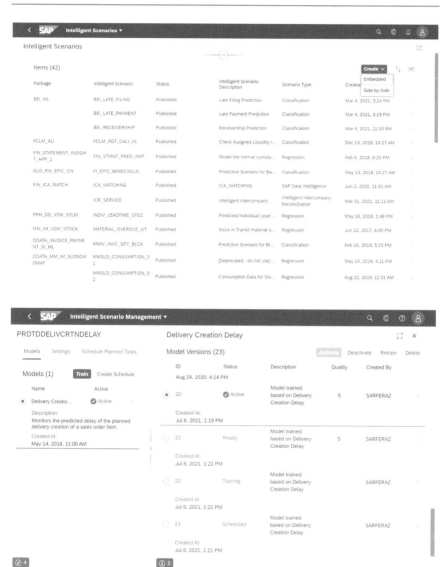

Fig. 24.10 Intelligent scenarios and intelligent scenario management

right ABAP package is installed on the system. The developer also needs to check if the ABAP class containing the machine learning logic is implementing the IF_ISLM_INTELLIGENT_SCENARIO interface correctly. After all prerequisites are processed, the procedure is very simple. Creating a new scenario is done by opening the Intelligent Scenario App on the Fiori launchpad and selecting the create button. A series of dialog boxes will guide the developer through the process, asking for any needed input, like name, description, and further configuration.

Managing Intelligent Scenario

Managing a specific machine learning scenario is done by opening the Intelligent Scenario Management application on the Fiori launchpad. The homepage of the application reveals a list of all the available scenarios that can be worked with. In order to appear on this list, a scenario needs to be made public by its creator or an authorized person. For finding a specific scenario appropriate filtering can be performed by type or creation date or searching for a keyword. After selecting a scenario, a list with its different versions is shown. Each version can be individually trained, deployed, activated, or deactivated. For each of these actions there is a specific workflow, which is not going to be discussed here. One of the most important advantages of the SAP Intelligent Scenario Management is that each of its workflows can be executed exclusively by interacting with the application's graphical interface, so that no specific programming knowledge is required.

Conclusion

As explained in this chapter, using the AI-enabled services in either their embedded or their side-by-side flavor can provide real added value to a business by improving existing processes and actively increasing the grade of automation in the company. SAP S/4HANA has lots of features with multiple customization possibilities, so that most of the use cases are being covered by default and require no complex programming skills to implement. If those standard features are not enough, the different integrated artificial intelligence libraries of SAP S/4HANA offer an out-of-the-box experience that suits every programmer's and data scientist's needs, allowing vast project implementations.

Internet of Things

25

The Internet of Things (IoT) defines a network of physical objects that have the capability to collect and exchange data through the network. These objects are equipped with embedded sensors that measure data from their environment and transmitters that enable the connection to the cloud platform. IoT based on SAP S/4HANA helps the user to transform the raw data collected by different object into valuable information for the business. That information helps improving the transparency and efficiency of different processes, like supply chain, production, or customer satisfaction. They can also help reduce maintenance costs, by constantly monitoring the devices and early recognition of problems. Thus, the foundation for Industry 4.0 is built. The SAP S/4HANA platform assists the customer and provides a comprehensive solution, covering IoT processes, from connecting the devices through data ingestion over to data transportation, storage, and interpretation.

Business Requirement

Manufacturing companies must increase productivity, produce individualized and high-quality products, mitigate the constantly changing environment, and meet the varying customer demand. For many companies Industry 4.0 is the response for turning those challenges into opportunities. Industry 4.0 respectively the industrial Internet of Things (IoT) refers to industrial transformation using new digital technology which allows gathering and analyzing data across machines and business systems, ensuring efficient processes to produce high-quality goods cheaper. Enablers for this are technology innovations like the IoT, edge and cloud computing, artificial intelligence, sensors, and robots. Thus, Industry 4.0 radically changes production across discrete and process industries toward autonomous manufacturing. Human work in production will be transformed with workers getting tailored information based on smart devices. Software solutions in production will be transformed from transactional execution to data-driven business process. Sensors, devices, machines, and ERP software will be connected.

© The Author(s), under exclusive license to Springer Nature Switzerland AG 2022
S. Sarferaz, *Compendium on Enterprise Resource Planning*,
https://doi.org/10.1007/978-3-030-93856-7_25

Application modules will be distributed between cloud and edge. Edge computing makes it possible to process application modules at the production site to enable reliability and avoid latency of business functions. Due to high level of connectedness, consequently the solution architecture must be secure, interoperable, portable, open, modular, affordable, and extensible. Often organizations consider Industry 4.0 as a manufacturing-, factory-, or distribution-center-focused approach. This is valid but not the whole story. Companies get the most out of Industry 4.0 by embracing it holistically across their entire organization. ERP systems like SAP S/4HANA have the potential to unlock the value of Industry 4.0, combining the intelligent manufacturing with end-to-end business processes across the supply chain. Industry 4.0 requires an industry-specific approach as challenges vary and there is no one-size-fits-all solution. The next figure shows the main themes of Industry 4.0 and provides also use case examples (SAP Industry 4.0 Strategy, 2021).

Industry 4.0 is based on four themes providing distinct value to the business. *Intelligent products* are manufactured and configured to fulfill customers' requirements. *Intelligent assets* are assigned dynamically to all processes. *Intelligent factories* are driven by data and machine learning for increasing the level of autonomous processing and delivering highly configurable products at scale. *Empowered people* are enabled for efficient decision-making and action execution due to availability of all the tools and information they need to do their best work. The digital twin is the common thread for Industry 4.0. The main idea is to provide a digital representation of a specific asset or system characteristics as they are designed, manufactured, and operated. This results in huge value as all information are maintained and updated consistently, for example, operating manuals, diagrams, service instructions and records, performance records, and failure modes. Thus, near-real-time processing across the network is enabled, and manual tasks are eliminated. With these data, organizations can implement capabilities that provide prediction for future states upon historical data, adopting the behavior or performance KPIs by changing variables, and performing what-is simulations by adjusting variables before instructing the physical system.

Those Industry 4.0 themes from Fig. 25.1 are implemented based on SAP S/4HANA modules like *R&D/Engineering*, *Manufacturing*, *Supply Chain*, *Asset Management*, and *Environmental Health & Safety*. Some solution capabilities of those SAP S/4HANA modules and their platform layering are illustrated in Fig. 25.2. From conceptual point of view IoT in terms of integrating sensor data into business processes is the new aspect from the SAP S/4HANA perspective. Thus, this is explained in the next sections.

Solution Capability

In this section the concepts for implementing IoT applications are explained. For this IoT applications, scenarios and architecture are depicted.

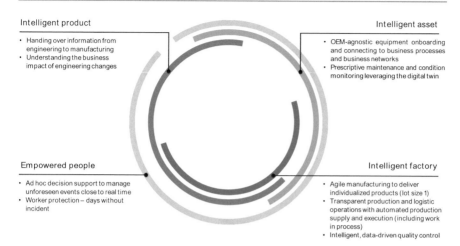

Fig. 25.1 Industry 4.0 themes and use case examples

Internet of Things Applications

Before coming to IoT applications, the basic terms should be clarified. In (ISO IEC JTC 1 IoT, 2015) the following definition for Internet of Things is given:

> An infrastructure of interconnected objects, people, systems and information resources together with intelligent services to allow them to process information of the physical and the virtual world and react.

Based on this, an IoT application can be described as software that provides intelligent services and algorithms, usually in combination with user interfaces for processing information coming from the interconnected objects, people, systems, and information resources for supporting organizations and human beings in solving a relevant business problem. It is typically based on technology components that provide generic capabilities to the application. Thus, an IoT application comprises many technical artifacts and interacts with a lot of different software components. Because of this, it is not always immediately apparent what actually belongs to one application. The granularity of an IoT application is defined by the perception of the customer: It is a set of services, user interfaces, and software components addressing one specific business problem and for which customers basically have the choice of using this bundle as a whole or not at all. Individual users however may only work with parts of the application.

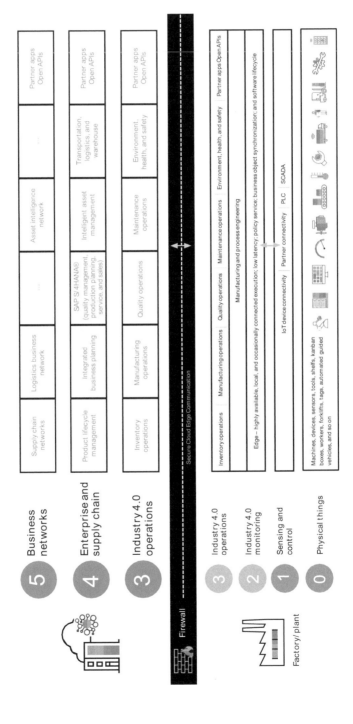

Fig. 25.2 Solution capabilities for Industry 4.0

Internet of Things Scenarios

Due to the generic nature of things and the growing technical possibilities, the domains addressed by IoT applications are very diverse—which is the reason for the enormous potential of IoT. Examples for IoT scenarios are:

- Monitor sensor data for machines, detect and predict possible damage so that parts can be replaced before failure.
- Manage moving assets (e.g., forklifts, cars) by tracking their location, state of operation, etc.
- Optimize inbound and internal traffic for logistics hubs, for example, ports, plants, production sites.
- Gain end-to-end visibility across the entire production process which is part of Industry 4.0.
- Access the quality of machined parts during production which is also part of Industry 4.0.
- Increase safety of critical processes by monitoring vital parameters of humans, for example, pulse in combination with other sensor data like acceleration.

Data Processing Scheme of IoT Applications

Most of IoT applications are based on the following processing of data (see Fig. 25.3):

1. Sensors that are part of or attached to a thing, for example, vehicle, machine, something wearable. The emitted data represent measurements of some physical parameter, for example, force, energy, speed, acceleration, frequency.
2. The sensor data are transferred to the IoT solution (i.e., the system on which the application is running) in a raw format that is defined by the manufacturer of the sensors or the components used for preprocessing the data. This information is stored as is on the IoT application system. In addition, information related to relevant events, for example, diagnostic trouble codes, key-on/key-off for vehicles, outages, detected issues, is also sent to the IoT solution.
3. By processing the sensor data, information in a domain specific format is derived and also stored on the IoT application system. In most cases, this derived data will be time series. The processing of sensor data is usually done in several steps, in which the content is parsed, and faulty information is corrected or taken out. Also, additional values may be computed like means based on a moving average and stored again as time series. Covering this process is a key capability of most IoT applications and often referred to as data ingestion. In some cases, SAP will not have access to the specification of the raw data format or to the data itself and hence depend on software from third party, for example, the manufacturer of the sensor or control unit creating/processing the data, for initially processing it.

1. sensors data is transferred to the IoT application
2. this raw data is received and stored
3. sensor data is processed and derived data/time series produced
4. on top of time series, aggregated data is created for analytics etc.
5. in some cases, the IoT application will automatically send information back to the thing for influencing its behavior
6. process steps are triggered in a business solution
A. master data is used for describing things, people, organizations (business partner) etc.
B. transactional business data can be combined with aggregated data for analytics

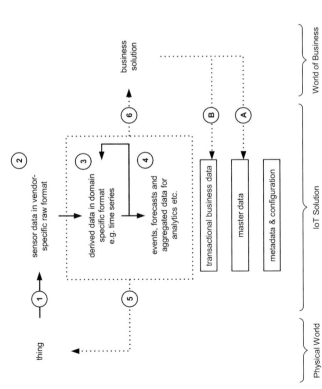

Fig. 25.3 Typical data processing of an IoT solution

4. Automated processing of, for example, time series leads to business-relevant information. This can be the detection of critical events, forecasts for the future, the prediction of upcoming values, and in most cases aggregated data with focus on analytics. Machine learning or mathematical models are often leveraged here. The goal is to give business users the most relevant information in a highly condensed form that they need for understanding if and what action is required.

5. In some cases, the IoT application will automatically send back information to the thing, for example, for influencing its behavior.

6. Based on the detected events, processes may be triggered on a business system like SAP S/4HANA that the IoT solution is integrated with. Additionally, other information, such as aggregated data may be transferred into the business system.

In all these steps, metadata may be used by algorithms for the interpretation of data from the various sources. Likewise, configuration data can be used for controlling the behavior of the algorithms involved in the data processing. Descriptions of things, devices, and sensors, for example, model or type information, can be subsumed under master data. Also, information on customers falls under this category. Transactional business data may be combined with time series and/or aggregated data in order to bring in the related perspective, for example, costs. Both the required master data (A) and transactional data (B) are often coming from business solutions like SAP S/4HANA, at least in parts. Master data specifically may have to be enriched on the IoT application system for covering all of the IoT-specific aspects. It is very well possible that some of the processing happens near to the things, for example, in a so-called edge component, and that other steps are performed in a central component. It depends on the specific use cases and the amount of data that can be transferred to a central component to what extent processing in decentral components is required. The next figure outlines the various processing steps and data involved.

Architecture of IoT Applications

Things are connected to the platform via the device connectivity component as shown in Fig. 25.4. It receives all the sensor data and hands it over to the message broker. Components consuming this incoming data are connected to message broker based on a publish-and-subscribe model. Most of the processing of sensor data is based on steps that operate on micro-batches that a streaming framework collects from the message broker. The latency for these steps can go down to around 1 s. For use cases in which faster response time is required, real-time processing steps can be connected to the message broker for one-at-a-time stream processing (Marz & Warren, 2015). In most cases, these steps raise events that are consumed by application services and forwarded to specific applications. Only in rare cases, real-time processing should lead to updates of aggregates because this increases the complexity of the consistent merging of these results with the outcome of micro-batch processing. If necessary, the timespan for streaming batches can be set to a

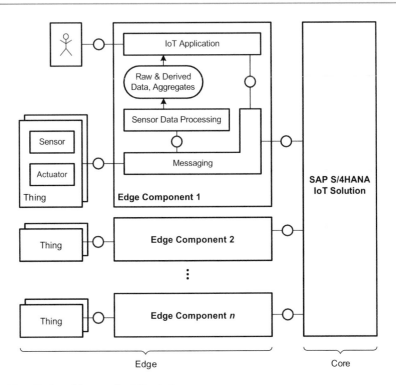

Fig. 25.4 Basic architecture for IoT solutions

longer period (e.g., 3 min), for which the term micro-batches may be misleading. However, the micro-batch processing of sensor data covers the following tasks:

1. All sensor data is stored as raw data (i.e., master datasets) directly.
2. Sets of derived data and time series are created or updated.
3. Aggregated information is updated.

The serving layer leverages different storage technologies for keeping aggregates, derived data/time series, and raw data. However, there should be one data processing and query layer that provides uniform access to all of these storage technologies of the serving layer. Users have access to analytics for inspecting aggregated information. The application services provide the foundation for all of the IoT applications. Both the server-side functionality of IoT applications and the application services are implemented as microservices hosted on a dedicated runtime environment.

In many cases, sensor data cannot be sent to a central IoT system directly. For instance, in production environments, computer numerical control (CNC) machines are usually not connected to the Internet but are rather part of a local area network (LAN) on the shop floor. Often, these machines don't support http(s) as communication protocol. For this reason, it is often required to use gateways that bridge between protocols and provide a secure connection between the components in the local network and the Internet. But this is not the only motive for having additional computing power at the edge (i.e., near the things). As mentioned previously, in many cases the volume of data that the complete set of sensors emit is too high or produced at a too high frequency for transferring it all to the central IoT system. Likewise, the feasible timespan for responding to critical events may be so short and require local action that a full roundtrip via the central system is not an option. In such scenarios, significant processing needs to be done on edge components for covering the following tasks:

(a) Filtering out the subset of data that should be transferred to the central IoT system (core)
(b) Detecting critical situations that require (local) action

Local action may also mean that the edge component sends back information to the thing, for instance commands to actuators that are part of a vehicle or machine. An actuator operates in the reverse direction of a sensor. It takes an electrical input and turns it into physical action. An electric motor is an example for an actuator. For performing the tasks described above, storing at least parts of the sensor data will be required locally. To what extent historical data can be kept in edge components depends to the system size and technology components that are feasible here.

The device connectivity component is the communication endpoint for all connected devices on the side of the IoT solution. It needs to securely identify each device, relate all incoming messages to one sensor as well as thing and via that also to a customer and tenant. This is required, because the subsequent processing steps are carried out within this context. All received messages are augmented with metadata and then handed over to the message broker. For ensuring secure data transmission between the devices and the IoT solution, which is the main task of device connectivity, the support of existing and evolving standards is crucial. Standards eliminate vendor-specific aspects and thus help simplifying the communication-related components. Most standards also define a solid approach for security. In this regard, one of the most relevant standards is the Unified Architecture by the OPC Foundation (OPC UA). Closely related to device connectivity is the management of devices. This provides the functionality which includes the automated software management (e.g., centralized software deployment for devices) for some of the devices and edge components.

Data ingestion refers to the incorporation and initial processing of new raw data for updating derived data and aggregates. As each type of sensor requires a specific treatment during data ingestion, the implementation needs to be extremely flexible and utilizes configuration data, so that it can be adapted without having customers to provide specific code. The complete processing must be based on small functional building blocks that customers can easily rearrange whenever necessary. For making this possible, it is required to provide a framework that allows users composing complex data processing flows out of elementary algorithmic steps that are then executed sequentially on each batch coming from the respective type of sensor. Processing results, for example, time series, are stored in the serving layer.

Intermediate outcomes of an elementary step are the input for the next step in the execution chain. The concept of defining a sensor-type-specific combination of processing steps and executing those on top of batches that are produced by a streaming framework is subsumed under the term ingestion pipeline. The sensor type in combination with configuration data influences the specific behavior of each ingestion step as well as the sequence of the steps as part of the ingestion pipeline. A special case of an ingestion step is the direct storing of incoming messages as raw data.

Exemplary IoT Application

For illustration of an IoT application in this section SAP Predictive Assets Insights is explained, which is part of SAP S/4HANA Asset Management. This solution is used by reliability professionals to assess, predict, and optimize the health of their assets. The application syndicates operational technology data (sensor data) and information technology data (maintenance data) to create digital insights for industrial assets. Today, maintenance and reliability experts have to automate operations and streamline maintenance and service processes. With SAP Predictive Assets Insights customers can predict equipment degradation and malfunction through advanced analytics, the Internet of Things (IoT), machine learning, and engineering physics-based models to deliver decision support. With advanced analytics reliability professionals can quickly determine top failure modes, understand leading indicators and thresholds, and capture equipment fingerprints. Real-time engineering simulations generate insights from virtual sensors based on multi-physics engineering simulation based on live IoT sensors and virtual sensors (Fig. 25.5).

Extensible machine learning (ML) predictive models are applied to determine failure probabilities and detect anomalies. IoT and ML help to monitor the health of equipment using an advanced alerting rules engine based on real-time sensor data, vibrations thresholds, and signals from machine learning and virtual sensors. The SAP Predictive Assets Insights extracts topics from the historical text data in the SAP Enterprise Asset Management notifications (i.e., long description texts from breakdown notifications) and matches these topics to the standard failure modes from ISO standards (e.g., ISO 14224) or from FMEA (Failure Mode Effect Analysis). The system also provides an optional step where the expert users such as reliability engineers can double-check the machine learning matching and provide feedback. With this feedback, the system then continuously assigns all notifications to specific failure mode. Based on these assignments, the system calculates metrics such as MTTF (Mean Time to Failure), MTTR (Mean Time to Repair), and MTBF (Mean Time between Failures) by different failure modes using the actual dates in the notifications as well as the keywords by failure modes to give insights on the frequencies as well as potential causes of these failure modes. Leading indicators are the indicators from sensor readings such as temperature or pressure whose specific conditions (e.g., temperature >90 °F and pressure <50 PSI) are correlated to breakdowns of an equipment or equipment model. Identifying these specific leading

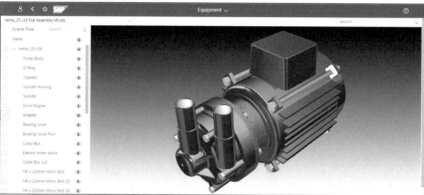

Fig. 25.5 SAP Predictive Assets Insights—equipment overview and details

indicators and conditions based on ML systematically can help customers determine condition-based maintenance rules quickly without pre-built models or data science resources. Dataset preparation capabilities allow to prepare data for machine learning, for example, aggregation periods, new features, null values. The creation of new datasets or the copying of existing datasets is also enabled. Tools to configure, train, and score models are provided. The solution facilitates to deploy custom algorithms into or perform machine learning outside of system in tool/language of choice. Finally, the simulation of virtual sensors is supported. A virtual sensor is a device that can be placed at a specific location on the product that provides a continuous reading of physical state at this location. Virtual sensors are required because of physical restrictions, unmeasurable quantities, lifecycle costs, and sensor calibration (Fig. 25.6).

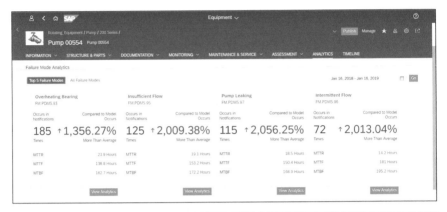

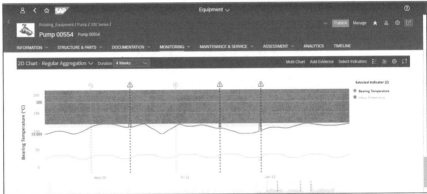

Fig. 25.6 SAP Predictive Assets Insights—analytics and monitoring

Conclusion

The Internet of Things (IoT) fuses the digital world and the physical world by bringing together different concepts and technical component. This is possible as everyday objects and machines have sensors that can communicate with each other over the Internet, making new models possible for business processes, collaboration, miniaturization of devices, and mobile communications. Thus, IoT connects people, processes, data, and machines to one another. The IoT facilitates new applications, businesses, and concepts such as Smart Grid, Industry 4.0, Connected Cities, Connected Homes, and Connected Cars. This network can be either online in the cloud or on premise.

Process Integration

Software applications and especially ERP solutions live in an interconnected world. The ability to integrate ERP into business processes encompassing multiple software applications, including those belonging to different organizations, is one of the fundamental requirements. This chapter focuses on process integration concepts and frameworks of SAP S/4HANA. Particularly, the use cases for process integration, the mediated and point-to-point connectivity types, API technologies like OData and REST, discovery and usage of APIs, monitoring and error handling are explained.

Business Requirement

Integration is becoming a key element for the digital transformation of organizations. There are various integration domains and scenarios that are encountered for integrating heterogeneous components and systems. Likewise, the systems to be linked typically *speak* different communication protocols and store their data in different formats and structures. The scope of integration is steadily expanding, with the introduction of cloud, mobile, and IoT scenarios to customer landscapes, and customers are urged to scale up their integration architecture to be able to effectively address these new areas of integration and exploit the wealth of opportunities these areas present. With the increasing demand for cloud technology and the accompanying introduction of innovations into it, customers are increasingly extending and integrating their existing on-premise applications into the cloud. Consequently, the expectation for customers that are already using cloud solutions is that SAP's on-premise and cloud solutions will provide integration with each other as well as non-SAP applications. The same, of course, applies to integration between business partners and enterprise networks, between enterprises and government agencies, and user-centric applications such as mobile apps with applications in the cloud or on premise to ensure an omnichannel user experience. To satisfy such growing integration requirements, customers and partners need a cloud integration

© The Author(s), under exclusive license to Springer Nature Switzerland AG 2022
S. Sarferaz, *Compendium on Enterprise Resource Planning*,
https://doi.org/10.1007/978-3-030-93856-7_26

platform with consistency and flexibility covering process, data, user, and IoT-related integration scenarios. This kind of platform is likely to reduce implementation effort, enhance control and compatibility, and lead to greater robustness, especially as upgrades are carried out.

There are two primary use cases for process integration:

- Application-to-application (A2A) integration: The integration of systems within an enterprise so that applications from different vendors can seamlessly connect to each other and support internal company processes. Integration is supported by exchange of messages and uses open standards for interoperability.
- Business-to-business (B2B) integration: The integration of systems across boundaries of an enterprise to enable cross-company processes. Such integrations must be in conformance with widely used industry standards like Odette and EDIFACT (electronic data interchange for administration, commerce, and transport).

Robust, reliable, and scalable communication is the backbone for remote coupling of processes. A well-known pattern that supports this is asynchronous message exchange. It decouples communication partners by eliminating the needs of a 100% simultaneous availability of involved parties and allows error handling at the places where the error occurs and could be handled best. In each involved platform a local process integration solution is required. It includes functional components for addressing, monitoring and error handling, data transformation (structural, value, and key mapping), integration configuration, web service runtime, and file exchange. The objective of end-to-end message monitoring is to ensure the connection between technical and business monitoring in order to allow a user to see the complete picture containing all involved information. All parts whatever they address—either technical, application-specific, or business process-related monitoring—shall store the monitoring information in the local system and expose relevant monitor information across systems. In asynchronous communication, there is no direct response so that the error monitoring and handling responsibility moves from the sender side to the receiver side. This concept is named Forward Error Handling (FEH). In order to execute an effective end-to-end error analysis, the error monitoring must be well integrated with other monitoring tools such as technical message monitoring or application monitoring. The error handling step must be user-role focused, so that the errors can be effectively solved by the right person responsible. The qualities of service (QoS) are set of characteristics like guaranteed delivery, duplicate detection, and delivery in right order, which define the behavior of communication. The sending application is primarily responsible for handling these characteristics, but in mediated communication the integration middleware handles QoS on sender's behalf. For example, during asynchronous message delivery if the receiver is not available to receive the message then integration middleware retries the message transmission to ensure guaranteed delivery. As shown in Fig. 26.1 there are various levels of integration starting with user interface to data integration. However, the objective of this chapter is on process integration only.

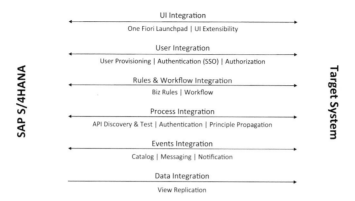

Fig. 26.1 Multiple levels of integration

Solution Capability

Enterprise architects defining the integration strategy in their company's system landscape usually try to find the best way to provide integration guidance across multiple teams, projects, and system integrators. For them it is important to look for the most suitable integration technology to approach new integration domains. The goal of the SAP S/4HANA integration strategy is to increase the straightforwardness of integration between SAP applications by aligning their processes and related data models, including the publication of APIs. The target is to simplify new integration solutions, especially for line-of-business (LoB) cloud integration scenarios, and to further deepen integration between SAP applications over time.

Communication Patterns

Two different patterns can be used to integrate processes as depicted in Fig. 26.2. The first is point-to-point and the second is mediated communication.

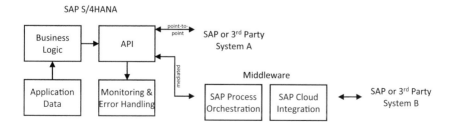

Fig. 26.2 Process integration patterns

Point-to-Point Integration

In point-to-point integration, different applications are connected directly to each other thereby enabling them to exchange data. The integration logic defines how to connect applications to each other. The logic is hardwired within each connected application at its endpoints. In point-to-point integration the connected applications can have their own data model, own databases, and this offers more flexibility than database integration. The interconnectivity among the applications having different data models is achieved by providing custom interfaces and custom mapping for each application that is connected. ERP systems like SAP S/4HANA are founded on functional rich technology platforms which typically support various API technologies for the type of communication. SAP S/4HANA offers for this connectivity option the direct connectivity, which is a go-to connectivity type, easy to set up used for SAP out-of-the-box solutions, as well as the SAP Cloud Connector, which is relevant only for SAP S/4HANA Cloud integration with SAP applications on premise and is secured by a *lightweight VPN* connection. The benefit of the point-to-point communication is low total cost of development (TCD) due to its simplicity and the reduced total cost of ownership (TCO) as no additional solutions are required. However, there are also limitations for the type of communication. If many applications are connected to each other, then the collection of such custom interfaces and custom mappings results in an unstructured, complex, and tangled integration landscape. Moreover, the complexity of such a landscape increases when either an existing application is upgraded with a newer version or altogether a new application is added to the landscape. Multiple mappings are developed to the same interface, and it is difficult to scale up such integration. Another additional problem in point-to-point integration is that any change required for connectivity to endpoints is difficult to manage and is error prone as the integration logic is distributed among the connected systems. Easy and effective change can be achieved when different systems are connected to a centralized connectivity solution rather than having direct connection. This enables creation of centralized integration logic. Mediated integration provides solutions to the problems of point-to-point integration. Moreover, this approach can very easily get out of hand as the number of connections increases to the square of the number of systems. Thus, monitoring and error handling can be complex.

Mediated Integration

In mediated integration, different systems are connected to the integration middleware. The integration middleware handles the integration logic and mediates the exchange of data between communicating peers. This eliminates the problem of distributed integration logic. An additional advantage of brokered integration is availability of connectivity endpoint details and interfaces at one central repository. This provides better control of change in connectivity requirements. Mediated integration provides more manageable, scalable integration landscape as any additional application can be connected to the integration middleware without affecting the existing integrations. By linking the systems via a central instance, all integration-relevant information is readily accessible in a central point. In addition, unlike the point-to-point approach, the number and layout of the connections remains manageable. For this connectivity option SAP offers the SAP Cloud Integration, which is the preferred process integration cloud-based middleware, available with prepackaged integration content (iFlows), and has extensibility options. In this regard, the SAP Business Technology platform is operated by SAP, and monitoring is carried out by the customer. Furthermore, SAP offers the SAP Process Orchestration, which is primarily an on-premise integration landscape, but can also be used for on-premise to cloud. This solution is completely operated by the customer. The drawback of the mediated communication is the increased TCO as additional middleware solution must be implemented and operated. For integration typically mapping between the source and target API must be provided. Thus, in case of the mediated connectivity such kind of content must be developed and deployed on the middleware product. Aspects like lifecycle management, extensibility, performance, or security become so more complex to solve as on additional technology stack is in place. The implementation of an application must not increase landscape complexity due to pure technical restrictions. This would be the case if the application programming model for integration relied on the presence of a middleware hub. On the other hand, a point-to-point programming model always allows customer to use a communication hub for scale-out and centralized administration. Therefore, the point-to-point communication shall be enabled by default. Support of easy-to-use mediated integration must be established by providing integration content from each application. For SAP S/4HANA provides numerous APIs which can be used for point-to-point and mediated integration. Those APIs and the underlying protocols are explained in the next section.

Application Programming Interfaces

Different kinds of Application Programming Interfaces (APIs) can be used to connect SAP S/4HANA with other SAP products, SAP Business Technology Platform, and third-party systems. The message delivery mode of APIs like synchronous delivery and asynchronous delivery defines the behavior of sender and receiver during message exchange:

- Synchronous delivery mode: In synchronous delivery mode, the sender sends a request message to receiver and expects an immediate response message from the receiver. The synchronous delivery mode is used when immediate continuation of further activities of sender is dependent on the processing of request message by the receiver. For example, a production planning process is dependent on delivery status of ordered raw material. So, the production planning queries the shipment status synchronously.
- Asynchronous delivery mode: In asynchronous delivery mode the sender does not wait for a response message from the receiver immediately on sending a request message. The asynchronous delivery mode is used when the processing of

message by the receiver can be decoupled from the sender. This decoupling allows the sender to continue immediately before having to wait for a response. For example, the supplier sends a notification of advance shipment to customer. The supplier can continue with the processing of next order without waiting for any response from the customer.

As illustrated in Fig. 26.3 there are different choreographies of single interaction between the communicating peers in the context of SAP S/4HANA.

Request-Confirmation is used for bidirectional communication. In this choreography, the sending application sends a request message to the receiving application. The receiving application performs the requested business action and returns a confirmation message to the sending application. Notification choreography is a unidirectional asynchronous communication. Here, the sending application sends a notification message to the receiving application. The notification message leads to data changes in receiving application. In contrast to Request-Confirmation, the receiving application sends no response to the sending application. Query-Response is a basic data provisioning pattern. In this pattern the requesting application requests some data from the provider application in read-only form, specified by a query. The provider application provides the data as response. Query-Response pattern can be either synchronous or asynchronous. Information choreography is another data provisioning pattern where sending application informs the receiving application about some changes. The difference to the notification pattern is that the information message is typically sent to a list of subscribed receivers, and the receivers are free to take immediate action upon the information received. In the following sections the different API types of SAP S/4HANA are described.

OData Services

OData (Open Data Protocol) is based on the OASIS standard that defines a set of best practices for building and consuming RESTful APIs. Therefore, it is designed to provide the standard CRUD access via HTTP(s). OData APIs are resource-oriented APIs that can be used to query and modify data models with entities that are linked by navigational relationships. OData enables the focus when creating RESTful APIs almost exclusively on the business logic by relieving the work of approaches for defining status codes or response headers. The OData services offered in SAP S/4HANA are currently only synchronous services in which the result of the operation is returned immediately in the body of the HTTP response. However, SAP is working on the option that asynchronous OData services can also be used in the future. OData is the preferred protocol for the use with custom UX, SAP Fiori, or SAP BTP applications.

SOAP Services

SOAP (Simple Object Access Protocol) is a network protocol for exchanging information in distributed environments that is based on XML to represent data and on Internet protocols to transmit the messages. Web Services Description Language (WSDL) is uses as a description language for SOAP-based interfaces

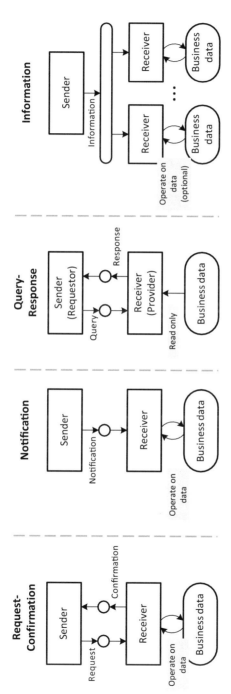

Fig. 26.3 API choreographies

and specifies the operations, as well the schemas for input and output data. SOAP services can be defined in the ABAP environment in the Enterprise Services Repository or in the backend repository of the ABAP application server. In case of custom services, there is also the option to generate SOAP services from existing ABAP function groups and BAPIs. The SOAP services offered in SAP S/4HANA are normally used for asynchronous, reliable communication, with messages that are typically one way, or don't need an immediate response. It's also possible to use synchronous SOAP services; however, they are only used in exceptional cases.

Remote Function Call

Remote Function Call (RFC) is the standard SAP interface for the communication among SAP systems and is utilized for the communication across applications of different systems in the SAP environment. This entails connections within SAP systems as well as those linking SAP systems to non-SAP systems. RFC is the traditional mechanism for remote communication which can also be performed over WebSocket instead of calling the remote-enabled ABAP function module. There are many differing kinds of RFCs, each having different characteristics and being used for a particular purpose. However, the most important are the synchronous, transactional (asynchronous) and queued (also asynchronous) RFCs.

BAPIs

Business Application Programming Interfaces (BAPIs) are a standardized programming interface for SAP business objects that are listed in the Business Object Repository (BOR) and are used for carrying out specific business tasks. Technically, BAPIs are implemented as RFCs and are typically called as synchronous RFCs. BAPIs have standard business interfaces allowing external applications to gain access to SAP processes, functions, and data. Client programs employing BAPIs to access SAP business objects can be part of the same SAP system, an external system, an HTTP gateway, or another SAP system.

IDoc

An Intermediate Document (IDoc) is a central standard SAP document format for asynchronous message exchange between SAP and non-SAP application. IDocs standardize the exchanged data independent of the used data transfer method. The transfer of IDocs is possible via transactional RFCs, via HTTP using an XML encoding, or via SOAP over HTTP. The IDoc interface is composed of the data structure definition as well as processing logic for this data structure. Additionally, exception handling can be defined in SAP Business Workflows with IDocs with no need for the data to already be present as SAP application documents.

SAP S/4HANA API Strategy

The current SAP Strategy is to focus on SOAP and OData APIs for new development. However, the traditional interfaces like RFC, BAPI, and IDoc are also supported in SAP S/4HANA. OData services will replace BAPIs for synchronous operations on resources, and SOAP services will replace IDocs for asynchronous messages. This strategy is already applied for SAP S/4HANA Cloud. Therefore, it is not planned to implement new BAPIs, RFCs, and IDocs for the cloud. However, to allow SAP customers to leverage existing and implemented integration scenarios, SAP released a controlled set of scenarios with traditional interface technologies (IDoc, BAPI, RFC) for SAP S/4HANA Cloud. In these scenarios, the SAP Cloud Connector enables RFC communication between cloud and on-premise systems in both directions.

SAP API Business Hub

The public APIs and several other types of content, like CDS views, are published in SAP's public directory SAP API Business Hub. Consequently, APIs that are not public are not listed here. In the context of SAP S/4HANA integration technology, that means that all listed APIs in the SAP API Business Hub have a compatibility contract and can't be changed or removed at any time. Additionally, it's possible for developers to experience the APIs via an API sandbox. To be able to consume the APIs from the SAP Business Hub the developers have to use the Communication Management and create Communication Scenarios and Communication Arrangements (Fig. 26.4).

SAP Application Interface Framework

SAP Application Interface Framework is a powerful framework for interface implementation, monitoring, error handling, and processing in ABAP-based systems. SAP provides the necessary interface configurations in the SAP Application Interface Framework for all asynchronous APIs in SAP S/4HANA Cloud. Therefore, these APIs are already integrated in the SAP Application Interface Framework for error handling and monitoring. For SAP S/4HANA On Premise this is only the case for a limited amount of applications. However, it's possible to configure those interfaces to be monitored, and developers can implement their own interfaces. The implementation of the interfaces is mainly done through customizing menus. Because different interface technologies come with different tools for monitoring and error handling, they might be hard to understand as a non-technology expert. SAP Application Interface Framework simplifies this process and provides uniform monitoring, alerting, and error handling. The interface components can be reused (e.g., checks or mappings), independently implemented, and tested. Furthermore, it supports variants of interfaces (e.g., exceptions), which can be tested independently as well. SOAP service, IDoc, and RFC are the supported technologies for asynchronous incoming and outbound calls. As an additional interface technology for outbound calls is OData supported. For synchronous OData calls, only error monitoring is provided.

Process Flow with the SAP Application Interface Framework

Figure 26.5 shows the conceptual architecture of SAP Application Interface Framework. Incoming calls are processed by the corresponding integration interface

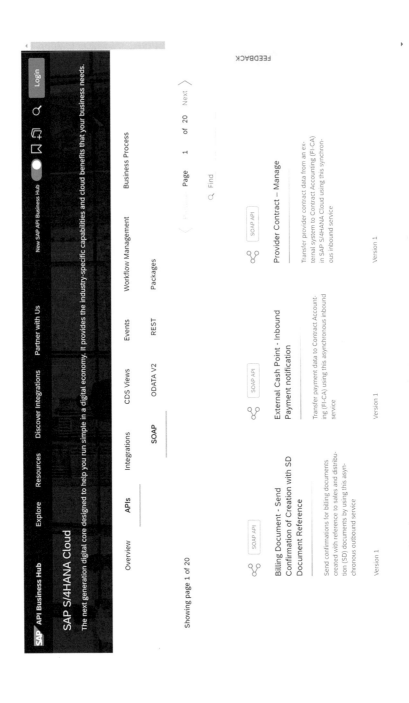

Fig. 26.4 SAP API Business Hub—https://api.sap.com

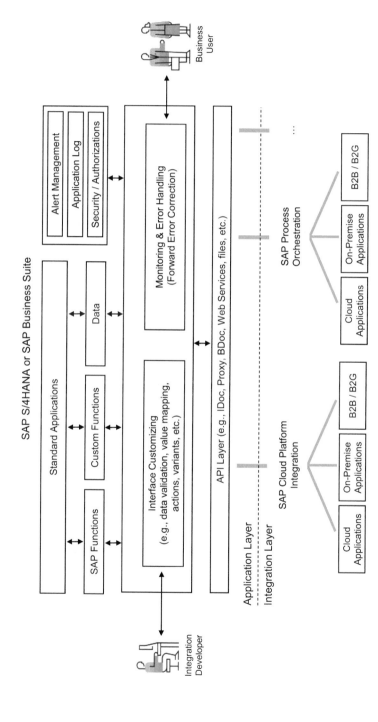

Fig. 26.5 SAP Application Interface Framework—architecture

runtime of the ABAP application server. The first step is that the interface runtime registers the call with the monitoring component of the framework, provided that the SAP Application Interface Framework is configured to be used for a particular interface runtime. Thereby the framework is notified of the call and is able to show it in the monitoring application. Next, the interface runtime invokes the actual application-specific request processing, and the application processes the request and records progress and errors in the application log. On completion or failure of the processing, control is returned to the interface runtime. In the event of error occurrences, the interface runtime logs the error information in its log. Afterward the interface runtime again calls the SAP Application Interface Framework to inform it about the status of the call. Subsequently the framework updates the status in its internal monitoring data and in the case of an error writes additional log messages. Additional configurations of the monitoring to trigger alerts to notify the user about errors are also possible. The users are able to read the details about errors and see the status of the call. Users can try to resolve error occurrences on the business level by, for example, filling missing data. The asynchronous messages and their payloads are stored in a user-friendly way in queues, so they can be edited and then be written back into the interface runtime. After solving the problem, the SAP Application Interface Framework notifies the runtime to reprocess the queued message. The process for outbound requests and messages is the same as the one described for inbound messages. THE SAP Application Interface Framework monitoring is notified prior to and after the sending of messages and requests. Then in case of errors, users can attempt to fix the problem and initiate the reprocessing of the message or request. Besides the monitoring and error-handling capabilities of the SAP Application Interface Framework, it is possible to intercept the processing of request and messages. Again, this can be specified for each interface runtime. As seen in Fig. 26.6 the interface runtime doesn't directly call the application-specific request processing but the request processing of the SAP Application Interface Framework instead. This allows the framework to perform checks and mappings based on the interface-specific configuration (e.g., value mapping). Identically, for outbound calls, the interface runtime invokes SAP Application Interface Framework processing before sending the request so that mappings and checks can be applied. The mapped request is returned by the SAP Application Interface Framework, which is subsequently sent by the interface runtime.

Integration Middleware

In addition to integrating SAP S/4HANA applications based on direct communication between them via aligned APIs, there are instances where dedicated integration middleware is preferred to mediate communication. The use of integration middleware is particularly useful when, for example, third-party products are to be integrated or messages are to be forwarded to different receiving systems.

Fig. 26.6 SAP Application Interface Framework—message monitoring

SAP Cloud Integration Service

The integration middleware SAP recommends for the cloud is the SAP Cloud Integration Service, which is available as part of the SAP Business Technology Platform. This is a multi-tenant service running on SAP Business Technology Platform which can be utilized for cloud-to-cloud integration as well as cloud and on-premise application integration. Messages coming from senders are processed by SAP Cloud Integration Service and relayed to receivers. Both senders and receivers are connected by adapters that implement the communication protocols the senders use. The incoming data from the sender's external protocol is converted to an internal message format by the sender adapter. This message format can then be used for further processing. The final outgoing messages are then converted by a receiver adapter from the internal format to the receiver's protocol. Besides the already offered adapters by SAP Cloud Integration Service for various protocols like SOAP, OData, HTTP/REST, it is possible to integrate a variety of third-party APIs with the Open Connectors capability in SAP Cloud Integration Suite. Thus, access is provided in a common way with standardized authentication, error handling, pagination, and data structures for third-party APIs from many cloud services. The routing and processing of messages is described by integration flows, which are also known as iFlows and are executed by the SAP Cloud Integration Service processing runtime. The description of iFlows encompasses the way messages are processed by senders and distributed to recipients and are visually modeled by means of the BPMN (Business Process Model and Notation) standard. For this purpose, design tools are integrated into the web-based user interface of SAP Cloud Integration Service. Predefined integration content from SAP is published on SAP API Business Hub and available for use in the customer tenant in the web user interface of SAP Cloud Integration Service. In other scenarios the offered integration content from SAP can be utilized as starting point for setting up a custom integration with SAP Cloud Integration Service.

SAP Process Orchestration

For on-premise deployment SAP recommends the integration middleware SAP Process Orchestration technology. SAP Process Orchestration has support for different installation options. Advanced Adapter Engine Extended is supporting connectivity via adapters for different protocols, routing of messages on the basis of routing rules, and mapping of message structures and values. For modeling and configuring integration content it also contains the Enterprise Services Repository and the Integration Directory. SAP Process Orchestration is an offering including an advanced adapter engine extended along with SAP Business Rules Management component and SAP Business Process Management software. Implementing application integration is distinguished in three distinct phases—the design time, the configuration time, and the runtime execution. The design time involves modeling the communication between applications at an abstract level—irrespective of the details of a particular system landscape. Later during configuration time, the communication model is adapted to run in specific system landscape. For example, the same model can be used irrespective of the physical environment of the IT systems involved. Finally, the runtime executes the configured communication model. SAP Process Orchestration architecture is composed of separate components that handle the integration tasks involved in each of these phases:

- Design time: Enterprise services repository (ES repository)
- Configuration time: Integration directory
- Runtime: Advanced adapter engine and integration engine

An integration expert uses ES repository to define and manage communication models. SAP also delivers predefined content for SAP S/4HANA within ES repository to enable out-of-the-box application integration for customers. SAP partners and customers can also extend and create new content in ES repository. The communication between applications is represented as a message. This could be, for example, a quotation or a sales order. Each message has a structure defined by the communication peers. The structure is represented as a message type in the ES repository. Applications participate in integration as either sender of messages or receiver of messages. The IT system landscape of a customer is not static. The existing IT systems are replaced or upgraded due to changing business requirements or relocated to a different network. For example, scaling up the performance of an order processing application may require upgrading the hardware of the IT system. Such changes may result in changes to the customer's existing configured communication. SAP Process Orchestration shields the existing configuration by differentiating between a technical system and a business system. A technical system is the physical server or individual operating system installation. A business system represents a communicating peer in communication. During configuration time, the integration directory refers to the business systems as communicating peer and not to the technical systems. This enables performing changes in technical systems like change of server address without affecting the configuration. The system landscape directory (SLD) offers a repository to define technical and business systems. Integration engine and advanced adapter engine use SLD information during message processing. Integration engine has the primary function of mediating the exchange of messages between communicating applications using the integration content from the ES repository and configuration objects from integration directory. The integration engine executes several services to process the incoming message. These services use configuration objects like receiver determination and interface determination and integration content like mapping objects. The services are called pipeline services, and they are executed in an appropriate sequence referred to as the pipeline (Fig. 26.7).

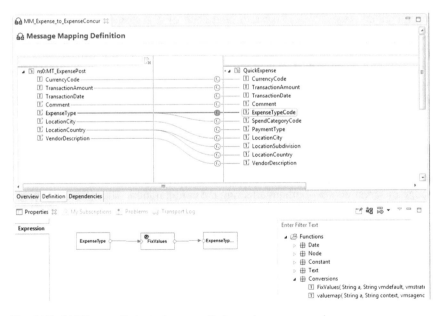

Fig. 26.7   SAP Process Orchestration—monitoring and message mapping

Conclusion

Process integration supports the chaining of business processes between two or more applications—a business process in one application initiates a supporting business process in another application. In contrast to master data synchronization, process integration does not typically require an initial load. It will not be appropriate anymore to speak of a *source* and *destination*. Examples of process integration include a service procurement process in SAP S/4HANA that initiates a contingent workforce process in SAP Ariba. SAP S/4HANA supports the point-to-point and mediated process integration. Furthermore, SAP S/4HANA provides thousands of APIs ensuring synchronous and asynchronous communication. For APIs different techniques and protocols are facilitated, for example, OData, SOAP, or RFC. Standardization for implementation and operations of APIs are enabled with SAP Application Interface Framework. For mediated integration SAP Cloud Integration Service and SAP Process Orchestration are provided as central middleware.

Data Integration

This chapter focuses on data integration concepts and frameworks of SAP S/4HANA. Particularly, the use cases for data integration, the data push and pull patterns, data replication framework, CDS-based data extraction, data transformation to data warehouse systems are explained.

Business Requirement

Application data is typically categorized as transactional data describing a single business event, or as master data, which is referenced in multiple business events. Data integration supports the synchronization of transactional and master data that is owned by source system but is also needed in the target system to enable analytics, machine learning, or the implementation of business processes. This includes both the initial load of the data from the source to the destination and the management of any changes that occur after this initial load. Examples include the synchronization of employee data between SAP S/4HANA and SAP Cloud for Customer. Usually, scheduled transfer of data from the source to the destination application is required, although near-real-time transfer might also be supported for delta changes. Bulk data transfers are demanded, although transfer of a single object may also be supported for near-real-time delta synchronization. Matching, mapping, or transformation of the data is needed before it is stored in the destination application due to differences in data models. Key requirements for data integration are:

- The data extraction solution shall support initial load: Initial load is the first step when an external application requires mass data from SAP S/4HANA. During an initial load a larger portion of instances is initially replicated from a source to a target at once. For this usually packing is required so that the data can be transmitted portion wise.
- The data extraction solution shall support delta load: If the overall size of a data source (# of rows x width of row) is small, then the data consumer can track

changes of the data source by a full reload of the source. However, this is only indicated for configuration data sources (e.g., code lists or similar) which are rarely changed. For other sources that regularly change (e.g., tables for transactional data) this approach is in general not feasible. To replicate such data sources, a delta handling is required that accomplishes the initial load by replication changes only the changes which occurred since the last data replication.

- The data extraction solution shall support resynchronization: Long-running collaboration, and data extraction is not an exception to this, tends to run out of sync. This means that the data source contains different data than the replicate, but the synchronization process does not show an error. Reasons for this are among others: Lost updates in the synchronization process, deletion at the receiver side, source objects falling out of scope if source object filters are used. Therefore, a resynchronization of the replicated data must be supported, either via complete reload of the data or via comparing and resolving the differences between source and receiver. The second approach requires more complexity, but for large data volumes a complete reload might not be feasible.

Further requirements concerning data integration are key/value mapping, transformation operations, staging area, data consistency, authorization and data privacy, extensibility and performance, monitoring, and error handling.

Solution Capability

Data integration means that SAP S/4HANA's data is transferred by a generic mechanism for various purposes like analytics, machine learning, or implementing transactional applications. Data integration itself does not trigger any business process steps. Different orchestration patterns and technologies for data integration are provided which are explained in this section.

Orchestration Patterns

In a *consumer-driven data replication*, the data consumer selects the data sources of a data provider which the consumer needs. The underlying technology then replicates the data of the various sources to the data consumer and fulfills the chosen qualities. From a business perspective, the data provider does not know who requests the data and for which purpose. A contrast to this is a *provider-driven data replication*. Here, the data provider knows the purpose of the data replication, defines the qualities, and is responsible to fulfill them. Master data replication from SAP S/4HANA to other applications is a typical representative of such kind of provider-driven data replication. Technically data integration can be implemented based on different patterns. The key data integration patterns in the context of SAP S/4HANA are illustrated in Fig. 27.1. There are two main approaches to replicate data from the source to the target system. With Push Data method, the source system

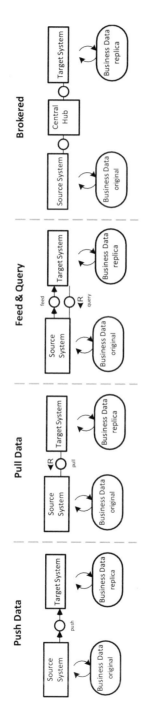

Fig. 27.1 Data integration patterns

sends all relevant data or changes via APIs to the target system. The source system as data provider monitors the data, and if it detects any changes, it sends the changed values to the target system as data receiver. The receiver acts passively and waits for new values. In SAP S/4HANA the Data Replication Framework (DRF) is based on push model.

In comparison to that, data pull runs at regular intervals, to pull the relevant data from the source system. A specific logic identifies changes in the source system and pulls it out and transfers it to the target system. In SAP S/4HANA the CDS Data Extraction is based on data pull. The pull model is usually implemented with a specific protocol, for example, for initial handshake and package wise transfer of data. Thus, the target system must also implement this protocol which results in closer coupling and additional development efforts. Furthermore, the source system must open a port so that the target system can recurrently pull data. For the setup of SAP S/4HANA systems this is a security risk which requires additional safeguard measures. Furthermore, the performance of the transactional processes in SAP S/4HANA could suffer, in case many target systems and high number of data sources are involved. The push model decouples source and target system very well. However, the data transfer responsibility is shift mainly to the source system. The push and pull method can be also combined as, for example, into the Feed and Query model. In this pattern, changes (such as employee ID, name, and e-mail address) are pushed from the source to the destination application initially as notification. If required, an additional, optional change feed may also exist, which provides a corresponding full object representation. These minimal attributes are referred to as feed in the above diagram. The destination retrieves additional data to update its local replica of the application data according to the notification. If required, a query can be also used, for example, to continue the business execution or to display to the end user in user interfaces. While the recommended approach is to retrieve additional data from the application layer using APIs, data integration tools may also be used to implement the transfer of application data from an API to a local schema. When data is being replicated, the initial load of the data can be performed by pulling the data from the source system. To minimize the data transferred after the initial load, only changed data should be transferred. An appropriate protocol mechanism (such as OData delta token) facilitates this. The Brokered Pattern is applied for applications that require advanced data transformation options, which are not available as built-in functions within SAP S/4HANA's data provisioning. Data consolidation, governance, and quality are also main reasons for implementing the brokered pattern based on a central hub. SAP Master Data Governance is an example for this pattern. The central hub usually supports push and pull capabilities.

Technologies Classification

Data integration technologies can be classified by organizational level and persistence handling. The organizational level considers if technologies are data-centric or application-centric. The more application logic and code can or must be deployed into a given technology to form a solution, the more application-centric it is. If, on the other hand, data structures and data storage aspects dominate the data integration setup, then a technology is rated as data-centric. The following levels exist:

- Manual Integration/Common User Interface: Users operate with all the relevant information accessing all the source systems or web page interfaces. No unified view of the data exists.
- Application-Centric/Orchestrated Integration: Integration logic moves from applications to a middleware or central hub layer. Although the integration logic is not developed in the applications, there is still the requirement for the applications to partially contribute into the data integration.
- Data-Centric Integration: Integration is accomplished by employing data-oriented technologies. These comprise message brokers like KAFKA, RabbitMQ, Solace. Another important group is replication, for example, SAP HANA SDI, SAP LT Replication Server, SAP Replication Server, and Mobilink.
- Virtual Integration or Uniform Data Access: This approach doesn't require data replication for the source systems. It defines a set of views to provide and access remotely the unified view to the customer. The data is not moved but remotely/virtually accessed during runtime.
- Physical Data Integration or Common Data Storage: A distinct system saves a copy of the data from the source systems to store and manage it independently of the original system. Technologies following the Extract-Transform-Load (ETL) paradigm are part of this level.

For persistence the data integration can be separated into copying (movement, replication) and non-copying (federation) paradigms. The following cases can be distinguished:

- Non-copying: No copy of data is made. Every query is evaluated against live data. Only the result of the query evaluation is sent back to the originator.
- Transitory copy: Message brokers usually store data in the payload part of a message temporarily to guarantee the requested quality of service. In replication technologies, the changed data is kept in shadow copies or stable devices.
- Copying: Data is copied and stored in another logical structure. This can happen inside the very same database, for example, in data marts.
- Moving: In contrast to copying, moving implies that the original data is deleted in the originating system after successfully completing the copy operation.

As a result, the following data integration technology groups are identified: Application to Application, Orchestration, Stream Processing, Message Broker, Replication, Offline and occasionally connected, Virtualization, Extract-Transform-Load, Migrations and Conversions.

Data Replication Framework

The SAP Data Replication Framework (DRF) as a local business object changes event processor which decides about the replication of the specific business object instances to one or more target system. It is used for data integration on business level and is a solution for data push pattern. Local change events are registered and connected to the corresponding outbound interfaces. It is used to define a replication model and check the filter conditions. The application informs the DRF about all changes in business objects. The DRF always sends complete business object instance via the given outbound. It is the event trigger for application data distribution with SAP Master Data Integration service.

Figure 27.2 shows the architecture of DRF after a business object change event in SAP S/4HANA. Customers can manage the whole data replication process to the specific target system in terms of which business objects shall be replicated through which interface and when. Using the Execute Data Replication (DRFOUT) option the whole data replication can be controlled, including initial data replication, delta data replication, or data replication on a one-off basis. The DRF is used for application integration on business level. As mentioned, customers can manage the data replication—decide which business objects are sent to which target system through which interface and to what time—using a push mechanism. Applications need to provide outbound interfaces like SOAP web service interfaces or ALE IDOC interfaces to use DRF. In the design phase the application connects their interfaces to DRF; afterward during the configuration phase the replication model can be created. The whole framework is completed by the key mapping framework and the value mapping framework, so it supports non-harmonized identifiers and code lists. The DRF offers several features. First of all, it is possible to connect all relevant data exchange technologies (Web Services, ALE, RFC, File transfer) and all relevant transfer modes (initial, delta, manual, direct) to the DRF. A powerful data filtering enables the customer to select objects by using configurable parameters, to reuse filters across business objects, and to use special system filter to avoid outdated copies in the target system. The DRF supports delta analysis and offers tracking and

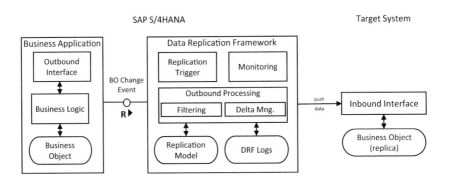

Fig. 27.2 SAP Data Replication Framework—architecture

monitoring capabilities (own logging, SAP standard tools for monitoring, core components for end-to-end monitoring). The pre-delivered SAP content can be extended by the customer, and it enables mass data. Outbound interface class depicted in Fig. 27.2 must implement the ABAP interface *IF_DRF_OUTBOUND*. The methods of this interface are listed in the table below. The most important method is *SEND_MESSAGE*, which pushes data from SAP S/4HANA to the target system.

Interface method	Description
INITIALIZE	Initialize method of the outbound implementation
ANALYZE_CHANGES_ BY_CHG_POINTER	Change analysis by ALE change pointers
ANALYZE_CHANGES_ BY_MDG_CP	Change analysis by MDG change pointers
MAP_DATA2MESSAGE	Map internal data to the message structure
SEND_MESSAGE	Send processed message
ENRICH_FILTER_ CRITERIA	Enrich filter criteria
ANALYZE_CHANGES_ BY_OTHERS	Change analysis by other parameters than change pointers
ANALYZE_CHANGES_ BY_MDG_CP	Change analysis by MDG change pointers
BUILD_PARALLEL_ PACKAGE	Build parallel package for message processing
READ_COMPLETE_DATA	Read complete data
APPLY_NODE_INST_ FILTER_MULTI	Apply node instance filter on multiple relevant objects
APPLY_NODE_INST_ FILTER_SINGLE	Apply node instance filter on single relevant object
FINALIZE	Finalize method for outbound implementation

Before starting with the replication as precondition DRF must be customized which includes:

1. Configuration of the data replication
2. Definition of filter criteria (for the use of external data replication filters)
3. Definition of the necessary authorizations

The customization of replication model defines which data shall be sent. This allows to specify which outbound implementations and filter objects shall be applied from the range of available services. These customizing activities are independent of the message target application. Together with the subordinate view maintenance, DRF supplies table entries that can be used as existing elements in the application configuration. In addition, corresponding classes for filter objects, filters, and service implementations are assigned to the delivered entries.

CDS-Based Data Extraction

The Virtual Data Model (VDM) is an executable, structured model of a HANA database view that provides direct access to the data of the business application in SAP S/4HANA at runtime. All existing tables can be transformed into an understandable, comprehensive, and executable data model that exposes all the business data. The VDM consists of CDS views. Core Data Services (CDS) are used to create persistent and semantically rich data models. Those data models can be consumed on database server and support conceptual modeling and relationship definitions, built-in functions, and extensions. CDS is an enhancement of SQL that can be used to define semantically rich database tables or views and user-defined types in the database. CDS views are managed by the data dictionary of the ABAP platform and executed in the database system. Those views are used in ABAP SELECT statements as the data source and only return data that the active user is authorized to access.

The CDS-based data extraction is a technical option for SAP S/4HANA On-Premise and Cloud concerning data integration. It replicates data from SAP S/4HANA into target systems like SAP BW4/HANA, SAP Data Intelligence, or third-party solutions. The CDS Data extraction is based on the data pull pattern. For different data integration scenarios, CDS provides several channels for a general data extraction model. Delta extraction can be performed using data extraction and delta element annotations of CDS views. To define these annotations, a delete element or a *pseudo delete* field, like a timestamp, is required. Figure 27.3 shows coarse architecture and an example for CDS-based data extraction.

Typically, CDS views are projections on database tables—the connection between view, table, table elements, and table key fields is modeled and can be reused by the underlying extraction framework. The SQL views generated during activation of the ABAP CDS views are used to read the access the data for extraction. The approach supports full and delta extraction from SAP S/4HANA with the following different API protocols:

- Operational data provider (ODP) offers the data extraction with the corresponding APIs and extraction queues. SAP BW4/HANA is using the method for replication of application data for data warehousing.
- Cloud Data Integration (CDI) is based on open standards and supports data extraction through OData services. This method can be used by arbitrary target system which implements the CDI protocol.
- ABAP CDS Reader Operator replicates the application data into SAP Data Intelligence and extracts afterward the data from the ABAP pipeline engine in the SAP S/4HANA system.

To enable CDS views for data extraction respective annotations must be specified. The key annotations are listed and explained below:

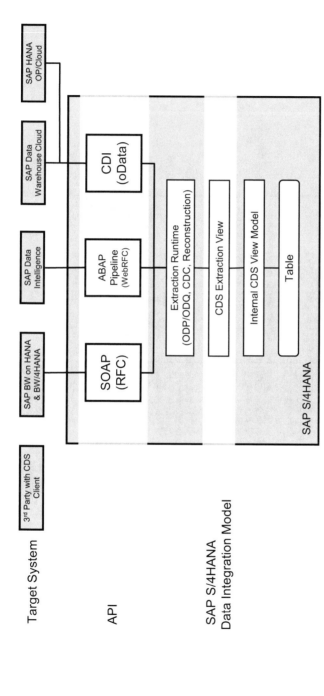

Fig. 27.3 CDS-based data extraction—architecture and example

```
1-@EndUserText.label: 'Sales Organization Data Extraction'
2 @VDM.viewType: #CONSUMPTION
3 @Analytics.dataCategory: #DIMENSION
4 @AccessControl.authorizationCheck:#CHECK
5 @AbapCatalog.sqlViewName:'SDSALESORGDX'
6 @Analytics.dataExtraction:{
7                enabled: true,
8                delta.byElement: {
9                    name: 'ChangedDate',
10                   maxDelayInSeconds: 300}}
11 define view C_SalesOrganization_DEX
12   as select from I_SalesOrganization
13
14 association [0..1] to I_Currency as _SalesOrganizationCurrency
15   on $projection.SalesOrganizationCurrency = _SalesOrganizationCurrency.Currency
16 association [0..1] to I_Currency as _Currency      = _Currency.Currency
17   on $projection.currency
18 {
19    @ObjectModel.text.association: '_Text'
20 key SalesOrganization,
21
22    @ObjectModel.foreignKey.association:  '_SalesOrganizationCurrency'
23    SalesOrganizationCurrency,
24    @ObjectModel.foreignKey.association: '_IntercompanyBillingCustomer'
25    IntercompanyBillingCustomer,
26
27-   //Company
28    @ObjectModel.foreignKey.association:  '_CompanyCode'
29    CompanyCode,
30    _CompanyCode.Country,|
31    _CompanyCode.Currency,
32    _CompanyCode.FiscalYearVariant,
33
34    //Associations
35    _Text,
36    _CompanyCode,
37    _IntercompanyBillingCustomer,
38    _SalesOrganizationCurrency,
39    _Currency,
40
41    //Delta
42    ChangedDate
43 }
44 where CompanyCode = _CompanyCode.CompanyCode
```

```
annotation Analytics {
      dataExtraction : {
          enabled : boolean default true;
          delta : {
              byElement : {
                  name : RefToElement;
                      @MetadataExtension.usageAllowed : true
                      maxDelayInSeconds : Integer default 1800;
                      detectDeletedRecords: boolean default true;
                      MetadataExtension.usageAllowed : true ignoreDeletionAfterDays :
                      Integer;
              };
              changeDataCapture : {
                  nodes : array of {
                          role : String(20) enum {MAIN; COMPOSITION;
                                                 LEFT_OUTER_JOIN; INNER_JOIN;};
                          // only one of the next 3 annotation may be used
                          association : associationRef;
                          entity : entityRef;
                          table : String(30);
                                      // only used if association is not specified
                          viewElement : array of elementRef;
                              // only used if association is not specified
                          logElement : array of elementRef;
                          filter : array of {
                              element : elementRef;
                              type : String(10) enum { EQ; NOT_EQ; GT; GE;
                                                      LT; LE; BETWEEN;} default EQ;
                              value : String(45);
                              highValue : String(45);
                              };
                      };
              };
          };
      };
```

- dataExtraction.enabled—Via this indicator the application developer can mark those entities that are suitable for data replication (e.g., for mass data it is necessary to provide delta capabilities). This capability is usually lost on the level of consumption views where joins, procedures, and aggregations blur the relation to the primary data. It is expected that an application will deliberately design a set of data provisioning views, which are suitable for consistent and redundant-free replication.

- dataExtraction.delta.byElement—The application developer can enable the generic delta extraction by this annotation.

- dataExtraction.delta.byElement.name—This is the element that should be used for filtering during generic delta extraction. This element can either be a date (ABAP type DATS) or a UTC timestamp.

- dataExtraction.delta.byElement.maxDelayInSeconds—There is always a time delay between taking a UTC timestamp and the database commit. The annotation defines the maximum delay in seconds. The standard value is 1800 s.

- dataExtraction.delta.byElement.detectDeletedRecords—By applying this annotation the system is going to remember all key combinations of the view that were extracted in delta mode. If a key combination doesn't exist in the view any more this is going to automatically generate a delete image in the extracted data.

- dataExtraction.delta.byElement.ignoreDeletionAfterDays—This   annotation
  makes   sense   only   together   with   dataExtraction.delta.byElement.
  detectDeletedRecords. The extraction will ignore deleted records if they are
  older than the specified number of days. The main objective is archiving. Example: If records are planned to be archived after 2 years then this value shall be less
  than 700. In this case, the deletion in the database tables will be ignored if the
  record is only less than 700 days.
- dataExtraction.delta.changeDataCapture.nodes—This annotation defines the list
  of tables that should be logged. Details regarding the attributes of this annotation
  are @Analytics.dataExtraction.delta.changeDataCapture.nodes List of tables that
  should be logged
  - .role Possible values:
    #MAIN The key of the extraction view corresponds exactly to the key of
      the logging table.
    #COMPOSITION There is a node with role #MAIN, and the key of the
      logging table is part of the key of the extraction view.
    #LEFT_OUTER_JOIN There is a left outer join but not all requirements of
      role #COMPOSITION are met.
    #INNER_JOIN There is an inner join to another table. Entries might
      disappear in the extraction view due to updates on the fields of the join
      condition.
  - .association Name of the association to the CDS projection on the table to be
    logged.
  - .entity Name of the CDS projection view on the table to be logged.
  - .table Name of the table to be logged.
  - .viewElement View elements of the equal join condition between the actual
    CDS view and the CDS projection view or the logging table.
  - .logElement Elements or fields in the logging table of CDS projection view of
    the equal join condition. Both arrays, *viewElement* and *logElement,* must
    contain the same number of elements. Additionally, the array *logElement*
    must contain exactly all key elements of the logging table without the client
    element.
  - .filter Filter on logging table:
    .element Name of the element in the logging table or view
    .type Possible values are: #EQ, #NOT_EQ, #GT, #GE, #LT, #LE,
      #BETWEEN
    .value The filter value
    .highValue Only used in combination with type #BETWEEN

  The delta handling for CDS-based data extraction is implemented based on
change data capture as depicted in Fig. 27.4. This approach uses database triggers
which are created for all database tables related to extraction views.
  Those triggers are implemented by the change data capture engine and depend on
the timestamp field to detect what has changed since a given point of time. The

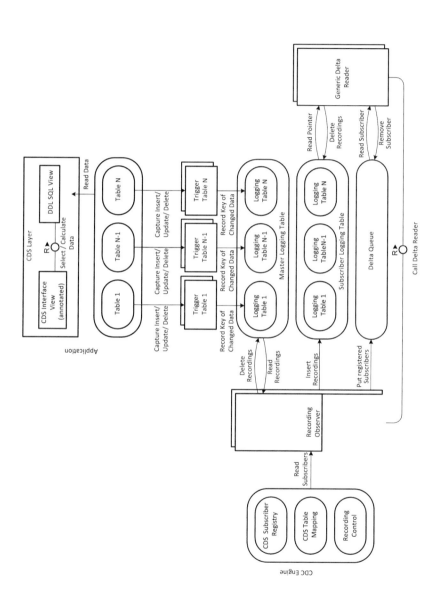

Fig. 27.4 Change data capture

corresponding change information is written into the change data logging tables. For this feature the CDS extraction views must be annotated accordingly. The change data capture framework provides information about the specific mappings between tables and views and can even do it automatically for simple cases. In regular periods of time the change data job is executed, and the logging tables are being filled. The change data capture engine uses them to determine if there were changes and what has been changed. Now the CDS writes the extracted data to the queues off the ODP framework.

Data Warehouse Replication

Replicating application data from SAP S/4HANA to data warehouse solutions is also very common use case. Figure 27.5 summarizes the key methods to extract data from SAP S/4HANA to SAP BW/4HANA in the context of cross-system analytics

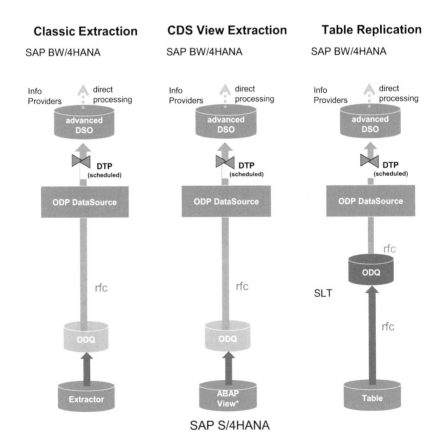

Fig. 27.5 Data extraction options for data warehousing

and historical reporting. SAP BW/4HANA supports direct access or a full data extraction and a delta extraction, including delta records. SAP BW/4HANA uses the ABAP CDS as a source. Based on the CDS view corresponding DataSource in the SAP BW/4HANA system is created. By using Operational Data Provisioning (ODP) source template, the CDS view is utilized to automatically fill the DataSource input fields. After saving and activating the DataSource, a Dataflow is created. The Dataflow contains the source system object and the DataSource itself. After creating a new persistent object with all fields of the DataSource, the object is copied to the new advanced Data Store Object (aDSO). Now the aDSO can be transformed using the SAP BW/4HANA techniques. There are options for the extraction of delta and full load. After choosing these options the aDSO can be executed to extract the data from SAP S/4HANA to SAP BW/4HANA.

In SAP ERP there are extractors provided for replicating application data to SAP BW. The majority of those classic extractors can also be used in SAP S/4HANA on premise. Due to simplification of the data model in SAP S/4HANA, some of the classic extractors have been deprecated. An additional data extraction method is the replication based on data base triggers using SAP Landscape Transformation Replication Server (SLT). A trigger copies modified rows to shadow tables or remote locations (e.g., for delta loading). The materialization is performed independently of the original transaction. While this reduces overhead, databases can get out of sync, which can lead to all sorts of problems for the information consumer. SAP Landscape Transformation Replication Server is based on this technique. In contrast to database triggers without transactions, triggers with transactions perform the materialization within the transaction. Because transactions are a well-proven method for guaranteeing the integrity of data modifications, this approach increases reliability of trigger-driven database replication. Of course, the cost of this increased integrity is reflected in decreased application performance caused by transactional overhead.

Master Data Governance

Master Data Governance (MDG) is also part of SAP S/4HANA and enables data replication based on the already explained Data Replication Framework (DRF). MDG supports in keeping master data consistent even in complex system landscapes that are distributed across various locations. MDG facilitates to adjust master data quickly to reflect legal changes, track changes, and respond flexibly to new requirements and to business transactions such as takeovers of other companies. MDG, central governance enables central ownership of master data in line with a company's business rules and processes. MDG provides domain-specific, out-of-the-box applications as well as a framework for custom-defined master data. MDG allows change request-based processing of master data with integrated workflow, staging, approval, activation, and distribution. MDG ensures to be deployed as a distinct hub system or co-deployed with SAP S/4HANA. Independent of the deployment option, MDG can use SAP and company-specific business logic to create master data for usage in an enterprise's business processes. Furthermore,

MDG consolidation offers functionalities to load master data from different sources, to standardize the master data, and to detect duplicates. For each match group, consolidation determines the best record from the duplicates in that group. These can be used in dedicated analytical or business scenarios. MDG combines consolidation and central governance to support various master data management scenarios, for example, initial load of master data as a starting point for central governance, consolidation of master data after mergers and acquisitions. With mass processing MDG facilitates to update multiple master data records at a time. To update records, the fields and records must be selected which have to be changed. The system then offers statistics on the updated fields and validates the data for business transaction use before activating the changes. MDG, data quality management applies rules to master data to determine errors and to trigger corrective measures. Rule mining allows to use machine learning for data analysis and for the creation of data quality rules from mined rules.

Master Data Integration Service

The Master Data Integration Service exchanges and synchronizes master data objects among business services. It creates and stores the data in their local persistence and distributes the master data objects and ongoing updates. It validates the incoming data on a basic level, writes all accepted changes to a log, and uses CDS view-specified master data models. When master data is created or changed in an application, this supplication calls the asynchronous change request API of the Master Data Integration Service. The customer can set different filters to influence what master data they want to get. The Master Data Integration Service supports the daily work of the employee and master data objects of the cost center.

Conclusion

Data integration transfers SAP S/4HANA application to target systems based on generic mechanism for different use cases, for example, analytics, machine learning, or implementing transactional applications. For data integration various patterns exist which are often also combined. SAP S/4HANA supports in this context pulling of data with CDS-based data extraction and pushing of data with Data Replication Framework (DRF). CDS views can be enabled for data extraction by adding specific annotation to them, for example, dataExtraction.enabled = true for full upload. DRF scenarios follow standardized class interface implementation for collecting and sending the application data. Initial load and delta handling are ensured by SAP S/4HANA data extraction technology.

In-App Extensibility

28

This chapter focuses on in-app extensibility concepts and frameworks which allow customers and partners to enhance the functionality of SAP S/4HANA. Particularly, adding database files and objects, extending application logic, creating forms/e-mail templates, exposing data, creating custom analytics, and the adoption of user interfaces are explained.

Business Requirement

Extensibility is the adaptation of standard software by partners, customers, or SAP, including the related integration into system landscapes, with the goal to add functionality for individual- or industry-specific needs. For customers, the most important use cases are Content Adaptability (UI, forms, analytics, documentation, individual terminology), Structure Extensibility (field extensibility, node extensibility), Business Logic Extensibility (new objects, business rules, application scripting, arbitrary complex extensions through coding), and Process Extensibility (workflows, process steps, integration). Figure 28.1 depicts the key use cases for the in-app extensibility.

Extensibility plays an important role in the context of business applications such as SAP S/4HANA or ERP systems in general. The software is supposed to be dynamically adjustable to the present businesses needs and the future ones too. Another benefit of extensibility is that software can be even more function rich, because add-ons could target a very specific or unique problem without bloating the core-software. It is important to distinguish at least two roles within the extensibility process: the line-of-business (LOB) expert and the developer (or sufficiently skilled IT expert). Extension projects are triggered and driven by business experts. Therefore, it is essential to incorporate them by providing suitable, non-technical extensibility tools. Still, certain tasks will require the involvement of the IT expert/developer. Key requirements concerning extensibility are:

© The Author(s), under exclusive license to Springer Nature Switzerland AG 2022
S. Sarferaz, *Compendium on Enterprise Resource Planning*,
https://doi.org/10.1007/978-3-030-93856-7_28

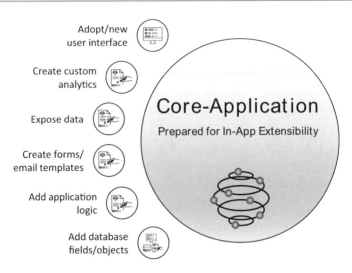

Fig. 28.1   In-app extensibility use cases

- Ensure Stability After Upgrades: Customers' and partners' extension must continue to work after patches and upgrades, without any manual or automated after-import activities.
- Enable Multilayer Extensibility: Multilayer extensions shall be supported in terms of allowing customer extensions on top of industry extensions.
- Avoid changing SAP delivered artifacts: Modification of SAP standard objects can be overwritten after updates and upgrades. Furthermore, using modified functionalities cut off customers from new innovations provided with updates and upgrades.

Solution Capability

In-app extensibility refers to extensions which can be implemented using predefined enhancement point within the core application. The core as well as extensions run on the same infrastructure allowing them to share the same database instance. The key difference is that the extension in nonintrusive, which means that there is no need to modify the core-software. Imagine extensions sitting on top of the core application, like a VM sits on top of an operating system as illustrated in Fig. 28.2 (Saueressig et al., 2021b).

Stability

Although extensibility offers a rich feature set and flexibility (even for non-developers), it also needs to meet certain stability criteria. Extensions therefore

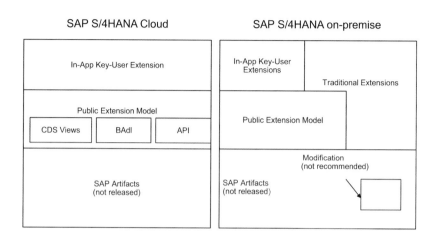

Fig. 28.2 Extensibility mechanisms

need to be future-proof, simple to maintain, and easy to operate. It's even more important for software as a service product, because of the limited abilities users have. In order to achieve these qualities, the development must be based on reliable interfaces, simplicity, and decoupling. For interfaces to be reliable they need to be technically and semantically stable across releases. Simplicity is achieved by providing tools which are easy to use by the end user. Loosely coupled software needs to be able to be updated without changing custom code, extensions aren't allowed to block any main software updates, logically and technically SAP S/4HANA core and extensions are separated, custom extensions have to access SAP S/4HANA through publicly released APIs only, and modifications of the core code aren't just not allowed, but not even possible.

Reliable Interfaces

To ensure the reliability of programming interfaces, like APIs, code enhancement points, or VDM views, they need to be kept stable across releases. To achieve that, only a few software artifacts are exposed to be extended, called, or referenced. In SAP S/4HANA only released artifacts are viable for use or extension. Other objects are hidden or visible for information purposes. Although useful for stability, only the new cloud version of SAP S/4HANA relies on that practice. The classic on-premise version allows for further modification, which could result in future compatibility issues, if used incorrectly. As shown in Fig. 28.2 reliability is at risk in on-premise systems, because extensions which aren't implemented through the public extension model could break after an update or modifications of SAP S/4HANA core.

Simplicity

Simplicity under SAP S/4HANA is achieved by generating technical objects, such as OData services, SAP Fiori UIs, custom code, view extensions and associations, and database changes, by tools rather than requiring further interactions from users, which leads to easy usability. The extensibility tools for the key user follow a no- or low-code approach.

Loose Coupling

In SAP S/4HANA loose coupling is provided for custom artifacts created with key user tools. To realize above-mentioned requirements, SAP S/4HANA and the custom extensions are coexisting in a stable runtime. Lifecycle on the other hand is separated to protect the SAP objects and allow future compatible development.

In the next sections different mechanisms of in-app extensibility of SAP S/4HANA are explained.

Field Extensibility

Field extensibility describes the ability to add custom attributes to data within applications. An example would be a remuneration statement with added lines for company specifics. In SAP S/4HANA key user in-app extensibility uses SAP objects to describe extensible applications. Those objects are used to describe structures of SAP S/4HANA applications. To be extensible and available in key user extensibility tools a given business object must be marked as such by an SAP developer through a business context which points to that particular business object note. The business context is also used to describe what is allowed to be extended in that note type.

Custom field extension refers to the capability of adding customer-specific fields to a business context of an application in a one-to-one relation or adding SAP fields that are available in tables and structures of the application. This approach is based on extension includes as illustrated in Fig. 28.3. An extension include is an almost empty include with a dummy field due to data dictionary (DDIC) restrictions. It is shipped by SAP as an anchor point for enhancements. The include is part of all necessary structures, for example, database, API structures, or service implementations. All enhancement fields are part of DDIC appends, which are a modification-free DDIC extensibility approach. The extension includes are the basis

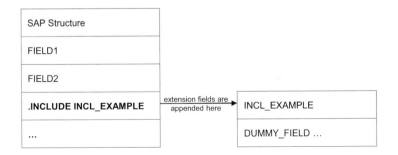

Fig. 28.3 Extension includes

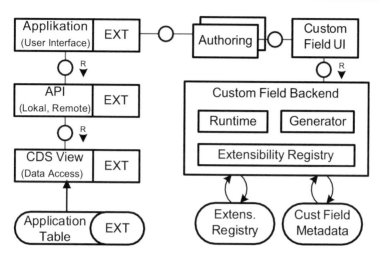

Fig. 28.4 Customer field extensibility

for the custom field extension which must explicitly be prepared by the application as shown in Fig. 28.4. In this context database tables and DDIC structures must be incorporated as extension includes to provide a stable anchor point for DDIC appends. Custom fields will be then added via DDIC appends. ABAP code in the application must generically transfer extension fields between structures/internal tables via move correspondingly.

Extensible CDS views for training data must provide as so-called extension include association to an extension include view. This is a CDS view on the database table containing only the key fields and later the custom fields from the extension include. The extension include view acts as a stable anchor point for CDS view extensions and makes the extension fields accessible on extensible CDS views via the extension include association. Custom fields will be added to the extension include view as soon as they are added to the persistency. The extensible CDS views will be extended when selected in the where used dialog of the Custom Field UI as not all consumers are able to traverse the extension include association to access the custom fields. The concept of field extensibility facilitates user to create new own fields or extend the usage of existing fields. For example, as shown in Fig. 28.5 on the user interface level the user is enabled for the following actions:

- Hide fields in a form, table, filter, hide groups, areas
- Add field to UI from field repository
- Rename labels of groups or fields
- Move field or groups, create new groups
- Combine fields into one line, split combined fields
- Define new filter and table variants

Fig. 28.5 UI adoption based on field extensibility

Integration and Data Source

Integration extensibility is important to allow customers and partners to connect SAP S/4HANA with other SAP or non-SAP systems like eCommerce solutions. It is essential in order to build highly specialized systems and custom solutions. SAP S/4HANA's integration extensibility allows for adding custom fields into standard APIs and exposing data through custom APIs as described in the last section. The data source extensibility can be used to create, edit, and delete data source extensions in order to enable the usage of existing fields in pre-delivered data sources. The data source extension feature enables the key user to enhance UIs, form data providers and reports by standard fields that the application did not provide there. The additional fields are read only. Write access is not supported.

Custom Business Logic

Custom business logic is enabled by the before-mentioned extensibility mechanism and aims to adopt software behavior. SAP S/4HANA offers a custom business logic tool which enables users to create their own calculations and algorithms, and validate certain SAP fields under their own criteria in which they can use several attributes, states, and/or external resources (Fig. 28.6). Technically the custom business logic extension is enabled via Business Add-Ins (BAdIs) which are object-orientated enhancement points. The key feature of Business Add-Ins is that they enable users to change the functionalities of well-defined business functions without making changes to the source code. Business Add-Ins aren't even limited to SAP S/4HANA development, which makes them versatile to use. They can be also integrated into customer application, which enables them to be customized by other customer applications. In case of SAP S/4HANA On Premise the ABAP tools like ABAP Eclipse can be utilized to implement Business Add-Ins. Thus, sophisticated development concerning Business Add-Ins can be leveraged. In the case of SAP S/4HANA Cloud, the implementation ability is restricted in order to avoid destabilization of the transactional processes due to incorrect or inefficient coding. Thus, only whitelisted ABAP statements are allowed, and no write operations are permitted. Nevertheless, customers can create own enhancement implementations by using ABAP for key users. They are able to implement their custom logic, test it, for example, with predefined test variants, and create filter conditions to define when an enhancement implementation is executed. Furthermore, customers can publish enhancement implementations to their test system, edit enhancement implementations that have already been published, and also delete enhancement implementations (Fig. 28.7).

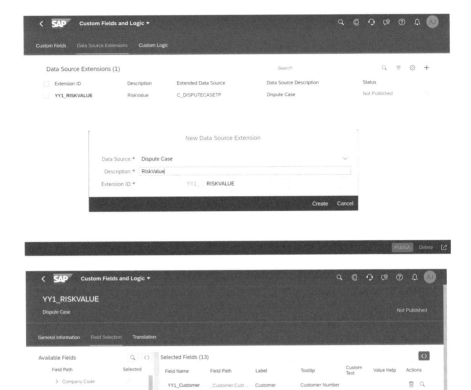

Fig. 28.6 Data source extension

Custom Business Objects

With custom business objects key users are enabled to manage data needed in extensions or process logic, which can work intendedly of the contexts defined by SAP S/4HANA. These objects give the need for new corresponding tables in the database. Much like in object-oriented programming languages, custom business objects can have a hierarchy with parent and child nodes, for example, for a marketing scenario own database tables are used. Furthermore, custom business objects can make use of user-generated, created, and updated OData services. Users

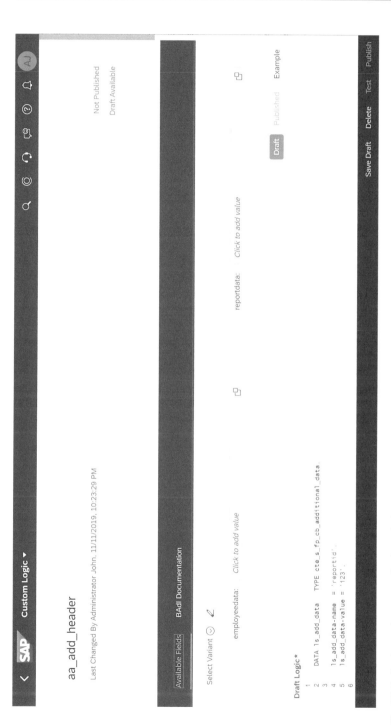

Fig. 28.7 Implementing custom business logic

also can copy already published custom business objects, generate UIs based on custom business objects, publish business objects, and edit published business objects. Furthermore, they are allowed to create subnodes for one business object, create custom logic on node level, reset business objects to their last published version, and even delete custom business objects that aren't in production yet. For custom business objects no instance-based authorization is provided and also no read access logging is supported. In addition, custom business object cannot be marked as relevant for data protection and privacy. Therefore, they cannot be blocked or deleted (Fig. 28.8).

Custom CDS Views

Custom Core Data Services (CDS) views build the foundation to create, read, update, and delete (CRUD) operations, OData services, and SAP Fiori applications. They are used to extend data models, custom analytics, and consuming data in custom logic. In the corresponding custom CDS views key user tool, users are able to build own CDS views based on publicly available CDS views for SAP S/4HANA. Furthermore, it is possible to join several CDS views, perform calculations and aggregations. The underlying concept for extensible CDS views is extension include associations to an extension include view. This is a CDS view on the database table containing only the key fields and later the custom fields from the extension include. The extension include view acts as a stable anchor point for CDS view extensions and makes the extension fields accessible on extensible CDS views via the extension include association. Custom fields will be added to the extension include view as soon as they are added to the persistency. The following example illustrates the extension of CDS views:

```
// SAP-defined View:
namespace sap.orgmgmt;

view EmployeesView as SELECT from Employee
{
  ID, name,
  salary,          // returns nested structure
  address,         // returns the association as itself
  {                // resolves :1 association and creates a structured type
        manager,
        name as orgunitName,
  } as orgunit
}

// Extension of SAP-defined View by customer "acme":
namespace acme.orgmgmt;

@EndUserText.Label: 'Extended Employee View' //adds a new label to the view
extend view sap.orgmgmt::EmployeesView
{
  // A new customer-defined field is added:
  acmeFlags,
  // the SAP-defined element "name" is extended with a new label text:
  @EndUserText.Label: 'Name of Employee'
  extend name,
  // SAP-defined structure "orgunit" is extended by the SAP-defined field "costcenter":
  extend orgunit { costcenter }
}
```

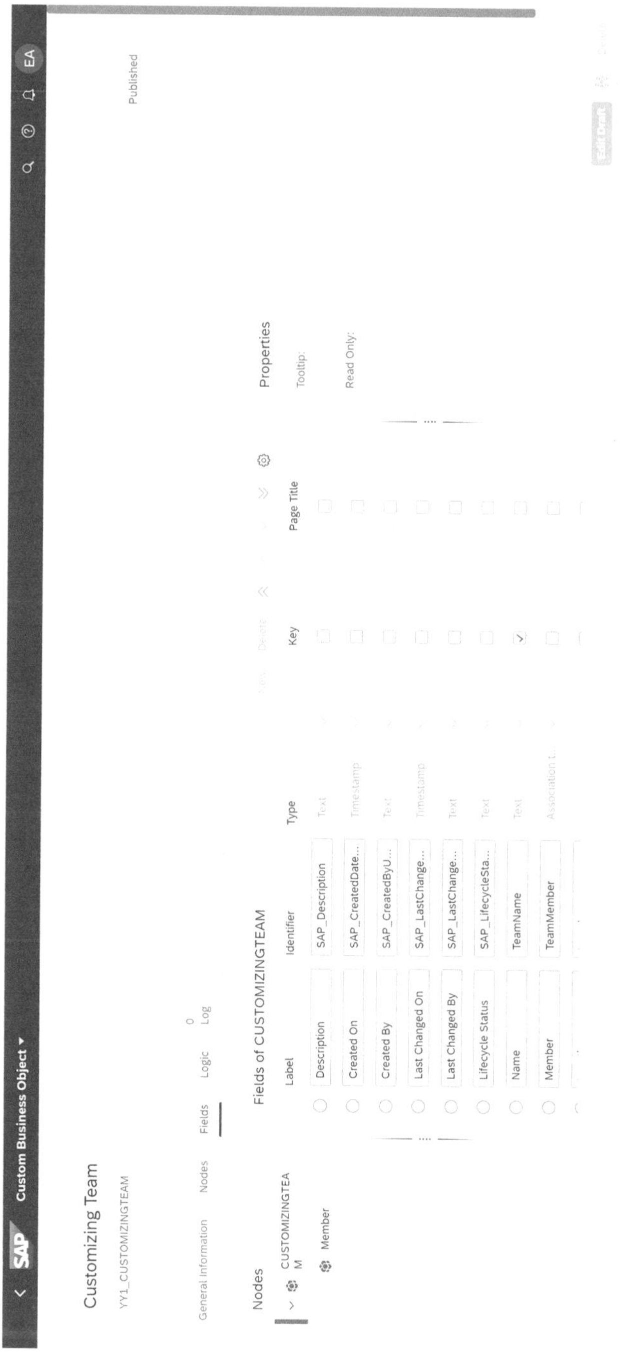

Fig. 28.8 Custom business object

The `extend view` statement leads on the one hand to the enrichment of the runtime object of the base artifact `sap.orgmgmt::EmployeesView` with the extension elements. On the other hand it leads to the creation of the name `acme.orgmgmt::EmployeesView`, which acts both as the name of the extension artifact and as an alias for the extended view allowing access to the base artifact together with all the extensions. This alias is equivalent to the effect of the following statement: `view acme.orgmgmt::EmployeesView as alias to sap.orgmgmt::EmployeesView`. The key user tool also supports exposing custom CDS view as read OData service for external usage. Another way to make use of Custom Core Data Services views is for the custom analytical queries which allows users to search and create new queries. The key user tool facilitates adding or removing custom fields in new queries. Additionally, it supports the creation of restricted measures, hierarchies, calculated measures, and user input filters. Custom CDS views can be leveraged as a data source on top of pre-delivered queries. Custom CDS view allow users to implement external APIs which are exposed with the OData protocol. The analytical scenarios make use out of cube or dimension CDS views. The View Browser gives a list of available CDS views and enables users to search and browse for views, view types, tables, and fields. The View Browser is accessible as the business role SAP_BR_ANALYTICS_ SPECIALST and is usually the starting point for custom CDS views (Fig. 28.9).

Custom Reusable Elements

Custom Reusable Elements are specified for custom code reuse. They enable users to modularize and structure custom code using methods organized in custom libraries. The most important features of Custom Reusable Elements are creation of new custom libraries and adding methods to libraries. Furthermore, adding details to those methods, testing of custom code, and saving/publishing custom code and methods are supported. Additionally, Custom Reusable Elements supports custom code lists which are reused in multiple custom business objects. A code list consists of code values and their corresponding value descriptions—for example, ['31.12.2020', 'Date']. Caution is advised when transporting a code list, because they can't be modified in any way afterward. The code value descriptions can also be translated. Another important aspect is the template approach which lets users' package and export extensions with the Export Extensibility Template App and import them elsewhere using the Import Extensibility Template App. This approach increases productivity with which users are able to develop certain extensions (Fig. 28.10).

Extensibility Cockpit and Inventory

The Extensibility Cockpit is comparable with a single point of contact. It shows users available in-app extensibility options of SAP S/4HANA Cloud at one place.

Fig. 28.9 Custom CDS views

Fig. 28.10 Custom Reusable Elements

Extendable objects can be displayed for selected business contexts. Furthermore, key users can list implemented extensions belonging to specific business context objects. They can also find links to objects and extensions like custom fields, APIs, and Core Data Services views. Extensibility Cockpit facilitates filtering on solution scopes, scope items, or business contexts. It adopts the appearance of a result list by sorting, grouping, and recording data. Furthermore, it allows to extend a search to extensible objects and choose the extensible objects that shall be included in a search. The Extensibility Inventory gives an overview of extensibility items and displays associations or dependencies between them. Furthermore, it shows how importing or exporting extensibility items affects other extensibility items. By clicking on an extension item, users can view additional information about it: The *header*, which contains the name, type, date of last change of an extension and the user who performed it, and information whether the item has been deleted, imported, and/or exported. *Uses* covers information about used extensions items by a given extension item. *Used by* works in a similar fashion, but it shows which extension items use the extension item in question. *Change History* gives a list of all changes made to a given extension item. The *Task Category* shows information about which category a given task is associated to. It can belong to deprecation, security, functionality, performance, stability, or error category. Finally, *Task Priority* shows information of whether an extension item is of low, medium, or high priority, depending on the urgency with which the item needs to be reworked. Furthermore, searching for names and descriptions of related extensible objects is supported. Information about the availability of a structural or logic enhancement for a business context is provided. Additionally, navigation to the SAP Best Practices Explorer for details about a scope item is enabled (Fig. 28.11).

Lifecycle Management

One aspect of lifecycle management is transporting extensions into different systems while remaining stable under mentioned criteria, whether it's a quality system to test or the production system. In the cloud variant of SAP S/4HANA the key user creates extensions in the test and configuration tenant, which afterward are transported to the production tenant. The Adaption Transport Organizer (ATO) is able to automatically perform this process without needing any administrative input while keeping the system stable. Another aspect of lifecycle management is the handling of SAP S/4HANA updates. It's demanded that all extensibility capabilities offered to customers must continue to work after an SAP software update without manual work, which makes updates independent of adaptions by the customer. For the on-premise deployment of SAP S/4HANA users need to manage updates through classical transport tools. Transport management can be used to export software collections, while being independent of system upgrades. Extended objects can be added in a software collection in quality system. To add dependent objects to a software collection, they can be provisioned accordingly. Once exported through the quality system, the software collection is imported into the productive system.

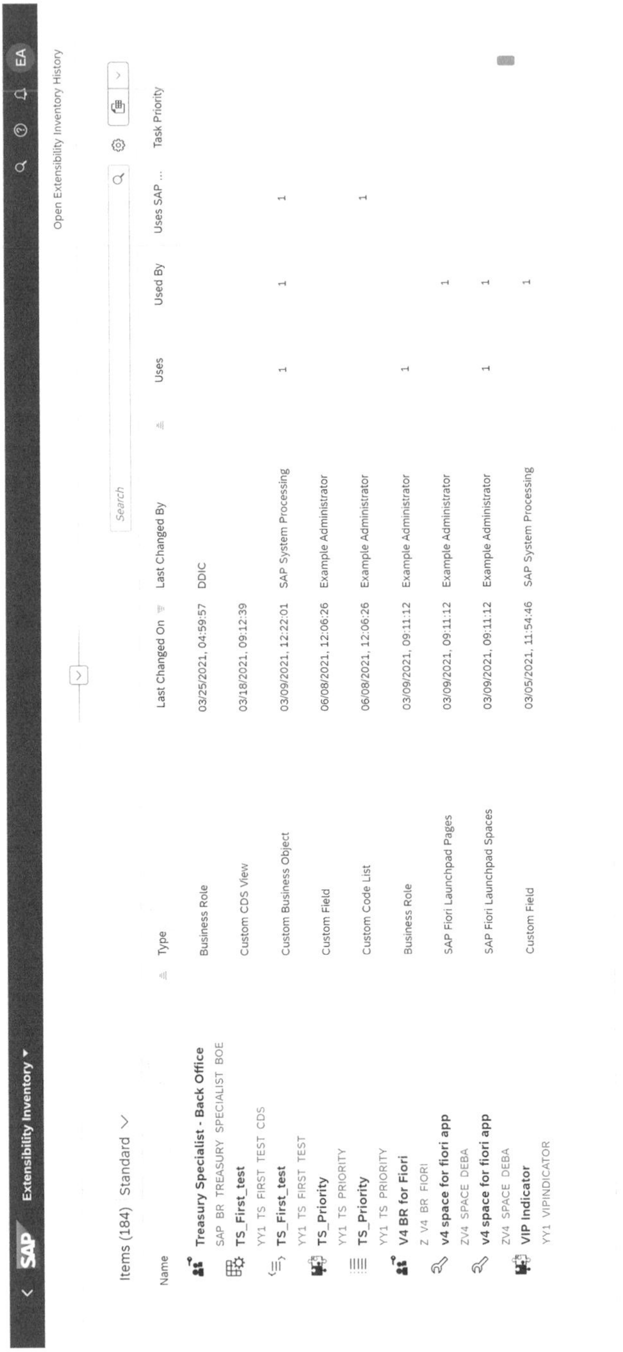

Name	Type	Last Changed On	Last Changed By	Uses	Used By	Uses SAP ...	Task Priority
Treasury Specialist - Back Office SAP_BR_TREASURY_SPECIALIST_BOE	Business Role	03/25/2021, 04:59:57	DDIC				
TS_First_test YY1_TS_FIRST_TEST_CDS	Custom CDS View	03/18/2021, 09:12:39					
TS_First_test YY1_TS_FIRST_TEST	Custom Business Object	03/09/2021, 12:22:01	SAP System Processing	1	1	1	
TS_Priority YY1_TS_PRIORITY	Custom Field	06/08/2021, 12:06:26	Example Administrator		1		
TS_Priority YY1_TS_PRIORITY	Custom Code List	06/08/2021, 12:06:26	Example Administrator			1	
V4 BR for Fiori Z_V4_BR_FIORI	Business Role	03/09/2021, 09:11:12	Example Administrator	1			
v4 space for fiori app ZV4_SPACE_DEBA	SAP Fiori Launchpad Pages	03/09/2021, 09:11:12	Example Administrator		1		
v4 space for fiori app ZV4_SPACE_DEBA	SAP Fiori Launchpad Spaces	03/09/2021, 09:11:12	Example Administrator	1	1		
VIP Indicator YY1_VIPINDICATOR	Custom Field	03/05/2021, 11:54:46	SAP System Processing		1		

Fig. 28.11 Extensibility Inventory

Furthermore, users have the option to merge different software collections into one software collection. Development objects are tracible, so the order of processed nodes and custom business objects are transparent. Furthermore, users are enabled to trace BAdl implementations or methods. Also, tracible are the values of input, output, changing parameters of validations, determinations, actions, and duration of execution. All those aspects are covered with the Custom Logic Tracing. To protect certain objects or functionalities, access to them can be restricted by associating them to catalogs through roles and authorizations. This is available for Custom Business Objects, Custom UI, and Custom Analytical Queries. To maintain roles and catalogs Identity and Access management applications can be used.

Conclusion

In-app extensibility is about extending the functional scope of SAP S/4HANA by relying on predefined methods and tools. In contrast to modifications customer's extensibility is safeguarded and continues to work after updates and upgrades. SAP S/4HANA offers a wide range of techniques to enhance the systems functionality from database tables to business logic and user interfaces, all while remaining stable under the criteria reliable interfaces, simplicity, and loose coupling. Key extensibility approaches were explained, for example, field extensibility, customer business logic and objects, customer CDS views. Furthermore, the lifecycle management requirements and solutions for extensibility were depicted.

Side-by-Side Extensibility

29

This chapter focuses on side-by-side extensibility concepts and frameworks which allow customers and partners to develop decoupled software modules for SAP S/4HANA. Particularly, developing dependent extensions and implementing own custom/partner applications are explained. The general structure of the SAP Business Technology Platform is described and illustrated with an example implementation.

Business Requirement

Every customer has additional use cases for enhancing the functionality of their ERP implementation. With extensibility for every specific use case an expert or even people without technical know-how can develop their own enhancements. These must be applicable for the cloud and on-premise ERP solutions. ERP systems are patched and upgraded based on a fixed schedule to remove security vulnerabilities, fix bugs, and improve experience by adding valuable new features. Thus, innovations are also delivered with patches and upgrades. However, this can take long and still may not meet the specific customer requirements so that extensibility mechanism must be always available. There are two types of extensibilities provided for SAP S/4HANA. The first one is in-app extensibility and the second one is called side-by-side extensibility. The in-app extensibility realizes an easy implementation for business requirements by key users. The key users don't have to be technical experts to implement simple extensions on their SAP S/4HANA system. The in-app extensibility comes with web-based extensibility tools for simplified lifecycle management. The side-by-side extensibility aims on technical experts using SAP Business Technology Platform (BTP) capabilities to extend SAP S/4HANA. By consuming SAP Business Technology Platform features applications can benefit from scalable technologies, for example, machine learning, analytics, or Internet of Things. These services can be accessed and modularly implemented on nearly all cloud-native programming languages. Side-by-side extensions are decoupled from

© The Author(s), under exclusive license to Springer Nature Switzerland AG 2022
S. Sarferaz, *Compendium on Enterprise Resource Planning*,
https://doi.org/10.1007/978-3-030-93856-7_29

Fig. 29.1 Side-by-side
extensibility use cases

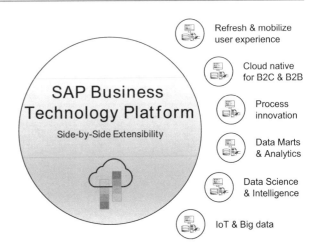

SAP S/4HANA and run as a side car to it. Thus, extensions that cannot be implemented using in-app extensibility are developed based on side-by-side extensibility. Huge software components representing new business processes which are not covered by SAP S/4HANA are an example where the side-by-side approach shall be applied. Figure 29.1 summarizes key use cases for the side-by-side extensibility.

Developers can build and test new user interfaces or mobile applications and may use cloud services to integrate external (non-SAP) users through social media or other channels. Technical experts are able to simplify enterprise processes and workflows by accessing application logic through APIs. Furthermore, developers can integrate their software with SAP Business Technology Platform applications and third-party solutions. It is possible for applications to trigger predefined events, like processes starting automatically or reporting functionalities if any sensor data reaches a certain limit. Customers can also build new standalone apps for their Internet of Things (IoT) infrastructure. This kind of application is independent and does not need additional services from SAP S/4HANA. Events or services can be triggered using APIs. The modularity enables highly scalable system infrastructures, which are independent of the SAP S/4HANA product lifecycle. Services can be activated or deactivated according to the customers' requirements. Developers can implement, test, deploy, and extend their applications with the SAP Web IDE, which runs on SAP Business Technology Platform. Side-by-side extensions also support hybrid scenarios in terms of implementing applications across the SAP S/4HANA On-Premise and Cloud systems.

Solution Capability

The technical foundation for side-by-side extensibility is SAP Business Technology Platform, which is a platform-as-a-service (PaaS). It is used to develop and integrate new applications or to extend existing applications through several extensions. Applications created within the SAP Business Technology Platform are available in the mentioned cloud computing environment which is managed by SAP. The platform contains many capabilities, for example, services focusing on security, data and storage, or analytics. With Java-based Software Development Kits (SDKs), the development of cloud-native applications is enabled. Customers can use SDKs to build their own application and cover their specific requirements. SAP partners can develop applications to sell them on the app store.

SAP Business Technology Platform

The SAP Business Technology Platform (BTP) is the foundation for side-by-side extensibility. Developers of applications and service providers build on SAP BTP as the single, unifying platform that provides the foundation of our cloud offerings to build, integrate, and extend. Over time, all capabilities in the intelligent suite will be consumable through this common platform, especially those that provide a benefit across products. To facilitate this, SAP BTP consists of three main parts, from an architectural perspective, as shown in Fig. 29.2: application plane, data plane, and foundational plane.

Plane Services

From an architectural perspective the application plane provides the client-facing entry point to the intelligent suite. The focus here is to achieve a harmonized approach to exposing the business domain model, business domain services, and flexible business processes. Consistent building blocks like user interface components, experience components (e.g., one-inbox), a central entry point, a marketplace, SAP Graph, and the underlying SAP One Domain Model all lead to a consistent user experience for a perceived homogeneous product suite. By being a centralized entry point, it also allows us to rethink our customer experience. This plane also enables a standardized approach to customization and extension. From an architectural perspective the data plane provides semantic and consistent access to all enterprise data across SAP systems/services, manifesting core principles of enterprise data management in the cloud. It combines SAP's entire portfolio of data-related cloud services into a single logical plane to provide, integrate, derive, and analyze data to enhance the value for the customer. It contains data management solutions, like managed SAP HANA services, SAP Analytics, SAP Data Intelligence, and SAP Master Data Integration. Data management technologies are mainly consumed by applications as managed services. Therefore, the data plane implements cloud qualities including elasticity, high availability, and cost efficiency to achieve the needed acceptance by applications. From an architectural perspective

SAP Business Technology Platform

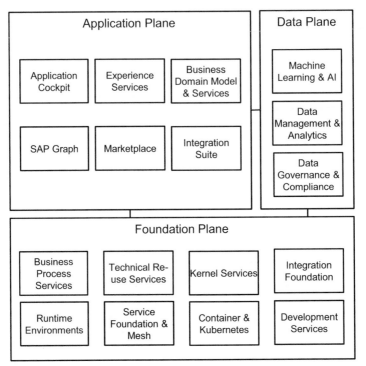

Fig. 29.2 SAP Business Technology Platform—functional architecture

the foundational plane establishes a common baseline of reusable services, as well as an open approach to grow an organic ecosystem of services. This plane includes the Kernel Services (identity service, audit log, event bus, subscription management, data privacy, and more), but also technical reuse services that drive synergies across the platform. The core of the foundational plane is a service management infrastructure, combined with a secure mesh for cross-service trusted communication. We strive for uniformity of the services with guardrails on API-based and event-based integration, but also UI integration. We expect service providers to offer cloud-native SLAs for their service, meaning committing to both measurable KPIs and a superior consumption experience (time-to-value) and successfully fulfilled quality criteria.

Development Services

Development services support the developer from SAP and its ecosystem. Providing solutions for developers who range from professional cloud-native developers to casual or citizen developers, this includes programming paradigms (ABAP in the cloud, CAP, RAP, etc.), SDKs, and a variety of development tools. Developers must target high availability, elasticity and scalability, pay-per-use consumption and trial, operability of services, etc. To avoid reinventing the wheel, best practices and patterns embodied in the development services result in higher development productivity, while aiming to remain flexible to break out where needed. SAP BTP also provides three distinct yet open programming model layers that define tool sets for different developer personas based on different needs and skills: A flexible cloud-native model with full control, a high-level coding model that offers conveniences for common business application development tasks, and a low/no-code model for citizen developer that features graphical extension, configuration, and customization capabilities. These layers complement each other and allow the combination of tools, such as the progression from low code to pro code. For the side-by-side extensibility the SAP BTP SDK, SAP Cloud SDK, and SAP S/4HANA APIs are the key building blocks. The SAP BTP SDK allows developers to create generic extensions with taking advantage of SAP backend datasets held in the SAP BTP system. Example use cases are expense reporting applications, business process workflow applications, or inventory management applications. The SAP Cloud SDK is based on the SAP BTP SDK and provides additional knowledge on the SAP S/4HANA processes and objects to build faster side-by-side extensions. It is a tool set for developers, which helps interacting with SAP S/4HANA when building cloud-native extension applications. It consists of various libraries (Java, JavaScript, ABAP) to support different types of programming languages. The SAP Cloud SDK provides predefined templates for specific projects to accelerate the development of extensions. The SAP S/4HANA APIs enable interactions between multiple software applications. It is available for both SAP S/4HANA Cloud and On Premise. SAP S/4HANA is used by developers to connect their enterprise with other resources. As a digital core it contains all applications offering programming interfaces for interaction.

Application Development

For side-by-side extensibility customers can develop applications or extensions for specific use cases. These applications are technically decoupled from SAP S/4HANA and integrated with APIs. Different domains must be considered in this context, for example, integration of UIs, users, processes, events, and data. The side-by-side extension programming model is comparable to an independent microservice consuming various contents from SAP S/4HANA. A custom-made application mainly consists of three layers: the UI layer, the application layer, and the database layer. The UI layer shows a well-designed interface of specific business processes to the user. The application layer covers the business logic and connects to SAP S/4HANA with APIs. The database layer contains the application data which is exclusive for the extension. Dependent extensions and customer applications can be implemented based on this approach as illustrated in Fig. 29.3.

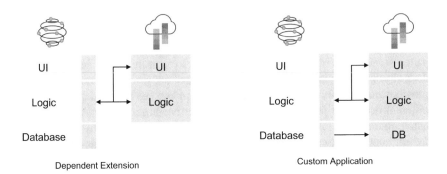

Fig. 29.3 Application development types

Development of Dependent Extensions

Technical experts develop dependent SAP BTP extensions if specific business process steps must be adapted. This adaption may result in a custom-designed user interface or in renewed business logics. A dependent extension consumes already existing assets of SAP S/4HANA as well as artifacts created based on in-app extensibility, for example, new OData service, new logic, or new data persistency. With the SAP Fiori launchpad it is possible to integrate the custom-built side-by-side extension as a new tile in the launchpad. The SAP Fiori launchpad is a landing page for all SAP Fiori applications as well as for classic UIs like SAP GUI. There are many use cases for dependent extensions. For example, customers can create proxy applications to secure the SAP S/4HANA system from the Internet. It is also possible to develop preprocessing and postprocessing applications. These can be helpful if data must be collected before a business process can be started in the SAP S/4HANA system or if the business process needs to trigger specific events based on the outputs of completed process steps.

Development of Custom Applications

Custom applications are running side by side on SAP BTP and are typically self-contained. They are used to provide new UIs for business processes, to deploy new business logics and also to create a new data persistency on SAP BTP. With Core Data Service (CDS) views application data can be replicated from SAP S/4HANA to SAP BTP. Events from SAP S/4HANA could also be consumed. The custom application could require new in-app extensions like new OData service or new logic and data. Just like the dependent extension, this application needs the SAP Fiori launchpad to integrate itself as a new tile in the SAP Fiori launchpad. There are many use cases for custom applications. They can be completely new to simplify a difficult business process, or they can substitute already existing business processes or single steps of these. In addition, businesses can build analytic applications. This is useful when connecting multiple data sources to one analytical database. Side-by-side custom applications are standalone apps.

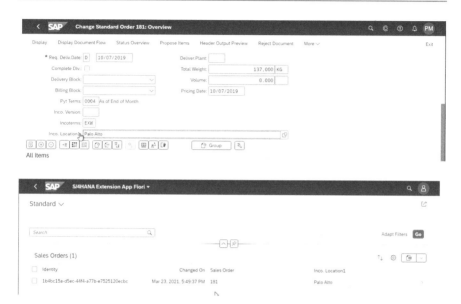

Fig. 29.4 Changing sales order in SAP S/4HANA and displaying sales order in SAP BTP

Development Example

The use case of the example application is about triggering an event when sales orders are updated in SAP S/4HANA and displaying the changes in the SAP BTP extension application as illustrated in Fig. 29.4. The user can update, for example, the *Inco. Location1* field of a sales order from *San Jose* to *San Francisco*. Thus, a change event is triggered in SAP S/4HANA. The example extension on SAP BTP shall receive the change event and notify all responsible employees about the update of the sales order. The extension application shall show the modified items in a sortable list as illustrated in Fig. 29.4. By clicking on an element, full details of the sales order shall be provided to the user of the extension.

Project Setup and Structure

To retrieve all object details from SAP S/4HANA Cloud and to view it in the SAP BTP application, the event trigger is used. The event can be by the API *SalesOrderChanged*, which can also be renamed. On top there is an SAP Fiori user interface as frontend. The application can be developed by using the SAP Business Application Studio. This framework contains template files for specific application types. The business system must be registered to connect the example extension with the respective accounts. The extension application requires instances for several services: SAP S/4HANA Cloud Extensibility and Messaging Events services. To access API endpoints, developers must request their own secret API keys on the SAP API Business Hub. To find the correct API key for this project, it is recommended to search for *Sales Order API* on the SAP API Business Hub. This API must connect with the SAP S/4HANA Cloud Extensibility service instance *Sales Order Integration*. Developers must choose a suitable runtime for their project. In this example it is the SAP Cloud Foundry. As development framework this project uses the SAP Cloud Application Programming (CAP) model, which includes languages, libraries, and tools for building enterprise apps. The SAP Business Application Studio allows developers to create applications through application wizards, which use predefined templates to easily create a new project. The developer must configure some general elements like the name of the application, language, API key connections, or destination paths for local testing purposes. By default, the connection is set up to a so-called sandbox, which is a secured testing environment container.

Any project created with the SAP Business Application Studio has a predefined file structure including all required files, methods, and settings for the app to run.

Figure 29.5 shows the general project structure as displayed in the SAP Business Application Studio. The project *example-extension-app* contains multiple directories and files. These files contain important information about connection and database configurations, the installed packages, and their versions. Furthermore, security restrictions, file paths, and dependencies are covered. Developers can follow this project structure to get a general overview of the project itself, and they can add, remove, or modify files. The project structure depends on the chosen template, which means that not every file shown in Fig. 29.5 is generated in every template

Fig. 29.5 General project structure

the SAP Business Application Studio offers. The *README.md* file contains a Getting Started Guide for a quick project overview. The most important files and directories will be described in the next sections.

Root Directories

The following root directories have to be considered:

- Directory: app—The app directory contains content for UI frontends, mainly for the SAP Fiori UI. For example, this directory contains key HTML files with general frontend structures of the project website.
- Directory: db—This directory contains database definitions and files for configuring the data model and other native models for the SAP HANA Cloud.
- Directory: srv—The srv directory contains business logics and files for connecting with external services, so applications can access data from these. It also contains the service-catalog.cds file with its entities. CDS files are design-time source files and contain definitions of the objects which the technical experts have to create in the SAP HANA catalog. In the following source code, you can see the sales order entity, which is available through using the API (Fig. 29.6).

For accessing data through APIs, there are script files, for example, the catalog-service.js file, which handle (database) connections, actions, and which can trigger specific events, like triggering a notification when a Sales Order element gets changed (see the following source code) (Fig. 29.7).

Fig. 29.6 Source code for srv/catalog-service.cds

 srv/catalog-service.cds

```
...
@readonly
entity SalesOrders
  @(restrict: [{ to: 'Viewer' }])
  as protection on
    API_SALES_ORDER_SRV.A_SalesOrder {
    SalesOrder,
    SalesOrganization,
    DistributionChannel,
    SoldToParty,
    IncotermsLocation1,
    TotalNetAmount,
    TransactionCurrency
    };

entity SalesOrdersLog
  @(restrict: [{ to: 'Viewer' }])
  as select * from db.SalesOrdersLog
;
...
```

```
●●●                          srv/catalog-service.js

 . . .

this.on('READ', SalesOrders, async (req) => {
  try {
    const tx = s4hcso.transaction(req);
    return await tx.send({
      query: req.query,
      headers: {
        'Application-Interface-Key': process.env.ApplicationInterfaceKey,
        'APIKey': process.env.APIKey
      }
    })
  }
  catch (err) {
    req.reject(err);
  }
});

 . . .
```

Fig. 29.7 Source code for srv/catalog-service.js

Root Files

The following root files have to be considered:

- File: .env—This file is important for local development purposes. Developers can put sensible data like secret API keys in there, and if they publish or upload their project, this file will get excluded as the definitions of file exclusions are stored in the *.gitignore* file.
- File: em.json—The em.json file is an enterprise messaging file in JSON format. It contains the configuration for how the enterprise messaging instance is set up.
- File: mta.yaml—This file describes the project structure and relationships. It defines all the different services and modules that are being used, how they communicate with each other, and how they will work together. An example of the HTML5 module is shown in Fig. 29.8.
- File: package.json—The package.json contains project metadata and configuration elements for different modules and services, for example, authentication or messaging services. An excerpt can be viewed in the source code of Fig. 29.9.
- File: test.http—This file contains useful statements and requests for quick local testing purposes. As the example in Fig. 29.10 illustrates, the file contains predefined requests for different use cases with standard authentication functions. Authentication contains multiple roles and rules, the standard role (called *Joe*) has minimum permissions, for example, only to read data.
- File: xs-security.json—Concerning the user authentication, the *xs-security.json* file is crucial as it defines different scopes of user authentication models which can be declared and used as templates. Figure 29.11 shows a corresponding example.

Fig. 29.8 Source code for
mta.yaml

```
● ● ●                              mta.yaml

  . . .

  # HTML5 APP REPOSITORY APP HTML5 MODULE
  name: example-extension-app-html5
  type: html5
  path: app/resources/html5
  builder-parameters:
    builder: custom
    commands:
      - npm run build
    supported-platforms: []

  . . .
```

Fig. 29.9 Source code for
package.json

```
● ● ●                           package.json

  {
    "name": "example-extension-app",
    "version": "0.0.1",
    "description": "Example Application",
    "dependencies": {
      "@sap/cds": "^4",
      "@sap/audit-logging": "^3",
      "@sap/hana-client": "^2",
      "@sap/xb-msg-amqp-v100": "^0.9.48",
      "@sap/xsenv": "^3",
      "@sap/xssec": "^3",
      "passport": "^0.4.1",

      "cf-nodejs-logging-support": "^6",
      "express": "^4"
    },

  . . .
```

Decision Matrix

Customers using SAP BTP for side-by-side extensibility must not take care of update routines anymore. The extensions are decoupled of SAP S/4HANA core with APIs and can be updated technically independently. Conversely, more flexibility is provided regarding lifecycle management. This advantage is not given for closely coupled extensions which usually should be better implemented on the SAP S/4HANA platform. SAP BTP is a platform-as-a-service offering which means that the lifecycle and operations of the platforms are managed by SAP. Thus, customers can consume the technology without being responsible for updates and upgrade tasks. Typically, SAP BTP has only one current version which gets updated every 3 months so that all needed libraries are updated regularly. SAP is responsible for the

```
●●●                          test.http

...

Send Request
GET http://localhost:4004/catalog/Sales
Authorization: Basic joe:

#-----

Send Request
POST http://localhost:4004/catalog/Sales(1)/CatalogService.boost
Authorization: Basic joe:
Content-Type: application/json

...
```

Fig. 29.10 Source code for test.http

Fig. 29.11 Source code for
security.json

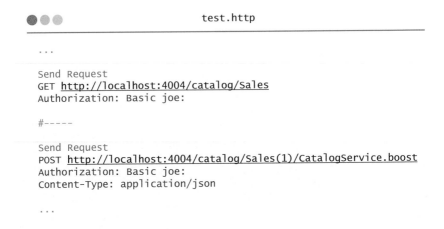

```
●●●                       xs-security.json

{
    "xsappname": "example-extension-app",
    "tenant-mode": "dedicated",
    "scopes": [
        ...
        {
            "name": "$XSAPPNAME.Admin",
            "description": "Administrator"
        }
    ],
    "role-templates": [
        ...
        {
            "name": "Admin",
            "description": "Administrator",
            "scope-references": [
                "$XSAPPNAME.Admin"
            ]
        }
    ],
    ...
```

operations of SAP BTP but also for continuous availability. Such kind of obligations are defined in a service level agreement (SLA). Therefore, customers must not care about critical errors, and SAP Support team must resolve issues. With the side-by-side extensibility, customers can build, test, and integrate their own applications and extensions. By using templates or predefined code snippets, technical experts can build business applications based on best practices efficiently. Git can be integrated as a software for version management. Developers can work together on their project

Extensibility Pattern	SAP S/4HANA (In-App)	SAP BTP (Side- by-Side)
Adapt existing Fiori UI	■	□
Create a custom user interface	■	□
Create a custom forms/ email template	■	□
Create a custom query	■	□
Add custom business logic	■	□
Create custom fields	■	□
Create custom business objects	■	□
Develop dependent extension	□	■
Develop your own custom application	□	■
Consume existing 3rd party apps	□	■
User Interface Integration	■	■
User Integration	■	■
Rules & Workflow	■	■
Events Integration	■	■
Process Integration	■	■
Data Replication	■	■

Fig. 29.12 Decision matrix

without any restrictions, because using SAP BTP every developer is able to own their instance. Being not restricted in development simplifies building extensions, for example, if a project has multiple branches, they can be easily merged. The total cost of development (TCD) can be reduced by taking advantage of SAP BTP and its SAP S/4HANA Cloud SDK. Developers and technical experts can use very time-saving features like third-party extensions to build their application. Less time in development means reduced costs, and with its simplified processes, also the effort to develop an application is decreased. The decision to use SAP BTP does not only have advantages but also drawbacks. The first disadvantage is its pricing. Customers must pay the platform-as-a-service licenses per user. The subscription relates to a fixed period of time; typically the period is 1–3 years long. Code snippets of on-premise systems cannot be copied and pasted right into SAP BTP. The code must be adapted to the platform; otherwise there will be syntax errors. It is not so easy for ABAP developers to reuse their previously backward compatible code and projects. However, this might be changed with *embedded ABAP* in future. As indicated in the table below, important to outline is that side-by-side approach shall be used for loosely decoupled and self-contained huge solution components; otherwise the in-app extensibility should be applied (Fig. 29.12).

In-app extensibility helps to enrich the core of functionalities, focuses on company-owned business documents, and offers variants of standard processes and business logics. The side-by-side extensibility is based on SAP BTP as well as third-party applications. Technical experts can integrate their dependent/custom applications to SAP S/4HANA. Developers can extend business core processes by triggering events before and after a certain process. It is also possible to develop custom standalone applications, which do not need any other services to run properly. These can be used, for example, in the Internet of Things (IoT). Digitalizing of business and sourcing out local resources to the cloud is an important trend. Customers mainly want new solutions, new software for their specific use cases; they don't want new software systems which act like those they already have. If a business changes, easily cloud customers can react to new market trends.

Conclusion

The side-by-side extensibility adds value to business processes. It simplifies extension and application development and reduces the costs of development by taking advantage of the SAP S/4HANA Cloud SDK. Technical experts can reuse assets as well as third-party extensions offered by SAP BTP, which is a platform-as-a-service. SAP BTP consists of application, data, and foundation plane. It enables the implementation of dependent extensions and custom applications. These are technically decoupled from SAP S/4HANA. Customers can access their data from everywhere and from any device as long as they have Internet access to securely connect to SAP BTP. However, in addition to the advantages, certain disadvantages should not be neglected. Using the platform-as-a-service can be expensive for small businesses and requires also additional developer know-how. Key decision criteria for applying side-by-side extensibility are to aim for implementing a huge self-contained software solution which is loosely decoupled from SAP S/4HANA.

User Experience

30

This chapter focuses on the user experience concepts and frameworks of SAP S/4HANA. Particularly, user interface design paradigm for consistent, integrated, and intelligent business applications is explained. Additionally, the architecture and development tools for user experience are depicted. First, the theoretical foundations of user experience are considered. From these the most important rules are derived that should be considered when developing user interfaces.

Business Requirements

People often think of user experience (UX) as something emotional rather than rational, making it difficult to create a business case for investing in good user experience. But in fact good user experience does have a monetary value, on top of the clear human value of making people happier. For example, a good user experience helps improve productivity, since people can get more done with system—ideally not just because they are more efficient, but also because they are more effective, because the system guides them with intelligence to what needs their attention most. Another important aspect is data quality: incorrectly entered data costs a lot later on in the process, so ensuring good data quality right from the beginning with a good user experience saves all these later data corrections. Easy-to-use software hardly needs any training, so significant training costs can be saved and subsequent support desk costs. If end users are included in the implementation, and it is ensured that the user experience suits their needs up front, the number of change requests from users requesting new or different features is decreased—changes to a deployed UI are more expensive than changes made beforehand. Also, user errors will be reduced—decreasing costs due to poor data quality and also support desk costs. On top of these quantifiable benefits, a good user experience brings clear human value benefits too—which are particularly important these days, when companies vie to attract the best talent, who want to work with cool modern tools rather than unattractive ones. A good user experience results in higher user satisfaction, allows inclusion of all employees, also those with disabilities, by supporting accessibility, and also helps ensure that people within the company actually use the software, rather than, for example, keeping data separate on their desktops as long as possible. If the applications are used by customers, then of course a good user experience will help build and increase customer loyalty. Finally, as an IT department, providing business units with software with a good user experience will help strengthen the relationship with them, since IT is providing software that their teams enjoy using.

Term Definitions

ISO 9241 is the fundamental series of standards of the International Organization for Standardization, which includes both the terms and the concepts regarding usability and user experience. This standard is used to derive the concept of human-centered quality, which plays a central role in the definitions of usability and user experience. The quality of a product or service is one of the key sales factors and is mostly divided into technical and human-centered quality. The human-centered quality is defined in the German version of the ISO 9241 standard—DIN EN ISO 9241-220 as the degree of fulfillment of the following dimensions in an interactive system: Usability, user experience, accessibility, and avoidance of harm from use. Many factors impact the human-centered quality, such as understanding of the involved target groups or the precise definition of objective criteria for measuring and evaluating user experience. Usability is a characteristic of interactive systems and describes the extent to which specific users can interact with the system effectively, efficiently, and satisfactorily. Effectiveness refers to the accuracy and completeness with which the target groups achieve their goals. An example of effectiveness in an ERP system is that a business user can maintain the goods correctly in the Warehouse Management. Efficiency, on the other hand, is based on the cost-benefit principle and attempts to achieve maximum output with minimum effort. Looking at the previous example, this means that the business user can process the orders using the ERP system with minimal effort, in the shortest possible time, without additional financial or material resources. The last aspect of usability is the satisfaction of the user groups. It deals with the physical, cognitive, and emotional reactions of the target groups that arise during or as a result of using the system. In particular, it addresses the needs and expectations of users and measures the extent to which they have met. Applied to the example, the business user's satisfaction would be high if the maintenance process is completed without error messages, delays, or other disruptive factors. The tasks relating to usability and their improvement can be derived from the explained aspects. On the one hand, a usability engineer needs to know its users, their tasks, and their application context. On the other hand, the usability engineer must use this knowledge to adapt the functional scope of the system to the target group and thereby develop the processes and procedures from the user's perspective. The user experience (UX) includes a user's perceptions and reactions resulting from the use and/or expected use of an interactive system. In this

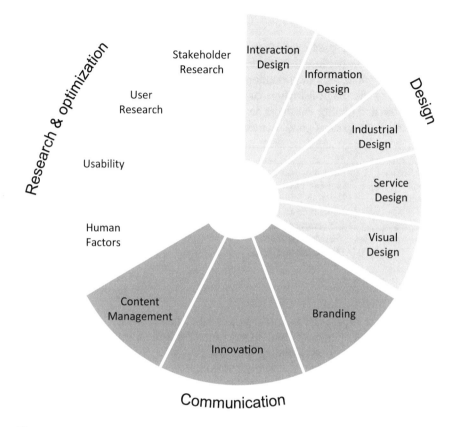

Fig. 30.1 User experience spaces

sense, UX is an extension of the objective concept of usability with a subjective dimension that reflects the user's view of the product. This includes both the expectations of the users and their experiences after the actual interaction with the system. The CPUX-F curriculum, which is based on ISO standard 9241, clarified the difference between usability and user experience. User expectations describe all personal perceptions prior to actual use, while satisfaction is generated from experiences during or after use. On the other hand, the user experience of an interactive system is divided into three areas that are interdependent and complement each other, namely design, research and optimization, and communication as illustrated in Fig. 30.1 (Robier, 2016).

In addition to usability and UX, accessibility is considered as a human-centered quality. This aspect is important for development as additional requirements must be taken into account. The ERP system must operate effectively, efficiently, and satisfactorily also for restricted groups. As a result of one or more physical impairments (e.g., auditory or visual), the ERP system should offer, for example, different font sizes or color settings or various sound volumes.

Relevance of UX

In recent years, the user experience has become increasingly important to the company's success because it influences many internal and external factors. These can be both monetary and emotional. The monetary aspects encompass all dimensions of the magical triangle of project management—both the direct costs and the time and quality that have an immediate impact on costs. The next table summarizes the impact of good user experience.

Time	Costs	Quality	Emotional
• Productivity ↑ • Onboard time ↓ • Development time↓	• Design and redesign/ development costs ↓ • Requests for change ↓ • Support costs ↓ • Maintenance costs ↓ • Teaching expenses ↓ • Documentation costs↓	• Data quality ↑ • Traffic ↑ • Service error ↓ • Learnability ↑	• Usability ↑ • User and customer satisfaction ↑ • Inclusion ↑ • Customer retention ↑ • Resistance to software ↓ (user acceptance ↑) • System trust ↑ • Customer recommendations ↑

A good user experience is based on human-centered quality and is thus fully aligned with users' workflows and needs, which leads to an immediate increase in workplace productivity by avoiding unnecessary clicks, hints, or error messages. During the definition of the requirements, the possible sources of error are identified in the best case and eliminated by the design, which results directly into the reduction of the operating errors. In addition, these standardized process flows improve data quality and traffic by collecting data faster and more accurately. The accompanying documentation during the requirement analysis and during the development of the UI can reduce documentation and development costs as well as the maintenance and support costs and change requests. A consistent design significantly shortens the time required to learn the software, making it easier to use and thus saves teaching expenses (training, working time, documents) for companies, but also reduces the development time and savings of design and redesign costs because proven components are used. The emotional effects of a good user experience are built on the monetary ones. If the user experience is good, the user experience increases, which increases both user and customer satisfaction, leading to better customer retention in the long term. Another aspect is that trust in the system increases over time and reduces internal company resistance to the software, as major changes do not take place. User experience enhances inclusion—this does not marginalize or prevent system users from working. All of these factors lead to positive feedback and increasing customer recommendations that are essential for the success of the company. There are computational formulas provided that enterprises can use to calculate the savings and profits through user experience. In general, the savings from user experience consist of three dimensions (Robier, 2016):

1. Cost due to error = (number of errors) × (Ø development time) × (employee costs) × (number of employees)
2. Development and maintenance costs = (number of changes) × (Ø hours/change) × (developer wage) × (4 if too late)
3. Costs resulting from increased productivity = (time saving) × (employee costs) × (number of employees)

As a result, the user experience has a high potential for savings, especially in applications such as the ERP systems, because they are used by many user groups and consists of thousands of transactions with respective user interfaces.

Solution Capability

The user experience concept of SAP is called SAP Fiori and is applied to all SAP software products with the aim of enabling the user to work easily and efficiently. Started in 2013 as a collection of applications with a new design, SAP Fiori has grown over time into an entire design system, which now includes a wide range of role-based features on multiple and different user devices. As an interface to the dimensions—people, economy, and technology—SAP Fiori aims to reduce unnecessary complexity and thus sets the modern standard for optimal user experience in SAP S/4HANA. Over the last 10 years SAP S/4HANA development has increasingly brought people, that is, the end users, into the equation. SAP has established a user-centered, design-driven development approach, where so-called design gates have to be passed to ensure that the necessary end-user research has been done and that the application design follows the SAP Fiori design guidelines. User centricity means being inclusive and taking care of all users, also those with disabilities. SAP Fiori is the single point where business and technology come together to best support users, helping them get their work done more easily.

SAP Fiori Design System

The goal of SAP Fiori is to ensure a uniform and qualitative user experience across all systems, thus differentiating their products from the competition. To achieve this coherence, the design system is based on certain core principles and values that are derived directly from the company's objectives and code and, on the other hand, from best practices that ensure the quality of the development processes. Practices conclude aspects like ensuring that user research is done, personas are defined, and guidelines are applied. The SAP Fiori design system allows us to provide the SAP Fiori user experience for a wide variety of technologies as shown in Fig. 30.2.

SAP Fiori aims to reduce software complexity based on five design principles:

1. *Role based:* The design or system development is based on specific roles within the company, such as business employees or accountants. This principle can be

Fig. 30.2 SAP Fiori design system

seen as a deepening of the human-centered quality described above, because the design is realized specifically for the workflows of a clearly defined target group which is defined here based on responsibility as role. Thus, role based means that the roles are considered which business users have, such as Accounts Receivables accountant, or Internal Sales representative, and the applications are designed for people in these roles.

2. *Adaptive:* Based on this principle, the applications that run on different devices such as notebook, tablet, or smartphone deliver the same user experience across multiple scenarios and use cases for the end user. This requires that they not only fulfill the requirement that they are responsive, but also allow teams to simplify the applications for mobile devices. Thus, adaptive means that applications can be used on different form factors such as desktop, tablet, or mobile phone. But adaptive goes beyond pure technical responsiveness, that is, ensuring that the same UI will run on mobile as well as desktop, by also allowing teams to build dedicated versions of desktop apps for mobile use cases.

3. *Simple:* This aspect can best be explained using the 2/20/200 s principle, according to which a user can recognize the status (situation) within 2 s, either good or bad. In about 20 s, the user should be able to identify the causes for this result, and in 200 s, the user should be able to see the exact reasons behind this in the form of detailed information. The screen should therefore always be minimalist, ordered, and contain only the most important information, but also serve as a fast access point for detailed information. Simple is easily said but difficult to do: Avoiding clutter on the screen, keeping only the important information in focus, having progressive disclosure to give users access to details as they need them.

4. *Coherent:* It is in human nature to get used to products and behaviors quickly. For this reason, users must always feel familiar with the system when operating the system. This can be achieved by avoiding repetition (consistent) and no gaps or illogical jumps (coherent) during use of different apps. Thus, coherent means that users of many applications feel that they all belong to the same family, that is, they behave consistently, and they feel coherent.

5. *Delightful:* The use of the software must be fun for the user to be able to build a positive emotional relationship with it. Non-functional aspects such as nice animations can help here, as an example of pure UI aspects which have nothing to do with features and functions for supporting the business. Thus, delightful means that users enjoy using the UIs, that they have a positive emotional connection to the software.

The SAP Fiori design system includes design languages for dedicated technologies: Web, native mobile, and conversational. Each design language specifies the look and feel, controls and floorplans, and common functions, and includes guidelines and stencils for designers and developers. SAP Fiori can be built using many technologies, with SAPUI5 being SAP's reference HTML5 web technology. There are two native mobile design languages: one for iOS and the other for Android. Existing products which have been built with other technologies cannot simply throw their UI technologies away and rebuild everything with UI5, so also other technologies are supported in providing an SAP Fiori user experience. Tools and reusable web components are provided to help development teams enabling a uniform user experience across all SAP S/4HANA applications.

SAP Fiori Design

SAP Fiori has evolved and improved continuously since 2013. With SAP Fiori 2.0 in 2016, a simple Web-based application for support cases became an application for the core functions in the company. In the following, SAP Fiori for iOS and Android was introduced, and since 2019, SAP Fiori 3.0 offers the comprehensive *whole* and is based on three properties—consistency, intelligence, and integration.

Consistency

Consistency means that the UI across all products is harmonized and unified by certain rules. These rules define the holistic design of the products, such as colors, themes, fonts, icons, layout (light and dark mode), as well as terms and settings. The aim is to provide the user with a continuously identical look and feel when interacting with the different SAP S/4HANA applications. SAP Fiori tries to solve the different semantics and design in the past, for example, in the shell header bar by unifying and optimizing the shell. This provides a comprehensive navigation option that enables the user to navigate anywhere and search across all applications using the search bar. Consistency is always worth keeping to a high level because it reduces errors, accelerates the speed at which users work, and therefore improves motivation in the workplace. The SAP Fiori Elements play an important role here because it enables to design recurring UI patterns such as lists or evaluations in a uniform way as shown in Fig. 30.3. SAP Fiori compresses everything that is relevant for a specific role using the Spaces and Overview Pages, whereby the various sections and tiles enable a minimized overview of the many functions.

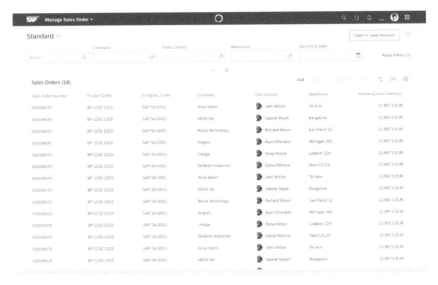

List Report

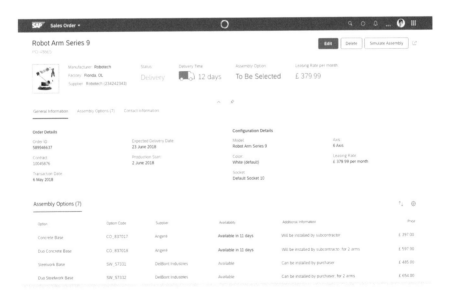

Object Page

Fig. 30.3 SAP Fiori Elements

Overview Page

Analytical List Page

Fig. 30.3 (continued)

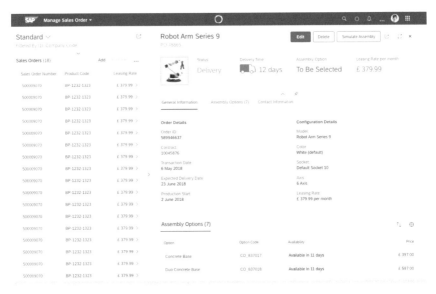

Flexible Column Layout

Fig. 30.3 (continued)

Intelligence

The intelligence of a system means that the system independently analyzes data and, on the basis of machine learning (ML) and artificial intelligence (AI), generates and displays recommendations and tips for the user over time. The goal here is to optimally guide the user and focus the attention on the highest priority tasks, for example, by notifications. SAP Fiori offers not only these notifications, but a wide range of other AI design patterns such as explanations, matching, rankings, recommendations, ideas, and actions for dealing with the given situation but also predictions and forecasts that facilitate the user's workflow. Figure 30.4 shows how intelligence works at SAP in the area of procurement. The overviews by main topics and the multiple information blocks established in SAP Fiori are intended to provide up-to-date and helpful information and suggestions for solving problems—which are compiled using AI and scoring models. Here, in the role of a Procurement Manager, it can be seen at a glance that the off-contract spend is quite high, that there are still overdue purchase order items given, and that the spend variance in procurement is quite high. To understand these facts, the user can choose the selected tile and then view the detailed information about the specific block.

If the Procurement Manager wants to know why the off-contract spend is so high and which materials are causing this, the person can navigate to the Monitor Materials Without Purchase Contracts view as illustrated in Fig. 30.5. At the top of the page a graph is showing which materials already have a vendor contract (green

Fig. 30.4 Applied intelligence for the Procurement Manager

Machine learning
used to calculate
ranking

Explanation
pop-over

SAP S/4HANA

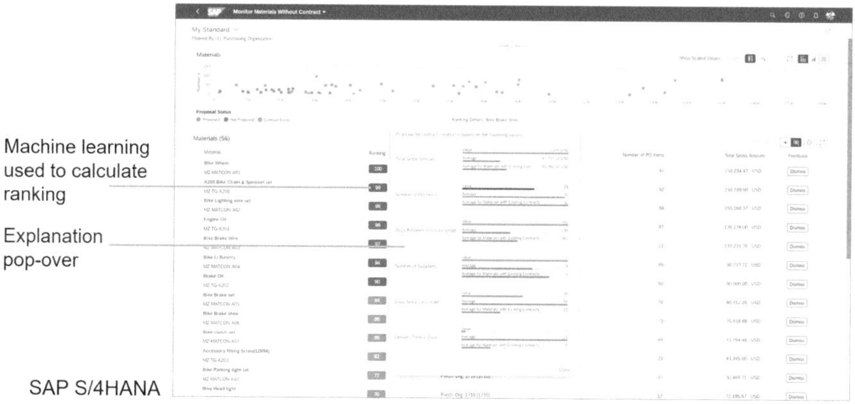

Fig. 30.5 AI-based recommendation for the Procurement Manager

bubbles). The bubbles in orange are the materials that have not been suggested by the system, the ones in blue are the ones that are recommended by SAP S/4HANA based on AI. The reasoning behind the recommendation is explained by the axes—on the X-axis the total gross amount spent on the necessary materials are displayed—here the user can see that the relevance increases as the gross amount grows. This makes perfect sense from the cost minimization perspective of a Procurement Manager. However, the SAP Fiori suggestions are not just based on the axes, but on additional factors that are displayed when a particular item is selected (see the central window in the figure below). These are listed in detail in the ranking lists and explained descriptively so that the user can get a sense of whether the suggestions actually fit or not.

Not only suggested solutions are offered, but also feedback on them, with the goal of being able to automatically evaluate the prediction of the methods and, in the next step, take that into account in the UI and adjust the influencing factors for the recommendations and explain them better afterward. Thus, the ranked lists include the basic and most important activities and remind what the user should do next.

These ranked lists not only increase the intelligence and predictive power of the interface, but also the speed of processing the user's tasks, because the user can just take the suggestions and continue to process them. At the same time, all the information for all the subsequent steps is stored and entered, so that the user should not make unnecessary entries and can complete the tasks more efficiently without distractions and loss of time. All of this creates an intelligent interface that makes it easier for the user to work and thus builds an even stronger relationship of trust with the system.

Integration

The SAP Fiori launchpad is the first point of contact and central access for all SAP applications. It allows access to the data of multiple applications. The launchpad depends on the role of the user and provides real-time information on all devices related to his or her workflow. They can personalize them by moving, deleting, or adding different tiles. Therefore, the SAP Fiori launchpad can be seen as the personal task area as a collection of to-dos with their priorities and access to all relevant activities in one place. Figure 30.6 shows the SAP Fiori launchpad and its elements.

The shell header and footer areas include icons and buttons for users to execute various actions, like search, a home page, SAP Jam interactions, and app navigation. There are two layout options to present the apps in the user's main working area. The classic home page displays application tiles and links which are arranged in groups. Spaces are used to integrate numerous related pages. The pages show related applications. Pages and spaces can be customized by the administrator and configured to suit the requirements of the users. There are user actions menu which allows access to user-related information and actions as well as personalization, profile settings, an interaction history, and the option to contact support, or give end user feedback. SAP Fiori launchpad is proactive and notifies users about important business tasks and requests that need their timely action or knowledge. The controls of SAPUI5 and the adaptive design of applications

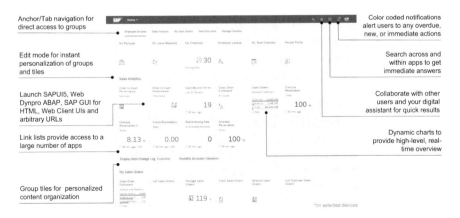

Fig. 30.6 SAP Fiori launchpad

facilitate the launchpad to run on multiple devices. The launchpad and its tiles take care about the resolution, image size, and scripting on the fly, as users switch between devices, allowing them to work how and where they want. Users can change the visual appearance of the launchpad by selecting standard themes, like SAP Quartz Light and Dark, SAP Belize, SAP Belize Deep, High-Contrast Black, and High-Contrast White. But also customer-specific themes can be created based on the SAP-delivered themes. The launchpad provides cross-app and in-app navigation, and enhances search capabilities and key user adaptation without the need of code. It is possible to integrate the launchpad with other UI clients, for example, SAP Business Client, SAP Enterprise Portal, SAP Fiori client, and Web browsers. For example, the launchpad can be run embedded in the SAP Business Client, which enables to call transactions in SAP GUI for Windows and then gain additional features compared to those provided with SAP GUI for HTML. The functional scope of the SAP Fiori launchpad can be extended with custom features using APIs, like adding new elements to the user interface. Furthermore, launchpad services can be consumed in SAPUI5 applications, for example, to develop navigation across applications.

Architecture and Development

In this section the SAP Fiori architecture is discussed in more detail. As illustrated in Fig. 30.7, the architecture can be roughly divided into three parts—back end, front end, and Web browser. The SAP Fiori front-end server acts as a Web server for all ABAP-based systems and contains the UI components (SAP Fiori launchpad, SAP Fiori apps, SAP Fiori Elements, and SAPUI5), the UI data (the roles and personal settings in the SAP Fiori launchpad), and the SAP Gateway (OData services).

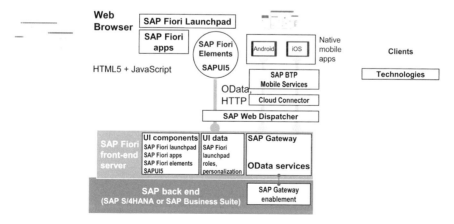

Fig. 30.7 SAP Fiori architecture

Therefore, the complete UI logic is defined here with the aim of achieving better scalability.

In the Web browser, the SAP Fiori apps and SAP Fiori launchpad are built using the HTML5 and JavaScript-based frameworks SAP Fiori Elements and SAPUI5. As soon as the user starts SAP Fiori launchpad in the browser, all required components and libraries are loaded from the SAP Fiori front-end server. The authorizations of the users are also considered by the front-end server, and the correct screens and role-dependent and personalized function are loaded. For additional security when communicating between the Web browser and the front-end server, the SAP Web Dispatcher is placed as an entry point for access. The OData services are the interface to the SAP back end that are provided by the SAP Gateway. The front-end server is depicted here as an add-on to the back-end system, which is the recommended deployment option for SAP S/4HANA. However, it can also be run as a standalone web server for SAP Fiori. In both cases, the SAP back-end system has a small enablement component for managing the communication with SAP Gateway. To use the mobile devices or to serve applications, this architecture is enhanced with the SAP Business Technology Platform (BTP) services for the mobile devices, which is securely reached via the cloud connector and works for both Android and iOS. The next step is to look at the architecture from the point of view of a developer and in particular to show the developer tools. This aspect is shown in Fig. 30.8.

SAP Business Application Studio is the new generation of SAP Web Integrated Development Environment (IDE). It facilitates the development process of SAP Fiori applications by supporting the complete development lifecycle through the

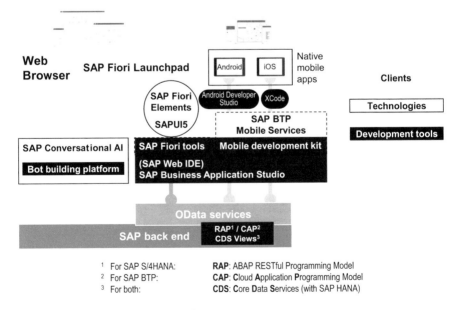

Fig. 30.8 SAP Fiori Development Tools

integrated SAP Fiori Elements and also running on the SAP Business Technology Platform (BTP). For mobile app development, an additional plug-in Extension for SAP Business Application Studio—SAP BTP Mobile Services—is offered. The advantage of SAP BTP Mobile Services for developers is that they only need to code once and can develop apps for both iOS and Android operating systems at the same time. Nevertheless, there are also monolithic solutions for mobile development—the SAP Fiori SDKs for Android and Android Developer Studio and XCode for iOS. SAP provides not only front-end developer tools, but also those for the back end, and tries to use the developer's programming flow for tasks such as reading or writing data to the back end. These include the RAP (RESTful Programming Model), CAP (Cloud Application Model), and CDS views. The CDS views can be used to model the application data that is stored in SAP HANA. The RAP and CAP, on the other hand, help developers create new services for OData and thus create SAP Fiori applications faster. The final step to an optimal UX is made by SAP Conversional AI technology, which includes the bot building tool for developers. This makes it easy to develop chatbots and other features with voice control. This technology is further developed by SAP CoPilot skills, which harmonizes the UX across all bots and usage platforms. These tools have a very important role in integrating modern enterprise assistants like Apple Siri, Microsoft Cortana, Amazon Alexa, and Google Assistant in the future.

SAP Fiori in SAP S/4HANA

For SAP S/4HANA all applications and transactions used are accessed via the SAP Fiori launchpad. The innovations of SAP S/4HANA come via SAP Fiori applications—so customers remaining on SAP GUI only would have a drawback. Also, selectively implementing individual SAP Fiori applications breaks the user experience and results in high implementation costs. By leveraging the SAP Fiori launchpad, all users can profit from SAP Fiori, including those users who still end up doing a lot of their work in the classic UIs such as SAP GUI and Web Dynpro. For the transition to SAP Fiori, SAP is not simply taking the old transactions and rebuilding them with new technology. Instead, user research is done to understand how people work these days and leveraging the new possibilities of SAP Fiori to build innovative new user interactions. SAP Fiori applications provide a new way of working and are the only way to profit from many innovations in SAP S/4HANA. Of course, SAP cannot replace over 100,000 transactions with SAP Fiori in a year or two, so these new SAP Fiori applications are supplemented with classic UIs as shown in Fig. 30.9. Nevertheless, over time the number of SAP Fiori apps available to customers is increasing.

SAP Fiori launchpad gives each user only those apps relevant to the roles assigned to them. Different roles have a different set of applications assigned—with some applications being used for multiple roles. The SAP Fiori launchpad provides the single-entry point for each user to access all their applications, as well as the shell services such as search and personalization. Finally, the SAP Fiori

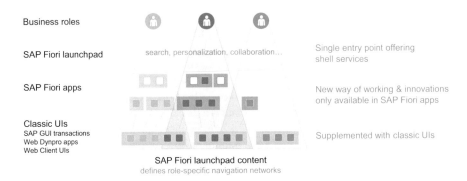

Fig. 30.9 SAP Fiori in SAP S/4HANA

launchpad content defines the role-specific navigation networks. This is very helpful and something which SAP S/4HANA provides out of the box via the so-called SAP Fiori launchpad content. Domain-specific information and actions are provided to the user. Thus, users quickly get an overview of what needs their attention with overview pages, list reports, and work lists, and can trigger quick actions or drill down to the next level of detail. Key and differentiating use cases are reimagined with the SAP Fiori user experience. All classic applications have the SAP Fiori visual theme. As already mentioned, SAP Fiori is how business users access SAP S/4HANA innovations. That means that customers who want to make the most of these innovations may need to activate 100s and in some cases 1000s of SAP Fiori applications and classic UIs. The recommended way to approach SAP Fiori activation of the SAP S/4HANA system is to identify the business roles that are relevant to customer's business in the SAP Fiori applications reference library (www.sap.com/ fiori-apps-library). This information can be found on all the standard SAP Fiori launchpad content delivered by SAP. In the next step, the relevant SAP Business roles using the Rapid SAP Fiori activation task lists are activated. This is the quickest way to get started, as they allow to enable all associated applications and generate a role and a test user per role in just one step. Hence, the standard business roles can be explored by experiencing them as a business user in the sandbox system. This will help customer's business experts gain a good understanding of how these roles work, such as what insights are provided and how a user navigates between SAP Fiori applications and classic UIs to complete their day-to-day work. Once there is clear idea of which business roles, which applications, and which app-to-app navigations is required to run in the system, the customer can start adjusting the SAP Fiori launchpad content. For a fast way to copy and customize the SAP business roles, customers can take advantage of the SAP Fiori launchpad content manager tool.

Conclusion

SAP Fiori is no longer just a concept, but a tool that has grown to meet the needs of users. With its variety of elements, it delivers an optimal user experience across all SAP products and thus also across all SAP S/4HANA applications. User experience has become significantly more important in recent years because companies no longer see it as a pure design function, but also as an economic benefit that promises long-term competitive advantages and high employee and customer satisfaction. For this reason, the continuous development and improvement of the user experience are indispensable. SAP Fiori makes this feasible through its innovative approaches and its architecture, which optimizes and simplifies the workflow of both the developer and the user.

Identity and Access Management

31

This chapter focuses on identity and access management concepts and frameworks of SAP S/4HANA. Particularly, secure access, managing users and permissions, identity authentication and provisioning service, business roles and catalogs, restrictions, and authorization objects are explained.

Business Requirement

Identity and access management (IAM) defines users' identities, manages what they can and cannot do, and provides compliance audits and reports based on this information. An IAM software solution should be able to create and manage user accounts, roles, and access rights for individual users in an organization to support these tasks. The solution typically includes user provisioning, password management, policy management, and identity repositories. As more businesses migrate to the cloud, their IT landscapes become more heterogeneous and diverse, frequently resulting in coexisting cloud and on-premise software systems—so-called hybrid environments. However, whether customers are dealing with cloud or hybrid environments, the requirements for identity and access management remain the same. Customers want to spend as little time as possible integrating systems while also providing their users with a seamless single-sign-on experience across systems and ensuring that system and data access is secure. IAM manages the interaction between different users with different roles, and the systems that comprise a company's IT landscape. System integration is considered successful when user interaction is smooth. Ideally, all systems in the IT landscape will behave as one from the user's perspective, which means that users will not have to authenticate themselves repeatedly when system boundaries are crossed. Security and compliance are also critical aspects of IAM. A solid IAM solution must ensure that legal requirements are met and company policies are followed. Furthermore, IAM must ensure that user authorizations are handled correctly so that users with specific roles can access only the services to which they are authorized. The same is true for data:

S. Sarferaz, *Compendium on Enterprise Resource Planning*,
https://doi.org/10.1007/978-3-030-93856-7_31

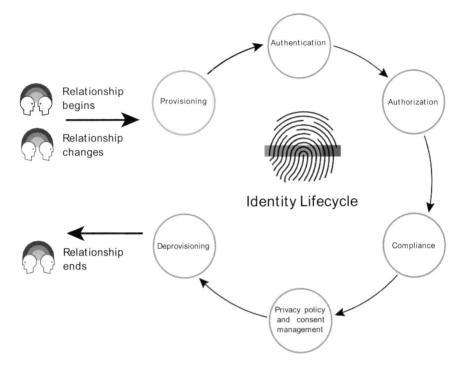

Fig. 31.1 Identity lifecycle

IAM must ensure that the right people have access to the right data. Figure 31.1 depicts an example of the identity management lifecycle, which includes all relevant administrative processes. Assume a company is considered that has a hybrid system landscape with systems both on premise and in the cloud. When a user and an enterprise form a relationship, the cycle begins. A user can be an employee, a partner, or a customer (or consumer). First, a user account is created in the company's central user store. The user data is distributed to all systems that are relevant to this user via provisioning. The user's role is an important factor in determining the subsequent processes and checks that apply. Aside from providing users with an appropriate account, the system may also provide users with a framework in which they can personalize services. Language settings and date and time formats are two common examples. Furthermore, the system may initiate workflows for business stakeholders to review and either approve or reject proposed changes to user profiles or access rights. During a person's relationship with the company, their role and tasks may change, for example, after a promotion or when responsibilities change. When this occurs, the person's user accounts must be updated to reflect the change. For example, new user accounts may be required, existing ones may need to be deactivated, or authorizations may need to be changed.

The authentication step validates the user's identity and determines their role. The application system where the user needs to work sends the authentication request to the identity provider system for this purpose. The latter then authenticates the user to the application assuming that the user is known to the identity provider. When this occurs, the application system is able to carry out the user's logon. In the authorization step, access rights are established and constantly monitored. Once a user has been authenticated within one system, authorization specifies which applications the user is permitted to start and use in that system, as well as the specific data the user is permitted to access within an application. In addition, the system handles procedures for treating, processing, and accessing private information in this step. At this point, the system performs controls to detect and respond to attempted security breaches. In order to reduce administrative overhead, self-services are established. Users, for example, can reset their passwords using self-service. Governance, risk, and compliance are critical components of the identity lifecycle. Compliance is the process of conforming to the requirements defined by laws, regulations, and policies. Segregation of duties, on the other hand, is a common case in governance. Certain combinations of activities within a system must not be performed by the same individual. For example, the same person should not be able to create and approve the same invoice. The use of personal data is becoming an increasingly important aspect of the identity lifecycle. A company's privacy policy specifies how private and personal information about its customers is handled. Users can confirm the personal information they are willing to allow the company to access and use based on predefined conditions using consent management. In this context, it is worth noting that the GDPR went into effect in May 2018. The GDPR, which replaces the Data Protection Directive 95/46/EC, aims to harmonize data privacy laws throughout Europe. Citizens will have more control over their personal data as data protection rules become stronger and more uniform. Businesses all over the world will benefit from having a single set of rules for operating in the EU. This regulation applies to parties who do business with an EU resident or deal with their personal data when goods or services are offered to them. It also applies to monitoring individuals' behavior within the EU. As illustrated in Fig. 31.1, when the user-enterprise relationship ends, the deprovisioning step occurs, in which the IAM system removes user access to applications and systems. Self-services are not depicted as part of the identity lifecycle in Fig. 31.1. Self-services are actions that users can perform on their own. A user, for example, can apply for new user accounts and authorization assignments; administrators and key users can configure their company's corporate branding. Thus, with Identity Management, IAM provides a solution for the provisioning and deprovisioning of identity for subjects. Only with the help of identity, other layers like authentication can operate properly. The second task of IAM is Access Management, which acts as a layer for providing authentication, authorization, and policy enforcement.

Solution Capability

After a brief introduction of the IAM use cases a further look is taken into the technical aspects of IAM focusing on the necessary services, concepts, and applications in the context of SAP S/4HANA.

IAM Services

The simplest implementation of IAM needs three services to operate which are explained in this section. Identity and access management services, also known as IAM services, comprise SAP BTP Identity Authentication and SAP BTP Identity Provisioning. This label is commonly used to refer to the combination of identity authentication and identity provisioning services.

Identity Management Service

Another major task of IAM is to provide identity to users. It manages the whole lifecycle of an identity in an enterprise. If someone is starting at a company, an identity gets created. Later on, it may get updated, if the roles or the person changes, and if the employee is leaving the company the identity gets deprovisioned. It should be as easy as it gets to ensure a complete identity cycle, because the identity itself enables a user to get access to sensitive resources. The SAP BTP Identity Provisioning service offers secure identity lifecycle management as a service, including provisioning and deprovisioning of identity and authorization. The following features are supported:

- Automatic creation and management of user accounts
- Administration of policy-based authorizations
- Capability to work with on-premise user stores as sources, such as the SAP Application Server for ABAP
- Capability to work with cloud user stores as sources, such as SAP SuccessFactors
- Compatibility with the SAP BTP Identity Authentication and the SAP BTP Integration service

These features enable customers to set up faster and more efficient user onboarding and offboarding administration. SAP BTP Identity Provisioning enables the centralized management of corporate identities in the cloud. It can also automate the provisioning of existing on-premise identities to cloud applications.

Authentication Service

The main quest of authentication is to answer the question of identity. IAM does not enforce a specific method to solve this problem. There are many possibilities, starting with a simple authentication via username and password or requiring multi-factor authentication or going as far as biometric authentication. This method is chosen by the developer of an authentication service, for example, based on the sensitivity of the underlying information. SAP BTP Identity Authentication is a product that provides authentication, single sign-on (SSO), user management, and on-premise integration services. It also offers convenient user self-services for employees and partners, such as registration and password reset. While SAP BTP Identity Authentication supports consumer and customer scenarios, the identity authentication service includes security features for protecting application access, the ability to define risk-based authentication rules, two-factor authentication, and delegated authentication to on-premise user stores and other identity providers. SAP BTP Identity Authentication is a central authentication service that is tightly integrated with SAP S/4HANA as well as non-SAP solutions. The following are the key features:

- Authentication for cloud and on-premise service provider applications that is secure (SAP and third party)
- Single-sign-on access from any device, at any time (Web and desktop SSO)
- Twitter, LinkedIn, Facebook, and Google social login
- Two-factor authentication using one-time passwords and password policies at the service provider application level
- Application of risk-based authentication to service provider applications, user group assignment, and Internet protocol ranges
- Self-services, such as self-registration and password reset, as well as the creation of custom privacy policies and terms of service at the application level

Authorization Management Service

It deals with the question of what can be accessed by a user. With the help of authorization policies, access to resources can be granted only if the user is entitled to view them. From an implementation point of view one of the main challenges is to provide a dynamic system which is extensible enough to ensure future use cases can be realized too. Additionally, the complexity of the system should be low enough so that custom policies can be implemented as well. So, policies build the foundation of granting access to resources with the IAM method. The ABAP authorization concept guards against unauthorized access to applications and services. A business user's authorizations determine which actions they can perform and which data they can access. In the ABAP authorization concept, authorizations are instances of authorization objects that are combined in an authorization profile that is associated with a role. The authorization profiles are assigned to business users through the associated roles, which are maintained using the role maintenance transaction PFCG. An authorization object is a collection of up to ten authorization fields. An authorization field can represent data as attributes of a business object or activities like reading or changing. During runtime, an authorization check is successful if one or more authorizations for an authorization object assigned to the business user match the required combination of authorization field values for this authorization object. An authorization object, for example, has a sales organization authorization field and a sales region authorization field. If a business user has one authorization for this authorization object for the combination of sales organization 100 and sales region

1000 and another for the combination of sales organization 200 and sales region 2000, this business user will have access to line items in sales organization 100 for sales region 1000 but not for any other sales organizations, such as 2000, during runtime. The business user in cost center 200 will only have access to line items for cost element 2000 and not to any other cost element.

IAM Implementation

The implementation inside SAP S/4HANA is relatively straightforward and is described in the following paragraphs. First of all, further details are provided concerning the authentication service implementation for SAP S/4HANA. This service is not directly integrated into the SAP S/4HANA Cloud tenant but provided by the authentication service of the SAP BTP itself. So, business users asking for authentication are signed in and verified against the SAP BTP authentication service and are then signed into the SAP S/4HANA Cloud system via Single-Sign On (SSO) using the Security Assertion Markup Language (SAML). SAML is an open standard and XML-based markup language to exchange authentication data and security assertions between the SAML service provider or application (in this case the SAP S/4HANA system) and the SAML identity provider (here the identity authentication service). As described earlier IAM does not enforce any specific implementation for identity provision and leaves the concrete implementation open for any system that aims to integrate IAM. In case of SAP S/4HANA this flexibility is forwarded to the end user. The customer gets the flexibility to configure specific password policies in the identity authentication service. A business user which shall have access to the SAP S/4HANA system must be created in SAP S/4HANA and registered in the user store provided by the identity authentication service. To provide an easy solution to customers for creating users and testing the correct functionality there are multiple helpers. At first there are two identity authentication service providers for a customer, one for productive use and the other for testing. This enables the customer to further test and integrate the desired behavior before influencing a production environment. Furthermore, numerous tools and integrations are provided to supply multiple (initial) users to the system. There are several communication scenarios to automatically replicate users from an external identity management system. The next required service from IAM is an authorization service. This service implements one of the core functionalities of IAM. This rather complex functionality shall be broken down into the following aspects:

1. Policy enforcement through business catalogs
2. SAP Fiori integration
3. Business role propagation

To start with the first bullet point, the following paragraph provides insights on how policy enforcement is implemented in SAP S/4HANA.

Fig. 31.2 Structure of business catalogs

Policy Enforcement Through Business Catalogs

To ensure a secure environment SAP provides *business catalogs* to its customers. The key task of a business catalog is to group applications and restriction types to define instance-based restrictions that belong together based on a business process or as a part of it. These business catalogs are regularly reviewed by ISAE 3000 audits to ensure no segregation of duty conflicts is present. Now the basic building blocks of a business catalog should be discussed. Afterward a big picture is generated out of these blocks (Fig. 31.2).

In the above figure the structure and the building blocks of a business catalog are depicted. To explain the relations, the authorization field is described first. The authorization field represents a low-level item in the ABAP authorization concept. To summarize, an authorization field determines which actions a business user is allowed to perform and which data the person is permitted to access. The authorization fields are internally grouped into authorization objects. These authorization objects are checked during runtime. A check is successful if a combination of one or more authorizations in an authorization object assigned to the business user meets the required combination of authorization field values for this authorization object. The exact propagation is discussed in a later paragraph. Restriction fields mask the low-level authorization fields as an authorization object for which restriction values can be defined by the customer. As restriction fields represent a core part of the policy enforcement, these fields are predefined by SAP and the customer cannot define their own fields. Restriction fields can afterward be combined into restriction types. Restriction types enable the business user to define *instance-based restrictions*. The main task of instance-based restrictions is to define which data records a user with a certain role is allowed to maintain. As for the restriction fields, the maintenance of customer individual restriction types is not supported. One or more restriction types can be assigned to a business catalog as described above. These concepts provide a solid basis for the implementation of an authorization service as described in the IAM standard. To provide a better UX to the customer SAP has built additional abstractions inside the authorization concept of SAP S/4HANA. With business role templates SAP has made a predefined set of common personas present in the customer's business. These presets enable the customer to quickly create customer-editable business roles, which can further be customized by the business user. With the abstraction of the underlying details the customer can focus on providing the right access to resources to business users, depending on their role inside the business. Business roles also work as an aggregation of one or more business catalogs. The business roles not only control the policies for the user, enforced with the help of restrictions, but also define which application are visible

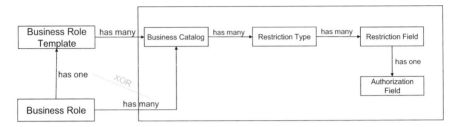

Fig. 31.3 Authorization overview

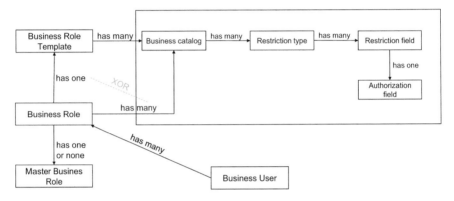

Fig. 31.4 Master roles in combination with business roles

to the user on the SAP Fiori launchpad. A customer is not forced to use the predefined SAP business role templates to create business roles. They can also be created by assigning one or more business catalogs manually to a new business role or starting with a clone of an existing business role. When using more than one business catalog, especially more than one restriction, a merging strategy is used to combine all restrictions available in the business catalogs. The concrete restriction values can also be maintained inside of a business role. To summarize a business role represents the main interface between the low-level policy enforcement tools and the customer. Therefore, it is a key part of IAM's authorization service working based on a *zero-trust principle*. The described relations are also visualized in Fig. 31.3.

To further enable ease of use, a concept named master business roles is provided in SAP S/4HANA. An existing business role can be marked as a master business role, which then enables the customer to derive other concrete business roles from the master role. The derived roles inherit all business catalogs and lock the defined restriction values in place. But the customer is free to add more restrictions to the derived role afterward (Fig. 31.4).

SAP Fiori Integration

As an extension to the above concepts, policies inside SAP S/4HANA are also enforced in SAP Fiori Pages & Spaces. So, business roles not only define access

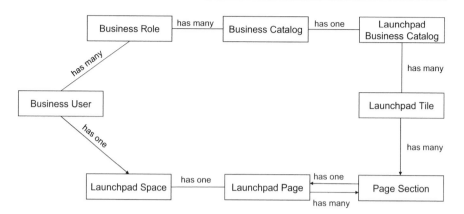

Fig. 31.5 Launchpad integration to authorization concept

restrictions, but also define how the UI is built for the specific business user. To enable this feature, every business catalog has its corresponding launchpad business catalog. This catalog describes which applications are visible to the business user, based on the assigned business catalogs. This feature improves the security level even further. This means, even if a user can somehow gain knowledge about the presence of other application, user's request is revoked by the server. To ensure interoperability between *business catalogs* and *launchpad business catalogs* the launchpad catalogs cannot be customized by the customer and come predefined by SAP. The SAP Fiori launchpad consists of page sections and launchpad tiles. Launchpad tiles are grouped into the above-mentioned launchpad business catalogs. Tiles belong to a page section on the launchpad, which can be further combined into a full launchpad page. A constructed launchpad page is then abstracted into a launchpad space. Each space has one or more corresponding business roles assigned. The above concept ensures that for every given business role, there is exactly one launchpad space, which represents the UI presented to the business user. To minimize the effort for the customer, SAP has corresponding launchpad spaces preconfigured for every business role template (Fig. 31.5).

Business Role Propagation

The last point aims to answer the question how business roles are propagated and translated into the corresponding SAP PFCG roles. As explained earlier, with simplification in mind, SAP provides abstraction layers on top of the low-level ABAP authorization concept. To efficiently and generally apply policy enforcement the ABAP authorization methods are used under the hood. The predelivery business roles from SAP, which provide the basis for the customer's own business roles, are equipped with their corresponding business catalogs. These business catalogs have SAP-defined PFCG roles for each business role. PFCG roles are not directly used by a business user, but instead generated out of the higher-level abstractions like business roles and their corresponding catalogs. Some of the authorizations are defined as *fixed values*. This means, the authorization values for the authorization object cannot be changed by the IAM administrator. To keep the simplicity high, these fixed values are not visible to the administrator at all. The core *activities* which define access to resources are called categories. SAP uses three main categories:

1. Read access groups all activities that do not change the object.
2. Write access groups all activities that perform change operations on an object. This includes, for example, creation, change, and deletion.
3. Value help groups' activities that are checked during value help functions.

With these fine-grained authorizations, every business object can have a field-level access control, which ensures a great segregation of duty.

The last major service defined in the IAM standard is the identity service. Its main task is to provide identity to user and manage the whole lifecycle of any subject regarding changes. For this task many services are in place which allow the management of business user individual business roles, as well as their corresponding business catalogs. There is also a central part deeply integrated into SAP S/4HANA, for example, if a new function or feature is present in the application suite, new business catalogs are provided out of the box, to ensure the policy enforcement in the authorization service is possible. There are many more lifecycle changes controlled by SAP:

- Changes to restriction types
- Changes to authorization default values
- Adding new applications to business catalogs
- Removal of applications from business catalogs
- Splitting/restructuring of business catalogs

To ensure a smoother migration process for each of these lifecycle changes, new or edited business catalogs are shipped, but switched off a release before they get activated, so that business user can assign the updated catalogs to all necessary users before the usage of the new catalogs is enforced. This process is even more simplified with the usage of business role templates, which described earlier are provided by SAP. These get automatically managed and updated as needed, so that the business users always have the correct authorizations. This covers the lifecycle management regarding the dynamic business environment. Another task is to provide a solution to user lifecycle management. For this task the IAM administrator is controlling which users can access which resources. The IAM administrator controls the assigned roles to a business user and can assign new ones if the lifecycle of the business users identity changes in a way that new processes or applications must be accessed by this user. There are also multiple user types present inside SAP S/4HANA, which can perform different tasks:

- There are business users which are the core of the user management. They can also be seen as real employees of the customer. They need to get explicit access from the IAM administrator.
- Administration and business configuration users are customer-specific users in the tenant. They are created as part of the tenant-provisioning process. Administration users own the authorization to create business users. The business configuration user is needed in the quality tenant only and is used for the configuration of the business processes.
- Communication users are only used for inbound communications in customer-managed communication scenarios. A communication user is assigned to a communication system.
- Printing users are the last available category of users. They are needed for the connection between the SAP BTP Print Manager and the printing queue web access service.

IAM Applications

To sum up the topic identity and access management in SAP S/4HANA some of the respective applications are briefly described.

As shown in Fig. 31.6, there are six applications specifically built to give easy control to the customer regarding the management of their users and their maintenance. In the following paragraph the objective of the key applications is shortly described and their connection to the concepts explained previously is outlined. Maintain Business Users application gives an overview of all business users which have access to the customers of the SAP S/4HANA system. Additionally, the business catalogs which are assigned to the business users are displayed. This enables the Administrator the easy visualization of which catalogs are assigned to which user. Also, the general maintenance of a business user is possible. Maintain Business Roles application provides an overview about all business roles present in the system. Here the administrator can monitor, filter, and manage all business roles.

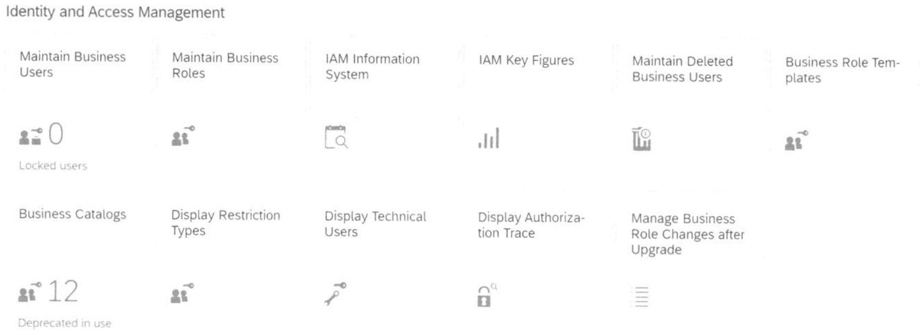

Identity and Access Management

Maintain Business Users	Maintain Business Roles	IAM Information System	IAM Key Figures	Maintain Deleted Business Users	Business Role Templates
⟐ 0	⟐	⟐	⟐	⟐	⟐
Locked users					

Business Catalogs	Display Restriction Types	Display Technical Users	Display Authorization Trace	Manage Business Role Changes after Upgrade	
⟐ 12	⟐	⟐	⟐	☰	
Deprecated in use					

Fig. 31.6 IAM applications inside SAP S/4HANA

The administrator is also able to see the assigned business catalogs. Additionally, new business roles can be created from scratch or with the use of business role templates to further simplify the creation of production-ready business roles. The management of restriction types can also be accessed within this application. The same features and functionalities provided for business users regarding the Display Business Users application are also implemented for the technical users present in SAP S/4HANA based on the Display Technical Users application. This includes, for example, locking and unlocking print or communication users, change username and password. The IAM Information System is designed to get insights into the usage and the interconnectivity between all aspects related to IAM in SAP S/4HANA. By applying filters, the customer can see which business roles are used by which user and can dig even further to display which concrete restrictions are applied. With the help of this application every authorization for every user can be visualized and IAM problem quickly be identified. The Business Catalogs application enriches the user experience with the introduction of management features to business catalogs. Within this application deprecated catalogs can be identified and migrated to their successors. Also, there are informative descriptions to every business catalog to further clarify their purpose. The Business Role Templates application brings the management of business role templates to life. Here, the customer can define their own, as well as review existing role templates.

This app provides a quick overview of critical issues affecting your business users and business roles. You can, for example, see if any business users are locked or if they have too many business roles assigned to them. The relevant data is displayed in detailed charts, allowing you to see the necessary figures at a glance. The IAM Key Figures application displays information like the number of business users who have been assigned to business roles, the month of the business user's most recent logon, the number of business users who are locked and unlocked, the business users' credibility, or the number of business roles with unrestricted access.

The Display Authorization Trace application enables an authorization trace for a business user. This allows to determine whether any authorizations are missing or insufficient. Key features are, for example, activation or deactivation of traces, displaying the results of authorization checks, including previously assigned authorizations and failed checks. Because a maximum of 10,000 datasets are possible, it is recommended to take this into account when defining the selection criteria, particularly the date range. If an authorization check yielded a filtered status, it can be investigated which business roles expose the affected restriction type. One possible solution is that the checked business user is not assigned to the required business role or that the demanded value has not yet been maintained (Fig. 31.7).

Conclusion

With an ever-growing usage of cloud-based services the need to provide a secure and controlled environment is steadily increasing. The huge variety of available on-premise and cloud resources demand a high flexibility to a framework which

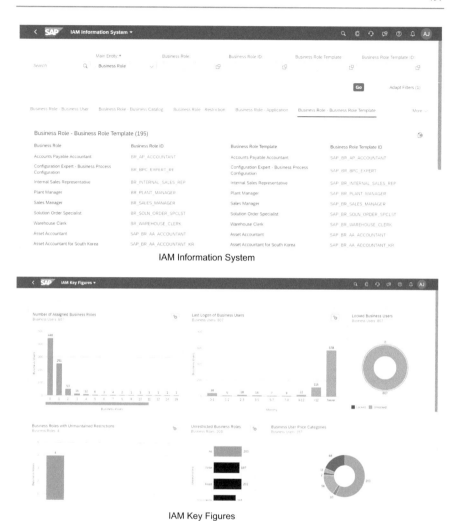

Fig. 31.7 IAM Information System and IAM Key Figures

aims to provide a unified layer of access control. Not only can IAM be used to provide granular control to resources available in the cloud, like IaaS or PaaS products, but its concepts can also be translated to provide security in SaaS solutions. Especially for highly flexible products like SAP S/4HANA with a big variety of use cases, it is crucial to have a security framework in place which is flexible enough to ensure users only get access to resources they are authorized to use. Also, products like SAP S/4HANA are working with sensitive information so the argument above weighs even stronger. IAM can be considered as a technique that provides an adequate level of protection to resources and data through rules and policies which are enforced on users via various techniques such as enforcing login password, assigning privileges to the users, and provisioning user accounts. So IAM decides who has access to what resources. Another task which evolves out of identity management is the responsibility to maintain the identity cycle, which includes creation, maintenance, updates, and deletion of identities.

Data Protection and Privacy

32

Data protection and privacy are important factors which need to be considered when working with personal data. There are different regulations which define relevant terms and set rules which need to be enforced. One of these regulations is the General Data Protection Regulation (GDPR). SAP S/4HANA Cloud and On Premise offer tools like the Information Lifecycle Management (ILM), Information Retrieval Framework (IRF), Read Access Logging (RAL), Change Management, and Consent Management, which take care of meeting the given requirements by following a holistic approach and handling data protection and privacy using a central solution. This chapter focuses on data protection and privacy concepts and frameworks of SAP S/4HANA. Particularly, general data protection regulation (GDPR) requirements, lifecycle of personal data, information retrieval framework, and read access logging are explained.

Business Requirement

The topics of data-sharing norms and personal data protection have evolved over the last years driven by the development of information technology. The first law which focused on these topics is considered to be first introduced in 1970 in the German federal state of Hessen. This law focused on regulating data-sharing within Germany and didn't address international data transfers. This resulted in data being processed and stored in other geographical locations and therefore jurisdictions where regulations were not that strict. Regulators needed to find a solution to this issue, and restrictions on international data transfer needed to be introduced. Afterward, one goal was to harmonize meaningful data protection across jurisdictions to enable the removal of transfer restrictions across national borders. The first two data protection frameworks were the Organization for Economic Co-operation and Development Privacy Guidelines (OECD) in 1980 and the Council of Europe Convention for the protection of individuals with regard to automatic processing of personal data in 1981, which is also known as Convention 108. Those regulations

S. Sarferaz, *Compendium on Enterprise Resource Planning*,
https://doi.org/10.1007/978-3-030-93856-7_32

allow transferring data to other participating states and even prohibit some restrictions on transfer for reasons of privacy between participating states. A newer approach on regulating data-sharing and data protection has been introduced by the European Union's Data Protection Directive in 1995, which led to the introduction of its successor in 2016: The General Data Protection Regulation went into effect on May 25, 2018. The topic of data protection and privacy has been around for decades and gained in importance over the last years. Regulations like the General Data Protection Regulation (GDPR) and Organization for Economic Co-operation and Development Privacy Guidelines (OECD) have a great impact on how personal data is handled and stored and SAP as a software provider needs to help their customers meet all given requirements with their products. There are two aspects which need to be taken care of when working with personal data. First it is important to ensure the data protection aspect and second companies need to meet all requirements in regard to the data privacy aspect. Data protection is about protecting information against unauthorized access through computing environments. For example, it is important to make sure that unauthorized users don't have the possibility to read or edit data. In the worst-case data could be lost, deleted, or abused, which could lead to further consequences. The information security officer is responsible for making sure that all requirements in this area are met. Data privacy is about protecting individuals with regard to the processing of personal data. Neglecting this topic could lead to the infringement of personal rights, which has high monetary penalties as a consequence. The data privacy officer is responsible for making sure that all requirements in this area are met. To meet the data protection and privacy requirements, technical and organizational measures (TOMs) need to be implemented. They ensure a level of security appropriate to the described risks.

General Data Protection Regulation

As already mentioned, the GDPR has been introduced in 2016 by the European Union as a successor of the first approach by the European Union's Data Protection Directive in 1995. The GDPR went into effect on May 25, 2018. Technically there were no major changes compared to the 1995s approach, but the GDPR has increased fines to up to 4% of the annual turnover of the company, which led to many companies caring a lot more about aligning to the given regulations. The highest given fine as of April 2020 was nearly 205 million euros. The GDPR is an approach which requires that any transfer to a country outside of the European Union needs to be made in accordance with a transfer justification. This transfer justification has to be approved in advance by the European Commission.

Personal Data

The GDPR introduces different definitions and principles. Personal data, for example, is defined as data relating to an identified or identifiable natural person ("data subject") who can be identified, directly or indirectly, in particular by reference to an identifier [...] or to one or more factors specific to that natural person's physical, physiological, genetic, mental, economic, cultural, or social identity. Therefore, personal data describes all data which identifies a person directly or can lead to a person being identified indirectly. Examples of information which identifies the person directly are:

- Names
- Postal addresses
- Telephone numbers
- e-Mail addresses

And in addition, examples of information which identifies the person indirectly are:

- Bank account numbers
- IP addresses
- MAC addresses
- Membership numbers
- License-plate numbers

An example of personal data in SAP S/4HANA is data related to the SAP Business Partner objects like its name, BP-ID, or address. Additionally, contracts which are made by the Business Partner use personal data like delivery addresses, billing addresses, bank account details, or contract numbers. All this personal data needs to be protected properly.

Principles

To improve data privacy standards, the GDPR defines a few principles for processing data in alignment with the GDPR. Those are:

- Lawfulness, fairness, and transparency
- Limitation of purpose
- Data minimization
- Accuracy
- Storage limitation
- Integrity and confidentiality

As a result, it is forbidden to process personal data if there is no proven and justifiable reason to do so. The purpose of processing data needs to be documented at any stage of processing. This baseline applies to complete sets of personal data and business partner records, but also to single pieces of data. Justifiable requirements to process personal data are met if:

- The data subject has provided consent
- The processing is required for the performance of a contract
- The processing is required to fulfill legal obligations

- The processing is required in the public interest
- The processing is required to safeguard a vital interest
- The processing is based on a legitimate interest

Consent is defined as any freely given, specific, informed, and unambiguous indication of the data subject's wishes by which he or she signifies agreement to the processing of personal data relating to him or her by a statement or by a clear affirmative action. Data processing is required for the performance of a contract when it is necessary or when there is an intention to enter into a contract. Examples for legal obligations could be tax reporting, income tax reporting, or reporting for social insurance in ERP software. Public interest is given when processing is necessary for the performance of a task carried out in the public interest or in the exercise of official authority. The processing should have a basis in Union or Member State law. Vital interest describes situations where data processing is essential for the life of the data subject or that of another natural person. Legitimate interests are fundamental rights and freedoms of the data subject.

Rights of the Data Subject
The GDPR defines a set of rights that can be enforced by the natural person (data subject). These include the following rights:
The data subject needs to be informed about how which data is processed and stored, with which purpose, and how long, prior to the process of processing. Data protection has been relevant in the design of products at SAP for very long and therefore, as already mentioned in the introduction, there are different relevant features for data protection which help the customer being compliant with GDPR in SAP S/4HANA. Those features are a central solution to data privacy challenges which reduce the effort that needs to put into conception for all SAP S/4HANA applications. The prior information-right is addressed by the information retrieval framework (IRF) in SAP S/4HANA, which will be introduced in one of the following chapters. Furthermore, the GDPR prescribes that the data subject has the right to request information on the data undergoing processing, which is also addressed by the IRF. Additionally, the data subject has the right to request deletion of personal data. Data has to be deleted when all retention periods have passed or blocked as soon as the primary purpose has passed, and the residence time has elapsed. The lifecycle of personal data in SAP S/4HANA must address this issue. Moreover, the personal data has to be accurate, kept up to date and be corrected (latest after request). This needs to be ensured within the applications. The data subject has the rights to restrict processing in certain cases and that automated decisions can become subject to manual interference, which also needs to be ensured within the applications. Last but not least the data subject has the right to request the stored, related personal data in a structured, commonly used, and machine-readable format. This process is again supported by the IRF.

California Consumer Privacy Act

The California Consumer Privacy Act (CCPA) is a law similar to the GDPR, which was implemented by the State of California Department of Justice in 2018. It gives consumers more control over the personal information collected about them by businesses. The law secures privacy rights for California consumers. These rights include but are not limited to:

* The right to know what personal information a company collects about them and how it is used and shared
* The right to have personal information collected about them deleted (with limited restrictions)
* The right to opt out of having their personal information sold
* The right to be treated fairly (non-discrimination) when pursuing their CCPA rights

Solution Capability

To align with the previously described data protection regulations (like the GDPR or the CCPA) SAP S/4HANA offers mandatory features which support meeting those requirements. For example, SAP S4/HANA offers features like

* Relevant security safeguards (as part of the technical organizational measures)
* Support for fulfilling data subject requests
* The ability to segregate personal data using organizational attributes
* Personal data deletion capabilities
* Inbuilt auditing capabilities
* Advanced authorization concepts

Additionally, SAP S/4HANA offers the following embedded data privacy tools which are intended to help the customer to meet all requirements. SAP is using a holistic approach by offering different generic tools like the Information Retrieval Framework (IRF), Information Lifecycle Management (ILM), and Read Access Logging (RAL) in SAP S/4HANA, which support the customer in meeting all data privacy and protection requirements. Those features and tools lead to security being integrated deeply into the company processes. They are described in detail in the next sections.

Information Lifecycle Management

Enterprises require a comprehensive information lifecycle management (ILM) strategy to keep up with the speed and complexities of data today. Furthermore, efforts to protect consumer identity have resulted in an increase in legal requirements. Various regulations, including the Sarbanes-Oxley Act, the Health Insurance Portability and Accountability Act (HIPAA), the California Consumer Privacy Act (CCPA), and the General Data Protection Regulation (GDPR), monitor and regulate data around the world. Additionally, there is an increasing need to manage aging systems, which consume ongoing storage, administration, and maintenance costs. These systems pose a legal risk because the data they contain must be accessible, for example, to tax auditors. Data accessibility becomes unpredictable as knowledge of old systems fades and old hardware is removed. Information management and retention have become so critical that an effective ILM strategy is now an essential component of an enterprise's overall strategy for dealing with the challenges of cost, compliance, and risk. Personal data, for example, must be deleted when it no longer serves a valid business purpose, according to privacy regulations. SAP has created an ILM approach that addresses the complex information management requirements of organizations. Policy, processes, practices, and tools are developed and used to align the business value of information with the most appropriate and cost-effective IT infrastructure—from creation to destruction of information. SAP provides a comprehensive and automated approach to ILM to assist in adapting to constantly changing regulations. SAP's ILM approach addresses various business scenarios, use cases, and challenges. In standalone ILM retention warehouses, the SAP Information Lifecycle Management (SAP ILM) component manages the data lifecycle of both live application systems and legacy data:

- Retention Management: SAP ILM tools and technologies support the entire information lifecycle, from creation to retention to destruction. These functions allow to enter various rules and policies that reflect various criteria, such as where data is stored, how long data is retained, and when data can and must be destroyed. These policies, which are typically based on external legal requirements or internal service-level agreements, can apply to both structured and unstructured data stored on various media types. The data is automatically archived into the appropriate storage area and given an expiration date based on the rules the customer created. Storage integration that is ILM-aware means that storage systems understand and can act on the stored data based on the rules customer defined. SAP ILM provides automated discovery functionality as well as legal and compliance-level information management. When the expiration date is reached at the end of the lifecycle, a destruction function permanently destroys the archived data.
- System Decommissioning: SAP ILM provides a comprehensive approach to shutting down legacy systems and bringing data from both SAP and non-SAP software into a centralized ILM retention warehouse. By decommissioning no-longer-used applications, customers simplify their overall system landscape and lower long-term administration and maintenance costs. SAP ILM provides a comprehensive approach to decommissioning legacy systems and consolidating the data into a significantly compressed retention warehouse. Native SAP software system integration, as well as data storage and loading capabilities, shortens implementation timelines. In addition, SAP ILM provides on-demand data access

Fig. 32.1 SAP ILM data destruction and archiving objects

and reporting options, allowing to view historical data even after the original system has been shut down (Fig. 32.1).

The lifecycle of personal data in compliance with the GDPR consists of three phases: processing, blocking, and deletion. In the first phase, personal data is processed based on the primary purpose, for example, as long as a contract needs to be fulfilled. As soon as this purpose no longer applies, the information can still be stored during the so-called blocking phase. During this phase the data needs to be blocked and access is granted only to authorized personnel. This means that data can be restored, for example, in case there are issues with the underlying contract or service. After a limited retention period, the data needs to be deleted without residue.

Fig. 32.2 Lifecycle of
personal data

The described lifecycle of personal data is illustrated in the following figure
(Fig. 32.2):

The ILM tool manages and automates these retention processes and is considered
as a complex part of data lifecycle management. It offers the SAP Fiori applications
which can be used to configure the tool, for example, by defining deletion rules.

Information Retrieval Framework

Data subjects have the right to obtain information about the processing of their
personal data, including the reason (purpose) for the processing. The Information
Retrieval Framework (IRF) is a tool in SAP S/4HANA which allows the user to
automatically search for and retrieve all personal data of a specified data subject. It
understands the connections between data from different tables and objects and
retrieves all connections and personal data. The merchant uses the SAP Fiori
application which collects all relevant data for a business partner. The search results
are displayed in a comprehensive, structured, and easy-to-read list. The following
applications are available through SAP IRF:

- Start Data Collection: This app facilitates to automate the retrieval of all personal
  data for a specific business partner. This app can be used to initiate a cross-
  application search for all personal data associated with a specific data subject. The
  selection criteria that can be used to narrow down the search are, for example,
  type of data subject ID (business partner), ID of the data subject (business partner
  number), the language of the data subject, the reason for which the data was
  gathered and processed. Customer can also select from a list of previously defined
  profiles to configure the collection, display, and download of personal data.
- Process Data Collection Results: This app allows to view and download the
  search results of the data collection process initiated by the Start Data Collection
  app. The application displays a structured, easy-to-read list of all personal data
  related to the specified business partner, subdivided by the purposes for which the
  data was processed. Furthermore, customers can use personalized profiles to tailor
  data collection to their specific needs, such as what data is displayed in the search
  results view. The data can be downloaded in various file formats to make it
  available to data subjects. This app can be used to view a list of all data collection
  requests that have been created with the Start Data Collection application, to sort
  and/or filter the data collection requests, to display all personal data (e.g., name,
  address, date of birth, employment, or creditworthiness data) of the specified
  business partner, organized by the purposes for which the data was collected and

processed. Furthermore, personalization profiles can be used to tailor data collection to customer-specific requirements. Profiles enable customers to save customized settings that affect the collection, display, and download of personal data. Change documents are written for each change in the search results display.

- Application Log for Information Retrieval: This app helps to search for and view application logs created during data model creation and/or data collection. Furthermore, the application allows to analyze log entries by obtaining more information about the logs and their messages. The application displays all logs generated during a data collection run with sub-object DTINF COLLECTION. For log entries additional information are provided, such as the start/end date of the collection process or the tables from which data was retrieved. The application also shows all logs generated by the DTINF GENERATE sub-object during data model generation.

Use cases of the IRF are tasks which are required to align with the data subjects' rights. For example, it is used to serve the data subject with information on personal data undergoing processing and the underlying purpose and retention policies. In addition, the IRF offers features which are used in other contexts (Fig. 32.3).

Read Access Logging

RAL is a tool which logs all read operations when personal data is accessed. It helps to clarify situations in case of abuse and makes sure that actors who might have access to data in the system, but weren't supposed to access this data, can be made responsible for possible consequences. RAL is frequently required to comply with legal regulations or public standards, such as data protection and privacy, for example, in banking or healthcare applications. Data protection and privacy are concerned with safeguarding and restricting access to personal information. Data protection and privacy laws in some countries even require that access to certain personal data be reported. Companies and government agencies may also want to monitor access to classified or sensitive data for their own reasons. If no trace or log is kept on who accesses data, it is difficult to hunt down the person responsible for any data leaks to the outside world. This information is provided by RAL. Read-only Access Logging is always based on a logging purpose that is freely defined according to an organization's needs (e.g., data protection and privacy). This logging purpose is then assigned as an attribute to each log entry, allowing log data to be classified and organized based on the logging purpose. Various archiving rules or reporting, for example, can be created based on logging purposes. Thus, the RAL framework can be used to comply with legal or other regulations, detect fraud or data theft, conduct audits, or for any other internal purpose. The RAL configuration is read when an application is launched. It indicates whether and to what extent the current function module, operation, or UI element is log relevant. Log entries can be organized based on their semantics. Predefined configurations may exist in SAP applications. However, in order to meet the legal requirements of organizations, the

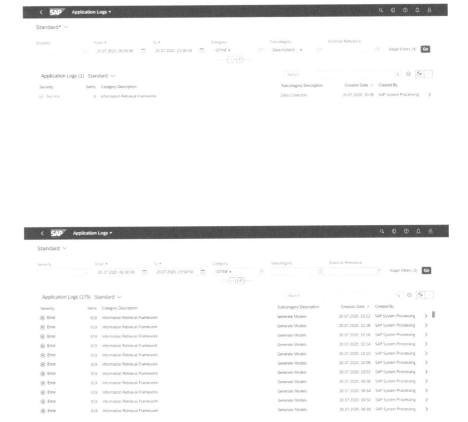

SAP IRF Application Log with different Filtering

Fig. 32.3 SAP IRF application log with different filtering

customer's key user is usually adapting them to company's needs. RAL can be used to monitor and log access to personal data. The information provided may include, for example, which business users accessed personal data from business partners and when they did so. SAP provides default configurations that assign log domains dedicated fields. A log domain is a category that groups data fields that are semantically identical or related. All fields displayed on the UI that are related to these domains are logged. The domain is shown in the log. In the RAL Configuration application, customers can activate or deactivate the available RAL configurations, as well as make changes. Customers should think carefully about which information is important to log. If a broad range of information is logged, customers will end up with a large amount of data that will be more difficult to process than if more specific logging is configured. Because they are only identifiable with this additional personal data, these log domains are logged with fields related to business partner (BP), customer (CUSTOMER), supplier (VENDOR), legal entity (LEGAL ENTITY), employee (EMPLOYEE), or student (STUDENT). TRADE_UNION data, for example, requires information about the EMPLOYEE. If necessary, log conditions are used to limit data logging (in technical terms, these fields are considered as conditions). For example, customs could configure RAL to log an employee-related field in a specific transaction only if the employee's religion is displayed. Access to this field is not logged if it is only visible on a tab that does not display the employee's religion.

By default, RAL is turned off. Customer can enable it in the RAL Configuration application's relevant section. With the Monitor application created logs can be displayed (Fig. 32.4).

Change Documents

Change documents is used for tracking all attribute changes to objects which have this feature enabled. For example, the date, time, old value, new value, initiator, and more parameters are logged. The tool offers various SAP Fiori application which can be used to view changes made to different objects. Many business objects are frequently changed. It is frequently useful, if not required, to be able to trace the changes made. If the changes are logged, customers can always find out what was changed, when it was changed, and how it was changed. This can assist in analyzing errors. Change documents are used to support auditing, for example, in financial accounting. A change document records modification to a business object. The document is created independently of any changes to the database.

Consent Management

Consent Management is a tool in SAP S/4HANA which helps managing consents of data subjects. It provides the SAP Fiori application which allows the user to import consents using a json file, enable the user to search and display consents, and view logs of previous import jobs. Any personal data collected or processed must be linked to a specific, predefined purpose, such as the performance of a contract or the fulfillment of a legal obligation. If customers need to obtain consent from the data subject before using their personal information, this consent data can be saved in the SAP system as consent records. Furthermore, the solution assists in handling consent data in accordance with applicable data protection regulations. It manages consent data retention, controls access to consent data, and aids in the blocking or deletion of master data. Consent administration allows to search for and view stored consent records, as well as import consent data from a file or through web services. Consent administration enables the following functions:

- Manage Consents: This application allows to search for and display consent records that have been previously imported from a file. The system provides a

Fig. 32.4 SAP RAL Metadata Extension Editor and Custom Metadata Extension

detailed list of consent information, such as the purpose for processing personal data, the responsible data controller, or third parties who may be involved.

- Import Consents from File: Customers can use this app to import consent data from a file. In order to do so, the data must be in JSON format.

The application allows selecting the appropriate level from the application log detail level dropdown list to specify the amount of detail customers want to log during the import process. Furthermore, by using the external reference ID field,

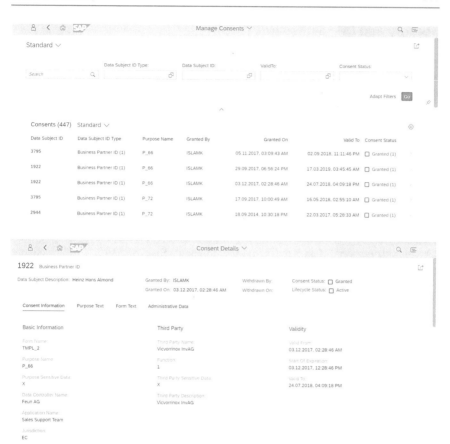

Fig. 32.5 SAP Consent Management—Manage Consents and Consent Details

own log ID can be created. This feature allows to easily search for and identify the logs relevant to customers when analyzing the import log in the Analyze Consent Import Logs application.

- Analyze Consent Import Logs: This application facilitates to search for and view the import logs generated during the consent record import process. Furthermore, the application allows to analyze log entries by obtaining more information about the logs and their messages. The tool enables viewing a list of all import logs that match the criteria you specified and narrowing down to the list of import logs (Fig. 32.5).

Security and DPP Safeguards (TOM)

As already mentioned earlier, technical and organizational measures (TOMs) need to be implemented to meet the data protection and data privacy requirements. SAP S/4HANA provides the TOMs described in this chapter.

Authentication describes standard authentication capabilities which enable system access based on personal authentication. For example, the SAP S/4HANA Cloud uses the Identity Authentication service of the SAP Business Technology Platform. Authorizations describe standard authorization concepts fine-tuned based on proper data separation. They define which data can be accessed and with which permissions. The SAP S/4HANA On Premise makes use of the existing ABAP authorization concept, and SAP S/4HANA uses role-based authorizations. Data Separation describes that personal data which has been collected for a specific purpose needs to be separated from personal data collected for other purposes. Changes to personal data need to be documented. SAP S/4HANA offers change logging capabilities like the previously introduced Change Documents tool. Encryptions ensure that personal data is not accessible by unauthorized parties during transit and at rest. Availability Control makes sure that personal data is available. This is achieved by implementing procedures like backup, disaster recovery, and business continuity. Examples for availability control measures are backups of SAP S/4HANA Cloud tenants. The transmission of personal data needs to be secure. The Transmission Control measures are guidance on how personal data should be transmitted to ensure a secure transmission of data. In SAP S/4HANA concepts like encrypted communication and using the Unified Connectivity (UCON) Framework come in place. The Job Control measure is about ensuring that the data processor is following the data controller's instructions and guidelines. It consists of some technical aspects but also organizational and contractual aspects. SAP S/4HANA Cloud fulfills several certifications, and SAP S/4HANA On Premise provides a range of audit functionality in regard to this measure. When pseudonymizing data, it is changed in a way that the data subject is not identifiable without using separately kept information. SAP S/4HANA offers procedures such as test data pseudonymization to apply pseudonymization. Disclosure Control is about logging all access operations to personal data. In SAP S/4HANA the previously described Read Access Logging (RAL) provides functionality to log all access operations. The goal of Physical Access Control is to prevent unauthorized persons from gaining access to data processing systems. In SAP S/4HANA On Premise the corresponding IT department and for SAP S/4HANA Cloud SAP as the operator need to ensure physical access control. For example, physical access control can be enforced by using access cards or by hiring a doorman.

Conclusion

Data protection and privacy are very important factors which need to be considered when working with personal data and come with different regulations which need to be met. SAP S/4HANA Cloud and On Premise offer different tools like the ILM, IRF, RAL, Change Management, and Consent Management, which handle data protection and privacy as a central component. As a result, the effort for conceptualizing new applications is minimized, and customers are able to be compliant with data protection and privacy laws. The chapter gave also an overview of the history of different data privacy regulations, described up-to-date data regulation laws, and showed how SAP supports their customers in meeting all requirements.

Secure Development and Operations

33

This chapter focuses on secure development and operations concepts and frameworks of SAP S/4HANA. Particularly, secure software development lifecycle with secure programming, threat modeling, code scans, and vulnerability assessments are explained. Additionally, secure landscape architecture and operations technics are depicted.

Business Requirement

Running a secure system landscape necessitates more than just secure software—system setup and system operation are critical components of a secure system landscape that provides a high level of protection against attacks and allows detection of such attacks to prevent downtime. IT Services and Operations Management (ITSOM) tools are important for security because they collect all necessary information about a system landscape, provide alerting mechanisms, and aid in the distribution of security patches to all systems that require them. Running and maintaining secure landscapes necessitates a plan. And with the growing need to collaborate with customers, partners, and employees at any time and from any location, a strategy that makes things easier to use and manage is required. A strategy necessitates a plan—an overall plan and thus a central controlling instance that executes—or at the very least keeps the plan up to date for everyone to refer to. If fighting a lot of small battles against vulnerabilities in a new setup, customers might win one or two, but they will lose in the end. Consider firefighters, public security, or even flood scenarios: all of the well-intended individual action, all of the uncoordinated help from motivated citizens may be useful on the spot, but it will never be able to keep an entire infrastructure or social system safe over time, let alone rebuild it. As a result, a central office must coordinate all measures and activities in order to provide them as efficiently as possible, at the right time, and in the right place. Thus, such a headquarters in IT landscapes in the form of a central solution for IT Services and Operations Management (ITSOM) is required—particularly in the SAP landscapes,

S. Sarferaz, *Compendium on Enterprise Resource Planning*,
https://doi.org/10.1007/978-3-030-93856-7_33

Fig. 33.1 Three phases for
ensuring security

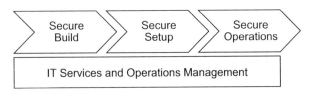

which are in many ways analogous to the real-world social systems and infrastructures from the preceding analogies. Aside from distributing goods or data and services, one of the concerns in such complex systems is always the system's security. Moreover, as with real-world systems, large areas of security are really aspects of monitoring and alerting, software lifecycle, and software logistics. As a result, security is frequently about knowing what is going on and understanding the landscape and its processes, which allows customers to identify issues and fix them quickly and with as much automation as possible. There are numerous ways to approach and subdivide the vast subject of software, system, and landscape security. First, secure software must be built, then secure systems and system landscapes in which this software runs must be set up, and finally, these landscapes must be kept secure in operations mode. Within these three main phases, the emphasis is on the aspects where IT Services and Operations Management (ITSOM) tools make a significant contribution to securing system landscapes (Fig. 33.1).

Obviously, security for software systems begins with what developers do. They are the ones who deliver code that is more or less secure. They are in charge of delivering security fixes as well as preparing interfaces for secure communications, monitoring, and alerting. Developers must answer questions like, Is the code well protected against manipulations and/or injections? Are interfaces designed to be secure? Where are the credentials hardcoded? Have the proper monitoring interfaces, alerting methods have been implemented? The first steps in operating a secure environment are to set up secure systems, system interactions, and thus system landscapes. Many tasks that must be performed only once during setup reoccur, on a regular or continuous basis, during the operations phase to ensure security, which is managed by an ITSOM solution. Setup is a critical phase because missing security is often invisible, especially in a new system landscape. If the configuration is not actively checked, security flaws are usually discovered during operations—often after some damage has already been done. Powerful ITSOM tools become mission-critical during the operations phase. This is true for many operations tasks, many of which play critical roles in maintaining the security of the operated landscape. What good is a secure configuration if changes to it go undetected? What is the point of obtaining security fixes if customers don't know where to apply them or how to assess their potential consequences? These are recurring tasks for IT Services and Operations Management (ITSOM)—the central management of information indicating potential vulnerabilities and attacks, as well as the coordination and routing of the corresponding fixes and defensive measures. Timing is a critical factor in security because the time between the occurrence of a new threat or vulnerability and its resolution defines the likelihood of damage. As a result, the ease and speed with which security issues can be fixed is critical, and the security of a system landscape rises directly proportionally to the speed with which fixes can be deployed across the entire landscape. This speed of fixing is affected by a number of factors, some of which are as follows:

- The landscape's homogeneity
- Completeness and consistency of landscape information
- Fixing method consistency
- Completeness and quality of information about landscape changes

Time is, of course, a critical factor on the business side of the equation. Security breaches and service outages can cost businesses millions of dollars in revenue. Preventative network and system security management and disaster recovery can help organizations avoid these losses and distinguish between profitability and non-profitability today. These effects are, of course, amplified by today's trend toward the cloud, which combines cloud and on-premise landscapes and provides an increasing number of solutions for remote and mobile access. Because many of the mechanisms are also applicable in these scenarios, they are not differentiated between these deployment options.

Solution Capability

SAP provides a Secure Operations Map that covers the three above-mentioned phases and serves as a reference to match the capabilities of ITSOM tools to the requirements for a secure system (Fig. 33.2).

The definition of IT Services and Operations Management (ITSOM) tools covers the tasks of the three phases: IT Services and Operations Management (ITSOM) tools are any products or services that aid in the monitoring of an IT landscape and all of its services, as well as the detection of any abnormal behavior. Any products

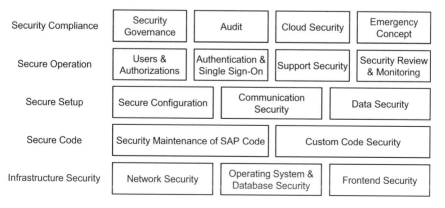

Fig. 33.2 Security map for development and operations

that improve control over the IT infrastructure (asset management, change management, configuration management), processes (job scheduling, workflow management), and service workflows are also acceptable (service and support desk, service-level management, business service management). On the tool side, SAP Solution Manager and SAP Application Lifecyle Management (ALM) are well-known offering in the ITSOM segment. In terms of security, it is accompanied by a suite of services provided by the SAP service and support organization, which are frequently controlled.

Secure Software Development

SAP has implemented a secure software development lifecycle (SDL) for software development projects, providing a framework for training, tools, and processes which can be also used by customers and partners. Because security is critical for anyone who uses SAP S/4HANA, and services for running critical business processes as well as storing and processing sensitive data, securely developed software is a requirement for secure operations. Following the secure SDL framework is a requirement for all the SAP S/4HANA product teams, for both on premise and cloud. This section provides an overview of secure SDL with a focus on the provisioning phases of a software product as defined in the ISO/IEC 27034-1 standard. Preparation, development, outsourcing, acquisition, and transition to operations are all covered by the standard. In the operational phases, when the software is deployed and used, the standard also covers activities such as software maintenance, extensions, and security response. In this sense, secure SDL encompasses the processes that describe how software is developed and maintained. Security is a primary concern for any global company, and as such, businesses expect solid and secure products and cloud offerings on which they can rely. As a result, SAP S/4HANA considers security throughout the software development lifecycle as shown in Fig. 33.3. To master this complex topic, the secure SDL consists of a well-chosen combination of methodologies, guidelines, processes, and tools. SAP is constantly improving those guidelines and tools as technology advances and the environment and threat landscape evolve. These activities are heavily embedded in the idea-to-market process framework as well as other corporate processes such as HR, product support, and cloud operations.

Security Training

Security is a cultural and organizational issue in which all employees must be aware of and embrace security requirements. As a result, security awareness and regular role-specific trainings are required for all roles involved in the development and maintenance of our software products. This includes knowledge and awareness of threats, common vulnerabilities, and attack patterns for product managers and development support roles. Knowing how to apply threat modeling and risk assessment methods assists all roles involved in deriving and deciding on application security needs, as well as planning corresponding requirements and application

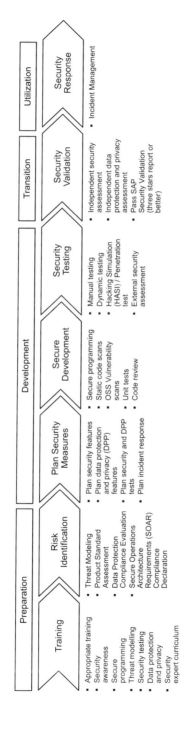

Fig. 33.3 Secure software development lifecycle (SDL)

security controls. Security training for architects and developers teaches them how to design secure software and write secure code. Security test methods and tools are taught to developers and quality assurance engineers. Furthermore, dedicated training curriculum are required as well as other learning opportunities for developing the role of security expert, such as security information sessions and local security summits. Participants in these training opportunities acquire or expand the subject-matter knowledge and skills required to become security advocates and support their teams during product planning, creation, and operation.

Risk Identification
SAP follows a risk-based approach to achieve security within economic constraints, taking into account the time and cost of product provisioning and operations. This risk-based approach enables targeted security investments that address all identified risks within the context of SAP S/4HANA. Product teams conduct a security risk assessment at the start of each new software development cycle to identify and analyze risks and rate their criticality. The security activities that are planned and carried out are based on the outcomes and decisions of the risk assessment. Product teams must first identify and classify the assets managed by the product as a prerequisite for the security risk assessment. These assets can be various types of data, but they can also be the availability of business processes as described by application specifications. Deep expertise is required to identify security risks from potential threats, assess these risks, and make informed decisions about how to treat each risk. Product teams at SAP S/4HANA benefit from using corresponding methodologies that have evolved over time within the company, with threat modeling being the most effective. Three modeling variants of risk assessment methodologies are used by developers. The first variant is threat modeling at the product level. It applies threat modeling to a broader product scope and architecture that includes a variety of parts and components, including self-developed, open-source, outsourced, and acquired components. It is an in-depth approach that provides a quick overview of the main threats applicable to the product and the risks associated with these threats. Scenario-based threat modeling is the second type of threat modeling. It is more similar to the well-known threat-modeling approach, and product teams use it for in-depth analysis of a specific product's components and supported scenarios. In cases where new planned features necessitate deeper investigation, the in-depth threat modeling of selected critical scenarios can be an outcome of the in-depth threat modeling approach. Furthermore, it can be used in the development of small applications or products with limited scope. The third variant, known as fast-track threat modeling, can be applied as a delta threat modeling approach. It can be used when applications use a well-defined architecture that has already been threat modeled, or when a new product version needs to be evaluated to see if an existing threat model from a previous version still applies. Fast-track threat modeling is based on a questionnaire that determines whether prior threat models' assumptions and dependencies are still valid. Following the completion of security risk assessments, a product team is tasked with determining which risks will be mitigated and managed further. This occurs during the phase of security planning.

Security risk assessments are a required task for SAP S/4HANA that adhere to the risk-based secure SDL, regardless of the supported deployment models.

Plan Security Measures

In addition to risk assessments, product teams must conduct a data protection compliance evaluation (DPCE) in order to properly plan features and controls that comply with legal requirements such as the EU General Data Protection Regulation. DPCE, in contrast to the risk-based approach to secure software development, has a dedicated compliance focus and requires strict adherence to regulatory requirements such as data deletion or consent management. However, ensuring effective personal data protection through the use of adequate application security controls is a topic of security risk management. The product team is asked to derive the security and privacy requirements applicable to the product based on the results of the risk assessment and the DPCE. The team should define a suitable security control for each applicable requirement, which includes a security activity, a verification measurement, and the time to apply it (see Fig. 33.4). The security plan for the product should include all applicable security controls that the product team decides to implement.

Security controls are classified into two types. To begin, security functions are those that the product team implements to enforce security within the software or that are used by an underlying application platform. Here are some examples:

- Access control is enforced through authentication and authorization functions.
- Encryption of data in transit and at rest.
- Message authentication code and integrity protection.
- Protection against click-jacking, request forgery, and secure session management.
- Data access and security events are logged.

Another set of potential security controls is defined by how a product team decides to prevent product vulnerabilities and achieve secure functions. For

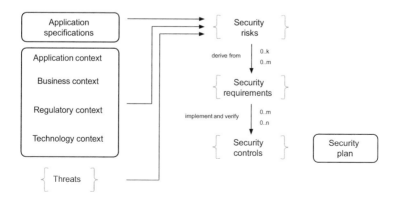

Fig. 33.4 Threats, risks, requirements, and controls

example, it is critical to address faulty input validation, corrupted memory errors, improperly encoded output, and gaps that allow privilege escalation. One or more verification measures are included in each security control. Verification measures could include:

- Architecture and code reviews, which help to ensure that the product team has placed and correctly implemented security controls.
- Static-code analysis, which can identify paths in the code where non-validated input can output, be injected into code or inappropriate database queries, or cause memory corruptions.
- Dynamic security testing, which can reveal unprotected access paths, indirect object references, or unexpected error situations that lead to privilege escalation.
- Penetration tests, which can confirm the expected security status or reveal new attack vectors.

SAP's Product Standard Security contains a supporting library of security requirements and security controls for product teams to use. This library contains a set of security requirements that can be used by product teams to help them mitigate security risks. Furthermore, it provides guidance on appropriate solutions and verification methods. The library, which has been accumulated and maintained over time, not only builds on SAP's experience as a provider of enterprise on-premise and cloud applications, but also incorporates content from valuable third-party and public sources like OWASP, SANS or CWE. Developing and maintaining a security plan is a requirement for all SAP standard software product teams. Furthermore, product teams are expected to have processes and plans in place to handle security vulnerabilities reported by third parties as soon as a product version is released.

Secure Development
Product teams design and implement a product's specified functionality and non-functional qualities during the development phase. SAP's Product Standard Security includes secure design principles such as *fail securely* in the event of an error, *secure by default, never assume trust, least privilege,* and *check authorization close to the resource.* The SAP S/4HANA product development teams are encouraged to use secure programming techniques, libraries, and tools that aid in the prevention of security flaws during implementation. The goal is to implement secure functions throughout the product, including application and security functions. It is critical that functions perform their intended functions and do not contain vulnerabilities that can be exploited. During this phase, the product team implements security controls outlined in the product's security plan, such as those built into the software. Developers also conduct design reviews, code reviews, additional threat modeling, and static-code analysis. The development team must adhere to the security plan, which includes plans for open-source, outsourced, and acquired components.

Security Testing

Product development teams perform a number of security scans as part of secure SDL, as described in the following sections:

- Static-Code Scans: The secure SDL methodology expects product teams to perform additional verifications of the implemented security controls through security testing, in accordance with the security test plan developed as part of the product's security plan. The secure SDL framework specifies a security testing approach that intelligently combines static and dynamic testing methods and tools. Static application security testing (SAST) tools are available and optimized for SAP's most popular programming languages. Development should, if possible, integrate these tools directly into the tool environment and use them on a daily basis. If this is not possible, the project team will run static-code analyzers on a daily or weekly basis and feed the results back to the developers for immediate audit and analysis during the development phase. The runs allow audited results to be carried over to subsequent source-code scans automatically. Static analysis is typically performed in an automated manner, allowing developers to process large amounts of code and potentially find many issues with specific classes. The use of static-code scan tools on SAP developed code, as well as auditing tool findings, is a required control in secure SDL that is independent of the identified risks.
- Open-Source Known Vulnerability Scans: As part of secure SDL, product development teams are required to scan their used open-source components for known vulnerabilities on a regular basis and to mitigate findings, such as patching to a secure version. The use of open-source known vulnerability scan tools on open-source components used by SAP, as well as auditing of the results, is the required control in secure SDL.
- Dynamic Static-Code Scans: Furthermore, as part of their risk-based security plan, project teams can plan and execute dynamic application security testing (DAST). Corresponding tools assist developers and quality engineers in dynamically traversing individual parts and scenarios supported by the product, observing actual application behavior, and potentially identifying additional security flaws. These tools are especially useful for testing the interaction and integration of components written in different languages or for incorporating components that are available only as binaries.

Security Validation

Product security validation ensures that SAP S/4HANA can withstand the rigors of real-world deployment. The security validation team works independently of the development and product-provisioning teams and serves as a governance instance for SAP's secure SDL. Security validation verifies that development teams have completed all mandatory tasks in SAP's secure SDL and runs its own security tests. The number and scope of these tests vary according to the importance and potential impact of security flaws in the product on customers. The scope of testing can vary from a simple process review to several days of active validation and penetration testing. The secure SDL requires all products developed within SAP's innovation cycle to go through the security validation process as a mandatory step.

Security Response

When developing secure products, preventing security vulnerabilities has the highest priority. Even the best security-assurance measures in place during development, however, cannot guarantee the complete absence of flaws or defects, especially when it comes to threats or insights discovered after a product has been released. As a result, SAP has a critical security response process. Following the release of a product or service—or any extension or modification to either—the product team must be prepared to receive vulnerability reports during use. In such a case, SAP must have contacts and the necessary technical skills on hand immediately to triage and investigate vulnerability reports and either confirm or reject the vulnerability. SAP is requested to provide timely security corrections to sanitize the issue based on the severity based on the internal target for a confirmed vulnerability. SAP's product security response team contributes to the high-quality mitigation of security vulnerabilities in shipped SAP software. This includes the following:

- Overseeing the responsible disclosure of vulnerabilities in SAP software reported by third-party sources such as security researchers and hackers
- Organizing the monthly security patch day
- Crisis management for issues such as SAP software breaches

Customers, partners, researchers, and others can submit vulnerability reports via SAP's online support tools or PGP-encrypted e-mail.

Secure Operations

It is not enough to have secure code to run a secure system. After deploying software, system configuration is critical to establishing a secure system from the start. Some security issues arise during the setup phase, when system components are deployed but not used and not checked. Secure configuration also includes the definition of security standards for systems against which subsequent changes can be validated. The ongoing business of operations is the primary focus of SAP Solution Manager and SAP ALM, and it is therefore critical to secure operations. Those solutions provide assistance to operators in all of their primary task areas. They offer an overview of the system landscape and its status, manage and monitor release and patch levels, and compare configuration changes to the compliant and secure baseline configuration defined by compliance activities and established during setup. Users and authorizations, authentication, and single sign-on (SSO) are typically handled with SAP Identity Management. However, SAP Solution Manager and SAP ALM support configuration validation, for example, data from the configuration and change database (CCDB) can be used to run queries like "all users with SAP

ALL access on a regular basis to monitor and verify compliance with SAP recommendations and corporate policies.

Secure Configuration

Based on information gathered in SAP Solution Manager and SAP Application Lifecycle Management (ALM), a set of services is provided to ensure secure configuration during initial system setup. Early Watch Alert (EWA) and the more detailed Security Optimization Service (SOS) compare customer settings (configurations and authorizations) with SAP-recommended standards. Based on the findings, a customer-specific security baseline that takes into account customer-specific conditions and security regulations can be developed. Any changes made during operations can then be monitored using configuration validation, ensuring that no unwelcome change goes unnoticed. In addition to regular monitoring, customers should run the complete SOS and/or EWA reports on a regular basis to ensure landscape compliance, as not only systems but also the threat landscape around the systems evolve and SAP recommendations may emerge over time. SAP Solution Manager and SAP ALM can monitor changes and configurations for interfaces in the same way that it does for changes and configurations, and they can assist in assessing the proper configurations for network communications with configuration validation in conjunction with support. It does not, however, play a role in traditional network security issues. SAP Cyber Defense & Response Center focuses also on SAP S/4HANA. Thus, all security events and incidents are logged and monitored, as well as security-critical events and incidents are mitigated accordingly. This monitoring is available 24 hours a day, 7 days a week, with an end-to-end security incident handling service in place. It is also possible to manually identify and analyze sophisticated attacks. This is mostly performed in case of complex attacks in order to identify the attacker and prevent future attacks, or to detect similar attacks faster and take appropriate security precautions to be better protected. Furthermore, SAP provides a process for customers to report security incidents.

Monitoring and Support

Support Security defines the policies for support personnel, secure support connections to customer systems, and support user roles, accounts, and authorizations. SAP ALM can assist in enforcing these policies through the mechanisms described in users and authorizations, authentication, and single sign-on (SSO). In light of the growing demand for data protection, this policy enforcement adds an additional layer of security and confidentiality to the system landscape. Customers' primary focus is on the ongoing process of reviewing and monitoring security. It is also a mission-critical area for SAP Solution Manager and SAP ALM, as they facilitate collaboration between the Operations Control Center (OCC) and the Innovation Control Center (ICC) on the customer side and the Mission Control Center (MCC) on the SAP side. The SAP Solution Manager and SAP ALM can be used as a central instance for all monitoring and alerting information within the customer's operations center, and—in an ideal setup—certain cases should be defined in which incoming alerts directly and automatically trigger the MCC at

SAP. Again, the information in the CCDB that will alert to any unexpected configuration changes in the landscape is mostly security relevant. These changes are detected and alerted by the SAP Solution Manager extension Enterprise Threat Detection. Periodic checks of the landscape against the configuration validation data confirm whether systems still adhere to the baseline configuration defined and implemented during the setup phase. This SAP Solution Manager and SAP ALM feature aid in maintaining a high level of security during productive system operations. Based on continuous monitoring, a single indication can already reveal a potential intrusion in progress, giving the administrator the opportunity to activate countermeasures. SAP Solution Manager and SAP ALM also handle problems and incidents and provide context-sensitive recommended actions (guided procedures) for these cases. As a result, those solutions play an important role in the security concept.

Landscape Architecture

To ensure secure operation of a platform such as SAP S/4HANA, SAP has considered a technically robust security architecture that divides the data and concerns and is legally capable at all times. On the other hand, SAP also uses a separation between the network and the customer and builds a layer in between to avoid vulnerability. Furthermore, SAP also uses many tests, hacking simulations, and scans to ensure security. Additionally, backup and recovery mechanisms are considered. Multitenancy architecture allows customers to share hardware without violating data protection and data privacy. Customer isolation takes place at application level using security groups, whereby each customer can be part of only one security group. Client isolation is incorporated in SAP HANA at database level. With these security groups, it is possible to establish communication between quality assurance system (Q instance) and production system (P instance). SAP can gain access to data and the system only by an administrator and multi-factor authentication. This prevents the use of hacked administration accounts and safeguards the data and the system. This is also used to run central lifecycle management tools to protect and maintain the cloud. However, the information from monitoring, incidents, and health checks is automatically considered into the SAP network to protect the systems and maintain them proactively if required. Customer access to cloud applications using the Internet is one of the most critical security challenges. The SAP S/4HANA Cloud applications can be consumed using HTTPS from anywhere, whereby customers have access via a central load balancer and Web Dispatcher. There are two interfaces: the UI interface, where the end user can work with the system via a UI, and an API interface, whereby this is used for system-to-system communication. The Web Dispatcher controls the message traffic in order to avoid, for example, distributed denial of service (DDoS) attacks. To ensure the security of applications and infrastructure, they must also be checked continuously. This involves performing various security tests such as penetration tests or hacking simulations on critical components.

Data Center Security

Since SAP's S/4HANA is also a cloud product, the security of the data centers around the globe must be ensured at all times. There are five important areas that are covered in this context: Physical security, network security, backup and recovery, compliance and confidentiality, and integrity. Physical security refers to the protection of servers, computers, and media from physical threats posed by third parties or natural disasters. This includes monitoring in and around the data center using surveillance cameras, motion sensors, and infrared sensors, among other things. Those utilities should display and log prohibited data center access so that security personnel can take appropriate countermeasures. Additionally, this also necessitates that the data center be constantly monitored and protected by security personnel. To prevent unauthorized access, also biometric sensors or access card readers can be used. The power supply must always be available so that the application services can be available, and no data is lost. If the power supply is interrupted, this must be mitigated by generators. Other physical threats include natural hazards such as flooding, fire, extreme heat, and cold. Countermeasures are, for example, reinforcing the data center's facade, installing ventilation and water sprinklers, and monitoring the temperature in the data center. Because the computers can be accessed from anywhere in the world, the connections must be monitored and managed as well. SAP uses data encryption in the transport layer (256 bits) to provide this security, makes use of several firewalls to protect the internal network from attacks, and deploys reverse proxy farms to obfuscate network tropology, and network operations are monitored all the time. When a system fails, backups are required to recover lost data. SAP performs a daily backup in which all data is saved. This also includes log file backups, which are replicated every 2 hours. If a data center completely collapses due to a fire, for example, backups can be obtained from another data center as SAP stores backups in several geographically separate data centers. Point-in-time recoveries are also provided. Backups, on the other hand, have a retention time of 4 weeks for production systems and 2 weeks for non-production systems. SAP allows to identify business transactions and track them down to their underlying source documents. In SAP S/4HANA, for example, it is not possible to delete posting-relevant data, but financial data can be changed of course. All changes to this data, however, are logged and the history is saved. Users often have access to more data and functions in applications than they require. This is a major security issue because users can have no access to sensitive data and functions. SAP has role-based access for this, which means that a user can consume only the functions and data that are permitted by the role. Thus, users' access to application features are limited to only what they require to for their tasks. User activities can also be monitored in order to detect unusual behavior and react appropriately in critical cases. The customer also has complete ownership of the data and can, for example, extract its customer data or gain access to it via read-only authorizations after the contract has expired. Customer data can be deleted only with the customer's permission. Through proactive, automated system monitoring, SAP S/4HANA can ensure data integrity and availability.

Conclusion

SAP strives to protect data and services as much as possible with the SAP S/4HANA security concept. On the one hand, SAP protects third-party data, data from within the company, and data from SAP itself. It will also make every effort to ensure that the cloud and its services are always in use. However, the greatest risk is posed by the employees and end users themselves, and no software is completely secure. SAP Solution Manager and SAP ALM serve as the focal point for a wide range of tasks and activities at the heart of managing a highly complex SAP S/4HANA system landscape. Those solutions are the tools of choice for defining, implementing, and maintaining a secure system landscape. The security of system landscapes is one of the aspects that such central management tools ensure. Overall, those operations' solutions are potent ITSOM tool.

Globalization and Localization

34

This chapter focuses on globalization and localization concepts and frameworks of SAP S/4HANA to enable country-specific regulations, languages, currencies, calendars, and time zones. Particularly, advanced compliance reporting, document compliance, and localization toolkit are explained.

Business Requirement

Globalization refers to any activity that brings different countries' people, cultures, and economies closer together. In the business world, globalization aims to practices that enable organizations to become more connected to their customers all over the world. This includes everything from product design to marketing in different national markets. Because of the rise of globalization, there has arguably never been a better time to build a business into a global company. Companies looking to expand have a plethora of options available to them, ranging from access to a global talent pool to an increased volume of information that can be used to position a business. Globalization primarily refers to the strategy of expanding business beyond national borders. It includes the processes that teach about international law as well as local regulations, how to create a multinational business environment, and how to connect with international partners to improve chances of success. In the past, globalization was more associated with large, complex organizations. But more enterprises of all sizes are going global due to new markets, foreign investment opportunities, ways to save on taxes, access to talent, gaining competitive advantage. Last but the not least, advancement in digital technologies have enabled them to become more global. As it becomes easier to enter new markets, there will be more product niches to exploit—and new customers to attract. However, truly going global necessitates extensive planning. Localizing the product is the most important steps in this process. Thus, localization fall under the umbrella of globalization. The process of adapting a product to a specific target market is known as localization. Localization is the process of adapting product to local markets by making it sound

S. Sarferaz, *Compendium on Enterprise Resource Planning*,
https://doi.org/10.1007/978-3-030-93856-7_34

and feel more native. It goes beyond simply translating the content. To create a product that meets the expectations of the locals, factors such as culture, religion, and local preferences must be considered. Localization entails customizing many elements such as currency, time format, colors, icons, and any other aspect of products that may appear foreign to target audience. This usually occurs after internationalization has occurred. Whereas internationalization creates a product that is easily adaptable to many different audiences in many different countries, localization takes that product and makes it highly relevant to a single market.

Companies need to comply with government regulations in a timely manner or pay hefty fines or worst stop operating in that market. Some typical compliance may include regular tax filing with tax authorities or in some cases generating electronic invoices that may need to be shared with the local authorities. On top, many of the customers/prospects have heterogeneous system landscape, and there's no single source of truth that makes their situation more complex involving huge reconciliation efforts. Figure 34.1 illustrates some of the examples of globalization and localization that organizations have to deal with. Enterprises need to support country official language—not just in the software but also in documents generated from the system shared with various authorities and partners. Taxes is another example for localization and globalization, for example, there are over 10,000 tax jurisdictions in the United States that have to be taken into account for the various transactions. Statutory reporting is a further instance as companies need to file timely financial statements and tax declarations. Thus, globalization, internationalization, and localization all have distinct characteristics. However, when expanding into emerging markets, each of these concepts is equally important. Skipping any step could cause to lag and prevent from developing a strong global brand.

Solution Capability

SAP S/4HANA helping organizations scale their business processes across the globe is a key differentiator. The ability of SAP S/4HANA to be used by multinational enterprises is referred to as globalization. Globalization consists of language support as well as support for local regulations such as tax management. The latter is known as localization. SAP has over 40 years of experience developing ERP software that is used in a variety of industries and countries. As part of SAP's i18N internationalization standards, SAP S/4HANA supports multiple languages, currencies, calendars, and time zones to address the global market. Because of the evolution and frequent changes in laws and regulations across countries, as well as different business practices around the world, product localization is critical if companies want to succeed in the international marketplace. SAP S/4HANA supports 131 countries, delivered more than 1500 legal changes, offers 64 local versions in 42 different languages with specific localization and legal features for countries and regions in the S/4HANA On Premise, and 43 local versions in SAP S/4HANA Cloud as of now, with the plan to achieve parity of localization between the cloud and on-premise editions within the next year. Localized business logic, such as tax

Payments

Country formats used to collect incoming and outgoing payment data

Taxes

Tax codes based on conditions or formulas for mandatory tax computation, taxation processes, exemptions

Master Data

Legally required information, VAT numbers, ID numbers, currencies, calendar

Statutory Reporting

Financial statements, tax declarations, EC sales list, document numbering

Invoicing

Country-specific invoicing process extensions

Benefits

Country-specific benefits, eligibility and admissibility rules

Languages

Country official language(s)

Time Data

Country-specific rules and formats

Validations

Country-specific format for address, IDs, bank accounts

UIX

Fiori Apps
Country-specific fields and features

Fig. 34.1 Examples of areas affected by globalization/localization

Product standard globalization is...

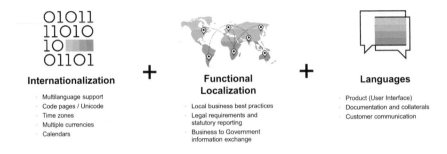

Product standard globalization is...

Fig. 34.2 SAP S/4HANA—globalization and localization buckets

calculations, and reporting capabilities are added to localized versions for application areas such as financial accounting, asset accounting, taxation, customer/supplier invoicing, procurement and sales, and master data validations. Localization features are typically added on top of standard functionality and are deeply integrated into the application logic. SAP S/4HANA supports globalization and localization through the three buckets illustrated in Fig. 34.2.

Languages cover not just the product but also the documentation, collaterals, and customer communication are offered in the local official language. Functional Localization offers out-of-the-box local business best practices complying with legal requirements and statutory reporting. Thus, business to government information exchange is ensured wherever it is required. Internationalization enables multiple language support, multicurrencies, and the ability to handle various calendars/time zones. Key applications and frameworks for localization are exemplarily explained in the next sections.

Global Tax Management

Managing indirect taxes such as VAT, GST, sales taxes, and use taxes, among others, has become a common challenge for many businesses as governments around the world have begun to implement increasingly sophisticated controls. Governments have done this not only by auditing fiscally relevant data but also by introducing more and more transactional obligations related to proof of delivery, by online validation of taxpayer registration, or even by real-time submission. As a result, companies must ensure that their enterprise management software models fiscally relevant entities correctly, makes accurate transactional tax decisions, submits tax information in real time, and records data in an audit-proof manner for consistent tax reporting. Scalable solutions that provide maximum efficiency

Global tax management A Holistic Approach to Manage Indirect Tax from a Single Source of Truth

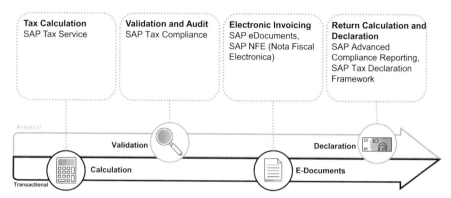

Fig. 34.3 SAP S/4HANA—global tax management

through automation and controls that enable global businesses to effectively manage eventual compliance risks are required. SAP S/4HANA resolves these challenges by offering global tax management. As finance organizations develop active engagement with their business operations and navigate changes to invoicing, collecting, paying, and reporting taxes, these solutions guide enterprises along their tax transformation journey. These capabilities are tailored to the needs of tax professionals, with an emphasis on four key areas of indirect tax management: Taxation determination, compliance with electronic documents, reporting on compliance, and tax administration. Global tax management is a comprehensive solution for managing indirect taxes. This act as a single source of truth is depicted in Fig. 34.3. There are many countries that have regulations to identify any tax evasion schemes or inaccurate reporting of information. Some even demand audit files with original document information on line-item level, master data, and in some cases supportive data like bank statements, inventories, or even production orders. This gives the authorities almost full transparency about the taxpayers.

To help enterprises to be able to pass audit and meet all the legal compliance, SAP S/4HANA has a complete solution covering tax calculation with SAP Tax Service, validation and Audit through SAP Tax Compliance, creation of specific electronic invoicing, for example, SAP eDocuments, SAP Nota Fiscal Electronica for Brazil, and Compliance reporting with SAP Advanced Compliance Reporting and Tax Declaration Framework. Customers can further customize many of these services to meet their unique requirements.

Global Payments

In recent years, there has been a concerted effort to replace bank-specific formats with standard XML formats defined by ISO 20022. Unfortunately, despite the fact that ISO 20022 increased standardization by defining the structure of these formats, differences persist. For example, some countries continue to use only a portion of the structure or expect the same information to be stored in different parts of the structure. Payment purpose codes, for instance, are used to categorize the type of payment (salary payments and payments for services). This information can be stored in some countries under the heading *Unstructured Remittance Information RmtInf>Ustrd>*, and in others under the heading *Regulatory Reporting RgltryRptg>* or *Instruction for Debtor Agent InstrForDbtrAgt>*. Based on the Common Global Implementation (CGI) initiative with country-specific changes, SAP S/4HANA provides predefined ISO 20022 payment format templates for each localized country. Credit transfers and direct debit formats are available. There are also local country formats available, for example, FEBRA-BAN in Brazil or Bacs in the United Kingdom.

Sometimes the SAP template format must be modified or a new format must be created. Map Format Data is an extended application functionality that allows to define or redefine structure and logic without programming. Figure 34.4 depicts the Map Format Data functionality's overview screen. The application allows to begin

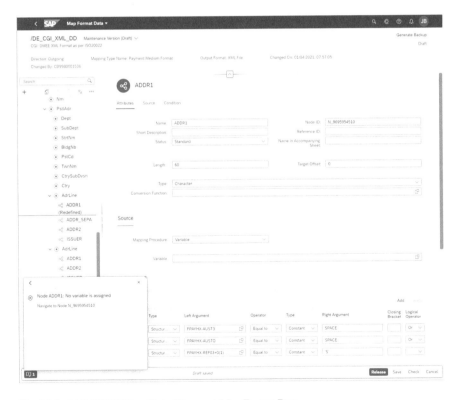

Fig. 34.4   SAP S/4HANA—Global Payment Map Format Data

with an existing template and restructure the format's structure and logic. The tool then performs consistency checks to assist in avoiding errors. It also facilitates to download the format definition and use it in another SAP S/4HANA system. Thus, the application enables the implementation of faster and less complicated payment formats through improved templates and an easier tool for changing or creating new formats.

Compliance for Reports

Global corporations and large organizations are frequently required to track time-consuming compliance processes. Because of digitalization and a rapidly changing economy, government laws and compliance requirements in the area of reporting, such as VAT/GST, EU sales list, SAF-T/audit, tax withholding, and ledger reports have evolved across countries. SAP S/4HANA for Advanced Compliance Reporting is a global legal reporting solution that meets country-specific reporting requirements. The Advanced Compliance Reporting consists of two applications: Run Advanced Compliance Reports and Define Compliance Reports. SAP has delivered over 240 reports that can be used with the Run Advanced Compliance Reports application to meet reporting requirements all over the world. The Run Advanced Compliance Reports application not only assists with report generation, but also allows for manual adjustments to prepared files, notifies of upcoming due dates, helps to view all of tasks holistically, and connects directly to government authorities for submitting legal reports online. The Define Reports application facilitates the implementation of reporting requirements in a country that have not yet been localized in SAP S/4HANA. To comply with constantly changing legal requirements, customers can either create own report or extend a standard report. Figure 34.5 shows the general layout of the Run Advanced Compliance Reports application, which displays a list of reports that are awaiting submission.

As shown in Fig. 34.6 the architecture of Advanced Compliance Reporting is based on three components: Business configuration, report definition, and report. CDS views, ABAP class methods, and analytical queries are used to consume application data. Knowledge Provider (KPro) is used to centrally store generated documents, and it also allows for the integration of a customer-specific document-management system. Adobe Forms is used to generate PDF documents. The report is prepared, generated, and electronically submitted to a government agency using report run. Embedded analytics is integrated into the advanced compliance reporting framework to help understand and explain the data shown in the reports, for example, to an auditor. It allows to drill down to the data that was read to generate the report, regardless of whether it was a line-item report (such as an audit file) or a totals-only report. Advanced Compliance Reporting includes workflow functionality, which facilitates reports to be sent for approval before being submitted to a government agency. The report definition component of Advanced Compliance Reporting includes the SAP Fiori application for building reports. The framework handles the majority of the business user-related aspects out of the box, allowing the

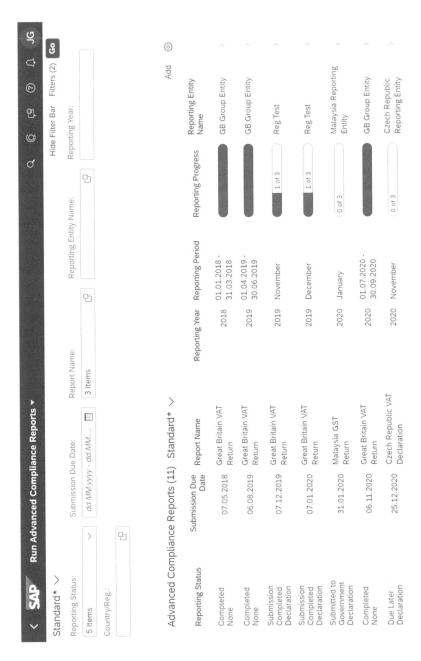

Fig. 34.5 SAP S/4HANA—Run Advanced Compliance Reports

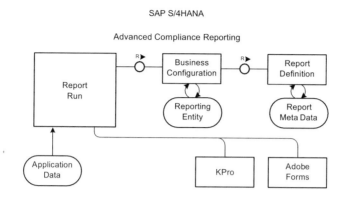

Fig. 34.6 SAP Advanced Compliance Reports—architecture

application developer to concentrate on the reporting requirements. In business configuration, a key user specifies which reports to submit, when they should be submitted, and for which reporting entity. At runtime, reporting tasks are generated based on this configuration, prompting the business user to generate a report. Additional report-specific data classification and aggregation may be required for each report, for example, the aggregation of tax line items with customer-specific tax codes into tax boxes for VAT returns.

Compliance for Documents

Many countries require registering business documents such as invoices and delivery notes with the tax authorities before issuing them. In other countries, public administration or digitalization bodies drive the use of electronic invoicing. SAP Document Compliance framework supports country-specific requirements for the exchange of electronic documents that use data from multiple applications. The extraction of relevant data, such as invoice data, is the first step in the process, which is triggered by a specific step in a business process, for example, the posting of the invoice. The submission process, which transforms this data into the target country-specific structure, is augmented by integrated cloud services that connect SAP S/4HANA with tax authorities or other receiving entities like a central invoicing platform or a service provider. Depending on the country, either SAP Integration Suite or the Peppol Exchange service of SAP Document Compliance is used to send, receive, and process relevant messages in accordance with technical requirements to ensure the data's confidentiality, authenticity, and integrity. The file's formatting is determined by criteria such as document type, provider/buyer country, tax information, and other master data, which are defined by the solution's configuration of a country-specific variation. The cloud service receives a corresponding response and returns it to SAP S/4HANA. In many cases, the response contains information such as an approval stamp or an official document number that must be saved in subsequent documents, such as accounting records. The document compliance framework's central application is the EDocument Cockpit, as shown in Fig. 34.7. This tool provides a unified user interface for monitoring and processing various documents, regardless of country or business process.

SAP Document Compliance includes functions in the SAP S/4HANA backend as well as services on the SAP Business Technology (BTP). The backend functions read the requested business data, generate eDocuments, and process received eDocuments. SAP Document Compliance sends and receives electronic documents using either integration flows in the SAP BTP Integration service or services built specifically for one document type, such as SAP Document Compliance. The architecture of the SAP Document Compliance backend functions is depicted in greater detail in Fig. 34.8.

The SAP S/4HANA backend contains all business logic. The Process Manager organizes the interconnected and related steps required to create the eDocument. Some steps are concerned with communication, while others are concerned with internal processing, such as creating and adding attachments. The eDocument Cockpit is used by business users to send the eDocument. Outbound messages are routed to the communication platform via the Interface Connector. In the Inbound Message Handler, inbound content is processed in order to be transformed into a new eDocument or a process step of an existing document. Through the Partner Connector, e-mails can be sent. The architecture is flexible, and these components can be used to build a variety of processes. This is accomplished by having configurations for each of the main objects like actions, processes, and interfaces. When the source documents are published, the corresponding eDocuments are generated and displayed in the Cockpit. Separate process steps are used to generate electronic messages in XML. The Interface Connector is responsible for mapping the source data to the message. The Cockpit displays a country-specific overview of the processes that the user is authorized to perform. A user may be authorized for Hungarian invoice registration and invoicing for Italy, but not for Hungary transport registration. By selecting the process, the eDocuments for that process are displayed in detail. Process-specific actions, such as sending, are displayed upon selection. BAdIs can be used to make specific changes to the content of eDocuments typically XML structures. Because these changes are usually scenario specific, the available BAdIs and their capabilities vary by scenario. There are also APIs that allow customers to access eDocument-related data, such as extracting received XML files for external archiving or further processing in another application. The APIs are available in the SAP API Business Hub.

Localization Framework

Geographic boundaries are blurring as global business expands, even as regional regulatory restrictions for businesses have become more pronounced. These trends

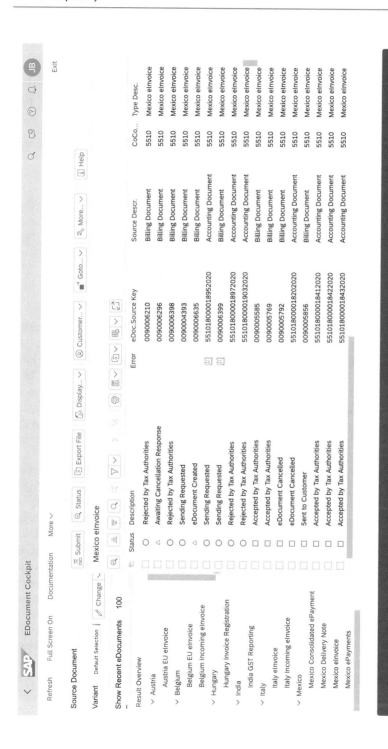

Fig. 34.7 Advanced Compliance Reports—architecture

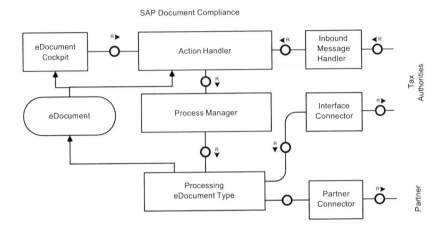

Fig. 34.8 SAP Document Compliance—architecture

point to the need for a comprehensive software solution that enables businesses to go global in a seamless manner. Configuration is the foundation for localization. Configuration examples include the factory calendar, currency, tax codes and procedures, fiscal year and general ledger settings, all of them allow to run basic processes in a specific country/region. However, there are additional legal requirements in a country/region, such as statutory reporting and specific invoicing or payment regulations. Thus, extensibility is required to complement the configuration. Extensibility is required when dealing with business-specific requirements that are not covered by a localization. Thus, configuration, functional localization, and extensibility layers enable 360-degree localization coverage.

The SAP S/4HANA Localization Toolkit consists of specific localization frameworks, for example, extensibility features provided by advanced compliance reporting and payment medium workbench, a tool provided by SAP to configure and create payment media sent by organizations to their house banks. It also provides generic extensibility features such as CDS view, OData, business logic, and UI. The toolkit covers these components and provides guidance on how to meet the requirements on top of the available localization features. Figure 34.9 depicts how the guidance spans several areas of the localization spectrum. The stack of underlying tools and technologies used in creating the guidance for localization-relevant extensibility scenarios is also visible. The guides that comprise the toolkit's core cover end-to-end scenarios for various localization areas. A scenario, for example, explains how to extend a tax reporting solution, display a custom field in a translated language, or adapt a form to meet a localization requirement. The toolkit collects several useful links and code snippets in one location, resulting in a faster imple-

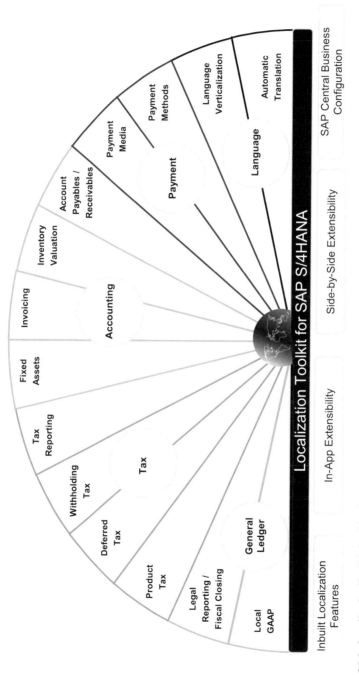

Fig. 34.9 Localization Toolkit for SAP S/4HANA

mentation time for partners and SAP S/4HANA customers. SAP offers an interactive community space dedicated to the localization toolkit, where partners and customers can access a variety of guides to check relevant scenarios and highlight their localization needs, which could be addressed through extensibility. It also serves as a platform for SAP localization development experts to share their best practices.

Multiple language support is in the context of localization of a prominent concept which is briefly explained in this section. In the focus of multiple language support are labels, short texts, and long texts which are displayed in the UI in the corresponding logon language of the user. To enable this, those language-dependent texts are stored in the database based on a specific data model. Language-dependent texts are saved in dedicated tables which have an identifier of the associated artifact, language key, and the text as structure. Thus, for each language key (e.g., DE, EN) the text is stored in the corresponding language. Those text tables are connected to the artifact tables with respective foreign associations. This is the foundation also for modeling CDS views and defining OData services which cover language dependency. Figure 34.10 illustrates a CDS view for sales order items that exposes material text as language-dependent attribute. The OData service on top reflects this accordingly by using adequate properties. In SAPUI5 application, multilingual capability are realized by maintaining the i18n*.properties files. i18n stands for internationalization. A separate i18n*.properties file must be maintained for each defined language. There must be also a default file which is used automatically if no explicit translation is specified. The i18n*.properties file is structured according to the key/value pair principle. This means that a value can be identified by specifying a keyword. It is mandatory that the keyword is unique. The structure of the keys is the same in all i18n* files.

Conclusion

SAP S/4HANA helping organizations scale their business processes across the globe is a key differentiator. This section provided an overview of selected localization capabilities that contribute to SAP S/4HANA being a global ERP system that can be used in almost every country. The ability of SAP S/4HANA to be used by multinational enterprises is referred to as globalization. Language support, as well as support for local regulations such as tax management, is all part of globalization. The latter is referred to as localization. Global Tax Management, Global Payments, Advanced Compliance Reporting, and Document Compliance were explained as exemplary applications that deal with highly country-specific issues. Allowing SAP customers and partners to develop their own localization extensions is also important for enabling the use of SAP S/4HANA in locations other than the 64 localized countries

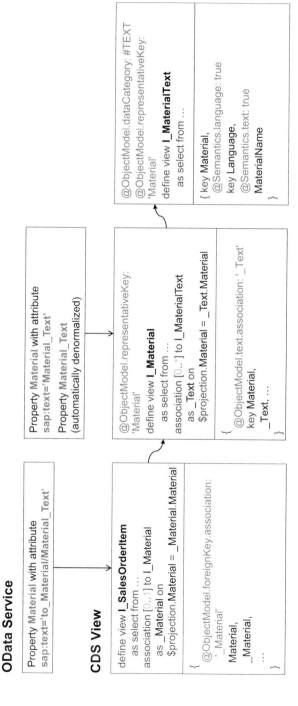

Fig. 34.10 Multiple language support

and regions. There are several tools and approaches available for this purpose, which are summarized under the Localization Toolkit umbrella. This toolkit was also discussed in this chapter.

Scalability and Performance

35

This chapter focuses on scalability and performance concepts and frameworks of SAP S/4HANA to ensure running the system with appropriated size and response time. Particularly, system sizing and clean-up, minimizing data footprint, scale up, and scale out are explained.

Business Requirement

It is particularly important for companies to be able to rely on the processes mapped in their ERP system. In times of digitalization, more and more processes are being digitalized or partially digitalized and mapped in ERP systems from various vendors. In order to be able to consistently deliver the services of a company in the same quality, companies are dependent on the availability and performance of high-quality processes. This requirement therefore also affects the IT systems which are implementing and controlling those processes. Key objective of ERP systems, besides providing the required functionalities, must be to ensure that systems of any size can perform the work in a reasonable response time. To fulfill this goal, the four pillars depicted in Fig. 35.1 have been identified:

Regardless of whether a legacy ERP is migrated to SAP S/4HANA or SAP S/4HANA is a company's first ERP system and is built on a greenfield site, SAP S/4HANA must be optimally planned. This includes all resources from storage to computing power and other issues such as hosting and tariff options. The answers to these questions are summarized under the keyword *sizing*. Too few resources usually means that the system will perform poorly. A system that is too large eats up money unnecessarily and pollutes the environment through higher power consumption without generating any added value for the company or the society. *Clean-up* covers various activities related to the lifecycle of data and storage media. Examples include housekeeping jobs, which can also be found in operating systems such as Windows or Linux. These are routine activities whose goal is to maintain the performance of an IT system. These include defragmenting file systems, deleting temporary data,

S. Sarferaz, *Compendium on Enterprise Resource Planning*,
https://doi.org/10.1007/978-3-030-93856-7_35

| Size System | Clean-up System | Minimize Network Traffic | Scale Hardware |

Fig. 35.1 Pillars of scalability and performance

and much more. Another example is the archiving of data that is no longer required. Another important issue takes place in the network. The use of cloud systems or other distributed systems that are not operated within an intranet increases the data throughput that must be transported through the public LAN or WAN lines from the actual server to the user. Since the public Internet lines are not the responsibility of individual software service providers, no optimizations can be made here. Nevertheless, to prevent problems in this area, there are some methods for reducing the *network traffic* of a system. These include avoiding sending data that is not required or separating historical and current data, which is usually required more frequently. Last but not least, the hardware used also plays a major role. It can be assumed that the performance requirements of a system will change over time. Since computing power is relatively expensive, there is a legitimate interest in keeping the costs of hardware as low as possible and wasting few resources. Accordingly, it is important to develop a system that can dynamically handle changing loads, and in addition to *adding and removing hardware* components such as CPUs or RAM, it also allows other scaling measures. Well-known service management frameworks, such as ITIL published and maintained by Axelos, also deal with these topics. For example, the practice called Service Capacity and Performance Management in ITIL V4 is responsible for ensuring that the services offered are available with sufficient capacity and that a balance is struck between a safety reserve and uneconomical excess capacity. A distinction is made between the following three disciplines (Axelos, 2019):

- Business Capacity Management (demands, trends, predictions)
- Service Capacity Management (workload management, monitoring)
- Component Capacity Management (resource and performance management)

Solution Capability

SAP S/4HANA performance is dependent on performance-optimized programming, adequate hardware sizing, and equitable resource sharing. The SAP S/4HANA Cloud offering is carbon-neutral thanks to the green cloud. In this section the use cases and solution approaches for sizing, scalability, and performance are explained.

System Sizing

System sizing basically means the translation of business requirements into hardware requirements. It concludes both the business throughput, the user concurrency requirements, and technological aspects. This means that the number of users using the various application components and the data load they put on the network must be considered. Theoretically, SAP S/4HANA could be deployed on a smartphone. However, the performance would leave much to be desired, especially for multiple users. The goal of most organizations is to minimize investment in inputs as well as operating costs while achieving the maximum throughput of their production systems, which optimally is also matched to customer demand. Sizing in general is an iterative process and is usually performed early in the project. There are existing sizing models for the product functionality with a reasonable number of input parameters and assumptions. There are specific size guidance for each SAP application. With those sizing procedures customers are getting help to determine the resources required by an application within their business context. In this case, relevant resources are the following:

- CPU
- Memory
- Data growth on disk
- Disk I/O
- Frontend network

In general, two approaches can be considered. These are *sizing by user* and *sizing by throughput*. Sizing by user is a linear approach which basically makes sizing very easy because the memory SAP S/4HANA needs is driven by user context, and users in generally are relatively easy to determine. However, it becomes more challenging when considering the determination of load patterns, the definition of a user, and the fact of sizing database growth by users. The basic advantages of sizing by throughput are the scenario- and transaction-driven view and the fact that sizing is based on actual business objects and scenarios. It distinguishes between peak and average sizing. Challenging is rather obtaining the right figures.

There are multiple techniques for Sizing an SAP System. Basically, a distinction can be made between those in which a system is built from the ground up (*greenfield sizing*) and those projects in which existing systems are enhanced with more functionality or for more users (*brownfield sizing*). The second category also includes migrations from older ERP systems to SAP S/4HANA.

Greenfield Sizing

Greenfield sizing is generally used in the context of new projects or implementations without or with inly little experience with SAP software. Within greenfield sizing, the following two methods can be considered. One is the hardware budget sizing method and the other is the advanced sizing method. In the following, the basic concepts as well as advantages and disadvantages are briefly described:

- Hardware Budget Sizing: This method is especially recommended for smaller companies and projects due to its ease of use. In this method, the selection of suitable hardware resources is mapped and supported by an algorithm. This algorithm contains assumptions and probabilities for different constellations and scenarios, taking identified risks into account.
- Advanced Sizing: This is a procedure for medium to large companies. Here, the size and the required hardware resources are worked out based on the estimated throughput of the new system. Questionnaires and formulas are used to collect the required data. At the same time, standard tools and guidelines are used. The focus of this method is always on the core business processes.

Brownfield Sizing

This approach refers to all projects that are not implemented on a greenfield site without framework conditions and dependencies. These include system upgrades for a higher number of users or shorter response times, the expansion of the system with additional functions, or the migration to an ERP system of a newer generation. Projects like these can exist for companies of all sizes and industries. In addition to the already known methods such as formulas and questionnaires, the data of the system monitoring and other statistics of existing SAP systems are also taken into consideration. The goal is always to increase the load or the function of an existing system. There are different approaches, depending on the stage of a solution's lifecycle. They can be one of the following:

- Re-sizing: Customer wants to add further users who will do the same as the current productive ones.
- Delta Sizing: Customer is live with SAP S/4HANA and wants to add additional functionality like EWM.
- Upgrade Sizing: Customer plans to upgrade to the latest SAP S/4HANA release.
- Migration Sizing: Customer wants to migrate from R/3 to SAP S/4HANA.

Quick Sizer is a tool based on the SAP Application Performance Standard (SAPS), which helps sizing the hardware of SAP systems. SAPS is a hardware-independent measurement method derived from the Sales and Distribution benchmark where 100 SAPS is defined as 2000 fully business processed order line items per hour. After completing this stage of the project, the hardware requirements are defined. The hardware itself can now be selected to meet the established requirements. There is no commitment to specific manufacturers or technologies, as SAP S/4HANA is platform independent and can therefore be operated on all systems. This enables companies to embed their new SAP S/4HANA system in their existing technology stack and therefore requires no additional knowledge and training when it comes to questions regarding the operation of the application. The SAP Quick Sizer tool is available online since 1996 and can be used free of charge. As of 2016 on average, around 35,000 new projects are carried out with the tool every year. There's a special SAP S/4HANA Cloud sizer available. Also included in the scope are sizing options for the following systems which can be calculated based on users and/or throughput: SAP S/4HANA, SAP HANA Standalone, SAP BW/4HANA, SAP Key applications. The tool uses structured questionnaires and can be used as input for greenfield sizing projects or as a check before Go live. Contact lists to hardware distributors and vendors are also provided. Quick Sizer calculates memory, CPU, disk, and I/O resources based on the described framework conditions.

Expert Sizing

Very large and complex projects, where, for example, several products and components are considered in one project, require the help of further tools and experts in the field of sizing. In this case, deeper and more far-reaching analyses are considered in addition to the results of a tool-supported sizing. There are no standard tools to perform expert sizing, but there is a wide range of possibilities for such additional analyses. Further handouts are provided, user-specific calculations are made, customer coding is analyzed, and sizing hints tailored to the customer are provided.

System Scalability

The scalability of a system is becoming increasingly important, especially in ongoing operation over a longer period of time. For most applications, the number of users and the volume of transactions can be expected to change over time. An IT system must also be able to cope with these changing parameters and handle workload fluctuations as well as load peaks. Within a certain time frame, increased demand can be buffered easily and quickly by using additional hardware. Too few hardware resources are usually associated with higher response times and, in extreme cases, lead to overload or even system failure. Since hardware is expensive, it is not attractive for companies to operate too many hardware components if there is no sufficient demand for them. However, hardware alone does not make an application scalable. At some time, a point is reached where no new hardware components such as additional CPU or hard disks can be installed. Even methods like virtualizing the CPU cores do not offer any performance gains beyond a certain point. For this reason, the application itself must also take some aspects into account in order to work efficiently and scale as well as possible. The following example shows how big the effects of supposedly small changes can be. Let us assume that through optimization measures the duration of a transaction can be reduced by 1 s. This means a saving of about 10 Joules per transaction. The absolute number is initially very small and leads to the conclusion that this optimization has hardly brought any advantages. However, if it is assumed that 1.5 million users carry out 20 transactions per day and that this is done on a total of 230 working days per year, this seemingly small optimization amounts to an electricity saving of 19 MWh at the end of the year. That is as much energy as 6000 two-person households consume in a year. The following four KPIs have been defined around S/4HANA that have an impact on scalability:

- *CPU time* of business transactions or tasks is measured to determine the number of processors required.
- *Disk size and disk I/O* are measured to determine the rate of database table growth and the file system footprint. This includes the number of insert operations for the database and write operations for files.
- *Memory* is measured in different ways depending on the type of application. For some applications, it's sufficient to measure the user session context, while for others it's necessary to also measure application-specific buffers and shared spaces and temporary allocations by stateless requests, among other factors.
- *Network load* measurements refer to the number of roundtrips for each dialog step and the number of bytes sent and received for each roundtrip. The measurements are used to determine the network bandwidth requirements.

To put it simply, it can be said that an ERP system is memory critical and that the focus here is primarily on memory. With analytics, however, it is the other way around. Here, the focus is usually on computing power and thus on the CPU. Since SAP S/4HANA combines analytical and transactional processing, both memory and computing capacity are relevant for these systems.

Scale Up

This approach is the easiest way to increase the utilization of a system. If there is an increased demand, hardware can simply be upgraded in the data center. This can be done, for example, by installing more CPUs or hard disks. The increased computing power in this way can be sufficient to satisfy the increased demand without having to accept a drop in performance. Since hardware components are usually kept in stock to a certain extent anyway in order to be able to replace defective hardware devices, the hardware already in stock can usually be used to expand the computing or storage performance within a very short time. For SAP S/4HANA projects, it is generally recommended to start the project with a single-node SAP HANA database (a node is an installation of an SAP HANA Index Server, a host is a physical machine with one or more deployed SAP HANA Index Server). This allows a better understanding of the workload and the growth of the data volume over time. With this method, currently 3500 CPU cores and up to 96 TB of main memory can be achieved for SAP HANA, since SAP Application Server for ABAP does not impose any limitations. When the system exceeds the available database capacity, the project should start scaling out. This approach can also be applied to all IT projects in general. Scale Up before Scale Out.

Scale Out

At some point, the scale-up tactic reaches a point where a server simply cannot be upgraded any further because all slots are already occupied and the best hardware on the market is already installed. Then, at the latest, a different tactic must be applied. Then scalability can be guaranteed only by a suitable IT architecture. In contrast to vertical scaling (scale up), there are no limits to horizontal scaling from the hardware point of view. However, the application design must be scale-out aware. Reaching hardware capacity limit with this pattern can cause one of the following options:

- Grow server sizes
  - (a) Increase the number of nodes
  - (b) Scale-up hardware
  - (c) Optimize sizing extrapolations during operations
- Add new servers
  - (a) Increase the number of servers
  - (b) Distribute tables across nodes

The SAP HANA database is currently available in a variety of host sizes ranging from 64 GB to more than 24 TB of physical RAM. It also supports virtualization with a variety of hypervisors or Infrastructure as a Service (IaaS) by multiple cloud partners can be used. In general, SAP HANA allows to distribute one database stretched across multiple physical hosts and provides a shared-nothing architecture with distributed database processing. This offers the following advantages:

- Support the need for very large databases
- Large volume handling beyond the limits of individual hosts
- Optimized workload distribution, using CPU of all multiple hosts
- Advantages regarding hardware cost and scalability

Figure 35.2 shows an example of the structure of an application with two application servers that access three SAP HANA databases.

Sharing data from an application across multiple databases must be explicitly supported by an application. This is the case for SAP S/4HANA. Since cross joins across multiple databases are very time-consuming and cost-intensive, the distribution of tables and data within the databases should therefore be planned and optimized. This is done, among others, by the SAP HANA Client Library and, on the other hand, by the developers who add new tables to a system. In practice, there are hardly any customers who need more than four fully equipped SAP HANA databases to work optimally with their SAP S/4HANA system.

System Performance

The performance of a system can also be viewed from both a technical and a user-centric perspective. Per definition response time is the time between when the user starts an interaction and when the application screen is ready for the next interaction. On the user side, the behavior shown in Fig. 35.3 can be observed with increasing response time. In the IT industry, sub-second response times are standard and are also in line with the perceived performance studies conducted by our usability team. What might be new is that the expected response time varies with the perceived complexity of a task. In the same way, the user behavior varies if the user's response

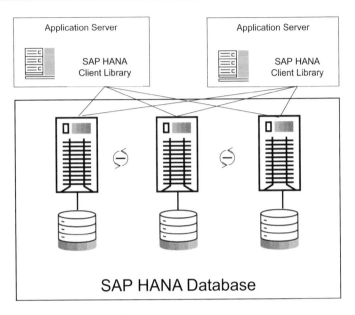

Fig. 35.2 The SAP HANA Scale Out

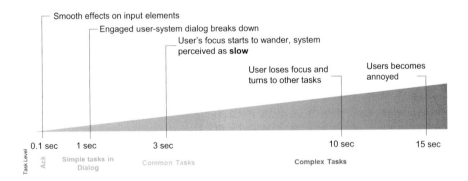

Fig. 35.3 Perceived performance

time expectations are not met. This is simpler than it may sound and worth looking at in more detail. First of all, users make assumptions about the complexity of each of their requests. Based on these assumptions, the users grant the computer system a corresponding amount of time to process their request. The time users allow for the system depends strongly on their perception of the complexity of the task. So, how can the complexity of tasks be described? The tasks most frequently handled by business systems can be divided roughly into three categories: acknowledging user input, presenting the results of a simple task, and presenting the results of a complex task.

A user input acknowledgment gives the user visual or acoustical feedback that the input has been received. Let's take a numeric input field as an example: when the user changes the focus or presses the enter key after typing in a value, the system checks the syntax of the input value and either produces an error indication or reformats the input value to the standard number format. Next, what is a simple task? A simple task is, for example, adding a new line item to a sales order or advancing to the next step in the wizard for a business process. Finally, complex tasks are navigations to another work center or the initial login to the system. In order to improve the performance of an application, there are a number of potential improvements that can be made. On the one hand, performance optimizations can be achieved through better hardware. However, since this point has already been discussed sufficiently in the section of sizing, it will not be taken up again at this point.

Performance-Optimized Programming

The first aspect to make the performance of a system as optimal as possible is the programming. Different methods for implementation can be found under the keyword Performance-Optimized Programming. In the context of *network and data*, the following relevant KPIs can be defined:

- Number of network roundtrips per user interaction step: The roundtrip time depends on the amount of network hops, which is basically the number of intermediate devices through which data must pass between source and destination and on the other hand latency that is the time from the source sending a packet to the destination receiving it. When data is sent over wide area networks (WAN) or global area networks (GAN), latency accounts for the largest share of roundtrip time. In the end, the conclusion is quite simple: The more roundtrips, the worse the application response time.
- Transferred data volume per user interaction step: Measures basically the data transferred between user interface front end and application server. The less data is transported over a network, the faster the transfer is handled and the faster the user can perform the next interaction with the user interface.

Figure 35.4 shows the decisive advantage of local area networks (LAN) over wide area networks (WAN):

Therefore, the following design principles are set for SAP product engineering:

- An application triggers a minimal number of sequential roundtrips and transfers only necessary data to the front end. The conclusion is obvious: the more roundtrips, the higher the impact of the network performance and the worse the application's end-to-end response time.
- An application transfers no more than 10–20 kB of data per user interaction step.
- Major strategies to optimize network performance include compression and front-end caching; both are implemented in and are part of standard SAP software.

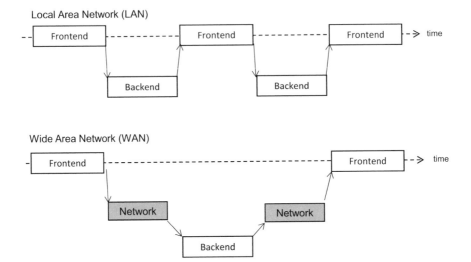

Fig. 35.4 LAN and WAN roundtrip

For *caching and buffering* SAP S/4HANA uses content delivery networks. The most important libraries of the frontend built with SAPUI5 are delivered via a Content Delivery Network (CDN). Further static resources are delivered by SAP S/4HANA Cloud Data Center. Both pieces of information are stored in the user's browser cache, so they are local and do not have to be shipped with every request. This saves a lot of data throughput so that the available bandwidth is used exclusively for dynamic resources such as business data, which is never cached in the front end. This approach decouples the dependency of the processing time on the amount of data to a certain extent. The design principle of nonerratic performance implies that there is a minimal underlying dependency on the amount of data or data constellation for the response time of an application. For example, if a month-end close is performed, the processing time essentially depends on the amount of data being processed. If a month-end close for October is performed which is a fixed amount of processed data, the processing time should remain constant and be independent of the amount of persisted data.

Another very important aspect concerning performance-optimized programming is the *database*. Very often, poor performance is caused by databases which are the bottleneck that needs to be widened. To remedy this situation, other factors must be considered in addition to the selection of the database technology. A first measure, for example, is the creation of replicas. A replica is the copy of a database or document that is updated at regular intervals and thus kept in sync. There is a database for all write operations, also called primary. All these actions are then transferred to the replicas. This has advantages for the availability, because if a primary node fails, a replica simply becomes the new primary node. On the other hand, it also has the advantage that read queries, which make up the largest proportion in an ERP system, can be executed on all nodes, regardless of whether they are primary or replica. This distribution of the load leads to considerable increases in performance. Another measure is the multi-temperature storage. Here, different storage technologies are used depending on the type of data. For example, most frequently used data is stored on particularly fast cache memories so that it can be processed and sent within a very short time. Since this type of memory is very expensive, not all information can be stored on it. For this reason, other types of storage are used, and decisions are made, for example, on the basis of the criticality and access frequency of the data as to where it is stored.

Another important factor that must be considered in the context of performance-optimized programming is the issue of the *system footprint*, especially the memory footprint. As already mentioned, possibility to reduce this is to swap application data from the cache to cheaper, less powerful memories. The efficient distribution of data across databases and tables also reduces the footprint of an application. However, the handling of old data is particularly relevant in the first place. In an ERP system, massive amounts of data accumulate over time. A system would therefore have to be able to scale massively without any further action. However, this is associated with enormous costs, which may not be offset by any added value. A distinction is made between the different types and states of data as depicted in Fig. 35.5.

As illustrated in Fig. 35.5, the data can be at different ages and goes through a lifecycle. The individual stages of the lifecycle have different effects on relevance and availability. For example, data that is in the Legal Hold section tends to be accessed infrequently. Accordingly, it does not have to be stored in a high-performance cache memory but can also be archived in compressed form on long-lived, inexpensive, and somewhat slower memory, since the speed of access is not an important KPI for this. Other KPIs and measures can be derived synchronously for other sections of the lifecycle in order to improve the storage effort and thus indirectly also the costs and performance in order to reduce the footprint of a system.

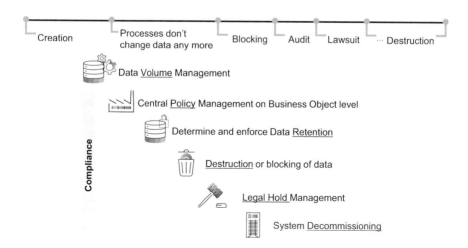

Fig. 35.5 Lifecycle of application data

In SAP S/4HANA it is ensured that old data is identified by tags/age column and thus treated differently. These tags are not visible to normal DB users but are managed by SAP HANA and ABAP implementations. In addition, SAP HANA allows individual columns to be transferred from main memory to other disks. This dramatically reduces the amount of data to be kept in main memory. The loading and unloading are partly automated by SAP HANA but can also be forced by the user. The data on the persistency layer on disk is not touched.

Furthermore, *code-pushdown* is applied for performance-optimized programming. In order to process data, it must be transferred between the application server and the database via a network. As already explained in the section network and data, this transfer is much slower than the server-internal transfer between main memory and the various caches. Especially hard disk accesses or other mechanical steps make this difference even more extreme. With SAP S/4HANA and its in-memory database technology, the last point in particular no longer applies. To minimize the impact of the network connection as a bottleneck, the ABAP programming paradigm code-pushdown can be used. Classically, the database is accessed for data which is needed for processing and calculations. These are then sent to the application server and processed there. This principle is also called *data to code*. However, this means that the request for data must first be sent to the database and the entire data must be sent from the database to the application server via a network. To save bandwidth and thus enable better performance, this principle was reversed. According to the motto *code to data*, calculations are performed only locally in the database management system. This shifts some of the load to the database server, but SAP HANA is designed to handle this. As a result, performance-intensive business logic, such as that found in Material Resource Planning (MRP) run, can be executed almost entirely on the database and not in the application server. For processing and calculations, mainly SQL views are used, which are associated with almost no costs. In addition, access to modularized database code using stored procedures written with SQLScript brings further performance advantages. The SAP S/4HANA semantic layer Virtual Data Model (VDM) applies the pushdown principle in a systematic manner. The VDM is made up of core data services (CDS) views that are defined on an ABAP level. When CDS views are activated, SAP HANA generates related SQL views automatically. When an SQL statement is processed on a CDS view, it is pushed down to the SQL view and handled on the database layer. When compared to a traditional SAP ERP application, where application data was loaded into the application server and looped for the relevant records, improved performance can be obtained. Finally, the drastically simplified data model comes into play. The data structure of SAP S/4HANA has been simplified compared to the classic SAP ERP, for example, by eliminating aggregate and index tables due to the usage of in-memory techniques of SAP HANA.

Elasticity and Fair Resource Sharing

If SAP S/4HANA is operated by the customer, then the customer can influence the applications capacity itself or via the contracted data center operator and determine which applications share common infrastructure components. If a company uses

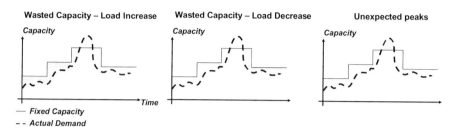

Fig. 35.6 Capacity scenarios

SAP S/4HANA in the public cloud and uses infrastructure as a service, handling of elasticity must be considered. Although the underlying techniques for elasticity could be partially used when customers operate SAP S/4HANA by their own, elasticity is the ability to fit the resources needed to cope with loads dynamically. Usually, this takes place in relation to scale-out measures, so that when load increases the hardware is scaled by adding more resources, and when demand wanes the hardware is shrunk back and unneeded resources are removed. Figure 35.6 shows three different capacity scenarios.

Three different challenges can be identified from this figure:

- Wasted Capacity—Load Increase: When the load increases more resources need to be added. To keep the wasted capacity as small as possible, it is required to elastically scale by adding more resources.
- Wasted Capacity—Load Decrease: When the demand wanes, resources need to shrink back. To keep the wasted capacity as small as possible, it is required to elastically shrink back and remove unneeded resources.
- Unexpected Peaks: With fixed capacities unexpected peaks cannot be covered with the existing resources. To prevent the impact of unexpected peaks it is required to elastically scale as close as possible to the actual demand while at the same time keep the wasted capacity as small as possible.

SAP operation uses its own developed Dynamic Capacity Management tool to elastically adjust the hardware capacity within an SAP S/4HANA multitenancy cluster. Two types of capacity planning are covered. *Tenant capacity planning* for enlarging tenant size, reducing tenant size, and moving tenant in (onboarding). *Landscape capacity planning* for moving tenant out to a different server (different multitenancy cluster) and to determine which tenant(s) should be moved if the server runs out of free memory so that the tenant requires more memory. The fully automated Dynamic Capacity Management tool sets limits on the resource consumption of tenant databases. On the one hand, it ensures that a tenant always has sufficient resources available and, at the same time, prevents one tenant from consuming too many resources and thus making the system too slow for others. In an SAP S/4HANA Cloud productive tenant, all database statements are monitored in certain quotas for response time, CPU time, and memory consumption. As soon as these are violated, they are subsequently processed by SAP development to further optimize such instructions. Sustainability is an important factor in the operation of IT infrastructures. Fair sharing of resources must therefore not be limited to the sharing of available hardware capacities but should also consider ecological aspects. For SAP S/4HANA the relevant factors for excellent performance are minimal response time, minimal resource consumption, maximal throughput, scalability, and simple sizing algorithms. Furthermore, consistent response time and resource consumption are key. The following cornerstones were defined in order to bring these defined goals into line with the sustainability targets set:

- In-memory computing rather than disk I/O
- Caches rather than CPU cycles
- Content delivery networks and code-pushdown rather than high data transfer and a large number of roundtrips

Conclusion

In times of ever faster growing requirements and increasing user numbers, a scalable application is of enormous importance. Especially for business-critical applications such as ERP systems, very high demands are placed on performance, in particular speed and expandability or scalability. A system with high response times not only limits the effectiveness, but also demotivates the users. Due to the immense number of potential use cases and industries that can map and integrate business processes in ERP systems like SAP S/4HANA, the scope of the software is very large. In order to meet the expectations of companies and users at the same time, measures must be taken, and intelligent concepts must be realized. This chapter explained performance and scalability of SAP S/4HANA and highlighted general problems as well as the concepts and architectures chosen to solve them. Greenfield, brownfield, and expert sizing approaches were described. Strategies for scale up and scale out were depicted. Methods for performance-optimized programming were elaborated.

Lifecycle Management

36

This chapter focuses on lifecycle management concepts and frameworks of SAP S/4HANA to support software deployment, upgrades, corrections, and decommissioning. Particularly, zero downtime options, multitenancy, and application lifecycle management tooling are explained.

Business Requirement

The software lifecycle encompasses all phases of a software product's planning, development, and use, as well as its eventual obsolescence or retirement. This process has many variable parts, but it can frequently be divided into several major components. This assists developers and others in comprehending how a product is created, implemented, and used. Planning phases are present in many of the most common stages of a software lifecycle. Professionals typically refer to requirements gathering or analysis, which is the process by which an undeveloped product is defined using criteria gathered. Next the product is analyzed and designed, followed by development. The final development stages of the lifecycle involve a product that has been released to a customer or other end user, at which point the product vendor is frequently involved in maintenance, problem-solving, upgrading, and other operations processes.

Figure 36.1 shows the lifecycle phases by grouping them into Development and Operations clusters. It is important to note that software does not always progress in a linear fashion through these stages of the software lifecycle. Rather, different parts of a product may evolve in different ways. Within the professional IT community, these are commonly referred to as iterations.

Software lifecycle management in ERP systems is about making the entire lifecycle of an ERP system as smooth as possible. Particularly important here is the stability of the transition through updates and upgrades. Organizations often underestimate the challenges occurring in the lifecycle of an ERP system, which can lead to failures or delays. Lifecycle management of an ERP system is an ongoing process as the solution

© The Author(s), under exclusive license to Springer Nature Switzerland AG 2022
S. Sarferaz, *Compendium on Enterprise Resource Planning*,
https://doi.org/10.1007/978-3-030-93856-7_36

ERP Lifecycle

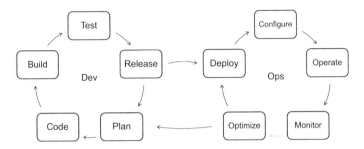

Fig. 36.1 Software lifecycle management

continues to evolve in the company. In comparison to other large software projects, the implementation of ERP systems often involves iterations. Organizations typically run on-premise ERP systems in a landscape of three interconnected systems: A development system for defining business configuration and expanding the application with custom developments, a testing system to ensure the quality and accuracy of newly maintained configuration settings and new custom developments, and a production system to run the organization's actual business processes. Business configuration settings and new developments (code changes) are transported through the system landscape. This is slightly different for cloud ERP systems where the provider operates the tenants. Cloud ERP systems must support a multitenant architecture that enables the SaaS provider to share storage and computing resources among tenants. The data of the tenant must be isolated and invisible to the other tenants. Usually, each cloud ERP subscriber receives a test and configuration, a production set of tenants, and, in most cases, a development set of tenants, similar to the three-system landscape track typically set up to operate on-premise ERPs. Cloud ERPs are hosted in data centers around the world. In general, there are two selection criteria to consider when selecting the right data center. First legal requirements, such as Chinese cybersecurity legislation or the European GDPR, which restrict data access to specific territories. Second latency requirements, such as ensuring good performance which is also impacted by the network communication to connect the customer's web browser to the ERP tenants. Therefore, a data center must be selected based on smart algorithms to minimize latency effects.

Solution Capability

Most of the lifecycle management concepts are well known or covered by other chapters, for example, development in Chap. 21, configuration in Chap. 37, or implementation in Chap. 38. Thus, this section concentrates on new approaches for SAP S/4HANA and therefore focuses on software maintenance, zero downtime, and multitenancy. Furthermore, the new available solution for application lifecycle management (ALM) is explained, which is referred to as SAP Cloud ALM.

Software Maintenance

ERP software must be compliant with the most recent laws and regulations, provide a new functional scope and innovative features, improve existing functionality, and, if necessary, correct errors. For this SAP S/4HANA must be regularly maintained, which is technically referred to as upgrade and update. While customers welcome new features and legal compliance, they do not want disruptions in their regular business operations. Examples of such disruptions are a request to test the customer's specific configuration with the updated software, a changed user interface that necessitates retraining users, or system downtime. As a result, SAP intends to manage the software lifecycle as smoothly as possible to avoid disrupting users. The only exception to this no user impact paradigm is a desired functional upgrade by the customer. During a maintenance event, SAP S/4HANA software and/or configuration is updated. If necessary, SAP applies corrections to all SAP S/4HANA Cloud tenants as a hotfix collection (HFC) every 2 weeks. If a single tenant fails completely due to a software error, SAP can apply an emergency patch (EP) as needed. SAP upgrades the SAP S/4HANA Cloud ABAP service to the next major software version every 3 months. Subscribers to SAP S/4HANA Cloud must plan for maintenance windows during which the tenant is unavailable. However, in order to ensure minimal business interruption due to maintenance, concept allowing zero downtime maintenance is provided. This approach follows the standard cloud architecture best practice known as blue-green deployment as illustrated in Fig. 36.2. The basic idea is to create a

Blue-Green Deployment

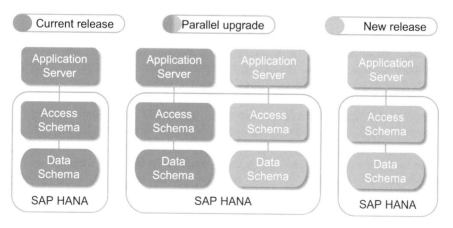

Fig. 36.2 Software maintenance based on blue-green deployment

temporary green tenant for software updates while users continue to work in the blue tenant. As a result, during the maintenance phase, these two tenants coexist for a limited time. When the maintenance phase is complete, all subsequent user logins are directed to the now-updated green tenant, and the now-outdated blue tenant is disassembled when no user is logged in. The blue-green deployment must solve several challenges, for example, configuring the additional green tenant with the same data as the blue tenant while business users continue to create new data. Once the update of the green tenant is finalized, all business transactions that occurred in the blue tenant in the interim are imported in the green tenant. Thus, all entered data can be preserved while the transactional processes run in the blue tenant.

To ensure this the blue and green tenants must share the same persistency. Technically, the ABAP application servers of the blue and green tenants share the same SAP HANA tenant database. Each tenant has its own tenant database in which the tenant's business data is stored. All the cluster's tenants have access to the shared database, which contains information such as software source code. The green tenant is the one where software and configuration changes are made during maintenance. As the blue and green tenants share the same persistency, the ABAP Dictionary (DDIC) for the green tenant must be updated while protecting the blue tenant from these changes. This is accomplished by introducing a new database schema—the access schema. This access schema serves as a bridge between application server coding and persistency. It conceals changes to database tables made by applications running in the blue tenant. If the data type of a table field changes during the upgrade process, this applied to the database's data schema. Hence, if a blue tenant application accesses the table, the access layer maps the data of this table field to the old, unchanged data type for both read and write accesses. When the same application from the green tenant accesses the table, the access layer returns data from the same table field with the new data type.

Zero Downtime

There are various approaches developed by SAP for downtime optimization during software maintenance. When it comes to the approaches shipped with the SAP Software Update Manager (SUM), there are three main approaches for applying support packages in SAP S/4HANA as shown in Fig. 36.3.

Both the standard procedure and the nZDM already offer some advantages with regard to downtime optimization. However, only ZDO can completely avoid a technical downtime. The technical downtime describes the time in which the system is actually down. Business downtime, on the other hand, stands for the time during which the system cannot be used by the users. The starting and shutdown of the system are also included. The main advantage of nZDM is that it significantly reduces business downtime compared to previous update approaches because more of the downtime-relevant update phases are executed while the system is still up and running for business users. During the uptime adjustment of table structure including conversions based on the *Record & Replay* technique is carried out in

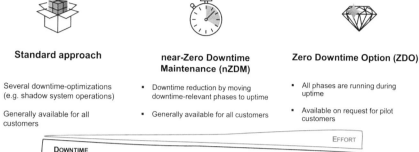

Standard approach

- Several downtime-optimizations (e.g. shadow system operations)
- Generally available for all customers

near-Zero Downtime Maintenance (nZDM)

- Downtime reduction by moving downtime-relevant phases to uptime
- Generally available for all customers

Zero Downtime Option (ZDO)

- All phases are running during uptime
- Available on request for pilot customers

EFFORT

DOWNTIME

Fig. 36.3 Downtime minimizing approaches

nZDM. This means that changes to the database during the uptime of the maintenance process generate triggers that record the changes. The recordings are only required for tables that are used for the shadow update/upgrade. The shadow tables are updated using the recording after the upgrade/update phases of the uptime. The majority of recording updates are performed during uptime. Only the delta must run in the downtime just before the switch. The Zero Downtime Option (ZDO) must be requested as a project and therefore cannot be used without restrictions. When selecting different procedures, note that procedures with a lower downtime automatically require a higher effort. Figure 36.4 shows that the technical downtime is eliminated completely with the ZDO, and there is an uptime on bridge instead.

The existing system runs partially in parallel to the upgraded instance. In the case of a normal technical downtime, the users would be logged out at a certain point in time, whereas during an uptime on bridge, the users are moved to another instance, a so-called bridge subsystem. This transition takes place in the background without any disruption of the users. This bridge is a copy of the main system but contains only the tables that are also affected by the upgrade. The ZDO procedure is divided into five different steps which are executed sequentially. First, the database content of SAP HANA must be migrated. SAP HANA Transport for ABAP (HTA) based on the SAP HANA Deployment Infrastructure (HDI) allows to develop content for the ABAP applications based on SAP HANA and transport the content (both the HDI and ABAP objects) together using the Change and Transport System of AS ABAP. This step migrates the native views from SAP HANA to HTA for HDI. In the second step, the compliance to the ZDO rules is checked and ensured. For this, development guidelines have been defined, and the SAP application developers must adhere to these guidelines. In addition, there are Support Packages with which the latest content for ZDO is distributed. Furthermore, known limitations of business applications are recorded in certain SAP documents. It should also be mentioned that third-party extensions are not supported by default. Therefore, third-party suppliers must contact SAP. In the second phase, ABAP Test Cockpit (ATC) can be used to perform compliance checks between ZDO policies and customer transports. In the third step, a table classification is carried out. The user's access

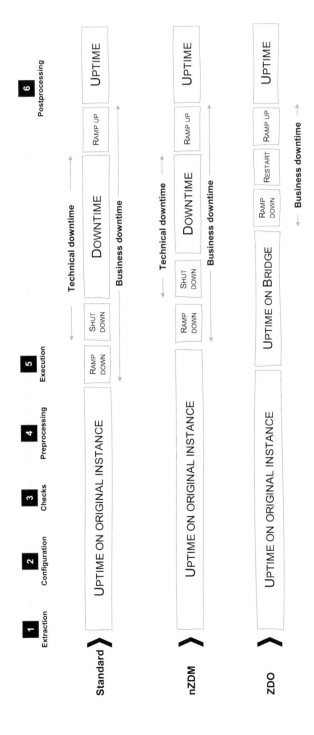

Fig. 36.4 Differences of the downtime approaches

to the various tables is checked. Here, the bridge mentioned above is used as a copy of the main system. This makes it possible to hide the changes on the upgrade system from the user of the production system. Thus, the tables are cloned so that the upgraded system has access to one instance of the table while the production system has access to another instance. In some cases, the cloned tables must be set to read-only. The access rights of business users during the bridge phase must be defined. The actual change to the tables is performed by the upgrade process, while the user can still access an instance of the system via the bridge. The classification is dependent on which actors process read and write operations on the table, whether content is imported into the table, and whether the table structure is changed. The tables can be divided into three different main classes. The first class is a *shared* table. These tables are not changed during an upgrade and must therefore only grant access to the connecting system during the upgrade process. There is a technical security mechanism behind this, which regulates the access of the upgrade instance to these types of tables. The second class is *clone* tables. These tables are changed during an upgrade and therefore cloned so that they can write and read rights to both, the bridge instance and the upgraded instance of a system. The third class of tables is *clone read-only* tables. These are also cloned. However, the bridge instance of the system has only read authorization here and no write access. Otherwise, issues may occur due to this type of table, if the bridge instance is written to the table during the upgrade. The *Impact Analysis Tool* can help identify these types of tables. In the fourth step, an impact analysis is performed using the SAP Software Upgrade Manager (SUM). The aim is to identify potential business impacts during the bridge phase. A sandbox system is used to which the new table classifications and the table data from the production instance of the system are transferred. In this way, at an early stage issues are identified which may occur in the future. For this, first current table statistics are exported from the connected system. After that, an impact analysis with all records is performed. Finally, the results of the different data records must be merged, evaluated, and interpreted. The fifth and final step in the ZDO process is the actual data migration. Here, the simplification of the data model is decoupled from the functional changes in the business applications. In addition, this step ensures compatibility by safeguarding that the new version of an application works with the old data model and the old version of an application works with the new data model.

Multitenancy

Multitenancy is a software architecture in which multiple tenants of a cloud service share software resources in order to distribute the associated costs and efforts across these tenants while still isolating each tenant from the others. All cloud services included in SAP S/4HANA Cloud are built with a multitenancy architecture. The SAP S/4HANA Cloud ABAP service's multitenancy architecture reduces tenant-specific infrastructure costs and operation efforts while providing tenant isolation on the same level as ensured by completely separate systems. Each tenant has its own dedicated ABAP application servers that run on its own SAP HANA tenant database

Multitenancy

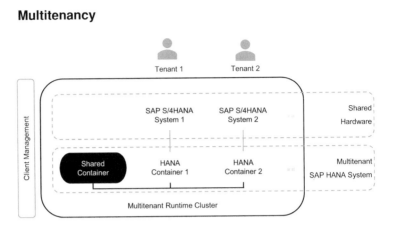

Fig. 36.5 Multitenancy architecture

as depicted in Fig. 36.5. Tenant databases are separate databases within a single SAP HANA database system that contain all tenant-specific application data and config-uration. In addition to these tenant-specific databases, each SAP HANA system has one more database that contains ABAP system resources that are by definition shared by all tenants, such as the ABAP source code delivered by SAP. This means that such resources are not stored in each of the SAP HANA's tenant databases, but only once in the shared database. The main components of an ABAP application stack are shared as a result, and the main components of an SAP HANA system are shared among multiple tenants. Thus, software is shared across all layers—on the SAP S/4HANA Cloud application layer, the SAP ABAP application server, and the SAP HANA layer—and joint software update events are held for all tenants on the same multitenant SAP HANA system. As each tenant has its own ABAP application servers and tenant database, it is completely isolated from the others. Each tenant is self-contained, so each tenant has its own database catalog, persistence, and backups, for example. SAP HANA's technical configuration prevents SQL-level cross-tenant database access and ABAP runtime write access to the shared tenant database. Only software updates and non-ABAP tools have write access to the shared database. With a one code line approach for SAP S/4HANA Cloud and SAP S/4HANA On Premise, the multitenancy architecture must be designed and implemented so that no existing installation is disrupted and the number of required changes on the application side is kept to a minimum. This is critical for minimizing the risk of any quality regressions. Each ABAP system in the SAP S/4HANA On-Premise system architecture is made up of a collection of ABAP application servers that are linked to a single SAP HANA database system.

The system architecture is the same for all system types, whether development, quality, or production. If multiple ABAP systems are running, they may share hardware. Depending on the required SAP HANA database size, several SAP HANA systems may run on shared hardware. Apart from the shared hardware, the

SAP S/4HANA systems do not share any other resources. Because of the shared-nothing software architecture, each new SAP S/4HANA system necessitates resources for a full ABAP system as well as a full SAP HANA database. Administrators must install, manage, and upgrade each of these systems on their own. With each new system, costs and efforts rise in a linear fashion. Cost-wise, this does not take advantage of any economies of scale, and in terms of effort, it quickly becomes unmanageable as the number of systems grows to thousands or more— which reflects the envisioned scope for SAP S/4HANA Cloud. The shared database allows all ABAP system resources which are by definition equal and immutable to be moved from the tenant databases into the shared database. Finally, the shared database contains all ABAP system resources that are identical across all ABAP systems and cannot be changed by customers in their tenants, such as the ABAP program source code, system documentation, code page information, or the standardized texts of error and success messages used in the SAP programs to inform end users of a specific processing status. The memory consumption of the tenant databases is reduced correspondingly by sharing these data in the shared database. Another advantage is that when upgrading to a new SAP S/4HANA Cloud release, all resources stored in the shared database only need to be upgraded once per the SAP HANA system, rather than individually for each tenant. This eliminates the need for tenant-specific upgrades. It is critical to note that an individual tenant cannot change or update any tables or data in the shared database because such changes would affect all ABAP application servers running on tenant databases in the same SAP HANA system. All tenant-specific data, such as transactional business data, configuration settings, or master data, as well as all types of tenant-specific extensions, is stored in individual tenant databases rather than the shared database.

Application Lifecycle Management

For handling the application lifecycle management (ALM) SAP offers among others SAP Cloud ALM. This tool allows to simplify the implementation and application of cloud-based solutions for customers. The offering is aimed at small, medium-sized, and larger customers who require a standardized cloud-based solution. As shown in Fig. 36.6, SAP Cloud ALM consists of two subareas, Implementation and Operation.

The Operation component of SAP Cloud ALM provides monitoring for applications, integration, users, and business processes. The Implementation component focuses on implementation projects and supports managing of processes, tasks, tests, and deployments. SAP Cloud ALM is integrated to existing frameworks based on the API hub. *Business process monitoring* provides transparency on end-to-end business processes within a distributed and hybrid solution landscape. It ensures uninterrupted business operations and improves the quality and performance of business process execution. Furthermore, it monitors the health of processes and detects anomalies during process execution, including drill-down into business documents. If necessary, it directly alerts users to process disruptions and provides

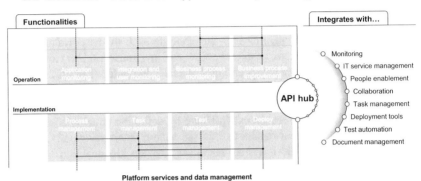

Fig. 36.6   SAP Cloud ALM—functional architecture

automated problem resolution via built-in operation flows. Business process monitoring delivers predefined process content, including auto-discovery of relevant
metrics that can be activated. *Integration and Exception monitoring* allows end-to-
end monitoring of cloud services and systems by correlating single messages to end-
to-end message flows. It helps in the monitoring of exceptions related to integration,
peer-to-peer interface support, as well as orchestrated integration. The solution
bridges the gap between business and IT during the problem-solving process by
alerting to notify responsible business and IT personnel of discovered integration-
related issues, searching for and tracking individual messages using exposed business context attributes such as order numbers, automation of operations to trigger
operation flows context-sensitively for automated problem correction. *Jobs and
automation monitoring* ensures that business operations run smoothly and improves
the quality and performance of business processes by monitoring the health of job
executions and detecting anomalies during job execution, notifying both business
and IT users of disruptions and exceptions, providing information at the job execution level to allow for fact-based root cause analysis and by reducing configuration
effort through the use of historical execution data. Job and automation monitoring
will be enhanced with operation flows to trigger corrective actions such as job
restarts, as well as job and automation analytics to enable trend analysis based on
historical data. *User and Performance Monitoring* provides transparency into
end-user performance as well as the use of business functionality. Performance
data is collected at the front end and server levels to determine the root cause of
performance issues. The use of the SAP Passport technology enables the correlation
of performance data measured at the front end, cloud service, and/or system level.
Health monitoring visualizes the health of cloud services and systems in order to
detect disruptions or degradations in service. It allows to run application health
checks for the SAP cloud services in order to check the status of persistency, jobs,
and connectivity. The solution supports health checks for customer-built cloud
services and on-premise systems, as well as trends and usage metrics. Embedded

analytics is provided to identify the root cause of a discovered problem. *Business service management* supports in the definition of customer-specific maintenance events at the business service level. Business service is defined as a grouping of technical services that represent business functionality. Externally communicated maintenance, disruption, or degradation events are propagated from technical services to business services as a result of business up/downtimes. The solution facilitates service time definition based on service-level agreements and service contracts on a business service level. *Problem Management* is divided into three subprocesses: problem identification, problem distribution, and problem resolution. SAP Cloud ALM is involved in all three subprocesses. Problem detection is implemented in SAP Cloud ALM by means of the options for monitoring the various components of the ERP system. The distribution of problems is implemented by SAP Cloud ALM through built-in alert management and intelligent event processing. Business automation, message management (e.g., chats, e-mails, or social media), and root cause analysis at technical and operational level help solve the problem. In addition, SAP Cloud ALM supports the ability for *performance monitoring*. This provides transparency on how the end user actually perceives the response time of the solution and how the business functionality is used. The performance is measured at the front end, at the network level, in the cloud service, and at the server level in order to identify the root cause of performance problems. Furthermore, SAP Cloud ALM provides tools for monitoring tasks and automated business activities. These improve the quality and performance of the execution of business processes. This is to be achieved by monitoring the execution of tasks and directly alerting both business and IT users when disruptions occur. Additionally, the configuration effort is reduced by using historical data about the execution of tasks.

Conclusion

Lifecycle management refers to all the phases of an ERP product throughout its planning, development, installation, usage, operations, all the way through to its eventual obsolescence or decommissioning. This chapter explained the approaches for software maintenance, zero downtime, and multitenancy. ERP software must be up to date with current laws and regulations, provide a new functional scope and innovative features, improve existing functionality, and, if necessary, correct errors. SAP S/4HANA must be maintained on a regular basis, which is technically referred to as upgrade and update. The blue-green deployment concept is used for software maintenance of SAP S/4HANA. For downtime optimization during the software maintenance of SAP S/4HANA the concepts for near-Zero Downtime Maintenance (nZDM) and Zero Downtime Option (ZDO) were described. The key idea of those approaches is to reduce downtime by moving downtime-relevant phases to uptime. The SAP S/4HANA Cloud multitenancy architecture was explained which allows tenants to share resources at the database, application server, and application levels. Multiple tenants share a single SAP HANA database system, which includes a shared database that stores application server and application data for all tenants in an equal and immutable manner. Each tenant has its own tenant database within the SAP HANA database system to keep all tenant-specific data completely isolated from all other tenants.

Configuration

37

This chapter focuses on configuration concepts and frameworks of SAP S/4HANA to allow customers and partners adopting the functionality by utilizing predefined variability. Particularly, authoring of configuration content and scoping of business configuration are explained.

Business Requirement

Configuration is the process of adopting ERP functionality based on predefined variability by customers and partners. It has always been a core strength of ERP products to provide a high degree of flexibility and thus a wide range of customizing options. This enables standard definition of business software to be adjusted and extended to meet the needs of each individual consumer. As of today, SAP S/4HANA offers thousands of individual settings for tuning an installation to meet the needs of a specific company. Which configuration combinations, however, are truly semantically correct? Which combinations produce a dependable business process? Which combinations achieve the best balance of diversification and efficiency? SAP has been providing reference content for more than a decade, allowing SAP customers to equip their solution with a consistent and reliable preconfiguration of all relevant business processes and supporting functionalities. This preconfiguration meets three important criteria:

- Rapid implementation: Preconfiguration enables to begin implementing the ERP system with a basic, consistent set of configurations. In many business areas, customers can start by accepting standard settings as the default and then define custom settings in focus areas. With this combination, customers can get started quickly with a fully functional solution and then further customize the application later. This lowers the initial total cost of implementation (TCI) and leads to a faster deployment and, as a result, a faster go-live.

© The Author(s), under exclusive license to Springer Nature Switzerland AG 2022
S. Sarferaz, *Compendium on Enterprise Resource Planning*,
https://doi.org/10.1007/978-3-030-93856-7_37

- Approach based on best practices: ERP vendors leverage their decades of experience to present a best-of-breed solution for an enterprise's core business processes. Best-practice content strikes a balance between high performance, solid flexibility, and country-specific flavors. This reference content is not rigid; it can be adjusted and extended at various points. The reference content, on the other hand, is a de facto standard that allows for a reliable and quick implementation.
- Compatibility across the lifecycle: The business world, and thus the reference content, is constantly changing. The rate of innovation adoption in ERP software is a key differentiator. New innovations must be readily available, simple to consume, and extremely dependable in terms of quality and performance. As a result, ERP vendors incorporate these changes into the reference content and regularly update the affected installations. However, these updates must not jeopardize the stability of customers' running productive landscapes. As a result, the reference content is enriched with lifecycle-relevant metadata to control how changes in existing implementations must be handled during the upgrade. This enables a secure, automated upgrade process, which is a critical quality. Changes that are incompatible with the software's and its content's lifecycle are avoided.

The function of a company's organizational unit determines a large portion of its required business functionality. What is the unit's purpose? Is it a sales office? Is it a legal entity or just a division of the company? Configuration must support multiple organizational units in a single tenant and divide them using dedicated company codes. As a result, the configuration and corresponding content must include the correct company code for the customizing settings to differentiate between the units. Furthermore, the scope varies depending on the purpose of the organizational unit. An organizational unit is typically associated with a physical installation and thus assignment to a legal space. The legal space also has an impact on the selection of correct configuration settings because country-specific settings that either support legal compliance or represent regional best practices must be chosen rather than global or general ones.

Solution Capability

As already mentioned, ERP systems like SAP S/4HANA are very rich in functionality that needs to be adopted according to the customer's requirements. That is why SAP created an application called SAP Central Business Configuration (CBC), which enables the user to configure a system systematically by using an existing pool of functions. This is ensured with different concepts and the two major components: Authoring and Consumption. Thus, guided procedure is provided to customize the entire system and get the most out of it for the customer. Unlike the extensibility management, which is about creating new extensions, the SAP Central Business Configuration enables a systematic implementation of the configuration from an existing pool of functions and maintenance of the SAP S/4HANA projects. It provides a consistent and simplified approach for customers and the SAP experts to scope business processes, select, and specify their solution configuration. The SAP Central Business Configuration introduces completely new possibilities to manage multi-product, multi-process, and self-service multi-user scenarios in one single intuitive-to-use and business-oriented, consistent solution. The system is already predefined and ready to use. Of course, these default settings must be tailored to the costumer's own needs, but customers can save so a lot of time. There are areas in which the preconfiguration is simply not sufficient, what means that customers must expand it. This can be done directly by the customer. It is also possible to enable delta deployment of scope extensions, for example, if the customer configured the system for Asia and now wants to deploy it in the United States of America as well. Due to the immense experience and the large number of customer project, ideal processes can be derived, which in turn are summarized in the Best Practices for the SAP S/4HANA content. This knowledge forms the basis for the preconfiguration. Thus, customers can access the experience of hundreds of thousands of projects.

Components Architecture

The SAP Central Business Configuration is a standalone service that registered users can use prior to provisioning a specific product or software package. Even before making a product selection, customers can use the configuration tool to browse through available business processes and fine-grained functions. The central scoping instrument, the business adaptation catalog, is structured purely according to business terminology and is updated whenever any of the products available introduces new innovations or changes in existing offerings. By assigning content to catalog entries, different products and solutions are available to realize the selected business capabilities. Customers can select not only a single product, such as SAP S/4HANA, but also fully integrated enterprise services from SAP and its partners' extensive product portfolio. The customer's demand is to focus on selecting the business processes that will be operated by their organization, rather than identifying required business content. The SAP Central Business Configuration identifies and deploys the appropriate content into the necessary software packages based on the customer's selections—boundary conditions, organizational structure, country footprint, and industry focus. This also includes the necessary integration settings. When performing self-service scoping, the SAP Central Business Configuration provides a compelling user experience. The scoping process is much more intuitive, transparent, easy to implement, and persona driven in design. It also takes into account potentially required authorization boundaries to ensure that not every user has the ability to change everything at any time, but areas of responsibility are also reflected in user profiling. As illustrated in Fig. 37.1, the SAP Central Business Configuration consists of the Authoring and Consumption components.

Business Application Factory (BAF) provides frameworks and services which abstract from the underlying SAP Business Technology Platform and provide security and technology guideline compliances. Using the SAP Business

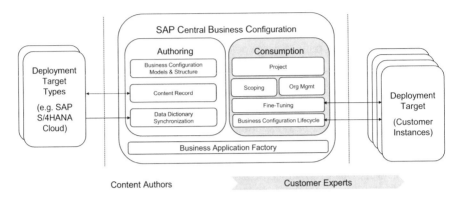

Fig. 37.1 The SAP Central Business Configuration—component architecture

Technology Platform based abstraction layer ensures that the Business Application Factory can be deployed on any Hyperscaler like SAP, Google Cloud Platform, Microsoft Azure, Amazon Web Services, and Alibaba Cloud. Kubernetes is used for this deployment. Business Configuration Lifecycle Management (BCLM) takes care of the central configuration lifecycle, ensuring that the business configuration performed in the central configuration system is always in a consistent state.

Authoring

The Authoring component deals with the maintenance of the configuration content. If a system is configured according to best practices, the configuration content is usually stored in separate tables. The basis is the Business Adaption Catalog (BAC), a hierarchical representation of all business-driven configuration decisions relevant for the customer. It defines the business scope of the customer's project in a clear and structured way. Decisions are displayed in a tree, and technical complexities are elegantly hidden. It sums up functionality as bundles of documented, selectable units and guides the customer through activities necessary based on their decision. SAP-delivered content is organized centrally, so it enforces overall consistency of delivered content. The Business Adaption Catalog consists of a hierarchy of structuring elements ending with fine-grained ones. It is possible to navigate in the catalog tree and scope through some available business capabilities. With the help of constraints, powerful instrument within the definition of the catalog, expressions of dependencies, and mutual exclusions of Business Adaption Catalog selection options are allowed. If the dependencies are identified, the customer should be able to make an informed and conscious decision for all necessary selections. The Business Adaption Catalog does not force choices on the customer; it just supports and secures. The basic structure includes a total of five layers, which can be divided into business content structure definition and business content data definition, as shown in Fig. 37.2.

A Business Area is a department within an organization, such as sales, purchasing, or human resources. It's only used to group Business Packages and not relevant

Basic Structure of the BAC

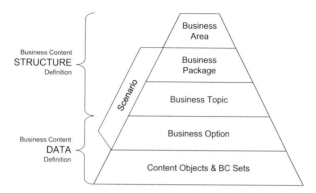

Fig. 37.2 Business Adoption Catalog (BAC)—basic structure

for the customer decisions. The next layer is the Business Package, which represents a logically definable subarea within the costumer's enterprise. It consists of capabilities that are required in that subarea, for example, the Sales business area includes a logical Contract Management (CM) subarea. Thus, the business package contains all capabilities for CM. Business Topic defines a logically subtopic within a subarea of the customer's enterprise. The business topic includes all capabilities required in that subarea. They can be grouped semantically. Business Option is the lowest level of decision. It represents a business variant or feature for a specific solution capability. Content Objects & BC Sets contain product-specific content packages. Business Adaption Catalog enables building more fine-granular configuration content, what leads to a much higher configuration flexibility. On the one hand the content development efficiency can be easily increased by getting rid of redundant content maintenance, for example, via templates and the mentioned layering. On the other hand, template-based docker instances enable a fast, flexible, low-cost setup of the SAP S/4HANA test environment. A much higher content quality is achieved by providing a more consistent authoring environment with Business Adaption Catalog authoring, for example, via branching. Every process of content authoring starts with the perspective and scoping of the customers. It's important to know the customer's vision and needs. Also, a scope-dependent approach is pursued, and Business Adaption Catalog considers changes. Giving partners the opportunity to create their own content for customers enables the scaling of Business Adaption Catalog. All these benefits are possible due to the back-sync process which is used to create the content for authoring. This includes the following steps:

1. Prepare the content and establish connectivity to the SAP S/4HANA system.
2. Scope in the authoring workspace by the creation of a defined configuration data context in SAP S/4HANA.

3. Update the authoring JSON file with the authoring workspace ID and staging ID.
4. Authorize the content by recording it via SPRO transaction and user-specific capturing of Implementation Guide Customizing (IMG) maintenance.
5. Push the recorded content from SAP S/4HANA to the Central Business Configuration with multiple back-syncs.
6. Identify those missing Data Dictionary (DDIC) artifacts and trigger a delta DDIC synchronization.
7. Store the content records in authoring workspace in worklist and create underlying temporary BC Sets.
8. Define related authoring views to be able to view a not yet abstracted BC Set using the specified authoring view.
9. Perform abstraction (templatization) to have the ability to view an intermediate BC Set after this abstraction.
10. Finalize the BC Set content, for example, resolving key clashes, and assign them to business options including country/region and sector assignment.
11. Perform tests via consumption workspace and deploy to an SAP S/4HANA test client. Correct errors either via Central Business Configuration directly or restart the process.
12. Close the authoring project/workspace and check the content for readiness.

The E2E processes available in the SAP S/4HANA solutions are described by *business process variant groups* and *business process variants*. Customers can preselect elements in the Business Adaptation Catalog based on a business process variant, giving a head start on the detailed decisions. Typically, a business process spans multiple business areas. For example, choosing the indirect material procurement business process variant would include the self-service procurement business package in the scope, but this package has financial requirements for accounts payable processing.

Consumption
Consumption, on the other hand, deals with the actual SAP Central Business Configuration, that is, projects are maintained, scoping is performed, and organizational structures are defined. This content is also stored separately and can be transported through the entire system landscape. No extensibility or configurations are directly made in the productive system to avoid error-prone situations. That's the reason why the content is defined in the development system, transported to a quality environment for testing, and if successfully validated, then transferred to the productive system. With the help of the reuse component Business Application Factory, standard functionalities such as authentication or correction are made available. The consumption is based on these five key components:

- Project Experience: This component manages configuration projects. The current focus here is on cloud applications, but the concepts are also suitable for all on-premise solutions.

- Scoping: This enables the definition of the objective for configuration projects. It follows a fit-to-standard analysis and starts with providing basic information about the company. It allows selecting and specifying countries and regions, business processes, and solution capabilities. Thus, relevant bundles and scenarios with predefined content can be suggested automatically. Each company is treated individually, so the system enables to make a series of business decisions to adjust the content and determine which of the available features and functions shall be integrated. This whole process is guided by built-in rules to ensure that the selected content is consistent and logical from a business and technical point of view. Starting this process launches the Business Adoption Catalog.

- Central Configuration: If the customer does not want or is not able to use the standard configuration, it is possible to make even more specific settings. It also allows to configure business processes based on the self-service configuration user interfaces (SSCUIs) and scope- and country/region-dependent configuration activities. For example, additional localizations can be added.

- Business Configuration Workspaces: With the help of business configuration workspaces, several implementation projects can be managed at the same time. Furthermore, templates can be used for future company rollouts. In this way, costs can be saved, and a standardization can be achieved. Company rollouts can be carried out quickly due to the parallelization of implementations and templates.

- Content: The aforementioned components are possible only through the SAP Best Practice preconfiguration content and the Business Catalog Adoption Catalog. Experience from hundreds of thousands of customer projects can be leveraged. In addition, the SAP Central Business Configuration introduces a completely new content structure, from scope items to business scenarios and from building block to business operations. Furthermore, configuration efforts of the pre-scoped workspaces can be reduced through fine-granular scoping.

Functionality and Concepts

From functional point of view SAP Central Business Configuration supports the project setup in terms of assigning team members to projects, the scoping of the required business scenarios, the execution of guided project activities. Furthermore, organizational structure management is facilitated, the execution of configuration activities is performed, and the lifecycle management is enabled including updates. In order to provide this functionality, concepts are required which are described in this section.

The *Project Experience* enables the customer to centrally manage all of their SAP implementations (Fig. 37.3). The dashboard shows the status of the entire system and the individual projects, whether they are still pending, in progress, or already completed. The user has a guided access to further applications like the scoping and a central access to SAP installations.

Project Experience - Explore

Project Experience - Realize

Fig. 37.3 Project experience—explore and realize

Fig. 37.4 Typical
configuration process

Prepare > Explore > Realize > Deploy

The typical configuration processes work with milestones and are depicted in
Fig. 37.4.

- Prepare: This step focuses on what is offered and what does the consumer need. The starter project is connected to a starter system and allows to explore the costumer's business processes with a preselected scope and example data before beginning the implementation project.
- Explore: The objective of this step is to define the scope und specify primary finance settings, request SAP S/4HANA license-dependent or non-standard scenarios, set up the organizational structure, and deploy settings to a quality system.
- Realize: In this phase, configuration activities for detail settings of the solution process are performed, also called *fine-tuning*. They must be carried out, and after finishing the release, they are transported from a quality to a productive system.
- Deploy: Current settings which need to be maintained directly in the production system are presented in this phase. Furthermore, manual rework on configuration activities is performed if required, and finally go-live is triggered.

The *Organizational Structure Management* facilitates to adapt and maintain the company's organizational structure and to activate the content data. It allows enhancing the organization structure when the customers have been using an activated solution already and would like to extend the organizational structure, for example, to add a new plant. Key features are the graphic view, which visualizes a scope-dependent and guided creation of organizational units and a table view that lists all organizational units in a table. As long as non-confirmed entities are waiting in the staging area, it is possible to change or delete them, because there is no instantiation of the org-related Business Configuration (BC) Sets into the workspace. All these Business Configuration Sets have a placeholder for the organizational identification (ORG ID), which gets filled with this particular ORG ID which shall be confirmed. After the deployment into the backend system those operations won't be able anymore. The *Business Configuration Lifecycle Management* supports the central configuration lifecycle and ensures that the business configuration performed in the central system is always in a consistent state. The goal is to make the content work not only at first, but also on a continuous basis. Customers can keep the SAP standard content as is or modify it to meet their needs. SAP Central Business Configuration calculates which content is used, what have been adapted, and which new content is available with each SAP update. Throughout the upgrade process, SAP makes improvements and corrections to the currently active scope. The SAP Central Business Configuration upgrade procedure ensures that customer's configuration settings are not altered. New innovations with additional scope elements, such as business process variants or business options, are made available for scoping and can be added after the upgrade via scope extensions. Without having to start from scratch, customers can get all of the latest innovations as additions to the standard content that they have adapted. As a result, an implementation project entails more than just managing configurations, so SAP Central Business Configuration is integrated with SAP Cloud ALM as part of the overall picture. SAP Central Business Configuration and SAP Cloud ALM are complementary tools: SAP Central Business Configuration manages configurations, while SAP Cloud ALM manages overall processes. Scoping decisions and activity statuses are synchronized

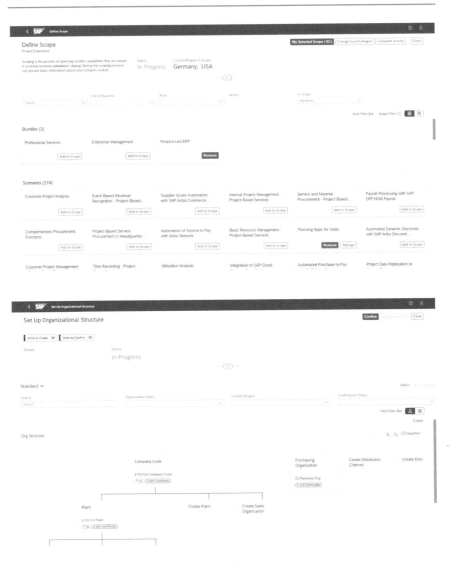

Fig. 37.5 Scoping and Organizational Structure Management

between the two tools as part of their planned integration, allowing to get the most out of SAP Cloud ALM and SAP Central Business Configuration (Fig. 37.5).

SAP Central Business Configuration adheres to SAP Activate implementation methodology and encompasses all configuration-related project phases. This tool focuses on activities in the workstream of application design and configuration. Initially, as part of the preparation phase, customers are given access to the SAP Central Business Configuration tool, where they configure their project, including naming the project lead and assembling the project team. In the starter project, customers conduct a fit-to-standard analysis as part of the explore phase. Simultaneously, customers create their implementation project in which they document the results of the fit-to-standard analysis, including the following information: Choosing a scope and countries/regions, configuring parameters for further system customizing, and defining the company's organizational structure. Following the completion of the explore phase, the settings are initially deployed. During the realize phase, customers can modify the preconfigured settings to better suit their business requirements. Depending on the project approach, SAP Central Business Configuration allows to use transports to release configurations in small, iterative steps or in larger chunks. During the deployment phase, customers perform cutover activities such as migration of their productive data. SAP Central Business Configuration assists in carrying out recurring activities, also known as current settings, to complete the project's go-live phase. Even after the project has gone live, customers can still make changes to it, such as expanding its scope, adding countries and regions, establishing new organizational units, or fine-tuning the business processes. Based on an integrated functionality to initiate changes, this expansion is possible. SAP Central Business Configuration also assists in adapting processes, features, and functions delivered by each solution upgrade. Thus, SAP Activate, SAP Central Business Configuration, and SAP Cloud ALM work in tandem.

Conclusion

Configuration is the process by which customers and partners adopt ERP functionality based on predefined variability. The ERP products' ability to provide a high degree of flexibility and thus a wide range of customizing options has always been a core strength. This enables standard business software definitions to be adjusted and extended to meet the needs of each individual consumer. SAP S/4HANA currently provides thousands of individual settings for tuning an installation to meet the needs of a specific company. Thus, SAP developed an application called SAP Central Business Configuration, which allows users to configure a system in a systematic manner by utilizing an existing pool of functions. This is accomplished through the use of various concepts and the two major components: authoring and consumption. As a result, a step-by-step procedure is provided to customize the entire system and make the most of it for the customer.

Implementation

38

This chapter focuses on implementation concepts and frameworks of SAP S/4HANA to assure successful implementation projects. Particularly, the activate methodology and tooling for discovery, exploration, realization, deployment, and running of SAP S/4HANA are explained.

Business Requirement

Traditional ERP software implementations have been built around extensive requirements gathered in workshops, followed by detailed design activities to create a *blueprint* for system implementation. This approach has resulted in systems that are completely tailored to the needs of the business, with extensive customizations and custom code, but are difficult to upgrade and maintain. Companies that implement software in this manner frequently discover that due to the level of customization in their system, implementing new capabilities can be a cumbersome and time-consuming process, preventing the adoption of these new capabilities in a timely manner. Furthermore, the goal of such implementation projects is to get the organization to the go-live phase, with the expectation that the software operations will be performed by IT or outsourced to an application management services provider. Modern implementation methods take a completely different approach based on maximum reuse of pre-delivered functionalities and applications, with a fit-to-standard mindset in solution deployment. The deployment strategy should be based on the use of agile techniques to reduce time to value and provide a working solution to business users faster than in traditional implementations. Deploying ERP systems is a continuous adoption journey that does not end with the first go-live but rather continues with the ongoing adoption of new capabilities that the solution already provides or features that are delivered in the solution's regular upgrades. Typically, after the initial go-live, organizations that use ERP solutions focus on the following two tasks:

© The Author(s), under exclusive license to Springer Nature Switzerland AG 2022   583
S. Sarferaz, *Compendium on Enterprise Resource Planning*,
https://doi.org/10.1007/978-3-030-93856-7_38

- Maintaining solution adoption by optimizing the solution to meet business needs on an ongoing basis.
- Adding new capabilities or expanding the solution's geographical footprint to serve more users across the organization.

The provisioning of best practices packages, which include preconfigured support for business processes and provide a great jumpstart for the solution's deployment, is a key accelerator for deploying ERP systems. These preconfigured supported processes are delivered in the system using a predefined chart of accounts and a predefined set of master data (organizational units, customers, vendors, materials, and so on). Because customers can self-enable the pre-delivered functionality, this asset enables project acceleration in the early stages. This allows to determine the fit of the standard solution and identify any delta requirements. The implementation methodology should cover the entire lifecycle from discovery to realize and run. Especially, the project team must be enabled in each phase to validate that the solution meets the demands of business users and, if necessary, to determine any needed configuration values and delta requirements, such as extensions, integrations, analytics requirements, or access-level authorizations. This activity is typically carried out by the project team in fit-to-standard workshops. The advantage of approaching deployment in this manner is the time saved by reusing pre-delivered process support and avoiding the expense and effort of rebuilding processes and content in an empty system. Organizations that take this approach and commit to the *staying close to standard* principle can benefit not only from time savings in initial deployments, but also from a built solution that is ready for the activation of continuously delivered new capabilities. This foresight is especially important in a cloud environment, where new capabilities are released at a faster rate than in a traditional on-premise environment.

Solution Capability

This section covers different aspects that are important within the overall SAP S/4HANA implementation process. The SAP Activate methodology is used in different implementation contexts, for which SAP solutions could be applied. Many cloud solutions focus on a greenfield approach, while new on-premise solutions are prevailed with brownfield situations, because many ERP systems are established long-lasting implementations that will sooner or later get deprecated. Therefore, the general SAP Activate methodology in this section is divided into two elaborations of this general SAP implementation topic. The first part covers the SAP Activate methodology for a greenfield SAP S/4HANA Cloud solution. The second focuses on the SAP Activate methodology, which is being used in transitioning to an SAP S/4HANA on-premise solution. Both approaches face different challenges, which will get addressed. The SAP Activate methodology in these different use cases can get enhanced and realized with SAP Cloud ALM, which is specifically designed to support customers in adapting an SAP solution into their business.

SAP Activate Methodology

Organizations that are just getting started with SAP S/4HANA can use the SAP Activate methodology to map out a detailed path that will structure the transition process. SAP Activate guides customers through the process of charting a strategy, planning, and scoping the transition, as well as activities to assess the solution's fit with the needs of the organization in fit-to-standard workshops, configuration, extensibility, integration, and testing, and finally production cutover and go-live. Following this process, business users will be able to benefit from using SAP S/4HANA in their daily business activities, and the organization will be able to continue to adopt new SAP S/4HANA capabilities to broaden the scope of the solution. SAP Activate is a set of three components that work together to support the SAP S/4HANA implementation: SAP Best Practices, the methodology, and the tools. The SAP Activate methodology delivers a manual for the implementation of SAP solutions. Customers may have different requirements regarding the adoption of an SAP solution. In general, customer requirements can be divided into three fields: Project, Process, and Task management. These need to be addressed and specified for specific solution practices.

It makes a huge difference, if a company is transitioning an existing SAP ERP into SAP S/4HANA or implementing SAP SuccessFactors into their otherwise independent system landscape. Therefore, the general SAP Activate methodology needs to be flexible for many distinct solutions. Nonetheless a fit-to-standard focus is present in every solution with an SAP Activate methodology implementation process. With the goal to fit a standard SAP solution into individual requirements of a customer, the steps shown in Fig. 38.1 are identified for the implementation process:

- Discover: Within the first phase of an SAP implementation process, it is important that customers come to an understanding of their individual requirements on a standard solution. They need to explore the given benefits, which an SAP solution offers. Therefore, key stakeholders need to be identified, which are also critical for a successful project kick-off. The potential total solution value is dependent on the recognition of individual stakeholder requirements. If they are not satisfied with their individual value, they may not support the further implementation of an upcoming project. Hence the involvement of every stakeholder group into the discovery phase of an SAP solution should have a high priority.
- Prepare: After customers got a detailed understanding of their individual requirements and got to terms with an SAP sales team, the prepare phase of the implementation begins. In this phase every aspect of a specific upcoming implementation project gets planned and prepared. The aspects fall into many categories. A project team needs to be assigned, the project plan needs to be finalized, and development systems need to be set up.
- Explore: In the explore phase the project team performs a *fit-gap analysis*. Therefore, the individual customer requirements are divided into fits and gaps. Fits are requirements, which are covered by the based standard SAP solution. On the other hand, gaps are requirements, which are not covered by the standard SAP

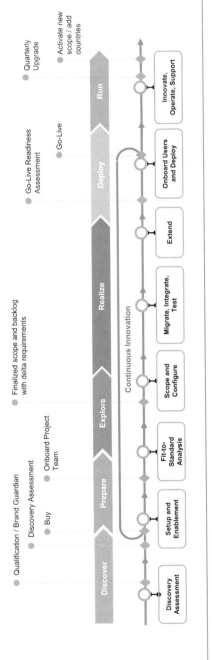

Fig. 38.1 The SAP Activate Methodology

solution out of the box. Gaps need to be specifically treated in the following realize phase. Every gap needs a detailed description and entry in the project backlog; hence these need to be individually covered and may be even implemented.

- Realize: The realize phase is characterized by different building and testing activities that build an individual system environment out of a generic SAP solution. Known fits and gaps are implemented, essentially to fulfill the customers' requirements in an adequate manner. Gaps need more attention in this phase, while fits are already identified as requirements, which are covered by default in the implementing SAP solution. These fits and gaps are implemented incrementally over different iterations to test the handling of each requirement thoroughly. Each iteration should bring new functionalities, to resemble the project progress over time. The outcome of this phase is an implemented SAP solution, which fulfills the customers' requirements and is ready to be deployed.
- Deploy: Within this project phase, the developed customer system gets its final touch before getting released into productional use, which is the first step of this project phase, but prior to that some final tasks need to be addressed. The customers' organization needs to be onboarded and prepared for the upcoming cutover. Therefore, planning support and training for end users is essential. Support processes for an operational use should also be implemented in this phase, to enable an optimal introduction of a new system as soon as possible. On the technical side final system tests need to be conducted, while every upcoming issue needs to be well documented.
- Run: In this final project phase, the implemented system is productively used. Main objectives of this phase are improvements of availability and system performance. Within this phase the defined value of the SAP solution gets realized, so that customer satisfaction is key. Therefore, opportunities for continuous learning and steady improvements should always be looked upon and evaluated. If potential for additional value is determined, these optimizations should get carried out.

In retrospect these different phases bring a form of consistency to every solution implementation, thus ensuring the right fitting of a standard SAP solution into specific customer requirements. Furthermore, the fit-to-standard focus gets carried out on the identification of fits and gaps in the explore phase. This phase's main objective is to evaluate given circumstances on the technical and business sides. At the end customers get a specifically configured SAP solution for their individual requirements. Thus, it is critical that individual use cases within the discovery phase have been identified. It is crucial to emphasize that the outcome of this methodology is customer value, which gets achieved by supporting business processes in the best manner possible. Hence, it is important that the run phase does not raise new and unknown problems and issues, which could impede dependent business processes. The SAP Activate methodology is divided into phases, deliverables, and tasks that are organized hierarchically. Each deliverable and task are also assigned to a workstream, which groups related deliverables and tasks together. The hierarchy organizes the deployment journey and is supplemented by accelerators, templates, documents, web links, and other assets that help you complete the task more quickly. SAP Activate's modularity allows organizations and SAP partners to replace specific sections of SAP Activate with their own processes and gates, as well as add their own processes as needed. SAP partners, for example, frequently offer their own flavor of program management or organizational change management (OCM) processes to use during the deployment. SAP Activate can be used in tandem with such procedures. If customers work in industries that have additional quality or validation requirements, they can use SAP Activate to overlay their required deliverables and quality gates (Q-gates) to comply with the processes and quality standards expected in their industry. SAP strongly advises keeping the SAP Activate components related to fit-to-standard, configuration, extensibility, integration, and technology in the resulting methodology in order to benefit from the strength of the product and content delivered with SAP Activate. SAP Activate's scalability enables to scale the approach to various project and organizational sizes. The methodology has been used successfully in SAP S/4HANA deployments in growing organizations in one country, as well as SAP solution deployments in multinational organizations operating in a diverse range of businesses across a broad geographical footprint. SAP Activate is designed to be scaled up or down based on the needs of organizations and the product being deployed. This scalability assists in deploying SAP S/4HANA with strict adherence to standard pre-configuration reuse to deploy solution in weeks and provides structure for organizations deploying the solution incrementally across a wide range of businesses.

SAP Activate takes the starting point of the customers into account and ensures greenfield approach for new implementation and brownfield for system conversion as illustrated in Fig. 38.2.

Greenfield Implementation

An SAP S/4HANA implementation follows the general SAP Activate methodology in many aspects but is specified for the cloud version of an SAP S/4HANA system. This approach depictures a greenfield situation, hence there is no need to take the transition of a preexisting SAP ERP system into consideration (see Fig. 38.2). Therefore, this approach can also be applied to a new implementation of an on-premise version of SAP S/4HANA. The previously declared general SAP Activate methodology phases for this greenfield situation for an ERP system are expanded by the following additions:

- Discover: The key activity within this phase is to deal with a trial SAP S/4HANA system to get a fundamental understanding of its functionalities. Out of these functionalities the customer needs to deduct his individual value propositions of this new iteration of ERP systems. After this phase the customer needs to know what value is provided by the SAP S/4HANA system.
- Prepare: The prepare phase is a straightforward phase for an SAP S/4HANA system implementation. Within this phase a base system needs to be set up and

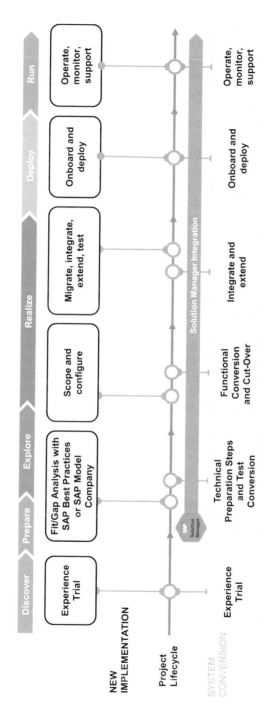

Fig. 38.2 SAP Activate for new implementation and system conversion

prepared for later configuration work. Additionally, some preparation work needs to be done within this phase for the fit-to-standard objective, which is mainly regarding design and configuration of the *to be realized* application. It is worth mentioning that data management, testing, and integration are not activities within this phase. Just out of the fact that a greenfield situation is preset, which does not involve any legacy ERP system with any relevant data or integration requirements.

- Explore: This phase is used to perform the fit-to-standard objective and to analyze the given SAP S/4HANA functionalities with already identified value propositions. Like in the general methodology, fits and gaps can thereby be identified, in which less gaps are desirable. Generally, many business processes and requirements need to be aligned with the given solution functionalities. Hence many design and developmental processes begin in this phase, as well as building a quality system (Q-System).

- Realize: As in the general SAP Activate methodology this phase brings the identified fits that need to be configured and gaps that need to be resolved to fruition. The main objective of this phase is a deployable productive system (P-System) that fulfills all customers' requirements. Therefore, identified consumer data and configurations get migrated, integrated, and tested in the prepared Q-System. These developments will later get transported to the P-System. This transport does not need to be carried out in a single action, but can rather be divided into an initial, instantiating transport and following ongoing transports. Business user can receive early access to an already partly functional P-System, so that the project team gets further information and feedback, which could be used to optimize the still developing P-System. Incremental iterations can carry out further development into the P-System, so that a useable, fully developed, configured, and deployable P-System is the final result of this phase.

- Deploy: The deploy phase is characterized by the productional go-live of the P-System and therefore of the SAP S/4HANA System. For that the final system tests are getting carried out, end-user trainings are getting run through, a cutover-plan for the carry-over of data in the P-System gets planned and accomplished, and post-live plans for end-user support gets realized, with the resulting processes being implemented. It is essential that the values of the declared value proposition are being realized so that the final custom-configured and implemented SAP S/4HANA solution can deliver on its proclaimed values, and customers are satisfied.

- Run: The run phase does not deviate from the run phase of the general SAP Activate methodology. It must be pointed out that an ERP system supports all business process, so that the solution performance in its run phase is critical to the long-term success of a company. Guaranteeing system availability is also key for delivering value as an ERP system. Furthermore, continuous improvement of availability and the general system performance should be a topic in the run phase of an ERP system.

Additionally, the described incremental iterations within the realize phase could also be applied to the adjacent phases from prepare to deploy. Therefore, it is possible for customers to iteratively add new functionalities or expand the previously identified project scope. Nonetheless such activities result in additional cost and time, which need to be outweighed by the resulting value of new functionalities. This can represent a good fallback-mechanism to add functionality after the solution went into productional use.

In summary, customers can rely on the SAP Activate methodology to successfully implement an SAP S/4HANA system, with a greenfield approach, which can be iteratively expanded. Thus, this procedure does not involve any conversion of already existing processes or data. As it has been already pointed out, such conversions are required for customers who already implemented another ERP system. Business processes are aligned with the long-lasting ERP systems, so that either a standardized solution needs a magnificent degree of customizability or business processes need to be realigned. Both endeavors are not easy to achieve; therefore, in some use cases a brownfield approach is inevitable. The following chapter focuses on this topic.

Brownfield Implementation

The transition of an existing and established ERP system and its corresponding structure renders a greenfield solution virtually impossible. Some sort of technical or business process-related legacies need to be carried over; hence a brownfield solution is required as shown in Fig. 38.2. Therefore, the following SAP Activate methodology focuses on a rather transitional implementation of SAP S/4HANA with its associated steps.

- Discover: This phase is like the corresponding previously described phases, although this phase is not the first step of an SAP S/4HANA implementation. In this step a business is already committed to a transition of their legacy ERP system to SAP S/4HANA, which requires a general understanding of possible benefits from this transition. The main purpose of this phase is to transform these recognized benefits into tangible value propositions and high-level requirements. Therefore, the individual customer business has a huge impact on specific, received values. An SAP S/4HANA implementation should fit into a larger, companywide digital transformation, which follows a digital transformation strategy. How and to which extent a modern ERP solution can contribute into this strategy should be clarified in the discovery phase.
- Prepare: Scope and goals have been declared so that a project team can be instantiated in the prepare phase. In this phase are all kinds of preparing transformation activities. These activities start with different prototype projects that each cover different parts of the overall transformation project to ensure its technical and functional feasibility. These findings should be used to guide to planning and preparation of the general transformation project. The main goal of this phase

should be an adequate preparation and foundation for the following project phases. Therefore, none of the, to this point, defined assumptions should be wrong, because they would lead to costly errors in the following project phases.

- Explore: This phase's main objective is to define and work out technical and functional details of the resulting SAP S/4HANA solution. Integration and configuration play a huge role within this phase, as to this point only possible solutions have been looked upon and existing business processes and functionalities have not been integrated into the project at least not at a detailed level. In this phase the fit-to-standard thought gets applied, while this may be more difficult than in related greenfield projects. Different fits and gaps are being identified, while it must be expected that more gaps are being identified than anticipated. Hence an on-premise SAP S/4HANA solution with a substantial share of custom development could be required to resolve these gaps. Within this phase a customer should get a good understanding of how the SAP S/4HANA solution is implemented, so that it fulfills its intended tasks and delivers its expected value.

- Realize: The realize phase is highly dependent on the outcome of the previous phase. A high number of fits lead to more extensive configuration work, which should be covered within the fit-to-standard focus, whereas a high degree of gaps leads to more custom solutions and therefore code so that the project deviates from the fit-to-standard focus. This mechanism needs to be understood and be a focus point in the previous explore phase. Gaps could be avoided by changing existing process or requirements. Gaps are more costly than fits because these do not need extra work and attention. If this phase in an SAP S/4HANA implementation starts aggregating more and more problems, these could have originated in the previous phase. Therefore, an extensive explore phase is key to minimize the probability of unknown problems, which will show up on a later point in the project. The realize phase should result in a nearly productional P-System, with a special focus on the cutover-plan. In a greenfield situation there is no legacy ERP system, which needs to be phased out. Thus, this fact needs to get special attention within the cutover-plan.

- Deploy: The deploy phase includes the go-live event and thus the production cutover. The developed P-System is put into productional use. This event needs to be extensively tested, so that no foreseeable mishaps could happen. As already described an ERP system is crucial for a business and its corresponding business processes. This means that not only the time immediately after a cutover is critical, but also weeks after the productional release need special attention. The so-called *hyper-care* phase starts after an SAP S/4HANA system went live and is in a useable state. Stability and availability are crucial. Hence the system needs to be closely monitored to expose potential optimization possibilities. The deploy phase ends together with its hyper-care phase.

- Run: All operational tasks fall within the run phase. As previously described the SAP solution delivers its value in its run phase, which justifies the system. The implementation project ends after the project team conducts no further improvement, but the run phase carries on. The responsibility regarding the productional system should get handed over to an operational team that maintains the solution over its lifetime. Within this phase further improvements and innovations could get implemented, but to a smaller extent.

SAP Activate provides project structure guidance and relies on a wide range of tools for configuration, application lifecycle management (ALM), identity and access management, data migration, extensibility, integration, testing, and tooling for user learning and user assistance. SAP Cloud ALM is one of the key tools for the SAP Activate implementation and therefore briefly depicted in the next section.

SAP Cloud ALM

An SAP Cloud ALM system can be summarized as a guiding, knowledge-rich, and best-practice emphasizing tool, which cooperates with the SAP Activate methodology. With SAP Cloud ALM upcoming customers can get supported in different aspects within their implementation journey. Overall, the whole SAP Activate methodology is represented. Therefore, SAP Cloud ALM is a crucial part in executing an SAP implementation project if customers do not already have thorough knowledge of the target-implemented SAP solution. Included SAP Cloud ALM capabilities range from foundational principles, like defining and classifying future users, project stakeholders, or system landscape, on the one hand, to Change and Deploy best practices, on the other hand. SAP Cloud ALM covers the whole customer journey of an SAP solution implementation, whereby problems can be dealt with quicker and uncertainties can be minimized. Especially a fit-to-standard focus is not a best practice anymore. It is rather an essential part of an SAP solution. This focus is critical for an SAP S/4HANA Cloud system, but also should not be ignored for an on-premise system. Nonetheless both approaches have a positive surplus on a fit-to-standard focus. This results in minimizing project implementation costs and achieving a better quality of the project outcome. Standard solutions are easier to maintain, better to expand, and do not need technical attention if some custom components need to be updated.

Out of these arguments, an SAP Cloud ALM should always be considered when implementing an SAP ERP system. Figure 38.3 recaps the functionality of the SAP Cloud ALM covering process and task support, the ability to handle tests, changes, and deployments. Furthermore, analytics capability is provided for project tracking and traceability. Some of the illustrated functionality is not already available with the current SAP Cloud ALM version.

Conclusion

This chapter explained concrete use cases of the SAP Activate methodology for the SAP S/4HANA implementations. ERP systems could get implemented as greenfield or brownfield solutions, so that two different SAP Activate variants were described,

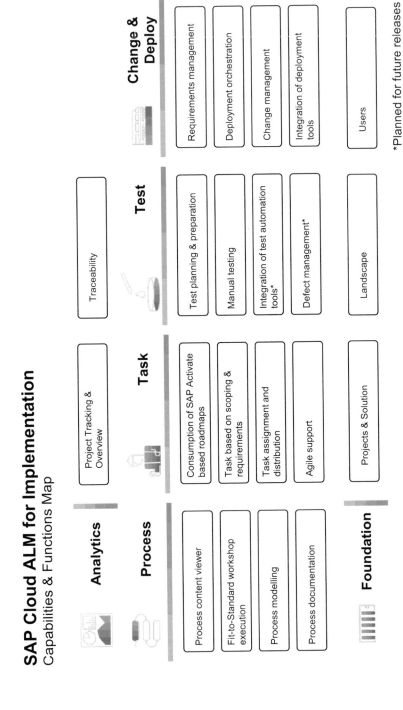

Fig. 38.3 SAP Cloud ALM—functional architecture

with each being able to use an SAP Cloud ALM solution to enhance their respective implementation. These elaborations follow different premises, a greenfield solution is preferably used in businesses that implement their first ERP system, whereas that is not always possible for businesses that have been using an ERP system for decades and always have some sort of legacy carry-over into a new ERP system. For these a brownfield solution is inevitable. Such brownfield situations rather need a transition instead of solely an implementation. These fundamental customer challenges of an SAP S/4HANA implementation are addressed within the different SAP Activate methodologies shown.

Appendix

This chapter outlines how to bring up own SAP S/4HANA trail system for exploring its functionality and concepts. Particularly, it is explained how to deploy a preconfigured system image on cloud platforms of Amazon, Microsoft, or Google. Thus, the underlying hardware is in the cloud, while the system is dedicated for personal use. Additionally, step-by-step guides for discovering SAP S/4HANA are provided.

Introduction

In order to deepen the understanding of the functionality and concepts which were described in the last chapter, exploring the SAP S/4HANA system is valuable. However, the deployment and configuration of an ERP solution is challenging and requires advanced expert knowledge. Furthermore, the provisioning of the demanded hardware is expensive, and the maintenance of application data is a sophisticated task. SAP Cloud Appliance Library (CAL) resolves these challenges and offers an appliance which is a preconfigured SAP S/4HANA system image with step-by-step tutorials.

SAP Cloud Appliance Library

SAP Cloud Appliance Library provides a quick and easy way to consume the most recent SAP cloud solutions, such as SAP S/4HANA, SAP HANA Express Edition, Model Company Solutions, or Industry Solutions. It's an online library of the most recent, preconfigured, ready-to-use SAP solutions that can be instantly deployed into customer's own public cloud accounts (e.g., Amazon Web Services, Microsoft Azure, and Google Cloud Platform) to get SAP projects up and running in a short time. A deployment of the preconfigured system image on on-premise hardware is also supported.

© The Author(s), under exclusive license to Springer Nature Switzerland AG 2022
S. Sarferaz, *Compendium on Enterprise Resource Planning*,
https://doi.org/10.1007/978-3-030-93856-7_39

SAP S/4HANA Fully Activated Appliance
The Software Appliance Concept

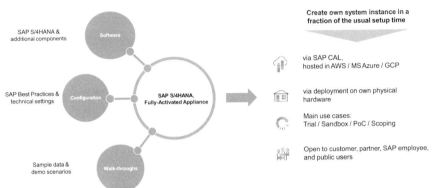

Fig. 39.1   The SAP S/4HANA fully activated appliance

As shown in Fig. 39.1 SAP CAL provides in addition to a preconfigured SAP S/4HANA also sample data and demo scenarios in the form of step-by-step tutorials. Thus, instantly the SAP S/4HANA business processes and frameworks can be explored. The SAP S/4HANA image consists of four single virtual machines that are coupled automatically into one solution instance. The appliance can be suspended and reactivated on an hourly basis. Calculator is provided to estimate the hosting costs for the different hyperscaler. For provisioning of an SAP CAL instance for SAP S/4HANA the following steps must be performed:

- Prerequisite: Obtain an account for Amazon AWS or Microsoft Azure or Google Cloud Platform.
- Step 1: Start the creation of personal trial instance.
  - Go to the trial landing page http://go.sap.com/cmp/oth/crm-s4hana/s4hana-on-premise.html
  - Choose *Start your trial now.*
- Step 2: Log on to SAP Cloud Appliance Library https://cal.sap.com/
  - You will get to the home screen of the SAP Cloud Appliance Library.
  - *Register* yourself as a new user (free of charge) for SAP CAL or *log on* with an existing SAP CAL username/password.
- Step 3: Accept Terms and Conditions for the 30-day trial period.
  - After you entered your user credentials and logged on you will be presented with the Terms and Conditions. Scroll down to read.
  - Choose *I Accept.*
  - Note: The 30-day trial period starts when you accept the Terms and Conditions and not when you create your first instance.
- Step 4: Enter your AWS/Azure/GCP account and create your personal SAP S/4HANA system.

- In the *SAP Cloud Appliance Library Instance Creation* page you have to specify your cloud provider account (see step 1).
- Click *"Create a new account"* (or click "existing account" if you have already entered a cloud provider account before).
- Enter *Instance Details* (this will become your personal S/4HANA system).
- Define the master *password* for your appliance (this will be assigned to various administrator users, e.g., SAP HANA SYSTEM user or Remote Desktop Administrator).
- Click **Create** (Note: If you need static IP addresses for your system, choose Advanced Mode).
• Step 5: Download private key for the instance (only needed for backend Linux operating system access).
- When prompted for the private key, choose *Store*.
- Note: The private key is a small .PEM text file, and it is needed only in case you want to access the Linux operating system of the trial landscape.
- The system will now be created in your AWS/Azure/GCP account. Time for this may vary depending on provider, region, and current system load (~1–2 hours should suffice in most cases).
- You may access the remote desktop earlier, but creation of the SAP S/4HANA system will take longer than the remote desktop creation (so even if you can enter the remote desktop already, the SAP S/4HANA system might not be responding yet).
- In general, the initial clicks in the system will be slow (until caches are pre-filled), as for all newly brought up SAP systems.
• Step 6: Instance is ready in *Instances* tab.
- After the deployment time your system is ready for logon.
- Clicking on the instance name lets you view the details of the instance.
- The *Connect* button provides direct logon access to
  Remote Desktop
  SAP GUI
  BI launchpad
  SAP NetWeaver administrator (JAVA)
- Fiori launchpad access works either via Remote Desktop or via local browser after hosts file mapping.

As already mentioned, SAP CAL provides demo scenarios to walk the user through a guided tour concerning the SAP S/4HANA capabilities. The user is free to step away from these tours. However, if users investigate additional features of the SAP S/4HANA system beyond what is provided in the demo guides, they may discover functions or processes that are not preconfigured and, as a result, will not provide a meaningful system response. To make those scenarios or functions work, users must configure them using SAP standard procedures. The demo scenarios can be found in Wolf (2021). The scope of the demo scenarios is centered on the SAP Best Practices content for SAP S/4HANA and is supplemented by additional scenarios, which vary depending on the exact release version of the appliance. To provide an impression of how the demo scenarios work, in the next section one example is described (Wolf, 2021).

Exemplary Demo Scenario

This scenario describes Financial Accounting Overview transactions and serves as a centralized, up-to-date reference for account rendering. Actual individual transactions can be reviewed in real time, with the original documents, line items, and transaction figures displayed at various levels. Investigate the following transactions:

• General Ledger Overview	• Cash Discount Utilization
• Journal Entries to be Verified	• Days Payable Outstanding Indirect
• G/L Account Balance	• Days Payables Outstanding Direct
• Quick Links	• Suppliers with Debit Balances
• Tax Reconciliation Account Balance	• Accounts Receivable Overview
• G/L Items Changes	• AR Aging Analysis
• Days Payable Outstanding Indirect	• Days Sales Outstanding
• Days Sales Outstanding	• Cash Collection Tracker
• Accounts Payable Overview	• Top 10 Debtors
• Payables Aging	

General Accounting Overview

What to Do	What You Will See
Open the Fiori Launchpad. User: **S4H_FIN**, Password: **Welcome1** Set Default Value for SAP Fiori Launchpad User Settings (Optional). On the SAP Fiori launchpad, go to User > Settings > Default Values.	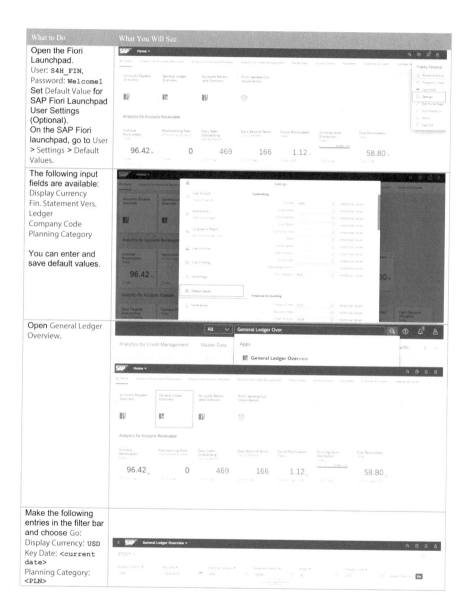
The following input fields are available: Display Currency Fin. Statement Vers. Ledger Company Code Planning Category You can enter and save default values.	
Open General Ledger Overview.	
Make the following entries in the filter bar and choose Go: Display Currency: **USD** Key Date: **<current date>** Planning Category: **<PLN>**	

What to Do	What You Will See
Statement Version: <YCOA> Ledger: <0L> Company Code: <1710>	
To customize the cards on the overview page, choose the User Icon on your home dashboard and choose Manage Cards.	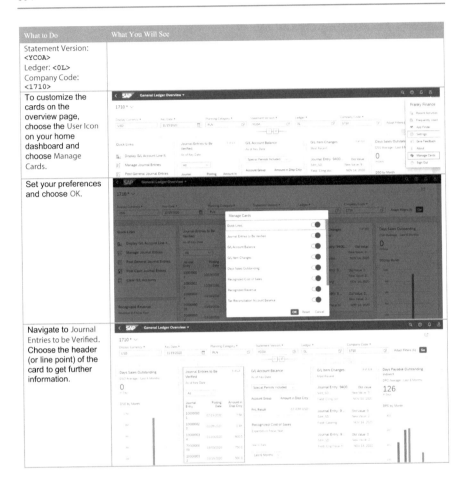
Set your preferences and choose OK.	
Navigate to Journal Entries to be Verified. Choose the header (or line point) of the card to get further information.	

What to Do	What You Will See
Navigate to G/L Account Balance. Choose the header (or line point) of the card to get further information.	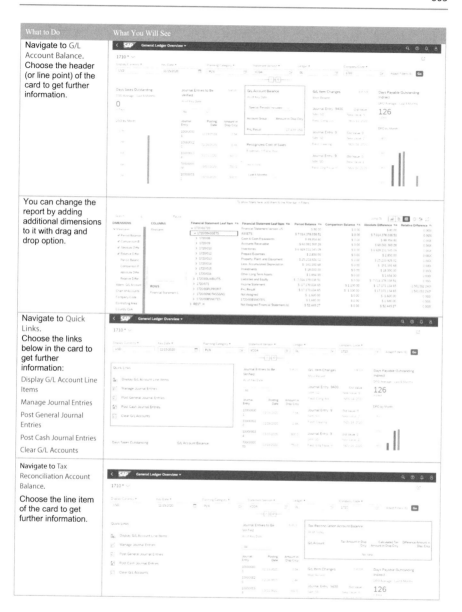
You can change the report by adding additional dimensions to it with drag and drop option.	
Navigate to Quick Links. Choose the links below in the card to get further information: Display G/L Account Line Items Manage Journal Entries Post General Journal Entries Post Cash Journal Entries Clear G/L Accounts	
Navigate to Tax Reconciliation Account Balance. Choose the line item of the card to get further information.	

What to Do	What You Will See
Navigate to G/L Items Changes. Choose the header (or line point) of the card to get further information.	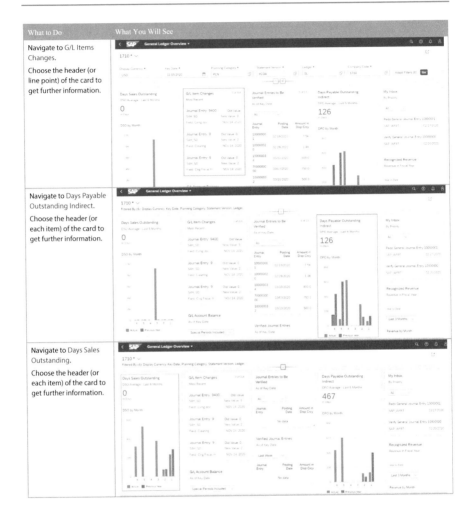
Navigate to Days Payable Outstanding Indirect. Choose the header (or each item) of the card to get further information.	
Navigate to Days Sales Outstanding. Choose the header (or each item) of the card to get further information.	

Accounts Payable Overview

What to Do	What You Will See
Open the Fiori Launchpad. User: `S4H_FIN`, Password: `Welcome1`	

What to Do	What You Will See
Set Default Value for SAP Fiori Launchpad User Settings (Optional). On the SAP Fiori launchpad, go to User > Settings > Default Values. The following input fields are available: Display Currency Fin. Statement Vers. Ledger Company Code Planning Category You can enter and save default values.	
Open Accounts Payable Overview.	
Make the following entries on the filter bar and choose Go: Display Currency: USD Company Code: <1710> Supplier: <any supplier> Country: <US>.	
To customize the cards on the overview page, choose the User button on your home dashboard and choose Manage Cards.	

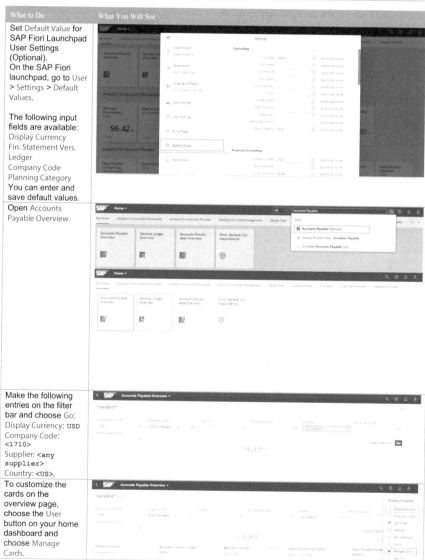

What to Do	What You Will See
Set your preferences and choose OK.	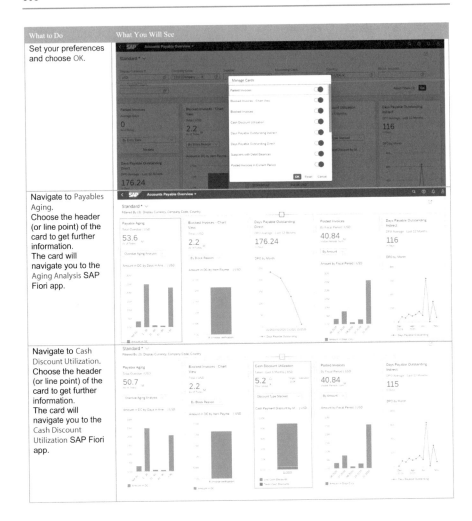
Navigate to Payables Aging. Choose the header (or line point) of the card to get further information. The card will navigate you to the Aging Analysis SAP Fiori app.	
Navigate to Cash Discount Utilization. Choose the header (or line point) of the card to get further information. The card will navigate you to the Cash Discount Utilization SAP Fiori app.	

What to Do	What You Will See
Navigate to Days Payable Outstanding Indirect. Choose the header (or line point) of the card to get further information. The overview page navigates you to the target apps. The global filter and header (and line point/bar item) information is carried over. The card will navigate you to the Days Payable Outstanding Indirect SAP Fiori app.	
Navigate to Days Payables Outstanding Direct. The overview page navigates you to the target apps. The global filter and header (and line point) information is carried over. The card will navigate to the Days Payable Outstanding SAP Fiori app.	
Navigate to Suppliers with Debit Balances. Choose the header (or line point) of the card to get further information. The overview page navigates you to the target apps. The global filter and header (and line point) information is carried over. The card will navigate to the Manage Supplier Line Items SAP Fiori app.	

What to Do	What You Will See
Navigate to Quick Links. Choose Approve Bank Payments (or My Inbox) of the card to get further information. The overview page navigates you to the target apps. Choose Approve Bank Payments. The card will navigate you to the Approve Bank Payments SAP Fiori app.	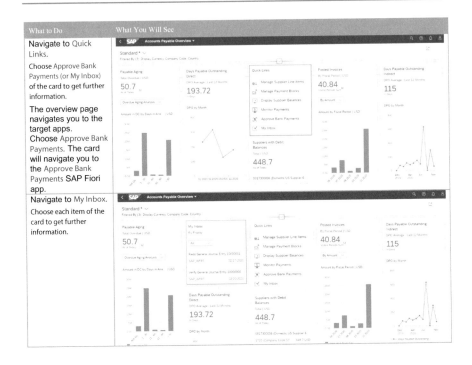
Navigate to My Inbox. Choose each item of the card to get further information.	

Accounts Receivable Overview

What to Do	What You Will See
Open the Fiori Launchpad. User: **S4H_FIN**, Password: **Welcome1** Set Default Value for SAP Fiori Launchpad User Settings (Optional). On the SAP Fiori launchpad, go to User > Settings > Default Values The following input fields are available: Display Currency Fin. Statement Vers. Ledger Company Code Planning Category	

What to Do	What You Will See
You can enter and save default values. Open Accounts Receivable Overview.	
Make the following entries on the filter bar and choose Go: Display Currency: USD Net Due Interval 1: <30> Net Due Interval 2: <60> Net Due Interval 3: <90> Company Code: <1710> If a default value is set in the SAP Fiori launchpad user settings, the filters have already been populated with the default values.	
To customize the cards on the overview page, choose the User button on your home dashboard and choose Manage Cards.	

Set your preferences and choose OK.	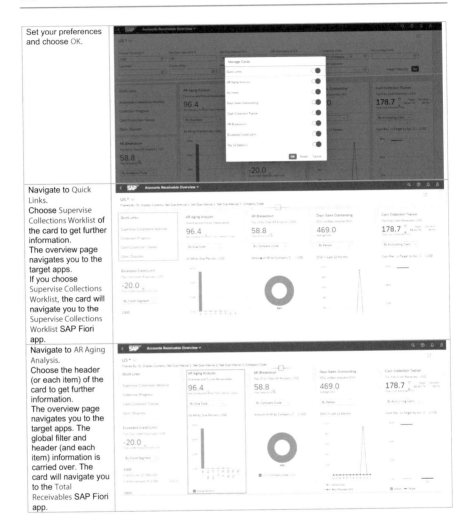
Navigate to Quick Links. Choose Supervise Collections Worklist of the card to get further information. The overview page navigates you to the target apps. If you choose Supervise Collections Worklist, the card will navigate you to the Supervise Collections Worklist SAP Fiori app.	
Navigate to AR Aging Analysis. Choose the header (or each item) of the card to get further information. The overview page navigates you to the target apps. The global filter and header (and each item) information is carried over. The card will navigate you to the Total Receivables SAP Fiori app.	

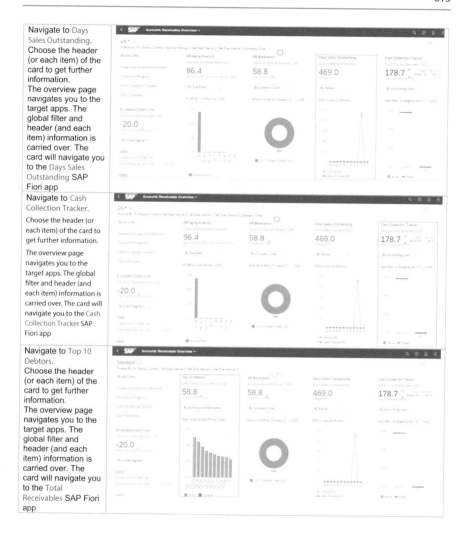

| Navigate to Days Sales Outstanding. Choose the header (or each item) of the card to get further information. The overview page navigates you to the target apps. The global filter and header (and each item) information is carried over. The card will navigate you to the Days Sales Outstanding SAP Fiori app |
| Navigate to Cash Collection Tracker. Choose the header (or each item) of the card to get further information. The overview page navigates you to the target apps. The global filter and header (and each item) information is carried over. The card will navigate you to the Cash Collection Tracker SAP Fiori app |
| Navigate to Top 10 Debtors. Choose the header (or each item) of the card to get further information. The overview page navigates you to the target apps. The global filter and header (and each item) information is carried over. The card will navigate you to the Total Receivables SAP Fiori app |

Conclusion

Exploring the SAP S/4HANA system is beneficial for deepening the understanding of the functionality and concepts described in the previous chapter. The chapter described how to set up own SAP S/4HANA trail system to investigate its functionality and concepts. It is specifically explained how to deploy a preconfigured system image on Amazon, Microsoft, or Google cloud platforms. This was achieved based on SAP Cloud Appliance Library, which in addition to a preconfigured system also provides step-by-step guides for exploring the SAP S/4HANA business processes and frameworks.

References

AXELOS Limited. (2019). *ITIL® Foundation ITIL* (4th ed.). TSO.

Balaban, D. (2019). *The ERP market is quickly growing.* Retrieved from https://blogs.sap.com/201 9/06/28/the-erp-market-is-quickly-growing/

Bitkom-Arbeitskreis Enterprise Resource Planning. (2016). ERP im Kontext von Industrie 4.0. Bitkom e.V. Retrieved from https://www.bitkom.org/Bitkom/Publikationen/Die-Zukunft-von-ERP-im-Kontext-von-Industrie-40.html

Bockstahler, M., Jurecic, M., & Rief, S. (2020) *Working from home experience. An empirical study from the user perspective during the corona pandemic.* Retrieved from http://publica. fraunhofer.de/dokumente/N-605596.html

Davidson, R. (2020). *Top ERP software vendors in 2020 | company comparison list.* Retrieved from https://softwareconnect.com/erp/top-vendors/

de Smet, A., Pacthod, D., Relyea, C., & Sternfels, B. (2020). *Ready, set, go: Reinventing the organization for speed in the post-COVID-19 era.* Retrieved from https://www.mckinsey.com/ business-functions/organization/our-insights/ready-set-go-reinventing-the-organization-for-speed-in-the-post-covid-19-era#

Essex, D., Diann, D., & O'Donnell, J. (2020). *ERP (enterprise resource planning).* https:// searcherp.techtarget.com/definition/ERP-enterprise-resource-planning

Gantz, J., & Reinsel, D. (2012). *The digital universe in 2020: Big data, bigger digital shadows and biggest growth in the far east.*

Gartner, I. (2019). *Gartner says 5.8 billion enterprise and automotive IoT endpoints will be in use in 2020.* Retrieved from https://www.gartner.com/en/newsroom/press-releases/2019-08-29-gartner-says-5-8-billion-enterprise-and-automotive-io

Gartner. (2021). *Presentation on enterprise resource planning software.* Retrieved from http:// www.gartner.com

Gaughan, D., Natis, Y., Alvarez, G., & O'Neill, M. (2020). *Future of applications: delivering the composable enterprise.* Gartner. Retrieved from https://www.gartner.com/en/doc/465932-future-of-applications-delivering-the-composable-enterprise

Gentner, A. (2020). Smartphone-Konsum Am Limit? Studie Zur Smartphone-Nutzung: Der Deutsche Mobile Consumer Im Profil. Retrieved from https://www2.deloitte.com/de/de/pages/ technology-media-and-telecommunications/articles/smartphone-nutzung-2020.html

Hackmann, J. (2020). *A brief review of SAP's current strategy.* Retrieved from https://www.sitsi. com/brief-review-sap-s-current-strategy

Iakimets, A. (2020). *What are packaged business capabilities?* Elastic Path Software Inc. Retrieved from https://www.elasticpath.com/blog/what-are-packaged-business-capablities

Jim Gray, A. R. (1999, August 2–6). *Transaction processing – Concepts and techniques.* Retrieved March 19, 2021, from Microsoft Research. Retrieved from http://research.microsoft.com/~gray/ WICS_99_TP/01_WhirlwindTour.ppt

© The Author(s), under exclusive license to Springer Nature Switzerland AG 2022
S. Sarferaz, *Compendium on Enterprise Resource Planning*,
https://doi.org/10.1007/978-3-030-93856-7

Lukic, J. (2015). Leadership challenges in the big data era. In R. Stankovic (Ed.), *Challenges to promoting entrepreneurship, leadership and competitiveness* (pp. 293–309). Faculty of Business Economics and Entrepreneurship.

Marz, N., & Warren, J. (2015). *Big data*. Manning Publications.

McKinsey & Company. (2019). *Industry 4.0: Capturing value at scale in discrete manufacturing*. Retrieved from https://www.mckinsey.com/~/media/McKinsey/Industries/Advanced%20Electronics/Our%20Insights/Capturing%20value%20at%20scale%20in%20discrete%20manufacturing%20with%20Industry%204%200/Industry-4-0-Capturing-value-at-scale-in-discrete-manufacturing-vF.ashx

Moore, G. E. (1965). Cramming more components onto integrated circuits. *Electronics, 38*(8), 114–117.

Pang, A., Markovski, M., & Micik, A. (2020). *Top 10 ERP software vendors, market size and market forecast 2019–2024*. Retrieved from https://www.appsruntheworld.com/top-10-erp-software-vendors-and-market-forecast/

Reinbolt, M. (2021). *Madeline, ERP market share and buyer trends for 2021*. Retrieved from https://www.selecthub.com/enterprise-resource-planning/erp-market/

Robier, J. (2016). *Das einfache und emotionale Kauferlebnis. Mit Usability, User Experience und Customer Experience anspruchsvolle Kunden gewinnen* (1. Auflage). Springer Gabler. Retrieved from http://gbv.eblib.com/patron/FullRecord.aspx?p=4098016

SAP Help Portal. (2021). *Product documentation for SAP S/4HANA*. Retrieved from http://www.sap.com

SAP's Industry 4.0 Strategy. (2021). Retrieved from https://www.sap.com/documents/2019/12/7eb945d8-777d-0010-87a3-c30de2ffd8ff.html

Sarferaz, S., & Banda, R. (2020). *Implementing machine learning with SAP S/4HANA*. SAP Press.

Saueressig, T., Stein, T., Boeder, J., & Kleis, W. (2021b). *SAP S/4HANA architecture*. SAP Press.

Shah, I. (2019). *Intro to data science: A step-by-step guide to learn data science*. Retrieved from https://towardsdatascience.com/intro-to-data-science-531079c38b22

Sridharan, V., & LaForge, R. L. (2000). Resource planning: MRP TO MRPII AND ERP. In P. M. Swamidass (Ed.), *Encyclopedia of production and manufacturing management*. Springer. https://doi.org/10.1007/1-4020-0612-8_818

Valutes Reports. (2020). *Enterprise resource planning (ERP) market size is projected to reach USD 60230 million by 2026* | Values reported. Retrieved from https://www.prnewswire.com/news-releases/enterprise-resource-planning-erp-market-size-is-projected-to-reach-usd-60230-million-by-2026%2D%2Dvaluates-reports-301127521.html

van der Aalst, W. (2016). Data science in action. In *Process mining: Data science in action* (pp. 3–23). Springer.

Vesset, D., et al. (2020). *IDC FutureScape: Worldwide future of intelligence 2021 predictions*.

Wight, O. W. (1984). Manufacturing resource planning: MRP II – Unlocking America's productivity potential (S. 53–54, Rev. ed.). Wiley. ISBN: 0-471-13274-8

Wolf, J. (2021). SAP S/4HANA Fully-Activated Appliance: Demo Guides. Retrieved from https://blogs.sap.com/2019/04/23/sap-s4hana-fully-activated-appliance-demo-guides/

Additional Bibliography

Abdelaziz, D. (2020). *SAP S/4HANA extended service parts planning 2020 development highlights*. Retrieved from https://blogs.sap.com/2020/10/05/sap-s-4hana-extended-service-parts-planning-2020-product-development-highlights

Alisch, K., Arentzen, U., & Winter, E. (2004). *Gabler Wirtschaftslexikon*. Gabler Verlag. https://doi.org/10.1007/978-3-663-01439-3_16

Antonova, R., & Georgiev, G. (2019). ERP security, audit and process improvement. In A. Al-Masri & K. Curran (Eds.), *Smart technologies and innovation for a sustainable future* (pp. 103–110). Springer International Publishing.

Badgi, S. (2007). *Practical SAP U.S. Payroll*. SAP Press.

Baltes, L., Spieß, & Wörmann-Wiese. (2017). *SAP - Materialwirtschaft.* SAP- Press.

Bennicke, M., Hofmann, A., Lewerentz, C., & Wichert, K.-H. (2008). Software controlling. *Informatik Spektrum, 31*(6), 556–565. https://doi.org/10.1007/s00287-008-0285-6

Box, G. E., Jenkins, G. M., Reinsel, G. C., & Ljung, G. M. (2016). *Time series analysis, forecasting and control* (5th ed.).

Bundesministerium für Wirtschaft und Energie. (2020). *GAIA-X: Die nächste Generation der digitalen Vernetzung in Europa.* Retrieved from https://www.bmwi.de/Redaktion/DE/Dossier/gaia-x.html

Bytniewski, A., Matouk, K., Rot, A., Hernes, M., & Kozina, A. (2020). Towards industry 4.0: Functional and technological basis for ERP 4.0 systems. In M. Hernes, A. Rot, & D. Jelonek (Eds.), *Towards industry 4.0—Current challenges in information systems* (pp. 3–19). Springer International Publishing.

CCPA. (2021). *State of California Department of Justice.* California Consumer Privacy Act (CCPA). Retrieved from https://oag.ca.gov/privacy/ccpa

Chang, S.-I. (2004). *ERP life cycle implementation, management and support: Implications for practice and research* (National Chung Cheng University).

Chugh, R., Sharma, S. C., & Cabrera, A. (2017). Lessons learned from enterprise resource planning (ERP) implementations in an Australian Company. *International Journal of Enterprise Information Systems, 13*(3), 23–35.

Common Weakness Enumeration (CWE). (2021). Retrieved from https://cwe.mitre.org/

Compa Mind Square. (2021). Retrieved from https://compamind.de/knowhow/sap-master-data-governance/

Computerweekly, Information Lifecycle Management (ILM). (2021). Retrieved from https://www.computerweekly.com/de/definition/Information-Lifecycle-Management-ILM

Cyber Security Training. (2021). *Certifications, degrees and resources, SANS.* Retrieved from https://www.sans.org/

Daehn, W. (2017). *The secret of SAP HANA – Pssst! Don't tell anyone!* Retrieved from https://blogs.sap.com/2017/12/01/secret-hana-pssst-dont-tell-anyone/

Destradi, M., Kiesel, S., Lorey, C., & Stefano, S. (2019). *Logistik mit SAP S4/HANA* (2. Hrsg.). Rheinwerk Verlag.

Doshi, K. (2020). *Reinforcement learning explained visually.* Retrieved from https://towardsdatascience.com/reinforcement-learning-explained-visually-part-4-q-learning-step-by-step-b65efb731d3e

Enterprise Resource Planning (ERP). (1999). In P. M. Swamidass (Ed.), *Encyclopedia of production and manufacturing management.* Springer. https://doi.org/10.1007/1-4020-0612-8_296

Feldmann, A., Zitterbart, M., Crowcroft, J., & Wetherall, D. (eds) (2003). *Proceedings of the 2003 conference on applications, technologies, architectures, and protocols for computer communications – SIGCOMM '03,* 2003, New York, ACM Press.

Furlanetto, D. (2016). *SCM APO demand planning (DP).* Retrieved from https://wiki.scn.sap.com/wiki/display/SCM/APO-DP

Ganesh, K., Mohapatra, S., Anbuudayasankar, S. P., & Sivakumar, P. (2014). *Enterprise resource planning. Fundamentals of design and implementation.* Springer (Management for professionals).

Gazet, A. (2010). Comparative analysis of various ransomware virii. *Journal in Computer Virology, 6*(1), 77–90.

Geis, T. (2019) Guido Tesch: Basiswissen Usability und User Experience. Aus- und Weiterbildung zum UXQB Certified Professional for Usability and User Experience (CPUX) - Foundation Level (CPUX-F).

George Saadé, R., Nijher, H., & Chandra Sharma, M. (2017). Why ERP implementations fail – A grounded research study. In *Proceedings of the 2017 InSITE Conference* (pp. 191–200), Jul 31, 2017. Informing Science Institute

Greenbau, J. (2016). *From two-tier ERP to the N-tier enterprise.* Retrieved from https://www.eaconsult.com

Hankel, M. (2015). *RAMI 4.0 – The reference architectural model industrie 4.0*. Retrieved from ZVEI: Die Elektroindustrie https://www.zvei.org/en/press-media/publications/the-reference-architectural-model-industrie-40-rami-40/

Hassler, M. (2017). *Digital und Web Analytics. Metriken auswerten, Besucherverhalten verstehen, Website optimieren*. s.l.: mitp Verlag (mitp Business)

History. (2019). *History.com: Industrial revolution*. Retrieved from https://www.history.com/topics/industrial-revolution/industrial-revolution

IBM Cloud Education: Artificial Intelligence (AI) and Machine Learning. (2020). Retrieved from https://www.ibm.com/cloud/learn/

Iliyasu, A. M., Bestak, R., & Baig, Z. A. (2020). *Innovative data communication technologies and application* (pp. 121–126). Springer.

Investopedia, Make-or-Buy Decision. (2021). Retrieved from https://www.investopedia.com

ISO IEC JTC 1 BD. (2015). *Big data, preliminary report 2014*. Retrieved from ISO http://www.iso.org/iso/big_data_report-jtc1.pdf

ISO IEC JTC 1 IoT. (2015). *Internet of Things (IoT), Preliminary Report 2014*. Retrieved from ISO http://www.iso.org/iso/internet_of_things_report-jtc1.pdf

ISO, ISO/IEC 9126. (1991). *Information technology—Software product quality - Part 1: Quality model*. Retrieved from http://www.cse.unsw.edu.au/*cs3710/PMmaterials/Resources/9126-1%20Standard.pdf

ISO/IEC 27034-1. (2011). *Information technology – Security techniques – Application security – Part 1*. Retrieved from https://www.iso.org/standard/44378.html

IT Jungle. (2018). *Marktanteile der führenden Anbieter am Umsatz mit Enterprise-Resource-Planning-Anwendungen (ERP) weltweit im Jahr 2017*. Retrieved from https://de.statista.com/statistik/daten/studie/262342/umfrage/marktanteile-der-anbieter-von-erp-software-weltweit/

Jalan, S. (2020). *Applications of data science in ERP*. Retrieved from https://medium.com/swlh/applications-of-data-science-in-erp-5e98347d4d07

Jax, B. (2018). *90 Jahre IBM Österreich – ein Grund zu feiern!* Retrieved from https://www.ibm.com/blogs/think/de-de/2018/05/90-jahre-ibm-osterreich/

Johnson, J. (2021). *Amount of monetary damage caused by reported cyber crime to the IC3 from 2001 to 2020*. Retrieved from https://www.statista.com/statistics/267132/total-damage-caused-by-by-cyber-crime-in-the-us/

KBMax. (2021). *KBMax – Lead to cash*. Retrieved from https://kbmax.com/cpq-term/lead-to-cash

Khiani, T. K. (2013). *Supply chain performance management overview*. Retrieved from https://wiki.scn.sap.com/wiki/display/CPM/Supply+Chain+Performance+Management+Overview

Kocian-Dirr, C. (2019). *Betriebswirtschaftslehre - Schnell erfasst*. Springer-Verlag (Wirtschaft - Schnell erfasst). ISBN: 978-3-662-54290-3. https://doi.org/10.1007/978-3-662-54290-3

Krämer, C. (2006). *Sven Ringling, Song Yang, mastering HR management with SAP*. SAP Press.

Krämer, C., & Lübke, C. (2004). *Sven ringling, HR personnel planning and development using SAP*. SAP Press.

Krishnan, V. (2016). *10 new requirements for modern data integration, database trends and applications*. Retrieved from https://www.dbta.com/Editorial/Trends-and-Applications/10-New-Requirements-for-Modern-Data-Integration-109146.aspx

Kurbel, K. E. (2013). *MRP II: Manufacturing resource planning. Enterprise resource planning and supply chain management. Progress in IS*. Springer. ISBN: 978-3-642-31573-2. https://doi.org/10.1007/978-3-642-31573-2

Lionbridge. (2021). *Localization, globalization, internationalization: What's the difference?* Retrieved from https://www.lionbridge.com/blog/translation-localization/localization-globalization-internationalization-whats-the-difference/

Management Study Guide. (2021). Retrieved from https://www.managementstudyguide.com

Managing Security with SAP Solution Manager. (2015). Retrieved from http://www.sap.com

Meleegy, A. E. (2017). *Optimiertes order promising: mit SAP S/4HANA Liefertermine effizienter planen und einhalten*. 28.03.17. Retrieved from https://news.sap.com/germany/2017/03/s4hana-order-promising/

Menon, S. A., Muchnick, M., Butler, C., & Pizur, T. (2019). Critical challenges in enterprise resource planning (ERP) implementation. *International Journal of Business and Management, 14*(7), 54.

MRP II. (2000). In P. M. Swamidass (Ed.), *Encyclopedia of production and manufacturing management*. Springer. https://doi.org/10.1007/1-4020-0612-8_602

Mueller, S. (2011). *Insert-only*. Retrieved from https://blogs.saphana.com/2011/09/14/insert-only/

Nebeling, N. (2020). *Seite an Seite mit ABAP in der cloud: Side-by-side extensions*. Retrieved from https://erlebe-software.de/abap-und-co/seite-an-seite-mit-abap-in-der-cloud-side-by-side-extensions/#:~:text=Wenn%20Sie%20in%20der%20SAP,by%2DSide%20Extension%E2%80%9C%20genannt

Nicolai, C. (2018). *Basiswissen Aufbauorganisation*. UVK Verlag. ISBN: 978-3-86764-835-6. https://doi.org/10.24053/9783739803869-1

Nissen, H. P. (2004). Von Wirtschaftssektoren zum Wirtschaftskreislauf. In *Das Europäische System Volkswirtschaftlicher Gesamtrechnungen, Physica-Lehrbuch*. Physica. https://doi.org/10.1007/978-3-7908-2659-3_2

OData. (2021). Retrieved from https://www.odata.org/

Oliver, R. L. (1980). A cognitive model of the antecedents and consequences of satisfaction decisions. *Journal of Marketing Research, 17*(4), 460. https://doi.org/10.2307/3150499

Open Web Application Security Project (OWASP). (2021). Retrieved from https://owasp.org/

Openbom. (2021). *BOM types. What are BOM types?*. Retrieved from https://help.openbom.com/get-started/bom-types/

Padia, D. (2019). *Downtime optimization approach – Let's talk all about different ZERO's*. Retrieved from https://blogs.sap.com/2019/10/11/downtime-optimization-approach-lets-talk-all-about-different-zeros/

Parasuraman, R., & Sheridan, T. B. (2000). A model for types and levels of human interaction with automation. *IEEE Transactions on Systems, Man, and Cybernetics – Part A: Systems and Humans, 30*(3).

Parikh, T. (2018). The ERP of the future: Blockchain of things. *International Journal of Scientific Research in Science, Engineering and Technology, 4*(1), 1341–1348.

Parthasarathy, S., & Sharma, S. (2017). Impact of customization over software quality in ERP projects: An empirical study. *Software Quality Journal, 25*(2), 581–598. https://doi.org/10.1007/s11219-016-9314-x

Phillips, M. (2018). International data-sharing norms: From the OECD to the general data protection regulation (GDPR). *Human genetics, 137*, 575–582. https://doi.org/10.1007/s00439-018-1919-7

Phrase. (2021). *Globalization vs. localization: Building a cohesive global growth strategy*. Retrieved from https://phrase.com/blog/posts/globalization-vs-localization/

Plattner, H. (2012). *In-memory data management. Technology and applications. With assistance of Alexander Zeier* (2nd ed.). Springer.

Plattner, H. (2013). *Lehrbuch in-memory data management. Grundlagen der In-Memory-Technologie*. Springer Gabler.

Profisee. (2021). *Master data management – What, why, how & who*. Retrieved from https://profisee.com/master-data-management-what-why-how-who

Rake, R., & Supradip, B. (2021). *ERP Software Market Outlook-2026*. Retrieved from https://www.alliedmarketresearch.com/ERP-market

Richter, M., & Flückiger, M. D. (2013). *Usability engineering kompakt. Benutzbare Produkte gezielt entwickeln* (3. Aufl.). Springer (IT kompakt). Retrieved from http://site.ebrary.com/lib/alltitles/docDetail.action?docID=10691416

Rumig, J. (2018). Multitenancy Architecture on SAP Cloud Platform, Cloud Foundry environment. Retrieved from https://blogs.sap.com/2018/09/26/multitenancy-architecture-on-sap-cloud-platform-cloud-foundry-environment/

Russell-Walling, E. (2011). *50 Schlüsselideen Management*. Spektrum Akademischer Verlag. ISBN: 978-3-8274-2636-9. https://doi.org/10.1007/978-3-8274-2637-6

Salahdine, F., & Kaabouch, N. (2019). Social engineering attacks: A survey. *Future Internet, 11*(4), 89.

SAP Activate. (2021). Retrieved from https://www.sap.com/uk/products/activate-methodology.html

SAP Cloud Appliance Library. (2021). Retrieved from https://sap.cal

SAP Cloud Application Programming Model. (2021). Retrieved from https://cap.cloud.sap/

SAP Cloud SDK. (2021). Retrieved from https://developers.sap.com/topics/cloud-sdk.html

SAP Extensibility Explorer. (2019). *SAP S/4HANA cloud extensibility overview.* Retrieved from https://extensibilityexplorer.cfapps.eu10.hana.ondemand.com/ExtensibilityExplorer/#/

SAP HANA Academy. (2021). *Building extensions for SAP S/4HANA cloud using APIs and events.* Retrieved from https://youtube.com/playlist?list=PLkzo92owKnVxiagp35AcwoxOlX0J4hLyY

SAP Insights. (2021). *What is ERP?* Retrieved from https://insights.sap.com/what-is-erp/

SAP Intelligent Asset Management Whitepaper. (2019). Retrieved from https://www.sap.com/swiss/products/supply-chain-management/asset-management-eam.html#pdf-asset=9e81308b-517d-0010-87a3-c30de2ffd8ff&page=1

SAP Official Website, SAP History. (2021). Retrieved from https://www.sap.com/about/company/history

Sarno, R., & Herdiyanti, A. (2010). A service portfolio for an enterprise resource planning. *IJCSNS International Journal of Computer Science and Network Security, 10*. Retrieved from https://www.researchgate.net/publication/267836036_A_Service_Portfolio_for_an_Enterprise_Resource_Planning

Saueressig, T., Gilg, J., Betz, O., & Homann, M. (2021a). *SAP S/4HANA cloud – An introduction.* SAP Press.

Schawel, C., & Billing, F. (2014). *Top 100 management tools. Das wichtigste Buch eines Managers Von ABC-Analyse bis Zielvereinbarung* (5. Aufl.). Gabler Verlag. ISBN: 978-3-8349-4690-4. https://doi.org/10.1007/978-3-8349-4691-1

Schewe, G. (2018). *Matrixorganisation. Definition: Was ist "Matrixorganisation"?* Gabler Verlag (Gabler Wirtschaftslexikon). Retrieved from https://wirtschaftslexikon.gabler.de/definition/matrixorganisation-39659/version-263061

Schick, U. (2017). *Side-by-side: Einfacher ERP-Apps entwickeln.* Retrieved from https://news.sap.com/germany/2017/09/sap-s4hana-cloud-sdk/

Schulte-Oversohl, H. (2019). Sales performance management. In M. Buttkus & R. Eberenz (Hg.), *Performance management in retail and the consumer goods industry. Best practices and case studies* (S. 385–403). Springer. ISBN: 978-3-030-12729-9. https://doi.org/10.1007/978-3-030-12730-5

Schuster, R. (2018). *SAP global track and trace: A new era in tracking and tracing.* Retrieved from https://blogs.sap.com/2018/06/28/sap-global-track-and-trace-a-new-era-in-tracking-and-tracing/

Searcherp. (2021). *Bill of materials.* Retrieved from https://searcherp.techtarget.com

Sethia, V., & Saxena, K. (2021). Automated ERP system with Internet of Things. *Innovative Data Communication Technologies.*

Soham, R. (2016). *Organizational management in SAP ERP HCM.* Rheinwerk Publishing. ISBN: 978-4-4932-1327-6

Sundaravaradan, S. (2020). *Supply chain & collaboration strategy.* Retrieved from https://blogs.sap.com/2020/01/28/supply-chain-collaboration-strategy/

Techopedia Dictionary. (2021). Retrieved from https://www.techopedia.com

Thompson, R. (2021). *Understanding data science and why it's so important.* Retrieved from https://blog.alexa.com/know-data-science-important/

Trienekens, J. J. M., Kusters, R. J., & Brussel, D. C. (2010). Quality specification and metrication, results from a case-study in a mission-critical software domain. *Software Quality Journal, 18*(4), 469–490. https://doi.org/10.1007/s11219-010-9101-z

Vahrenkamp, R. (2021). *Enterprise-resource-planning-system.* Retrieved from https://wirtschaftslexikon.gabler.de/definition/enterprise-resource-planning-system-51587/version-2 74748

Vahs, D. (2019). *Organisation. Ein Lehr- und Managementbuch* (10. Aufl.). Schäffer-Pöschel Verlag. ISBN: 978-3-7910-4281-7. https://doi.org/10.34156/9783791042831-141

van der Aalst, W. (2014). Data scientist: The engineer of the future. In *Proceedings of the I-ESA conference* (Vol. 7). Springer.

Varga, E. (2019). Introduction to data science. In *Practical data science with python 3: Synthesizing actionable insights from data* (pp. 1–27). Apress.

Vector Solutions. *What is environment, health, and safety (EHS) & why is it important?* Retrieved from https://www.vectorsolutions.com/resources/blogs/what-is-ehs-and-why-is-it-important/

Weber, W., Kabst, R., & Baum, M. (2014). *Einführung in die Betriebswirtschaftslehre* (9. Aufl.). Gabler Verlag. ISBN: 978-3-8349-4676-8. https://doi.org/10.1007/978-3-8349-4677-5

Wellers, D., & Koch, C. (2021). *Circular economy: The path to sustainable profitability.* n.d. Retrieved from https://insights.sap.com/circular-economy-sustainable-profitability/

Werner, H. (2008). *Supply chain management. Grundlagen, Strategien, Instrumente und Controlling* (3. Aufl.). Gabler. ISBN: 978-3-8349-0504-8. https://doi.org/10.1007/978-3-8349-9549-0

Wilson, K. (2019). *Understanding SAP global track and trace.* Retrieved from https://blogs.sap.com/2019/05/14/understanding-sap-global-track-and-trace/

Wöhe, G., & Döring, U. (2000). *Einführung in die Allgemeine Betriebswirtschaftslehre* (20. Aufl.). Verlag Franz Vahlen (Vahlens Handbücher der Wirtschafts- und Sozialwissenschaften). ISBN: 3800625504

Yuhanna, N., Owens, L., & Cullen, E. (2015). *The Forrester Wave™ enterprise data virtualization.* Retrieved from https://www.forrester.com/report/The+Forrester+Wave+Enterprise+Data+Virtualization+Q1+2015/-/E-RES117844, Forrester Research.

Jnited States

. Taylor Publisher Services